D0875179

VEBLEN

VEBLEN

The Making of an Economist Who

Unmade Economics

CHARLES CAMIC

HARVARD UNIVERSITY PRESS

Cambridge, Massachusetts

London, England

2020

First printing

Library of Congress Cataloging-in-Publication Data
Names: Camic, Charles, author.
Title: Veblen : the making of an economist who unmade economics / Charles Camic.
Description: Cambridge, Massachusetts : Harvard University Press, 2020. |
Includes bibliographical references and index.
Identifiers: LCCN 2020018113 | ISBN 9780674659728 (hardcover)
Subjects: LCSH: Veblen, Thorstein, 1857–1929. | Economics—United States—History. |
Exploitation. | Leisure class. | United States—Economic conditions.
Classification: LCC HB119.A2 C266 2020 | DDC 330.092 [B]—dc23
LC record available at https://lccn.loc.gov/2020018113

to Caroline and Susannah

&

to Beth

CONTENTS

VEBLEN

INTRODUCTION

E conomic news and information are the stuff of everyday life in the United States and around the world today. Smartphones ping alerts about the latest figures for unemployment and housing starts within seconds of their monthly release by government agencies; news media headline trade accords, executive compensation packages, and the interest rate policies of the Federal Reserve Board; editorial writers describe the data and statistical techniques of economists from Harvard and the Paris School of Economics; and we are all engulfed by the regular outpouring of information on oil prices, averages on the Nasdaq and Nikkei stock indexes, consumer confidence levels, and the price tag of government programs. To imagine our atmosphere purified of these elements is to warp ourselves into another galaxy.

Our forebears, going back a century and a half, would easily recognize our situation, not in fine detail of course, but certainly in its broad outlines. As the United States and the nations of Western Europe industrialized in the second half of the nineteenth century, their elites and citizens were on the watch—though with fewer quantitative tracking measures than we now have—closely attuned to tariff regulations, the currency standard, railway rates and surcharges, court rulings on the structure of corporations, the prices of summer and winter wheat, and the division of shares of the country's wealth. On these issues—which filled the national newspapers, urban immigrant newspapers, and local town papers—hinged the outcomes of high-stakes electoral contests.

Yet no more than now did "raw" economic data then speak for themselves. Almost without exception, the brute facts arrived before the public prepackaged, accompanied with an intellectual guidebook as to their meaning—with an interpretation that served to convert the voiceless information about the economy into economic *knowledge*. And, perhaps predictably, these interpretations ranged widely in content, some deeply tinted by the agendas of sharply divided political and social groups, others wanting to maintain more distance from the intergroup conflicts of the age. All the same, whether they preferred a hands-on or arms-length style of intervention into the public arena, most economic writers, including most occupants of the newly established position of the academic economist, had problems closer to home to deal with at the same time. These were their recurring struggles with one another over the proper manner in which to interpret the bare facts of economic life in order to produce the right kind of economic knowledge.

A mild-mannered lion in these struggles over economic knowledge was Thorstein Veblen. Preeminent British economist (and near-miss Nobelist) Joan Robinson once categorized Veblen as "the most original economist born and bred in the USA"; and her encomium—one of scores of similar tributes paid to Veblen over the past 125 years—invites a fundamental question about the relationship between new forms of economic knowledge and the life of the intellectual innovator.[1] This book pursues that question through a historical study of the connection between Thorstein Veblen's economic ideas—the distinctive type of economic knowledge he created—and how he was born and bred intellectually.

THE PROCESS OF VEBLEN'S coming-into-being as an economist was a prolonged one, which lasted from the pre–Civil War period until the final decade of the nineteenth century. Described by present-day historians as the era of the "making of modern America," these years witnessed massive immigration to the country by northern Europeans, the settlement of the prairies of the Midwest and the mechanization of agriculture, explosive urbanization and industrialization, and the metamorphosis of the country's institutional infrastructure. Veblen was closely aware of all these changes. Not yet the abstractions of historical monographs, they roiled the places where he lived, as he made his way—by the unbridled invention of the age, the railroad—from a Norwegian immigrant community in rural Minnesota to long-settled areas of the East Coast, and then to Chicago, which (with a population of more than a million and a half) was already the nation's Second City, as well as the locus of its meatpacking, grain, and lumber industries, its emerging corporate form of capitalist enterprise, and its devices for stimulating mass consumption. Every one of these great historical developments threaded through Veblen's life experiences, and all of them feature in his fin de siècle writings.

Even so, everyday experiences are multilayered and concatenated, and for much of the time from his boyhood until the end of the nineteenth century Veblen viewed the panorama of his age through the windows of classrooms, at a succession of schools where he was a star student. Initially those schools were local, though with a twist; for, just by luck, Carleton College—newly founded but already academically well-equipped— was only a few miles from his family's farm, so Carleton was where his parents sent him when he finished common school. Then, following his college graduation, Veblen entered graduate school, studying at four of the leading American universities of the period, one, Yale University, antique but undergoing major intellectual renovation, the other three—Johns Hopkins University, Cornell University, and the University of Chicago— epicenters of the transformation in higher education that had recently begun in the United States. Not only this, but it was for the explicit purpose of advancing his education that Veblen left the farmstead and moved several times afterward; the forceful pull of the university and the attraction of particular professors occasioned all the major geographical moves he made (except for a timeout back home due to illness).

In the course of all these moves, Veblen gradually became an economist, and a highly original one.[2] Economics was not his intended destination; at the outset, Veblen aspired to a career as a philosopher, but this plan proved temporary, and soon he was reconsidering his options. One purpose of this book, then, is to follow his intellectual journey step by step, examining Veblen's pivot into economics and his transformation into an innovative economic thinker as he proceeded—amid the swirling economic and social changes of his age—from the local schoolhouse to Carleton College, Johns Hopkins, Yale, Cornell, and the University of Chicago.

Measured in units of time, this trip was a lengthly one. Among the social scientists of Veblen's generation, no other figure clocked in so many years as a student and apprentice within America's higher-educational institutions.[3] In the instance of Veblen, moreover, that long expanse of time was heavily saturated with intellectual repetition—in particular, with the form of repetition I will call "repetition-with-variation" (a notion I borrow from European philosophers and the American sociologist Robert Merton). Viewed solely in terms of formal coursework, the schools Veblen attended varied significantly from one another. At each, he studied different academic subjects with different professors, whose teachings differed in important ways. Despite these variations, however, these institutions all bore a strong family resemblance; at one school after another, Veblen's teachers, nearly all of them German-educated, did their work by using intellectual practices that were analogous to one another. In this way, they equipped Veblen with equivalent skills, resources, and other intellectual tools—or, in other words, with a similar repertoire of concepts, critical and constructive arguments, and techniques for formulating arguments. This repertoire overlapped, furthermore, with experiences Veblen had beyond the walls of the academy; his formal education and his informal education reinforced each other over the course of many years. Talented student that he was, Veblen learned the intellectual repertoire he was taught, mastering that repertoire so well that he was able subsequently to expand it and to refine it in order to address issues different from those that concerned his teachers.

Sociologists and nonsociological readers alike are likely to find a study of several decades in the life of a nineteenth-century economist an odd project for a sociologist to take on, and perhaps it is. Nonetheless, in the spirit of the African adage that "it takes a village to raise a child," my aim is to show that this astute sociological principle also applies to knowledge producers, even to a creative knowledge specialist like Thorstein Veblen. The development of an intellectual innovator, no less than the raising of a child, involves social processes that link the elders of a village to the youth of the next generation. To be sure, this analogy goes only so far, because the "village" inhabited by young intellectuals typically exceeds the physical boundaries of a particular geographical location to encompass multiple locales, just as happened in Veblen's case. But this widening of intellectual space that has been underway for the last century and a half has not diminished the role of the tribal elders of the academic world. In recent times, the number of those elders has actually grown and, as often as not, their impact on academic newcomers has expanded.

This intergenerational dynamic operates differently in different cases, of course. Repetition-with-variation is only one element in the story of intellectual growth and creativity. As far as I know, however, it is an element that sociologists and other social scientists have all but overlooked. More important, it is an element that we would not expect to play a positive role in the development of thinkers who become innovators. After all, repetition by the village elders of *their* ideas is the antithesis of new knowledge, is it not? That, at any rate, is what previous writers on

Veblen's work have assumed. But the historical evidence laid out in the following chapters shows that repetition-with-variation may have the opposite effect: the effect of stimulating and facilitating intellectual innovation. And if this statement applies to the extreme case of Thorstein Veblen, it likely holds in other instances too. At the least, the process of repetition-with-variation turns a new light, I hope, on the persisting puzzle of how novel cultural forms can arise from preexisting forms.

THIS INTERPRETATION OF THE RELATIONSHIP between the way Veblen was "born and bred" and his later economic ideas departs from the interpretation that has shaped our understanding of Veblen for close to a century. Originating earlier but engraved in Joseph Dorfman's imposing 1934 biography *Thorstein Veblen and His America*—still regarded as the definitive account of Veblen's life—this interpretation of the development of Veblen's economic thinking presents him as an "outsider" to the intellectual mainstream, a "detached" thinker marginal to the academic village of his era, a poorly adjusted creature from a remote cultural planet.[4] This marginality, in Dorfman's telling, "alienated" Veblen and engendered the "Olympian aloofness" that enabled him to formulate his heretical economic ideas and his vituperative criticism of the economic dynamics of his society in *The Theory of the Leisure Class*.[5]

This perspective on the origins of Veblen's economics has had a wide following. Reducing Veblen's oeuvre mainly to *The Theory of the Leisure Class*, several generations of prominent intellectuals—some writing in admiration, others in derision—have latched onto this figure of Veblen as the aloof academic outsider, enlisting him in support of each writer's own point of view. For C. Wright Mills, Veblen stood as the archetype of "the outsider, and his work [is] the intellectual elaboration of a felt condition" that transformed him into "the best critic of America that America has produced."[6] For John Kenneth Galbraith, Veblen was the rugged, antiestablishment "frontiersman," whose "cool and penetrating" gaze called forth the maverick economic analysis found in *The Theory of the Leisure Class*, "the most comprehensive [tract] ever written on snobbery and social pretense."[7] For Cornel West, Veblen, along with fellow marginal man C. Wright Mills, represented the tradition of "cultural criticism" vital to "left oppositional thought and practice."[8] In contrast, according to David Riesman, Veblen's social marginality produced "a system of analysis [that] now appears over simple, and not adequate for understanding contemporary society" and its economic workings.[9] Later, Theodor Adorno flayed Veblen's work as "one big joke" that misfired because of the "spleen" of the outsider.[10] And John Patrick Diggins invoked Veblen's "marginal status" to explain his hardened tendency "to negate everything and affirm nothing."[11] This Veblen-as-outsider thesis brims with synonyms: Veblen as an "inscrutable misfit," Veblen as a "stranger" in the academic corridors of his time—these are also common descriptors.[12]

Interrogated, most of these claims break down; their terms lack precision, while the assumption that Veblen's heterodox ideas arose from his social marginality rests heavily on circular reasoning. Further, these claims square poorly with much of the biographical evidence, as Veblen scholars have begun to recognize.[13] British sociologist Stephen Edgell quips, for instance, that Veblen "was white, Protestant, male, and in due course famous—hardly a major contender for the marginal-man title."[14] It is true, as proponents of the marginality thesis like to emphasize, that Veblen did enter the world of higher education with a Norwegian immigrant background, in contrast to many of his teachers and academic contemporaries, who were of Anglo-Saxon descent. But there are many other career features to consider. For example, in an era when a scholar's first professional job placement carried long-lasting implications (even more so than today), Veblen's peers sometimes started out their academic careers at obscure teaching colleges or, in luckier cases, at cash-poor state universities barely on the map; Veblen's career began at one of the nation's richest, most distinguished private universities. What was more, in an academic context where prominent scholars, even those with positions at research-oriented universities, spent semester after semester teaching introductory courses to bored college students in other disciplines, Veblen mainly taught courses on research topics in his own specialty area for advanced students aiming to become researchers in the same field. In a period when leading academics were often lured into publishing knockoff writings—elementary textbooks, newspaper articles, and so forth—Veblen published his work almost exclusively in professional journals targeted at economists.

For the purpose of understanding Veblen's intellectual development, this last fact is the most revealing. This is so because, first and foremost, Thorstein Veblen was an *academic economist,* a specialized professional scholar in a historical era when academic knowledge producers—and knowledge producers specializing in economics—were just beginning to make their appearance in the United States. Entering the emerging academic world during the last quarter of the nineteenth century, Veblen became an early prototype of the "professional academic"—that species formerly referred to as "academic man."[15] Rather than an outsider to the American academy, Veblen was actually an accomplished member of the first cohorts of university-based social scientists, scientists, and humanists who took part in shaping the model that, in many ways, is still found up and down the corridors of the twenty-first-century academy.[16] This is one reason the connection between his academic life and his ideas is worth examining.

I've commented that Veblen turned to economics in the course of his schooling, not as a result of looking down on economic life from the Olympian heights of an outsider. But his education in economics involved more than simply going to school. At Carleton, Johns Hopkins, Yale, and Cornell, Veblen gravitated to the subject of economics with the guidance and support of men who themselves were "political economists" (to use the job title that was standard up to the 1890s) and who were also among the driving figures in the emergence of economics as a specialized area of study within US institutions of higher education. Furthermore, not only were these men the academic institution builders, they were, between them, the leading American representatives of all the major "schools" of late nineteenth-century economic thought—classical economics, historical economics, and marginalist economics. Veblen thus learned economics studying face to face with the country's marquee figures. From these impressive beginnings, he then moved almost immediately, for a fourteen-year stay, to a faculty position at the University of Chicago. Here he taught graduate-level courses on economic theory and the history of political economy (in seminars that included several prominent future economists), translated a classic German economic treatise, served as managing editor of a premier economics journal, and formed cordial professional relations with three generations of economists.[17]

This rich set of experiences carried Veblen far out into the choppy waters of late nineteenth-century economics, submersing him in the profession's theoretical and empirical literatures, its past and present controversies, its festering in-house debates—and signposting for him the field's dead ends and promising areas for exploration, the cold and hot spots, the closed questions and the open ones. It was to the hot questions that Veblen then turned, setting after them with the whole repertoire of practices he had learned and fine-tuned in the course of his education. Tellingly, of the seventy articles and book reviews Veblen published in the years covered by this study, all but one fell squarely within the compass of academic economics, as did his two books from the period, *The Theory of the Leisure Class* (1899) and *The Theory of Business Enterprise* (1904).[18] Veblen himself situated *The Theory of the Leisure Class* in this same category; and academic reviewers, writing about the book before it acquired its popular reputation as an outsider's manifesto, explicitly greeted it as a contribution to economic theory.

It is true that Veblen's intervention into economics drew on literatures that lay far afield (in philosophy, ethnology, psychology), and that he sharply attacked many received economic doctrines. But economists of his era engaged in conduct like this all the time; most of them read widely outside of economics, and many hurled strong criticisms at other economists. Veblen may have taken such behaviors to a new level, but informed contemporaries still regarded him principally as a professional economist—in fact, as one of the leading professional economists of the age.[19] In a letter in April 1899 (a month after the publication of *The Theory of the Leisure Class*), J. Laurence Laughlin—the conservative classical economist who chaired Veblen's department at the University of Chicago—described him as "one of the brainiest, deepest economists we have" in the world of higher education.[20] In letters from spring 1906, when Veblen was a candidate for a professorship in the Department of Economics and Social Science at Stanford University, well-informed marginalist economist Allyn Young reported to Stanford president David Starr Jordan that, among leading figures in the American economics profession, "there is general agreement that no better selection" could be made for the position than that of Veblen. And Young himself shared this view, telling Jordan, "I do not think that [Veblen] has an equal among American economists in breadth of scholarship and subtlety of analysis."[21] On the basis of recommendations like these, Jordan hired Veblen, only to have to ask for his resignation three years later as the result of allegations about his domestic life. But, as late as 1911, Jordan's judgment remained that Veblen "is one of the highest living authorities [on] economic theory."[22]

IN THIS BOOK I piece together Veblen's educational career in order to bring Veblen-the-academic-economist into the foreground and to interpret his work in this context. By viewing Veblen in this way, I also aim to make a small contribution to adjusting the balance in current perceptions of late nineteenth-century American thought. During the past quarter century, major studies of this subject have focused attention primarily on

American philosophical thought, reducing economic thought and, in particular, Veblen's writings to ciphers.[23] To take only the most influential of these studies published in the past twenty years, Louis Menand's *The Metaphysical Club* tells "a story of ideas in America," from the late nineteenth century to the early twentieth century, by presenting a collective biography of four professional philosophers—William James, John Dewey, Charles S. Peirce, Oliver Wendell Holmes—the group "more responsible than any other group for moving American thought into the modern world."[24] In this account and others like it, Veblen and most other academic economists of the era melt into the background, although "moving American thought into the modern world"—into "the Modern Industrial System," as Veblen called it—called forth intense and far-ranging discussions about economic knowledge, discussions in which Veblen participated and interceded.[25]

Because my main concern is with Veblen's training for this intervention into the economic debates of his time, my account will stop when Veblen was just shy of fifty years old and fully formed as an academic economist. The book thus differs from biographies that cover an entire lifetime, plumb the inner mental recesses of the person under study, and describe biographical episodes that have little bearing on the person's ideas. My account also brackets those dimensions of Veblen's work that have led some commentators to portray him as a secular prophet, a political thinker, an epistemologist, an aesthetician, a cultural anthropologist, or a social psychologist (although I will nod to these other dimensions when they relate directly to Veblen's economic writings). Depending on what a twenty-first-century reader wants to learn about Veblen's life and ideas, my neglect of these topics is more or less serious; but I have found such elisions necessary in order to examine, in greater detail than is available elsewhere, Veblen's education and how it prepared him for his career as an academic economist.[26]

In the background of my account is the premise that we cannot adequately understand Veblen's economics by synecdoche, by taking a small part of his oeuvre—his first book, *The Theory of the Leisure Class*—for the whole, as many commentators have unjustifiably done. More illuminating than this one-text approach has been a body of scholarship that spotlights the Janus-like character of Veblen's economic writings as a totality. According to this interpretative tradition, Veblen was concerned with both the past and future of economic theory. Looking to the past, Veblen savaged (say these scholars) the economic theories of his predecessors for their atomizing analysis of economic activity, as well as for their claim that economic action is similar in form regardless of when in time or where in location it occurs. Obversely, according to this scholarly consensus, Veblen sought to lead economics towards a future in which it simultaneously redesigned itself as an evolutionary science of the origins and growth of economic institutions and reconceptualized economic activity as the conduct of socially embedded human beings with attributes that change in the course of evolution.

As far as it goes, the consensus is right to locate these themes at the center of Veblen's work. They are there, they are prominent, and they are significant (for Veblen, as well as for his legacy), and in this study I discuss them in detail. But they also had a convoluted history antedating Veblen's writings. Every one of them was sufficiently commonplace that contemporary economists sometimes described these themes as "trite."[27] More than that, we can find every one of these themes in the work of Veblen's teachers, where they were repeated to him, in different ways, in the course of his schooling. Even Veblen's writing style—his iconoclastic prose—was a standard piece of equipment in the intellectual toolbox handed down to him.

What awaited was an occasion for him to put these intellectual tools to good use, and Veblen recognized his opportunity when it came along. His father was an accomplished carpenter who adapted the skills he acquired as an apprentice in Norway to the challenge of turning acres of forested wilderness in the American Midwest into rolling fields of wheat; and his sixth child was no less adept at appropriating and recalibrating the practices he learned during his education to what he saw before him at the frontier of economics. That sight was a controversial idea and theory rapidly gaining acceptance and stature among European and American economists during the years when Veblen's professional career was beginning. Called "productivity theory"—or "marginal productivity theory"— this idea had already found a broad range of applications in the work of economists attracted to it. However, towering over nearly all these other uses was the application of marginal productivity theory to the centuries-old problem of economic distribution.

This was the problem of explaining the allocation of shares of a nation's wealth to different social groups, or (what amounted to the same thing) answering the question of why different "factors" of production receive different economic returns—smaller versus larger slices of the national income pie—for their contributions to the production process. Usually, economists focused this question on the economic returns netted by rival social classes, Capital and Labor in particular (both usually written in capital letters). In the tumultuous closing decades of the nineteenth century, this question, long tucked away in economic treatises, suddenly acquired urgency both inside and outside the academy. Faced with this uproar, many American economists seized on marginal productivity theory, which appeared to offer a compelling new way to make sense of the distribution of national wealth among rival claimants. For, as arcane economic theories went, the marginal productivity theory of distribution furnished a simple answer to the riddle. The theory asserted—to quote its leading American exponent, John Bates Clark—that so long as markets are competitive, "the distribution of the income of society is controlled by a natural law [which efficiently allocates] to every agent of production"—Capital included—exactly "the amount of wealth [that it] has specifically produced."[28]

This bold and confident assertion of a direct correspondence between productivity contributions and the distribution of wealth and income was anathema to Thorstein Veblen in the aftermath of his intellectual experiences up to this point. But the assertion was also an opening for him, an opportunity to repurpose the intellectual equipment and practices in his tool kit to dismantle the productivity theory of distribution and to construct an alternative approach. This is the reinterpretation of Veblen's work this book proposes. I hope to demonstrate that Veblen's writings constitute an all-out assault on the premises, reasoning, and empirical claims of the marginal productivity theory of distribution, as well as a formidable effort to turn this theory upside down.[29] Veblen signaled this ambition in many of the writings that commentators have looked past. But he was also forthright in *The Theory of the Leisure Class,* which deflated any notion that shares of national income accrue to society's wealthiest groups because of their "productive contribution." This comforting platitude Veblen's book replaces with a relentless analysis of the wealthy as wasteful social parasites who live by means of behaviors that are "predatory, not productive"—behaviors that rest on the economic institutions that the productivity theory of distribution ignored.[30]

Veblen's rethinking of the relationship between "who produces" and "who reaps the benefits" was the core issue that arched over and motivated his work in the years examined in this book. Yet, this issue gets lost insofar as we overlook Veblen's immersion in turn-of-the-century academic economics and the education that enabled him to join the knotted discussion about productivity theories of distribution. And that loss goes further, because when we neglect the innovative position Veblen formulated in the productivity debate, we also miss other fundamental facets of his intellectual contribution both to his contemporaries and to us as well.

One aspect of this contribution is Veblen's insight into the duplex nature of economic life. In his view, economies involve, at root, activities that are "productive" and activities that are "unproductive," or (as he liked to say) "nonproductive." Day in and day out, both kinds of activity carry enormous consequences for human well-being and the functioning of society. According to his critique, though, economists devoted themselves almost exclusively to the study of production; by long-standing practice (if not definition), economics was the "science of the production of wealth."[31] Nonproductive activities, objected Veblen, had no more than a toehold in this intellectual tradition (or elsewhere in the social sciences). Now and then, anxieties about unproductive behaviors and unproductive social classes might seep out from the crevices of political economy—most often from the conceptual crack named "consumption"—but that was all. For Veblen, however, economists' myopic handling of nonproductivity all but denied its existence, preventing them from grasping its importance, its pervasiveness, and its essential connection with production. The phenomena of productivity and nonproductivity, Veblen held, cannot be severed.

Here is a further instance where interpreters who go no further than *The Theory of the Leisure Class* come up short. Fixating on the vivid picture of "conspicuous consumption" that Veblen drew in the book, they characterize him as the theorist of excessive spending behavior, not the theorist of nonproductive economic activities more generally, let alone the theorist of nonproductivity in relation to productivity. On these themes, Veblen's other turn-of-the-century writings were more plainspoken. In them, he amplified his larger argument that nonproductivity—regardless of whether it takes the form of conspicuous consumption, indulgent leisure, or wasted work efforts—depends on a range of predatory activities that occur right alongside productive activities. In more oblique terms, however, this argument was already present in *The Theory of the Leisure Class*, where Veblen insisted on moving nonproductivity from the outer periphery of social-scientific thought to the center in order to examine its interplay with the process of economic production. This bifocal perspective distinguishes Veblen from many other social thinkers.

A second facet of Veblen's contribution is his distinctive, doubled-barreled *historical* approach. Political economists and other social theorists of Veblen's era have often been portrayed by their critics as ahistorical thinkers. In recent decades, however, researchers have challenged this stereotype; they have found that many late nineteenth-century and early twentieth-century American thinkers were imbued with a strong "historical sensibility." (I take this expression from intellectual historian James T. Kloppenberg, who used it to describe young philosophers of Veblen's generation.)[32] Broadly speaking, this historical sensibility came in two diverging forms, both of which had begun to infiltrate economics before Veblen entered the field.

One of these was the panoptic perspective exemplified in the various evolutionary doctrines that American thinkers drew from the natural sciences during the final decades of the nineteenth century, and wanted to import into newly emerging academic fields like psychology, anthropology, and sociology. To do so, members of these fields set about to study the origins and development of phenomena such as mind, culture, and society—and it wasn't long before economic theorists (some of them, at least) followed suit. They turned their attentions to the great transformations that had occurred in economic life over the course of millennia, as humankind gradually progressed from its "savage" beginnings to the glories of industrial "civilization." This concern with the *longue durée* differentiated the historical sensibility of evolutionists within economics from the orientation of a different group of economic scholars. This group consisted of economic historians, who divided the past into much smaller units—a few decades or, at the extreme, a few centuries—and sought to examine the particular activities and institutions that had caused particular changes in the organization of economic production and distribution.

Part of Veblen's achievement was to fuse these two historical vantage points, integrating the evolutionist's unbounded sense of the past with the economic historian's more localized view. As I have said, interpreters of Veblen have long recognized the evolutionary dimension of his thinking; but here again the tendency has been to allow one aspect of his work to overshadow others.[33] There is no question that Veblen was a vigorous advocate of Darwinian evolutionary theory; he pleads for it, urging economists to resist the lure of ahistorical productivity theories by using Darwinian concepts to analyze epochal changes that had occurred in the processes of economic production, acquisition, and distribution. Yet

Veblen exhibited as well the economic historian's determination to confront the particularity of historical change. Among his contemporaries, Veblen was the economist who compiled annual statistics on the upswings and downturns of American wheat prices; who chronicled the economic demands of a band of unemployed men marching to Washington, DC; who thoroughly combed thousands of pages of US government reports on the activities of specific American corporations; and who moved from place to place toting fat anthropological bulletins on the particular economic institutions of different American tribes.

In Veblen's writings these two historical strands—the evolutionary claims and the analysis of particular times and places—go together. Each closely informs the other, as his general evolutionary theorizing gives focus and direction to his specific historical inquiries, while those same historical inquiries specify how his evolutionary generalizations operate on the ground. This novel synthesis of "nomothetic" and "idiographic" approaches is something that Veblen's distinguished student Wesley Mitchell recognized when he credited Veblen with "blending historical research and theory more perfectly" than any previous figure in the history of economics.[34] But Veblen's superiority over his predecessors in achieving this blend is a comparatively minor issue, because his double-stranded historical sensibility carries a larger meaning for readers. With intent, Veblen ruthlessly destabilizes the economic world as an object of knowledge by continually unsettling the taken-for-granted order of things: hurling all things economic into the flux of short-term processes nested in long-term processes; infusing all economic realities with historicity writ small and large; and insisting that every present economic moment will dissolve in time, just as all past historical moments (whatever their duration) had done, and just as all future moments would do. Veblen's historical vision accepts no other possibility.

In the chronology of Veblen's intellectual career, all these themes in his work—his confrontation with the marginal productivity theory of distribution, his demand that economists study productivity in relation to nonproductivity, his two-toned historical sensibility—took shape side by side with one another and in tandem with his critique of the assumptions of past economic theories and his campaign to transform economics into an evolutionary science of institutions. No one of these elements was the originating Big Idea that impelled Veblen subsequently to formulate the others. As I will point out, these elements all emerged together, as he skillfully adapted the intellectual practices he learned during his long education to the challenges he faced as an academic economist in the United States at the end of the nineteenth century and the start of the twentieth.

WHEN I BEGAN THIS STUDY of Thorstein Veblen many years ago, I had no inkling of this interpretation of his work or this argument about his intellectual development. About both issues, I had a wait-and-see attitude. I am a historically oriented sociologist of knowledge, and my research interests have always been in the relationship between lives and ideas, and in the ways social processes connect the life experiences of intellectual innovators with the kinds of knowledge they create. Whose lives, which ideas, what patterns of connection—I have filled in these blanks with different historical answers in different writings. Before starting this study, I decided to focus on Veblen mainly because of the coincidence of his high reputation as an original social thinker and the existence of a gap in the biographical literature—the fact that a single, now almost ninety-year-old book remained the one general biography of Veblen's intellectual development.[35] At the outset, I had almost no familiarity with most of Veblen's work, and I had no interpretation of it in mind. Buying into the notion that Veblen was an academic outsider, I did not see him as an academic economist; and had I realized that I would eventually be sucked so deeply into the marsh of nineteenth-century economics, I probably would have picked another biographical subject.

Only after reading more of Veblen's work did I become interested in the type of economic knowledge that he constructed and in the puzzle of how his life experiences equipped him for the job. Throughout my research, however, my slant was that of a sociologist of knowledge; scholars approaching Veblen from other angles would, almost inevitably, have noticed other aspects of his work and proposed different accounts of his intellectual development. Even after I narrowed my focus down to the development of Veblen's economics, my research continued to involve many different historical threads: material on Veblen's schools and teachers; books and articles written by or about his contemporaries in economics, philosophy, anthropology, and biology; and information about national and local social, economic, and political conditions during the era I examine. Excluding the subject of his teachers and schools, these topics belong to bulky historical literatures, from which I have learned a great deal. Even so, the size of most of these secondary literatures is too large for anyone but the historical specialist to digest, and I have had to be selective. So, like other researchers in my situation, I "sampled"—not randomly of course, but by selecting primary and secondary sources closest to the questions I am asking. This research method was less than foolproof, I know; but the only alternative I could think of was not to complete the project.

Because this book is a historical study, it does not analyze at any length how Veblen's writings can help us understand economic conditions today—turbulent financial markets, global economic crises, predatory corporate and state actions, the human assault on the environment, rampant consumer spending, and so on. In recent years, these topics (every one of which Veblen prised open) have become subjects of a robust body of scholarship, thriving in several subfields of economics and sociology, that uses Veblen-inspired ideas to examine contemporary economic problems.[36] This book follows Thorstein Veblen's long path to the kind of economic knowledge we see in these ideas.

IN CHAPTER 2, I lay out the sociological argument I use in later chapters to examine the relationship between the features of Veblen's life and work I have just flagged. The chapter describes the theoretical and historical scaffolding that undergirds my argument, introducing a few general ideas about time and place, and then tailoring my concepts to accommodate Veblen's historical era. This argument draws on, but differs from, existing sociological approaches as well as existing biographical approaches to the question of how new knowledge develops. Because outlining these approaches entails some explicit theoretical discussion, however, nonsociological readers may prefer to skip past the beginning section of the chapter. Doing so should not interfere with reading the rest of the book, since I try otherwise to keep the theoretical details in the background.

Chapter 3 covers the first two decades of Veblen's life, examining his parents' Norwegian origins and the farming communities of the Upper Midwest where the family set down roots in the 1850s and 1860s. The chapter describes Veblen's education, focusing on his experiences in rural common schools and especially at Carleton College, in Northfield, Minnesota, where the curriculum during the 1870s spanned from the classics of antiquity to the findings of the modern evolutionary sciences. Chapter 4 continues this narrative by discussing Veblen's studies at Carleton in the fields of philosophy and political economy under the guidance of John Bates Clark, who was then on the brink of international renown as an economist. Chapter 5 details the next phase of Veblen's education after he left the Midwest, in the early 1880s, to attend Johns Hopkins University and Yale University, with the intent of becoming an academic philosopher. Here I examine the ideas of the seven preeminent scholars with whom Veblen studied during this period: at Hopkins, Herbert Baxter Adams, Richard T. Ely, George S. Morris, and Charles Sanders Peirce; at Yale, Noah Porter, George T. Ladd, and William Graham Sumner.

Chapter 6 pauses the narrative of Veblen's schooling to discuss the lengthy interval (1884–1891) when he was back in the Midwest, convalescing from a debilitating immunologic disorder. His career on hold, Veblen witnessed the transformations going on around him in American society. The chapter describes some of the economic and cultural dimensions of these changes. It also examines the growth of institutions of higher education and the emergence of specialized academic disciplines, in particular the field of economics at a tumultuous moment in its intellectual history.

In Chapter 7 my biographical account resumes with Veblen's return to university life in the 1890s. This chapter starts with the period Veblen spent at Cornell University as a graduate student in political economy and history, studying with heavyweights James Laurence Laughlin, Herbert Tuttle, and Moses Coit Tyler. Next the chapter follows him to the University of Chicago, where he continued his work under Laughlin, amid the scene of the university's founding and the economic chaos of a city rising from the ground. At the University of Chicago, Veblen transitioned from graduate student to junior faculty member, his ears open to the consensus among local authorities in the social sciences, the humanities, and the biological sciences, who were rallying around a set of ideas (about history, society, and science) that strongly reinforced the lessons of his past experiences.

The subject of Chapter 8 is Veblen's work as an economist in the milieu of the University of Chicago. In this chapter, I examine Veblen's writings up to the time of his departure from Chicago in 1906, including *The Theory of the Leisure Class* and *The Theory of Business Enterprise*. The chapter situates Veblen in the context of the theoretical and methodological debates taking place among late nineteenth- and early twentieth-century American economists. I discuss how his own writings were creative interventions into these debates, built from the extensive repertoire of practices and resources he had acquired by repetition during the previous four decades. By the end of this period in his life, Thorstein Veblen had formulated his major ideas and stood as an admired member of the field of economics.

In Chapter 9, I chronicle Veblen's vacillating academic fortunes after his departure from Chicago. Here, I return to the Veblen-as-outsider thesis to discuss the developments in Veblen's later life that brought him his reputation as a marginal man, even though he had been an academic insider long into his professional career. Veblen himself, as I show, took a hand in this fashioning of his image, although other forces also played into the result. By way of concluding, I circle back to the book's argument about the relationship between repetition and the development of new knowledge.

SOURCES AND ABBREVIATIONS

Understanding the development of Thorstein Veblen's ideas has long been hampered by a lack of materials of the kind intellectual biographers ordinarily rely on, namely surviving documents from the thinker's own pen or typewriter. When the biographical subject is an academic of Veblen's era, these documents typically include professional and personal correspondence, private journals and miscellaneous jottings, logs of meetings and other daily activities, course syllabi and lecture notes, early drafts of later publications, unpublished manuscripts, and so forth.

In the case of Veblen, most of these cupboards are empty. Within the archives of the universities where he was a student or faculty member, there are modest collections of letters written by or to Thorstein Veblen, plus a few sets of notes by graduate students who took his courses, but that is all. A more substantial source are the letters Veblen's colleagues, friends, acquaintances, teachers, students, and family members wrote about him either to one another or to Joseph Dorfman in reply to queries he sent when he was researching his biography of Veblen in the late 1920s and early 1930s. The major repository of these letters is now the Joseph Dorfman Papers, which I abbreviate in the endnotes as JDP—Joseph Dorfman Papers, Rare Book and Manuscript Library, Columbia University. Aside from this collection, my account draws on several other primary sources, both archival and published.

ARCHIVAL SOURCES

AVP   Andrew A. Veblen Papers, Minnesota Historical Society.

AV-*Fam*   "The Veblen Family: Immigrant Pioneers from Valdris," c. 1915, AVP.

AV-Gen   *Veblen Genealogy: An Account of the Norwegian Ancestry of the Veblen Family in America which was Founded by Thomas Anderson Veblen and His Wife Kari Bunde Veblen.*

> Andrew Veblen had this 150-page typescript privately printed in 1925. It is now available through the HathiTrust Digital Library, https://www.hathitrust.org/.

CCA   Carleton College Archives, Laurence McKinley Gould Library, Carleton College.

DCGP   Daniel Coit Gilman Papers, Special Collections, Sheridan Libraries, Johns Hopkins University.

DSJP   David Starr Jordan Papers, Department of Special Collections and University Archives, Stanford University Libraries.

EARP   Edward Alsworth Ross Papers, Wisconsin State Historical Society.

ESP   Edwin Seligman Papers, Rare Book and Manuscript Library, Columbia University.

EVOM   "Memoirs of Mrs. Sigurd Olsen," Norwegian-American Historical Association.

> Mrs. Sigurd Olsen was the married name of Thorstein Veblen's older sister, Emily Veblen.

FWTP   Frank W. Taussig Papers, Harvard University Archives, Harvard University.

GFP   Gregory Family Papers, Bancroft Library, University of California, Berkeley.

GHMP   Mead, George Herbert. Papers. Special Collections Research Center, University of Chicago Library.

HBAP   Herbert Baxter Adams Papers, Special Collections, Sheridan Libraries, Johns Hopkins University.

HNP   Herbert Newton Papers, Manuscripts and Archives, Yale University Library.

HTP   Herbert Tuttle Papers, Division of Rare and Manuscript Collections, Cornell University Library.

JBCP   John Bates Clark Papers, Rare Book and Manuscript Library, Columbia University.

JCBP   John Casper Branner Papers, Department of Special Collections and University Archives, Stanford University Libraries.

JFJP   J. Franklin Jameson Papers, Manuscript Division, Library of Congress.

JLP   Jacques Loeb Papers, Manuscript Division, Library of Congress.

JPER   Records of the *Journal of Political Economy*. Special Collections Research Center, University of Chicago Library.

JWP   Jacob Warshaw Papers, State Historical Society of Missouri.

LCA   Luther College Archives, Preus Library, Luther College.

LFWC   Lester Frank Ward Collection, Manuscript Division, Brown University Library.

OLEP   Orrin Leslie Elliott Papers, Department of Special Collections and University Archives, Stanford University Libraries.

OPR-UoC   University of Chicago. Office of the President. Harper, Judson and Burton Administrations. Records. Special Collections Research Center, University of Chicago Library.

RBAP   Rasmus B. Anderson Papers, Wisconsin State Historical Society.

RHP   Herrick, Robert. Papers. Special Collections Research Center, University of Chicago Library.

RTEP   Richard T. Ely Papers, Wisconsin State Historical Society.

TV-CCA   Thorstein Veblen Collection, CCA.

TV-CU   Thorstein Veblen, Cornell University Graduate School Record and Administrative Correspondence, Division of Rare and Manuscript Collections, Cornell University.

TV-UoC   Veblen, Thorstein. Papers. Special Collections Research Center, University of Chicago Library.

TV-YU   Thorstein Veblen Folder, Manuscripts and Archives, Yale University Library.

WGSP   William Graham Sumner Papers, Manuscripts and Archives, Yale University Library.

WRHP   Harper, William Rainey. Papers. Special Collections Research Center, University of Chicago Library.

In endnotes that cite correspondence from these collections, I also abbreviate the names of the letter writers or recipients I refer to most often.

AV   Andrew A. Veblen

JD   Joseph Dorfman

TV   Thorstein Veblen

PUBLISHED SOURCES

Books by Thorstein Veblen

The following abbreviations are for those books of Veblen's that I cite by page numbers in the text. In the endnotes, I reference many of his other publications. JD*TV* (519–524) provides a complete bibliography of Veblen's books, translations, articles, and reviews.

AO   *Absentee Ownership: Business Enterprise in Recent Times; The Case of America* (New York: B. W. Huebsch, Inc., 1923).

HL   *The Higher Learning in America: Memorandum on the Conduct of Universities by Business Men* (New York: B. W. Huebsch, Inc., 1918).

IG   *Imperial Germany and the Industrial Revolution* (New York: B. W. Huebsch, Inc., 1915).

IW   *The Instinct of Workmanship and the State of the Industrial Arts* (New York: Macmillan, 1914).

TBE   *The Theory of Business Enterprise* (New York: Charles Scribner's Sons, 1904).

TLC   *The Theory of the Leisure Class: An Economic Study in the Evolution of Institutions* (New York: Macmillan, 1899).

> Reissued in 1912 under the title *The Theory of the Leisure Class: An Economic Study of Institutions.*

College and University Publications

CarltAC *Annual Catalogue of the Officers and Students of Carleton College.*

CornlUR *Cornell University Register.*

JHCir *Johns Hopkins University Circulars.*

UoC-AR *Annual Register* [of the University of Chicago].

UoC-Bull *University Bulletin* [of the University of Chicago].

UoC-QC *Quarterly Calendar* [of the University of Chicago].

UoC-UR *University Record* [of the University of Chicago].

YaleCat *Catalogue of the Officers and Students of Yale College.*

Professional Journals

AJS *American Journal of Sociology.*

Annals *Annals of the American Academy of Political and Social Science.*

JHS *Johns Hopkins University Studies in Historical and Political Science.*

JPE *Journal of Political Economy.*

QJE *Quarterly Journal of Economics.*

Biographies

JDTV Joseph Dorfman, *Thorstein Veblen and His America* (New York: Viking Press, 1934).

> When quoting from this book, I cite the revised seventh edition (1961), as reissued in 1972 (Clifton, NJ: Augustus M. Kelley Publishers). This is the final edition of the book, and it contains a few items of information Dorfman was unaware of when he published earlier editions. Otherwise, the first and final editions are essentially the same.

JDTVR   Joseph Dorfman, *Thorstein Veblen: Essays, Reviews, and Reports* (Clifton, NJ: Augustus M. Kelley Publishers,1973).

JJTV   Elizabeth Watkins Jorgensen and Henry Irvin Jorgensen, *Thorstein Veblen: Victorian Firebrand* (Armonk, NY: M. E. Sharpe, 1999).

Although inaccurate in their interpretations, these biographies nonetheless contain letters and other documents that are available nowhere else. For biographical information on Thorstein Veblen and the Veblen family, however, the writings of his older brother Andrew Veblen are the best single source. These include AV-*Fam* and AV-*Gen* (listed earlier), as well as some two dozen detailed letters Andrew sent to Joseph Dorfman between 1925 and 1932 (located in JDP). These consist of Andrew's answers to questions Dorfman asked him, plus several angry critiques of a draft of Dorfman's biography. In addition to these materials, Andrew authored several short publications (which I cite in endnotes) about the Veblen family.

I have drawn heavily on these items from Andrew's pen, although I have tried to use them cautiously. In historical research, as in news reporting, it is less than ideal to rely on one informant, especially when the informant, like Andrew, is not a neutral bystander but closely connected to the people and events being described in retrospect. That said, Andrew Veblen's writings have several strengths.

First, Andrew was a professional scholar, trained to be careful about factual details. (He did postgraduate work in physics at Johns Hopkins University, and he spent his career as a professor of physics at Iowa State University.) In AV-*Fam,* AV-*Gen,* and elsewhere, he drew on official documents about the Veblen family's genealogy, local land transactions, and so forth. To avoid depending simply on his own recall, Andrew conducted extensive conversations about his family's history with other members of the Veblen clan, including a formal interview with his father in 1895. In addition, Andrew had at his disposal information about his family that dated back to the years when the events he chronicled actually occurred. An indefatigable collector, he began, as early as adolescence, to compile scrapbooks and to keep daybooks relating to his family. Because Andrew was older than Thorstein by nine years, these documents cover much of Thorstein's childhood and schooling.

Second, Andrew was a witness to major episodes in Thorstein Veblen's education. Despite being older, Andrew began his formal education at a later age than Thorstein, so the schooling of the two brothers overlapped not only during their precollege years but also for much of their time at Carleton College and Johns Hopkins University (and then again during Thorstein's hiatus in Iowa in the late 1880s). This extended time together gave Andrew Veblen direct contact with Thorstein Veblen for the first thirty-four years of Thorstein's life; these are years that coincide with the period treated in this book. Early in his correspondence with Dorfman, Andrew did strike a modest note about the time he spent with his brother, saying that, after Thorstein's first three years at Carleton, "I have been in touch with him only by correspondence except for short visits now and then."[37] However, six years later, Andrew shed the modesty out of exasperation with Dorfman's misunderstandings, chiding Dorfman: "When it comes to understanding my brother's character, I do not acknowledge that any one knows better than I do. And when it comes to telling about the history of the family, its condition economically and socially, its environment, and all that went into my brother's development of personality. . . . I do not yield to any one. And I can not be expected to abate from the position I take. You can not possibly get more authentic information or understanding of our family's history than I possess. . . . For I am fair and I have lived an intelligently observant life."[38]

Third, Veblen scholars who have subsequently investigated the Veblen family's moves, property holdings, and so on have come across very few errors in Andrew's statements. As economist William Melton wrote in 2000 (after combing through government documents relating to the Veblens), "When it has been possible to check [Andrew Veblen's] account through other sources, he has been almost unfailingly correct."[39]

On the basis of these three factors, I have felt justified giving weight to Andrew Veblen's words about his family and his younger brother.

CHAPTER 2

THEORETICAL AND HISTORICAL
SCAFFOLDING

W here new economic knowledge comes from is not a new question. It was already under considerable discussion in Veblen's time among writers interested in the field of political economy. Witnessing the rise of new economic doctrines and the decline of long-established ones, academic economists and popular commentators attributed this intellectual shift to causes that ranged from unresolved technical problems in existing economic theories to far-flung changes in the capitalist economy. In his turn-of-the-century writings, Veblen himself weighed in on the topic.

In the twentieth century, when most economists lost interest in the history of economics, historians stepped in. They brought economic knowledge into the large family of human knowledge, examining the history of economic ideas in the same way they examined the development of other branches of the family, such as philosophy, social theory, and psychology. During the past thirty years, social scientists have also been drawn to questions about how social knowledge develops and have hammered out a set of concepts useful for addressing those questions. With an eye to the case of Thorstein Veblen, the first part of this chapter introduces a few of these concepts, fills in some of the blank space between them, and puts together the theoretical scaffolding for this study. In the second part of the chapter, I arrange this scaffolding to fit the historical era of Veblen's early intellectual career and propose an argument about how Veblen arrived at the type of economic knowledge he formulated.

1.

When we go on a trip, people advise us to travel light. Following this rule of thumb with the aim of understanding Veblen's development as an economist, it will be useful to pack four concepts.[1]

FIELDS

Traditionally, historical studies of the origins of new knowledge revolved around a dichotomy: the distinction between "internalist" and "externalist" explanations of intellectual change that fueled heated debates among scholars during the middle decades of the twentieth century. On the "internalist" side of the debate were those historians and social scientists who viewed the development of new ideas as the immanent outgrowth of the preexisting state of knowledge in some area of learning, the natural next step in the working out of the theories (and other knowledge claims) that characterized the area just before the new ideas appeared. In contrast, "externalist" accounts emphasized the causal role of factors other than the state of knowledge, such as the economic, political, and religious forces present in the larger historical context outside the realm of ideas.

If I were writing during the heyday of this debate, social scientists and historians would have expected this study of Veblen's ideas to take sides (or to propose a compromise). By now, however, this dichotomous way of thinking about the origins of new ideas has been superseded, and this book reflects that change. The change grows out of a critique leveled by scholars in the interdisciplinary area of Science Studies, who have argued that the separation between internalist and externalist explanations is an artificial and muddy division that exhausted its value long ago.[2] In place of this division, researchers have increasingly shifted attention away from the debate over internal versus external forces and toward the analysis of the institutions that *bridge* those two set of forces. This shift in focus has led to the study of the specific organizational sites, or settings, where knowledge experts *do their work*. And what work is that? It is the work—the multifaceted work—of "making knowledge": of stating what is known (or regarded as "known" at any particular time), reproducing that knowledge, packaging it, communicating it, and disseminating it to various audiences, extending and applying it, and even creating it in new forms. Science Studies scholars have used different words to name the places where these knowledge-making activities occur. For the sake of parsimony, however, I will stick primarily to one of these names in this book, following the lead of researchers who call these locations "fields." This is a concept social scientists have applied to sites of knowledge production that range from science laboratories at small local colleges to richly financed international research consortia. In this study, however, I will apply the term "field" mainly to a type of site that has existed (in some form) for the past 130 years: namely, the academic discipline.[3] I mention the concept at this point to have it on hand when I turn in later chapters to the fields of philosophy and economics as they operated in Veblen's time.[4]

When social scientists use the terminology of "field," they invite us to think of modern societies as carved up into separate spheres, each with a life of its own. As social scientists characterize it, a field is a relatively autonomous social microcosm, which is built around a network of relations among the men and women who belong to it. In contemporary societies, there are many of these spheres: economic fields, political fields, cultural fields, religious fields—as well as academic fields organized for the purpose of knowledge production.[5] This way of picturing societies has been worked out most fully by French sociologist Pierre Bourdieu and his followers, but many other social scientists have formulated versions of it. In the United States, sociologist Randall Collins has been a leading advocate of the idea.[6]

"Field," of course, is a metaphor. Like any metaphor, its value lies not in itself, but in what features of something else it throws into relief. In this book, that "something else" is Veblen's intellectual development; for examining this, the field metaphor is helpful in highlighting two aspects of Veblen's intellectual world. First, the people who make up a field are cognizant of other group members and relate to one another around the issues that define the field. To quote sociologists Neil Fligstein and Doug McAdam, the members of a field "are attuned to and interact with one another on the basis of shared (which is not to say consensual) understandings about the purposes of the field [and] their relationships to others in the field."[7] Second, a field has an internal structure, typically a hierarchical structure. According to scholars who use the metaphor, a field consists of an arrangement of positions organized in a ladder-like manner, such that men and women on higher rungs command more than lower-placed people do of the valuables that field members care about and compete over. Further, what matters to field members varies from one social field to another; in some fields, the desideratum is wealth, in others political power, in others celebrity status, and so on.

In the knowledge-making fields where Veblen was situated, we will see the workings of these two features of social fields, but with modifications specific to his own historical period. Like economic, political, and religious fields, knowledge-making fields operate in somewhat similar ways, though not identical ways, in different times and places. That said, what makes a field into a *knowledge field* is that its participants are (according to field theorists) primarily involved in "truth-seeking" rather than in the pursuit of wealth, power, or celebrity. Above and beyond other objectives they may have, members of knowledge fields want to formulate the "correct" theory of certain phenomena in nature or society, or the "proper" method of scientific research, or the "right" set of empirical research findings.[8]

Despite this goal, however, most academic disciplines are shot through with opposing claims about which theories, methods, or findings constitute the truth and which do not; and these competing truth claims are the issue that subgroups inside the field fiercely fight about in hopes of winning the high-stakes war of words that divides them. Victory means that one subgroup has succeeded (for the time being) in establishing the validity of its truth claims over rival claims, at least according to the general opinion of most people inside the discipline at any particular time. With this achievement primary, the energies of field members are sometimes directed toward other fields as well, inasmuch as the intellectual boundaries of their own field—like the boundaries of the fields Veblen took part in—are porous, open to currents flowing in from neighboring fields. What is more, knowledge fields generally depend on economic, political, and cultural supports (the "external" forces of old) in order to maintain themselves as relatively autonomous intellectual microcosms, and the availability of these supports varies historically. When they are in short supply—as in Veblen's era—knowledge producers may need to appeal for material backing and cultural legitimation to people in surrounding fields.[9]

But how do these field conditions bear on the development of *new* forms of knowledge? Decisive here is the role of newcomers who are moving into entry-level positions in an intellectual field.[10] According to Randall Collins, new entrants face a choice if they want to attain positions where their voices—their truth claims—are heard and accepted by other field members: either they "find a topic someone else [in the field] is talking about and agree with it, adding something which extends the argument," or they "pick a quarrel with someone else, contradicting what the other is saying" and successfully defending a new set of claims.[11] Aside from these two options (or finding a way to blend them), there is no alternative in this situation. But either way, the newcomers begin with the status quo. They take their point of departure from the available state of knowledge in their field and from the ways its members have already defined the field's problems, concepts, references, and so forth (paraphrasing Bourdieu).[12] It is this base of knowledge that cooperative field members try to extend and that quarrelsome field members try to upend.[13] Except among intellectual innovators who are not situated in a specialized knowledge field but rather in the political field, the religious field, or the like, new types of knowledge take shape in direct relation to conditions in the field of knowledge where the innovator-to-be is located.

KNOWLEDGE PRACTICES

What is this thing called "knowledge," though? Or, better, what is it for the purposes of this book? Researchers in the area of Science Studies point in a helpful direction.

Before the mid-1980s, historians and social scientists who studied the intellectual development of the natural sciences, the social sciences, and the humanities often viewed knowledge as a string of *statements* that thinkers from the past arrived at during their ruminations.[14] The features of these statements—and what made them worth the historian's time—differed from case to case. The statements of historical interest might be descriptive or normative, concrete or abstract, empirical or theoretical, correct or incorrect, and so forth. Regardless, historical researchers tended to group these statements under the rubric of "ideas," and I will sometimes use this shorthand expression. The book is, after all, concerned with many of the statements that Veblen set down in his writings.

All the same, to have knowledge in statement form presupposes knowledge in other forms. As the work of Science Studies scholars has shown, knowledge consists of far more than finished sentences on a page. It entails as well *practices* and *resources*—a pair of terms convenient for drawing a (loose) distinction between some of the main factors that combine into knowledge statements.[15] The "resources" of knowledge producers are their skills and their equipment: their basic abilities (cognitive, linguistic, mathematical, physical, and so on), plus the whole array of materials at their disposal—for example, laboratory instruments and preset ways of problem solving (in the case of natural scientists); or canonical texts and theories, documents and monographs, and commonplace observations and information (in the case of social scientists). "Practices" are the activities that make use of these resources: the ways of doing, seeing, thinking, and judging by which knowledge makers wield their instruments and skills when going about their work.[16] These activities span the continuum from mundane hands-on techniques (performing bioassays, combing through documents, putting marks down on a page); to tasks that entail significant amounts of improvising (building an argument, applying a set of concepts); to deep-wired modes of perceiving and classifying whatever falls in the knowledge maker's path. Some of these practices are ones that knowledge specialists formulate in words and explicitly agree (or disagree) about, while others go unspoken, covering a field so completely that its members do not realize they are engaging in them.

An integral part of these practices—and of especial interest as we look ahead to Veblen—is the practitioner's intellectual posture: the image that knowledge producers project by their style of argument and communication, the tone of their authorial voices, the attitude they show toward the work of other scholars, and so forth. Ordinarily, this intellectual persona draws its features from one of several stock characters that contemporary audiences recognize as soon as it comes onto the stage—the experienced authority, the curmudgeon, the indefatigable researcher, the skeptic, the rebel, and so on. (Different eras have different casts of characters.) By wearing the demeanor of one of these familiar figures, members of knowledge fields signal how they want readers to perceive what they are saying and to interpret the gist of their statements.

These practices and others, combined with the resources that are on hand, furnish members of a knowledge setting with what Science Studies scholars call a "repertoire," or "tool kit," that enables them to carry out their work. However, even with a tool set of this kind all ready to go, it is a separate question whether field members will actually do what their tools enable them to do. No matter how complete it is, a knowledge-making repertoire lies inert, gathering dust, until someone opens it up, sifts through it, takes some things out, and puts them to work. Intellectual resources and know-how come to life, in other words, only inasmuch as knowledge specialists marshal them to reach an objective they want to attain. In this respect, the world of knowledge exactly parallels other areas of human culture, as cultural sociologist Ann Swidler described in an oft-cited passage: "All people know more culture than they use" or could possibly use; in order to function, individuals mobilize "diverse cultural materials" in different ways, "appropriating some and using them to build a life, holding others in reserve, and keeping still others permanently at a distance."[17] To winnow among these different alternatives, Swidler continued, "people run through different parts of their cultural repertoires, selecting those parts that correspond to the situation or exemplary problem that currently holds their attention."[18]

Here Swidler's concern was with "people" in general, not specifically with those who, like Veblen, become major innovators in knowledge fields; but directing her observation to these people requires only minor adjustment. To make this adjustment, it is helpful to borrow a page from the theory of human conduct formulated by the American "pragmatist" philosophers of Veblen's own era and more recently elaborated on in the work of "neo-pragmatist" thinkers. This theory is relevant here because it draws a fundamental distinction between routine situations, in which people are able to achieve their goals as they have in the past, and situations that confront them with unexpected, unfamiliar complications that interfere with reaching their original objectives. From the pragmatist viewpoint, situations of the second type serve as significant catalysts of innovation because, as neo-pragmatist Hans Joas has explained, they are "situations which call for solutions"; they prompt individuals to launch a "creative search for new possibilities"—a search that, typically, homes in on a feasible solution only gradually, as the individuals involved struggle to define and overcome the problem by tapping some of the resources they have available.[19] These nonroutine situations occur, according to pragmatists, in all domains of social life. So, when they arise in knowledge fields, it follows that innovating knowledge producers, too, will seek to address the situations before them by sifting and sorting from among the instruments they have on hand—as these lie, as John Dewey put it, "waiting, like tools in a box, to be used by conscious resolve."[20]

In proposing this theory, pragmatists warn against treating what falls under the headers of "problem," "solution," and "tool" as if these were separate entities, neatly partitioned from one another and frozen in time. What constitutes a "problem" for a particular person is not some hard stone set off from the repertoire of resources and practices he or she has on hand. Situations crystallize into defined problems only in relation to the available stockpile of instruments; without this, individuals lack the wherewithal to conceive the complications they meet *as* problems amenable to solutions. The converse holds as well. "Solutions" are not a set of ready-made keys waiting for people to come looking for them. They are improvised and continuously revised courses of action that depend on how individuals have parsed problems, on which tools they have at their disposal, and on what kind of outcome they count as an acceptable solution—a Band-Aid, a revolution? Besides that, even tool sets lack fixity. The same implements that serve to accomplish today's tasks may fall short tomorrow, prompting users to adapt and modify their tool kits. "A tool," wrote Dewey, is "something to be improved by noting how it works."[21]

These pragmatist insights dovetail with the newer conception of knowledge that Science Studies scholars have proposed and that I adopt in my account of Veblen. Underpinning what knowledge specialists produce—their statements, or the problem solutions they eventually reach—are the practices and resources, the bundles of equipment and know-how, that knowledge specialists use to spot a problem situation and to attack it from the angle of their objectives. In this way, the processes involved in their innovations and the innovations themselves go hand in hand. The concept of "knowledge" involves both.

FIELD ENTRY

These observations conjure up a scene of knowledge makers working to solve problems—sometimes routine, sometimes novel—in their academic field by using the practices and resources they have available. Watching this scene, we may be interested in following the story forward in time, and we may also be intrigued about what led up to it, especially if we have good reason to believe—as we do in the instance of Veblen—that the backstory bears on the developing one. If knowledge involves repertories of practices and resources, where and how do knowledge producers acquire these repertories, and why do they differ from person to person? And if knowledge making involves tackling problems that arise in a particular field, how do aspiring knowledge producers wend their way to that field to begin with?

Social scientists who study knowledge fields have usually taken up their analysis in the middle of this sequence. Departing from this midpoint, they have tracked the story of knowledge specialists forward in time by examining their role in the struggles underway in their discipline over opposing truth claims. On the other hand, only rarely have researchers looked backward to earlier moments to understand why different knowledge producers have different intellectual repertoires at their disposal, how they land in their particular disciplines, and what forces shape these developments.

These questions concern what we might call *field entry*. This is a concept I want to introduce in order to direct attention to features and phases of the early careers of knowledge makers like Veblen. These include the processes that carry men and women to the entryway of their knowledge field and enable them to cross the threshold and go inside; they also involve the processes that prepare these new entrants to become full-fledged field members, participating in the intellectual battles taking place in their discipline. About these processes scholars who study knowledge making know relatively little, because their concern with disciplinary controversies has overshadowed research on what led up to the knowledge specialist's involvement in those controversies.[22]

We find this imbalance in the writings of both Pierre Bourdieu and Randall Collins. Focusing their theories of knowledge production on internal field struggles, the two authors skimp when it comes to earlier moments in the lives of knowledge producers—although they do touch on the topic.[23] Bourdieu observes, for example, that before individuals reach the field they will eventually occupy, they are already endowed with "dispositions" that set them on their "trajectory" and give them the intellectual and social "competence" to participate in their field once they arrive.[24] This is a valuable insight, but not one Bourdieu does much to develop. On his account, the individual's endowment of dispositions is an inheritance that is "principally determined" by general social background factors such as the individual's place of birth and the income, occupation, and religion of his or her parents.[25] Factors of this kind, however, are far too generic to shed much light on the origins of the particular intellectual tool sets that particular knowledge makers acquire in the course of the field-entry process.

Collins, for his part, digs deeper into this aspect of knowledge production.[26] His historical analysis of the field of philosophy shows that philosophers who formulated innovative ideas started out, almost invariably, as students at the feet of philosophers who themselves were major figures. (What drew either the students or their teachers to enter the field of philosophy in the first place, Collins does not say.)[27] By associating with eminent mentors, according to Collins, novice philosophers developed a feel for which philosophical issues mattered and which did not, a sense for which problems in the field had been solved and which were still open, and an understanding of how to build and dismantle a philosophical argument.[28] On these points, Collins's theory converges with recent research in Science Studies that likewise emphasizes the ways in which "educational infrastructure helps to shape the world of ideas" through the "formative training" that fledgling knowledge makers undergo in different historical periods.[29] One of these ways consists of apprentice-type relationships, which expose neophytes to "the intellectual and personal qualities" of a "charismatic" master.[30] Another pedagogical mechanism involves immersing novices in intensive drill work, so that they gain practice using the instruments, mechanical as well as theoretical, needed to participate in their discipline. According to Science Studies scholars, these educational experiences do more than transmit existing knowledge from one generation to the next; depending on the circumstances of the case, they can also call forth novel forms of knowledge.[31]

Despite these illuminating arguments, however, Collins and researchers in Science Studies take us only so far toward understanding the field-entry process, because they typically overlook the inescapable *time dimension*— the inherent temporality—of social experience.[32] Master-pupil relations, drill work, and other forms of training all have a duration on the clock, which is sometimes brief and sometimes long, sometimes continuous and sometimes interrupted. Not only that, but the start time of such pedagogical experiences sometimes happens early in the careers of future knowledge producers, while in other cases the start time occurs later. Further, pedagogical events are sequenced; they are preceded by and then followed by other educational experiences, which may convey congruent or discordant messages. We know from scholars in the area of "life course" research that the duration, timing, and sequencing of life events have lasting consequences for those who experience these events. We know, too, that the nature of these temporal elements varies for different individuals, for different social groups and generations, and in different historical eras.[33] Yet, so far as I am aware, none of these time factors has previously been specifically included in the study of knowledge production or related to the question of why knowledge producers bring particular repertoires with them when entering an academic field and joining the ranks of its members.

Faced with this void, we might take a lesson from life course researchers, who point out that capturing temporality requires the sociological study of biography: the "recognition that lives are influenced by an ever-changing historical and biographical context."[34] In making this point, life course researchers are not writing specifically about knowledge producers, but the researchers' argument provides, nevertheless, a useful bridge to the subject of intellectual biography. This is convenient at the outset of a book on the development of Thorstein Veblen's economic ideas, because if there is any area of scholarship where one might expect to learn how knowledge makers come to command the practices and other tools of their trade, biographical narratives would seem to be the place.[35]

The literature of intellectual biography disappoints these expectations, however, at the same time as it brings in its trail additional problems. If we go back to the 1970s and 1980s, intellectual biographies were an endangered species among social scientists and the humanists, who relentlessly attacked them for treating biographical subjects as unified entities separated from the cultural discourses and social institutions of which they were a part. More recently, however, the species has, in the assessment of historian Malachi Hacohen, "returned with a vengeance in most fields of history," dusted off and updated to address these critiques.[36] While this positive assessment probably exaggerates the revival of intellectual biography, there has been a wave of renovated studies of the lives of several major figures in the history of economics, and of other academic pioneers of Veblen's era, if not of Veblen himself.[37] As soon as we open them up, however, we find that most of the newer biographical accounts are thin when it comes to basic questions about how these men and women initially made their way into their intellectual fields and how they acquired the intellectual tools to innovate there. Moreover, many of these biographical accounts actually obscure those issues by lapsing into debatable narrative moves, which have also handicapped biographies of Veblen.[38]

For one, there is a marked tendency for biographies of economists and other social thinkers to abbreviate the education of these figures almost to the vanishing point. This holds true for education in the sense of formal schooling, as well as for informal learning experiences in the family, the local community, and so forth. Of these two components of education, the informal has fared slightly better, because it is standard practice for biographies of nineteenth-century intellectuals to include a few paragraphs on the personalities of the parents of the hero (or heroine) and their religious and social attitudes, as well as on conditions of the town where the subject grew up.[39] From this background information, the reader can sometimes make an informed guess about the intellectual resources the protagonist acquired before entering the wider world. Formal schooling, however, has received even less attention. The typical intellectual biographer will, to be sure, acknowledge that the protagonist received *some* early schooling, perhaps adding that the college he or she attended exuded a certain atmosphere (usually a conservative religious one), but often that is about all. For instance, in historian John Milton Cooper Jr.'s monumental biography of Woodrow Wilson, we hear only that, from childhood through college, the schools that Wilson attended "did not challenge his mind" and that in law school as well his "classwork bored him." One learns nothing about the substance of Wilson's studies until the fledgling political scientist, approaching age thirty, entered graduate school studying history at Johns Hopkins University (where, coincidentally, Veblen, who was Wilson's junior by one year, had studied the year before).[40] Historian Robert Westbrook's authoritative study of John Dewey (who was two years younger than Veblen and was another Hopkins graduate student) follows the same template. Although explicitly concerned with Dewey's intellectual "making," Westbrook's study suffices with observing that the "curriculum of the Burlington public schools" that Dewey attended was "woeful."[41] The entire subject of schooling then drops away until Dewey's later enrollment at the University of Vermont, where he was an undergraduate for a four-year period that Westbrook covers in as many paragraphs. It would be easy to cite other examples.

Sometimes the neglect of formal education makes sense because the protagonist did not attend school until late adolescence or early adulthood. This was the case with philosopher William James (Veblen's senior by twelve years), as well as with statistician and sometime economist Karl Pearson (Veblen's English contemporary, exactly his age). But home-schooling (even in elite families, like James's) was a dying institution in the United States in the postbellum era, when college attendance, along with postgraduate study, was on the rise among men, like Veblen, who were aiming for academic careers. Among those in *this* group, not only did formal education start in childhood (the "timing" factor of life course researchers), but it continued uninterrupted through a succession of schools (the "sequencing" factor) up to early adulthood (the "duration" factor), for a combined total of approximately twenty years. Although that total is slightly less than the total for academics today, the figure equals roughly a third of the life span of white American males who survived to age five in the second half of the nineteenth century.

Intellectual biographers give no rationale for treating these long formative years as ciphers, and it is hard to imagine how these scholars could defend the practice on substantive grounds, although there may be other reasons for its persistence. Cultural historian Louis Menand has observed that "biographers often operate on the . . . assumption that what is most private is most revealing," and biographers who study nineteenth-century thinkers may tacitly operate on this same assumption.[42] School lessons, after all, are no match for hidden secrets, so why drag readers through the tedium of the classroom? Then too, the intellectual biographer's preferred method of research is to hunt down and comb through the protagonist's unpublished writings and personal correspondence. Because future academics, even of the introspective nineteenth-century variety, rarely produced much material of this kind during their school years, this period necessarily slips through the mesh of the biographer's net, precluding a careful look into the phases of the field-entry process.

Beyond this nonchalant handling of education, moreover, biographies of economists (and other social thinkers) founder because they often superimpose onto the early lives of their protagonists certain standard plotlines that beg more questions than they answer about the relationship between the knowledge these men and women created and the years leading up to their academic careers. We observe this if we sort these standard plotlines into categories, which I will do here by differentiating *river narratives, watershed narratives,* and *overhang narratives.* Although no intellectual biographer speaks of "field entry" per se, each of these three biographical narratives amounts to a way of addressing the question of how knowledge producers are drawn to their fields and acquire the tools they eventually use to create new knowledge.

A *river narrative* depicts the early life of its protagonist as an onrushing stream of events, a deluge that sweeps up whatever lies in its path, or whatever in its path catches the biographer's eye: the religious affiliation of the protagonist's parents, the ideology of the political parties of the time, the titles of books popular with contemporaries, and so forth. Depending on the biographer's industriousness, a river narrative can easily become an everything-but-the-kitchen-sink account held together by the implicit assumption that when diverse currents meet something new somehow rises to the surface. Recent biographies of Veblen's younger contemporaries, economists John Maynard Keynes and Joseph Schumpeter, illustrate this approach.[43] But, again to quote Menand (writing about river-type accounts), "we may wonder whether the bits and pieces on which biographical narrative are often strung are not a little arbitrary."[44]

By comparison, *watershed narratives* are more chronologically organized. They center attention on some formidable rock that interrupted the cascading river of the hero's life and permanently altered its course. In particular, watershed stories spotlight the transformative event, circumstance, or "influence" that abruptly jolted, or more gradually veered, the protagonist into the fresh ways of seeing and thinking that subsequently defined his or her intellectual contributions. This narrative structure is another common trope in biographies of nineteenth- and twentieth-century economists.[45] Humanist Jeremy Adelman encapsulates it when he observes: "Biographers—indeed their subjects—often latch onto a formative moment, a turning point, an *eclat* after which the subject has changed and whose future consists of its direct effect. This can be a trauma, a book, an external event." Adelman criticizes this form of biography for its "tendency [to] oversimplify" the story of the hero's intellectual development and to overlook the less dramatic, more incremental "stockpiling" of resources in which he or she was engaged.[46]

Overhang narratives offer another familiar story line. What distinguishes them is that they situate the protagonist on a promontory point, at a high remove, social and intellectual, from his or her philistine contemporaries. According to this third trope, the protagonist is a spectator who (as a result of socially imposed or self-imposed isolation) stands apart, viewing the flotsam below with the onlooker's sharp-eyed detachment and declaiming heretical ideas that depart from the mainstream. Among Veblen's contemporaries, his teacher, philosopher Charles Sanders Peirce; his close friend, physiologist Jacques Loeb; and social psychologist Charles Horton Cooley have all been characterized by their biographers in these terms.[47] Versions of the overhang narrative have also been commonplace in the broader literature of intellectual historiography, where the metaphor of the detached outsider—or the marginal man, the stranger, the misfit—has been invoked to explain just about every innovation in the modern history of ideas.[48]

Now, there may be historical times and places that suit each of these plotlines. Considering them as accounts of the field-entry process, the three narratives (whether used singly or in combination) do accord, sometimes, with the early lives of innovative knowledge producers. More often than not, however, these biographical narratives miscarry because the biographer superimposes his or her story line onto the historical evidence without taking sufficient account of the temporality of life: without considering, for example, the sequencing of the episodes in the narrative, or at which point during the protagonist's early years these episodes occurred, or how long they lasted. Whether an experience occurred intermittently over a two-month period or ran uninterrupted for a decade, whether it started at age seven or age twenty-seven, whether it was bookended by similar or by dissimilar experiences, river-style biographers do not say—and apparently do not care. Indeed, so little do timing factors matter that most of the events in river narratives might just as well have happened all at once rather than in temporal succession. Rescramble the ordering of events A, B, and C, or allow them to happen concurrently instead of one after another—what difference does it make for understanding the protagonist's maturation into a producer of new knowledge?

Overhang-style accounts suffer from similar defects. They draw no distinction between whether the protagonist's time as an onlooker lasted for months or for years, or whether the time gazing down from the overhang was interspersed with periods when he or she was *not* situated at a distant remove from contemporaries. And only superficially are watershed narratives any more sensitive to time. To speak of a watershed is, of course, to acknowledge a sequence: prewatershed, watershed, postwatershed. But biographies of this type usually take no account of the start time or the relative duration of these chronological units—as if such time factors had no bearing on the story.

In none of the three narratives, however, is the omission of temporality a trivial oversight. For, whatever else it is, knowledge production is a process that happens in time and hinges on time. It does not occur apart from the hours, days, months, and years when future knowledge makers acquire their stockpile of intellectual tools and the know-how to go out on the disciplinary field and tackle new challenges. But what fills up this time?

REPETITION-WITH-VARIATION

Part of the answer to this question is *repetition,* which is a process stored in time. By definition, repetition is the reoccurrence at a later point in time of an experience that is the same as (or similar to) an experience that happened at a previous point. Without the inherent temporal element—without a division between before and after, or previous and later—repetition has no meaning.[49] When we speak of repetition, we mean that Experience 3 comes *after* Experience 2, which comes *after* Experience 1. If these experiences occur simultaneously, we are dealing with an entirely different situation. Speaking for a long tradition of continental philosophy, French philosopher Gilles Deleuze observed, a half-century ago, that experiences that are repeated do not simply "add a second and a third time to the first, but carry the first time to the 'nth' power."[50] Iteration 3, in other words, is not a discrete experience that we can understand on its own, as if it occurred outside the longer time series to which it belongs. Iteration 3 "echoes" (to use Deleuze's verb) Iteration 2 and Iteration 1, *and* it sounds as well Iteration 2 echoing Iteration 1—and onward and outward, as Iteration 4 echoes Iterations 3, 2, and 1, and also echoes each of these *as* each one (except the first) resounds each of its predecessors, as they resonate each of their predecessors, in a temporal snowball that gathers force with each successive repetition.

Continental philosophers have talked about repetition in the abstract—that's their job. Because this book is concerned with knowledge making by a real historical figure, however, I want to borrow the concept of repetition and put it to a more specific use. I want to examine the relationship between the *repetition of knowledge practices,* as this repetition occurs during the education of future knowledge producers, and the knowledge they produce after they become members of an academic field. In proposing this argument, I will be viewing field entry as a process during which novice knowledge makers encounter and apply certain knowledge-making practices repeatedly, cumulatively, raised to the nth power. As the novices do so, their use of those practices becomes something much more than an occasional experience; it turns into an everyday routine. Plied over and over again, those practices become the novice's way of tackling problems akin to problems where she or he has seen those practices used before. The repeated practices also equip the neophyte with tools to attack novel problems when they arise.

These effects are intensified when repetition occurs in the form that I will call *repetition-with-variation.*[51] I draw this expression from scholarship in the humanities that points out that only rarely are repeat experiences "mere" copies, or "exact" replicas, of prior experiences. Instead, although successive iterations may be roughly the same—that is why they are repetitions—they may still differ from one another, and in several ways. This is easy to see when we are talking about poetry, painting, or musical compositions. Setting side by side two artistic productions—from, say, the same artist or the same historical period—we notice their similarities at the same time as we spot their dissimilarities: repetitions combined with variations.

This situation has many analogues in the world of knowledge production. Consider the simplified example of a team of scientists that works away in its laboratory, day in and day out, using (let us say) Practice 1 to investigate Problem A. Here we have an instance of repetition, pure and simple (although each day still presents something a little different from the day before). But then the team wins a generous grant to study Problem B and another to study Problem C. Knowledge making hereafter takes on a new cast, as the scientists in the lab work to adapt Practice 1 to Problem B and then again to Problem C—so that when the scientists use familiar

Practice 1, they necessarily modify it, varying it this way, that way, another way. For there is actually no end to the twists that practice variations can take, no more than there are limits in poetry, painting, or music to possibilities for thematic variations.[52]

Increasing these possibilities further is the *spatial aspect* of knowledge production.[53] For novices, this is an especially important factor. Academic newcomers can train in one place—in, say, the laboratory of one mentor, conducting research in one disciplinary field, at one institution. Alternatively, newcomers can study with several mentors, crisscross different fields, and transfer from institution to institution. When geographical and intellectual movements like the latter take place, they have major ramifications for the process of repetition-with-variation, depending on how well aligned—how consistent with one another—different mentors, different disciplines, and different educational institutions are in their knowledge-making repertoires. Practice-wise, any two locations may be as unlike as night and day; but, then again, they may be more or less congruent, so that the knowledge practices the newcomer encounters at one destination echo the practices he or she has met at previous stopping points—though always with variations, because different mentors are *different* mentors, different disciplines are *different* disciplines, different institutions are *different* institutions.[54]

When repetition-with-variation occurs in this fashion, the novice learns that the practices and other knowledge tools used at one site are not unique to that particular site but are elastic. They have the capacity to stretch from one setting to another and to serve multiple intellectual purposes. From the neophyte's viewpoint, in other words, the tools apply not just to Problem A, Problem B, or Problem C; instead, they are transferable and transposable across a wide range of problems. And the more the novice meets variants of the same practices at one location after another, the more natural those particular practices become for the novice—until, sooner or later, they congeal into a kind of academic second nature, which the budding knowledge maker increasingly takes for granted as the right way to construct knowledge, regardless of the problem at hand.

One corollary of these points is that repetition is not the dead drag on creativity that the word often connotes. According to its everyday meaning, repetition is a process that perpetuates established ideas; by its very nature, it looks backward, not forward—it *repeats* what is already there. "Tradition," "conservation," "reproduction": these are the phenomena that sociologists and others typically associate with repetition, and rightly so in some situations.[55] But repetition-*with-variation* is something else again. Seventy-five years ago, sociologist Robert K. Merton called attention to the relationship between repetition-with-variation and the emergence of novelty—an insight that has since all but vanished from the social sciences.[56] I propose, however, that in regard to the question of how new knowledge originates, Merton's insight remains valuable. Insofar as repetition-with-variation conveys to novices that certain knowledge-making practices and resources are pliable, extendable, multipurpose tools, repetition-with-variation gives novices the means to try to overcome new obstacles where they arise—handing them the wherewithal to innovate.[57]

CASES LIKE THESE SUGGEST another biographical metaphor: not that of a river, or a watershed, or an overhang, but that of a *reservoir*. Out in nature, a reservoir is a catchment area that impounds the water and silt that flow into the area though many rivulets, which the rains have carved into the earth by the force of repetition. Once this occurs, the reservoir lies, waiting, until living creatures withdraw from it to meet their needs.[58] Sometimes future knowledge producers develop new ideas in a similar way, storing up the resources and practices that cumulatively come their way, through different channels of experience, by the process of repetition-with-variation. As the occasion arises, knowledge producers draw from this reservoir to confront the intellectual challenges before them. How and where they carry the water and sediment they draft remain for them to decide.

2.

The usefulness of the reservoir conceit for understanding the development of new knowledge depends on the presence of historical circumstances conducive to the process of repetition-with-variation. In post–Civil War America, such conditions were rife, especially at the places in the nation's landscape where Thorstein Veblen moved about. This is why the reservoir trope provides a helpful means to describe his making as an economist.

Previous biographies of Veblen have not taken this approach. Instead, they have depicted Veblen's intellectual development using river, watershed, and overhang narratives—most frequently the last of these three.

We see this in the grandparent of all accounts of Veblen's life and work, Joseph Dorfman's daunting (three-hundred-thousand-word) book, *Thorstein Veblen and His America*. First published in 1934, and still the most widely read study of its subject, this book interprets Veblen's oeuvre as the achievement of a socially "detached" academic "misfit," who lived in a state of "alienation" from his peers and functioned as a maverick and iconoclast: as a "spectator viewing life from a detached position" and with an attitude of "Olympian aloofness."[59] Or, as Dorfman worded this interpretation in some of his many later reiterations of it, Veblen was the archetypical social "outsider" who held a "Man from Mars vantage point" and scorned the perspective of the "Man in the Mainstream"; occupying a position at the margins of the "web of [his] society," he "was able to see it with unusual clarity, as a whole, from the outside."[60] Sometimes Dorfman attributed Veblen's social marginality—and resulting intellectual originality—to his upbringing on a culturally isolated farm of impoverished immigrants who spoke only Norwegian.[61] Other times Dorfman ventured that, from early childhood onward, Veblen was an "untamed and unconforming" personality, destined for "tragic maladjustment" to his surroundings.[62] And sometimes Dorfman reversed the order of the elements in his account by suggesting that Veblen's iconoclastic mind was the cause, rather than the consequence, of his social alienation.[63] Most often, however, Dorfman sufficed with the bald claim that "the particular kind of original, fundamental speculations offered us by Veblen" would not have happened "had he sprung from the main stream of our society" rather than from its remote margins.[64]

This interpretation long carried weight because of its vintage. Dorfman began research on his book in the mid-1920s when he was a graduate student in economics at Columbia University, where his mentors encouraged him to write as his dissertation an intellectual biography of Thorstein Veblen. Veblen was still alive, living and occasionally teaching in New York City, and most people familiar with him saw him through the lens of this period.[65] Characteristically, Veblen would not cooperate with the project; wanting no biography of himself written, he simply did not respond to Dorfman's letters.[66] Despite this rebuff, the resourceful doctoral candidate was able, as no later scholar would be, to interview and correspond with scores of people who knew Veblen personally, including family members, friends, and professional associates (many of whom quickly tired of Dorfman's leading questions).[67] The result of this research was a trove of material so voluminous that it seems sometimes to have overwhelmed Dorfman, leading him to resort, for large portions of his book, to a dizzyingly river-style narrative, in which he tossed all sorts of undigested information (and misinformation) about Veblen's life and times. Apparently the result did not entirely satisfy him (or his dissertation advisers); so to give the material the semblance of a unifying interpretation, Dorfman grafted onto it his Veblen-as-outsider thesis, which came to dominate his tome—and nearly all subsequent studies of Veblen.

In fact, from the mid-1930s to the mid-1990s, Dorfman's thesis stood as dogma, repeated nearly verbatim by dozens of authors attempting to explain the distinctive features of Veblen's thought. Some of these authors regarded Veblen as a thinker of rare insight, who made major theoretical contributions, while other commentators repudiated his theories as ill conceived and deeply flawed. But all parties agreed that to mention Veblen was to speak of an iconoclast whose heterodox ideas were shaped by his social position as an aloof outsider. We find this notion (as I mentioned in Chapter 1) in the work of prominent intellectuals like C. Wright Mills, Theodor Adorno, John Kenneth Galbraith, and Cornel West.[68] Over the years, we notice it as well in the writings of leading scholars such as economist Robert Heilbroner, who depicted Veblen as "an American by birth but a citizen of nowhere"; sociologist Daniel Bell, who summed Veblen up as "the 'outsider' all his life"; and the dean of American intellectual historians, Dorothy Ross, who characterized Veblen as "the only true outsider" of his intellectual generation.[69] As late as 1999, historian John Patrick Diggins recycled this interpretation, attributing Veblen's "iconoclastic" disposition and "originality" of mind to the fact that he was an enigmatic "misfit," an "intellectual wanderer" consigned to a "marginal" existence— "one of the strangest creatures ever to walk in the groves of academe."[70]

By this same date, however, both watershed-style and more elaborate river-style accounts of Veblen's intellectual development were becoming increasingly common, and this trend has continued. Historian Rick Tilman and his collaborators, for instance, have by now spent more than three decades developing the contention that Veblen's thought arose from a diverse "multitude of sources," including "the big sweep of American industrialization," the utopian writings of novelist Edward Bellamy, the lab experiments of physiologist Jacques Loeb, and so on.[71] Other scholars, meanwhile, have singled out some particular watershed episode in Veblen's career—for example, his encounter with the ideas of Charles Darwin, or Herbert Spencer, or anthropologists E. B. Tylor and Franz Boas (and so forth)—as the decisive turning point, or influence, in the evolution of Veblen's ideas.[72]

Strong attacks on Dorfman's narrative have also been launched by scholars aiming to revise his error-laden depiction of the Veblen family as culturally isolated, monolingual, and poor, as well as his "pathography" of Veblen as a psychologically maladjusted personality.[73] Significantly, however, it is at this point that the revisionists have generally wound down their assaults on Dorfman's marginality thesis. In doing so, they have kept alive variants—some stronger, some weaker—of the now almost ninety-year-old contention that Veblen was an academic outsider. We see the tenacity of this claim in Tilman's continuing characterization of Veblen as "a marginal man and perennial outsider," as well as in the persisting efforts of leading Veblen scholars to attribute his ideas to his status as a "misfit"—a "stranger" in the academic world of his time.[74]

A crippling feature of many of these accounts, going back to Dorfman's original, is the haziness of their central argument. Like the intellectual biographers discussed above, Veblen's interpreters have ignored the historical clock, neglecting the duration, timing, and sequencing of experiences, such as his encounter with Darwin, his contact with the "big sweep of industrialization," and so forth. In addition, these accounts often are nebulous about which aspect of Veblen's thought they are seeking to explain. Like many nineteenth-century writers, "Veblen's thought" was an amalgam of philosophical premises, ethical presuppositions, political and social commentaries, historical and ethnological information, and views on a wide range of biological, psychological, sociological, and economic subjects. To try, as Dorfman and many other authors have done, to subsume all these different strands under a single all-purpose explanation of the connection between Veblen's life and ideas obscures more than it clarifies.[75]

IN THIS BOOK, I am concerned not with Veblen's ideas en bloc, but specifically with the ideas at the center of his writings in the field of "political economy"—or "economics," as we would now say. Turning the spotlight here focuses attention on the subject that Veblen, as well as his contemporaries, saw as his main interest; and, on this point, the majority of later interpreters have agreed, even when their own emphasis has fallen elsewhere. Because of my concern with Veblen's economics, I construct my narrative with an eye out for the practices and resources that underpinned this specific pillar of his work; my aim is not to track all the other intellectual acquisitions he picked up in the course of his education. To come at the story from this angle is not, however, to impose a teleology on the development of Veblen's work in political economy. For had contingent historical circumstances (opportunities, obstacles, and choices) landed him in a field besides economics, as they could well have done, Veblen might never have used these practices and resources at all, and certainly not in the ways he did.

Even in terms of his work in economics itself, moreover, the equipment Veblen wielded consisted of many diverse pieces—many more than I discuss in this book. My analysis is selective, among other reasons because if there is any general consensus among scholars who have studied his ideas, it is that Veblen, in building his economics, relied heavily on *four knowledge-making practices:*[76]

1. The practice of viewing the world—whether the natural world or the social world—as continually undergoing *change* rather than as timeless.
2. The practice of perceiving the world in *holistic categories* rather than in atomized units.
3. The practice of valuing *productive work* above other types of human activity.
4. The practice of esteeming *new forms of human knowledge* over traditional forms.

Later chapters will put some meat on the skeletal words that I have italicized here, though I would warn against trying to attach a single, uniform meaning to any of them. Every one of these concepts has taken on different meanings and associations in different historical contexts. In Veblen's own work, we will see specific versions of these ideas when he writes about (1) *evolution,* (2) *organic social institutions,* (3) *productive activities,* and (4) *modern science.* At this point in the book, I mention these ideas only to flag them for special notice as the narrative unfolds.

BEFORE VEBLEN APPLIED THESE intellectual practices in the field of political economy, however, he already had them firmly in his grip as a result, in part, of the process of repetition-with-variation. That is my argument. From childhood onward, these were intellectual tools he encountered again and again—in different forms, to different degrees, and with different valances attached—and he met them wherever he went. These reiterations happened, furthermore, not simply because the four practices were, as historians used to say, hanging "in the air" (although in some ways they were). More consequently, these practices constituted Veblen's terra firma; they soaked the intellectual ground he traipsed, day in and day out, at the places where he was schooled and as he moved from place to place. What is more, these recurrences were not coincidental; they had strong historical foundations. It is because Veblen grew up when and where he did that his experiences were saturated by repetition-with-variation to an especially high degree.

We see this most directly when we consider his education, and his formal schooling in particular. Curiously, this is not a subject that previous accounts of Veblen's development—whether structured as a river, watershed, or overhang narrative—have examined. Like intellectual biographers generally, most Veblen scholars have preferred to skip school, dispensing with the long formative years of Veblen's life in a few paragraphs, sometimes in a few sentences.[77] Yet, when we probe these early years and view them in the context of American society in second half of the nineteenth century, we observe how much repetition-with-variation marked Veblen's time and place. This was so for several reasons, three of which I want briefly to preview here.

First, in this era teachers still relied heavily on what they called the "method of recitation." They organized instruction around standardized "readers" in subject areas such as grammar, history, geography, science, and mathematics, expecting that students would learn about these subjects by memorizing textbook passages and then "reciting" them—repeating them—while teachers watched for accuracy and then posed a few basic questions about sentences in the texts. Deep into the nineteenth century, this ancient method of learning by rote was the dominant pedagogical technique in American educational institutions at all levels (common schools, classical schools, most colleges, and even certain postgraduate courses), and students whose schooling lasted several years, as Veblen's did, typically walked away imbued with the ways of thinking displayed in the readers they had memorized and regurgitated. In the case of Veblen, this learning experience would seem to count against my argument that his education helped equip him with tools he eventually used in his writings, since repeating passages from the texts that made up traditional curricula would hardly appear to offer relevant preparations for a career of intellectual innovation. As we will see, however, sometimes these curricula were more pliable, more in sync with the times, than our historical assumptions lead us to expect.

Second, changes in American higher education that took place in the last three decades of the nineteenth century were favorable to repetition-with-variation: most significantly, the emergence of research universities and, as part of this development, the establishment of postgraduate programs in an ever-expanding number of academic fields. Under other historical circumstances, organizational changes of this kind would scarcely have caused an increase in repetition of the four knowledge-making practices listed earlier. But this increase is exactly what did happen, as university growth unleashed a frenzy of cross-institutional imitation. American university presidents were driven to this behavior because they lacked models for how to organize a research university. Faced with this problem, they looked to one another and, more importantly, to Europe—to Germany in particular, which was then the leading exporter of blueprints for university building. Conveniently, too, young scholars eager to import the German model stood ready; for, before postgraduate programs were up and running in the United States, college graduates seeking advanced research training had little choice but to go abroad to continue their studies. So, from the 1860s onward, American students flocked to Europe, where they found—especially when working with members of the flourishing German historical school—a repertoire of knowledge practices that revolved around evolutionary change, the organic nature of society, the value of work-oriented activities, and the importance of new scientific knowledge. When these German-educated students returned to the United States and assumed faculty positions, they inevitably carried this repertoire into America's new universities, stocking all of them with similar intellectual tools. This transformation proved consequential for Veblen, who stayed in the United States for postgraduate training and studied at four different universities that were built along German lines and dedicated to German ideas about knowledge making.[78]

A third conduit of repetition-with-variation was the national stage. Evolution, society as an organic entity, the imperative of work, and the value of scientific knowledge: these were more than items in a tool set imported from German universities. In America during the postbellum era, they were staple themes in a wide range of social and cultural debates, which were carried on in the press, in meetings of political and religious groups, and in everyday conversations in local gathering spots. Modern historians have, in fact, characterized the final decades of the nineteenth century, variously, as the "Age of Evolution," the age of "the Discovery of Society," the age of "the Primacy of Work," and the "Age of Science."[79]

All the same, one has to be cautious about overreaching with these expressions, since many Americans of that time were out of step with these ways of thinking, if not oblivious to them. How specific individuals responded to the views that were circulating about evolution, society, and so on, differed according to their personal life histories—and here Veblen had a distinctive one. His long years of training in a particular set of intellectual practices effectively primed his own reaction, raising the salience of these ideas when they echoed in newspapers, magazines, books, and other channels of public discussion and debate. For him, these media served as another mechanism for repetition-with-variation.

THESE ASPECTS OF VEBLEN'S historical context bring us back to the subject of a writer's intellectual persona: the style and demeanor that authors project to their audiences. Veblen came of age as a scholar during what his contemporaries often called, proudly, the "Age of Iconoclasm."[80] The mantra was telling; for we ordinarily think of iconoclasm as an oppositional stance, adopted by isolated outsiders who train a critical eye on the accepted conventions of people on the inside of the institutions of their society. Overhang-type narratives of Veblen illustrate this agonistic conception of iconoclasm. In Veblen's own time, however, iconoclasm was not a deviant posture that inherently went against the intellectual grain; it was a style of argument and expression that formed an established convention in its own right, at least in prominent intellectual circles, both lay and academic. As gentleman scholar George Rogers Howell explained in 1895: "This may be called the age of iconoclasm because it dares to attack any and all questions in the physical universe, and in mental and moral philosophy; the age takes nothing for granted."[81]

Some contemporaries recoiled from this combative, controversialist approach, sharing the opinion of jurist Irving Browne, whose 1885 book *Iconoclasm and Whitewash* despaired that "the iconoclast . . . has undertaken to demolish the whole human race" by knocking over all of its historical heroes (from Homer to Columbus to Washington) and replacing them with, among other false gods, the evolutionary theories of Darwin and his followers.[82] But the majority of American intellectuals trumpeted iconoclasm as a practice that actually produced new knowledge and spread its fruits. Speaking for this contingent in the 1889 issue of the *North American Review,* for example, Percy Douglas, a popular essayist, celebrated iconoclasm as the "national idiosyncrasy" that had made America "the most progressive nation on the face of the earth." This triumph Americans had accomplished, in Douglas's view, by "destruction and revision . . . two most potent weapons of progress," the instruments that raze "outworn ideas and ideas," "old institutions and traditions," and clear the way for "the newer thought of our own age." Even so, according to Douglas and like-minded writers, unfinished business remained, because "there is still a great work for the American iconoclast to do in politics, art, science, commerce, sociology, and religion."[83]

This opportunity was not lost on university presidents and the members of their faculties as they set about to make their young institutions places for the production of new knowledge. For this "great work" was exactly the objective they aimed to achieve, in tune with the "spirit of iconoclasm."[84] As Veblen commented midway into his career, the ideal university is (or should be) the preserve of iconoclasm, in the natural sciences and the social sciences alike.[85] Still further, it was a knowledge practice that Veblen's teachers, both traditionalist and antitraditionalist, espoused and used in multiple knowledge fields, as he witnessed firsthand. In this way, an iconoclastic style became a component in Thorstein Veblen's own knowledge-making repertoire, not because he was a detached outsider but rather because he was an experienced insider to the academic world of his time.[86]

CHAPTER 3

BEGINNINGS

1.

A half-century before Thorstein Veblen sat writing about the foundations of economic theory in a comfortable academic enclave on the South Side of Chicago, a flat new city already fraying with industrial decay, Thomas and Kari Veblen, his parents, lived unsettled and uncertain, surrounded by immovable mountain ranges, in the ancient Valdres region of south-central Norway. Newlyweds with dim economic prospects in their thickly forested birthplace, they were looking elsewhere to build their future lives. So, in spring 1847, they secured from their local Lutheran minister permission to leave the region and to join with two other couples from the Vang Parish about to set out for America. Departing almost immediately, Thomas and Kari arrived in the United States some four and a half months later, after a brutal four-thousand-mile trip.

These dates of travel place the Veblens early among the nearly seventy-eight thousand emigrants from Norway who moved to the United States before the end of the Civil War. In this period, only Ireland sent more, though it was not hunger but a severe shortage of arable land that motivated the Norwegians to emigrate.[1] Theirs was a peasant economy with little tillable acreage still available for those who aspired to be independent farm owners: *bønder,* as they were called. Between 1815 and 1865, Norway's population doubled in size while its area stayed the same. This disparity prevented the offspring of landless families from moving up into the *bonde* class and forced downward children of propertied families who were not inheritors. In this way, the land shortage threw many Norwegians either into the intermediate class of *husmenn* (cotters leasing small plots on *bønder* estates) or other tenants, or into the swelling ranks of day laborers who worked in the fields (or in lumbering, mining, or handicraft).[2]

The country's rising agricultural productivity and expanding foreign trade ensured that few people went hungry; but, despite signs of capitalist development in urban areas and coastal districts, midcentury Norway remained a predominately rural society, still based more on barter than on monetary exchanges. Its economic opportunities paled when compared with those the mountaineers heard about in the missives they received from the advance team of countrymen who had already gone to America. Passed from household to household, copied hundreds of times, these "America letters" unleashed "America fever"—these were contemporary expressions—as friends and relatives in the United States told those back home about how "fertile fields lie uncultivated in America," and about how "every poor person who will work diligently and faithfully can become a well-to-do man here in a short time," to quote a letter from one Knud Syalestuen, writing in 1842 from Vernon, Wisconsin (only eighty miles from where the Veblens would settle seven years later).[3]

Added to the push and pull of economic opportunities was the growing antipathy many ordinary Norwegians felt toward the people at the top of their country's recently reshuffled social hierarchy. Prior to the nineteenth century, the boundary between *bønder* and *husmenn* (and other lessees) was relatively loose. *Husmenn* might rise to *bonde* status, for example, by clearing and claiming uninhabited land in the north of Norway, just as *bønder*, when burdened with debt, might fall in social position as they sold off their properties.[4] Besides, as a consequence of strong traditions of communalism, *bønder, husmenn,* and day laborers might work and eat side by side during peak agricultural seasons, and all of them might pitch in to lend mutual assistance in times of need.[5] However, these customs and practices were fast retreating in the early nineteenth century. By this time, as historian Lowell Soike has observed, "a wide social gulf separated those who owned land from those who did not," and, in some regions of the country, "no servant, laborer, or cotter had much hope of ever rising to become a *bonde*." What is more, large cracks were developing within the *bonde* class, as it bifurcated between peasant freeholders, who cultivated modest plots of land by themselves or with the help of a few men and boys, and the wealthy owners of great estates, who relied on the work of dozens of *husmenn* and farm laborers.[6]

Exacerbating these social divisions, and also pushing the landless in the direction of migration, was the political structure that took shape following Norway's forced union, in 1814, with Sweden (under the Swedish crown). With the political unification of the two countries came a new constitution for Norway that devolved state power and authority onto a small echelon of high-ranking state officials, university-educated professionals (lawyers, clergymen, and so on), leading industrialists and merchants, and owners of large landed estates.[7] From the viewpoint of the broader Norwegian populace, subjugation to this elite was a chronic affront, felt most directly through government policies that favored special elite interests.[8] But even more galling to the commoners, the people who belonged to the country's upper tier openly flaunted their superior position, brandishing their status by prominent displays of their cultivation and education (their "refined" speech, etiquette, and manner of dress), as well as by their lavish spending and aversion to hands-on labor.[9] An 1850 article in one of the country's leading newspapers captured growing public perceptions of the elite when it caricatured the wealthy landowner as a *sofabonde*—couch *bonde*—and decried the economic and social inequalities that made possible these offending lifestyles. The article read: "We literally live in a topsy-turvy world. Not only do those who work hardest get least, but what is even more striking: those who do everything are abused and called tramps, wretches, etc. He who sits immobile in his sofa and smokes tobacco and otherwise does nothing, lives so well that he gets sick."[10] According to historian Peter Munch, part of America's appeal to mid-nineteenth-century Norwegians was the promise of "freedom from conventional differentiations of status" that were hardening in their own society.[11]

THIS MEDLEY OF MOTIVES, which would subsequently drive legions of these men and women to migrate to the United States, was already at work in the thinking of Thomas Anderson Veblen (age twenty-nine; born 1818) and Kari Bunde Veblen (age twenty-two; born 1825) by early 1847. Writing to Joseph Dorfman many years later, Andrew Veblen—Thomas and Kari's oldest son and Thorstein Veblen's oldest brother—explained Thomas's calculus. "Father often spoke of the reasons for his emigration. He looked for better opportunity for himself and mother in America, materially, socially, politically, and intellectually. (Socially, because in the old country there was not any real chance of getting ahead materially.)"[12] Filling in the backstory to this explanation, Andrew traced both branches of his family to native *bonde* roots that went back before the Reformation: for generations, the Veflen and Bunde farms had loomed large on the Valdres landscape—the names of the two families were carved into the side panels of the front pews of the local church. Moreover, according to Andrew's genealogy, men from both sides of the family always "stood well in the esteem of the community [and] belonged to the specially industrious and dependable portion of the body of citizens."[13] This is a statement one probably should treat as little more than a family legend, but a legend that Andrew and his siblings evidently regarded as a historical fact.

By the late eighteenth century, however, younger sons on both sides of the family fell from landowners to renters because of primogeniture rules combined with deteriorating economic conditions, which left them unable to purchase lands of their own. In this way, Andris Veblen—Thomas's father and Thorstein Veblen's paternal grandfather—"lost his patrimony and became a poor man," who never rose from the precarious status of a lessee.[14] Even so, he made sure that Thomas attended common school until age fourteen (the age of confirmation). At twenty-two, Thomas entered five years of required military service, and in the years in between he learned the trade of carpentry and cabinetmaking, by which he mainly supported himself. The whole time, Thomas had, Andrew tells us, "only his two hands as capital."[15] When he partnered to do carpentry work with his army friend Steffen Olsen Helle, Thomas was initially too poor to buy his own tools, so he had to rent Steffen's. Sizing up their long-term economic prospects if they remained in Norway, Steffen and Thomas laid tentative plans to emigrate to America. Steffen, the more prosperous of the two, then undertook reconnaissance, traveling to the United States in 1846 to scout out possibilities in southern Wisconsin, which he probably heard about through a few Norwegians already in the area.[16] Once there, Steffan almost immediately acquired land and began proselytizing on behalf of his new country, spreading "America fever" to Thomas and dozens of others back in Valdres just as fast as the virus would carry.

In the same year, Thomas, saving up for the cost of transatlantic passage, married Kari Thorsteinsdatter Bunde, whose distinguished family line had also been on a choppy downhill economic course (although Kari too had attended the local common school). Starting out, the young couple leased a crofter's farm, situated on traditional Veflen lands, and awaited the birth of their first child, a son who died in infancy in April 1847.[17] A few days later, Thomas and Kari left Valdres for Drammen, a seaport on Norway's southeastern coast, where they joined the other emigrating couples from the Vang Parish.[18] From there they sailed on *Den Gode Mening* ("The Good Intention") to Hamburg, Germany, where the ship's captain, who had promised them passage across the Atlantic, abandoned the Norwegians, leaving them stranded until the captain of a small whaling tub, *Haabet* ("The Hope"), agreed to take them on to Quebec. This portion of the journey, most of it on violent seas, lasted for another three months, during which time the group's food supplies nearly gave out and all the young children on board died. When the vessel finally reached Quebec, the Veblens were both seriously ill; Thomas so much so that he was almost quarantined. Still, once past customs officials, he and Kari (and their travel party) resumed their journey, going by boat across the Great Lakes to Milwaukee, Wisconsin, where they landed, in mid-September 1847, with their resources down to $3 ($97 in 2020 dollars).[19]

2.

Without a break in the action, this drama of a hard-driving immigrant family then continued, almost as if it were scripted to illustrate the mythology of the Great Atlantic Migration to the United States. From the time of the Veblens' landing, moreover, there already coursed through the saga many of the defining currents of nineteenth-century American economic history: industrialization (concentrated still in the northeast and mid-Atlantic states, but spreading fast); technological invention and the mechanization of production (in factories and farms); urbanization (along inland waterways); westward territorial expansion (made possible by the wholesale destruction of native peoples and the natural environment); and mass immigration, not only from Scandinavian countries, but in even greater numbers from Ireland and Germany.[20] Gaining strong momentum at the time Thomas and Kari Veblen arrived in the Upper Midwest, these insistent changes would always be a part of their daily lives and those of their children.[21]

Most immediately, however, the Veblens had their sights set on farming, which was then the dominant sector of the American economy and would continue as such until after the Civil War. During these years, farmland was both cheap and abundant in the territories on the nation's frontier, such as Wisconsin and Minnesota, because federal land policies were designed to keep land prices low and to limit the size of homesteads. Under the terms of the 1841 General Preemption Act, buyers could acquire 160 acres (the maximum amount) of pristine land for a cash payment of $1.25 (=$38) per acre. It was under this generous policy that Steffen Helle, Thomas's former carpentry partner, acquired his landholdings in the newly recognized state of Wisconsin, and the Veblens soon did the same, although they had a rougher time coming up with the necessary cash.

Even so, history dealt them an unprecedented hand, at least if we take seriously the research of scholars concerned with the distribution of wealth within societies. Researchers who write about our own society tell us, for instance, that in the middle of the second decade of the twenty-first century, the wealthiest 1 percent of Americans held roughly 40 percent of the nation's wealth, while the top 5 percent held 67 percent. Historians who study the colonial period give different (though somewhat similar) figures: in 1774, the richest 1 percent claimed a 28 percent share of the country's wealth, and the richest 5 percent a 63 percent share.[22] The statistics for these two periods are not comparable because they are based on different kinds of data and analyzed by different statistical methods. Several years ago, however, economic historians Jeremy Atack and Fred Bateman calculated, for the pre–Civil War period, two pairs of statistics that are comparable because they derive from the same data and methods. Using information from the federal manuscript census of 1860, Atack and Bateman found that, in the United States as a whole at this date, the upper 1 percent claimed roughly 25 percent of the nation's wealth, and that the upper 5 percent held 54–57 percent; whereas in the rural Upper Midwest (where the Veblen family then lived), the top 1 percent of the population had 11.2 percent of the wealth, while the top 5 percent had 30.1 percent—a much flatter wealth distribution, comparatively speaking. Now, a society in which the richest 5 percent commands nearly a third of the wealth is, quite obviously, a far cry from a world where wealth shares are equally divided among the members of the society—if we take that form of wealth division as our gold standard (as we might want to do on various moral grounds). Nevertheless, thinking of societies not as they might be arranged but as they actually have been arranged over the course of history, Atack and Bateman reached a striking conclusion from their statistical analysis:

> Equality was a nineteenth-century American watchword. Nowhere were conditions riper for attaining the egalitarian ideal than in the antebellum rural North. *Was it achieved? Probably.* [The situation was] not perfect, [since] even the egalitarian economy had its blemishes. That should not detract from the basic reality . . . that the ideal was *more nearly realized in the rural northern United States than elsewhere in human history* about which we have substantial knowledge.[23]

We may certainly doubt that there was anyone on America's farmlands in the nineteenth century who walked around knowing this quantitative fact—if we accept all of Atack and Bateman's statistical evidence. All the same, it is useful to bear in mind that Thomas and Kari's son Thorstein—who was born shortly before 1860 and whose later writings center on making sense of wealth-share differences—grew up in a milieu that was a historical outlier both in its pattern of wealth distribution and in the direction of more, rather than less, equality of distribution.

Probably unique in this way, midwestern farming in the mid-nineteenth century had another distinguishing feature, which was not quite so unusual from a wide historical angle, but is pertinent for understanding the Veblens and the work of their son. A future critic of classical and marginalist economic theories that rested on atomistic premises, Thorstein Veblen grew up in a period when agriculture in the Midwest hinged on an economic institution that, scholars argue, significantly confounds those theories. That institution was the "self-sufficient" family farm that produced what household members needed to feed, clothe, and house themselves (with some level of comfort), while also producing surpluses of grain, meat, dairy items, and so forth for sale on the market.[24] Simple-sounding enough, this institution had two noteworthy features. First, as Atack and Bateman explain, the self-sufficient household farm was "an engine of family and social organization."[25] Working for the benefit of the family as a collective unit, it functioned in ways that deviated from the individualistic model of "the quintessential economic man."[26] Second, according to sociologist Harriet Friedmann, the self-sufficient family farm "involves only one [social] class, which both owns the means of production and provides the labor power to set them in motion." As such, it is an arrangement that slips through the economist's differentiated "cost categories" of wages and profits, exposing these categories as applicable to only one form of economic production: "capitalist production."[27] Thorstein Veblen, in his turn-of-the-century writings, would press a similar critique.

But, then again, Veblen had the self-sufficient family farm in his blood. It is what his parents worked to build when they came to the United States, and it is where they would raise him. During their first two years after arriving in Milwaukee, Thomas and Kari Veblen moved four times (helped sometimes by Steffen Helle), as they climbed upward economically. In late 1849, they relocated for a fifth time, moving to a property in Sheboygan County, Wisconsin, where they intended to settle. By the time of this move, their son Andrew had been born, and the family had been joined by Thomas's brother Haldor, a bachelor, who became a permanent member of their household.[28] However, as the result of complicated land transactions, Thomas and Haldor found themselves with a 160-acre parcel in a remote and heavily forested area of Sheboygan County that proved too difficult to clear for extensive farming. Even so, as Andrew Veblen recounted, the Veblen brothers managed, within a few years, to "develop . . . the land into a farm that was yielding a good living, and which was considered a model farm."[29] They were able to realize the substantial sum of $1,600 (=$51,800) when they sold the property in 1854.[30] This allowed the family to move further north to the recently settled and fast-growing township of Cato, in Manitowoc County (forty miles shy of Green Bay), where they eventually owned a two-hundred-acre homestead and farmed for the next eleven years.[31] Here, after two daughters and another son, Thomas and Kari's sixth child, Thorstein Bunde Veblen, was born on July 30, 1857.[32]

In one of his letters to Dorfman, Andrew described the farm that the Veblens built in Cato, Wisconsin:

> The farm was a "self-supporting unit." . . . All farms were more or less such, if well handled. It depended on the native and acquired skill and ingenuity of the farmer, how far this ideal was carried out. My parents were both rather more skilled than their neighbors, in the various processes that such a system of farming called for; and theirs was an outstanding case of "self-sufficiency." . . . In Norway the farms were particularly "self-sufficient units," and thus the immigrants were well trained in this system, [giving them] a distinct advantage over many other pioneers, that had less of this method of preparation.[33]

In recent years, Andrew's account has been corroborated by economist William Melton, whose research clarifies that "self-sufficient" was not the same as insular.[34] The Veblen farm was also deeply embedded in external market relationships, something about which people from rural Norway knew almost nothing prior to emigrating to America.[35] Like many other midwestern farms, though, the Veblens' farm, as soon as it was up and running, began producing more wheat (its primary product) and other foodstuffs than family members could consume. This left surpluses available for sale on the market. Behind these surpluses were Thomas's "interest and energy [in] the business of farming" (Andrew again), combined with soil conditions that, once cultivated, were ideal for growing wheat, oats, and other cereals.[36] As Andrew recalled: "The policy followed by Thomas Veblen was to get the land to . . . yield as much as possible. I have heard him characterized as the sort of farmer who made every square foot of available soil produce."[37] To accomplish this, not only did he and Haldor take on the rough physical labor of clearing, planting, and harvesting their acres, but Thomas also harnessed other people in the household to work alongside them. These included his sons, when they were of the right age and not in school, and a number of newly immigrated Norwegian men—some two dozen of them over the years—whom the Veblens took into their household and helped acclimate to the United States, while the men provided extra hands in the fields.[38] In addition, Thomas kept abreast of new farming technologies, taking the local lead in adopting inventions, such as the "combined thresher and winnower," which streamlined wheat production.[39]

As a midwestern grain grower, however, Thomas's connection to the economic universe beyond the rural hinterlands did not end with his purchases of new farm equipment. By the time his family moved to Cato, this remote frontier area, like scores of others, was already enmeshed in the international economy. This was because, as historian William Cronon has shown, the farmlands of the Upper Midwest were by then functioning as leading suppliers for markets in the Northeast and in Europe. These farmlands were (seemingly) limitless sources of the lumber and the grain that populations outside the Midwest demanded, and which the waterways and railways were increasingly capable of transporting from the outback to the entrepôt of Chicago and, from there, to all points east.[40] Just two years before the Veblens arrived in Cato, for instance, one nearby village shipped logs equivalent to ten million feet of lumber to the Chicago market, while wheat exports from the county rose 630 percent during the decade the Veblens lived there, even without any available railroad connection to Chicago.[41]

We do not know, of course, how much of this local growth was attributable to the Veblens' own farm, nor how directly involved the Veblen brothers were in exporting wheat to the Chicago market. Most likely their involvement was relatively modest, especially compared with what it became after they moved in the mid-1860s to Rice County, Minnesota, which was linked to Chicago by rail.[42] All the same, regardless of the intensity of the contacts between specific midwestern farmers and the Chicago market, the centripetal forces of this "speculative boomtown" proved unstoppable. On an almost daily basis, the city sucked rural wheat growers into the capitalist whirlpool of industrial and financial empire builders, owners of grain elevators, traders in "futures" on the Chicago Board of Trade, and the growing phalanx of midlevel business managers and commercial middlemen.[43] Rare, moreover, were farmers who welcomed these changes. Just the opposite: farmers routinely denounced them, in the spirit voiced by Joseph Medill, the Chicago newspaper editor, who wrote in 1870 about how the members of Chicago's grain establishment "form the grand ring, that wrings the sweat and blood out of the producers, [as] the great, laborious, patient ox, the farmer, is bitten and bled, harassed and tortured, by these rapacious, blood sucking insects."[44]

This suspicious way of thinking about the new economic realities outside the self-sufficient farm came naturally to rural Norwegian-Americans in the mid-nineteenth century.[45] Such thinking fit with the hostile attitude they brought with them from Norway toward capitalists and other elites, and echoed the warnings about unsavory speculators sounded in popular Norwegian-language guidebooks for American settlers.[46] And it accorded with what historian Laurence Larson has described as the Norwegian-American's ingrained sense "that he was being exploited by the native element," that "too often the banker, the lawyer, the wheat buyer, and other 'smart' business men coined good money from his ignorance of American ways."[47] This belief was a strong theme in the Norwegian-American newspapers found around the Veblen household.[48] And it was a belief underscored by Thomas's own dealings with slippery Wisconsin land speculators and small-town merchants and millers, as well as with local government officials who, for example, imprisoned Haldor for several months on charges of a theft he did not commit.[49] Adding to these grievances was what Andrew Veblen called the "robbery" of the Veblen surname, when local tax collectors, poll-list keepers, and other county agents, confused by Norwegian naming practices, "forced on father"—for the entire duration of the family's time in Cato—the unwanted name of Thomas *Anderson*.[50]

In addition to the larger economic factors that led the Veblens to uproot from Sheboygan to Cato, there was what Andrew described as the family's "racial isolation." Or, as he elaborated:

> The country all about the Veblens [in Sheboygan County] became settled by immigrants from Holland. . . . Of course these were most excellent people and formed a model community. But among them

the Veblens found themselves strangers, who could have no inter-course with their neighbors, except in their own very limited En-glish, of which the neighbors knew even less than they. There was no prospect that the difficulty ever would be much mitigated so far as their own generation might be concerned. And for the children who were to be reared, the outlook was culturally and socially dis-couraging. . . . There were no opportunities for satisfying religious and spiritual needs of such observations as the grownups had been trained to look on as essential or had become traditional.[51]

Regarding these needs, though, Cato had much more to offer them. Like many international migrants today, most nineteenth-century Norwe-gian immigrants came to the United States not on solo missions but as members of interlinked social groups. Their movements followed a pat-tern in which a small band of pioneers emigrates to a new country and, once settled in an area, encourages and assists others back home—relatives, friends, friends of friends—to migrate to the same area, thereby spawning a second, usually larger, cohort of immigrants, which then entices a third cohort of settlers to move to the area, and so on. Fueling this process, in the case of Norwegians, were the "America letters," plus the actions of first movers like Steffen Helle, who attracted Thomas and Kari Veblen to Wisconsin and soon lured others from the same Valdres region of Norway. By the end of the 1840s, many of these Valdres migrants had settled in Manitowoc County, Wisconsin, alongside groups of German, Irish, and New England pioneers, who before long were joined also by Scottish, En-glish, French Canadian, and Polish immigrants.[52] (Politically, the poly-glot county was more homogeneous, voting mostly for Democrats but supporting the new Republican Party's antislavery platform.) The Nor-wegians concentrated in the midsection of the county, which eventually became so well populated with *Valdriser* that local government authori-ties eventually made "Valders" its official name.[53] This area of Norwe-gian settlement abutted Cato, where the Veblens moved to be close to families from their region of Norway.[54]

Ethnic settlements like this held a strong appeal for families from Norway and enabled immigrants to accomplish two valued objectives at once. One was the goal of economic assimilation, which they pursued, just as the Veblens did, by building farms that produced surpluses that netted profits on world markets. The other objective was cultural solidarity, which they hoped to achieve by adapting their traditional community institutions to the conditions of their new country.[55] These institutions included Lutheran churches and parochial schools, in which Norwegian was the spoken language, as well as gatherings of groups of neighbors to socialize on Sundays and holidays, and to provide practical support, when needed, on one another's farms. By means of such "community projects," according to historian Odd Lovoll, Norwegian immigrants drew the "strength and solidarity . . . to endure the hardships of pioneer life," while staying the course toward economic assimilation.[56]

Religion, the hard backbone of Norwegian communities like those in Cato, also contributed to ethnic unity, though in a more roundabout way. Almost from the day they landed in America, emigrants from Norway fell into theological conflicts that originated back home but grew in intensity in the more pluralist religious environment of the United States.[57] At the center of these controversies were two opposing ecclesiastical blocs, which formed the main intellectual factions within nineteenth-century American Lutheranism. One of these was the "High Church" faction, aligned with the Norwegian Synod, which aimed to maintain the doctrines and ceremonies of the state church of Norway, while leaving it to those in the church hierarchy to address religious problems posed by the American context. The other camp was the "Low Church" party, associated with the so-called Eielsen Synod, which opposed state-church hierarchies and formalistic rituals, and sought a revival of pietism and a fundamental spiritual reawakening. Across decades, the two factions fought bitterly over a maze of issues, which sociologists John and Ruth Useem summarize: among them, "the use of lay ministers, retention of the structure of the Old World church, the perfectibility of men, the imminence of the end of the world, the annihilation of the wicked, the establishment of secular schools."[58] Despite these many points of conflict, however, the battle between the two groups focused everyone's attention on the same cultural issues; as such, it promoted ethnic cohesion directly in the midst of religious dissension.[59] Moreover, as Lovoll has pointed out, believers on both sides were tied to one another to by their "strict adherence to [Luther's] confessional writings," including his teachings about the importance of the religious community itself.[60] As well, both factions were puritan to the core in their intellectual and moral commitments, tireless in exhorting the virtues of working hard and avoiding luxury and other material temptations.[61]

When the Veblen family arrived in Cato, it became a part of a Norwegian colony where this infrastructure of community institutions was already developing; this was one of the attractions drawing the Veblens to the area. Here they experienced the ethnic solidarity missing in Sheboygan County, at the same time as they remained involved in an economy that extended far beyond the local Norwegian-American community. In Cato, next to other groups of pioneers, were fellow *Valdriser* who regularly interacted with one another, and here too was a Norwegian church that gave Kari and Thomas the institutional means they sought "for satisfying religious and spiritual needs" of their children. Cato, as Andrew Veblen recounted, "provided great opportunities for social contact." He wrote: "The distances between homes and surrounding clearings was small, and intercourse was easy to keep up [in] all seasons." Also, "this accessibility . . . invited and promoted social intercourse; and naturally made for public spirit . . . in the community."[62] Embodying this spirit, Thomas and Haldor helped their neighbors (Norwegian and not) with various labor-intensive farm tasks, even though the two of them—industrious, intrepid, and in command of the labor of their household borders—rarely needed their neighbors' help in return.[63]

The Valdres church that the Veblens attended in Cato was affiliated with the Norwegian Synod and adhered to High Church ideas and practices. During the family's first five years in the parish, the church pastor was Jakob Aall Ottesen, an outspoken young intellectual, descended from one of Norway's most distinguished clerical families, who was rapidly emerging as a leading voice—and leading religious knowledge maker—on the traditionalist side of the theological battles raging within midwestern Lutheranism. "A tenacious controversialist and grimly purposeful leader" (in the description of historian Theodore Blegen), Ottesen became a presence in the Veblen household; he made frequent calls on the family, although, as he later told Andrew, he "never felt satisfied that he had [Thomas's] full support."[64] But Andrew had a simple explanation; namely, his father "did not care about religious controversies or cults." He and Kari earnestly upheld Lutheran beliefs and rituals as parts of their ethnic heritage, and they wanted to pass them on to their children; but Thomas "never was excited about his own or anybody's religion," so he and Kari never sided, theologically, with Ottesen, or his controversialist successor (L. M. Biørn), or the pastors of the Valley Grove Lutheran Church that the family joined after its move to Minnesota.[65]

Regardless of Thomas's and Kari's own feelings, however, polarizing religious controversies filled the air of the Norwegian ethnic communities where they settled. Whether through the words of local clergymen, or conversations among parishioners, or polemics in the Norwegian-American press, the heat of sectarian belligerence made its way right inside the household where Thorstein Veblen lived until mid-adolescence (and where he lived, intermittently, in later years). And this intellectual heat no doubt affected him, though in what specific ways it is hard to know. The American studies scholar R. Laurence Moore has plausibly speculated that nineteenth-century religious controversies caused the "intellectual quickening of young Americans," especially those who subsequently be-came social scientists, by furnishing them in childhood and adolescence with "the first stimulants" to abstract reasoning, argument, and debate—and this "quickening" hypothesis may well hold for Veblen, although there is no direct documentation of this.[66] Less speculatively, however, what we notice is that the practice of intellectual controversy—so much a part of Veblen's eventual work as a knowledge producer—encircled him as he grew up and as he first observed intellectual life in action.

INTELLECTUAL CONTROVERSY WAS A FEATURE not only of the Veblens' years in Cato but also of the next (seventh) installment of the family's long westward migration. The family had moved to Cato because cultural and economic conditions there compared favorably with those in Sheboygan, but by the early 1860s Thomas and Kari felt that conditions might be better still in Minnesota. Influencing their thinking was the pull of an ex-panding colony of some three hundred Norwegians living in the south-eastern region of the brand new (largely Republican) state: a colony made up of Cato neighbors who had just relocated to the area; of new immi-grants from the Veblens' parish back in Norway; *and* of members of Kari's immediate family, including her mother, her brothers, her stepfather, and her stepsiblings.[67] Visiting this branch of the family in 1863, Thomas rec-ognized the economic attraction of the area, which offered acres of cheap, fertile prairie land, well suited for the cultivation of wheat in a decade when wheat was king.[68] As his daughter Emily (Andrew's and Thorstein's sister) recalled: "My father had never seen the prairies before, and fell in love with them at once. . . . He wanted to sell out in Wisconsin and move to Minnesota, and would not rest before he accomplished it."[69] But a Civil War was raging (Thomas narrowly escaped the draft), so the family, by now including eight children, waited until July 1865. Then, by wagon, rail, and steamboat, the Veblens moved to Wheeling Township, in booming

Rice County, Minnesota, where Thomas acquired a 290-acre property, which he, Kari, and Haldor developed into another self-sufficient, efficient family farm, situated in the local Norwegian community but also incorporated into the larger economic world around it.[70] It was this farm that became the family's final homestead, and the economic and cultural milieu of Thorstein Veblen from ages eight to seventeen—his immediate environment, almost every day, throughout this long stretch of time. Here, too, Thomas reclaimed the family name of Veblen.[71]

By the time they got to Minnesota, the Veblens had prospered. Their Cato, Wisconsin, farm was the township's second largest (and the largest among Norwegian farms) and placed second also in terms of its economic valuation. When they sold it in 1865, the Veblens cleared roughly $4,500 (= $73,700), a threefold increase in their wealth in the decade since they had moved from Sheboygan.[72] Then, in Rice County, Minnesota, they replicated their success, even in the face of the widening predatory practices of business interests in Chicago, as well as in nearby start-up towns. In 1870, only five years after they arrived, the Veblens owned $8,000 (= $164,000) in real estate and personal property—the second-highest figure in Wheeling Township—and by 1880 they had more than doubled that figure.[73] For much of their time in Cato and early on in Rice Country, the family benefited from the overall uptrend of the US economy and from the fact that the international and national markets for wheat, the Veblens' main crop, remained strong even during economic downturns.[74] By the late 1860s, however, grain prices were declining, and Andrew recalled that "the economic situation was therefore a rather hard one for father."[75] Despite some lean years ahead, though, the family's wealth continued to grow because of Thomas's proactive measures, such as adopting practical scientific innovations (he introduced the county's first harvester) and diversifying production (he supplemented his wheat crop with corn, eggs, and milk).[76] Writing to Dorfman, Andrew commented on how his father carefully followed "changes in farming conditions, such as differences in marketing, greater diversification, changes to stock and milk production, and the like. He was a progressive farmer and always one of the first to meet the new needs" and new demands of the turbulent American economy in the second half of the nineteenth century.[77]

These economic accomplishments gained Thomas and Kari prominence and admiration both in Cato and in Rice Country, where their social status was enhanced by attributes of another kind. Known for their industriousness (even within communities of hard-working people),

Thomas, Kari, and Haldor were known too for the craftsmanship of their work. When Thomas emigrated from Norway, he carried along his training and abilities as a carpenter, and he put his trade to use during his years in the United States, mostly for his family, now and then in answer to requests from his less skillful neighbors. Among many examples of this, Andrew wrote to Dorfman: "Father hewed the square-timber of the barns that he built, did all the work of building the dwellings, made much of the furniture"—"chests, bureaus, built-in cupboards"—plus sleighs and wagons.[78] Living in a time and place where small log cabins were the norm, Thomas twice built spacious two-story frame houses: the first one, in Cato, so well designed and appointed that Andrew found it almost "pretentious"; the second, in Rice County, a "jewel of craftsmanship," according to modern architectural historian Jonathan Larson.[79] (The second house still stands, and has been recognized as a National Historic Landmark.) And Kari was no less adroit in her own areas of expertise, spinning, knitting, weaving, sewing, and fitting garments, at a skill-level that put her work in constant demand in the community.[80] She also served in the role, common in Norwegian-American settlements, of folk doctor, the practical physician who neighbors called on when medical needs arose.[81]

The same dedication that Thomas and Kari brought to their work they also channeled into the upbringing of their children, at least according to the memoirs of Andrew and Emily and the more fragmentary recollections of some of their siblings. In addition to insisting on the children's formal schooling, Kari taught her daughters her craft skills, while Thomas involved his sons (including Thorstein, whom his brothers accused of sneaking off to read) in farm chores from their early years through their college years—although the Veblens, unlike many other Norwegian-American parents, did not hire out their offspring to work on other farms. Cozy scenes like the following, moreover, recur in the adult memories of the children:

> It was the gathering of the family in the long winter evenings that was particularly memorable. In the large living room, it was a busy semi-circle that gathered about the blazing logs or blocks in the large fireplace. The women spinning or sewing, [while] the men would be doing repairs on gloves, leggings, shoes and the like; or they might be whittling axehandles either to replace broken ones or to sell. No one sat exactly idle. Some one might be reading aloud from the newspaper. . . . Some one would relate one of the

old [Norwegian] tales while others would give close attention. . . .
The arrangement in our house invited all to share the society of the
whole household together, [with] solidarity and community of
sentiment.[82]

This was Andrew's own rendition of events, deeply tinted, no doubt,
with sentimentality. But the accounts provided by Emily, sister Mary, and
brother John Edward (Ed) brought out the same themes.[83] So, if the heart-
warming moments do not correspond with how a detached observer
would have described them, they probably convey the shared *perception*
the Veblen children had of their comfortable upbringing and the warm
atmosphere of their home. The tellers of Norwegian folktales to whom
Andrew's comment refers were some of the houseguests (the new immigrants, as well as some down-and-out locals) to whom the Veblens provided a temporary home; and the reader was usually Thomas, reading
from the weekly Norwegian-American newspapers and the serialized
novels of the left-wing writer (and future Nobel Prize winner) Bjørnstjerne
Bjørnson. Aside from his reading choices, though, Thomas typically did
not, according to Andrew, "express opinions at all freely on economic or
other topics, either in farmer problems and politics or in general political
questions. He talked very little and expressed practically no opinions on
the church or the social order. . . . He never 'preached' in his own house
or anywhere." With Kari, it was the same: she "was not given to giving
her opinion except in matters of her immediate province of mother and
housekeeper."[84] All the same, Emily, Mary, and Andrew all recount instances when their parents' opinions came through in their actions—most
visibly in their contacts with neighboring "Indians" (Chippewas and
Menomonees), with whom Thomas and Kari seem to have exhibited the
patronizing and racialized attitudes of nineteenth-century European immigrants toward Native Americans.[85]

We can only speculate, however, about the impact these local surroundings had on Thorstein—whom it is admittedly hard to picture sitting rapt
in a family circle around the fire. Whether or not that happened, in his
later writings Veblen did speak of two "instincts" that "conduce directly
to the material well-being" of humankind. One of these he named the
"sense of workmanship," the propensity that drives an individual to
seek "economy and efficiency for the common good and disapprov[es]
of wasteful and useless living"; and the other he called the "parental
bent," which is "an ever resilient solicitude for the welfare of the young

and the prospective fortunes of the group."[86] It is unlikely Veblen would have identified these instincts as pervasive realities if he had not observed behaviors like them during his own youth. Regardless, Thorstein Veblen remained close to his mother and father throughout their lives, and Andrew Veblen says that his brother agreed with the consensus of the siblings that their parents possessed exceptional intelligence.[87] An apocryphal story comes down that Thorstein Veblen attributed the ideas in *The Theory of the Leisure Class* to childhood conversations with his father, and he later wrote about the formative role played in human evolution by the "phenomena of motherhood."[88]

Still further, American farmers showed up in Thorstein Veblen's work, both early and late, although with Veblen's attitude toward them changing, depending on whether he was speaking about farmers like his parents or those of a different make. In the early 1890s, when he was beginning his career as a professional economist, Veblen made American wheat farming the subject of two of his earliest articles. At that point, he had yet to formulate his own economic theory, so he used the concepts of classical economics to depict wheat farmers in the Midwest, in the period from the 1860s to the 1890s, as an economic success story. He argued that, during these years, wheat famers generally netted high profits, in part because of "fortuitous" international market conditions but also because of the "systematic human effort" of farmers who introduced new agricultural "methods and appliances"; these are innovations Veblen described from firsthand knowledge, all the way down to granular details about harvesting spring wheat on Minnesota fields.[89] Then, a half-dozen years later, when developing his own economic theory in *The Theory of the Leisure Class,* he was careful to grant farmers a small exemption from his otherwise critical treatment of American spending and buying behaviors. "Conspicuous consumption," he observed, "claims a relatively larger portion of the income of the urban than of the rural population, and the claim is also more imperative. . . . So it comes, for instance, the American farmer and his wife and daughters are notoriously less modish in their dress, as well as less urbane in their manners, than the city artisan's family with an equal income."[90]

But, in subsequent work, Veblen's analysis of American farming darkened more and more, reaching night pitch in his late works, *Imperial Germany* (1915) and *Absentee Ownership* (1923), where he flayed midwestern farmers—along with land speculators, absentee owners, small-town businessmen, commercial middlemen, and on and on—for their "spirit of cupidity," their destructive "passion for acquisition," and their deceptive maneuvers "to come in for as much of the free income [from the land] at the cost of the rest of the community as the law would allow."[91] Dissecting what he sarcastically called the "American plan" for the agricultural expansion in the Midwest, Veblen sketched an almost unbroken history of settlement based on "the seizure of fertile soil" and "debauchery and manslaughter"—horrifying evidence, in his view, of the "sclerosis of the American soul."[92] Yet twice he interrupted this wrenching account, making exceptions carved from his own experiences. In the first instance, he differentiated the kind of pioneers who moved to the Midwest from New England from the breed of pioneers who came as part of the "large immigration from northern Europe" in the mid-nineteenth century. Elaborating, he remarked, bitterly, that "the foreign immigrants did the work necessary to the reclamation of this stretch of fertile land, and the native-born in the towns did the business, [which] was directed to getting something for nothing at the expense of the foreign immigrants."[93] And, later, Veblen interrupted his narrative a second time:

> Through the greater part of its history the visible growth of the country has consisted in the extension of the cultivated area and the increasing farm output, farm equipment, and farm population. This progressive taking-over and settlement of the farming lands is the most impressive material achievement of the American people, as it is also the most serviceable work which they have hitherto accomplished.[94]

Both interruptions jolt. They insert into a grave history of pillage a quiet, but felt, tribute to people just like Veblen's own parents: people who had emigrated from Europe to shoulder the hard work of farming in the Midwest, people who had accomplished the "most serviceable" and "most impressive material achievement of the American people."[95] Veblen wrote these words just before and shortly after he turned sixty, but they attest to the long reach of his upbringing—to the imprint of many early years, each one echoing the others, spent on his parents' midwestern farm.

3.

Reluctant, ordinarily, to voice opinions on the social and political issues of the day, Thomas and Kari Veblen took a strong stand on education.

They were committed to schooling their children, and they made sure that happened. In this way, they embraced the belief in education that was widespread among Norwegian immigrants at the time, though the Veblens ratcheted it up several degrees.[96]

Estimates by historians of rates of school attendance in the nineteenth century vary widely, depending on date and region of the country. At mid-century, enrollments were lower in newly settled rural areas than else-where, because parents needed the labor of their children to help bring wild fields under cultivation. For example, on the basis of 1860 records from Manitowoc Country, Wisconsin, where the Veblen children began their schooling, Edward Ehlert has calculated that only around 50 percent of school-age children attended a public school—a "common school"—for some length of time.[97] Beyond that point, enrollments declined further at each higher step on the educational ladder, as this extended upward to the later years of public school and to different forms of higher educa-tion, since the costs of climbing onto the upper rungs outweighed their practical benefits, at least in the thinking of many midwestern farm par-ents. But the Veblens were an anomaly. Of the nine Veblen children who survived infancy, eight (five boys, three girls) completed the common-school curriculum, seven enrolled in the classical track of a college prepa-ratory program, four attended college, and three graduated from college.[98] Of those three, one (Emily) was the first Norwegian-American woman to receive an American college degree; the second (Andrew) went on to do several years of postgraduate work in physics; and the third (Thorstein) received a doctorate in philosophy and nearly earned a second doctorate in political economy.[99] This was a record of educational attainment that few (if any other) large nineteenth-century American farm families ap-proached. Andrew told Dorfman: "Father . . . was the driving force to get us schooled. He did not simply 'allow' us to go, . . . but he could be aggressive about it. Mother seconded him, of course; she generally up-held him if we [the children] differed with him."[100]

The parents started early. As soon as Kari felt that one of her sons or daughters was ready, she began teaching the rudiments of reading, aiming to cultivate the early literacy that was so prized in Lutheran communi-ties. But as the children entered the kindergarten years, and as the size of the Veblen brood kept growing, Thomas arranged for a succession of tutors—Norwegian men who had come to the United States with some higher education—to live with the family for several months each year and give the older children regular instruction in reading and math (and

Figure 1 Thorstein Veblen's parents, Thomas Anderson Veblen and Kari Bunde Veblen

religion). The Veblens chose this option because, when they first moved to Cato in 1854, the township had no common school, so they let their home serve this purpose—to the point that, as Andrew recollected, the family's "living room was immediately arranged as a classroom, . . . and some of the neighbor children got permission to come to the 'school.'"[101] This was Thorstein Veblen's milieu in the early years of his life, before the scene of his formal education shifted to the common school that had opened in Cato in the meantime. Precocious, Thorstein began attending the school in 1862, shortly before he turned five; and, when the family resettled three years later in Rice Country, Minnesota, Thomas and Kari again sent him to the local common school, which he attended for a three- to four-month winter term and a shorter summer term over the following nine years, until he enrolled at Carleton College in 1874.

During this period, his education was infused heavily with the teachings of Lutheranism as spelled out in the two canonical texts of Lutheran pedagogy: Martin Luther's *Smaller Catechism* (1529) and the commentary on it by Erik Pontoppidan in *Truth unto Godliness* (1738), which Norwegians referred to as the *Explanation.* Found in the Veblen household from its earliest years in the United States, these books were the tools Kari and the family's live-in tutors used to teach religion to the children. The two texts also provided the basis for the religious instruction Thorstein and his siblings received from pastors in Sunday school and from teachers in the parochial schools the children sometimes attended (in addition to common school).[102] In these venues, the standard method of the instruction was recitation: teachers required pupils to memorize and correctly repeat back to them mandatory answers to fixed questions that the books listed. Religious educators regarded this method as the ideal way of instilling moral and mental discipline, while also inculcating Lutheran doctrines.[103]

Many of the questions in these books had to do with abstruse points of theological doctrine, in particular Luther's teachings about "sanctification" and "redemption," which were remote from the economic ideas Thorstein Veblen later formulated. But the two catechisms also furnished answers to ethical questions, laying down principles of moral conduct that expressed a distinctive way of thinking about human life and judging what is right and wrong. One of these principles was Luther's condemnation of "sloth" and "waste," a prohibition rooted in his conviction that virtue "breaks down owing to the resistance of the Devil and the lust of the flesh, and also to greed and luxury."[104]

This animus toward excess and indolence is, of course, an attitude we expect to find in the teachings of a leader of the Protestant Reformation. But its predictability from the perspective of our own notions about Protestantism does not mean that nineteenth-century Norwegian-American children took the proscription casually; neither, conversely, does it mean that their religious education included all the other provisions of what we think of as the "Protestant Ethic." To the contrary, despite our tendency to associate Protestantism with individualism, in Luther's moral universe a Christian lives and attains worth only as a member of established social institutions.[105] The *Smaller Catechism* insists on this point when it interweaves its prohibition against waste and idleness with another moral principle, the obligation Christians have to one another because of the "stations" they occupy in society as husbands, wives, parents, children, masters, servants, laborers, and political subjects.[106] Discussing these stations one by one, Luther's *Catechism* outlines specifically what each one demands of its incumbents.

This understanding of human conduct as oriented to the fulfillment of duties toward other community members bears little resemblance to the conception, post-Luther, of action as the rational pursuit of the self-interest of separate individuals. Instead, as the historian of religion Heinrich Maurer explained nearly a century ago, "the Lutheran is social in being a Christian, a Christian by staying put and performing in his station in the best of faith. . . . Whatever his station, he may not be sufficient unto himself. He is not an agent, he is an organ, . . . a splinter of a larger whole, [of a] society [that] is not an aggregate but an organism—God's wonderful work."[107] True, accomplishing this exalted work was a moral mission without end because of the temptations of sin and the incapacity of reason to clear the way to duty. But taking the human condition as it is, the Lutheran primers of the nineteenth century adopted the practice of downgrading "reason" in favor of an alloy of the emotions of "fear, love, and trust in God" as the foundation of the Christian life. This practice was one that Thorstein Veblen observed again and again in the religious literature of his childhood and adolescence.

He read this literature in Norwegian. In the Veblen household, the primary language spoken was Valdris, the dialect of the region of Norway from which Thomas and Kari had emigrated. But Norwegian was the language of the local church and its sacred scripts (the Bible, as well as the *Smaller Catechism* and the *Explanation*), so the Veblens had no option but to teach their sons and daughters in Norwegian, at the same time as the children were picking up English from other sources. Because of this, the children grew up "bilingual" (as Andrew and Emily Veblen liked to say), and Thorstein was no exception—although Dorfman, as part of his "outsider thesis," claimed Veblen was deficient in English until he went to college.[108] Before he was even born, however, Thorstein's older siblings had acquired the new language by interacting frequently with English-speaking children in their multicultural neighborhood. As a consequence, according to Andrew, their little brother "could not but help learning English as early as he could articulate words." In addition, he actually learned to read in English before he was able to read in Norwegian.

(Accounts differ over whether Thorstein carried into adulthood a slight Valdris accent when speaking.)[109]

As usual, Kari and Thomas played a significant role in this development, while learning, along the way, to speak and read English themselves.[110] Living in a period when some Norwegian-Americans were dead set against an English-language-based education, Thorstein's parents held the opposite view. Despite their standard practice of staying out of public controversies, they sided strongly with one of the two camps in the dispute over schooling that riled Norwegian-American communities of the Midwest from the mid-1850s to the late 1870s. This dispute set supporters of the Norwegian Synod's top clergymen, who denounced common schools as pagan institutions and urged Norwegian-only parochial schools, against public school proponents, who saw secular education as an essential step toward their goal of assimilation.[111] The Veblens fell in the second camp, and to push the cause at the local level, Thomas, in a rare move, stood for and won the position of treasurer on the Cato District Board, where he worked successfully, over several years, to establish common schools in the area.[112] It was at one of these schools that Thorstein Veblen began his formal education in 1862; conveniently, another public school was already up and running for him and his school-age siblings when the family moved to Rice County in 1865.[113]

Because common schools were *common* schools, historians and biographers have often overlooked their effects on boys and girls who were, in adulthood, *exceptional* in some walk of life. How much, after all, can something typical tell us about someone atypical? Before jumping to the obvious answer here, however, we need to look inside these mundane places of learning. Mid-nineteenth-century American common schools differed from the age-graded public schools in the United States today. They were "common" schools in that, in principle, they were open to all (white) children within a particular community. But they were not necessarily free, they did not generally have state-mandated attendance requirements, and they did not usually separate students by age. Built on lands the federal government had set aside for school construction, and maintained and supervised by local school boards, common schools might have pupils ranging in age from four to twenty-one, and most students simply entered and left as their parents saw fit.[114] In rural areas particularly, such schools were nearly always bare-bones arrangements. They consisted of one spartan classroom under the charge of one teacher, often a young man or woman, employed on a year-to-year basis, who was scarcely better educated than the more advanced students in the room.[115] Commenting on these conditions as they related specifically to the education of the Veblen children, Andrew wrote to Dorfman about "the very primitive common schools of Wisconsin and Minnesota of that time."[116]

A process of learning still goes on, though, under primitive conditions—it has throughout history. Humble though they were, common schools of the mid-nineteenth century had a curriculum, and that curriculum had a content (however unimpressive it may be by our standards). We can form a fairly good picture of that content by examining school textbooks from the period. Admittedly, schoolbooks are not always to the point in intellectual-historical research. For instance, in circumstances in which knowledge transmission is mainly oral—centered on what the teacher says in lectures—textbooks may sometimes be irrelevant. In terms of common schools, on the other hand, they carried great weight because of the way teachers conducted instruction once students could sound out the alphabet and count. Standing opposite a classroom of pupils who differed widely in how much they knew beyond the basics, teachers fell back again on the venerable method of recitation. They called students aside one by one, or in small batches, and asked them to repeat passages they had memorized from "readers" that corresponded roughly with the level of proficiency the students had reached in some subject area. (In an area like math, the teacher slightly adjusted this method by requiring students to memorize algorithms and then complete sample problems or exercises.) Using this technique, teachers who did not know much about a subject could still manage to "teach" it. All they had to do was to follow along in a text and check whether the student had memorized assigned passages accurately. In no other method of instruction have schoolbooks played such a salient role.[117]

Almost inevitably, this way of teaching spawned textbook editions by the hundreds, as publishers rushed in to take advantage of a market that was rapidly expanding as a result of the opening of scores of common schools in newly settled areas of the country. Textbooks are textbooks, however; not unlike textbooks today, schoolbooks of the mid-nineteenth century tended to closely duplicate one another, giving them "a startling similarity," according to historian Ruth Miller Elson, whose research examined more than a thousand different schoolbooks from the period.[118] This similarity is significant for our purposes because it tells us that the themes and practices found in these schoolbooks were almost certainly present, to some extent, in the texts that Thorstein Veblen and his siblings studied. Andrew told Dorfman that, in Rice County, the Veblen household contained "the full complement of text-books used in the Minnesota public schools."[119] Although we do not know the specific titles of the schoolbooks his younger brother read, it is hard to imagine that they deviated from the hundreds of look-alike texts out there on the market.[120]

WHAT, THEN, WERE THE THEMES that ran through the kinds of schoolbooks that came into Thorstein Veblen's hands? Elson's study (corroborated by later research) identifies several that are pertinent as we track Veblen's intellectual development.[121] First, and most obviously, the textbooks took every opportunity to decry idleness, waste, extravagant display, and ill-gotten acquisitions, and to contrast these derelictions with the cardinal virtues of honest labor, frugality, and self-denial—drilling in the precept that life's rewards should be earned, not fleeced.[122] Reflecting the generic Protestantism of the age, this theme surfaced in all the main subject areas, fine-tuned to their peculiarities but leaving few topics untouched.

In popular storybook series, such as Jacob Abbott's *Rollo at Work; or, the Way to Be Industrious* and in Reverend William McGuffey's moral tales of Hugh Idle and Mr. Toil, for instance, the theme blared itself out as early as the title and cast of characters.[123] Poems, a favorite genre in readers, kept to the script. In one, the poet observes that "the rich man's son inherits lands, and piles of brick, and stone and gold," while the son of the poor is the "king of two hands," who "does his part in every useful toil and art." In another, the young reader heard: "Let vapid idlers loll in silk around their costly board; Give us the bowl of samp and milk, By homespun beauty poured!" And another, addressed to an imaginary pupil facing the choice between becoming a farmer and becoming a lawyer, compared the two occupations, marshaling the dichotomy between the productive man, who works for what he has, and the nonproductive man, who lives as a parasite:

> To fit up a village with tackle for tillage
>   Jack Carter he took to the saw,
> To pluck and to pillage, the same little village
>   Tim Gordon he took to the law.

This short lesson, one of hundreds just like it, functioned as part of a larger morality play that was the stock in trade of common-school reading assignments: the inspiring tale of the self-made man, whose hard work and thrift earn him the reward of material success in a society respectful of private property. As schoolbooks reenacted this play, though, the story unfolded as something more than a paean to the rugged individualist, because the self-made man never stands alone. In the poem, Jack Carter is concerned for his village, and, like him, the self-made men of the books labor in the service of family, church, community, and nation. Summarizing this motif, Elson comments that, in the readers, "God does not entrust wealth to the successful man for self-indulgence but for the benefit of the community."[124] This emphasis on the good of the community repeated, undisguised, ethical teachings already familiar to the Veblen children from the time they spent memorizing Luther's *Smaller Catechism*—and from participating in the Norwegian-American communities where they were growing up.

This "social" theme in the school texts had another dimension to it, moreover. At the same time as the books insisted that individuals labor for their communities, the texts urged the complementary idea that the social community—writ large in the form of nationalities and races—shapes the individual, even when the individual is a trailblazing historical figure. In the familiar manner of books targeted for children and adolescents, the texts of the period engaged in outsized hero worship. But they then demoted their heroes in relation to the imperial forces of race and nationality, defending the demotion by means of intellectual practices that show nineteenth-century American culture in its most disturbing light. Opening up a geography or history book from Veblen's school years, we find a vocabulary that, first, describes all human beings as the carriers of nationality traits that embody variations on the attributes of their "race." This vocabulary then characterizes "race" by using a classification scheme that sorts humankind (on the ground of external physical characteristics) into groups, bearing names like "Caucasian, Mongolian, Malayan, Negro, and American Indian," and next arranges those groups into a fixed hierarchy that places "Negro" on the bottom and "Caucasian" at the top, with the last category sometimes divided into a lower tier for nationalities from southern Europe and an upper tier for the northern European (the "Teutonic" or "Aryan") race.

Associated with these different races were the different kinds of conduct that anchored the school morality tales. Commonly used books taught, for instance, that "the Asiatics are in general luxurious, indolent, effeminate and servile," whereas members of the northern European race exhibit "industry and thrift." These characteristics, according to this account, gave a decisive edge to northern Europeans, Americans in particular, when it came to economic growth, new scientific discovery, and the development of "Useful Knowledge"—something Elson describes as "the primary intellectual value embodied . . . in the schoolbooks."[125] Averred one textbook writer: "We [Americans] are scholars in the useful; and employed in improving the works of nature."[126] Another author asserted that members of the northern race "have carried to their fullest growth all the elements of active life with which nature is endowed. They have perfected society and morals, literature and art, the principles of philosophy, [becoming] the rulers of history."[127] What is more, they accomplished this triumph not just by the singular efforts of formidable individuals, but because of "the genius of our [American] institutions," "institutions, blessed and blessing in their influence": "useful institutions," "free institutions," most of them "kindred institutions" shared by the British and American peoples.[128]

Folded into this way of thinking was a conception of the history of humankind. This conception was a by-product of the sharp dichotomies the schoolbooks set up between work and indolence, productive and unproductive activities, just and unjust rewards, the individual and the community, and so on, because these polarities had a temporal dynamism built into them. They geared into motion whenever any one of two poles pulled against the other, as they were almost fated to do. This polar tension enabled textbook writers to spin a tidy historical narrative that they could overlay onto the development of individuals and nations both: the rich man's dissipated son sinks into ruin because of extravagance and sloth, while the poor man's industrious, provident son makes his way upward to benefit his community; powerful nations (such as Rome and Portugal) decline over time as their institutions are corrupted by luxury and indolence, while hungry settlers in a wilderness slowly build a great nation by laboring hard and saving long. Regardless of the specifics, these recurring historical accounts assumed, as Elson observed, a "teleological evolution instituted by God to perfect man's world" by ultimately rewarding virtuous conduct and eradicating vice.[129] Running counter to the way Thorstein Veblen subsequently parsed social evolution, the textbook accounts took as their premise that major historical changes occur as productive human activities struggle to make headway against unproductive activities.

Nineteenth-century text authors did not invent this set of intellectual practices—the ways of thinking about and judging human conduct that we find in the schoolbooks. These were derivative all the way down. In designing school lessons as they did, these elementary books were channeling to captive young audiences an intellectual repertoire that was in wide circulation beyond the spare walls of the common school. The effect was to reinforce and strengthen the repertoire, as recitations inside the classroom made pupils, like the Veblen children, practice the textbook practices, across a variety of subject areas, during all the years they attended school.

For Thorstein Veblen, those years totaled twelve. That number was at the extreme high end for students in the Upper Midwest in the 1860s and 1870s; but if Veblen had complaints about common schooling, there is no evidence of them. Just the opposite: his one (known) comment about the common-school curriculum offered a favorable impression. In *The Theory of the Leisure Class,* Veblen drew an invidious distinction "between the instruction offered in the primary and secondary schools, on the one hand, and in the higher seminaries of learning, on the other." As he sizes them up, the "higher seminaries"—mainly, the colleges of New England—teach cant. In contrast, "primary education in its latest development in the advanced industrial communities"—the category in which he placed midwestern farming communities like those of his youth—"is directed chiefly to proficiency or dexterity, intellectual and manual, in the . . . employment of impersonal facts, in their causal . . . incidence."[130] These words are not Veblen at his clearest, but they amount, even so, to a strong tribute to common schools from a thinker who regarded the "causal" analysis of "impersonal facts" as among the great achievements of modern science.

When Veblen offered this positive assessment, he was referring, most likely, to instruction at the higher levels of the curriculum in Minnesota schools in the years after the family's move to Rice County. Before that, when the Veblens were still in Wisconsin, the school curriculum in their county consisted of the standard fare of reading, arithmetic, and writing-cum-spelling, with some history and geography tossed in—just as in the textbooks.[131] In Rice County, these remained the principal subjects in the first years of schooling, and Thorstein cooperated with the regime, at least to judge from Andrew's admiring recollection that his brother "knew every word in the 'National' spelling book, and synonyms and opposites of every word, [and] he could not be spelled down on any word in the series of readers and spellers used."[132] But Minnesotans, at least on paper, were not satisfied with a curriculum that stopped with the usual subjects. During the period when the Veblen children were attending the local school, school districts in the state began testing applicants for teaching positions not only on a very long list of the basics: "orthography, reading, writing, mental arithmetic, written arithmetic, English grammar, composition, rhetoric, geography, natural history, physical geography, and history." Prospective teachers also needed to demonstrate their knowledge of more advanced sciences: "botany, natural philosophy, geology, astronomy, physiology, political economy, chemistry, algebra, geometry and trigonometry, surveying and navigation."[133]

That any of Thorstein's own teachers would have covered all these areas, or even known what most of them were about, is extremely unlikely. Andrew did remember, however, that some Rice County teachers were able to take students "beyond the elementary subjects." Then, too, some teachers presumably included in the program a smattering of the natural sciences in their first principles and applications; otherwise Thorstein Veblen would have had no ground for later asserting that the common schools cultivated "proficiency or dexterity, intellectual and manual, in the . . . employment of impersonal facts." At these subjects, however, the Rice County school curriculum reached its upper bound, and it would not have carried Thorstein any further into the advanced subjects. Besides, as Andrew recalled (in a backhanded compliment to his brother's teachers), Thorstein "was toward the last the most advanced pupil in the school, and I believe the teachers were closely enough put to it to keep ahead of him."[134]

Well before Thorstein topped out in this way, furthermore, the demands of the common school were light enough, and the school year abbreviated enough, that he was left with plenty of time to read and study on his own. As he did, he was limited by the paucity of reading materials at home and in the farming community, but he grabbed what he could. During the family's Cato years, this consisted mainly of religious literature and issues of the Norwegian-American weekly *Emigranten*. But in Rice County, increasingly, there was more around the household to read, including the popular New York political and literary magazine *Harper's Weekly*. According to Andrew, Thorstein's tastes ranged widely during his common school years. He read novels and dime novels, among them many from the best-selling "Beadles Dime Novels" series of Wild West adventures.[135] At the other end of the intellectual spectrum fell what Andrew described as Thorstein's "extensive reading of . . . history, and mythology, and general science—the foundation of his universal or general information, for which he became known wherever he went." Some of this literature was in English, some in Norwegian, but, in these years, Thorstein taught himself German also by working through the small library of a German neighbor, becoming proficient enough that he was able to read the thick prose of Immanuel Kant. But he leavened philosophy with poetry, reading verse and composing poems in both English and Norwegian.[136]

We do not know what specific ideas Veblen took away from this eclectic assortment of writings. But when it came to the popular literatures of Norway, contemporary and classical, there was one strand he cannot have missed as he sat reading this work on his parents' thriving immigrant farm, in midst of the capitalist economy of the American Midwest. That strand was the long movement of history, the brute fact that humankind had a past that differed from the present. The years of Veblen's youth coincided, for example, with the period in *belles lettres* when both of Norway's literary lions, Bjørnstjerne Bjørnson and Henrik Ibsen, were writing plays, short stories, and poems that not only were set in the past (usually Norway's past) but also used the past as a counterpoise to the present. In doing so, they intentionally built on folk materials they drew from the past, especially the plots and styles of the ancient Norse-Icelandic sagas, in order to create mighty Viking warriors whose valiant deeds reflected the barbarous conditions of the dark ages in which the stories occurred.[137] According to Andrew Veblen, "Thorstein knew," as early as his common-school years, "such of the works as were out and available in the book market of Bjørnson and Ibsen"; even more, he knew the texts of great Norse-Icelandic sagas themselves, which he returned to throughout his lifetime.[138] (In the late 1880s, as Chapter 6 will discuss, he translated one of these sagas into English.) For him, these were more than storybooks. Dating from the twelfth and thirteenth centuries, when anonymous writers set them down from oral traditions, they were an experience of immersion into the political and economic circumstances, and the religious and household customs, of an epoch more than a half-millennium removed from his own. They stretched his time horizon outward from the present and backward to raw conditions of life in real societies of the High Middle Ages, and back further into the antiquity the saga writers depicted.[139] This stretching outward and backward dramatically temporalized Veblen's own society, making America in the second half of nineteenth century only a moment in a vastly extended process in time. This historical outlook comported with a sense of the world already chiseled into the immigration and settlement saga of the Veblen family itself.[140]

81

4.

Why Thomas and Kari Veblen wanted their children to continue their educations once they were done with common school is a matter for speculation. Coming from rural Norway, they carried with them negative associations between universities and the country's despised ruling elite, and in America they observed little interest in higher education during the first decade or more after they arrived. On the eve of the Civil War, only 3 percent of white males between the ages of eighteen and twenty-one were enrolled in some form of higher education, and the percentages were even lower in other demographic groups.[141] In the Midwest, transplanted New England farmers resisted sending their sons to college in hopes of keeping their hands on the land, and many immigrant farmers shared this attitude.[142]

On the whole, though, Norwegian-American parents took a different tack. As historian Theodore Blegen has explained, they actively encouraged "the younger generation to . . . push on to academies, colleges, and universities, [in order] to make careers in the professions."[143] Very likely, Thomas and Kari shared this mentality up to a point—judging, for example, from the fact that none of their sons remained on the farm in adulthood. (Two became academics; the other two, businessmen.) Andrew Veblen remembered an 1864 conversation in which his father "talked . . . a good deal about my future, and his desire that I should have the advantage that he lacked of an 'education.'" Andrew also told a story that, when he and his siblings were attending the common school in Manitowoc in 1863–1864, their teacher—one Ira Jerome—"was a college graduate, and was undoubtedly a man of great and varied attainments. . . . He was the first to tell father that he must 'educate' me; that is send me to college. . . . I believe this suggestion from Mr. Jerome, was the germ that grew into the ambition that father came to cherish, of putting his boys and girls through college."[144] That this particular teacher played a role in the family's plans is probably true, but only because Thomas and Kari had already succumbed to the educational germ as they thought ahead to their children's futures.

But this opened the question of what to do next. In this era, there was as of yet no standard template for parents to follow, and students wanting to continue their education after finishing common school might go next either to a public high school (where such a thing existed), or to a college, or to a hybrid of the two—an "academy," which was a precollege preparatory program that might be grafted onto the front end of a college program to make up for the shortage of high schools. (There was little uniformity among the schools in any of these categories.) Thomas considered all three possibilities, trying them out on Andrew, who was sixteen when the family moved to Minnesota in 1865. At this date, higher-educational institutions of all types were scarce in the Midwest, although the next decade would witness a vigorous growth spurt. So Thomas opted to send his eldest son to the Norwegian college that had just opened in the region, Luther College, in Decorah, Iowa. The Veblens' minister in Rice County wrote an enthusiastic recommendation to the college, expressing the hope that Andrew's talent would "find its proper development and calling"; but Andrew never actually started there because of a serious illness that kept him away from school and other exacting activities for the next five years.[145]

At the end of that period, Thomas veered in a different direction, deciding to send Andrew to a high school in the neighboring town of Faribault, Minnesota. But this arrangement lasted only fourteen months, after which Andrew taught common school for several months before changing course again. At the relatively advanced age of twenty-three, he enrolled at a small college in nearby Northfield, Minnesota, a thriving wheat- and flour-exporting town with fifteen hundred inhabitants.[146] The college had opened in 1867 as Northfield College, but its trustees had renamed it Carleton College in 1871, when Boston brass manufacturer William Carleton gave the school an unrestricted cash gift of $50,000 (= $1.1 million), the largest single contribution up to that time made to a Midwestern college.[147] That fall, Andrew began the "classical course" in the new institution's preparatory academy, moving into the "college department" in 1874, graduating in 1877—and making Carleton the natural choice when his parents came to pick a school for his siblings. Brother Orson entered Carleton (for a short stay) in 1872, and sister Emily followed in 1873. The next year, straight out of common school, Thorstein joined them, enrolling (with fifty other students) in the classics division of the college prep academy from 1874 to 1877, and then continuing (as part of a fast-shrinking group of thirteen) in the college program from 1877 until his graduation in 1880.[148]

Northfield was twelve miles from the Veblen farmstead, and its proximity was apparently a large part of Carleton's appeal to the family.[149]

But, whatever Thomas and Kari's reasoning, Carleton turned out to be a fortuitous choice for their sixth child. Viewed only from the outside, the school (aside from its large endowment) was nothing out of the ordinary, just another among the several dozen small Protestant denominational colleges founded in these years.[150] Its own affiliation was with the mainline Congregational Church, and in its early years many of its students were Congregationalists, with New England family roots, from Northfield and the surrounding areas. The school's first president, James W. Strong, came to the job in 1870 from a position as minister of the Congregational Church in nearby Faribault, and the young pastor had few qualifications for his new job other than an interest in creating "a true Christian College" (in the words of the school's *Annual Catalogue*). For Strong, this meant establishing "an institution . . . aiming directly and avowedly to promote those moral and religious ends which Christianity sets forth as the highest," and strict religious observers credited him with accomplishing this mission in short order. Reporting to a Congregational oversight committee in 1879, M. McG. Dana, a pastor from St. Paul, wrote: "This Christian college is the place where . . . the light of a godly example shines in the lives and teaching of instructors . . . and where the worship of God is avowedly a part of the daily life."[151]

Still, in part because Strong and the college's trustees had somewhat more money to work with than officials at other denominational schools, they took steps that set Carleton apart from the rest of the pack. For one, despite its Congregational roots, the college operated from the outset on the principle that it was "not denominational." Its student body included, by the time of Thorstein Veblen's arrival, fewer Congregationalists than students from other Protestant denominations, Scandinavian Lutherans among them.[152] Besides diversifying in this way, Carleton innovated with regard to its academic program, since another of Strong's goals was to build a school "inferior to none in its standard of scholarship."[153] That ambition put it at the vanguard of the emerging trend toward what historian Roger L. Geiger has called the "multipurpose college."[154] This was an institution that provided the traditional classical curriculum of the northeastern men's colleges, but also included precollege programs *and* college-level courses in the natural sciences and the modern languages— and, still further, admitted women into its ranks. From its early years, Carleton did all of this and, to mount and maintain the ramped-up program, Strong hired a staff large by 1870s standards. Between Veblen's enrollment in 1874 and his graduation six years later, the Carleton faculty grew from eight members to twelve (eight professors, four instructors).[155] Further, outstripping the qualifications of teachers at the New England colleges, almost all of Carleton's professors had master's degrees (then the top credential for college teaching), and nearly all of them were young and attuned to recent scholarship in the subject areas they taught.[156]

DURING HIS YEARS AT CARLETON, Veblen experienced most of what the curriculum had to offer.[157] His point of entry was the study of the classics, and he took courses in Latin or Greek (or both) for seventeen of the eighteen terms he attended. At the time, Carleton's precollege and college programs were both divided into tracks, and as he moved through them, Veblen enrolled every term in the classical track.[158] In going this route, he was following what contemporaries commonly regarded as the path to a career in one of the learned professions.[159] But in mid-nineteenth-century America, a classical education gave students a benefit greater than the gentleman's level of literacy in the ancient languages.[160] This benefit is something most intellectual biographers have overlooked. When writing about a historical figure who had a classical education, the modern-day biographer's tendency has been to treat it as the boring study of the grammars of dead languages, not finding in it any larger *intellectual* significance. William James's biographer Robert Richardson writes, for example, of the future philosopher's time at Harvard College: "The curriculum was largely fixed and uninteresting, consisting mainly of the classics"—and, with that, the classics altogether vanish from James's life story.[161]

But who hasn't learned something from experiences that are uninteresting, especially when they occur, day in and day out, for years on end? In Veblen's time, a good classical education did not cease with the study of Latin and Greek vocabulary, grammar, and oratory—though there was plenty of that. Involved, too, was the young classicist's movement "from words to worlds": a long jump from the student's own time and place into the historical contexts of the ancient authors and the subjects they wrote about. Making this leap happen was the explicit aim of mid-nineteenth-century classical educators, who, as historian Caroline Winterer has argued, stood "among the most innovative of American scholars" of the time, as they substantially broadened classical education beyond language textbooks to the writings of Latin and Greek authors (as well as to new scholarship on ancient societies). Writing in 1870, Yale philosopher and classicist (and future Veblen mentor) Noah Porter explained:

> The student of Virgil and of Homer cannot painfully translate a few books of the *Aeneid* or the *Odyssey*, without entering into the thoughts and sympathizing with the feelings, and living somewhat of the life of human beings greatly unlike those whom he has ever known or imagined. Their thoughts and feelings . . . open to him a new world of sentiment and emotion.[162]

Carleton's young faculty embraced this new conception of the classical curriculum. So, over six years, Veblen spent many hours reading and translating texts from the Roman canon by Virgil, Cicero, Caesar, Livy, Tacitus, Horace, and Juvenal; and, from the Greek canon, by Homer, Plato, Xenophon, Herodotus, and Thucydides. These writers lived more than a millennium earlier than the authors of the medieval Norse sagas, and their work transported Veblen into societies even more remote from postbellum America. What is more, the majority of these ancient authors were men who wrote not plays, not poems, but histories—or, more accurately, what they intended as histories, either of their own era or of previous epochs. In Greek, Veblen read, for example, Herodotus's *Histories,* a semiethnographic account of societies that fell victim to Persian imperialism; Thucydides's *History of the Peloponnesian War,* a causal analysis of Hellenic empire-building; and Xenophon's *Anabasis,* a firsthand description of the defeated Greek army's march homeward from Persia and its encounters en route with "barbarian" tribes and customs. In Latin, Veblen read parts of Livy's 142-volume historical narrative of Rome's growth and expansion; plus Tacitus's *Germania,* an ethnographic study of the "barbarian" peoples east of the Rhine.[163] Amplifying these sources, Veblen's program included classicist William Smith's influential *Smaller History of Greece* (1866) and *Smaller History of Rome* (1869), which traced the centuries-long development of the "political institutions," "religious institutions," and "national institutions" of ancient societies, along with their changing economic and military foundations, especially Rome's increasing dependence on foreign conquest, plunder, and "the institution of slavery."[164] Veblen spent an entire term on each of Smith's histories.

In the classical curriculum, this practice of historicizing social life, rather than taking social forms as timeless and unchanging, went together with certain ways of evaluating human conduct. We see these practices in the classical authors' recurring criticisms of individuals, groups, and epochs that succumbed to greed, luxury, ostentation, and indolence. Illustrative of this attitude was Cicero's terse lament to his contemporaries that "we have corrupted our souls with shady seclusion, luxury, leisure, idleness and sloth." In classical histories of Rome in particular, the "leisure" class—that elite whose members did nothing productive—came in for strong denunciation. As well, the classical authors heaped ridicule on society's "parasites": a word that natural scientists would apply, centuries later, to dependent biological organisms, but which the ancients used (in texts Veblen translated) to describe individuals who lived "on somebody else's loaf"— like the despised character of the freeloader in Greek and Roman plays.[165] Further, lest students skip over the basic moral message, William Smith drove it home as he blamed the decline of Roman civilization on the corrosive influence of "enormous fortunes" ill-gotten, and on the accompanying vices of "indolence," "idleness," and the "love of luxury."[166]

In singling out these behaviors for condemnation, the texts in Carleton's curriculum inevitably extolled others. For his part, Smith hailed the Greeks for being "temperate," "self-denying," "simple in manners," and willing to make "heroic sacrifices" for their community; and he praised the early Romans because they were "hardy, industrious, . . . and lived with great frugality."[167] This depiction of ancient society none too subtly transformed noble pagans into good Protestants, thereby reinforcing the values of the midwestern farms and towns where students of the classics came from. Yet, on the basis of expurgated editions of the ancient texts used in the college program, few students—Veblen included—would have realized the anachronism or have been able to overlook textual passages that dramatized the moral practices that Carleton upheld. During the last year of the curriculum, for instance, students worked through Plato's *Apologia,* where they listened to the aging Socrates, legendary for the simplicity of his own lifestyle, decry the chase for "money, reputation and place" and defend the heroic pursuit of a philosophical life, devoted above all to the unending search for "knowledge."[168]

Wrapped up in the classical education, too, was a distinctive intellectual stance, a caustic style that had several facets. For one, the classical authors, as critics of society, often wrote in a heretical manner that Veblen could not have missed. In his final year at Carleton, for example, his study of the classics centered on the poet Juvenal, who had famously adopted and polished the literary form of satire to castigate his Roman contemporaries for their economic follies: their class divisions, wealth accumulations, squandered leisure time, and conspicuous expenditures.[169]

But the ancient writers did not just attack their societies' mores. They made a routine practice of also railing against one another. "Indefatigable controversialists" (to use the descriptor of historian Peter Gay), their modus operandi was that of the intellectual dissenter, fighting fiercely to promote their ideas over those of other writers, living and dead.[170] Not only this, but in Veblen's student days, American and European classicists were using some of the ancients' same argumentative practices as they themselves battled over the so-called Homeric Question. This was the contentious issue of whether or not there existed an individual poet "Homer" who composed the *Odyssey* and the *Iliad* (a text used at Carleton) and, if not, whether these two foundational texts of "Western civilization" were produced by many hands working over many centuries, as revisionist research into the sociohistorical context of the poems suggested. An esoteric question meant (we might well think) for specialized scholarly publications, it came to Carleton via Smith's *Smaller History of Greece,* which introduced students to the disputing parties in this "great controversy" before aligning with the side of the iconoclasts.[171] So, in case Veblen somehow failed to notice the practice as he listened in on the religious controversies then occurring inside the Norwegian-American church, the classics curriculum offered further demonstration that scholars, modern as well as ancient, worked in a confrontational mode. That is how knowledge makers did business.

BESIDES THE STUDY OF classical literature, Veblen's program at Carleton included courses on English and American literature, in which instruction was carried out using recent textbooks rather than the original writings of literary figures.[172] Among these textbooks were Truman Backus's *Shaw's New History of English Literature* and John Hart's *Manual of American Literature.*[173] The two authors were mainstream academic writers (Backus a professor at Vassar College; Hart a professor at the College of New Jersey, or Princeton as it was soon renamed), and their books consisted mainly of capsule summaries of the work of dozens of literary figures on both sides of the Atlantic—just as we might expect of introductory surveys, whether then or now.

Ordinary as they were, however, these books too were soaked through with a sense of history and society. Aside from being chronologically arranged, they both rested on historical arguments that expanded "literature" beyond the exclusive bounds of imaginative writing and then embedded literary developments within a drama of social change that arched over individual authors. To his college readers, Hart explained, for instance, that it was "with the increase of material wealth" in antebellum America that there "came a corresponding growth in the department of letters"—a department he saw as including, next to the usual litterateurs (novelists, poets, and authors of short stories), philosophical and political writers, plus some of the latest "scientific writers" and "writers on political economy."[174] Backus went further, elongating the historical time line of the drama. Picking up where the ancient authors had left off, his text followed English literature forward from the Roman conquest of the "primitive Britons," whose "habits were nomadic and predatory" and preliterate, to the Teutonic and Norman invasions. Through this tracking, Backus aimed to show how "the character of a conquest determines its effect upon the language of the conquered"—or, in other words, how different literatures "were evolved from social confusion." Continuing the story, Backus analyzed the writings that resulted from the decay of feudalism and the "great transition from the old order to the new order" associated with the Reformation, which was the defining event in "the social, religious, and political annals of our race," as well as in the growth of its social "institutions" and its "dazzling progress" in scientific knowledge. Unexceptional statements, no doubt, to Thorstein Veblen, who was already familiar with this kind of social and historical thinking; but here, in the literature on literature, was yet another repetition of these intellectual practices.[175]

JUST DOWN THE ACADEMIC corridor there were further variations that involved more of Veblen's time at Carleton and left a stronger imprint. These came his way through courses in the natural sciences, which formed an integral component of the school's curriculum. At Carleton, students studying the classics had direct contact with the hard sciences in a period when higher-educational institutions often segregated the sciences from the classics. In some areas of the country, for example, the growing popular demand for practical training in the hard sciences was met by building independent technical and agricultural colleges; and in older institutions, like Harvard and Yale, by creating separate "scientific schools" placed outside the traditional college program.[176] In 1876, however, when President Strong and his faculty organized Carleton's collegiate curriculum, they established a "scientific" track alongside the school's freshly delineated classical and literary tracks, making it a regular part of the school's pre-paratory and college programs. Further, they *required* classics students to take a range of courses in the natural sciences.[177]

Several other new midwestern colleges tried this design too. But Strong's initial cash advantage, and his persistent fundraising efforts, enabled him to recruit young scientists for his faculty and buy them the latest scientific equipment, so that his science program was thriving within a decade of the college's founding. By 1879 the *Annual Catalogue* was crowing—and with good reason—that "the Scientific Department of the College will not be excelled by that of any similar institution" in the Upper Midwest. As evidence, the catalogue pointed to the college's extensive "chemical, physical and anatomical apparatus" and its brimming "cabinet of specimens in the departments of Geology, Mineralogy and Natural History," including hundreds of rocks, minerals, fossils, and "casts of rare and fine extinct [life] forms." In astronomy, Carleton boasted an up-to-date observatory, sufficiently advanced in the technology of planetary measurement that it was then *the* central node in the process of standardizing time in the United States—sending out, every day at noon, the time signals by which railroads and other businesses throughout the Midwest synchronized their clocks.[178]

This state-of-the-art equipment underpinned a state-of-the-art science curriculum that kept Carleton students up-to-date in an era of constant scientific change in Europe and the United States. Unencumbered by the deadweight of old professors teaching from antiquated textbooks, Carleton was a conduit of newness, funneling down to its little population ideas flowing from not one or two but nearly all the hotbeds of contemporary scientific theory and research—geology, zoology, botany, astronomy, as well as from more settled areas like physics and chemistry.[179] So far as we can reconstruct Veblen's coursework, he studied all of these subjects (plus math, up to the level of calculus), using textbooks by leading scientific authorities at major universities and colleges.

Reading these texts for hours on end gave him, while he was still green in the sciences, a great deal of specialized scientific information (a stockpile he drew on in his later writings). But the texts also showed him, and accustomed him to, the intellectual equipment and know-how that produced this information and gave it coherence. Not limited to any one subject, this equipment consisted of the knowledge tools—the accepted ways of conceptualizing nature and doing science—that were then being applied, both explicitly and tacitly, by scientists working in different areas.

At Carleton, exposure to this repertoire was unavoidable, since it was on exhibit in science courses term after term, drilled in daily by repetition—a method Carleton clung to because of its (presumed) positive effects on inculcating moral discipline in students and helping them absorb their academic lessons. Nationally, in this era some American educators were starting to question the pedagogical wisdom of the recitation technique, but their critique had yet to produce much change. As a rule, colleges still retained the method in nearly all their courses, and Carleton did likewise, although its professors were beginning to supplement recitation, at the edges, with lectures and, in science classes, with hands-on lab exercises.[180] Regardless, mastery of the text remained the pedagogical objective, as the *Annual Catalogue* made clear, for instance, when it described final exams: "The last week of each term is devoted to examinations, [in which] about one-fourth of the text-book used during the term is taken up each day" for the purpose of recapitulation.[181] In this situation, there were knowledge practices that science students could scarcely overlook. As regards the development of Veblen's own intellectual tool kit, three of these practices stand out, especially because he had already encountered them in other forms.

The first concerned the activity of science itself. Before Veblen entered Carleton's science courses, he had watched local farmers adopt new scientific technologies in agriculture; he had read, in common-school history books, about the progress of knowledge through scientific discovery; and he had heard ancient writers celebrate the unceasing quest for knowledge— *scientia* in Latin. It is hard to know how he would have defined "science" before his coursework in the natural sciences, however, since the word meant different things to different people—classical authors versus local farmers, for example. But the science program at Carleton clarified the nebulous, giving "science" the double meaning of a particular method *and* a particular form of knowledge that resulted from that method. We find the first of these meanings in frequent textbook statements about "the scientific method of arriving at truth," or, what amounted to the same thing, "the method of observation." For the scientist-authors, here was the fountainhead of science: "the primary facts . . . at the basis of astronomical science were obtained . . . by observation"; botany rests on "these [several] observations and a thousand others"; the physical sciences rely on "the method of observation," and so forth.[182]

Still (as many of the Carleton texts continued), the scientific method fell short until it actually produced new knowledge of nature's "laws." For this purpose, the books insisted on the importance of induction: scientists had to look up from their raw observations to identify general phenomena—"generalized facts"—and find the pattern that connected one type of phenomena to another, ideally in a causal manner. Science, said one of Veblen's textbook authors, meant "the discovery of the laws which govern these phenomena, and of the grand chain of causes and effects which explains the mode of their occurrence."[183] Said another: "Science then is not a mere knowledge of disjointed unreconciled facts or truths, but a knowledge of these facts as mutually related ... under all-inclusive principles and laws [by which scientists can] ascertain their causes. Towards this state all knowledge tends in proportion as it tends to perfection."[184] According to some of the scientists read by Carleton students, that perfection occurs only by God's hand: God put the laws of nature in place and God enables scientific investigators to discover them.[185] Other authors in the curriculum were quieter on the role of the Divine (and on the scientific status of biblical knowledge). All the same, every one of the textbook writers presumed that science entails the task of finding laws.

This way of understanding science meshed with a second practice that ran deep through the science textbooks. This was the assumption that nature is never at rest: nature's laws are dynamic laws that have to do with change—change in all of nature's kingdoms. Veblen did not need Carleton's science classes, of course, to tell him that change happens. The felt reality of change was already in his bones, not only as a result of the experiences of his family (immigration, frequent geographical moves, the ups and downs of the capitalist world economy, even a family surname lost and reclaimed), but also as a result of his own intellectual experiences (reading literatures that transported him to events that took place generations, centuries, millennia back in time). Still and all, these episodes must have seemed to him, initially, as little more than a collection of particular historical moments. In the Carleton science courses, on the other hand, singular moments were an anathema; change occurred according to the workings of general laws. "Matter is every-where subject to change," wrote physicist Sidney Norton, as he laid out Newton's "laws of motion." In the same spirit, botanist Alphonso Wood described "laws of growth" in plant tissue; astronomers Simon Newcomb and Edward Holden, "laws governing the motions" of heavenly bodies; and zoologist James Orton, the "great law of reproduction" by which every generation in the animal world is succeeded by another.[186]

Central among these dynamic laws were the "laws of evolution," which the Carleton text writers included in order to account for changes that occurred over the vastness of history. What particularly cried out to them for explanation were unsettling new discoveries by geologists and astronomers that had radically altered the scale of time, giving nature an antiquity that some people found hard even to comprehend. According to Newcomb and Holden, the universe was twenty million years old. Geologist Joseph LeConte gave thirty million as the age of the earth alone. Geologist James Dana spoke casually of a world "thousands of millions of years" old.[187]

Making sense of this enormous historical expanse led several authors to bring into their textbooks laws that were explicitly "evolutionary"— although no two Carleton texts interpreted evolutionary principles in the same way. At one end of the spectrum of contending interpretations there was, for instance, Dana's theistic, teleological view of the "evolution of the earth." This was the idea that "the earth [came] to its present condition through a series of changes or progressive formations, and . . . although Infinite Mind has guided all events toward the great end—a world of mind—the earth has, under this guidance and appointed law, passed through a regular course of history of growth." Then, in the middle of the interpretive spectrum fell evolutionists like LeConte, who sought to retain theism but to knit it together with ideas that contemporaries associated (not always accurately) with the names of European thinkers such as Lamarck, Darwin, and Spencer (discussed further later). Waving the word "evolution" more insistently than any other author in the curriculum, LeConte depicted evolution as a teleological process of "progressive change" that culminated in the "reign of man" over nature, but that in earlier historical periods involved a hard "struggle for life" among lower species, during which "the fittest only survived." And at the far end of the continuum, Newcomb and Holden presented a chilling, nonprogressivist account that concluded that earth, "like all other organisms we know of, must come to an end in consequence of those very laws of action which keep it going. . . . It must end in a chaos of cold, dead globes . . . when the sun and stars shall have radiated away all their heat, unless it is re-created by the action of forces of which we at present know nothing."[188]

This evolutionary way of thinking about the earth and the stars spawned a third practice: the practice of extending the laws of evolution to encompass humankind. This extension reflected the assumption of several scientist-authors that to study nature was to study human beings too. Making this point from the angle of a geologist, Dana sought to include in his science not only the development of "valleys, rivers, and plains" but the entire "system of life [that] began in the simple sea plant and the lower forms of animals, and ended in Man." The province of Dana's subject, in other words, was "the earth in reference to man" and "all productions that pertain to man's welfare." In another variant of this viewpoint, zoologist Orton held that "man himself is developed on the same general principles as the Butterfly"; each originated as a "homogeneous globule" that slowly speciated by means of "the very gradual process of 'natural selection.'"[189]

The "Man" in these passages was not individual man, however. For Dana, Orton, and the other evolutionary scientists who belonged to the Carleton curriculum, "Man" served as a shorthand for mankind, the human species, or other collective bodies in which the individual was only a fleck. The prominent physical geographer Arnold Guyot, for example, used the inclusive expression "Human Family," though "race" was his preferred group concept. So he split the human family into six distinct races, associating each one with a different period of evolutionary origin, and with different mental and physical traits. Fixing on group differences in physique, Guyot (using grotesque facial sketches) depicted the peoples of the southern hemisphere as exhibiting "deformity and ugliness," while "Caucasians" possessed the "greatest beauty" and developed into the world's most "cultured and progressive people." LeConte voiced similar views. He presented Man as necessarily part of a "social organism," divided into races, which evolved (or failed to) through long stages: the Stone Age, the Bronze Age, and the Iron Age. These LeConte distinguished from one another by their systems of economic production, as well as by their weapons, forms of plunder, and decorative "ornaments"—group attributes that indicated their level of "social development."[190]

In acclimating students to these ways of thinking about nature, science teachers at Carleton were moving in step with Americans outside the academy. This may surprise us when, a century and a half later, many men and women deny any form of evolution. Yet, the leading historian of evolutionary thought, Peter Bowler, has observed that "America . . . experienced a full-scale Darwinian revolution in the early 1860s"—a revolution that, with ups and downs, continued for the rest of the century, according to other historical researchers.[191] True, the story was a complicated one, rife with mutual misunderstandings among the parties involved. Evolutionary concepts met firm resistance in certain quarters of the public, and many people willing to accept some evolutionary doctrines rejected Charles Darwin's own claim that the evolution of life-forms occurs principally through a nonteleological mechanism: namely, the "natural selection" of variations in plants and animals that arise by chance in the organic world. (I elaborate on this idea in Chapter 6.) Against this view stood numerous teleological theories of evolution that wore the label of "Lamarckian" (after the early nineteenth-century French naturalist Jean-Baptiste Lamarck) and offered more directional accounts that involved the mechanism they called the "inheritance of acquired characteristics." These conceived evolution as a process through which a species acquires, by means of the repeated use of certain behaviors, advantageous characteristics that their offspring directly inherit, so that each successive generation becomes better adapted to its external circumstances. (In Lamarck's classic example: giraffes, short-necked early on in the course of evolution, made their necks longer by stretching them as far as possible to reach the leaves of tall trees; doing so, the short-necked creatures bequeathed slighter longer necks to their progeny, who did the same over generations, progressively bringing forth the long-necked giraffes of the present.)

In the literature of the day, the lines between Darwinian and Lamarckian theories were soft and permeable, and eclectic combinations of the two approaches commonplace. Darwin's own work sometimes incorporated Lamarckian elements (the notion of the inheritance of acquired characteristics), and some self-identified Lamarckians returned the favor. But the most polyphonic voice in the conversation was Herbert Spencer, an English writer who became the best-selling evolutionist in America in the second half of the century though a series of books in which he ranged from philosophy to biology, ethics to political economy, and beyond—and in which he frequently changed his arguments. Branded in his lifetime as everything from a theist to an agnostic, a proponent to an opponent of teleological thinking, a descendant of Lamarck to an ally of Darwin, Spencer attracted both ardent admirers and strident critics.[192] (Then and since, the opinion of most informed commentators has been that Spencer belonged to the Lamarckian tradition.) Despite different contemporary reactions to Spencer (and to most evolutionists), however, from the 1860s onward evolutionary ideas quietly made their way into America's educational institutions, infiltrating high schools and colleges through new or revised textbooks, just like those used at Carleton and other religiously affiliated schools.[193]

Perhaps because Carleton itself was a Congregationalist institution and Congregationalism was the denomination "most influential in interpreting and propagating" evolutionary ideas (to quote historian James Moore), Carleton students received a heavier dose of evolutionary doctrines than students elsewhere.[194] But this comparison is less important than the fact that teachers and students who were on the ground at Carleton in the 1870s recognized that evolutionary ideas warranted serious attention. The science professors demonstrated this clearly by their choice of textbooks, and other members of the faculty strongly reinforced the point.[195] "Evolution," wrote Andrew Veblen to Dorfman, "was often spoken about at Carleton in my day and discussed; and no one appeared to question its validity. I heard no one say anything against the theory."[196]

THIS ACADEMIC SETTING formed Thorstein Veblen's intellectual world during his six years at Carleton, and we can be certain he was wired into it. The recitation method of instruction demanded that students master the contents of their textbooks, and Thorstein's transcript shows he earned top grades in almost every academic subject—science, literature, Latin and Greek, and so on. (For all eighteen terms, he also received high grades—several times a perfect grade—in "deportment," a subject that apparently required students to attend "devotional services in the Chapel" and "public worship on the Sabbath" and to refrain from "intemperance, profanity, playing at cards or billiards, dancing, and whatever hinders the highest mental and moral culture.")[197] At the end of his first three years at Carleton, Thorstein won the Atkins Prize—in the generous amount of $80 (= $2,000)—for his knowledge of subjects taught in the preparatory program.[198] He ranked first on the entry exam into the college program proper. The strong performance then continued in his college-level courses, even in his third and last year when he took a double course load, after deciding to squeeze Carleton's junior and senior requirements into a single year.[199] Economist John Bates Clark (who taught at Carleton from 1877 to 1881) remembered that Veblen, at the end of that year, "passed an exceptionally good examination." In a letter to Dorfman years later, Clark added: "I always spoke of Veblen as the ablest man that Carleton had graduated during the time that I was familiar with conditions there."[200]

Outside of his coursework, Thorstein Veblen also took an active part in campus life. Replying to a question from Dorfman, Andrew described this aspect of his brother's time at Carleton.

He was generally considered a good member of the college community by both students and faculty. Naturally his unquestioned brightness and ability attracted favorable consideration among some students and teachers. Perhaps some regarded him with some admiration. [I do not recall] what he said on any one matter in particular. Th., as most of us, doubtless made earnest statements in what came up in discussions of all sorts—in our small, intimate groups, in debates, literary society, etc.[201]

Following Andrew's example, the literary society Thorstein joined was the classically styled Philomathian Society, a large student group that met weekly for "debates, essays and orations," sometimes serious, sometimes the opposite.[202] Thorstein belonged to the Philos all through Carleton, playing a visible enough role that a columnist in the *Northfield Mail* complained that "some of T. B. V.'s [literary] productions" had nothing in them besides "trifling wit."[203] (The *Northfield Mail,* one of the town newspapers, was apparently hard up for copy. Apparently, too, by 1877 "T. B. V." was a known figure.) Asked years later by Dorfman whether Thorstein Veblen's personality caused any "antagonism" with other students, his college classmate Rudolf von Tobel said: "I never knew that [Veblen] engendered [restrictive] any such." (What he remembered instead was that Veblen had a "dry humor that was likely to break out on almost any occasion, especially a solemn one.") Pushed further by Dorfman about whether he could recall "any cultural antagonism between Norwegians and New Englanders" in the Carleton student body, von Tobel replied: "None whatever."[204]

For Carleton students in this period, events outside of the college did not attract much attention. Republican Northfield was a very placid town, except on September 7, 1876, when it grabbed national headlines as the scene of a violent raid on the First National Bank of Northfield by the outlaw gang of Jesse James and Cole Younger, in what became the legendary gang's last stand. (Gang members killed two townsmen, townsmen killed two gang members, and in the ensuing manhunt the rest of the gang was captured, except for Jesse James and his brother.) On the day of the botched robbery, Thorstein Veblen was, according to family accounts, threshing wheat on his parents' farm, rather than watching the mayhem in town; but an echo of the incident appears in *The Theory of the Leisure Class* when he discussed the "recrudescence of outlawry" in America in the 1870s.[205] What Veblen may have been involved in more directly was work on behalf of the Independent "Greenback" Party, a political organization that was then mobilizing in the run-up to the 1880 national elections. In a context shaped by popular reaction against the brutal government crackdown on workers during the Great Railroad Strike of 1877, the Greenbacks were growing fast, using what historian Nell Painter has described as an "anticapitalist and antibanking rhetoric," which was based on an invidious contrast between party members "as 'producers' and bankers as parasites." In an item about Carleton in the *Rice County Journal* in November 1879, the writer speculated about Thorstein's late return to school for the fall term: "We supposed he has been too busy furthering the interests of the Greenback Party in regard to the election to come soon." But from the tone of the remark, it is hard to tell whether this was a campus in-joke or a factual statement. Regardless, the rhetoric Veblen heard from the Greenbacks was nothing new to him at this point.[206]

Veblen's years at Carleton had a more private side as well. It was here he met his first wife, Ellen (Nellie) Rolfe. Two years younger than Thorstein, she began the classical track of Carleton's college prep program with Thorstein in 1874, and they continued together through the college program until his early graduation in 1880. (She graduated in 1881, delivering an oration on the historical progress of society.) Ellen was the niece of Carleton's President Strong, and the daughter of a wealthy Stacyville, Iowa, family; her father, Charles Rolfe, was a prominent and successful businessman with commercial holdings and financial interests throughout the Midwest.[207] Like Thorstein, Ellen was an excellent student: von Tobel described her as "easily the most intellectual member of the class" of '81, and he recalled "her sparkling and, at times, slightly caustic wit."[208] These were Veblen's traits as well, and the two soon developed a close relationship. According to Ellen's subsequent account, Thorstein "told me he loved me 'as dearly as he could' when I was only sixteen and he eighteen. I refused him then as I continued to do. . . . But because of his love of me, I felt bound to him in a sense, and did not expect to marry anyone else."[209] (Ellen was not always accurate, but this statement comes as close as we can probably get to the details of the early relationship.) Still, because of Thorstein's problems with health and employment in the decade ahead, the marriage did not happen until 1888. Many marital agonies followed for Ellen and Thorstein, however, and the couple were legally divorced in 1913.

During his years at Carleton, Thorstein stayed in close contact with his family. The family farm was nearby, and in Northfield he shared a house with several of his siblings. This was a modest house that Thomas

Veblen built by hand in 1873, on a lot he bought in the town to accommodate the growing number of offspring attending Carleton, plus some of the younger children in the family, whom he and Kari had decided (for the sake of convenience, presumably) to send to public schools in Northfield before they were old enough for Carleton. According to Emily Veblen, this setup also cut down on overall expenses.[210] It also kept Thorstein Veblen embedded in his family as he was making his way intellectually, socially, and perhaps politically into new territories outside the kin group.

This living arrangement gave big brother Andrew an especially large role as a kind of surrogate father to his younger siblings. Age twenty-six when Thorstein entered college at age seventeen, Andrew set the example Thorstein would follow when he chose his academic program at Carleton (and afterward). What is more, Andrew was a man of strong opinions, even during his twenties. For the most part, these early opinions have left no records, but two traces have survived, though one is no more than a three-sentence summary of Andrew's 1877 commencement oration. If we take the two records together, however, we can detect a distinctive perspective on the social world, which shows Andrew generalizing from particular moments in the history of his own family.

The first of these items, his Carleton graduation address, titled "The Literature of the North," looked backward and forward in history, in an encomium to his family's Norwegian heritage. Speaking to an audience with few Scandinavians sitting in it, Andrew used the occasion to celebrate "what the literature in prose and poetry of the Scandinavian nations has done, is able and destined to do for Englishmen and for all mankind," because it contains cultural "treasures we could not afford to be without." In contrast, the second item, a short article, dealt with the present, as Andrew criticized current social conditions in the country where his family had settled. Titled "Poverty or Luxury Most Productive of Crime?," and appearing in the *Northfield Standard* in 1872, the article began with the hackneyed dichotomy, right out of common-school readers and Lutheran catechisms, of the rich man and the poor man: the first living in "luxury" and "consequent idleness," taking advantage of others in society, the second "obligated to labor." But, in an expansion of the usual story, Andrew pictured these characters as they appeared in the eyes of those in the society around them: we "all detest" the poor man, recoiling because "he is not polished," while we "admire . . . the man whose mansions ornament our towns," for it is "natural for us to be dazzled by show and display." The result, Andrew observed, is that although the rich man probably commits more crimes, he has the wherewithal to better conceal them, whereas the poor man is always punished, in an example of the "corrupt logic" that is destroying, by means of the "increase of wealth," the society built by the industrious, "virtuous pilgrims." But Andrew then issued a historical reminder, one straight from the home and hearth: "The great and good men of our county have, almost without exception, been the children of poverty rather than of luxury."[211]

To imagine that Thorstein Veblen's later work was "influenced" by these particular statements by Andrew is farfetched—Thorstein's phenomenal memory notwithstanding. All the same, Andrew's two brief writings provide a quick measure of the intellectual pulse of the mentor with whom Thorstein lived daily for the three years when the brothers overlapped at Carleton. What Andrew's statements indicate is not "influence" but the existence of another social space in Thorstein Veblen's life where the practices of thinking in terms of historical change, seeing the individual as part of a social whole, and valorizing work over idleness were practices as natural as tending the surrounding wheat fields.

Of course, Thorstein Veblen grew familiar with many practices besides these in the course of his upbringing. He learned the skills needed, for example, to carve wood; maintain good deportment; solve calculus problems; and read books in English, Norwegian, German, Latin, Greek, and French. Likewise, he became acquainted with other ways of thinking about and evaluating the social world—some of them occasionally divergent from the practices emphasized in this chapter, some of them simply off on other tangents. But with none of these *other* knowledge practices did his experiences start so early in life, continue for so many back-to-back years, and recur in so many different contexts—family, community, church, common school, college, and so forth. Even with this rich accumulation, however, all that any of these practices amounted to, throughout these early years, were resources in a holding area, lying in wait until Veblen felt that some of these stored materials, rather than others, might enable him to accomplish what he wanted to accomplish. And to get to that point would still take him time.

MANY YEARS AFTER receiving his A.B. from Carleton in 1880, Veblen spoke out about American colleges, usually critically. Drawing on his impressions of undergraduate life at Yale University (where he was a graduate student in the early 1880s), Veblen derided the country's most distinguished colleges as leisure-class havens, islands where the offspring of the wealthy collected souvenirs of privilege that served no socially productive purpose. He counted participation in college sports as one of these status markers, but his primary example was the worthless study of the classics. "The ability to use and to understand certain of the dead languages of southern Europe," he remarked in *The Theory of the Leisure Class*, "serve the decorative ends of leisure-class knowledge" by a display of "conspicuous waste": they "consume ... the learner's time and effort in acquiring knowledge which is of no use."[212] This is a theme he frequently returned to, and we might interpret his statements biographically, as evidence of a lingering distaste for his own classical education. The inference is plausible, for whenever the subject of classical education came up in his later writings, "useless" was Veblen's immediate verdict. (To repeat, though: just because someone calls his or her earlier experiences "useless" does not mean that they were. "Worthless" college courses often teach us more than we realize.[213])

Even so, when Veblen looked beyond undergraduate programs at Yale and other large universities, he offered a more positive assessment of some American colleges that were classics-based. What provoked much of Veblen's ire about the classics programs he criticized was that they were organized to keep students away from the pursuit of science, which held the promise of knowledge that actually was worthwhile. As Veblen knew, however, some colleges did not throw up this barrier; instead, they actually prepared students for scientific research. In a book he drafted around 1904, he wrote:

> It is coming to be plain ... that, for the advanced work in science and scholarship, the training given by a college of moderate size commonly affords a better preparation than is had in the very large undergraduate schools of the great universities. This holds true ... in spite of the fact the smaller schools are ... working against the side-draft of a religious bias ... and are under-rated by all concerned.[214]

What Veblen was referring to here, approvingly, were colleges much like Carleton, and the curriculum at colleges of this kind—colleges with a religious side draft—nearly always involved the study of the classics.[215] He had experienced that firsthand at Carleton, yet studying the classics there had not been at odds with learning modern science. Carleton had a classical track *and* a science track, and its program required classicists to take a range of science courses. Not only that, but the two tracks converged in their use of knowledge practices that Veblen himself would later draw on. Perhaps for these reasons, he held Carleton in special regard. For instance, replying in 1917 to a request from Carleton trustee Hiram Scriver to contribute to a fundraising campaign to enlarge the college's physical plant, Veblen answered that a contribution was "out of the question," because growth would ruin the institution. "The endeavor to make Carleton a big college or a pseudo-university," he told Scriver, was a "deadly mistake," which would "throw away its opportunity to do the work for which its place and character fits it." Staying its established course, Carleton "was a good small college": "one of the best, in fact."[216] The statement was high praise—Veblen did not get more enthusiastic than this. This small college a few miles away from his parents' midwestern farm had left its mark.

CHAPTER 4

ENTERING AND LEAVING

1.

Carleton College gave a great deal to Thorstein Veblen. In his six years there, he mastered Latin and Greek, inhaled the natural sciences, scored academic honors, earned an A.B. degree, and met his future wife. He also started to make his way toward a career.

It is hard to know what occupation his parents initially envisioned when they sent him off to Carleton. And as a seventeen-year-old farm boy when he enrolled in Carleton's college prep program, Thorstein probably did not have much of a clue either—perhaps even less of one than most seventeen-year-olds today have. In the 1870s, a classics-based college education mostly functioned, as it had traditionally, as a gateway into a career in one of the established professions—the ministry, medicine, law, or government service.[1] But as much as Thomas and Kari Veblen may have wanted their children to be college educated, it's unlikely they ever expected bookish son Thorstein to pursue one of these careers: *none* of their sons did.[2] The remaining option, aside from a career in business, was to become a teacher on some rung of the educational ladder. The parents knew college graduates who earned their livings as common-school teachers; and not only had Andrew Veblen taught at a local high school before he went to college, but right after his graduation from Carleton he was offered (and accepted) a job teaching Latin and English at Luther College in Iowa.[3] That was in 1877, the same year Thorstein finished prep school and was moving up into Carleton's college program.

So perhaps a teaching position of some kind was the destination the Veblens had in sight for Thorstein once he completed college, their hopes fanned by the opening up of more common schools, preparatory academies, denominational colleges, and state universities in the Upper Midwest throughout this period.[4] Still, no one in the family, Thorstein included, could have imagined for him a future position as a university-based educator engaged in specialized scholarly research. Few college freshmen today aspire to this peculiar line of work, and in the 1870s no one did—positions of this type were unheard of in the United States. Indeed, outside of the natural sciences, educator-researcher positions in universities were nearly nonexistent until the final decade or so of the century, when employment opportunities began improving for young men waiting in the wings. This fluid situation offered Veblen a chance to become part of the new generation of Americans who were in the process of creating and defining the "professional academic"—the American version of the professional academic—and establishing that pursuit as a recognized career on the country's social landscape. By his last year in college, Veblen, without the slightest idea of what was ahead for American higher education, was inadvertently equipping himself to respond to this historical opportunity with one final set of courses he took at Carleton.

These courses were in philosophy and its satellite areas. Veblen studied philosophy in a period when "philosophy" had a wider ambit than it does today; within the curriculum of the typical nineteenth-century college, philosophy included all branches of knowledge aside from the ancient and modern languages, mathematics, and the natural sciences. By pedagogical convention, college textbook writers divided this large subject matter into two halves: "mental philosophy," which included epistemology, logic, metaphysics, and psychology (or the nature of "mind"); and "moral philosophy," which dealt—prescriptively—with personal ethics and conduct in the social world. Carleton followed this standard division, making courses in moral philosophy and mental philosophy requirements for seniors in the program. In Veblen's final year he took both courses, and during his last two years at Carleton he took several related courses.

In the area of moral philosophy, he used a series of textbooks that offered elaborated and sophisticated versions of doctrines and practices that went back to his childhood, presenting these ideas in new renditions that refashioned the themes of Lutheran catechisms and common-school primers in order to fit midcentury America. Leading the lineup here were James Fairchild's *Moral Philosophy* and Mark Hopkins's *Evidences of Christianity*. (Both authors were Protestant divines who, like Carleton's President Strong, rose to college presidencies: Fairchild at Oberlin College; Hopkins at Williams College.) Representing one of the dominant strands of nineteenth-century ethical theory, the two books introduced Veblen to the anti-individualist "doctrine of disinterested benevolence."[5]

This moral doctrine—to cite Fairchild's representative formulation—taught that actions are wrong when they arise from selfish "desires and passions" but virtuous when they heed the Bible's commandment to "love thy neighbor." It was from the "practical outworking of benevolence" (in this biblical sense) that there arise, according to Fairchild, the duties of parents to children, teachers to pupils, rulers to subjects, and so on—all of these specific social obligations manifesting the general "duty of usefulness" to one's community. In Fairchild's view, meeting these obligations is facilitated for moral agents by certain unselfish attributes of human nature, including "the powerful instinct of parental affection" and "the impulse to usefulness." Regardless of these helping instincts, "industry, employment, is a duty," and "a life thus devoted stands opposed to a life of self-indulgence—a nursing of one's own ease, or comfort, or pleasure."[6]

So far, Fairchild's teachings simply rehearsed the platitudes sounded in childhood textbooks. But, in a move that surprises us today, Fairchild overlaid the doctrine of disinterested benevolence with a jeremiad about the corrosion of benevolence in his own society, voicing a social critique that pinned blame for the new immorality on newly ascendant economic forces. Good Protestant pedagogue that he was, Fairchild held that "wealth"—*provided* it "has been honestly made"—"is to be regarded as a means of usefulness, to be employed conscientiously and benevolently." But, in his own society, he lamented, it "is often found easier to acquire wealth, than to use it wisely, [because] the struggle for acquisition not rarely perverts the character" of the wealth chaser. What was more, inasmuch as people care "to be held in esteem by others," they are increasingly devoting "large expenditures" to satisfy "the arbitrary demands of fashion and ostentatious display, [which] are a bottomless abyss, swallowing all resources, and yielding only emptiness." Still further, observed Fairchild, wealth often is not honestly earned, but amassed by adopting "the ordinary business maxim"—the maxim of self-interest—that "makes the simple [person] the prey of the shrewd." From an ethical standpoint, however, "there are things that cannot properly be appropriated." Historically, for example, it was "preposterous [for some social groups] to take possession of the unoccupied land of a continent, and exact rent of all others who enter upon it"; and no less morally reprehensible was the contemporary "effort to raise or depress prices, by shrewd management, as in securing a monopoly, or producing a glut [in order to make] a profit out of the loss of others." But Fairchild sternly asked his college readers: "What good account can [a person] give of himself, whose business is speculation in Western lands, or in Wall-street stocks?" Warning them that "no business can be approved which does not contribute to human welfare," he handed them an ethical ideal to strive for: "A perfect civilization involves an exact distribution of the result of labor among the various parties that have contributed to the result."[7]

Running through Fairchild's moral, economic, and historical analysis was an explicit concern with the nature of "social institutions" and their "origin and historical growth"; and in drawing out these social themes, Fairchild was again a representative author. Mark Hopkins's treatise, *Evidences of Christianity,* similarly described for Carleton students the "institutions that enter into the fabric of society."[8] Still, for neither Fairchild nor Hopkins was this topic the main focus. By the date of their texts (the 1860s), American moral philosophers had mostly handed off the topic of society's workings to historians and political analysts, who had shaved off "social institutions" as a subject more or less separate from the rest of moral philosophy—although still something to moralize about. To these writers, the notion of "social institutions" came naturally; best-selling authors had already put it into wide circulation as a means to describe the features of American society and to compare them with the characteristics of other societies. The terminology of "institutions" appeared, for instance, in contemporary histories of the United States by patrician historians like George Bancroft, Francis Parkman, and William Prescott, and it was a strong presence also in popular sketches of the nation by foreign visitors such as Alexis de Tocqueville and Frances Trollope. In volume 1 of his eight-volume *History of the United States of America, from the Discovery of the American Continent* (1834–1878), Bancroft, for one, spoke of "ancient institutions," "feudal institutions," "aristocratical institutions," "free institutions," "communal institutions," "popular institutions," "political institutions," "civil and religious institutions," "the unequal institutions of society," and so forth.[9]

By these channels, the topic of social institutions made its way into postbellum college texts, and Carleton's curriculum—synced, as usual, with the contemporary textbook market—contained leading examples of this genre of institutional history. Most likely, Veblen's exposure to it began in 1879, partway through his sophomore year, in a course titled "Analysis of Civil Government," where the assigned text was a book with the same name by "counselor-at-law" Calvin Townsend, which was dense with the vocabulary of "institutions" and purported to provide a "theory of our institutions."[10] On this score, however, Townsend's text offered nothing to compare with François Guizot's *General History of Civilization in Europe, from the Fall of the Roman Empire to the French Revolution,* which formed part of the curriculum of Veblen's combined junior and senior year, when he took Carleton's History of Civilization course. Guizot's opus was by then an established classic; written by a prominent, colorful French (Protestant) historian and politician, it appeared in French in 1828 and in many later English-language editions, frequently used in American colleges before and after the Civil War. Looking backward in 1928, intellectual historians (and sociologists) L. L. Bernard and J. S. Bernard gave Guizot's text principal credit for pointing American scholars toward the systematic study of "the history of institutions in the third quarter of the nineteenth century"—an exaggerated assessment, but testimony, nonetheless, to the preeminence of the *History of Civilization* in that period.[11]

In the book, Guizot presented a nimble drama that foregrounded ways of thinking about and judging society that had been coming at Veblen from many directions. Spanning fifteen centuries of Western European history to highlight "the grand crises [involved] in the development of modern society," the drama sought to demonstrate and redemonstrate how social institutions—"political institutions," "municipal institutions," "religious institutions," and on and on—are "continually changing," always in a state of "chaos" and "unfixedness." Taking in the panorama, Guizot believed that Western civilization had experienced enormous "progress" and would continue to do so; he opined that "a special law of Providence" guaranteed this development (which was still in its "infancy"). Even so, Guizot held that the historian's interest was not with the divine law of progress but with tracking the earthly "chain of causes and effects." For this purpose, he decomposed history into forces that promoted progress and forces that hindered it. Invoking the familiar Protestant moral metric, he rated "lassitude and inactivity" as hindrances, "activity" and enterprise as agents of progress—but agents with two different faces. One of these Guizot saw manifested throughout history in "avarice," "pillage," "predation," and similar selfish actions, while the other form of activity embodied "productive principles" operating through industry and science. Between these bald alternatives, Guizot left Carleton students in no doubt about the right choice. In line with the rest of the moral philosophy curriculum, his *History* instructed Veblen and his classmates that virtuous

conduct entailed productive activity aimed toward the "perfection of social relations."[12]

Communicating this real-life lesson (and others like it) gave moral philosophy textbooks a lofty mission in nineteenth-century American colleges. But perhaps because the subject boiled down to glorified common-
places, moral philosophy lost its draw among postbellum educators in
comparison with the more urgent subject of "mental philosophy." This
development is counterintuitive; moral philosophy dealt with passions, duties, and actions, while mental philosophy concerned the interior workings of the mind. So how could mental philosophy become a matter of
urgency? The answer has several parts. The men who taught philosophy
during the two decades after the Civil War fell into two groups: an upper
tier of philosophers who had done postgraduate work in Europe and, following their return to the United States, wrote treatises on mental (and
moral) philosophy for scholars and advanced students; and a lower tier of
homebred college teachers and textbook authors who filtered ideas
drawn from these treatises down to larger student audiences. This arrangement gave American philosophy a strongly European flavor in an era
when British and continental philosophers had become preoccupied with
epistemology, logic, and metaphysics (the rubrics shifted around). That pre-
occupation stemmed from what scholars and other philosophically minded
people, who were then attempting to ride the waves of unanticipated, often
unsettling, discoveries in the natural sciences, assumed to be the close relationship between scientific knowledge and mental philosophy.[13]

At the base of this assumption was the conviction, shared among intellectuals, that to qualify as "knowledge," statements about the natural
world required the imprimatur of philosophy. This was so because, going
back to antiquity, philosophers commanded the authority to determine
what counted as knowledge—*Scientia*—as opposed to opinion (or fiction
or fabrication).[14] In early modern Europe, this long-mooted issue took a
sharp turn in the wake of Isaac Newton's discovery of the fundamental
laws of physics and astronomy, and the cascade of natural scientific discoveries that followed, because there was little doubt (among the people
concerned about this issue) that those discoveries offered something more
than opinions: they actually *were* knowledge. But what made them so?
Or, as mental philosophers phrased this question: What was the source
of scientific knowledge?

In the two centuries that separated Newton from Veblen, European
men of letters spilled many arcane and polemical words as they hammered

out responses to this question and broke apart into contending philosophical schools—several of them relevant to Veblen's education.[15] To take these positions chronologically, the earliest was English "empiricism" as it was formulated by Newton's friend John Locke (1632–1704), who held that knowledge, properly so-called, is rooted in the observation of objects and events external to the knower—that is, in the sights and sounds that the knower experiences. Presented to the mind as ideas, these sense impressions provide the materials from which the knower—legitimately, in Locke's view—induces those uniform patterns of causal connection that are stated in natural scientific laws. Locke's account here was relatively straightforward, and this made it easy prey for David Hume (1711–1776), the disturbing voice of "skepticism" in this period. According to Hume, there was nothing scientifically legitimate about Lockean induction. To the contrary, what the would-be knower takes to be a causal connection between objects or events is actually nothing more than a conjunction of ideas or impressions that he or she has come, by force of habit, to associate with one another. In Hume's view, we have no warrant for treating our customary mental associations as descriptions of real causal processes in nature, since our minds have no way to grasp hold of those real processes on the basis of our contingently connected ideas. This limitation, on his account, undermines any and all efforts to differentiate knowledge from opinion.

Two vigorous replies followed. One of these was that of the German "idealist" Immanuel Kant (1724–1808), who proposed that the human mind comes naturally equipped with an internal structure, or (in our terms) a basic operating system. This structure Kant spoke of as a set of "categories," meaning by "categories" not boxes in the brain, but a universal set of mental processors that organizes the knower's sense impressions and constitutes objects in nature as causally connected—"causality" being one of the mind's basic categories. Knowledge—the desideratum— is made possible, according to Kant, by the operation of these categories on the sensory materials that come from the knower's experiences in the world. That said, however, Kant was quick to add a qualifier: human knowledge is always at a remove. Because the mind can never turn off its categories in order to look into what may lie behind them, human knowledge deals only with objects as they *appear* on the knower's mental screen, not with "things-in-themselves"—Kant's term for the realities that knowers are unable to grasp and that, therefore, must remain permanently unknowable.

The second retort to Hume was the "realist" position of Scottish philosophers Thomas Reid (1710–1796) and Dugald Stewart (1753–1828), who balked at setting Kant-like limitations on the mind's ability to know the natural world. Rejecting Hume's depiction of the mind as a bundle of mental associations, and disavowing Kant's notion of unknowable realities, the Scots maintained that the mind is endowed (by the Author of Nature) with powerful "faculties." These include certain cognitive principles— certain taken-for-granted "principles of commonsense"—that enable the knower to have a direct perception of external objects as they are in-themselves and in their real causal relations. It is due to these first principles, claimed Reid and Stewart, that the knower can validly arrive at scientific knowledge by the use of induction.

Among these approaches, the Scottish commonsense perspective dominated the teaching of mental philosophy in American colleges deep into the nineteenth century, at the same time as the other approaches (except for Hume's) were also widely aired. Carleton in Veblen's day was no exception. In the Logic course he took in his junior/senior year, for example, the assigned text was the *Manual of Elementary Logic,* an extremely popular work by Lyman Atwater (professor of philosophy at Princeton Theological Seminary), who held to the Scottish philosophical tradition and joined in its defense of scientific knowledge based on induction, telling readers that induction "is the principal instrument of scientific progress, and of all advance in human knowledge, except through Divine Revelation, within the realms of actual being."[16] Carleton's *Annual Catalogue* for the year did not list which other mental philosophy texts students used, but in this area, too, the local faculty kept them abreast of certain wider contemporary developments, as we see in the case of Veblen. At the end of his junior/senior year, when it came time to choose a subject for his graduation address, he picked nothing less than "Mill's Examination of Hamilton's Philosophy of the Conditioned."

Veblen's formidable title flagged what was *the* central dispute in mental philosophy in the 1870s (at least in the eyes of philosophy teachers in American colleges). The "Hamilton" in the title was Scottish philosopher Sir William Hamilton (1788–1856), whom many regarded as "the greatest metaphysician of his age," while "Mill" was John Stuart Mill (1806–1873), the preeminent English philosopher of science (among his other credits).[17] In the controversy between the two, Hamilton had the first word. His philosophical project, as he summed it up in lectures published in the late 1850s, was to reconcile and integrate Scottish realism and German idealism. To this end, he accepted the Scots' contention that mental faculties make knowledge of reality possible, while he also agreed with Kant that things-in-themselves are unknowable because they are inaccessible through the categories of the mind. Toggling between these positions, Hamilton maintained that the mind's faculties, or categories, do allow direct perception and knowledge of reality so far as the mind's powers extend, but these powers do not extend to things-in-themselves. Hamilton worded this claim by saying that our knowledge of the natural world is always "conditioned" by our limited mental faculties, so that absolute, "unconditioned" knowledge is impossible. Despite this limitation, he held that we can know by inference that things-in-themselves do have certain real effects and that we can nail down the scientific "laws which govern the appearances of the material universe [and regulate] the phenomena of organic and inorganic bodies." In addition, according to Hamilton, we know there are some things we cannot know, first among them God—who is "at once known and unknown."[18]

To Mill, Hamilton's position was logically incoherent, as he elaborated with hostile zeal in his six-hundred-page *Examination of Sir William Hamilton's Philosophy*, which first appeared in 1865. Dissecting Hamilton's writings passage by passage, Mill convicted him of the mortal philosophical sin of inconsistency. This inconsistency, as Mill described it, had to do with Hamilton's colliding claims about the human mind: the mind has powers that allow it to perceive and know reality directly; but then again the mind cannot have such knowledge because its powers are "conditioned" and things-in-themselves are unknowable; but yet again the mind can draw correct inferences about things-in-themselves. Pulling back from these conflicting assertions basic to Hamilton's realist-idealist defense of scientific knowledge, Mill invoked Locke's empiricism. He strongly reaffirmed, as philosopher John Skorupski has summarized, that "the whole of science . . . is built from the materials of experience," as these give rise to the "sensations" that underwrite the "inductions" that are the basis for formulating general causal laws.[19]

The fact that Veblen picked the recondite Hamilton–Mill controversy as the subject of his commencement address is telling.[20] He had thousands of other options. The speeches of the two other young men who graduated with him from Carleton's classical course, for example, were titled "Development of the English Language" and "Man, a Seeker after Truth."[21] But Veblen went in a more esoteric direction when, in the nearly ninety-degree heat of June 24, 1880, he spoke to an audience that included not only faculty, college trustees, and family members but also Minnesota's superintendent of education and its Republican governor (businessman John Pillsbury, founder of the famed flour company). Later that day, the *Rice County Journal Extra* reported: "Veblen, son of Thor, in spite of the heat, hammered away blow upon blow, and with no mean skill, at a subject the bare name of which was almost an overdose for the average hearer. He held, in a word, that the case of Mill vs. Hamilton was clearly one of *sequiter* [*sic*]."[22]

Aside from this short news item, nothing is known about the content of Veblen's address; there are no copies or other accounts of it. For this reason, whether he aligned himself more with Hamilton or with Mill is a matter for guesswork.[23] If we consider Veblen's attitudes toward his intellectual ancestry in the immediately following years, either alignment seems plausible. All the same, it's a good bet that his speech came down on the side of Hamilton. What suggests this is that Veblen was entering the debate after Mill had attacked Hamilton, not the other way around; there would have been no need for Veblen to deal Hamilton another blow, especially when most philosophical pundits thought Mill had bested Hamilton. That victory disappointed American educators, who revered Hamilton (because of his fusion of science and religion) and who had no affection for Mill (the notorious agnostic). For Veblen to champion Mill in this context would have been an unpopular move in front of members of the audience who were Hamilton admirers, but the *Rice County Journal Extra* did not hint at any griping about the substance of the speech.[24]

Whatever side Veblen took, his oration put him in the thick of a dispute in which the two opposing parties were actually on the *same* side in their stance toward scientific knowledge. Despite their differences, both Hamilton and Mill upheld the prevailing practice among philosophers of accepting, defending, and extolling natural science. By this era, when the two men were the reigning philosophical authorities, that practice was a matter of course, so that Veblen would have been drawn into it over and over. Joining the Hamilton-Mill controversy meant engaging in the practice and using the tools that were part of it: the concepts, canonical texts, points of reference, and so forth that made up the Western philosophical tradition. These tools were new ones for Veblen the college boy, but the practice itself was not. Farmers in the audience, businessmen, teachers: all these familiar people were promoters of scientific knowledge in more mundane ways, as Veblen had been observing for years. When he spoke about Hamilton and Mill, he was dealing with internationally known mental philosophers who were in sync with these down-home boosters of science.

Joining the debate also gave Veblen hands-on experience with the techniques philosophers used to construct and present their arguments. He had previously seen some of these techniques in the theological controversies flaring in the Norwegian-American church, and he had also seen them in the way Greek and Roman authors treated their adversaries, but now he was engaged in them more directly. In 1879, the year before Veblen's graduation, G. Stanley Hall, a young American philosopher off in Berlin to learn about laboratory methods for studying the human mind, grumbled that the philosopher's research method often consisted of nothing more than a "hypercritical" posture toward the work of earlier philosophers. Hall did not name Hamilton or Mill as illustrations of this practice, though he might have, for their modus operandi, too, was to focus on the writings of previous philosophers and to attack.[25] Mill described (almost as a compliment) how Hamilton had leveled "very serious charge[s] against the great majority of philosophers" and succeeded as "a most unsparing controversialist"; and Mill then followed suit, tearing into Hamilton's texts chapter and verse, using the "iconoclastic rhetoric" he is known for.[26] And Veblen, it seems, was quick to learn by example and to pick up the practice of the philosophers he was dealing with in his graduation speech, in which—to quote the *Rice County Journal Extra* again— he "hammered away blow upon blow" at *their* arguments.

This practice had another one conjoined to it. Hamilton and Mill, like many philosophers before them, aimed high. They both sought to intervene in a long-standing controversy among the giants of mental philosophy concerning what they all regarded as the problem of securing the foundations of human knowledge. And, once again, Veblen picked up his cues, charging into this headlining dispute and confronting two of the leading philosophers of the age and the latest philosophical innovation, the doctrine of the conditioned. He was twenty-two years old, just graduating from a small midwestern college—and this immodest ambition to arbitrate and advance a debate at the cutting edge of Western philosophy shows his youth as well as some of the personality traits he had acquired by then.[27] But what this ambition captures also is Veblen in the process of learning the intellectual ropes, practicing the techniques by which scholars did their work.

2.

At Carleton, as in most American colleges, Moral Philosophy and Mental Philosophy were capstone courses taught by the college president. In Veblen's junior/senior year, however, President Strong was frequently away from Northfield on fundraising campaigns, so he delegated the two subjects to another faculty member, John Bates Clark (1847–1938), professor of political economy and history (and college librarian).[28] In both areas, Clark apparently stuck to the subject matter as Strong had mapped it out, introducing his students to the texts, themes, and practices described in the previous section. At the same time, Clark taught his own regularly assigned courses, including one titled Political Economy, which rounded out Veblen's program at Carleton. Packed into his busy final year, this course nevertheless grabbed Veblen's attention, as Andrew Veblen recalled: "Economics became of great interest to [Thorstein] at Carleton. Prof. Clark was a very inspiring teacher" in his eyes.[29]

How much Veblen's attraction had to do with the force of Clark's intellect, and how much with the intrinsic appeal of political economy to someone with Veblen's life history up to that point, is impossible to parcel out. Less than a decade after Veblen left Carleton, Clark stood at the forefront of American economics, and to this day he ranks as one of the most important economic theorists America has ever produced.[30] While at Carleton, Veblen did not know that renown was just ahead for Clark; but Veblen probably spotted that, unlike the rest of the college's able faculty, Clark was a productive scholar in his own right, publishing articles on economic topics in prominent East Coast periodicals and carrying the students in his classes beyond textbooks and into theories of his own invention that he was still thinking through. Many years later, Clark told an interviewer that "some of his early ideas"—those at the core of his later work—"were being worked out while he occupied a chair at Carleton College, with a weekly requirement of twenty hours teaching."[31] At the time, Clark was only in his early thirties—he was born a year before Andrew—and he and Veblen were in regular contact. All told, Veblen probably took a half-dozen different courses with Clark (including Analysis of Civil Government and History of Civilization, mentioned earlier), and in these the combination of small class size and one-on-one recitation sessions made for close interaction.[32] And just as Veblen admired Clark, Clark returned the praise, writing in a recommendation letter a few years later that Veblen was "a student of remarkable diligence, ability and success" and that "the work which he accomplished in studies taught by me led me to entertain the hope that he would become not merely a successful teacher, but an earnest and successful investigator, especially in Philosophy and Political Economy." The connection between the two men lasted throughout Veblen's career, and Clark continued to send recommendations for his former student even after Veblen publicly attacked Clark's later writings.[33]

In terms of background, Clark fit the emerging prototype of the American academic scholar.[34] He came from a prosperous New England family, of old colonial stock and devout Congregationalist beliefs, and received the standard-issue classical education at Brown University and Amherst College. In his family line were ministers and other professional men, and when his father, a commercial engineer, became ill and relocated to Minneapolis, Clark put his college studies on hold to move with him and help support the family by working as a partner in a machine shop that sold farm equipment. His career goal, at that point, was to become a minister, but when Clark finally graduated from college, he decided to follow his developing interest in the subject of political economy and go abroad (like dozens of other Americans wanting advanced training) to study the subject at the universities of Zurich and Heidelberg, where he received the equivalent of a master's degree. Returning to the United States after three years in Europe, however, Clark was unable to find an academic position on the East Coast, so in 1875 he became a lecturer at Carleton. Poor health prevented him from beginning full-time teaching there until 1877, the year Veblen entered Carleton's college program.[35]

By then Clark's title was professor of political economy (and history), and in creating this position Carleton was far ahead of the national curve. Prior to 1877, only Harvard (in 1871) and Yale (ambiguously in 1872) had established professorships in political economy; other American colleges were slow to follow. Courses in the subject went back to the 1820s, but these were typically given by college presidents teaching moral philosophy or by moonlighting businessmen. Either way, the subject was in the hands of men who were not trained scholars and who shackled "political economy" to its original meaning as "*political* economy": advice for legislators and other elites about policy issues such as free trade, tariffs, currency reform, and so forth.[36] Why Carleton College broke away from this tradition of having amateurs teach political economy is unknown, although the move was probably related somehow to the connections Clark had previously made in the Minnesota business community,

Figure 2 Veblen's professor at
Carleton College, John Bates Clark

whose members were well represented on Carleton's board of trustees
(and who may have urged President Strong to hire Clark to teach political
economy).

Whatever the backstory to Clark's professorship, his Political Economy
course provided an unconventional point of entry into the topic. As he
introduced political economy as a subject, Clark simultaneously chipped
away at it with running criticisms of the doctrines Americans associated
with the subject. In this way, he presented Veblen with an eviscerated political economy, tainting the young man's first encounter with the field with
a heretical attitude toward the very thing he was learning about. During
the middle decades of the nineteenth century, the men who taught political
economy in American colleges typically relied on textbooks that retailed
stronger or weaker versions of the so-called classical or English school of
political economy. Up to a point, Clark continued this pedagogical convention at Carleton. During his first two years teaching Political Economy,
he assigned Englishman Henry Fawcett's *Manual of Political Economy*
(1863), which followed the well-marked classical path of defining concepts such as "labor," "capital," and "wealth," and then laying out "the
laws that determine the production, the distribution, and the exchange of

wealth." (Fawcett was among those economic writers who slighted the subject of the "consumption" of wealth.) But in the following year—the year Veblen took the course—Carleton's published list of required books omitted Fawcett's text, perhaps as the result of oversight, but more likely because Clark stopped assigning it.[37] Still, in his lectures that year, he included John Stuart Mill's *Principles of Political Economy* and spoke about the "works of English Economists."[38] So, by way of one text or another, Clark exposed Veblen to the tenets of "classical economics."[39]

Clark, however, interspersed these textbook materials with strong objections to classical economics. Clark kept lecture notes (that by luck have partly survived) of his Political Economy course when Veblen took it— Veblen's name is even scrawled in Clark's handwriting in the margin of the notes. The notes are only outlines, but because these closely tracked Clark's publications from 1877 to 1881, combining the two sources (plus Clark's notes for other courses he taught around this time) gives us a fairly full view of his ideas when Veblen encountered them.[40]

As Clark would have been the first to admit, many of these ideas were imports he had just carried back from Germany, where he had come under the spell of the historical school of economics. As a graduate student in Heidelberg for two years, Clark had studied with Karl Knies, one of the school's founders, who regularly flayed classical political economy on several counts: first, for depicting individuals as creatures of "self-interest" alone, rather than as psychologically complex, anthropologically mutable human beings motivated by "material" and "nonmaterial forces"; second, for severing individuals from the social groups to which they belonged, neglecting the economic and noneconomic aspects their "communal life"; and, third, for eliding "the process of historical development" by postulating "unconditional and constantly uniform" economic principles that failed "to take account of the great differences and developmental stages existing in human civilization." Holding as an article of faith that "the horizon of political economy [must be] extended beyond the perspective of Adam Smith," Knies insisted to his students that the "economic *forces* and *phenomena* of the present day are to be comprehended as a mere *historical fragment, and are neither to be treated as entire and universal for all economic phases and evolutions, nor as typifying such phases and evolutions.*"[41]

In 1879 and 1880, Clark communicated these precepts to Veblen, transposing onto the study of economic life the same ways of thinking Veblen was seeing in different guises throughout the Carleton curriculum.

"The accuracy of the conclusions of Political Economy," asserted Clark in good controversialist form, "depends on the correctness of its assumptions with regards to the nature of man," but "the assumed man is too mechanical and too selfish to correspond with the reality." He was speaking of the reality of human beings who are "actuated" by a "multiplicity" of "psychological forces," extending all the way from "the greed of gain," "the desire for personal adornment," and "love of display," to "higher wants"—"unselfish" and "spiritual"—for what is "true, beautiful, and good." Making things worse, "the great fact that society is an organic unity has been, for the time, forgotten [by political economists], and the attention has been fixed on individuals and their separate . . . actions in valuing and exchanging commodities." To rectify these errors, Clark proposed what he thought of as a complete overhaul of political economy: "The science . . . needs to be built on a permanent foundation of anthropological fact" and to recognize that "economic man" has been formed and transformed through "ages of social development." Illustrating this claim, Clark described for his students how human needs had evolved across time with the transition from hunting and gathering to agriculture and then to industry as the economic basis of society. In other lectures, he filled in this evolutionary scheme with historical specifics by examining the economic, political, and religious "institutions" of the "Celtic Period," the "Roman Period," the "Saxon Period," the "Norman Period," and so forth.[42]

Clark's historical charges against the classical English economists fit with his dual role as Carleton's professor of history, as well as political economy. But, in addition, he had heavy charges to level against classical political economy as a body of theory, charges aimed at breaking free from its "mazes of logical wandering," deconstructing its concepts, and formulating an alternative economics.[43] (Veblen may have noticed the irony that, in the same breath that Clark was scorning the English economists' conceptual tangles, he was creating an elaborate theoretical maze of his own.) Among the theoretical defects Clark found in the literature of political economy, one particularly galled him. This was the conceptual distinction economists, going back to Adam Smith, drew between the "productive" and the "unproductive": between productive versus unproductive *labor*, between productive versus unproductive *consumption*. In his *Principles of Political Economy*, Mill plied this dichotomy to confer value on human labor when it increases society's stock of physical goods or "*material* objects," but not otherwise; and he used it to contrast consumption that "goes to maintain and increase the productive power of the community" from "unproductive expenditure[s that] tend to impoverish the community."[44]

But Clark, in his Carleton lectures and early articles, insisted that these distinctions were misconceived. By his accounting, "all labor is productive," physical and mental alike; this is the reason economic competition dispenses "compensation" to workers and capitalists both (legitimately awarding owners of capital a large cut of the social pie). Likewise, according to Clark, not just some but all consumption diminishes the resources of a society, although all of it simultaneously spurs production, thus growing society's wealth.[45] In later years, Clark and Veblen both wrestled further with these issues. In the process, Clark formulated a theory of value and distribution that set him apart from both the English classical economists and German historical economists, whereas Veblen worked hard to explode that theory. During their time together at Carleton neither man was thinking that far ahead; yet in the way Clark packaged the subject of political economy and handed it to Veblen, it was already a body of knowledge focused directly on the issue of what was productive for a society and what was not. By adopting this focus, Clark's teachings sharpened for Veblen a way of perceiving—a way of construing the social world and making sense of what was happening in it—that he had been accustoming to throughout his youth.

Grafted onto Clark's teachings, moreover, was a searing commentary on his own society.[46] In the tour he gave his students of successive stages of history, Clark brought out two themes: the growing productive potential of societies to satisfy the expanding wants of their populations; and the role played in history by wars of conquest, episodes of plunder, forms of slavery and subjugation, and other rapacious acts. Modern industrial societies, Clark believed, reveal the same countervailing features. In them, "the number of new wants and the ability to satisfy them . . . increase[s] indefinitely" as a result of the progressive development of new productive forces and social institutions, such as market-based competition and free labor.[47] And yet, in Clark's shattering depiction, "predation" continues insidiously to return.

We do not enslave men now-a-days. The emancipation proclamation ended all that, did it not? We offer a man a pittance, and tell him to take it and work for us from morning till night or starve; but we do not coerce him. It is at his option to choose whether he will work or not; he is free, you observe! We do not eat men—precisely. We consume the product of their labor, and they may have virtually worked body and soul into it; but we do it by such indirect and refined methods that it does not occur to us that we are cannibals. We kill men, it is true; but not with cudgels in open fight. We do it slowly, and frequently take the precaution to kill the soul first; and we do it in an orderly and systematic manner.[48]

To Clark, this "latent brutality" called out for diagnosis by political economists and for remedies. Its cause, according to his report, lay in economic changes gone awry, as evidenced, for example, in the way "many small, . . . scattered mercantile industries have largely been superseded by centralized establishments," which are "owned by a few men [with] a dense population of operatives," or workers. These changes, in his assessment, "are favorable to the quantitative increase of wealth," but they "are not favorable to its equal distribution" between owners of capital (or other types of private property) and their workers. Furthermore, these changes foment mass discontent from the side of the workers—malignant "socialistic tendencies," "communistic agitations," and other "social disturbances" that endanger an economy based on private property ownership.[49] Even so, Clark pointed out, blueprints were available for more benign forms of socialism, less menacing to the status quo, that were worth considering and perhaps implementing:

There are measures for securing that union of labor and capital in the same hands, which would effectually prevent discord between them. There are measures for the securing of small landed properties by laboring men, which would give them the benefits of property ownership, and commit them to the maintenance of social order. There are plans for cooperative societies of different kinds, some of them in successful operation, which secure an identity of interest between employers and employed. . . . There are some voluntary organizations which acquire their property legitimately, and are attempting to test the practicality of a new mode of living. . . . There are methods yet undiscovered, waiting for intelligent men to develop and test them.[50]

In Clark's view, not only would adoption of such methods tame the threat of communism, it would also restore morality to its preeminent position in economic life, thereby galvanizing action to ameliorate the "evils of poverty and ignorance."[51] These reformist ideas were, as Clark knew, associated with the contemporary "Christian Socialist" movement, with which he strongly identified during this stage in his career. Doing so brought socialist ways of thinking onto the Carleton campus—with, apparently, no protest from his colleagues or students (or even the college's trustees).

Significantly, Clark laid the responsibility for developing a reformist agenda primarily on the shoulders of economists, which was exactly where the German historical school had placed the burden. In an article, "The Scholar's Duty to the State," published in the June 1878 issue of the Carleton newspaper, he likened the economist to a chemist whose research develops agricultural methods that improve soil conditions for millions of farmers: "So the economist who can devise a means of removing the causes of extreme poverty will" (with the collaboration of the state) "do more than many charitable associations for the permanent benefit of the poor." Yet first things first. Because the "applier" of scientific knowledge always follows and depends on its "discoverer," "then economic investigation is our duty of the scholar; the application of the results of past investigation is a second duty." These were motifs in his "Political Economy" lectures as well, and in sounding them Clark added his authority to the many other voices Veblen had heard welcoming the advance of scientific knowledge. But Clark added a twist: unlike chemistry, "economic science" was a "young science"; it had "the work of investigation"—the "first and highest" of the scholar's responsibilities—still before it.[52] So here was a mission awaiting, an invitation to something new, something challenging, something important—and better yet, it was a standing invitation that did not require an immediate commitment from the student.

3.

By some point in his junior/senior year, if not earlier, Veblen had a tentative plan for himself: he would continue his education. On the day of his graduation, the *Rice County Journal* ran an item unusual for a small-town newspaper in 1880. "Thorstein B. Veblen intends," it reported, "to enter upon a post-graduate course at Yale next year." Not for another eighteen months did Veblen carry through on this particular plan, but the idea shows what he had in mind at the end of college. His sights were set on getting some kind of academic job.[53]

What mix of factors played into Veblen's reasoning? From a practical standpoint, he had few obvious career alternatives. Discounting the ministry, law, and the other traditional professions, the default option (mentioned earlier) was teaching—though not, in his own thinking, at a common school or a high school.[54] His principal role models at the time, Clark and brother Andrew, were college teachers; and, as Clark's example showed, it was possible to combine teaching with scientific "investigation" and publishing. To Veblen, that probably looked like an appealing package, well suited to his aptitudes and budding interests in mental philosophy and political economy. His teachers were encouraging him to continue, as Andrew recalled. When Thorstein was at Carleton, wrote Andrew to Dorfman, "I think he always hoped he might take a graduate course. Doubtless the influence of J. B. Clark and the faculty generally at Carleton went toward the growth of this idea."[55]

Deciding to pursue a "graduate course" left many logistical issues for Veblen still to figure out, however, and that did not happen all at once. In 1880, there was no standard road map for him to follow. The norm that a college teacher would acquire a doctorate in his or her academic subject area was just starting to take shape, and before it did the key to an academic job was not a postgraduate degree but being in the right place at the right time. To quote historian Laurence Veysey, in nineteenth-century American colleges, a professor "was likely to be appointed as a result of casual social contacts (or religious loyalty), rather than in recognition of academic competence," let alone because of advanced research training in a specialized academic field.[56] By the 1870s, standards were rising in some of the new colleges that were opening up, including Carleton, where most members of the faculty had master's degrees they earned by taking extra courses at one of the colleges in the region, as Andrew did.[57] In addition, young men on the East Coast who aspired to become academics often went to study for a few years in Europe (as Clark had done), and some of them (but not Clark) returned to the United States with a doctorate—though Veblen does not seem to have considered going abroad.[58] This suggests that he may at first have envisioned going no further than a master's degree, which would make sense given that American doctorates were still extremely rare. By 1879, only some two hundred of them had ever been awarded, and it is hard to imagine that anyone in the Veblen household, Thorstein (and Andrew) included, had more than the haziest notion of what the degree was. (It baffles many college students and their parents even today.) On the other hand, Yale was, at this point, the largest American producer of doctorates, so Veblen was probably aware that it was the place to go should he want to continue that far.[59]

Even so, most of the doctoral degrees previously awarded in the United States had been in the natural sciences (including medicine), followed by classics. In the areas Veblen had gravitated toward at Carleton, the numbers were minuscule: seven in philosophy and three in political economy.[60] These numbers reflected the dismal job outlook in philosophy and the near nonexistence of professorships in political economy. Clark's failure to secure a position on the East Coast, even with a respected German master's degree in hand, illustrates the problem. Writing from the ground in 1879, G. Stanley Hall commented that "there is very small chance that a well-equipped student of philosophy in any of its departments will secure a position of a teacher of the subject." Modern historians have corroborated Hall's assessment—with the qualifier that the academic job market started to improve in the late 1880s and 1890s at some of the new research-oriented universities.[61]

Still, in his junior/senior year, it is unlikely Veblen was counting the number of job vacancies in philosophy. In the classical curriculum, at Carleton and elsewhere, philosophy continued to command the preeminent position it had long held in the Western intellectual tradition: it was the center of the intellectual universe, the premier forum where great intellectual issues were debated, the hotbed of intellectual excitement. So, like some of his scholastically inclined contemporaries, Veblen was pulled in, quickly and deeply. This attraction was not at the expense of political economy, since philosophy still included political economy within its boundaries. Clark, after all, whose degree was in philosophy, taught both subjects, bringing Veblen up to the minute in mental philosophy (up to the Hamilton-Mill controversy), while also inviting him to the forefront of political economy. In his graduate program, Veblen hoped to pursue both topics, leading off with philosophy.

By the time Veblen reached this point, he had entered an intellectual field. He had transitioned from a college boy memorizing warmed-over textbooks to a junior scholar absorbed in the specialized questions that groups of contemporary philosophers were grappling with and arguing over in their continuing conversations with one another—and he could hardly wait to join them, as his commencement address showed. This transition was facilitated by many years of practice that schooled him in the ways of thinking that were conventional in philosophy and equipped him with some of the materials of the philosopher's craft—the esoteric vocabulary, the list of unresolved problems, the knowledge of who's who in the field, and so on. Even at that, though, his apprenticeship was incomplete, and there was more in store: gaining more experience with the equipment he had available, amassing more resources and skills, and finding opportunities to put his intellectual tool kit to work—as well as weighing other career options, since starting out in an intellectual field was not a commitment to staying there. For the time being, however, Thorstein Veblen was in the field of philosophy at the entry level.

FOR VEBLEN, field entry involved a geographical departure, leaving quiet Rice County, Minnesota, for a yet unseen university out east. Before going too far away, however, Veblen detoured to Madison, Wisconsin, where he had taken a job as a schoolteacher for the 1880–1881 academic year. His motive, as Andrew remembered, was financial: Thorstein hoped to save some money for graduate school. The job was at Monona Academy, a small, private, coeducational high school attached to a theological seminary run by the Norwegian Lutheran Synod. Andrew, who was active in the Synod's midwestern operations, had helped arrange this position for his brother.[62]

From one angle, this move meant evident changes for Thorstein Veblen. Madison was a city more than six times the size of Northfield, a state capital, Republican-controlled, that had yet to rebound from the economic depression of the 1870s. From another angle, however, the move also meant further involvement in the Norwegian-American community, which prolonged Veblen's exposure to relentless theological infighting. Historian J. R. Christianson has argued, in fact, that Thorstein's hiring at Monona Academy, shortly after Andrew's hiring at Luther College, shows that "the Veblen brothers . . . were clearly being recruited into the church-based elite of the Norwegian-American community."[63]

Whether or not that was the case, Veblen's year in Madison put him at the storm center of the most acrimonious of all the controversies that engulfed the Norwegian-American church in the nineteenth century: the controversy over predestination, the doctrine of "God's election of men to salvation."[64] This belief split the Norwegian Synod into two factions so hostile that their adherents reportedly tore into disputes with one another "on the streets and in the alleys, in stores and in saloons, and through a continuous flow of agitating articles" in the press (according to one of several contemporaneous accounts). At stake was the cardinal question, almost mandatory for a maturing philosopher to consider, of the place of human agency in human destiny. In answer, one Synod faction maintained that eternal life rests solely on God's inscrutable gift of grace to wayward mortals, while the other faction urged the less determinist view that, in the redemption of sinners, humankind's own conduct also plays an important role. As it happened, the leading spokesmen for both camps taught at Monona Academy and Seminary, making the environment so openly acrimonious during Veblen's time there that the Academy closed right after he left in 1881.[65] How he navigated his way through the school year is unknown.

Outside the school, Madison provided some counterbalance—if not from controversy at least from theological controversy. Monona Academy stood across town from the University of Wisconsin, small and floundering at the time, where Veblen made several faculty connections, among them a close (and long-lasting) friendship with another Norwegian-American, Rasmus B. Anderson, America's first professor of Scandinavian studies. When Veblen met him, Anderson was in his early thirties (the same age as Andrew Veblen and Clark), but he was already renowned. His name was familiar throughout the Norwegian settlements of the Midwest and beyond, where his prolific and combative writings, according to his biographer Lloyd Hustvedt, "had made him . . . the most generally respected man in Norwegian-American affairs" in the country and earned him "the romantic mantle of an upstart rebel."[66]

Anderson relished this reputation and cultivated it, most confrontationally in his 1874 book *America Not Discovered by Columbus,* in which he argued (though his claim was not new) that tenth-century Norsemen, not the Italians of legend, were the first Europeans to reach the Americas. As Anderson explained in his autobiography, he intended the book to be "thoroughly sensational and defiant," and he was delighted that readers perceived him "as a fearless iconoclast." His purpose, in the book and in public lectures and other writings, he said, was to jolt his contemporaries out of the present day and hurl them back into the past, both recorded and unrecorded. Conversant with evolutionary ideas, Anderson discussed, for example, the "hoary age" of the earth and how the American continent had "emerged from the watery waste that encircled the whole globe and became the scene of animal life." But what interested him more than theories about these earliest beginnings was the historical information contained in Norse-Icelandic mythology, which he translated, popularized, and drew on to describe and analyze "the early institutions of Norway."

In doing so, he aimed to lay the groundwork "for elucidating the history and institutions of . . . contemporary nations."[67] For Anderson, this was a project ready to take off.[68]

NONE OF THESE SOURCES WERE, by themselves, indispensable for getting Veblen ready to become the knowledge maker and intellectual innovator he became: not the ancient philosophers or the modern scientists, not Mill or Hamilton, not the school primers or textbooks, not the religious iconoclasts or academic ones, not Andrew Veblen or Rasmus Anderson. When Thorstein Veblen boarded a train for Baltimore in fall 1881, he was an outsider to the East Coast (for the moment), but one who carried an insider's heavy store of up-to-date knowledge-making tools, a rich sampler of the ideas of the age. Yet few of the sources he had encountered would have meant much had they been one-off acquisitions. Practically considered, many of these materials were, by the time of his departure, almost interchangeable with one another. The one exception would be Veblen's studies with Clark, which pointed him directly to the field of philosophy (and political economy), but only after years of priming before he became Clark's student. Subtract any other individual experience, however, and there would have been little difference in the makeup of the intellectual tool set Veblen had in tow when he left Madison.

Consequential for him, in other words, was not this source or that one, but the steady laying in and layering on of so many analogous ones deriving from so many different contexts: the recurring enactment of a set of practices and the stockpiling of a set of resources through a process that began early in his life and continued, without interruption, over the span of two decades. That the world is in temporal motion, that parts depend on wholes, that worth inheres in work, that knowledge inheres in science: these ways of thinking were among the implements that the knowledge builders whom Veblen encountered were putting to use, whether they were up against the rock of natural knowledge, the marrow of philosophical knowledge, or the mud and wet sand of historical and social knowledge. Veblen became skilled and flexible in using all these implements as he moved from place to place, subject area to subject area; for, in the course of this rotation, he learned that these tools were not single-purpose instruments but multipurpose and adaptable to different problems. As I mentioned previously, these tools did not tie Veblen's hand or prevent him from picking up plenty of other equipment besides. Still, most of the other bits of equipment later acquired lacked the thick weight of biographical time and constant repetition, the accumulated force of all the practice Thorstein Veblen had behind him when he set off on the next leg of his trip.

GLOSSARY ON ECONOMIC SCHOOLS

In this chapter and those that follow, I refer to different "schools" of economic thought using names that warrant more explanation than I provide when they appear. The purpose of this glossary is to fill in and tie together some of this background information.

Among the school names prevalent among economic writers in the United States when Thorstein Veblen was a college and graduate student, the two that crop up most frequently are the Older School and Younger School of political economy, although "economics" was beginning to displace "political economy." ("Political economy" went back to the seventeenth and eighteenth centuries, when it referred to treatises that advised monarchs and legislators on husbanding state resources, wealth, and revenue. Wanting to shed this antiquated connotation, professional academics in the closing decades of the nineteenth century often substituted "economics," though not all the time. Some scholars treated the terms as roughly synonymous.)[69]

Postbellum American political economists used "Older School" and "Younger School" to designate different traditions of economic thought, and with each tradition they associated different authors, theories, research methods, and attitudes toward social policy. In our own time, historians of economics have shown that many of these alleged associations were incorrect from both textual and contextual standpoints; if we want historical accuracy about these subjects, this modern scholarship is the place to look. For the task of following Thorstein Veblen's intellectual development, however, more relevant than present-day research is how writers of his own era understood, typified, and judged the different theoretical schools, because those interpretations were the ones that made up Veblen's milieu and provided intellectual resources for him. Among Veblen's teachers, Richard T. Ely (at Johns Hopkins), William Graham Sumner (at Yale), and James Laurence Laughlin (at Cornell University and the University of Chicago) all wrote explicitly—from the slant of the different traditions they represented—about the history of the major schools of economic thought, so Veblen did not need to go far to learn their versions of the story.[70]

Lining up these schools by historical birth order, Veblen's teachers and other chroniclers typically began their accounts with the "Older School," although names like the "Old School," the "classical school," the "orthodox school," the "English school," and the "deductive school" were also commonplace—and largely interchangeable. (Whether or not the names were capitalized varied by author and publisher.)

According to contemporaneous historical accounts, the Older School originated, for all intents and purposes, in 1776 with Adam Smith's *The Wealth of Nations*. As Laughlin told the story, Smith's treatise developed "a connected set of ideas on production, distribution, and exchange" (with production taking the lead), and it successfully formulated those ideas as principles or laws that had nearly universal reach; as such, it supplied a rich store of concepts and topics that gave political economy its substance. Laughlin summarized:

> Seeing distinctly that labor was the basis of all production, [Smith showed] that the wealth of a country depends on the skill with which its labor is applied, and upon the proportion of productive to unproductive laborers. The gains from the division of labor are explained, and money appears as a necessary instrument once society has reached such a division. He is then led to discuss [the] distribution [that] takes place among the factors of production, [from which] he is brought to wages, profits, and rents. The functions of capital are explained in general; and he discusses . . . the accumulation of capital, money, paper money, and interest.[71]

Among British authors, this paradigm—or so the story went—continued early in the next century with Thomas Malthus and David Ricardo; and, while increasingly under siege, it was still going strong in the 1870s in works by classical theorists such as J. E. Cairnes (later a foil of Veblen's).[72] Along the way, books popularizing Older School teachings—and sometimes aligning them with laissez-faire doctrines opposed to government intervention into the economy—found a substantial readership. (Henry Fawcett's *Manual of Political Economy*, which Veblen may have encountered at Carleton, fell in this category.)

A standard fixture in this formulaic account of the Older School was the work of John Stuart Mill, especially his *Principles of Political Economy*, which was first published in 1848 and remained the most widely read book on the subject for decades. Writing here (and in companion pages of his 1843 *System of Logic*) in a more systematic manner than was typical for the classical authors, Mill characterized the "field of Political Economy" as a deductive science built on the inductively generated premise that individuals are universally motivated by "the desire of wealth," or "the desire to obtain . . . the greatest quantity of wealth" (of "useful or agreeable things") "with the least labor and self-denial." From this starting point, and several correlative theoretical principles, the political economist, Mill argued, could arrive at knowledge of the natural "laws of production and distribution"—with production still holding analytical priority. This idea led him to assert, along with Adam Smith, that not only is "labor . . . an indispensable condition to every productive operation" but it is also the primary factor determining the cost and normal value of economic objects.[73] Mill likened economic laws to the "invariable" causal laws of physical sciences, maintaining with confidence (though also with qualifiers) that "whoever knows the political economy of England, or even of Yorkshire, knows that of all nations" throughout recorded history. Further, although Mill regarded economic theory as wholly scientific and untainted by moral judgments, he asserted that theoretical principles have practical consequences, once removed. Insofar as policymakers themselves take the lead and knock on the economist's door looking for means to achieve policy ends, he said, the theorems of political economy can then lend technical assistance. Appealing to this (self-professed) nonpartisan stance, Mill and other classical theorists frequently claimed to separate their field from any particular political programs and to license it to serve agendas that ranged from laissez-faire to socialist.[74]

After spelling out these tenets of the Older School, Veblen's teachers and other commentators then described the opposing ideas—which different narrators deemed better or worse—of the "Younger School": the so-called "inductive school," "new school," "ethical school," or (most often) the "historical school" or "German historical school." The last two expressions tended to be amalgamated, reflecting that most Americans who went to Europe for graduate work during the second half of the nineteenth century studied in Germany (as previously mentioned). From this experience, many formed the impression that the historical approach to economics was an almost exclusively German pursuit, rather than a line of research active elsewhere as well (particularly in England).[75]

In the context of German scholarship itself, the historical school of economics was a relatively late offshoot of a much broader intellectual movement known as "historicism." Reaching back to the eighteenth century, this movement, by the mid-nineteenth century, sprawled over the fields of biblical studies, theology, classics, philology, philosophy, and jurisprudence, instilling in all of them the credo that "everything in the human world . . . is made by history," and "that nothing has an eternal form." To the mind of German historicists, the aim of science, therefore, was to understand this perpetual historical movement, by means of inductive research based on original historical documents when possible.[76]

During the 1840s, historicism spread to the study of political economy through the work of Wilhelm Roscher, Bruno Hildebrand, and Karl Knies, whom nineteenth-century commentators retrospectively lumped together as the "first generation" of German historical economists.[77] (Subsequently, Veblen did combat with all these figures.) As one of the most prolific teachers of future America economists, including Veblen's first two mentors in the subject, Karl Knies received particular attention because of his unremitting attack (quoted earlier in this chapter) on classical economics for its atomizing, ahistorical emphasis on individual wealth seeking and its failure to formulate "developmental laws of the economy."[78] Rather than abstracting the economy from the larger social world and professing neutrality from political causes, Knies and other members of his generation aimed to link the economy organically to the evolving institutions of the state and, by doing so, to suggest measures to promote the "general welfare" of the population under modern conditions.[79] To accomplish those purposes, these scholars called for inductive research on the nature of economic life at different stages of human history.

In the opinion of many economists at the time, this call fell flat until the emergence in the 1870s of the "second generation" of the German historical school. Spearheaded by Gustav Schmoller, the members of the second generation continued the first generation's onslaught against classical economics but contributed archival and statistical research in a raft of studies of the organization of economic activity in different areas of Europe during different eras. Second-generation researchers hoped these empirical studies would push economic theory in an evolutionary direction, although critics in Europe and the United States dismissed their work as too descriptive to generate theoretical laws (of either a developmental or a transhistorical kind). Undeterred, Schmoller and his colleagues believed they had solid historical support for "the idea of the State as the guardian and leader of the social and industrial interests of the people." (These words were those of visiting American W. E. B. Du Bois, who studied with Schmoller during the 1890s and sent home the message that "the German professors have preached socialism.")[80] Expanding on this idea, second-generation historicists held that "the course of history shows a slow but steady progress toward higher forms of economic organization" under the supervision of the state and the historical economist.[81]

The disagreements between the older classical school and the younger historical school formed the main fault line in the stock narrative of the development of political economy that students encountered in American colleges and universities in the decades after the Civil War, sometimes with subplots tossed in. Occasionally, for example, narrators—Ely and Laughlin among them—also mentioned a Marxist school (or a socialist school, or both), which some of them connected to the classical school (because of Marx's emphasis on production and labor) but others associated with the German historical school (because of Marx's concern with laws of historical development). These topics added a few twists.

However, far more important—at least when we think ahead to Veblen's economics—was the remapping of the field of economics that began in the late 1880s and early 1890s with the arrival in United States of what English-speaking writers referred to as the "Austrian school." This tag was attached chiefly to the work of three Viennese economists who loomed over economic theory throughout the turn-of-the-century period: Carl Menger (the school's principal), Eugen Böhm-Bawerk, and Friederich Wieser. In the eyes of many British and American economists, the Austrian school appeared to be a departure from both leading economic schools. It appeared to break from the Older School by repudiating the classical economists' strong emphasis on production (to the neglect of consumption and the marginal utility conception of value), and from the Younger School by rejecting the historicists' commitment to inductive methods and antipathy to abstract theory. (I elaborate on these points in Chapters 7 and 8.)

Going forward in time, the school signs became even more complicated. By the end of the nineteenth century, most American economists saw the Austrian school as one of four distinguishable branches of a larger—and internally contentious—family of economic theories that economists were starting to refer to as the "marginal utility school" or (later) "marginalism."[82] The other three branches of the family were recognizable strains as well: the work of John Bates Clark (from the mid-1880s on); the work of English economist William Stanley Jevons and French economist Leon Walras, whom contemporaries bundled together as the "mathematical school"; and the work of Englishman Alfred Marshall, author of the acclaimed *Principles of Economics* (1890) and progenitor of the "Cambridge school" of economics. By the turn of the century, Veblen himself was using these same divisions to identify different economic theories and set the stage for his critique, which focused particularly on Clark's marginalism and that of the Austrian school. (American economists' interest in the mathematical school and the Cambridge school lay mostly in the future.) In 1900 Veblen even contributed his own terminological invention, "neo-classical," to label Alfred Marshall's approach, which combined principles of marginalism and classical economics.[83] (A generation later, some of Veblen's students launched, in opposition, what became the "institutionalist" movement in American economics.)[84]

But the terms and the topography remained in flux, as economists frequently redrew theoretical boundaries and reshuffled name cards, just as economists do today. Notably, economists did not put Veblen's "neoclassical" coinage into general circulation until the period between the two world wars, at which point their tendency was to treat neoclassicism and marginalism (en bloc) as one and the same.[85] Still later, however, discussion of the different schools of marginalism returned as economists witnessed a discipline-wide proliferation of discernable schools of economic thought. According to some historians of economics, modern neoclassical economics emerged only after World War II, when economists refined and extended Alfred Marshall's late nineteenth-century version of marginalism to encompass new substantive topics, analytical concepts, and statistical techniques. As they did so, they renovated neoclassicism and consolidated its position within so-called mainstream economics, at the same time that other marginalist schools with nineteenth-century origins—in particular, the Austrian school, which had occupied Veblen's attentions—assumed satellite-like positions.[86] By the time these developments occurred, Veblen was long gone from the field of economics.

CHAPTER 5

YOUNG PHILOSOPHER

1.

At some point in the year between his Carleton graduation and the end of his teaching stint at Monona Academy, Veblen decided against enrolling at Yale and redirected his graduate school plans to Johns Hopkins. The university was enticing: founded just five years earlier (in 1876), it was an overnight sensation, a mecca for college graduates throughout the country who sought to pursue graduate work at an institution that was being touted, in and out of the academic world, as America's first "real University." Writing to a friend in 1884, Woodrow Wilson—a history graduate student at Hopkins and a young man nearly impossible to please—enthused that the university was "the best place in America to study." Accolades like this were commonplace.[1]

During Veblen's junior/senior year in college, he had resisted the pull, perhaps because Yale, with a longer history behind it, seemed like a safer choice. But during his year in Madison, Johns Hopkins took on features that increased its appeal. For one, the university claimed to be expanding its program in the subject areas Veblen wanted to pursue: philosophy and political economy. For another, word was circulating that "the better colleges," when they were hiring new teachers, "were increasing looking for faculty from 'the Johns Hopkins,'" and this information (as Andrew Veblen recalled) gave Thorstein Veblen "a good opinion of the status of J.H.U."[2] Finally, there was the fact that Andrew Veblen was heading to Hopkins to study physics and mathematics. In fact, just as Thorstein was finishing his work in Madison, Andrew resigned his position at Luther College and moved to Baltimore, in September 1881, with his wife, two children, and sister Emily. For Thorstein, the balance of factors now tilted in Hopkins's favor, so he joined the family migration.

The result of this decision was a crammed five-month stay in Baltimore, a city that bore little resemblance to Northfield, Minnesota, or Madison, Wisconsin. With a population of more than 320,000 (thirty times that of Madison), Baltimore was the sixth-largest city in the United States and one of its great polyglots: a jittery mix of descendants of the antebellum Southern aristocracy, newly arrived European immigrants (from Germany, Poland, Russia, and Italy), and a segregated caste of African Americans (among the largest concentrations in the country) relegated to menial jobs as servants or as unskilled workers in the expanding industrial workforce. While the Upper Midwest where Veblen had grown up had one of the most egalitarian patterns of wealth distribution in European and American history, mid-nineteenth-century Baltimore was one of the three most unequal US cities in the distribution of wealth. The top 1 percent of the population held 40 percent of the wealth and the top 10 percent more than 80 percent—statistics indicative of disparities comparable to those we find in American society today. Such disparities translated into conspicuous differences in lifestyle that were often condemned in the press. The local newspaper, the *Sun,* for example, editorialized: "The poor become poorer, the rich grow richer; money flows in streams; waste and extravagance and parade and ill-taste, and bad manners obtrude their random and graceless forms everywhere."[3]

Behind the statistics and editorials was a prospering urban economy built on commerce (international as well as national), manufacturing, and financial speculation. In terms of capital holdings, the Baltimore and Ohio (B&O) Railroad dominated the city, sometimes with explosive consequences. When the company imposed a 10 percent wage cut on its employees in summer 1877, railway brakemen walked off their jobs, halting rail traffic in several states and setting off mass protests on Baltimore's streets until government authorities called in a federal militia to break the strike.[4] (In a large rock-throwing confrontation, the troops killed ten people.) Watching the unprecedented scene, news reporter James Dacus called it "a spectacle that made one feel as though it was a tearful witnessing . . . of the last day, when the secrets of life . . . shall be laid bare in the hideous deformity and ghastly shame."[5]

This was just four years before Veblen arrived in the city, and there is no record of his own reactions to economic conditions during his time there. Regardless, we should avoid thinking of the economic sights and sounds of a place—whether Baltimore or any other location he lived at as a young man—as somehow "causing" Veblen's later ideas. The most likely upshot of any reactions he did have to capitalism in Baltimore would have been to reinforce the impressions he had already picked up about capitalism in the Midwest; those reactions would have added to the pile of observations he was storing up for the future. For the time being, Veblen's attentions were on his academic work, as well as on his family. During his months in Baltimore, he roomed in boardinghouses; but (as Andrew wrote to a friend) Thorstein also spent "a considerable part of his time" with Andrew's family, which had become involved in the city's Norwegian community—an active "Norwegian colony," according to Emily Veblen's description. Consisting of men Andrew knew from his time at Luther College, along with a network of Norwegian sea captains and their families (located in Baltimore because of its heavy export trade with Europe), this community provided Thorstein Veblen with sturdy social attachments as he figured out the new city and its university.[6]

Johns Hopkins University owed its existence to the B&O Railroad; the money that built it derived from a $3.5 million bequest from Johns Hopkins, one of the company's long-time directors and, eventually, Baltimore's wealthiest citizen.[7] The sum, equivalent to roughly $780 million today, was the largest ever given to an educational institution, and the trustees of Hopkins's estate decided to use it to create a new kind of educational institution, one explicitly devoted to increasing "the world's stock of literature and science." Uncertain how to achieve this, the trustees appointed as president Daniel Coit Gilman, a German-educated physical geographer who had launched curricular reforms at Yale a decade earlier and welcomed the opportunity to build on a grander scale in Baltimore, where he set to work adapting the German model of higher education to the American environment. To Gilman, this meant establishing a nonsectarian institution that would give America its own center for postgraduate training and, at the same time, stand committed to the "encouragement of research" conducted to make possible "the discovery and advancement of truth."[8] Four years later, the philosopher Charles Sanders Peirce, who had a front-row seat to these developments, described the result. Speaking to a French audience about intellectual life in America, Peirce reported that "the members of this little university" had already published a large number of "original researches, some of them of great value, [which] are fairly equal to the sum of what all the other colleges in the land have done . . . in the last twenty years."[9]

This record reflected Gilman's knack for identifying intellectual hot spots and recruiting faculty members who were specialists in these areas.

Figure 3 Thorstein Veblen, early 1880s

Initially he concentrated his efforts on seven areas, which he organized into protodepartmental units. (I will refer to these units simply as departments, although "department" was not typically used in this way until the 1890s.) In the semester Veblen enrolled, Hopkins had departments of biology, chemistry, physics, mathematics, "History and Political Economy," "History of Philosophy, Ethics, etc.," and "Logic."[10] All of these Gilman regarded as "sciences"—or as areas that should be upgraded into sciences—and he sought to furnish all of them with the facilities, equipment, and materials they needed to carry out scientific research in ways suited to their particular subject matter. The widely circulated *University Circulars* advertised this feature of the school, and graduate students were well aware of it. A couple of months after arriving, Andrew Veblen, for one, wrote: "The university answered quite closely to my expectations: able teachers and plenty of them, a choice library, costly and excellent apparatus for physical and chemical work—a good place for hard work."[11] Those in the social sciences and the humanities shared this perception, as we see in the letter by Woodrow Wilson (quoted earlier) and in many other contemporary accounts. Philosopher Josiah Royce, who earned a doctorate at Hopkins shortly after Veblen arrived, evoked the scene: "The beginning of the Johns Hopkins University was a dawn wherein 'twas bliss to be alive.' . . . The air was full of rumors of noteworthy work done by the older men of the place, and of hopes that one might find a way to get a little working-power one's self. . . . The University wanted its children to be, if possible, not merely well-informed but productive, [and] one longed to be . . . a creator of his own infinitesimal fraction of a product."[12]

At the time, the "noteworthy work" causing all this buzz had a signature characteristic. This research was openly and proudly evolutionary in bent, not only in the natural sciences but throughout the university—although "evolution," almost inevitably, took on different meanings as it moved around the campus. In the year Hopkins opened, Gilman arranged for a public address by English biologist Thomas Huxley, who was the leading contemporary spokesperson for Darwinian ideas. Gilman also appointed H. Newell Martin, Huxley's collaborator, as the head of Hopkins's biology department, which Gilman authorized Martin to design so as to encompass Darwin's most controversial theory: the doctrine of descent by natural selection. The department and the university tolerated many competing evolutionary theories, as well as the research practices that went with them.[13]

Thorstein Veblen observed this attitude toward evolution in the course of his own studies, which followed an unusual path. At a time when nearly all graduate students at Hopkins worked primarily within a single academic unit, Veblen officially attached himself to two units: philosophy and political economy. In a December 1881 letter to Gilman, he explained: "I intended at the time I came here to take up Philosophy as my principal study. Since then, however, I have thought it best to give more attention to Political Economy, so that, while attending all the courses of lectures by Dr. G. S. Morris, most of my work has been under the direction of Dr. R. T. Ely."[14] The statement captures Veblen at a segue. At Hopkins,

Figure 4 Veblen's professors at Johns Hopkins University *(from top, left-right):*
George Sylvester Morris, Charles Sanders Peirce, Herbert Baxter Adams, and Richard T. Ely

because political economy was separated from philosophy, he could follow the dual interests he formed at Carleton only by locating in two intellectual fields simultaneously, which was a unique way to pursue a graduate degree in philosophy. His decision to do so brought him into regular contact not only with the two professors mentioned in his letter, philosopher G. S. Morris and economist R. T. Ely, but also with two other faculty members whose courses related to his interests: H. B. Adams, a historian in the joint department of history and political economy, and C. S. Peirce, the sole member of the logic department. Except for Peirce's, these names are not familiar today but they stood large in the American academic world of the time, and Veblen became closely acquainted with all but the aloof Peirce. (Hopkins's small number of graduate students and 9:1 student–teacher ratio enabled close contact.) In a coincidence of timing, all these scholars were then in their prime.

With George Sylvester Morris (1840–1889), Veblen took his heaviest load: History of Greek Philosophy, Ethics, and a special course of lectures based on Morris's forthcoming book, *Kant's Critique of Pure Reason*. In these, Veblen encountered, from different angles, the labyrinthine position Morris had just formulated after a decade of pondering the central issues in mental philosophy. The son of a prosperous Vermont business family, Morris had attended Dartmouth College and Union Theological Seminary (he originally planned to become a minister) before heading to Germany to study with members of the philosophical wing of the historical school. This was during a period when the never-ending debate over the foundations of human knowledge had moved beyond the Hamilton-Mill controversy that preoccupied Veblen at Carleton and pivoted to the idea of legitimating scientific knowledge by historicizing it—a move derived from the influential critique German philosopher G. W. F. Hegel had leveled against Kant's theory of knowledge early in the century. By the 1880s, however, Kant's viewpoint, refurbished, was gaining renewed attention and acceptance as a result of the clamoring "back to Kant" movement then underway in Europe and America. (I will describe this movement in Section 2.) Pushing back against neo-Kantians and holding firm to Hegel's earlier critique, Morris formulated a philosophical stance that Herbert Schneider, the historian of American philosophy, once called "dynamic idealism."[15]

In Morris's view, when Kant postulated that the knower has knowledge of the external world only as the result of the mind's internal structure (the mind's "categories"), he overlooked that the connection between the human mind and the objects of knowledge is an inherently mutable and "organic" one. It is a relationship, said Morris, that fundamentally transforms both the knower and the knowable over the long span of human history, eventually reaching the point where the unknowability of "things-in-themselves"—as Kant had described the problem of knowledge—is a limitation knowers transcend. These knowers are not separate atoms, but members of an evolving "social organism," a "community of consciousness," where "the individual . . . is organically one with a larger life," which is embodied in the state. This developmental process occurs under the teleological guidance of "Absolute Spirit" (Morris's Hegelian word for God), who carries humankind slowly to science—or Absolute Knowledge—which is predicated on "historic intelligence" about the movements of the Spirit through the ages.[16]

From this interpretation of history it followed, Morris maintained, that the natural sciences were incomplete insofar as they stayed locked into scientific models from the recent past, as British philosophers had done. In one of his more straightforward statements, Morris asserted:

> At the beginning, in the seventeenth century, of the modern period in philosophy, the modern mind . . . sought . . . to insulate itself . . . from all connection with that historic past, from which it was in fact itself but an historic growth. The attempt was made to effectuate a solution of intellectual continuity, by placing the past under a ban of disgrace. This solution, breaking-up, or analysis, had . . . its relative and temporary justification; and that as a step in a process which could become complete only in a final synthesis, enriched . . . by all the acquisitions of modern science, but not excluding the riches of the past. . . . British thought has to the greatest extent, until recently, remained in that "irretrievably analytic" frame of mind, which [has] all the quality of a disease. . . . And this insulation . . . is necessarily connected with excessive devotion to the methods of mechanical analysis. Thus it is that in our day one of the most urgent . . . needs is the revival, in philosophy, of the historic sense.[17]

Operating in the Hopkins context, Morris was careful not to set philosophy, as he here celebrated it, over against the natural (or social) sciences, but to connect them as moments in a more encompassing process of historical change. "Philosophy," he stated, "may be fitly described as the science of the whole, . . . the study of and search for the truth, the universal truth, to which all special orders of truth or 'sciences,' and orders of 'science,' are organically related."[18]

This conception of philosophy as the über-science ran through Morris's courses at Hopkins, and he tried to impress it on President Gilman (who was growing uncomfortable with such metaphysical flights in a modern university), explaining that his aim was "primarily to represent philosophy . . . as a definite science, . . . the 'bond of all sciences.'" Here was Morris's rationale for devoting so much of his energy to the study of the history of philosophy, for only in this way did he think one could demonstrate that science was a historical growth. In the course Veblen took on Greek philosophy, for example, Morris sought (according to his course description) to provide, by starting with the ancients, "an exposition of the nature, methods, and results of philosophic thought, . . . [with] constant reference to the results of modern research in science and philosophy."[19] In substantive focus, this course, as well as the other two courses Veblen took with Morris, had next to nothing in common with the field of political economy (at Carleton or Johns Hopkins), and yet in the philosopher's Hegelian outpost, too, Veblen found a style of thinking infused with an unmistakable sense of the mutable, the organic, the scientific.

This way of thinking stood out also in the work of polymath Charles Sanders Peirce (1839–1914), who taught logic at Hopkins, on a part-time basis, from 1879 to 1884. Compared with Veblen's experiences with Morris, his contacts with Peirce were fewer and thinner. In a December 1881 letter to Gilman, Veblen wrote that he had been attending Peirce's course on elementary logic "latterly"—that is, since some point midway into the academic semester—and that was the extent of their direct interaction.[20] This logic course was the first half of a sequence many graduate students found incomprehensible. John Dewey experienced it that way, and Andrew Veblen (who took the "advanced" half of the course after his brother had left Hopkins) observed that it "called for an extensive knowledge of formal mathematics, and I do not think Th. would have enjoyed it."[21] Presumably Thorstein did not face the same impediment in the "elementary" part of the sequence, although Peirce was a notoriously off-putting classroom teacher, riding on his reputation as a "master mind."[22] (Peirce was the precocious son of a renowned Harvard astronomer and mathematician, who homeschooled the boy before sending him to Harvard. There and afterward, Peirce studied mental philosophy, mathematics, and the natural sciences, and was attracted, ambivalently, to Darwinian evolutionary theory. As the result of his many eccentricities, however, Peirce's academic career continually foundered, even as he published widely and produced a series of seminal articles that shaped the development of American pragmatism. To support himself, for many years he conducted research in astronomy, chemistry, and physics for the United States Coast and Geodetic Survey.)[23]

In the *University Circulars* for 1881, Peirce described the lecture course Veblen attended as concerned with "logic, deductive and inductive, including probabilities"—topics that were the themes of his recent publications. Designed in this way, the course introduced Veblen to some of the principal ideas from this period in Peirce's career, and these turned out to be a combination of intellectual practices old and new to Veblen. The glorification of modern science, already so familiar to him, pervaded all of Peirce's teachings. As Dewey wrote in reference to Peirce's course: "By Logic, Mr. Peirce means only an account of the methods of the physical sciences."[24] Peirce took this approach because he wanted to raze the ancient notion that logic was "the art of thinking" and to reconceive logic as the study of the triumphal methods of modern scientific research. In his view, during the previous quarter century, these "methods had created modern science" in areas like astronomy, physics, and chemistry (his own areas) but still needed to be formalized and generalized so that researchers could tailor these methods for fields that were lagging behind as recognized sciences. Peirce believed that "the higher places in science in the coming years are for those [scholars] who succeed in adapting the methods of one science to the investigation of another. That is what the greatest progress of the passing generation has consisted in." Even so, by his account, "professional logicians . . . have been slumbering through ages of intellectual activity, listlessly disregarding the enginery of modern thought"—and thus coming up short in their efforts, from Locke to Mill, to establish the foundations of human knowledge.[25]

So Peirce looked elsewhere, taking some guidance from Charles Darwin in *On the Origin of Species,* which had been published twenty years earlier. In doing so, Peirce gave Veblen his first direct opportunity to see Darwinian thought in action. (Veblen had, of course, already been exposed to evolutionary ideas.) From Darwin—or, more accurately, from the interpretation Peirce gave to Darwin's work—Peirce drew two fundamental principles of scientific knowledge.[26]

The first of these was a social-evolutionary principle. In response to Kant's thesis that human knowledge presupposes the operation of the mind's "categories," Peirce argued that these categories are long-term evolutionary products. Asserting that "the mind of man is strongly adapted to the comprehension of the world," Peirce asked: "How are we to explain this adaptation?" His answer: "The great utility and indispensableness of [the mind's categories] are such as to suggest that they are the results of natural selection," because living beings possessing these categories "would have an immense advantage in the struggle for life."[27] (This Darwinian answer contrasted with Morris's claim that the historical development of human knowledge was due to the teleological actions of Absolute Spirit.) This natural selection process occurs, moreover, at a collective level. "To make single individuals absolute judges of truth" about reality is, according to Peirce, a philosophical fallacy because, considered in an evolutionary light, the role of the individual is negligible. "Reality depends on the ultimate decision of the community"; it is "that which, sooner or later, information and reasoning would finally result in, and which is therefore independent of the vagaries of me and you."[28] Or, more elaborately (and eloquently):

> Logicality inexorably requires that our interests [in knowing] shall *not* be limited. They must not stop at our own fate, but must embrace the whole community. This community ... must not be limited, but must extend to all races of beings with whom we can come into immediate or mediate intellectual relations. It must reach, however vaguely, beyond this geological epoch, beyond all bounds. He who would [do otherwise is] illogical in all his inferences, collectively. Logic is rooted in the social principle.[29]

Besides this principle, Peirce borrowed another from Darwin. This was the insight that scientific laws are probabilistic statements. In Peirce's view, the methods of modern science—"observation of facts" and "induction" (complemented by other techniques)—serve effectively to discover the "Order of Nature": "the universal subjection of phenomena to laws."[30] But he interpreted Darwin as saying—and Peirce agreed—that *general* laws map on to *particular* instances of such phenomena only probabilistically. In other words, a general law tells us neither *to what degree* that law covers any individual case, nor *how* the general law operates in the individual instance. These are questions, according to Peirce, that scientists cannot answer simply on the basis of inferences from a general law, but only when also taking into account the specific facts of each case. Peirce made the point in the following way:

> Mr. Darwin proposed to apply the statistical method to biology. . . . Darwin, while unable to say what the operation of variation and natural selection in any individual case will be, demonstrates that in the long run they will adapt animals to their circumstances. Whether or not existing animal forms are due to such action, or what position the theory [of evolution] ought to take, forms the subject of a discussion in which questions of fact and questions of logic [or logical inference] are curiously interlaced.[31]

Historian of biology Michael Ghiselin clarifies this aspect of Darwin's reasoning by a contrast with the thinking of his forerunners: "Darwin's predecessors had grossly overestimated the extent to which laws of nature might account for the observed phenomena, or, what is much the same thing, they had underestimated the amount of historical contingency that is necessary to provide a proper scientific account of this world." As an expert on probability, however, Peirce was one of the few philosophers of his time who grasped Darwin's doctrine of the probabilistic relationship between the general laws and historical particulars. How much of this doctrine Veblen took in when he attended Peirce's lectures is unknown. But the topic of Peirce's course was, explicitly, the place of probability in scientific laws, and Veblen was an attentive student, studying at Hopkins to build up his stock of intellectual resources.[32]

So motivated, Veblen loaded onto his coursework in philosophy two other courses, one from each wing of the department of history and political economy. These were Sources of Early European History, with Herbert Baxter Adams (1850–1901), and History of Political Economy, with Richard T. Ely (1854–1943)—courses and teachers with much in common.[33] Adams and Ely both descended from old Yankee lineages, Puritan in belief and successful in business; both attended a classical academy and an illustrious Eastern college (Amherst in Adams's case; Columbia in Ely's); and both received German doctorates (Adams in history and political science; Ely in political economy), in both instances from the University of Heidelberg, where they studied with historical economist Karl Knies. In these ways, they were formed from the same mold as Veblen's mentor at Carleton, John Bates Clark, who was a personal friend of Adams going back to their days together at Amherst. (According to Adams,

Clark brought him and Veblen together. Before Veblen went to Hopkins, Clark contacted Adams to recommend Veblen "in the highest terms.")[34] Like Clark, Adams and Ely brought back with them from Germany a deep interest in the historical evolution of economic life-forms, and they carried this interest directly into their classrooms at Johns Hopkins. When Veblen took courses with the two men in fall 1881, he heard lectures by a historically oriented economist playing in sync with lectures by a historian who was concerned with economics.

What was more, Adams and Ely both centered their teaching on the topic of "institutions"—a concept they waved enthusiastically. Presenting their work this way fit with the practice of Karl Knies, and with President Gilman's preferences as well. When laying out his blueprint for Hopkins, Gilman (who had once taught history) envisioned a curriculum that would include courses on "the early history of institutions" and "the development of institutions," and that was exactly what Adams and Ely delivered. Together, as historians Philip Ethington and Eileen McDonagh have documented, the two men made their department a training program in "historical institutionalism"; they aspired "to place the study of society on a scientific footing by tracing the course of economic, political, and other institutional developments over the historical period since antiquity."[35] Graduate students understood this. When Woodrow Wilson arrived at Hopkins in 1883, he wrote to his fiancée: "When I got within range of these professors here, . . . I found that they wanted to set everybody under their authority to working on what they called 'institutional history.'" Facing the same pressure, Frederick Jackson Turner, another graduate student (and a future giant of the American historical profession), felt he had "to conform to the institutional interpretation so favored at Hopkins." And young historian J. Franklin Jameson, a classmate (and friend) of Veblen's, recorded in his diary, in December 1881, that Adams was urging him "to do some work in institutional history." A year later, Jameson complained about the almost single-minded focus, "at the J.H.U., . . . on the hist. of Institutions (with a large I)."[36]

In Adams's "Sources of Early European History," Veblen encountered this practice on a weekly basis.[37] Judging from Adams's (chaotic) lecture notes, the course covered the period from the final days of the Roman Empire through the settlement of the British Isles by Saxon tribes in the Late Middle Ages. To expand the time frame, Adams included backward glances to the Stone and Bronze Ages and a few forward glances to the Americas. His central narrative was the drama of the centuries-long westward migration of "the great Germanic race" (the Aryan or Teutonic race, as he also called it) and its social institutions, as a consequence of population growth, the need for better methods of production, and the "love of war and adventure." While unfolding this story, Adams sought also to make students aware of recent research on earlier "stages" of European history by archeologists and ethnologists. (He was especially keen about research on the different head shapes of different European "races.")[38]

Adams's interest in this early period in European history was inspired by his larger interest in American colonial history, which was the subject of his research publications in the early 1880s and several talks he gave in a departmental seminar series Veblen attended. In these, Adams marshaled archival evidence to demonstrate how the industrious English colonists bequeathed their own Germanic inheritance to the New World by successfully transplanting their community-minded social institutions, their "free" political institutions, and their commercially oriented economic institutions. Summing up his position, Adams wrote:

> In [the] provisions [that colonial settlers made] for local government, schools, churches, hospitals, freehold land tenure, and commons for public use, we recognize the leading institutions which have entered into the town-life of New England. The idea of all these institutions originated in Old England. . . . Even the Yankee disposition to truck and trade . . . was inherited from a nation of traders and adventurers, and by them from their Germanic forefathers. English commerce and English colonies sprang primarily from the amber-dealing tribes of the Baltic and sea-roving, colonizing bands of Northmen. The spirit of Saxon and Norman enterprise dawned upon New England from shores beyond the ocean.[39]

Adams intended this argument—which represented what modern historians have called the "Teutonic thesis"—as a critique of classical political economists who regarded this "disposition to trade" as a timeless characteristic of human nature, rather than the product of social evolution.[40] He pressed this critique in order to show that the work of historians was in accord with Darwinian ideas, or at least Darwinian terminology. American history should, Adams urged, "be viewed and reviewed as an organism of historic growth, developing from minute germs, from the very protoplasm of state-life" by means of a process that is still ongoing: "This country and all its institutions, though they adopt the best which the Old World can teach, will constitute a New World still by natural selection, and by independent organization [that will reach] harmony with a new environment," in part as the result of "a struggle for existence." Writing to a friend in 1880, the year before Veblen arrived at Hopkins, Adams boasted, in seriousness, that his research on colonial villages "will be for town history what [Thomas] Huxley's work on the crawfish is for biology." To Gilman, he put the assertion just slightly more modestly the following year when he described himself as "a door-keeper in the house of Science."[41]

Economist Richard Ely, who joined the Hopkins faculty on a trial basis that same year, replayed these themes in a course that was the final addition to Veblen's heavy schedule—the addition that caused him to swerve from philosophy and "give more attention to Political Economy" (as he told Gilman). This course was History of Political Economy, which Ely taught using a template he had recently acquired in Germany. The template gave Veblen a distinctive slant on the history of economics and better acquainted him with some of the big names in its canon. In course lectures, Ely examined the doctrines of Adam Smith (and his predecessors and successors) through the lens of an invidious contrast between classical economics and historical economics. Channeling his teacher Karl Knies, Ely's account reproached Smith and his accomplices for making "universal self-interest the preponderating cause of economic phenomena," eliding motives such as "generosity, love of mankind, a desire to see those about one happy, pride, sentiment, etc." Further, these "*a priori* economists" (as Ely called them, to paint them as armchair speculators, not inductive scientists) treated society as "simply the sum of individuals"; they failed to recognize that "we are inextricably and organically bound upon state and society." And to top off these defects, classical economic theory assumed that its propositions had the force and the "dignity of natural laws" that held true "for all places and for all times"—fatally overlooking that "'human institutions . . . modify [these] pretended natural laws,'" since economic phenomena, like all "social phenomena, [are matters of] growth and development, changing with society."[42]

As someone who had studied with J. B. Clark at Carleton, Thorstein Veblen had heard these criticisms before, almost verbatim, so Ely's assault on classical economic theory probably carried little news value. Other students found the critique stale. Veblen's friend, Jameson, arriving to class late one day, joked he "'didn't miss much. [Ely] fought his man of straw, the *a priori* economist, over again, and demolished him much as usual.'" All the same, Ely's lectures conveyed, more clearly than Clark's had, the fact that political economy consisted not only of different theories but also of opposing factions of economists who were actively waging war over these theories. In this way, Ely mapped out for Veblen the social terrain of the *field of economics* as it looked at the time (at least to Ely and many other observers). Presenting students with this field map made his course more than a synopsis of economic ideas from the past, as we might expect to find in a course on the "history" of political economy. Besides précis, the lectures offered students a guided tour of a combat zone divided, according to Ely's stylized account, between the Older School of classical economists and the Younger School of German historical economists. Ely's purpose for the tour was not to mediate or compromise. As a soldier himself in the struggle between right and wrong he was depicting, Ely left students in no doubt that right-minded economists followed the intellectual practices of the Younger School. Jameson, in another report on Ely's lectures, wrote that Ely's "narrow little narrow mind has become so steeped in German prejudices that he can't see any good in the English economists."[43]

Jameson perhaps overstated Ely's biases, though there is ample evidence of them in his published writings also. In any case, for the second time in a row, Veblen's coursework in economics took place under the direction of an economist who was highly critical of classical economics. At Carleton, Clark had attacked the classical doctrines; at Hopkins, Ely, who was scrappier, pushed the attack harder, leaving Veblen short, once again, of an orthodox education in the subject. But for a second time, too, Veblen had a teacher who was extending an invitation to participate in the development of a new approach. Older School partisans, said Ely, had once thought that political economy was "perfect and complete," although, as the situation stood in the early 1880s, "everything in political economy seems unsettled." In his view, though, this disarray carried with it a large opportunity to construct "a higher and more advanced political economy" by joining forces with "the younger men in America [who are] abandoning the dry bones of orthodox English political economy for the live methods of the German school." Doing so was incumbent on the economist, Ely believed, because "the topics he discusses are so vital."[44]

Among these vital topics, Ely's own emphasis fell on socialism, as Veblen was quick to notice. Ely featured this subject in several of his lectures in History of Political Economy (and in his books from this period, which grew out of those lectures).[45] It was in this course Veblen received his first systematic introduction to the subject of socialism, which

Ely, along with the majority of other contemporary economists, located squarely within the purview of economics. This was true among members of the Older and Younger Schools alike; for, despite deep differences of opinion about socialism as a form of society, economists concurred that analyzing the economic dimensions of socialism ranked high on the research agenda of their field. For Ely, this task involved assessing the validity of the grievances that motivated socialist movements in Europe and the United States, as well as evaluating "the practicability of . . . the measures they advocate[d]" to redress their grievances.[46]

As to the merits of the case, Ely judged that "the complaints of the socialists are often but too well founded." "Wealth," he stated, "has a dangerous tendency to accumulate . . . in accordance to [property] inheritance, privilege, and class," rather than "in proportion to useful intellectual and physical labor performed." Then too, "the tendency of our time is to conduct all business on a large scale, and crush out the 'small man.'" Still further, he observed, "a specific vice of our time, and one which political economists of all schools condemn, is extravagance and luxury. It is waste of economic powers, injuring those who indulge in it, and exciting envy and bitterness in the minds of those who are excluded."[47]

Recognizing these injustices, Ely accepted that broad-scale reforms were needed to secure the "public interest." But he objected to reckless socialist programs that sought the "violent" overthrow of the status quo; he favored "peaceful" socialist measures that preserved "republican institutions" and some forms of private property. To effectuate these measures, Ely looked to "three chief agencies": "Science, the State, and the Church." He enlisted the church because Christian morality had the spiritual power to implant "sound ethics" into economic life. (This idea was the basis of Ely's commitment to Christian Socialism, which had also attracted Clark.) But beyond this palliative, Ely, who was eager to denounce the laissez-faire doctrines of the Older School and propagate the statism of the Younger School, put store in the "central authority" of the state—a "people's state"—to regulate capitalist excesses and institute mechanisms for the downward redistribution of wealth and other economic resources. His reasoning here was straightforward: "If there is anything divine on this earth, it is the state."[48]

Even so, on Ely's account, neither church nor state could pursue effective socialist reforms when would-be reformers were lost in "dense ignorance." Progress depended, he held, on "a better education in political, social, and economic science," which, in turn, depended on the continual growth of scientific knowledge itself. Vesting this kind of faith in science aligned Ely with President Gilman, who was resolute that—besides producing knowledge for its own sake—the university should "advance the public interests," disseminating scientific knowledge so as to bring about "a better state of society, [with] less misery among the poor, less ignorance in schools, less bigotry in the temple, less suffering in the hospital, less fraud in business, less folly in politics."[49] Hopkins faculty members, nearly all of them, embraced this elevating vision, shaping it to fit their specific disciplines. Reclusive George Morris gave well-attended public lectures on "Topics Historical and Practical in Ethics," while Herbert Adams devoted much of his career to educational outreach programs that he believed would "lead . . . the Republic to a more thoroughly democratic state of society, with fewer artificial distinctions of culture," and would demonstrate, too, that "the higher learning is not for the benefit of a favored few, but that it is beneficial and accessible to the sons of citizens of whatever station."[50] These were modest initiatives in comparison with Ely's socialism, but Gilman (who was no friend of socialism) accommodated all of them in the spirit of open intellectual inquiry.

Where Veblen himself stood in the midst of these intellectual currents shows through in a fragment of a paper he wrote during his semester at Hopkins, probably in November 1881. The paper grew out of his course with Ely, who required graduate students to prepare "essays on assigned topics."[51] Veblen's topic was "J. S. Mill's Theory of the Taxation of Land," and no full copy of the paper has ever been located. In early 1882, however, an unsigned synopsis of it, almost certainly written by Veblen, appeared in the *University Circulars*:

> With the advance of society the rent of land increases. This increase is independent of any effort on the part of the landlord, being the product of the activity of the community. The State should, therefore, by a peculiar tax, appropriate this "unearned increment" and not permit it to go to the owner of the land. To obviate all injustice to owners who have bought land with the expectation of being permitted to enjoy the future increase of its rent, the State is to offer to buy the land of the owners at its market price as an alternative to their keeping it and paying to the State the increase in rent. As a consequence of such an alternative, land having a speculative value would be sold to the State in order to avoid loss to the owners. The measure would . . . lead to an almost universal na-

tionalization of land; differing, however, from generally entertained schemes for the State's getting possession of land, in that the expense of the change would be more equitably distributed on all classes of the community.[52]

Reading these sentences now, they come across as extreme. Graduate students in the social sciences today do not write course papers that advocate nationalizing landownership, taxing all income derived from speculation, or distributing wealth equitably across social classes. In the second half of the nineteenth century, however, these subjects were common debate topics among American and European economic writers (socialist and otherwise)—standard items in the "generally entertained schemes" mentioned in Veblen's abstract. His own entry point into this debate about wealth distribution was a thirty-year old chapter in John Stuart Mill's *Principles of Political Economy*. In it, Mill proposed the concept of an "unearned increment" to describe "a kind of income which constantly tends to increase, without any exertion or sacrifice on the part of the owners" of income-generating properties. Mill applied this notion—a variant of his concept of "unproductive labor" (discussed in Chapter 4)— to the economic returns that arise from the capacity of landowners to extract ever higher "rents," not because of improvements they make to their properties, but because the demand for land has a natural tendency to increase as the population and wealth of a society grow over time "due to the exertions of the whole community." Mill observed that the consequence of this tendency was that landlords "grow richer, as it were, in their sleep, without working, risking, or economizing."[53]

Invoking the "principle of social justice," Mill asserted the unearned increment was a historical wrong that needed to be righted. He cautioned, however, that correctives had to fit the times. In the long term, land nationalization and other socialist measures might provide ideal redistributive solutions, but for the present a more feasible alternative, in his opinion, was to raise land taxes so the state could appropriate the "unearned increment" for the benefit of society. Issued on Mill's high authority, this proposal drew reactions from all sides of the intellectual and political spectrums. Classical economist Henry Fawcett, for instance, raised the possibility of the state buying up land from property owners, though he then ruled this idea out as financially and administratively unworkable. More important, just before Veblen entered Hopkins, Henry George, a San Francisco journalist and liberal reformer, floated another taxation plan in his book *Progress and Poverty* (1879), which soon became a national best seller (as well as one of Ely's favorite texts). George accepted Mill's contention that the material progress of society brings landlords unearned gains in the form of increasing rents, but went further to link those gains directly to speculation on the part of landowners who withheld land from immediate use "in expectation of increased value in the future." Fixated on this aspect of the economic inequality, George (who liked to issue commandments) exhorted: "Abolish all taxation save that upon land value." He believed that by this one targeted intervention—his so-called single-tax plan—"every member of the community would participate in the advantages of [land] ownership."[54]

To judge from Veblen's abstract of his paper, it is clear that during his time at Hopkins he was playing off against these leading economic writers, but not straying too far. For the most part, he simply concurred with them, sharing their alarm that landowners were accruing an unearned income increment by means of illegitimate rents. Where Veblen's position differed slightly was in supplementing tax-based remedies (like those of Mill and George) with a state buyout option under which landowners could avoid taxes on rents arising from land speculation by ceding those lands to the state in exchange for compensation. This roundabout way of nationalizing landownership was, Veblen thought, something previous political economists had generally overlooked—though, going forward in his career, he did not spent much time on compensation schemes either. When he returned to the subject a quarter century later, Veblen shrugged off landlord compensation plans as historically backward-looking; his youthful belief that the state might work on behalf of "all classes of the community" barely outlasted his time at Hopkins. While there, however, he confidently rested his buyout proposal on the agency of the state, loyally accepting the statism of Ely (and Morris and Adams). Further, when Veblen formulated the plan, it had a strong agrarian flavoring, redolent of the Upper Midwest of his youth. We see this in his emphasis on landlords—rather than industrial capitalists, or property owners generally—and in his scruples about imposing any "injustice" on landowners. These specific features of his paper were not ideas he held on to in his future work. All the same, the paper's main point always stayed with him, reshaped and expressed in many different ways. Years later, he encapsulated it simply and severely: "America has been . . . *the land of the unearned increment.*"[55]

But setting aside Veblen's later work, his synopsis shows him already using the intellectual practices he had been learning for almost twenty years: thinking in holistic terms ("society," "community, "classes of the community"); viewing the social world as an entity in motion (undergoing "advance," drastically altering its property relations); and extolling work over its opposites (commending changes that are "the product of activity" versus gains that are "independent of any effort on the part of the land-lord" and are "unearned"). These ways of thinking, seeing, and judging were practices in full force at Hopkins, sounding up and down the hall-ways, echoing and reechoing in different tones throughout the different subject areas Veblen was studying.

For his part, Ely liked Veblen's paper on Mill—unsurprisingly, since Veblen wrote it for Ely, using Ely's ideas. Some time later, Veblen told Jameson, "Dr. Ely advised me to send [the paper] to a periodical to have printed." (He added, "I sent it and, as might have been expected, the 'periodical' died of it.") In addition, Veblen immediately got to work on a sequel, informing Gilman in December 1881 that he was "planning and preparing for a paper on the Relation of Rent to the advance of Population," and that he intended to "have it completed about the end of the present semester" (January 1882)—although there is no evidence this second paper materialized.[56] Veblen did, however, present a version of the first paper at a meeting of one of the seminar series on campus. (His précis synopsized this version.)

His involvement in the series formed an additional tie-in to the intellectual milieu at Hopkins, where seminars were a conspicuous presence. Another of Gilman's German-inspired innovations, seminar series were, in fact, a major feature of the apparatus Gilman built in order to carry graduate education beyond classrooms, where professors lectured about what was already known, and into forums where researchers—veterans and neophytes alike—met to extend the bounds of knowledge through "free enlightened controversy" (as Josiah Royce, an early witness to Gilman's seminars, described them).[57] In Veblen's time, these venues included the Mathematical Seminary, the Philological Association, and the Metaphysical Club, along with the seminars Adams and Ely organized in the department of history and political economy. Attending seminar meetings formed part of Veblen's busy schedule and intensified his interaction with his professors and other young men from around the country who were fellow graduate students. His paper "Mill's Theory of the Taxation of

Land" was one of four papers presented at the gathering of the department's Historical and Political Science Association on December 21, 1881. Jameson, who was there, wrote in his diary entry that the session was "dull"—and that was all he had to say about it. (This reaction is additional evidence that Veblen's ideas about land nationalization and so on were standard fare.)[58]

"Dull" or not, the meetings of the Historical and Political Science Association and other departmental activities gave Adams and Ely additional mechanisms to promote their training program in historical institutionalism.[59] Adams, for example, explicitly organized the history seminar Veblen attended as a "scientific laboratory" for the development of "original studies in American Institutional History."[60] Adams also brought to campus, with great fanfare, popular English historians who had written on the subject; as a result, Veblen heard lectures by James Bryce, speaking on English political and legal institutions, and by Edward Freeman, expounding Adams's sacrosanct Teutonic thesis on the origins of American institutions. In this period, too, Adams, tireless in his cause, launched (under his own editorship) an influential series of monographs—stiffly called the *Johns Hopkins University Studies in Historical and Political Science,* whose aim, in his words, was to cultivate "American Institutional and American Economic History." Generously salted with references to the "evolution" of economic institutions, one of the first volumes in the series carried the title (nearly duplicated in a title Veblen later used) "Institutions and Economics."[61]

Still and all, none of these local attractions, nor his gallery of teachers, were enough to hold Veblen at Johns Hopkins for more than one semester. The reasons for his early departure were (it seems) principally academic ones, although finances were also on his mind. Andrew Veblen explained to Dorfman that, if Thorstein had been on his own, he would have had "nothing to go on" to pay for a graduate school education. So his family had stepped up: "Father and our brother Orson, joined in providing money for his three years in graduate work."[62] (Orson Veblen, a middle brother, was by then prospering in the Minnesota lumber business.) In an era when graduate school was a completely unknown quantity, this outlay was an unheard-of show of family support, though Andrew did not say how much it amounted to. In any case, Thorstein stayed on the lookout for additional sources of support and, within weeks of arriving at Hopkins, appealed directly to Gilman, asking for "an abatement of tuition" because of his "lack of means."[63] The appeal failed, but two months later Veblen upped

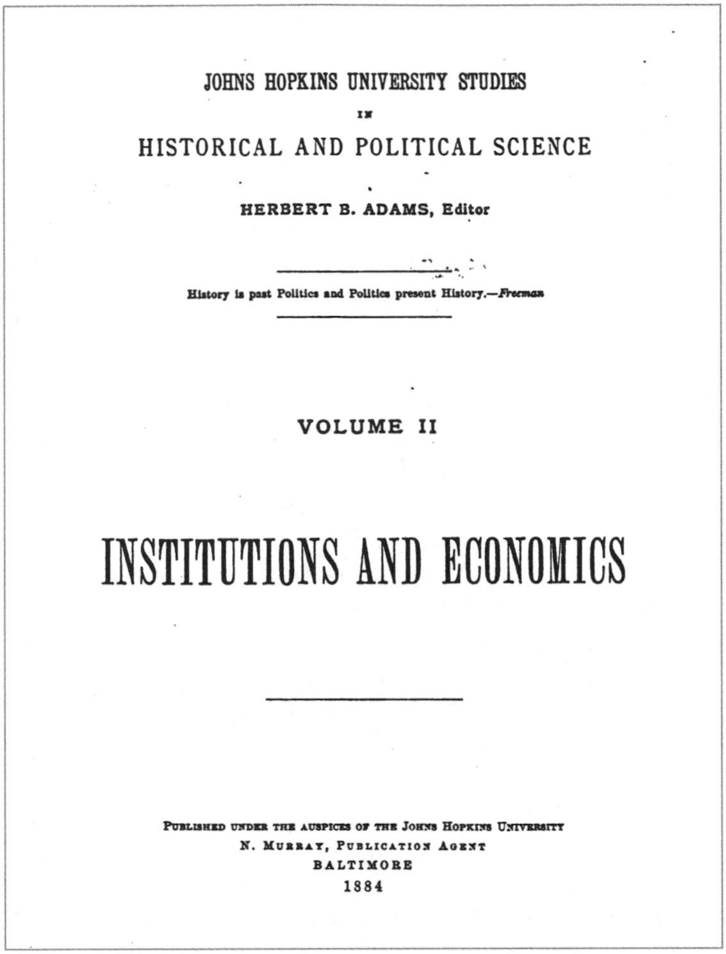

JOHNS HOPKINS UNIVERSITY STUDIES

IN

HISTORICAL AND POLITICAL SCIENCE

HERBERT B. ADAMS, Editor

History is past Politics and Politics present History.—*Freeman*

VOLUME II

INSTITUTIONS AND ECONOMICS

PUBLISHED UNDER THE AUSPICES OF THE JOHNS HOPKINS UNIVERSITY
N. MURRAY, PUBLICATION AGENT
BALTIMORE
1884

Figure 5 Monograph series for research on institutional history

his request and applied for one of Hopkins's coveted graduate fellowships. These were another Gilman invention, since research fellowships for graduate students were all but unknown in the United States in this period. But Gilman established twenty of them—with stipends in the grand amount of $500 (=$13,000) per year—and the competition was stiff. Swamped with strong candidates, Gilman turned down Veblen's request, just as he rejected the applications of John Bates Clark, John Dewey, Woodrow Wilson, and several other heavyweights, during the first decade of the fellowship competition. Still, Hopkins tuition charges and local room-and-board costs were lower than elsewhere, so graduate students usually managed to meet expenses without a fellowship. In another letter to Dorfman, Andrew Veblen wrote: "I do not think [Thorstein's] not receiving a scholarship had anything to do with his going from Baltimore to New Haven"—once he decided to revert to his earlier plan to study at Yale.[64]

Those who knew Veblen had another explanation for his fairly sudden about-face (which occurred between mid-December 1881 and mid-January 1882). Many years later, Archibald Maynard, a onetime student of Veblen's, recalled him quipping that the *University Circulars* that had piqued his interest in Hopkins proved, after he was on site for a while, to be "circulars of misinformation" about its program.[65] The statement roughly corresponds with Andrew's recollection that his brother moved from Hopkins to Yale because "he expected to find more nearly what he wanted there. I do not think there was any other reason."[66] These recollections do not say what exactly Veblen found wanting at Hopkins, but Jameson, who talked with Veblen while he was making his decision, was more specific. In his diary entry for Saturday, February 4, 1882, Jameson wrote: "Veblen came to see me about trains to New Haven, whither he is going Monday, probably. It is undoubtedly a far better place to work in political economy." (He added: "Still I am sorry to have him go.") This account points to a reversal in Veblen's thinking about working further with Ely, most likely because he had come around to Jameson's opinion that, as a mentor in economics, "Ely himself is not particularly valuable." That studying political economy was the main factor driving Veblen's choice to relocate meshes with a letter he sent to Jameson from Yale fifteen months later, after he had reapplied for a fellowship in philosophy at Hopkins and was prepared to return to Baltimore (before Gilman turned him down again). Veblen said: "I am still of the opinion that on the whole Yale is preferable to J.H.U. so far as Political Economy goes."[67] This criterion is perplexing, considering Veblen was still pursuing a doctorate in philosophy. But, then again, he was a young philosopher with intellectual range.

2.

Veblen transferred to Yale in 1882 because he wanted to study with members of its graduate faculty, not because of an interest in the local surroundings. Yale College and the city of New Haven were just so much background noise—although that noise was plainly audible.[68] New Haven, Connecticut, a city only a fifth the size of Baltimore, was undergoing its own makeover, as it crawled out from the economic depression of the 1870s and entrusted local government to successful (Democratic) businessmen, rather than scions of patrician families. These changes reflected the growth of industry on a scale modest when compared with Baltimore or Chicago, but sufficiently large to fill the city with nearly six hundred small- and mid-sized factories, dependent on immigrant labor and specializing in the manufacture of locks, clocks, carriages, corsets, and cigars. Two months after Veblen arrived, he told Jameson he "found things [in New Haven] pleasanter than I had expected." Two months after that, forgetting himself, he wrote to Jameson again: "I am beginning to like New Haven better lately than I did when I first came."[69]

Yale College itself was mired in conflict, though not over issues that affected Veblen directly. Unlike at Hopkins, where undergraduate training occurred in the shadows of the towering graduate program, at Yale undergraduate education took precedence—an institutional fact that kept some of the college's main stakeholders at odds with one another from the 1860s to the 1880s. The discontent was fomented by the "Young Yale" movement, a group of alumni and faculty that sought to modernize the college and wrest control from diehard Yale traditionalists. Under contention was a range of overlapping issues, some concerning esoteric rules of academic governance, such as whether there should be lay members on Yale's clergy-dominated board of trustees. Others, more fundamental, had to do with the college's curriculum, particularly whether its ancient, lockstep, classical program—heavily overlaid with Congregationalist religious doctrines but relatively thin on science—should be updated and secularized to include more courses in the natural and social sciences (and to allow students to take some courses as electives). Because of Yale's visibility throughout the country, these in-house conflicts gained national attention, provoking literally hundreds of articles in the press, which stamped the institution with a sharp identity. As Yale's trustees handed victory after victory to traditionalist forces, the college became known (as one contemporary summed up public opinion) as "the leading representative of more conservative tendencies in [American] education."[70] When Veblen moved to Yale in the early 1880s, this was its reputation, and observers widely assigned blame (or credit) to Yale's (supposedly) antireformist president Noah Porter (1811–1892), with whom Veblen soon began to study.

Veblen, in other words, was not dissuaded from going to Yale by the conservative reputation of its undergraduate program. Andrew Veblen told Dorfman that his brother actually enjoyed the change of scenery and that "he was interested as an observer of Yale life." Thorstein Veblen's one known contemporaneous comment about the college pertained not to its curriculum but to its athletic program (which was then in its glory days). After the 1882 Yale-Harvard baseball game, Veblen joked to Jameson: "It has been some surprise to me to see how kindly the puritan of today takes to Baseball and circuses. I noticed a Prof. from the Theological Seminary at the Baseball game. Athletics . . . is decidedly the most characteristic virtue of Yale, and perhaps of New Haven, and I am afraid it covers a multitude of sins." Only years later did Veblen expand this thought into a critique of "gentlemen's colleges"—Yale College writ large—as leisure-class preserves (or "penal settlements") held together by an atavistic mixture of religious indoctrination, useless classicism, and athletic tribalism.[71]

More immediately, however, Veblen's focus was on Yale as a place for postgraduate work. Shortly after enrolling, he told Jameson that he found Yale "an improvement on J.H.U." and that he "like[d] the school and the teachers very well."[72] Before the meteoric rise of Hopkins, Yale had been (as I have mentioned) the premier site for graduate education in the United States. It had conferred the first American doctoral degrees in 1861, and by the time Veblen arrived it had awarded dozens more, mainly in the sciences. Administratively, these degrees came through the department of philosophy and arts, an organizational unit Yale authorities had grafted onto its undergraduate program in order to bring together college graduates seeking advanced training and research-oriented faculty members interested in working with graduate students. Under this arrangement, Porter's predecessors succeeded in recruiting to the Yale faculty a number of internationally renowned scholars in the sciences and the humanities. Strengthening this roster were scientists appointed to the faculty of the Sheffield Scientific School, a satellite of Yale College that had been set up at midcentury, though gifts from private donors, to offer students (who were not enrolled in the college) courses in the natural and social sciences. (Daniel Gilman, before he became the president of Johns Hopkins, was a member of the Sheffield School and the chief architect of its program. He left Yale after the trustees passed him over in favor of Porter for the presidency of Yale.) Combining the faculties of the college and the Sheffield School, Yale stood, as historian William Barber has written, at "the forefront of American science" when Porter took office in 1871. Further, although Porter devoted Yale's resources mainly to undergraduate education and Hopkins soon surpassed it in many specialty areas, Yale remained a nationally recognized center for scientific research well into the 1880s.[73]

From this position, Yale, like Hopkins, displayed an earnest commitment to advancing scientific knowledge. And at Yale, too, "science" stretched to encompass not only the study of nature but also the study of the social world and the world of the humanities. Whether the topic of research fell in one of the natural sciences (geology, paleontology, zoology, or botany), or in history or politics, or in art history or Greek, Yale scholars were determined to cast themselves as "scientists" who used methods of observation to study empirical facts. This attitude spread even to the remote field of philology, which was in the hands of the eminent philologist William Dwight Whitney. As his biographer has emphasized, "Whitney wanted fervently to see language study achieve parity of status with the most advanced sciences, [and] he regarded the vindication of his field's scientific standing as one of his most important tasks."[74] What was more, most Yale's scientists, again like those at Hopkins, championed evolutionary doctrines, even Darwinian varieties of evolutionism, at least circumspectly (to the extent they allowed God a role of some kind in steering human evolution in a progressive direction). Whitney's "science of language," for example, was a philology that examined the evolution of language from its first beginnings, drawing on Darwin's work just as Darwin drew on Whitney's. (The two were professional friends.) Likewise, Yale paleontologist Othniel Marsh carried out research on the evolution of the horse and the great-toothed bird, which Darwin, writing in 1880, hailed as providing "the best support to the theory of evolution that has appeared within the last twenty years."[75]

In the corners of Yale where Veblen decided to study, these ways of thinking were also in daily use. As he did at Hopkins, Veblen split his time between two departments, or "groups" as they were called at Yale: "Intellectual Philosophy; Ethics," and "Political Science and History." Political economy, the subject that brought Veblen to Yale, was quartered in the second of these groups, which was the home base of William Graham Sumner (1840–1910), a professor of political and social science, whose teaching portfolio consisted heavily of courses in political economy. He was one of the three men with whom Veblen studied at Yale; the two others belonged to the Intellectual Philosophy; Ethics group: Noah Porter himself and George Trumbull Ladd (1842–1921), who joined the faculty

Figure 6 Veblen's professors at Yale University *(clockwise from top left):* Noah Porter, George Trumbull Ladd, and William Graham Sumner

the same year Veblen transferred to Yale. Veblen's work with these scholars ran for an intensive two-and-a-half year period, until he received his doctorate in June 1884. During this time, he continued to receive financial support from his father and brother, and he perhaps did some tutoring, though he was never worry-free on this count. In September 1882, Porter wrote to the administrator of the Philosophy Department about Veblen's situation: "His means are very limited, and he hoped when he came to obtain [remission?] of the charge for tuition. . . . Cannot something be done for him? At least cannot he be allowed to go & the payment be deferred [?] till his commencement?" Porter added: "He is a very able & accomplished student." (It is unknown whether Porter's request was approved.)[76]

When Veblen was studying with them, Sumner, Ladd, and Porter all occupied places on the national intellectual stage. Here, "Billy" Sumner eagerly assumed the role of the heavy, the gladiator, who publicly assailed everyone and anyone who clashed with his staunch beliefs. In social background, he differed from Veblen's previous mentors. Sumner's father was an immigrant from England who had worked as a railway repairman in Hartford, Connecticut, where his children went to public schools. By a twist of financial fortune, his son William Graham Sumner managed to attend Yale College and then to go abroad to study ancient languages, history, and theology for three years, during which time he came under the influence of biblical scholars from the German historical school. These experiences led Sumner to a short-term job at Yale as a tutor, then to several years outside the academy serving as an Episcopal minister, and finally to his appointment (a decade before he met Veblen) as Yale's all-purpose professor of social science.[77] This position gave Sumner wide latitude, and during his long career on the Yale faculty, he taught, besides political economy, courses in history, philosophy of science, and anthropology as well as sociology. (After the turn of the century, writers increasingly labeled him as a "sociologist," but he was always larger than the pigeonhole.)

During Veblen's time at Yale, Sumner concentrated principally on political economy, offering two graduate-level courses on the subject each year, which he taught using lectures and recitations (still a favorite teaching method, even with graduate students). Veblen took both courses, and in both cases student lecture notes have been preserved. These were taken by another Yale graduate student, J. C. Schwab, who attended the two courses only four years after Veblen, so his notes are likely a close approximation to what Veblen heard.[78]

The first of these courses was Political Economy, a course that departed from what its title might suggest to us, although Veblen knew what he was getting into. Summer regarded himself as an orthodox economist in the tradition of the English school, and when he taught the subject to undergraduates he relied on the standard textbooks of classical economics, supplementing these with a short text of his own that gave students problems to solve by applying the principles of political economy. Even so, Sumner's graduate course covered material that had far more in common with the German historical school than with the English school, because he designed it to follow the development of economic life forward from hunting and gathering groups, to societies based on pasturage and agriculture, to the emergence and expansion of industrial society. En route, Sumner examined population growth and migration, foodstuffs and methods of production, and changes in land tenure systems and consumption patterns—tossing in lengthy asides on cannibalism, the "idiotic character" of Roman luxury, medieval guild regulations, and dozens of other topics.[79]

Underwriting his discussion of these details about thousands of years of world history was Sumner's conviction that the doctrines of the classical economists were riddled with defects. This was the third time in a row Veblen studied with an economist who rolled out this critique; as of yet, not one of his professors of political economy was satisfied with the theories of the Older School. Clark and Ely had introduced Veblen to economics by means of a strong dissent from the tenets of classical political economy, and Sumner was now airing his own dissent—and he *was* a classical economist (and proud of it). But this allegiance did not stop Sumner from sounding very much like Clark, Ely, and critics everywhere, who faulted the English economists for conceptualizing human beings as selfish monads and assuming that the laws of economics applied universally. In his first lecture in Political Economy, Sumner told his students otherwise: the laws of political economy "only deal with . . . the highest level of civilization. There is, however, also an economy at the level of hunting, pastoral etc. tribe." Furthermore, "the individual by himself is unthinkable, and can only be thought of as a unit in society." From these claims, Sumner had only a short step to take before he was urging the creation of a new science—sociology—whose purpose was to study "the structure and functions of the organs of society" and the processes by which "social institutions grow and change." On this view, "the essential elements of political economy are only corollaries of special cases of sociological principles," as tailored to fit the "material" aspect of industrial societies.[80]

For the most part, these sociological-cum-economic principles had yet to be formulated—or so Sumner said in a nod to his Yale colleagues and others who held that knowledge must wait on careful scientific research. But he believed that the development of the social sciences was actively underway and that the era had arrived for knowledge-producers to reject claims about social world that were "founded on authority, tradition, arbitrary invention, or poetic imagination" and to turn to "scientific methods," modeled after those in the natural sciences, to uncover the "facts and laws" of society. Flagging this project as urgent for students, Sumner felt social-scientific research had, nonetheless, already gone far enough to demonstrate that the laws of the social world were "evolutionary" and built on what he glossed as hard Darwinian principles, such as the "struggle for existence" and the "survival of the fittest" (as he loosely interpreted these). In Sumner's view, there were "no bounds to the scope of the philosophy of evolution" as applied to social life; he regarded this proposition as established, once and for all, by Herbert Spencer's rendition of the doctrine of evolution.[81] Unlike Yale's theistic evolutionists, Sumner made no effort to soften Darwinian or Spencerian strains of evolutionism with comforting assurances that history was progressing in a divinely anointed direction. "Under our so-called progress," he wrote, "evil only alters its forms, and we must esteem it a grand advance if . . . good has gained a hair's breadth over evil in a century." Or, with less pathos: "The scientific view of the matter is that a thing exists for reasons which lie in its antecedents and causes, not in its purposes or destiny."[82]

To find these antecedents and causes, Sumner not only tracked evolutionary processes over the long term but also dealt with historical changes that occurred over shorter intervals of decades and years, which were the time units Veblen watched Sumner use in the second course he took with him, Politics and Finance in the History of the United States.[83] In this two-year course, Sumner focused his lectures on a relatively narrow interval of the recent past, the period from 1776 to 1876, and on a discrete set of events in American history, mainly the economic effects of federal legislation on tariffs, taxation, banking, and currency.[84] These financial issues were controversial topics of social policy throughout the nineteenth century, and Sumner presented students with a detailed narrative of the historical figures who had been involved in them and the surrounding economic and political institutions. Like several of Sumner's publications from the 1870s and 1880s, the course made the subject matter of economics nearly synonymous with economic history, illustrating that the economist's interest lay in historical specifics no less than in general evolutionary laws. To underscore this theme, Sumner provided students (in both of the courses Veblen took) with long lists of supplementary readings that included dozens of monographs on American and European institutional history.

In addition, Sumner's analysis of the financial history of the United States had an ulterior purpose: to lend scientific credence to the doctrine of laissez-faire. Although his political economy lectures adopted ideas from the German historical school, Sumner voiced nothing but disdain for German socialism and its "paternalist" state programs, which he regarded as intellectually misconceived and socially pernicious. In contrast, the policy of laissez-faire was, for him, nothing less than science itself speaking in policy tones, broadcasting the practical implications of Darwinian principles of struggle and survival. Extrapolating from these principles, Sumner maintained that "competition is the law of nature, [and nature] grants her rewards to the fittest." Because of this brute fact, interferences with nature's processes—most abhorrently, government policies to assist the needy—necessarily result in "the survival of the unfittest," the perpetuation of "the hopelessly degenerate members of a society," to the long-run sacrifice of the "general interest." In statements like these, callous in their wording even for Sumner, we see what would subsequently be called his "Social Darwinism," a stance repugnant to many of his reform-minded contemporaries.[85]

All the same, Sumner's main target was not society's down-and-out but the corrupt at the top who expected "something for nothing" (a favorite barb of Sumner's and later of Veblen's). Getting their hands on this "something" was the overriding objective of the "plutocrats," despised by Sumner, who used their wealth and influence to capture the state for selfish purposes, in particular to impose tariffs to protect some business enterprises (their own "consuming institutions") at the expense of other industries ("producing institutions"). Sumner counted this as an egregious contemporary instance of the "plunder and robbery" committed throughout history by the "privileged classes," the "idle rich" and the lawyers, soldiers, clergymen, and politicians who did their bidding. Wreaking havoc with the laws of nature, these predations also violated the moral maxim (repeated by Sumner at every turn) that society's rewards belong to the "industrious and the frugal," not to the "parasites" who "live in exemption from labor" and seek "gain, not by the legitimate fruits of industry and enterprise, but by extorting from somebody a part of his product under guise of some pretended industrial undertaking." Throwing open "the doors of waste and extravagance"—the opportunity for the wealthy to "squander and spend," while people who labor hard are racked with "jealousy of wealth"—this form of extortion lay, according to Sumner, at the core of American protectionism, and he reviled it as destructive "jobbery." (The epithet, subsequently adopted by Veblen, was a mid-nineteenth-century coinage.) Surveying the many defects of his era, Sumner placed this brutal knifing of the social organism above all the others: "The greatest social evil with which we have to contend is jobbery."[86]

These were Sumner's staunch views during the period when Veblen was at Yale, and Veblen reacted favorably to his teacher (whatever he thought of Sumner's attitudes toward the destitute). Andrew Veblen told Dorfman that Thorstein, who was not required to do so, devoted "all or most of [his] time at Yale" to studying with Sumner. Almost immediately after arriving at the university, Veblen wrote to Jameson that he was "very well pleased" with Sumner's Political Economy course, and a year later Veblen continued: "Prof. Sumner's two years' course of lectures on US political and financial history will [soon] be completed. . . . I have liked the lectures very much and think they have grown more interesting the farther they have gone."[87] Standing on Sumner's ground too, Veblen wrote a paper that, in 1884, earned him—"over some very strong competitors"—what was then Yale's highest (and only) university-wide award: the John A. Porter Prize for Best English Essay. With an eye on the prize's cash award of $250 (= $6800), Veblen chose, from a list of designated topics, "The Distribution of Surplus Revenue in 1837," which required applicants to "investigate the history and theory of the distribution" of federal monies to the states, with reference to financial legislation passed during the presidency of Andrew Jackson. The Jacksonian era was a period in economic history Sumner covered at length in his lectures and writings, and the subject of state revenue distribution fit also with Veblen's paper at Hopkins on the state's redistribution of the unearned increment. What Veblen actually wrote in his prizewinning essay we do not know, however, because no copy has been found. For his part, Sumner regarded it as "a very important thesis."[88]

DESPITE HIS GOOD EXPERIENCES at Yale with Sumner and political economy, Veblen held to his initial plan to continue toward a doctorate in philosophy. Writing to Sumner several years later to ask for a letter of recommendation, Veblen prompted: "As you may remember, I graduated from Yale . . . as Ph.D. in Philosophy and Social Science." Both men understood, however, that "social science"—that is to say, Sumner's sociology-laced political economy—had taken the back seat for Veblen. A couple of years afterward, when Veblen was applying for admission to graduate school at Cornell (in order to get a second doctorate), he stated, more accurately, that at Yale he had taken "Philosophy as a primary and Economics and Social Science as a secondary course."[89]

Why he stuck with philosophy, when political economy was the subject that had actually drawn him to Yale, is not hard to construe. His original reasons for entering the field of philosophy still pertained. His education at Carleton had placed philosophy at the apex of human knowledge, and his teachers at Hopkins and Yale kept it there—George Morris most obviously so, with his belief that philosophy was the master science that unified all other domains of knowledge. Further, as a practical matter, insofar as *any* new academic jobs were opening up (outside the natural sciences and the study of foreign languages), these were in philosophy, which afforded, in the subfield of "moral philosophy," at least some space for pursuing work in the social sciences. During Veblen's time at Yale, doctoral degrees in political economy simply had no takers at all (Veblen's was only the fourth Yale PhD in philosophy), and Sumner did not produce PhDs until the 1890s. His own chair was in "Political and Social Science," rather than in "Political Economy"; and when Arthur Hadley, soon a luminary in American economics and later Yale's president, joined the Yale staff in 1879, he was relegated (as Veblen would have seen) to serving as a foreign language tutor for four years before college officials allowed him to offer, for no salary, a course in economics. Under these circumstances, it is unlikely Veblen wavered long over whether to pursue a degree in political economy or a degree in philosophy.[90]

Besides, the field of philosophy continued to attract him intellectually, and he valued working with the two faculty members who made up Yale's division of "Intellectual Philosophy; Ethics"—the local name for "mental and moral philosophy." Of the two, George Trumbull Ladd was not someone Veblen initially intended to study with, if his name had even entered Veblen's awareness when he was deciding whether to leave Hopkins. (Ladd was appointed to the Yale faculty just one semester before Veblen's move, mainly to lighten President Porter's teaching load at the undergraduate level in the areas of philosophy relating to psychology.) A Congregational minister turned mental philosopher, Ladd had family roots that went back to the Mayflower; his immediate forebears had settled the Western Reserve region of Ohio, where his father was a well-respected, modestly successful businessman. Ladd's schooling, unlike that of Veblen's other mentors, did not involve a sojourn in Europe. After graduating from Western Reserve College, Ladd attended Andover Theological Seminary, where he was drawn to the biblical scholarship of the German historical school, as well as to the works of Kant and those of University of Berlin philosopher-psychologist Hermann Lotze. These experiences left Ladd with a wealth of German ideas he would mine years later when he joined the Yale faculty.[91] During Veblen's own time at Yale, Ladd was not yet teaching graduate-level courses. Advanced students studied with him one-on-one, however, as Veblen did once he realized that he and Ladd had overlapping interests. Andrew Veblen told Dorfman, "Thorstein so often spoke of Ladd that I have the impression that he worked with him a good deal."[92]

When Veblen's association with Ladd started, the philosopher was just completing a 1,500-page book titled *The Doctrine of Sacred Scripture: A Critical, Historical and Dogmatic Inquiry into the Origin and Nature of the Old and New Testaments*.[93] The ample subtitle was Ladd's way of conveying, even as he tackled a subject far afield from what other Yale scholars were researching, his commitment to some of the same intellectual practices—and ways of thinking about scientific knowledge, holism, and the inherency of change—that natural and social scientists on campus were using in their work. For, devout Christian though he was, Ladd aimed to show that the Bible, rather than being the simple product of divine inspiration, was "an historical growth, which must be traced and understood, in large measure at least, as are other growths of history." To accomplish this, he asserted, "the Bible must now be reached by the inductive method" of modern science; in other words, "he who wishes to know the true story of the origin and nature of the Bible must first of all ascertain as many as possible of the facts," including those discovered by the evolutionary sciences (geology, paleontology, archeology, anthropology, ethnology) about the age of the earth, the origins of the human race, and so forth.[94] Melding together the findings of these sciences, Ladd disputed that God created the universe in the manner depicted in the book of Genesis and that Moses authored the Pentateuch, as well as many other fundamental tenets of biblical historiography. Still further, Ladd disputed the antiquity of the Bible as an actual text, marshalling evidence that the book was actually "constituted" during the era of the Reformation as a result of "supremely important causes" of a secular kind that were "not the intentional work of any individual minds."

> The revival of a general interest in literature gave to men a partic-
> ular interest in the literature of the Bible, which had for so long a
> time been, like that of Greece or Rome, buried in manuscript edi-
> tions of the palaces and cloisters. The discovery of printing had made
> it possible actually to give the Bible to the race. . . . Commercial
> interest and adventure were . . . brought to bear upon the propaga-
> tion of the Bibles. . . . But, above all, the sense of moral unrest—of
> dissatisfactions with the present, and of longing after something
> better and more like a celestial ideal—had grown strong in the heart
> of the nations.[95]

In an era of American history dominated by literal interpretations of the Bible, Ladd's views set off years of public outrage, and it is unlikely Veblen tracked the fight. But in the early 1880s, Ladd was already absorbed in a second line of work (closer to Veblen's interests in mental philosophy), in which he repurposed the intellectual tools he used in his biblical writings. This second line, as Ladd described it, involved applying the methods of science to the internal workings of the human mind. German philosophers, Ladd knew, had already initiated this project: they were creating the "new psychology," wresting the structure and operations of the mind from armchair speculators, and subjecting the nervous system and the five senses to experiments designed to copy those in the high-flying field of physiology. So Ladd followed the Germans' lead straight into the laboratory. Extending their "materialistic" approach to mind—while preserving "spiritualistic" phenomena such as "consciousness," "volition," and choice"—was the purpose behind his seven-hundred-page *Elements of Physiological Psychology: A Treatise of the Activities and Nature of the Mind from the Physical and Experimental Point of View*, published in 1887, which he was researching and writing nearly full-time when Veblen was his student.[96]

This timing gave Veblen another prolonged occasion to observe "science" and "evolution" colonizing a wide territory. Ladd summarized his rationale:

> We do most confidently believe that modern psychology is amply
> entitled to be called a science; and even—if you please—"a natural
> science." It is a science, because it has a sufficiently well-defined [set]

of phenomena, which it undertakes to describe and to explain [just] like every other genuine inductive science . . . [In order to explain,] the science of psychology has the task of tracing the evolution of mental life, [i.e., its] genesis and development.[97]

This assertion about mental evolution was one Ladd pressed from two sides: first, by considering the ages-long development of the human species (as divided up into races); second, by advocating the study of "the history of the mental life of [the] human being, from the cradle (or even from its embryonic existence) to the grave," treating that history as a process that "unfold[s] itself in a regular order, in which all that comes at all comes in due sequence and acknowledged dependence upon what has preceded." In fleshing out this evolutionary view, Ladd maintained that the individual's reflexes, habits, and other attributes form a "living unity": that the human being is not an agglutinated "mass of nervous matter," but (as Ladd's biographer has summarized) "a dynamic organism" engaged in conduct that is "purposeful" and strives toward "the solution of practical problems of living." What is more, the development of this "real being" was, for Ladd, "dependent on the *relations* in which it is placed to other real beings" in the social world.[98] Critics of Ladd, in the late nineteenth century and since, have faulted him for proposing a less penetrating account of mind than William James formulated a few years afterward in *The Principles of Psychology,* but between 1882 and 1884 Veblen was not yet thinking about James's writings. Through his work with Ladd, he was experiencing new iterations of intellectual practices familiar to him by this time.[99]

Veblen's other mentor in philosophy at Yale was President Noah Porter, seventy years old, internationally eminent as a scholar, locally controversial as an administrator. A descendant of early colonial stock and a long line of New England ministers, Porter had attended Yale College and its theological department (the future Divinity School), and served for ten years as a Congregational minister before joining the Yale faculty in the late 1840s as professor of moral philosophy and metaphysics. Later, at the mature age of forty-two, he spent a year's leave in Berlin, studying with philosophers and other scholars from the historical school, before returning to Yale, where he wrote a series of prodigious treatises (which became a mainstay of postbellum American philosophy) and succeeded to the presidency in 1871 as the favored candidate of the Yale trustees who wanted to maintain the classical curriculum.[100]

Judging Porter in his role as president, Yale historian Brooks Kelley once described him as "the wrong man at the wrong time": a stubborn traditionalist focused single-mindedly on undergraduate education and staunchly opposed to contemporary intellectual trends.[101] More recent assessments, though, have been much more flattering, agreeing with historian Louise Stevenson that Porter was deeply committed to "new German scholarly methods" and determined to make Yale "the home of scholarship"—a place for the production of new knowledge.[102] It was Porter who hired both Ladd and Sumner, and he supported their research and that of other faculty members. In early 1880, however, Porter came under public fire after the *New York Times* hyped an incident in which he and Sumner clashed over Herbert Spencer's *The Study of Sociology,* a tract Porter objected to allowing Sumner to assign to Yale undergraduates because of the English evolutionist's polemical attack on religion as "theological bigotry" that "distorted facts" and caused "perversions of opinion [that stood] in the way of Social Science." Eventually Porter and Sumner reached a compromise about the book and the flap died down, but not before Porter gained a reputation as a benighted opponent of science and evolution—a charge that would bedevil him for more than a century. (According to later scholars, the overblown "Sumner-Porter controversy" was a minor battle of personalities, not a major war of ideas.)[103]

Porter's dedication to science ran long and deep. Throughout his academic career, his devout classicism went together with reverence for "the magnificent sciences of Nature" and "the splendid achievements of modern science," and he preached scientific principles even in his metaphysical writings. At the start of his principal work, *The Human Intellect,* he immediately raised the banner. Declaring his intention "to adhere most rigidly to the methods of true science," he aimed to transform mental philosophy into "psychology," which he defined (in a strained but sincere effort to combine his descriptive and normative interests) as "the science of the human soul." In agreement with the new psychology of the Germans, he then laid out a detailed analysis of the senses and other "internal states," including instincts, habits, and dispositions. Because Porter, unlike Ladd, conducted no experimental research himself, he was left to base this analysis on the research of others; but this limitation did not alter his conviction that psychology "is, like all the sciences of nature, a science of observation," predicated on "the inductive method" and "subject to those rules of investigation and of evidence which are common to them all." Further, these methodological rules pertained as well in "political and social science," a science he welcomed to deal with the natural fact that "man is a social being, and that he is formed for and must exist in organized society."[104]

Porter readily acknowledged that laws of evolutionary change might extend to include psychological and social phenomena, and he said so not just to appease his critics. In allowing for this extension, he did insist that scientists not overstep their evidence and inflate evolution so as to shrink the role of "an intelligent Creator" in any of the realms of nature. But, on Porter's view, science and religion, properly conducted, were not opposed, and "we have no fears from either." Consequently, Christian men and women, he maintained, should stand "ready to reexamine every question of faith in the light of the newest researches, . . . and, if need be, to modify our belief by the issue." Adhering to his own unorthodox advice, he ploughed through the literature of the physical and biological sciences, singling out Darwin's research and asserting, apropos of "the operation of the struggle for existence and the survival of the fittest," "this theory is perfectly legitimate as an hypothesis, and is supported by the unquestioned and unquestionable presence and operative forces of [these] two tendencies or laws" in nature. What was more, although Porter rarely associated these forces with the social world, he accepted that societies are subject to "the operation of evolution" and undergo "stages of development."[105]

Of more pedagogical importance to Porter than the grand theory of evolution, however, were historical changes on a human scale—and the lessons these offered. His brief on behalf of classical education turned on his conviction that the writings of the ancient authors would (as noted in Chapter 3) open the student's eyes to "the life of human beings greatly unlike those whom he has ever known or imagined." A grasp of human history, in Porter's view, brought to life "the morning of the race" and its subsequent moments, illuminating the changing "manners and institutions" of past ages, up to and including "the origins and growth" of the "free institutions" of the Anglo-American people.[106]

In addition, according to Porter, institutional history provided knowledge about the social conditions that encourage virtue. As a moral philosopher, Porter was a strong proponent of the "doctrine of benevolence" that Veblen had been introduced to at Carleton; Porter upheld the principle that "every man is morally bound to feel and act for the highest well-being of his fellow-men." For individuals to live up to this sacred duty requires of them "industry and foresight" rather than "slackness and indolence," moral choices that—as history instructs—are partly shaped by the presence of virtuous rather than "vicious institutions." In Porter's estimate, however, "the complications of modern society" heavily favored institutions of the vicious kind. These fed "the love of money and fashion," engendering "speculation in stocks, grains, and other provisions," along with "social inequalities, defective education, bad government, and bad religions," all of which made it hard "for millions of the depressed classes to supply themselves even with daily bread." By no means did Porter intend this heartfelt litany as a plea for new economic order; he accepted as natural the "institution of property," inasmuch as it enabled property owners to fulfill the duty of benevolence. All the same, he condemned property that was "gained and held in the spirit of robbery," and he railed against the laissez-faire notion that "the individual and the community will thrive most effectively when . . . each man looks out for himself." Contrasting the capitalist regime of property ownership with a regime that would abolish private property to promote greater social "co-operation," Porter—a septuagenarian at the helm of Yale, no less—kept open the historical options in the hope that, going forward, capitalism could learn something from alternative institutional arrangements:

> [Although] we find overwhelming reasons to conclude that communistic principles can never take the place of separate ownership of property, . . . the evidence is constantly accumulating, that the principles of co-operation may be safely and wisely applied in ways which are as yet untried, and with a success which has never yet been dreamed of.[107]

How deeply these ways of thinking tinted Veblen's interactions with Porter is unknown, though the timing was right. Porter published most of the writings I have just quoted within a year or two of Veblen's graduation from Yale, so they almost certainly conveyed his ideas when Veblen was at Yale between 1882 and 1884. Moreover, Porter—who, in interaction, was "learned and simple, kindhearted and sociable" (in William James's description)—formed a regular presence in Veblen's academic life during this period.[108] In an April 1882 letter to Jameson, for instance, Veblen told his friend: "I am taking . . . two classes in Philosophy under Pres. Porter." (About them he added: "[I] am very well pleased.") A year later, in February 1883, he sent an update: "I have eleven hours a week this term, mostly in Philosophy" with Porter. There is no record which of Porter's courses Veblen was referring to; the *Yale Catalogue* states only that, in these years, Porter's graduate-level courses rotated across "psychology, philosophy; history of philosophy; and ethics." Regardless of the specifics, however, after a run of no fewer than three of Porter's courses, plus frequent one-on-one contacts with him, Veblen could not have missed the president's overall views on science, history, and society.[109]

Exactly what else these courses offered Veblen is hard to say since Porter gave Veblen leeway to pursue his own interests (up to a point). As Veblen wrote to Jameson: "Just now, Hegel is all the rage, that is with me, and, by consequence, with Pres. Porter. . . . The president does not agree with Hegel, but so far I have not let myself be disturbed by that."[110] Veblen's attraction to Hegel (which proved temporary) was a direct carryover from his time at Hopkins, where he had observed George Morris's contorted Hegelian efforts to set human knowledge on solid philosophical foundations. As Veblen knew, securing those foundations was also an overriding concern for Porter. Unlike Morris, however, Porter cleaved mainly to the Scottish "realist" position, which he overlaid with some of Kant's distinctive vocabulary. Doing so had pulled Porter closer to Kant's views on knowledge, although only by a few steps, because Porter's larger aim—front and center during Veblen's time at Yale—was to defeat Kant on his own terrain by affirming the "knowableness" of "things-in-themselves" and the power of human cognitive faculties to achieve real knowledge of nature and society. From these assertions followed Porter's claim that scientific knowledge could be—and necessarily had to be—built on the basis of induction.[111]

What kept these timeworn epistemological issues in the limelight for philosophers in the early 1880s was the "back to Kant" movement then underway on both sides of the Atlantic. The movement was sparked by the centennial in 1881 of the publication of Kant's *Critique of Pure Reason* and the upcoming centennials of the other two parts of his vaunted trilogy, the *Critique of Practical Reason* (in 1888) and the *Critique of Judgment* (in 1890). Centennial events included international conferences, special issues of philosophical journals and reviews, and a spate of books and articles both by champions and by critics of Kant's ideas. In these forums, philosophers outdid one another in their appraisals of Kant's significance (positive or negative): E. G. Robinson (of Brown University) averring, for example, that "it is hardly possible to overstate the necessity of a right understanding of Kant on the part of any one who would criticise modern thought intelligently," or John Coyle (of Princeton) calling the "revival of the zealous study of Kant . . . the one movement that will most benefit philosophy." Dissenter from Kant that he was, even Noah Porter shared the general opinion, agreeing that "no writer repays study so well" as Kant. Indeed, when the Chicago publishing house of S. C. Griggs & Company launched in 1881 a series of books on Kant's trilogy, Porter authored the volume on Kant's second *Critique*. This book followed a volume on Kant's first *Critique* by the series editor, the eminent George Morris himself. According to the series announcement, Robert Adamson (of Victoria University, in England) was lined up to write a final volume on Kant's third *Critique,* although his never materialized. Elsewhere, however, Adamson described the third *Critique* as "undoubtedly the hardest of Kant's writings."[112]

Here was a ready-made opening for an ambitious young scholar seeking to stamp his mark on the field of philosophy, and Veblen did not hesitate to take it. In his Carleton commencement address four years earlier, he had thrown himself into the star-studded Hamilton-Mill dispute, and he now moved, with assurance, onto the latest scene of the philosophical action, writing an essay that became his first article: "Kant's *Critique of Judgment.*" Appearing in July 1884 in what was then America's premier philosophical journal, the *Journal of Speculative Philosophy,* the article was the first English-language study of Kant's third *Critique*. With it, Veblen aimed to fill (as far as fifteen journal pages permitted) a crying void in scholarly literature on Kant and to win himself a recognized place in the philosophical debate du jour. Writing about Kant's *Critique of Judgment* gave him the chance to go head-to-head with the recently resurrected German philosophical lion, and to do so at a moment when both of his philosophical mentors, Porter and Morris, were writing books on Kant's *Critiques*. (As Veblen knew, Ladd and Peirce were also Kant aficionados.)[113]

In content, Veblen's article followed Porter's approach to Kant, though Veblen's tone was less critical. Unfazed by Kant's challenging German, he confidently swept through the *Critique of Judgment,* depicting it as a book concerned with the foundations of human knowledge. Laying out just a few of Kant's concepts and propositions, Veblen reformulated these to lend support to Porter's modified Scottish realism, particularly the thesis that "the faculties of the intellect" make possible the process of induction by which "knowledge of reality"—and of the causal laws of nature—can legitimately be attained. Elaborating, Veblen held that "hardly any part of our knowledge except that got by induction" has practical value and that it was for this reason that "today any attempt, in any science, which does not furnish us an induction, is counted as good for nothing." This argument showed Veblen drawing, for the purpose of tackling contemporary philosophical problems, from the repertoire of intellectual practices he had been stockpiling: valorizing scientific knowledge, thinking in holistic terms (he described objects of knowledge as forming an "organic whole" and a "connected totality"), and focusing on processes of change (on the "cumulative character" of scientific evidence and on the cognitive "unrest [that] drives the mind" continually to search for causal patterns). And evident in his article, too, was Veblen's belief that general scientific laws apply to particular cases only more or less, only with greater or lesser degrees of probability, not with complete certainty—a claim he made into one of the article's main themes. An "abstract law," he wrote, can "never get so far as to afford us ground for asserting . . . that a given cause will produce a given effect" in any concrete instance, because "there is always an element of probability, however slight, in our knowledge of particular causes." This viewpoint reflected Peirce's teachings when Veblen was at Hopkins, although he almost certainly heard the same doctrine from Porter, who also emphasized the "probabilistic"—or "contingent"—nature of general laws when they are applied to individual cases.[114]

Porter, as well as making an intellectual impact on Veblen's first article, also oversaw Veblen's 1884 doctoral dissertation. The title of this, as handed down for decades by Veblen scholars, was "The Ethical Grounds of a Doctrine of Retribution"—and Veblen perhaps did write a thesis by this name and on this subject. The words "doctrine of retribution" raise an immediate flag, however, because the expression was commonly associated with evangelical Protestantism and an esoteric debate about divine judgment that pitted the "doctrine of retribution" against the "doctrine of forgiveness." Students in the Yale Theological Department were involved in this debate, but it was extremely remote from Veblen's course of study (as far as we know about it). What is more, nowhere else in his oeuvre did Veblen mention the "doctrine of retribution" or even the concept of retribution, or anything of the sort. In their writings, Porter, Morris, and Ladd discussed "retribution" very briefly, and so did Kant, Mill, and Spencer, but almost as asides. Speculating about Veblen's relation to the topic is moot, however, because the piece of evidence that would decide the issue is missing. In 1925, when Dorfman asked Andrew Veblen about getting a copy of "The Ethical Grounds of a Doctrine of Retribution," Andrew could not recall ever seeing something of that description; and Wesley Mitchell, Veblen's student and close friend, said the same a few years earlier.[115] More significantly, when Dorfman requested a copy from the Yale Library, the only thing the librarians could produce was a title, which they probably copied from an official listing, compiled in 1915, of all known "Doctors of Philosophy of Yale University."[116] It was on this list that "The Ethical Grounds of a Doctrine of Retribution" first cropped up as the title of Veblen's dissertation. But the list was based on information cobbled together thirty years after Veblen received his doctorate, and it has not been authenticated. Any number of clerical errors in Yale's then haphazard record keeping could explain how a fluke title, perhaps originating in the theological department and unrelated to Veblen's dissertation, crept onto the 1915 list. The familiar requirement that PhD recipients deposit a physical copy of their dissertation in their university library was not introduced at Yale until 1893, a decade after Veblen graduated— so "The Ethical Grounds of a Doctrine of Retribution," if it actually existed, probably never made its way into the Yale Library system.

There is, however, another possibility: that Veblen's dissertation was the same as his article on "Kant's *Critique of Judgment.*" In the 1880s, Yale's doctoral requirements consisted of two years of coursework, a final exam, and a "thesis," with "thesis" meaning something different from the behemoth dissertation of today.[117] At Yale and elsewhere, theses were often short. Porter's first PhD student, for instance, earned his doctorate with a twenty-four-page review article. In this context, it would have been natural for Porter to count Veblen's Kant essay as his "thesis" and to encourage him to write the essay for this purpose; it is hard to fathom why Porter would have expected Veblen to produce something more. An added consideration is chronology. Scholarly journals in the late nineteenth century were fast-moving operations; typically, editors acted on submissions as soon as they arrived, immediately putting accepted papers into production, so there would be enough copy for the next issue. The fact that Veblen's article on Kant appeared in July 1884 means that he probably submitted the manuscript of the article to the *Journal of Speculative Philosophy* (a bimonthly) a month or so beforehand. This chronology places that submission date just around the time Veblen completed his thesis (in order to graduate in June 1884) and, therefore, would have had the manuscript ready to submit. Finally, there was Veblen's schedule. We know that from December 1883 to May 1884, he was busy writing his prizewinning paper "The Distribution of Surplus Revenue in 1837" and that during these months he was also writing "Kant's *Critique of Judgment.*"[118] Squeezing in the work of researching and writing a dissertation on the separate topic of the "ethical grounds of a doctrine of retribution" world probably have been too much even for an intellectual workhorse like Veblen—though it remains possible. Either way, his long schooling as a philosopher was now concluded.

CODA: TAKEAWAYS

Whether they were philosophers, historians, or political economists, Veblen's seven professors at Johns Hopkins and Yale presented their ideas in a similar manner. Living in the Age of Iconoclasm, they regularly adopted a confrontational posture, seeking to topple their predecessors by assaulting their premises, attacking their conclusions, and doubting everything in between. In a different time and place, some of these men might have dressed as explorers of uncharted intellectual territories, architects of an intellectual synthesis, or dispassionate commentators on conflicting ideas: knowledge makers can don many different identities. But Veblen's teachers opted for the role and the style of the controversialist, seeing themselves as rebels fighting in opposition to error and cant, raining down skepticism, even heresy, on citadels of misguided and dangerous ideas.

Some of the seven even boasted of this style of argument and expression. Proudly, Ely depicted himself as "a born rebel and a skeptic"; Peirce trumpeted his "heretical principles of philosophical research"; Ladd basked in "his career as a skeptic" who always stood at the center of controversy. Characterizing Adams (as he came across to students in the period when Veblen knew him), Jameson observed: "All his work is the product of a desire to be iconoclastic and cynical." Readers of Morris and Porter saw some of this style too, for even as the two philosophers drew from their forebears—Morris from Hegel and Porter from many classical and modern sources—they relentlessly battled the orthodoxies of accepted authorities (British ones in particular) who held contrary views. And Sumner had no peer; ready to spring to attack whatever the occasion, he was, in his biographer's description, "one of his century's great controversialists"—America's premier "iconoclast."[119]

For every one of Veblen's professors, this style enwrapped similar ways of perceiving and understanding the phenomena they taught and wrote about: their practice of viewing these phenomena as undergoing historical and evolutionary change; their practice of thinking about them as components of a larger organic whole; and their master practice of regarding science as the touchstone of knowledge about these phenomena. (Among his Hopkins and Yale professors, not one defended a static, atomistic, or nonscientific point of view.)[120] Inasmuch as Veblen's teachers dealt with the subject of human conduct, they also uniformly commended work-based—productive—activities over other forms of behavior. By the time Veblen walked into his mentors' classrooms, these practices were so much a part of their work, so taken for granted, that using them was a matter of course. Those practices were the gears that slipped into place whenever one of the seven got down to the routine of formulating and communicating his ideas. Still further, this intellectual machinery functioned in a multipurpose manner. Veblen's professors brought it to bear in the analysis of a broad range of substantive topics: the fundamentals of epistemology, the text of the Bible, the composition of the psyche, the principles of political economy, the nature of socialism, the history of American financial institutions, the history of colonial settlements, and on and on.

In this way, graduate school became, for Veblen, an experience that combined the extended repetition of certain knowledge practices with multiple variations on those practices. Indeed, not only did these practices turn up in the context of different substantive topics, they repeated themselves across different universities (one long-established and one new); across different intellectual fields (philosophy, political economy, history, and "social science"); and across men very different in piety, politics, and personality. Seen together, the ways of knowing that Veblen accustomed to in any one setting he then practiced in another, as he soaked up the words and example of his teachers while they were handling (in lectures, writings, and meetings) the routine and novel intellectual problems that came their way. Furthermore, rather than discrete episodes, these practice modules—training sessions in each professor's intellectual workshop—formed cumulative moments, each flowing into the next, enhancing one another, with the uncompromising force of time as their ally. As mentioned in Chapter 2, sociologists have documented that the impact of life events depends significantly on the duration, start time, and sequential ordering of those events. We see this effect when we realize that Veblen's experiences in graduate school with knowledge practices relating to evolutionism, organicism, and the importance of science were prolonged experiences over an intensive three-year period, which followed—with no break—on the heels of years of preparatory training back home in the same intellectual habits that every one of his teachers at Hopkins and Yale used. Counted on the clock, this was an apprenticeship nearly a quarter century long.

THERE REMAINS, HOWEVER, a further difference among Veblen's professors that would seem to challenge my claim that their knowledge practices constituted repetitions that were reinforced by variations caused by the fact that these men came from different fields, wrote on different topics, and differed in social location and character traits. This additional difference was that what some professors regarded as "historical change," "organic," and "science" was not what other teachers meant when they used these conceptual tools, which (one might argue) were the "same" only superficially, exhibiting nothing more in common than a few words. This divergence of meaning would suggest that what may initially look like an instance of repetition-with-variation was actually an abyss of incommensurables—the kind of impasse you and I might find ourselves in if your notion of, say, "energy" had nothing in common with mine, or conflicted with mine, or could not even be compared to mine because we were both obscure when we said "energy." Sumner's Spencerian understanding of historical change as a natural evolutionary process, for example, was not only different from but also antithetical to Morris's Hegelian conception of history as the teleological movement of Absolute Spirit: neither man would have counted the other's "history" *as* history. Similarly, what Morris called science—namely, philosophy perfected—would have been anti-science for Sumner, as well as for Ely and Adams. And the entities Veblen's professors described as "organic" diverged from one another, as we notice when we compare Peirce's transhistorical, organic "community" of reasoners with the "living unity" Ladd spoke of when discussing humankind's organic mental states, or with the historically specific organic web of "social institutions" that interested Adams, Ely, and Sumner. Put these thinkers in a room and they might well have talked past each other, if they did not come to blows (always a possibility with Sumner in the room).

Discrepancies such as these occur often within and across scientific fields, in some cases driving a wedge between one group of scientists and another, but other times creating a "trading zone" in which similarities that are only superficial nevertheless allow productive intergroup dialogue to take place.[121] A version of this situation happens when a scientist-in-training (or a neophyte social scientist or humanist) crisscrosses different specialty areas, studying with experts who do talk past one another, while the trainee has to listen to all of them on a regular basis. Hearing about "energy" from you, from me, and from other specialists, the trainee learns that energy—whatever else it may be—is a notion vital for all the experts, a conceptual tool we all wield, even as we forge it differently and apply it to different purposes. From the perspective of any one of us, absorbed in our specialty areas, your "energy" may appear incommensurable with mine. Yet, from the viewpoint of the trainee, who cycles from your workshop to mine, trying to cobble together his or her own tool set, "energy" is a common piece of knowledge-making equipment that no expert functions without. Taking on different shapes and sizes, it serves as an element in the specialized work that goes on in every workshop.

During his long apprenticeship, Veblen's situation resembled this hypothetical trainee's. As Veblen moved back and forth across the intellectual worlds of Morris, Peirce, Ely, Adams, Sumner, Ladd, and Porter, he experienced, from every direction, knowledge practices that entailed viewing the world as subject to change, as organically configured, and as demanding scientific study. Reaching far and wide, pliable, easily transposable, these ways of thinking then came naturally to Veblen when he got down to his own work—as we see already in his youthful writings on Mill's theory of land taxation and Kant's theory of knowledge.

These practices were not Veblen's only takeaways, moreover. Few knowledge makers could get very far with the meager tool kit I have described, and Veblen's teachers all had much more than this to offer him. As experts, the seven had ready at their side a battery of the techniques, assumptions, and bits of practical know-how that were commonplace in the subject areas in which they worked. Morris and Peirce knew, almost instinctively, which issues in mental philosophy posed open questions and which were moribund; Adams and Sumner were versed in the methods of historical research; Ely had a sense of how to fight with political economists; Porter and Ladd shared the belief that the human mind consists of habits, reflexes, and instincts. What was more, all these men had stockpiles of materials in their intellectual workshops: field maps, models for problem solving, stylized constructions of the canon, volumes of factual information, and much more. In these stockpiles, Veblen found probability theories, discussions of human mental faculties, accounts of hunting and gathering societies, monographs on eighteenth-century and nineteenth-century economic history, attacks on jobbery and unearned increments and other forms of economic plunder, arguments about socialism, proposals for social reform—and many other resources he tapped into, selectively as needed, when he confronted the problems dealt with in his later work. Hopkins and Yale did not shortchange him.

We would be wrong, however, to think of Morris, Peirce, Ely, Adams, Sumner, Ladd, and Porter as isolated voices in a wilderness into which Veblen stumbled. Taking an aerial view of the 1870s and 1880s, we see like-minded men and women in many crevices of American culture (as I will elaborate in the next chapter). Evolutionism, organicism, adulation of science: these were familiar points of view, and often accepted ones, on the American intellectual landscape in the last quarter of the nineteenth century. Veblen's seven professors had no monopoly on these perspectives; their intellectual equipment corresponded with ways of seeing that were then gaining cachet among Americans far beyond the walls of Yale and Hopkins.

Training inside the academic walls differed, nevertheless, from on-again, off-again encounters with these ideas in the larger social context. For young men like Veblen, studying at Hopkins and Yale meant studying with teachers who, as faithful descendants of the German historical school, were vocal exponents of the practices I have described, intent on adapting their knowledge-making tools to the problems in contention in philosophy and political economy in the early 1880s. Further, because their jobs involved teaching graduate students one-on-one, Veblen's professors were in a position to transfer their intellectual skill set directly and to give their pupils regular practice in using the tools of their trade. With the exception of Porter, Veblen's mentors belonged to the first generation of American scholars hired by the academy for the twin purposes of conducting specialized research and training postgraduate students to do likewise when their turn came. This first generation was the outcropping of the post-bellum expansion of higher education that would, by the early decades of the twentieth century, make the United States a nation of universities. But, in the early 1880s, there was only a smattering of these institutions, with Hopkins and Yale at the head of the pack. Veblen's teachers secured professorships at these schools—a very unusual accomplishment in itself, much envied by peers—as a result of contingent personal and institutional circumstances; and similar biographical circumstances led Veblen to Hopkins and Yale, just at the time these men were teaching there. But the movements of these individual men presupposed the transformation then happening in American higher education and, as part of it, the emergence of the university as a breeding ground for young scholars (mainly white, male, and Protestant) who carried out research and mentored postgraduate students, who would become researchers mentoring postgraduate students, who would, in turn, carry on, passing the job forward from generation to generation—and putting into place what is still a large part of the job description of the professional academic.

As one of the first dozen men to earn a doctorate in philosophy from an American university, Veblen arrived at the birthing hour of this development, and he saw the opportunity. Indeed, he stretched that opportunity about as far as possible by means of multipliers: working in political economy, while earning his philosophy degree; moving from Hopkins to Yale, so he could better pursue both fields at once; and managing to study with not one or two, but seven intellectual giants (after already studying with John Bates Clark). Among Veblen's professors, in fact, every one was a visible and highly productive scholar, and most were barely older than Veblen. (Ely, for example, was three years older than Veblen, Adams seven years.) And all of them were serious about postgraduate education, committed to producing the scholars of the future (and giving them license to develop their own ideas). This was true even for the recluses in the mix, Morris and Peirce, although Veblen did not move in their circles.[122] At the other extreme, Ely and Adams labored zealously (and successfully) to inspire graduate students to heed the call of "historical institutionalism," and both of them actively encouraged Veblen to pursue his research. Sumner and Porter did the same.[123]

Returning to the Upper Midwest in summer 1884, Veblen carried a pedigree that had no match. No young scholar educated in the United States in the 1880s—whether in philosophy, political economy, history, or social science—surpassed Veblen in the combined voltage of his teachers, and more was still to come from most of these men.[124] Porter, Morris, and Peirce were already philosophical luminaries when Veblen studied with them, but they did not remain on the scene. (Peirce left academe in 1884; Morris died in 1889; and Porter died in 1892.) Each of the others, however, brandishing his iconoclasm, had greater eminence in store. Three years after Veblen left Hopkins, for example, Adams spearheaded the founding of the American Historical Association, where he served as executive officer for sixteen years until his death. In 1885, Ely, together with Clark, founded the American Economic Association; Clark served as its third president (in 1894) and Ely as its sixth (in 1900). Ladd was the second president of the American Psychological Association (in 1893) and the fifth president of the American Philosophical Association (in 1904); Sumner was the second president of the American Sociological Society (in 1908). To this day, American intellectual historians rank Veblen's professors among the prime movers of the academic world fin de siècle. An education any more in the academic mainstream than his would have been hard to accomplish in three years' time.

CHAPTER 6

TRANSITION

1.

From the start, the professional academic has faced employment problems. The academic job market has existed in the United States for nearly 150 years, but for most of this time it has afforded too few job openings to accommodate all the young scholars wanting academic careers. Occasionally, opportunities have been better: during wars and postwar periods; in eras of demographic transition; in times when new research specialties, thin in personnel, have emerged to address national needs. In these moments the demand for academics has outrun the supply. But more typically, particularly in philosophy and many social sciences, there have been just enough positions available to flame newcomers' hopes of finding academic jobs despite unfavorable odds.

This imbalance between supply and demand was already an acknowledged fact when Veblen was in graduate school, and he saw it directly in the life stories of his teachers. Clark, Morris, Peirce, Adams, Ely, Sumner, Ladd, and even Porter: not one of them had an easy entry into an academic career. The Yale men on this list secured their faculty positions after they had first served years as parish ministers, while the nonclerics (a more relevant point of comparison for Veblen) got their professorships only after an anxious waiting period when they worked either as tutors for wealthy families or as temporary academic adjuncts. Even in philosophy, which (as I mentioned in Chapter 4) was better situated than many of the younger disciplines, academic jobs were acutely scarce in the 1870s and 1880s, so much so that budding philosophical giants like William James, G. Stanley Hall, and Josiah Royce were forced to live years in occupational limbo before they finally landed faculty positions, which owed at least as much to their personal connections as to their scholarship. In 1884, the year Veblen earned his doctorate from Yale, he was one of five men in the United States receiving a PhD in philosophy. Of the five, only one went straight into an academic job—and that one was John Dewey, who was hired by the University of Michigan because his dissertation adviser (George Sylvester Morris again) was assuming a full-time position there and wanted to bring Dewey along.[1]

Veblen had nothing equivalent to Dewey's situation in the background, however. So he returned to his family's farm in Minnesota in summer 1884 to bide his time until he got wind of faculty openings he could try for, presumably at institutions where he had connections. That was the way Andrew Veblen had secured his positions at Luther College and, subsequently, at the State University of Iowa; and, like Andrew, Thorstein probably had his future prospects pinned on some of the state universities or small local colleges then opening up in the Upper Midwest (though none too fast from the angle of the job seeker). So that he would be ready to prove that he actually had earned a doctorate when he was out East—in case a local college president wanted to know—Veblen carried a glowing testimonial from Noah Porter, dated June 28, 1884.

> It is with great pleasure that I certify that Mr. Thorstein B. Veblen, B.A. Carleton Coll. 1880, Ph.D. Yale College 1884, has been a student in the Graduate Department of this college for 2½ years. . . . He has prosecuted special studies in Political and Social Science and in Speculative Philosophy, Ethics, Psychology, etc. I can give confident testimony to his faithfulness and the critical ability which he has evinced in all his studies. I have in all my experience had few pupils with whom I have had greater satisfaction, or who have made more rapid or more satisfactory progress. . . . I can confidently recommend him as a very accomplished scholar and a very able man, who ought not to fail of occupying a commanding position in some higher seminary of learning.[2]

Before he could make use of Porter's recommendation, however, Veblen's academic plans were thrown off course by an incapacitating health problem of a somewhat mysterious kind. According to his younger brother Ed, when Thorstein "came home after graduating [from Yale], he complained of ill health, and [looked] peaked and weak"; and Andrew recalled that, for several years after that point, Thorstein's "health was not robust enough to allow him to pursue academic work either as student or teacher."[3] In 1890, after he had recuperated, Thorstein told Rasmus Anderson that he had "suffered an attack of Malaria." But this label may have been his own retrospective diagnosis; for, according to Andrew, when Thorstein was in the throes of the problem, he "never mentioned" malaria (which was then a poorly understood condition).[4] Because an epidemic of malaria was raging across New England when Thorstein Veblen was at Yale, it is certainly possible he contracted the disease at the time.[5] Based on what little is known about his symptoms and the course of his illness, however, an immunologic condition, such as Addison's disease, seems a more likely diagnosis than malaria, at least according to present-day medical knowledge.[6] Without fuller information about the ailment, its true identity will probably remain unknown.

Still and all, by his own account, Veblen was "disabled for serious work" for a five-year period, running from mid-1884 to mid-1889. During this lengthy convalescence, he lived mostly on his parents' farm in Rice County, Minnesota, "assisting in the farm operations as his strength allowed" (Andrew's recollection) and offering "rather impractical theories about running the farm" (Ed's recollection).[7] In winter 1885–1886, he stayed with Andrew's family in Iowa City, Iowa, site of the state university (and the self-styled "Athens of Iowa"); and after his marriage to Ellen Rolfe in April 1888, he lived for nearly three years with her family in the hamlet of Stacyville, Iowa. Both towns were surrounded by farms involved (like his own family's farm) in corn, wheat, and dairy production. These locales provided a change of scenery that reimmersed him in the agrarian world he had left when he moved to the industrialized East Coast. Looking back a few years later on this extended career time-out, Veblen described his feelings about it in a letter to his graduate student (and love interest) Sarah Hardy: "I once 'lay low' for several years, [and these were] some of the most enjoyable times I have had."[8] The hiatus gave him an unencumbered opportunity to read and to observe.

2.

To nineteenth-century Americans interested in economic life, the US economy of the 1880s offered a lot to witness, and Veblen was primed by his previous experiences to take in a wide swath of the panorama. The phenomena he observed did not cause him to formulate his economic theories—or there would have been thousands of thinkers like Veblen, for thousands of intelligent and thoughtful contemporaries saw much of what he saw, either firsthand or through reports in national newspapers that reached towns across the country by rail almost daily. All the same, Veblen's observations carried heavy weight in his thinking. They were reliable resources with up-to-date information about the state of the nation's economy, piling up for him to use when and how he decided to do so. Although most of these materials were probably a jumble when Veblen first came across them, for the purpose of this chapter it is helpful to view this information as pointing up four features of the turbulent American economy in the last quarter of the nineteenth century.

First, the age was marked by a huge expansion in industrial production and, right alongside it, a whiplash of macroeconomic convulsions that shook contemporaries immediately. Using international comparisons, historian Walter Licht has described the speed in economic growth: "In 1860, . . . the United States still lagged behind Great Britain, France, and Germany in industrial output. Just forty years later, . . . industrial production in the United States would dramatically surpass the combined manufacture of its three main rivals. Between 1860 and 1900, American industrialists recorded on average a more than fivefold increase in production." This transformation involved a permanent shift in the locus of production from the workshops and small manufacturing firms of antebellum America to sprawling factories that produced new industrial goods (such as iron, steel, and machinery), consumer staples (such as textiles, lumber, and milled grain), and other commodities in great qualities. This development went together with the geographical spread of production sites from the East Coast to the midwestern heartland (Chicago and its environs in particular), and a fivefold increase in the size of the industrial labor force as a result of foreign immigration and heavy internal migration from rural to urban areas of the country.[9] Accompanying these changes were severe macroeconomic fluctuations, careening more often in a downward than an upward direction. Even as economic output rose, rates of growth regularly declined, halting boom times and plunging most of the country into two major depressions (1873–1878, 1893–1897) and a serious recession (1882–1885), in a rocky slide that economic historians characterize as a "Great Depression." Contemporaries experienced this tumult in high rates of unemployment (above 30 percent in some years), sharply declining firm profits, and a record number of business failures.[10]

These changes drew widespread public attention, igniting controversy about the causes and consequences of economic growth, about who benefited and who suffered from the recurring economic cycles, and about what, if any, policy measures the federal government should adopt under the circumstances. This debate occurred in a political context in which the Republican and Democratic parties, at the national level at least, tilted toward poles opposite from those we now associate with them: Democrats championed a laissez-faire position and a small-government approach to economic growth, while Republicans favored a more activist stance and state interventions to stimulate the economy.[11]

A second fundamental feature of the postbellum economy, inevitably intertwined with the first, was the emergence of the "corporation" as the organizational form of the private business firm.[12] Prior to the Civil War, most firms, whether workshops or manufactories, were proprietorships belonging to individual capitalists or family-based partnerships managed by their owners. To build and operate the much larger manufacturing and transportation firms of the postwar era, however, required greater financial resources than these traditional sources could mobilize. So capitalists legally "incorporated" these new firms (or business enterprises, in the argot of contemporaries) as joint stock companies, which were owned by multiple shareholders and investors. This ownership arrangement, although it may sound like little more than a legal technicality, had the far-reaching effect of breaking the previous tie between owning and managing a firm—except in cases in which the founder of a firm continued to direct the corporation (as the result of large stockholdings), as did John D. Rockefeller at Standard Oil and Andrew Carnegie at United States Steel. Otherwise, though, direct control of the firm passed from company owners to salaried executives and top managers, a new species of economic actors, first hatched in the railroad industry, who were hired to set policies and execute plans to ensure the viability and profitability of their companies in a competitive economy.

During the last quarter of the nineteenth century, these corporate managers—"captains of industry" as Carnegie called them—worked to accomplish those objectives, using everything from predatory trade practices; to violent crackdowns on workers; to federal monetary and tariff policies; to the rulings of high courts; to monopolistic measures to consolidate firms through cartels, trusts, or mergers. Through these mechanisms, successful managers grew and diversified their firms, integrating the activities of mass production and mass distribution to forge the giant business enterprises that would dominate the economy of the nation (and the world) long into the future. Midwestern farmers had an unobstructed view of this process of growth in the dense infiltration of their region by the railroad industry, as well as in the appearance during the 1870s and 1880s of the "bonanza" ranches of Minnesota and the Dakotas, where corporate managers oversaw armies of migrant laborers cultivating wheat on vast acreages owned by absentee investors. From the late 1880s onward, the same ownership and management arrangement also underwrote the development of the lucrative ore mining industry in the Mesabi Iron Range of northeast Minnesota.[13]

This "incorporation of America," as historian Alan Trachtenberg has called it, was accompanied and facilitated by several interlaced developments.[14] These included the establishment of specialized financial institutions with the economic capacity (and political clout) to support the heavy costs of industrial expansion, and in particular the creation of investment banks and their intricate devices for carrying on speculation in stocks, bonds, and other securities. These instruments were among the standard operating methods of the financers and speculators—J. P. Morgan being the prototype—whom some observers were already beginning to characterize as "robber barons." Another allied development was a proliferation of scientific inventions: a constant flood of technological innovations that mechanized and streamlined large-scale factory production, overhauled the nation's system for transporting raw materials and finished goods, and designed and marketed a cornucopia of new commercial and industrial products. (Between 1860 and 1890, the federal government issued patents, to amateur inventors and experts in the fast-expanding corps of professional engineers, for more than four hundred thousand new inventions, among them hundreds of labor-saving machines and thousands of consumer attractions.)[15]

Alongside these developments, business firms increasingly became bureaucratic organizations, in part because corporate executives needed (or felt they needed) elaborate infrastructures. So, with the advent of top managers, who directed the corporation as a whole, came middle managers charged with overseeing specialized units within the corporation; then lower-level managers tasked with running subunits; and then scores of subaltern accountants, salesmen, and clerical workers—all stacked in a hierarchy of administrative control. By and large, these fine gradations inside the business world were a new historical phenomenon—one that historians see as contributing to the emergence and internal stratification of the American middle class. We glimpse the width of this new economic ordering in statistics from 1890, which economist Charles B. Spahr published a few years later. According to Spahr's data, the annual income of families in the "middle classes" (where lower-level managers, senior clerical employees, and low-status professionals fell) ranged from $500 to $5,000 (= $14,600 to $146,000), whereas the income of "well-to-do" households (the families of higher-level managers, independent businessmen, lawyers, and doctors) extended from $5,000 to $50,000 (= $146,000 to $1.46 million). For "wealthy" households (families of industrialists, substantial merchants and real estate owners, top executives, and elite professionals), Spahr's data give no upper-income bound; but other data from 1890 show that the top 1 percent of the US population then held 51 percent of the nation's wealth, while the top 12 percent held 86 percent. The top two hundred families—those headed by the owners of the largest manufacturing and commercial firms, leading financiers and investment bankers, and heirs of great estates—had fortunes exceeding $20 million (= $585 million).[16]

These immense income and wealth differentials were dramatized to contemporaries by a third salient aspect of the American economy during the closing decades of the century: its strong pivot toward consumerism. Historian William Leach has described this era as "the crucial formative years of . . . a society preoccupied with consumption, [and] luxury, spending, and acquisition."[17] Leach attributes this development to the encroachment of profit-seeking corporations into the activities of retailing and heavy product advertising, while other historians point to the desire of the nation's wealthiest families to flaunt their financial success by means of palatial homes, expensive entertainments, custom-designed accoutrements, and so on. Whatever the reasons, the market for consumer goods swelled not only among the richest Americans but also among women and men lower down the social ladder. These people could now find mass-produced versions of the luxuries and conveniences they coveted (fashionable clothing, cosmetics, home furnishings, and appliances) within arm's reach in the alluring department stores then sprouting up in cities and towns: "goods suitable for the millionaire at prices in the reach of millions," as an 1887 ad for Macy's department store put it. Beyond buying portable goods, moreover, upper-middle- and middle-class families often had the financial resources to purchase larger homes in more attractive suburban areas, to give their children more years of schooling, to participate in more exclusive social circles, and so forth.[18]

This emulation of lifestyles turned in two directions. For, just as these prosperous families took their consumer cues by looking up to the rich, so too the less well-off aspired to copy men and women in the middle. Store clerks were known, for example, to take out loans so they could afford stylish clothing, restaurant dining, and even music lessons. (By the 1880s, the amount of private debt was estimated by contemporary economic reporters at $25 to $30 billion.) And rural Americans too willingly joined the feast, as Chicago-based mail order houses like Montgomery Ward and Sears, Roebuck—the world's two largest merchandising organizations by 1900—flooded the countryside with mail-order catalogs offering tens of thousands of items for sale, delivery, and display.[19] However, urbanites and suburbanites were the people who most insistently chased yet another of the envied ornaments of the consumer society: leisure time. This unmistakable emblem of wealth glistened in the decorative use of household servants, the elites' Newport holidays, and the summer vacations of the middle classes, as well as in shortened work weeks, outings to beaches and museums, and attendance at concerts and sporting events—the social desiderata out of the reach of people of lesser means.[20]

Still, not everyone cheered the new consumerism. The situation was just the opposite: for every eager Macy's shopper and Sunday afternoon beachgoer, there was another contemporary unnerved that the pursuit of leisure and luxury would sap the nation's "commitment to the moral primacy of work" (to borrow the expression of historian Daniel Rodgers). Traditional though it was, this conviction that "work was the core of the moral life" fueled public discourse throughout the nineteenth century, uniting religious and secular voices, the political left and the political right, in condemning the loathsome figure of the social "parasite" who was "too lazy to earn his living by his own toil."[21] Here was the villain of scores of sensationalist reports in the press about the excessive spending by the rich on costume parties, stables, yachts, and marriages into the European aristocracy; and one of the trademarks of the era was the newspaper cartoon of a porcine millionaire, wearing a diamond stickpin and lolling in comfort, surrounded by servants, clerks, and other underlings.[22] Fiction writers, for their part, seemed never to tire of lacerating the same upper crust. The moral failings of the wealthy, the extravagant, the indolent, and the improvident filled the popular novels of William Dean Howells, Henry James, Edith Wharton, and Theodore Dreiser, as well as Mark Twain's and Charles Dudley Warner's satire The Gilded Age: A Tale of Today (1873). Sticking to this motif twenty years later, Warner penned an essay titled "The Leisure Class," in which he opined that "in a republic there is no room for a leisure class that is not useful." (In a flourish, Warner added that "the sociologist might begin to study the effect of this leisureliness upon society.")[23]

These critical attitudes meshed with a fourth feature of the American economy in the closing decades of the nineteenth century: the widespread eruption of economically inspired protest. In urbanized areas, populated by growing legions of wage workers, sometimes organized by trade unions, this protest took the form of strikes and other work stoppages, which occurred at an astounding rate of five hundred incidents per year during the first half of the 1880s and one thousand per year during the second half of the decade. In the mid-1880s, more than twelve thousand businesses experienced these disruptions, and this figure also grew significantly in the next decade, with strikers and employers both coming away with their share of victories and defeats. Some of these strikes (including some nearby to Veblen in Chicago, as I will describe in Chapter 7) involved thousands of organized laborers and community sympathizers, and federal, state, and local law enforcers—and captured national notice. Other job actions were spontaneous, local responses by workers to wage cuts and hardship conditions on the job.[24] The hostility workers felt toward their employers ran deep, feeding a well of economic discontent that gave them common cause with American farmers, hit hard by the periodic economic downturns and harboring grievances over high railway freight charges and steep lending rates by national corporations, as well as by profiteering on the part of local merchants and bankers. (During Veblen's years back in farm country, Minnesota and Iowa farmers complained bitterly as they struggled to make fixed mortgage payments when farm commodity prices were falling. In terms of the Veblens themselves, however, Thomas Veblen had paid off his family's indebtedness years earlier).[25]

Rather than strike, however, farmers organized, over a million strong, in a succession of grassroots movements: the Greenback Party, the Grange, and the Farmers' Alliance—the latter a national federation of more than a thousand local organizations that went by the name of "cooperatives."[26] These were small, voluntary associations that groups of local farmers established to transact their purchasing, processing, and marketing activities jointly or collectively, thereby reducing their dependence on what they saw as cabals of railways barons, grain elevator operators, bankers, and other sinister "monopolists." Blanketing the Great Plains and Midwest, cooperatives abutted the Veblen family farmstead in the 1870s and 1880s, when several of them operated out of nearby Faribault and Northfield, Minnesota.[27] In the early 1890s, the Farmers' Alliance, which up to then had defined itself mainly in terms of its collectivist economic program, assumed a more political identity when it transformed into the People's or Populist Party. In this capacity, it continued (until its electoral defeat at the end of the century) the cause of establishing farmers' cooperatives, while simultaneously fielding candidates for elective office in the hopes of advancing a national agenda for monetary reform and state ownership of railways and public utilities.

These items on the farmers' agenda were much more than demands of the hour. Like many later protest movements, the Farmers' Alliance, the Populist Party, and their cousin associations—for convenience, I lump these together here as "populism"—rested on an encompassing worldview, a distinctive set of intellectual practices that were at once critical and constructive. From its critical side, populism provided, as historian Charles Postel has written, "one of the most intense challenges to corporate power in American history."[28] Populism crossbred two older strains of American thought: on the one hand, a credo of "producerism," which harkened back to the belief of the Founding Fathers that society's producers, and they alone, deserve the fruits of their labor; and, on the other hand, the postbellum belief that corporations are predatory forces responsible for the great wealth disparities across social classes. The second was a recurrent theme in farmers' newspapers of the 1870s, 1880s, and 1890s, including the sheets that were issued from the incendiary Norwegian-American press.[29] Popular writer (and prominent Minnesotan) Ignatius Donnelly illustrated the combination of these two strains in his 1892 "Preamble" to the platform of the Populist Party:

> We meet in the midst of a nation brought to the verge of moral, political and material ruin. . . . Our homes [are] covered with mortgages, labor impoverished, and land concentrated in the hands of capitalists. [T]he fruits of the toil of millions are boldly stolen to build up colossal fortunes, unprecedented in the history of the world. [Meanwhile, the old] political parties . . . propose to drown the outcries of a plundered people, . . . so that corporations, national banks, rings, trusts . . . and the oppression of usurers may all be lost sight of. They propose to sacrifice our homes, lives, and children on the altar of mammon; to destroy the multitude in order to secure corruption funds from the millionaires.[30]

Determined to stem this calamity and reverse the recent course of American history, populists grafted onto their critique a constructive plan for social reorganization via an overhaul of economic institutions: the "establishment of co-operative institutions, productive and distributive."[31] According to the blueprint of populist architects, these institutions would draw their design, at the same time, from the rural cooperatives of the kind the Farmers' Alliance had already built *and* from large private corporations, inasmuch as corporations were innovating methods for organizational consolidation and efficiency. As populists conceived of these renovated institutions, they would operate across state and regional lines, enabling farmers and other producers to corner the market on their products and, with government help, centralize the distribution of these products to consumers, thus circumventing third parties, such as capitalist owners and corporate middlemen.

The fact that this proposed institutional redesign never became much of a reality did not deter populists (and their cousins) from envisioning society as a social organism that was on the move to a future beyond capitalism. Crop growers by day, farmers connected to the movement were intellectuals by night, working with many of the same knowledge tools then in use in academic circles. The Farmers' Alliance, for example, sponsored thousands of evening lectures and seminars on the latest scientific and social-scientific topics, while also putting into wide circulation inexpensive reprints that carried the theories of leading evolutionary thinkers right into the nation's farmhouses. In this way, there arose among many populists what Charles Postel has called an "evolutionary imagination" and a "belief in progress, science, and technology"—ideas that were reinforced by a range of socialist writings infiltrating the countryside at the same time.[32]

At the head of this socialist reading list was a manifesto titled *The Co-operative Commonwealth*. Authored by Laurence Gronlund, a Danish-born freelance writer working in the United States, this 1884 book became (at sales of more than a hundred thousand copies) the bible of late nineteenth-century populism—as well as one of Thorstein Veblen's reference points in the years ahead.[33] Addressing the economic discontent of the era, the book denounced the rise of large corporations and the motivating principles of modern capitalism. In Gronlund's prose, "he is . . . a 'capitalist' who possesses wealth that brings him an income *without any work* on his part" but simply because he belongs to the "fleecing class": a class whose members devise mechanisms of private property ownership that allow them to thrive, just like "parasites and vampires," on the blood of farmers and other producers. To Gronlund's historical relief, however, this craven system was only a historical way station en route to a resplendent socialist future: "A cooperative commonwealth . . . in which all important instruments of production have been taken under collective control; in which the citizens are consciously public functionaries and in which their labors are rewarded according to results." Gronlund regarded this future as far more than a populist fiction, because socialism is "the natural heir" of capitalism, "a higher stage of development," the necessary "culmination" of an epochal process of "evolution" that finds realization in "a whole people united in one body politic," working under the aegis of the "State [as] a living organism." This evolutionary process, according to Gronlund's account, constituted a movement governed by "laws indwelling in our social organism:" laws discovered by the unrivalled "scientific method of studying Society."[34]

It is not known whether Veblen read *The Co-operative Commonwealth* during his several years back in farm country; likely he did, given the book's popularity. He did include it when he taught his "Socialism" course at the University of Chicago in 1894, devoting several lectures to critiquing Gronlund's conception of socialism and his populist brand of statism and producerism. Insofar as surviving course notes indicate, however, Veblen did not discuss Gronlund's evolutionism, organicism, paean to social science, or attack on the fleecing class.[35] But, then again, Veblen had no reason to associate such ideas specifically with Gronlund, or even with the larger chorus of voices of economic protest, because these ways of thinking were, by the 1890s, already thoroughly familiar to him from other sources (as we have seen and will continue to see). During Veblen's time away from the academy, with his ears open to the noises of the changing American economy, here these practices were sounding again.

3.

Meanwhile, the organizational transformation of American higher education that started after the Civil War, and that Veblen had observed firsthand at Johns Hopkins and Yale, continued, pushed by institution builders with a range of economic, political, religious, and purely intellectual interests.[36] Years later Veblen would critically dissect these interests in his book *The Higher Learning in America,* but as he recuperated from his obscure illness in the mid-1880s what drew his attention was the changing national academic landscape.

Foremost among the changes (from the viewpoint of a PhD holder without a job) was the expansion in the sheer number of institutions of higher education. In the Midwest, in particular, the 1880s saw the founding of forty new colleges, boosting the total by a third, from 120 to 160.[37] The majority of these were small denominational colleges of the type described in Chapter 3—namely, "multipurpose" colleges. In these years, too, state universities increased in number and capacity, while specialized vocational schools opened to cater to students interested in engineering, architecture, agriculture, forestry, and other applied subjects. This growth spurt required substantial financial resources, which were furnished by federal land grants to states, contributions from local organizations and small private donors, and the largesse—often conspicuously ostentatious—of the country's industrial and financial titans. Growth also required teachers and created new faculty positions, though positions remained in comparatively short supply. When hiring faculty members, most colleges continued to expect little in terms of specialized training or credentials, perpetuating a situation in which the number of men and women available to teach outstripped the availability of academic jobs.

In tandem with the rising number of higher-educational institutions came the further development of one subspecies: the research-oriented university.[38] Historians of education count six research universities (Hopkins, Yale, Harvard, Cornell, Columbia, and Clark) as operational by 1890, with another eight up and running by 1900.[39] Although that figure was only a fraction of the total number of higher-educational institutions in the country (and one made up almost exclusively of sons of white families of means), observers at the time immediately anointed this small subset of schools as the pinnacle of the academy and zenith of American learning. This elevated position made these institutions, as we have seen in the instances of Hopkins and Yale, the mecca for prominent scholars (and those aspiring to prominence), as well as the destination of choice for postgraduate students, like Veblen, who were unable to study abroad for financial or other reasons.

Situated in this commanding position, research universities also took the lead in supporting, sometimes even encouraging, a new way of organizing knowledge. This development, which Veblen had also experienced in nascent forms at Hopkins and Yale, was to partition human knowledge into separate "containers"—intellectual boxes that contemporaries were starting to refer to as "academic disciplines" or "academic fields."[40] (These expressions entered circulation in the late nineteenth century.) This partitioning appealed to university presidents as a means to coordinate graduate training with undergraduate instruction through specialized administrative units, or "departments." It also appealed to faculty members who wanted to upgrade their role from that of a teacher of miscellaneous subjects to that of a knowledge specialist: a member of a recognized "profession" of fellow experts embedded in intellectual networks woven into associations (regional and national) that sponsored journals and meetings to facilitate communication among specialists. Academic fields, academic disciplines, academic departments, academic professions: these overlapping organizational entities henceforth constituted the infrastructure of American higher education, both for Thorstein Veblen and for scholars down to the present.[41]

Certainly there were institutional variations. Competing among themselves for limited external resources, each university sought to broadcast to the public (and potential benefactors) its own distinctive infrastructural strengths and characteristics. Even while doing so, however, all universities announced and embraced the same primary mission, as Veblen had already seen: "to advance knowledge" or, what amounted to the same thing, "to advance science." For men and women in other historical eras, this equation of knowledge and science would not have been so automatic. Again, the post–Civil War period was unlike past ages in this respect. "By the 1880s and 1890s," writes historian of science Daniel Thurs, "it was not uncommon for authors [in and out of the academic world] to reflect that the 'nineteenth century has been an age of science' or that they lived in a 'scientific age' in which the 'scientific spirit' was gaining in strength."[42] To be sure, "science" remained an elastic notion; at the time, it referred to different activities and held out different promises for members of different social groups. To captains of industry, science meant better technologies of production and distribution (and more commercial patents); to farmers, improved methods for breeding and planting (and new designs for populist social reconstruction); to the devout, a wider window out onto nature as God designed it; to guardians of democracy, a stronger foundation for civic discourse (and for informed public debate about economic and political issues): champions of science were everywhere. And together, despite their differences, they threw their support behind everything from local science fairs and science museums, which drew Americans by the tens of thousands during their newfound leisure time, to expansions in the federal budget to fund massive research initiatives like the Agriculture Department's Division of Entomology and the US Geological Survey.[43] The new research universities, with their overriding commitment to the growth of scientific knowledge, served as the flagship.

4.

In this milieu, the subject of evolution dominated the intellectual dialogue. For, if "knowledge" widely connoted "science," "science" widely connoted the study of the organic process of "evolution." This was the view both outside the academy and inside the offices, laboratories, libraries, and classrooms of higher-educational institutions.

Among members of the public at large, interest in evolution, strong in America before the Civil War, soared during the last quarter of the nineteenth century, carried upward by newspapers and magazines that retailed different conceptions of evolution and different attitudes toward them. Adding to this literature were abridgments of the books of Charles Darwin and Herbert Spencer, mass-produced in cheap editions that (as we have seen) even distressed farmers were able to afford. Sales of Darwin's 1871 *Descent of Man,* which brought the human species itself into the evolutionary drama he began in 1859 in *On the Origin of Species,* were "almost unprecedented," although they were quickly exceeded in sales by Spencer's many volumes on evolution.[44] Popularizations of evolutionary theories by big-name English and American science writers sold in the United States by the tens and hundreds of thousands. (This is to say nothing of the writings of evolutionary socialists like Laurence Gronlund.)[45] All the same, the public's engagement with the topic of evolution was nothing compared to what went on inside the new research universities, where presidents outdid one another in their efforts to promote the scientific study of evolution. Within the constraints of their limited budgets, they spent heaviest on building up departments in the biological sciences, staffing their faculties with scholars in physiology, morphology, zoology, botany, paleontology, geology, and related fields—the disciplines most closely involved in inductive research on plant and animal populations.[46] In the eyes of university presidents, these fields provided—by their combined practices of inductive research, organic thinking, and evolutionary analysis—explicit role models for upstart disciplines outside the natural sciences to follow, inasmuch as those disciplines wanted to gain admission to the house of science.

AGAINST THIS BACKDROP, controversies about the study of evolution in the biological sciences quickly rippled out into other academic fields, as

Veblen saw when he subsequently returned to the academy and heard the loud rumble of two controversies in particular.[47] The first and smaller of these concerned animal and plant classification. Going back to antiquity, naturalists relied heavily on taxonomic practices; their research depended on procedures for determining the similarities and differences among animals (or plants) x, y, and z, so that these forms of life could be appropriately named, categorized, and ordered relative to one another (in species, genera, and so forth). Among botanists and zoologists of the late nineteenth century, these classification practices continued (sometimes updated) to attract practitioners, but evolutionists often objected to work in this vein, finding taxonomic categories too static and too ahistorical to capture and contain the life of life-forms. This was the criticism leveled in 1891, for example, by botanist J. M. Coulter (soon to be Veblen's colleague at the University of Chicago) when he attacked scientists for squandering their energies on "pigeon-holing" and the "juggling of nomenclature." Far more necessary, said Coulter, was "genetic" research aimed to uncover inductively "all the facts of plant origin, structure, and life," always treating each plant as a "whole organism" that functions "in connection with others."[48] Scholars in other fields did not need much coaxing to see that this type of critique had a long reach. As early as 1884, Richard Ely, for one, complained that Older School economists had engaged in useless "wrangling concerning nomenclature and verbal quibbling concerning definitions."[49]

The second, more foundational, controversy had to do with the process—the "means or machinery"—by which evolution occurs. (I take these words from Cornell University botanist L. H. Bailey, writing in 1894.)[50] A subject of much speculation going back to the 1860s, the topic gained focus in the new universities during the 1880s and 1890s, when biological scientists threw themselves into research projects that homed in more precisely on the mechanisms that cause evolutionary movement. More often than not, these projects took Darwin's account (often misconstrued) as both their jumping-off point and their foil. According to Darwin's analysis in simple form, evolution takes place in nature through a "two-step process of *variation* and *natural selection*."[51] As the members of any one generation of an animal or plant species reproduce, slight variations arise randomly in the physical traits of their offspring; thereafter, the natural environment—working glacially over millions of years—selects those traits that confer adaptive benefits on some individuals in the species, thus enabling those organisms to survive and reproduce when pitted in competition and struggle against less favored offspring. Charles Darwin sometimes glossed this outcome, in battlefield language, as the "survival of the fittest," although he did not intend to convey any necessarily victorious progression to higher life-forms, since "survival" was keyed to local and changing environments. (The random variations that prove adaptive in one environment may not have that effect under altered conditions.)

For contemporaries, the most disturbing feature of Darwin's analysis was his claim about the role played in organic evolution by purely random variations, a claim many biological researchers rushed to refute by constructing accounts that harkened back to the ideas of Lamarck and maintained that the "inheritance of acquired characteristics" was the principal mechanism of evolution. (Recall the giraffe examples in Chapter 3.) By the 1870s, these accounts typically were referred to as "neo-Larmarckian"; they held that environmentally adaptive traits do not develop by blind chance but as a result of an organism's own (purposive) behaviors, which become, through repeated use, fixed habits that are then inherited by its offspring, who improve on them by further use and exercise, passing them down across generations. During the last quarter of the nineteenth century, theories of this teleological type had great appeal in an out of the county's research universities, and they largely prevailed over the Darwinian perspective until their defeat in the early twentieth century. In the interim, the two theories spawned variations and combinations by the score, most of them accepting the evolutionary premise that, as Bailey summed it up: "All forms of life are mutable."[52]

Factoring into this debate, too, was research on one other evolutionary mechanism, which nineteenth-century naturalists called "symbiosis" or "mutualism." Here, they drew on the ideas of the Belgian zoologist Pierre-Joseph van Beneden, who sought to scotch Darwinian notions—about natural selection, species competition, and so forth—by demonstrating the evolutionary significance of codependencies between one species and another. What van Beneden had in view were phenomena like the organic connection that emerges between the lobster and the worms inside of it: the worms live on the lobster's dead eggs and the lobster survives because the worms cleanse it of decomposing matter that could be fatal. Scientists in this tradition saw the development of such mutually beneficial codependencies as necessitating a revision of versions of Darwin's theory that foregrounded competition and conflict when "analog[izing] the animal world and human society." For, rather than portraying humans as if they were bellicose animals, these scientists represented even the lowest of animals as if they were cooperating human beings engaged in "social life" centered on mutual aid. Inversely, however, these researchers found that cooperative symbiosis could shade over into relationships in which one species behaves like a "parasite . . . who lives at the expense of another," contributing nothing to the survival of its host. Such parasites, said van Beneden, "are very commonly found in nature" and have human analogues "in the ancient as well as the new world"—for example, in the "great nobleman" of the past or the modern "knight of industry" who "lives solely on blood and carnage, [surviving] by cunning, by audacity, or by superior villany [sic]." In the last two decades of the nineteenth century, American naturalists carried out research on the symbiotic underpinnings of organic evolution under the rubric of "parasitology," a subject then beginning to take its place within the biology programs of the country's universities.[53]

NONE OF THESE ISSUES remained confined within the walls of the biological sciences, as the instances of Hopkins and Yale show. With university administrators (and just about everyone else) holding these disciplines up for veneration and emulation, they inevitably cast a spell. They gripped scholars in many other precincts of the academy with the conviction that their fields too could meet prevailing expectations if they adopted the knowledge-making practices of the biological sciences. Taking this step, these scholars correctly reasoned, was the surest way to raise a field's scientific status and vest it with the legitimacy required to persuade university presidents to recognize its independence from mental and moral philosophy. So this strategy became the path academics followed en masse. Historian Jeffrey Sklansky has shown, for example, how would-be social scientists of this era shifted deliberately away from older, individualistic notions to explicitly "organic" concepts that emphasized social relations, social interdependence, and social selves. (Sklansky's study included the fields of sociology, anthropology, economics, political science, and psychology.)[54]

Still more pronounced than this shift toward organicism was the diffusion into the budding social sciences of the biological scientists' practice of thinking in evolutionary terms, taking it for granted that the world is always in motion and that change is the sine quo non of life itself. This presumption was shared across the spectrum of the social sciences, even as these disciplines fought to distinguish themselves from one another. For instance, in the field of psychology, which fell at the experimental end of the social science spectrum, the period saw the spread of the "new psychology" that Veblen had encountered in rudimentary form when studying with George T. Ladd at Yale. Subsequently pushed further by philosophers such as William James and John Dewey (and by other members of the Chicago school of pragmatism, which I discuss in Chapter 7), the new psychology expressly aimed to formulate evolutionary theories of mind and behavior. Its ambition, as James trumpeted it, was the application of "the natural-science point of view," and in particular the "evolutionary point of view," to the study of the development of consciousness, habits, and instincts—including "social" instincts, such as "our desire to attract notice and admiration, our emulation and jealousy, our love of glory, influence, and power."[55]

This agenda of the new psychology matched the program of the discipline of history, which fell closest to the humanities end of the spectrum of the social sciences. That historians would have a professional interest in what happens between Time A and Time B, that we expect. In the late nineteenth century, however, that interest, as historian Peter Novick has shown, dovetailed with a new interest in turning historical scholarship into a "science" based on the "scientific method" of observation and inductive fact-gathering. Not only that, but most historians in this era went so far as to accept some version of evolutionism, particularly the "Teutonic thesis" about the early Germanic beginnings of American institutions, to which Herbert Baxter Adams had introduced Veblen at Hopkins. Such theories did not lead the new scientific historians to articulate evolutionary "laws" per se; then as now, historians were too concerned with historical specificity to do that. Nevertheless, their research revolved around evolutionists' themes of origins and development, especially as applied to political and economic institutions. (These institutions appealed to historians in part because they were amenable to scientific observation, in a roundabout way, through public documents.) Surveying the state of American historiography in 1891, J. Franklin Jameson (Veblen's friend from Hopkins) wrote: "Never was there a time . . . when so great a proportion of the best historical work was devoted to the subject of the history of institutions"—to the study of their "genesis," "growth," "movements and changes."[56]

Psychology and history: two different disciplines focused on two different subject matters (mind and behavior versus political and economic institutions), yet united by a similar way of thinking—thinking of social phenomena as constantly changing. Every other late nineteenth-century American social science adopted the same viewpoint, although one field especially warrants mention here because of the fascination it held for contemporaries and for Veblen himself.[57] This is the field of "anthropology," the last of the social science fields to take form as a separate academic discipline or even to acquire an agreed-upon name. (This delay had to do with the fact that so many other fields laid claim to what became the material of anthropology. At Carleton, Veblen came across some of this material when he studied geology, for example.) Speaking broadly, the subject matter of late nineteenth-century anthropology was humankind as it existed outside the time and space bounds of so-called Western civilization.[58]

The time dimension of this "outside" area was enormous. Anthropologists (to use their eventual name) were leading figures in accomplishing by the late nineteenth century what historian Thomas Trautmann has spoken of as "revolution" in thinking about human time. This they did by building on several midcentury archeological discoveries of prehistoric remains in order to extend "human history indefinitely backward, for tens of hundreds of thousands of years or more." "Very suddenly," according to Trautmann, "the bottom dropped out of history"—the "recorded history" of historians—on the basis of strong evidence of the antiquity of humankind and of the immense transformations that carried it up to the present time.[59]

While this anthropological revolution in time was underway, the spatial dimension of change also gained great academic visibility through publications in "ethnology." In this subfield of anthropology, scholars dealt with the lives of non-Western peoples, usually by drawing on numerous reports about the world's indigenous populations that had been compiled by Western missionaries, colonial administrators, explorers, and so forth. By the late 1880s, when English anthropologist E. B. Tylor, for instance, sat down to examine the "institutions of marriage and descent," he had at his disposal data on the customs of more than 350 different peoples. This figure seems large, but it expressed the ethnologist's working principle that social institutions mutate substantially as one circumnavigates the globe. This was the belief also of Herbert Spencer, who (as his friend Francis Galton recalled) "went to great cost . . . to obtain a collection of the customs of all available nations . . . for the purposes of intercomparison." Relying on such information, Spencer devoted several of his tomes to the comparative analysis of the "industrial institutions," the "political institutions," the "domestic institutions," and the "ceremonial institutions" of Western versus non-Western societies. (The quoted words are titles of a few of Spencer's books.) In the 1870s and 1880s, America's premier ethnologists Lewis Henry Morgan and J. W. Powell applied the same method to investigate how the "institution of property" differed in different places.[60]

Anthropologists' efforts to stretch the time and space boundaries of humankind were not disconnected activities, moreover. Typically, ethnologists intertwined the temporal and geographical aspects of change to formulate evolutionary laws that equated the living indigenous populations of the nineteenth century with prehistoric tribes. This sleight of hand enabled ethnologists to assert that both types of society represented the early stage—the "lower" or "primitive" stage—of a forward-marching developmental process. In the view of most ethnologists, this early stage constituted the first in a sequence of three stages. To all three they applied telltale labels: "savage" to designate peaceful, seminomadic bands of hunters and gatherers; "barbarian" to refer to tribes that settled in villages, engaged in farming and animal husbandry, and used iron weaponry to fight intertribal wars; and "civilized" to describe nations characterized by the advent and growth of cities, science, and industrial production.

In the second half of the century, most ethnologists made an elaborate show of imposing these same labels onto different "races"—understanding "races" as physical-cum-cultural categories ordered in a hierarchy of intellectual and moral superiority. From this angle, as historian George W. Stocking Jr. summarized it, "the 'lower' races were . . . the 'uncivilized' or 'savage' ones, the races with darker skins; civilization, on the other hand, was . . . synonymous with European society, which was the society of . . . large-brained white men" who exemplified the mental prowess of the "Aryan" race.[61] Depending on their proclivities, anthropologists couched these evolutionary claims in "Darwinian" or "neo-Lamarckian" vocabularies (or some compound of these). These different evolutionary notions surfaced, too, among anthropologists who opted to replace the "savagery-barbarism-civilization" schema with alternative stage models. These included Herbert Spencer's popular distinction between societies of a "militant type" (organized around warfare and "predatory" activities) and those of an "industrial type" (based on peaceful, coordinated systems of factory production). This dualism underpinned Spencer's argument that as social evolution advances, "the militant type yields place to the industrial type" (barring "reversions" to militarism). In due course, Veblen put all this conceptual equipment to use.[62]

THE DEVELOPMENTS UNFOLDING IN PSYCHOLOGY, history, and anthropology had parallels in the field of economics, although because this field came out of the academic starting gate earlier and under different auspices, its story differed somewhat. Courses in "political economy," distinct from "moral philosophy" courses, began infiltrating the curricula of American colleges as far back as the Jacksonian era, often with a spur from local merchants and bankers who wanted their sons and other wealthy young men educated to think properly—that is, in terms of classical laissez-faire principles—about economic policy questions. (Frequently, these local men of affairs taught the college course in political economy.) After the Civil War (as I have pointed out), the demand for economic expertise then rose dramatically, as a torrent of new economic issues— violent economic downturns, government regulation, monetary reform, the emergence of the corporation, the prospects of socialism—seized the attention of the public, which had grown larger, more divided over policy matters, and hungrier for economic knowledge.[63]

College and university presidents were closely attuned to this demand and responded by taking steps that accelerated the development of the field of economics.[64] We see this in a contemporary report by economist J. Laurence Laughlin. Drawing on a survey of sixty higher-educational institutions, Laughlin found that, between 1876 and 1892, "the aggregate hours of instruction [in political economy increased] more than six times" overall, thus demonstrating that "the study of Political Economy [had] entered upon a new and striking development."[65] What was more, although adding more hours of undergraduate instruction did not require college presidents to create separate faculty positions in political economy (because teaching economics could be off-loaded onto instructors in other subject areas, if not onto local businessmen), such positions began to be created. According to a study by historian John B. Parrish of twenty-eight leading colleges and universities of the late nineteenth century, the number of professorships in political economy grew from a meager three prior to 1880, to twenty by 1890, to fifty by 1900. Considering the modest size of American higher education at the time, these were strong numbers, even if not strong enough to accommodate every aspiring economist looking for a faculty appointment. Nonetheless, academic employment opportunities in political economy exceeded those available in the other social sciences.[66]

This comparative advantage came wrapped in a liability, however. The widespread popular interest in economic problems that prompted higher-educational authorities to create more courses and jobs in political economy compromised its standing as a legitimate science. To some college and university heads, political economists were what the label said: they were men who, when they taught about the "principles of political economy," slanted them to lend support to one versus another side in ongoing policy debates. (Which side a would-be economist upheld was, at some institutions, the deciding factor in whether the person was appointed to a faculty position in the first place.) Because of their partisan views, political economists of this garden variety bore little resemblance, in the eyes of research-minded university presidents, to the kind of scholars they were looking for: scientists who dealt not in politics but in facts, just as natural scientists did. At the same time, like Daniel Gilman at Hopkins, presidents wanted their professors to serve the public as long as they held to the methods of science.

University presidents found different ways of trying to satisfy these different demands. Some turned to the small contingent of men who had received doctorates in political economy in the United States (usually from Harvard, site of the first American professorship in the subject) and who upheld the approach of the English classical economists, favoring a separation between scientific laws and evidence, on the one hand, and social policy, on the other. In the view of these old schoolers, economists should analyze economic life, while leaving it to policy makers to seek out their research in order to inform the development of policy measures. (In practice, men from the Older School often violated this norm.) Other presidents chose to hire scholars from the Younger School: economists who had earned doctorates in Germany, where political economy was both a recognized science *and* a project with an ethical commitment to the cause of progressive social reform. These men, who numbered roughly five dozen by the turn of the century, served as direct carriers of the knowledge-making equipment of their mentors from the German historical school. In this way, these scholars transmitted intellectual practices that rejected classical economics and regarded economic life as part of a web of social institutions that evolved, like a growing organism, over the long course of history. Among Veblen's teachers, John Bates Clark and Richard T. Ely were both men of this type.[67]

For these Younger School economists, as well as for a few members of the Older School, political economy was more than an undergraduate teaching area, and they were more than schoolteachers. To them, political economy was a scientific discipline, and they were specialized researchers working to advance the state of knowledge in the field. To this end, they sought to organize their discipline in the way a scientific discipline was organized in Germany—namely, as a community of scholars communicating with one another about the theories and research topics they had in common as knowledge specialists. Making this kind of intellectual community a reality was one of the reasons for the launch of several academic journals in the field in the 1880s and 1890s, as well as for the founding of the American Economic Association (AEA) in 1885 in a move initiated by Ely, Clark, and other representatives of the Younger School. Established to promote intellectual back-and-forth among economists, these forums also immediately became sites of intense in-house controversy, including conflict between social reformers associated with the Younger School and conservatives from the Older School, whose members at first felt unwelcome in the AEA. In spring and summer 1886, this conflict spilled over into a very public battle, spread across several issues of *Science* (a popular national weekly), in which soldiers from the two camps went at one another as they advocated for their different views of economic knowledge. (Because of the visibility of this incident in the press, Veblen might well have gotten wind of it in the Midwest.) For a time, the controversy confounded economists' hard-fought efforts to elevate the field into the ranks of the sciences, though the quarrel proved short-lived, in part because the two schools found ways to compromise. By the time Veblen left the Midwest four years later, economists were more absorbed in other controversies.[68]

5.

When Thorstein Veblen, writing to Sarah Hardy several years after his recovery from his mystery illness, told her that he had "enjoyed" his hiatus in the hinterlands, he was not expressing any general affection for bucolic countryfolk. Excepting immigrant farm families like his own, Veblen (to judge by his later writings) saw the "pioneer-farmers" of the Upper Midwest as driven by "an indefinitely extensible cupidity, . . . with a view [to] getting a little something for nothing" from the land and from their neighbors: "Nowhere and at no time [have they] been actuated by a spirit of community." Still more contemptible, in Veblen's view, were small-town businessmen—a breed familiar to him from his frequent day trips during his convalescence to Northfield, Minnesota, to do "marketing and buying" for his parents' household and from his longer layovers in Iowa City and Stacyville, Iowa.[69] On Veblen's account, which echoed some of the rhetoric of movements such as the Farmers' Alliance and the Populist Party, small-town merchants and bankers—aiming likewise at "getting something for nothing"—exerted a "strangle-hold on the underlying farm population," extracting from it "an inordinately wide margin of net gain." This windfall swelled further the more local businessmen fell "under the dominion of those massive business interests" that were the pillars of America's corporate economy.[70]

Apart from occasional rhetorical echoes of this kind, however, Veblen steered clear of populism—both its ideas and its activities—during his recuperation and subsequently. In one of the first articles he wrote after his return to academic life, he placed populism among those reform programs of the time that were "nearly farcical" in their deficient understanding of how "the economic structure of society grows and changes form." Springing from "an intellectually undisciplined populace," populism, like other movements that looked to the state for salvation, was the bruised fruit of "the paternalistic tree of life."[71] (Veblen repeated this assessment at several later points in his career.) Describing the period when Thorstein Veblen was still recuperating on his parents' farm, Andrew Veblen told Dorfman: "I do not think he took any part in political discussion, except perhaps that he may have talked with neighbors about the questions that were in men's minds at the time. [The Northfield area] was a community in which political meeting [sic] were seldom held." Extending this account through Thorstein Veblen's time in Iowa, brother Ed went further, saying that Thorstein "took no part in politics except to turn Father and the rest of us democratic. We all had no taste for politics or public affairs of any kind."[72]

What Thorstein was mainly doing during this time-out period of his life, according to Andrew, was "upbuilding his health." As Ed explained, this involved a little drama. In a letter to Dorfman, he gave details: a "theory which obsessed [Thorstein] was that the Veblen [family] health and more especially his own, was absolutely on the bum. He theorized and theorized [about it] and dieted and talked . . . that we were all short-lived, tubercular, and generally no account physically"; he even "had to have his food cooked different, etc. etc."[73] This obsession aside, in another letter to Sarah Hardy, Thorstein wrote "You asked what I did during my years off. That is precisely the point. I did nothing." By this he meant "nothing" beyond reading as the mood struck him (and as the books he wanted to read were available locally, sometimes from a university library).[74] It was this idyllic condition Veblen probably had in mind when he asserted years later that humankind possesses an "instinct of idle curiosity . . . by the force of which men, more or less insistently, want to know things, when graver interests do not engross their attention."[75]

STILL, VEBLEN'S OWN ATTENTIONS remained partly engrossed by scholarly interests, or at least literary ones. In early 1885, for instance, the alumni section of *Carletonia* ran an entry (which probably traced to him, since he was living in the Carleton vicinity) stating that he was "writing periodicals"—though the item gave no more information. When Dorfman was researching his biography, however, he told Andrew Veblen that he had "found out that [Thorstein] Veblen spent a few years after his return from Yale writing articles for distinguished gentlemen for the North American Review." Andrew, who usually jumped to correct Dorfman's mistakes, did not contest this account, which has a ring of plausibility. As one of the leading East Coast monthlies, the *North American Review* published articles on contemporary social and economic issues by public figures who sometimes paid ghostwriters to put words in writing for them. Because of his Yale and Hopkins connections, Veblen may have gotten occasional work of this kind. When asked about the source of Thorstein's income when he was staying in Stacyville a few years later, Andrew Veblen himself speculated: "There may have been something earned by writing; though I have no sure clues."[76]

Another project from Veblen's hiatus years is certain: his ninety-thousand word translation of *The Laxdæla Saga,* an Icelandic epic composed in the thirteenth century and set in the heroic Viking age from the ninth to the eleventh centuries. Veblen's motive for taking on the task, which entailed many hundreds of hours of close work, was probably growing popular interest in the Norse-Icelandic sagas, combined with the fact that scholars considered *The Laxdæla Saga* the most important of the great sagas yet untranslated. Further, the *Saga* (as described by Rasmus Anderson, among others) belonged to the history of the "Teutonic Race." Veblen finished the translation in April 1890, but it was not published then because, as he told Anderson, he was "unable to make any advance toward paying for the expense of publication" (as publishers expected him to do).[77] When a version of the translation finally appeared in 1925—by then Veblen's renown made his publisher willing to bring it out—Veblen added an introduction that mustered this story of medieval blood feuds to illustrate his views about human society. *The Laxdæla Saga* was, he felt, "an ethnological document of a high order," illuminating the "archaic phase" of human culture and the "institutional innovations" that accompanied it and brought about a "revolutionary change" in "civil institutions," as well as religious ones. What was more, the epic showcased "institutional hold-overs": social arrangements that with modifications were handed down from the past and eventually relayed to the present. Because "the Viking age was an enterprise in piracy and slave-trade," it presaged, according to Veblen, the modern "business enterprise," each system "forever driven by its quest for profits" and reliant on "getting something for nothing by force and fraud" and by "cumulative privation and servility on the part of the underlying population" that supplied the epoch's "resources of man-power and appliances."[78] For Veblen, translating the *Saga* entailed seeing the social world through these sharp lenses, viewing it as a complex of changing social institutions commandeered by armed thugs pillaging people who toiled. As such, carrying out the translation meant plying—now in a very different context—intellectual tools he was accustomed to using long before he began the translation.

Dovetailing with his translation work were two other encounters Veblen had around this time. One was with a massive ethnological trove, the annual *Reports of the Bureau of American Ethnology.* Veblen owned a complete set of these volumes, running from 1881 (when the series started, while he was at Johns Hopkins) until 1907. Sponsored by the Smithsonian Institution, the aim of the *Reports* was, as the bureau's director (J. W. Powell) explained, to study the "great departments of objective human activities: viz., arts, institutions, languages, and opinions"—and the series lived up to its billing. It published a stream of fine-grained anthropological accounts of the indigenous peoples of North America, among them Franz Boas's still-respected 1888 monograph, "The Central Eskimo," which examined several tribes on Baffin Island, Canada, comparing their economic activities and social customs (including their modes of dress).[79] Veblen heavily annotated his copy of Boas's study, approvingly citing it (and other reports in the series) in his later writings.

A second notable encounter during this period involved a slim book published the same year as Boas's report. This was journalist Edward Bellamy's short fiction *Looking Backward, 2000–1887* (1888), one of the

great popular bestsellers of the century. The novel depicted the inhabitants of a late twentieth-century economic utopia as they retrospectively
sized up the American economy of the nineteenth century, horrified by
what they saw in that "most unhappy century." To explain their dismal
verdict, Bellamy filled the mouths of his characters (wooden, all of them)
with long speeches that added up to a digest of contemporary critiques of
the economic status quo: a jeremiad against "prodigious wastes," "utter
idleness," and "wanton luxury"; against "corporate tyranny" and "great
consolidations of capital"; and against a society in which a few predatory men and their families live "from the labor of others, rendering no
sort of service in return." On the reverse side of this critique, Bellamy
sketched the unfolding story of the "process of industrial evolution" that,
by the year 2000 on his calendar, would transform "modern social institutions" for the better, creating an organically ordered industrial army that,
because of "the progress of mechanical invention," would satisfy society's
material needs—under state supervision by a board of benevolent elders.
Given Veblen's disdain for "the paternalistic tree of life," this statist design
for the future could not have appealed to him, although Veblen scholars
are correct when they detect similarities between the details of Bellamy's
economic analysis and the details of Veblen's a decade afterward. Specifics
aside, however, Bellamy's way of thinking about society (as evolving, as
holistically made of institutions, and as a matter of work rather than idling
or preying) was more of the same for Veblen: a fictionalized rendering of
intellectual practices he had been carrying around for years.[80]

IN APRIL **1888,** Veblen married Ellen Rolfe, whom he had courted on
and off since their student days together at Carleton a decade earlier. According to an account written by Ellen in 1897—unfortunately, the only
account we have of the courtship—it was at Carleton that Veblen first told
her he loved her (and, by implication, wanted to marry her), but she rebuffed him. Afterward, "after leaving college, he engaged himself to a new
acquaintance whom he 'did not love nor ever told that he loved.' He broke
this engagement while at Yale." Then, in 1885, when he was back home
convalescing, Veblen formally proposed to Ellen, who accepted, but
quickly grew disappointed when he almost immediately postponed the
wedding date. As Ellen recounted: "When we had been engaged six months
and he told me it would be three years before we could marry, and made
no move to provide the means for our marriage even at that distant day,

I broke the engagement hurt beyond words." But, sometime after that, she again changed her mind and the wedding ceremony took place—despite that "both families were against it," according to biographers Elizabeth Jorgensen and Henry Jorgensen. From then on, until Veblen's move to Ithaca, New York, in January 1891, he and Ellen lived in Stacyville, Iowa, in the Rolfe family's large summer home.[81]

Ellen wrote that Thorstein Veblen called these two-and-one-half years "the sweet Stacyville days," and she too saw them as happy ones. Due to a rare anatomical abnormality, Ellen was unable to have sexual intercourse, but (according to the Jorgensens' research) the two shared a variety of intellectual and social interests. Veblen scholars have accepted Dorfman's claim that Ellen read Bellamy's *Looking Backward* along with Thorstein, and that she said: "I believe that this [experience] was the turning-point in our lives . . . because it so affected me." (I have been unable to confirm Dorfman's story).[82] These were the years, too, when Veblen was caught up translating *The Laxdœla Saga*. Because Ellen had a modest investment income from her father, businessman Charles Rolfe, the couple was able to support themselves in what Ellen's half-sister later described as a "bohemian" lifestyle.[83] In 1889, however, the Rolfes were hit economically by the financial collapse of the giant Atchison, Topeka, and Santa Fe Railroad. Charles Rolfe was heavily invested in the company through its president, his brother-in-law—and Ellen's maternal uncle—corporate titan William Strong (younger brother of Carleton's president James Strong), who was fired that year for company mismanagement. This severe setback, according to Ed Veblen, forced the men of the Rolfe family "to get out and hustle." This occurred shortly after Thorstein Veblen had decided to wind down his long hiatus and begin trying to find a job.[84]

All of his tries proved to be false starts, however. In 1888, shortly after Ellen and Thorstein married, and while William Strong was still the head of the Atchison, Topeka, and Santa Fe Railroad, someone in the family apparently hatched a plan for the company to hire Thorstein as its in-house economist, but that did not happen. (Likely the plan never got off the ground because of a lack of interest on Strong's or Veblen's part.)[85] What was clearly on Veblen's mind was finding academic work, and between summer 1889 and summer 1890 he made several attempts to land a college teaching post. Almost all of these attempts were in the Upper Midwest, where he had family connections to college officials. Because of the continuing shortage of jobs in the area of philosophy, however, none of his known search efforts was for a position in philosophy itself, the field in which he had earned his doctorate.

In July 1889, Andrew sought to use his connections at his own institution, the State University of Iowa, to get a position for Thorstein in political science instead. To increase the chances of that happening, Thorstein asked Herbert Baxter Adams, Noah Porter, and William Graham Sumner to send recommendations attesting to his abilities in the subject, and they all obliged with strong letters of support, but to no avail.[86] Around the same time, Andrew also contacted administrators at Michigan Agricultural College (now Michigan State University) about a position in economics for Thorstein. Andrew wrote as well on his brother's behalf to the Universities of Michigan, South Dakota, and Wisconsin (all state universities), and to Gettysburg College in Pennsylvania—although it is unclear whether these schools actually had job openings in the social sciences. Andrew even tried to get Thorstein some kind of "position in high school."[87] As Thorstein wrote to Rasmus Anderson in May 1890, all of these attempts were "fruitless." The next month, he told Anderson, he applied "for a place to teach Economics and Social Science in the Indiana University"; and the following month he tried for a long-shot position as an instructor of "natural science" at St. Olaf College, a tiny Lutheran institution in Northfield, Minnesota, where his older brother Orson served as a trustee.[88] Thorstein had no success at either institution or elsewhere. Andrew conjectured that "other candidates were better backed, perhaps, than he," and Ed summed up that Thorstein "could get nothing in the way of teaching."[89]

As a matter of pure speculation, we might wonder whether Thorstein Veblen of the late 1880s would have become Thorstein Veblen, the renowned economic theorist, if he had secured any of these local teaching jobs, rather than (as events later played out) a position in economics at a premier research university, where he took up questions he might not otherwise have been drawn to. Would he have stayed in one of the jobs he applied for in 1889 and 1890? Perhaps not: to judge from comments he made a decade and half later, Veblen looked down on state universities as shallow "quasi-'universities'" that were organized not "by men of scholarly or scientific insight" but by "practical politicians with a view to conciliate . . . a lay constituency clamouring for things [that are] pecuniarily gainful."[90]

Still, fifteen years earlier, some of these same institutions seemed a lot more attractive to him. If we go by his letters at that time, Veblen would probably have taken (at least for a while) a teaching position at one of the nearby state schools had any of them actually made him a job offer. After losing out for the Iowa State position, he wrote to Anderson, with disappointment: "I built my hopes" on it. Regarding the Indiana job, he stated, as late as June 1890, "the work is exactly what I want, and I am very anxious to secure it."[91] Veblen knew these jobs were not designed to encourage or enable faculty members to produce new knowledge; but, as interested as he was in the subject of political economy as far back as his college years, he was apparently not champing at the bit to write anything on the subject during the 1884–1890 period. Neither his health nor his marriage prevented him from taking pen to paper and tackling economic topics—had he wanted to do so.[92] But, most likely, he did not yet know exactly what he wanted to do going forward, apart from obtaining a suitable academic position or, in his words, "finding work as a teacher of such a kind as I believe I could do serviceably and creditably to myself" (as he wrote to William Graham Sumner in reference to the year 1890–1891). Responding in January 1891 to an inquiry the previous year from T. R. Ball, an administrator at Johns Hopkins, Veblen explained himself: "It is some time since I received a postal from you inquiring about my present occupation. . . . I neglected to answer at the time on account of uncertainty as to what my occupation was to be for the year."[93] Veblen was in his mid-thirties when he sent back this dispirited admission.

As in the past, however, Andrew Veblen took a guiding hand in what came next. According to Ed, "after several futile attempts to get [Thorstein] placed in some academic position," Andrew "prevailed on him to reenter academic life by matriculating with some University as a student." Andrew later described how he and Thorstein appraised the situation: "After having been in rustication so long, . . . it seemed that it was wise to get into academic relations by going somewhere and taking up work."[94] The plan was to resuscitate Thorstein's stalled academic career by means of additional postgraduate training, concentrated this time primarily on economics. From the brothers' perspective, this was the logical choice because, by then, Thorstein was no longer engaged in the field of philosophy, although he *was* equipped to move into the field of political economy, in which he had made a solid start back at Carleton, Hopkins, and Yale. So, several biographical pieces now snapped into place. Veblen had prepped in the subject; he knew, from working with Clark and Ely, that political economy was a scientific hot spot calling out for new researchers; and he was aware that the growing popular interest in economic issues was spurring university presidents to create more jobs in the area. Landing one of these positions was no certainty, as his failed applications at Iowa and Indiana proved, but he and Andrew reasoned that entering the field of economics was probably the surest way out of Thorstein's occupational impasse.

Factoring into the decision, too, was Andrew finding out (perhaps during a trip to Ithaca, New York, in 1889) that Cornell University, although it was a state-supported institution, was also an expanding research university—and one that awarded fellowships in political economy to advanced graduate students. What was more, attending Cornell would, Thorstein realized, offer the opportunity to broaden his credentials in political economy; it would complement his previous coursework with economists of the Younger School by studying with the leading American economist of the classical school. Still, he considered other universities before finally settling on Cornell, and that did not happen until two months after the 1890–1891 academic year had already started. In late November 1890, he wrote to the registrar at Cornell to ask "if there is anything to hinder the admission of a new graduate student to a regular graduate work from the beginning of the winter term."[95] Presumably the registrar's answer was "no," because by January 1891 Veblen was living in Ithaca (without Ellen, for the time being). His six and one-half years of "rustication" in the Midwest were over.

CHAPTER 7

YOUNG ECONOMIST

Returning to graduate school at age thirty-four for a second PhD was a daring move for Veblen to make. Even today it is rare for a woman or man with a doctorate in one field to decide to pursue a doctorate in another field. In 1891 this step was almost unheard of, and Thorstein Veblen may well have been the first person in US history to receive a PhD from one American university and then go back for another doctorate at a different university.[1] The second effort yielded better results, however, bringing him back into the academic mainstream and steering him toward problems in the field of economics that, in the years immediately ahead, called forth his principal contributions to economic knowledge.

1.

The classically named university town of Ithaca, in south-central New York State, was sprinkled, like New Haven, Connecticut, with small manufacturing firms. In Ithaca, these firms specialized in the production of glass, salt, furniture, and paper, and the town was smaller and less developed than New Haven; at ten thousand residents, it was the size of Madison, Wisconsin, when Veblen was teaching there back in 1880–1881 and was not incorporated as a city until 1888. "A brilliant prison" was how economist Henry Carter Adams described the town when he lectured there back in the early 1880s, although by the time Veblen arrived a decade later, Ithaca boasted trolleys, electric street lights, home telephones—and the nation's third-wealthiest institution of higher education (outranked only by Harvard and Columbia).[2]

The university carried the name of its multimillionaire benefactor Ezra Cornell, cofounder of the Western Union Telegraph Company, America's first telecommunications giant. A member of the New York Senate in the 1860s, Cornell, with the help of fellow senator Andrew D. White, leveraged federal land-grant monies to establish, on property Senator Cornell donated to the state, a nonsectarian college "to teach such branches of learning as are related to agriculture and the mechanic arts [for the benefit] of the industrial classes."[3] White, a German-educated historian (previously on the faculty of the University of Michigan), became the school's first president, promising in his 1868 inaugural to build an institution opposed to elites "for whom Greed is God and Moneybags his prophet."[4] Subsequently, however, after a leave of absence to serve as US ambassador to Germany, White raised his sights. By the early 1880s, he aimed to replicate the model his friend Daniel Gilman had instituted at Johns Hopkins and to create a research-oriented institution dedicated to the growth of new knowledge. White's successor, historian Charles Kendall Adams, who occupied the presidency when Veblen was at Cornell, continued this project.[5]

In putting this model into place, Cornell's first two presidents designed a university with features already familiar to Veblen from his previous educational experiences. As at Hopkins and Yale, science was the idol of the local residents, who saw themselves as inductive researchers studying the process of evolution in botany, zoology, physiology, geology, chemistry, physics, and adjacent fields. Looking beyond these areas, university administrators expected other fields of scholarship, whether old or new, to emulate what the natural scientists were doing. When Andrew White mapped out the curriculum for the program in "history and political science," for instance, he insisted that the instructor's "first step . . . is to enable the student to secure some adequate general knowledge of the simpler facts in the evolution of man and of society in the past which best aids in solving the problem regarding the evolution of both in the future"; for this purpose, "efforts [must] constantly be made to trace back important events and institutions through the various stages of their development."[6]

By the time Veblen entered Cornell, it was administratively divided into "schools," which were subdivided into department-like units.[7] During the five terms he spent there, from winter 1891 to spring 1892, Veblen enrolled in the School of History and Political Science, which comprised several of these de facto departments, history and economics among them.[8] These were subjects in which Andrew White had taken a special interest, and historians of higher education credit him as the first university president to propose a separate department of political economy and to arrange for regular coursework on the topic. As a spur to postgraduate education in the area, Cornell, which was tuition-free for all graduate students, also offered a small number of fellowships to defray living expenses, including two earmarked for "Political Economy and Finance." During the 1891–1892 academic year, when he was among the seventeen graduate students in the School of History and Political Science, Veblen held one of these fellowships. This additional income enabled Ellen to join him in Ithaca, where she enrolled as a graduate student in Cornell's Botany Department. Otherwise, Veblen relied on a loan (apparently never repaid) that he received from his father, in another exceptional show of parental support in an era when graduate school was terra incognita.[9]

Cornell required graduate students in all its divisions to declare a "major subject" and two "minor" subjects. On forms he filed with the university registrar in January 1891, Veblen listed "Economics" as his major, and "American History" and "English Constitutional History" as his minors. To judge from his official university record, he concentrated during his first two terms on classes in history and did not take any in economics, although the record appears to be incomplete.[10] In any case, American and English history made sense to Veblen as another area to study formally. It meshed with some of the coursework he had done at Hopkins and Yale, and he may have thought that more history courses would improve his job prospects at midwestern colleges.[11] Whatever Veblen's thinking, Cornell's demarcation between the "departments" of economics and history gave institutional reality to a major change that was beginning to infiltrate American higher education: the move toward dividing economics and history into separate academic disciplines. Fueled by the trend toward specialization within American universities, this move took off, paradoxically, in the same decade (the 1880s) when economists of the Younger School and their allies were working to transform political economy into a field concerned with the historical growth of economic institutions. Back at Hopkins, Veblen studied in a combined department of "History and Political Economy," where Richard Ely and Herbert Baxter Adams moved easily between the two fields; and at Yale he had worked with William Graham Sumner, whose writings and lectures blended the two subjects. But at Cornell, the two disciplines were institutionally differentiated from each other (with topics in economic history floating between them), showcasing a developing split Veblen observed as he cycled between his major and his minors.[12]

On the history side of his program, Veblen studied with Moses Coit Tyler and Herbert Tuttle.[13] In American history specifically, his mentor was Tyler (1835–1900), then a towering figure in the discipline of history in the United States—and a man whose life was a mixture of features found in the biographies of Veblen's previous teachers. Descended from colonial stock, Tyler grew up poor as the result of his father's business failures, but a stroke of fortune carried him to Yale College and Andover Seminary. Afterward, he pursued a career in the ministry, until a psychological breakdown. Seeking an alternative, he moved to England and found work lecturing and writing on American civilization. He parlayed this experience into a faculty position at the University of Michigan, where Andrew White lured him away to Cornell in 1881, offering him the country's first professorship of American history.[14]

Like Herbert Baxter Adams, Tyler expected historians to adopt "the attitude . . . of scientific investigators," devoting themselves to the "disinterested" study of historical records. He also wanted students of history to take cognizance of the long sweep of human evolution and the historical nature of human traits that were often misconceived as eternal. Toward this goal, Tyler's foundational course at Cornell, War for Independence, began (as he described it) with "prehistoric times" and with "the native races, especially the mound-builders and the North American Indians, [and] the pre-Columbian discoveries," before going on to examine "the development of the ideas and institutions of the American colonies with particular reference to religion, education, industry, and civil freedom." In the winter and spring 1891 terms, Veblen took the two courses that followed in Tyler's course sequence: American History from the End of the War for Independence and American Constitutional History. Although lecture notes for Tyler's courses have not been preserved, we can gather the gist of his teachings from his published writings, which dwelt on the "origin and growth" of American institutions, the "evolution of thought," the "unfolding of the American mind," and other "evolutionary" processes. Tyler's work also challenged ahistorical notions of "individualism," "natural rights," and the "pursuit of wealth." All of these, he sought to show, were phenomena that arose and mutated over the course of centuries.[15]

Tyler's specialty was the history of American literature, which in his view was inseparable from cultural, social, economic, and political history. Individual writers were not solitary wordsmiths but featured players in the drama of the country's "spiritual moods, its motives, [and] its passions"—or, more simply, its shifting state of "public opinion," as conditioned by its "social organization." Tyler gave the illustration of colonial New England and Virginia: "the social structure of New England was that of [population] concentration, the social structure of Virginia was that of [population] dispersion." Culturally speaking, the result was that Virginians were "less enterprising, less industrious, more self-indulgent," and more inclined to "literary barrenness," while New Englanders demonstrated more "enterprise and thrift," more hard work, and more literary accomplishment. Magnifying this difference, Tyler argued, was the contrast between democratic, public-spirited New England and aristocratic Virginia, dominated by "a class of landowners, haughty [and] indolent," and rutted in a tradition of "no schools; no literary institutions, . . . no public libraries; no printing-press; no intellectual freedom; no religious freedom."[16] On none of these points were Tyler's ideas original, at least not to Veblen; but in voicing them, Tyler recharged ways of thinking about the social world that Veblen had practiced at Carleton and Hopkins a decade or more earlier.

Herbert Tuttle (1846–1894), Cornell's professor of modern European history, did likewise. Cut from the same fabric as Herbert Baxter Adams, Richard Ely, and John Bates Clark—Puritan roots, Yankee business heritage, classical education, attendance at an Eastern college (the University of Vermont)—Tuttle had gravitated to the field of history during a ten-year career in journalism that took him to Europe and pulled him into the orbit of German historicism. Through personal connections, this background landed him a visiting faculty position at the University of Michigan, and from there White recruited him to Cornell the same year that he hired Tyler. The exact nature of Veblen's work with Tuttle is not known. When Veblen submitted his "outline of proposed course of study" to Cornell's registrar in January 1891, he wrote that he planned to enroll in Tuttle's course The Growth of the English Constitution, and Tuttle's gradebook for the term listed Veblen's name, although there is nothing in Veblen's official record to show he completed the course. All the same, on the basis of as many of Tuttle's lectures as Veblen attended, as well as from Tuttle's writings, Veblen would have recognized the Cornell historian as another determined practitioner of the "historical institutionalism" Veblen had heard Herbert Baxter Adams and Richard T. Ely espouse at Hopkins.[17]

Tuttle's course English Constitution was actually the second part of a three-part series of courses he taught under the signature title "History of

Institutions." Tuttle offered this series frequently, sketching out his lectures in legible notes that still survive. These show his strong interest in teaching students that social institutions are neither "direct Divine creations" nor the product of a "voluntary contract" among individuals seeking "utilitarian" ends. Rather, institutions are coordinated parts of the "organism" that is human society; they are "matter[s] of habit & usage" that undergo a "constant process of development," an evolutionary transformation "strikingly like [the] rise & fall of living nat[ural] organisms, whether animal or vegetable." The special task of the historian, according to Tuttle, was to extend the "inductive" methods of the natural sciences to tailor general evolutionary laws to fit the "historical, concrete" aspects of individual societies. In the course in which Veblen enrolled, Tuttle used this approach to analyze the English constitution not as a written document but as the "sum of accepted usages" (land tenure, trial by jury, and so forth) that emerged through a process of "natural growth, from the earliest times to the present," as invading armies of Romans, Normans, and Saxons successively molded the customs of the British Isles. On Tuttle's account, this development occurred through "stages of plunder, settlement, conquest, domination, decline, and overthrow," eventuating in the "inst. which make [the English-speaking people] a free people."[18] (This was Tuttle's rendition of the Teutonic thesis.)

Similar themes appeared in Tuttle's published writings during his time at Cornell. These included his acclaimed *History of Prussia* (1884–1896), a four-volume work of archival scholarship that tracked the development of the political and economic "institutions" of eighteenth-century Prussia back to "primitive and medieval" conditions in central Europe and then forward in time. Tuttle characterized this development as a tumultuous "process of evolution," a process defined by acts of "wanton robbery and violence" that noblemen perpetrated for centuries against "easy prey," such as the peasants who worked their lands.[19] In addition to this scholarly opus, Tuttle (the erstwhile journalist) wrote highbrow magazine articles that mixed his academic ideas with a reformist political stance. This he formulated in a more temperate manner than Veblen's previous teachers—Ely on the left, Sumner on the right—although he focused on similar issues, socialism in particular. In an *Atlantic Monthly* article in 1883, for instance, Tuttle defended the "law of social evolution," applying it to "the history of many political institutions," but objected to the claim associated in the public's mind with the teleological view of Herbert Spencer that evolution was necessarily accompanied by "progress" and "improvement."

Figure 7 Veblen's professors at Cornell University *(clockwise from top left):* James Laurence Laughlin, Herbert Tuttle, and Moses Coit Tyler

As a counterinstance, Tuttle cited the rocky history of socialism, which he depicted as a "movement . . . that may be provoked by the just complaints of an oppressed class, by the inevitable inequality of fortunes, or by a base jealousy of superior moral and intellectual worth." Whatever its source, though, socialism entailed, he argued, the insidious growth of a centralized state bureaucracy—"paternal government"—that, in the context of the period, increasingly favored tariffs and other protectionist measures over the free trade principles of the past: a shift in policy that endangered the "principles of society and government common to all the English peoples." Tuttle pinned the intellectual blame for this ruinous change on the diffusion into the United States of the statist doctrines of economists of the German historical school and their assault on the English school of political economy. Because of the rift between these camps, he asserted, America "is now passing through an important crisis"—a crisis that could only be resolved by advances in economic theory.[20]

2.

Towering over Veblen's work with Cornell's historians was his training with the head economist on its faculty, James Laurence Laughlin (1850–1933), a man only seven years older but a generation ahead in his career and already recognized in and out of the academy "as one of the country's greatest defenders . . . of the classical tradition in economics" (to quote his biographer).[21] Laughlin's presence at Cornell had been one of the university's main attractions for Veblen. By late 1891, with his hopes set on becoming a bone fide economist, Veblen wanted, according to Andrew Veblen, "to hear and get in touch with men of different views from his own and different from his former teachers."[22] Knowing that his professors at Carleton, Hopkins, and Yale had taught him classical economics by way of a relentless critique of its assumptions, Veblen expected that Laughlin would present the subject in a more favorable light, thereby supplementing and rounding out his preparations for entering the field of economics.

With that as the plan, Veblen arrived at Cornell intending to take three of Laughlin's courses, two of them survey-style and devoted mainly to "current economic issues" (currency reform, tariffs, and so forth), and the third a seminar in which students carried out "critical studies of economic problems." From Veblen's official record, though, it is again unclear how far he followed through on this plan. Laughlin's survey courses fell among

Cornell's combined undergraduate-graduate courses, and it seems unlikely that, with so much prior coursework in economics under his belt, Veblen would have attended, more than occasionally, introductory lectures and discussions with students half his age. Laughlin's own preferred teaching method, in any case, was to create what he regarded as a "laboratory" setting in which he worked one-on-one with advanced students like Veblen, pushing them to become "economic scientists" who would conduct "independent research" and "think independently."[23] Veblen may not, at first, have expected Laughlin to drive students in this direction, since Laughlin had a notorious (if exaggerated) reputation for adhering single-mindedly to classical economic doctrines. But, regardless, at the personal level, Laughlin tolerated and encouraged intellectual dissent, lending support to generations of graduate students—men and women both—even when they broke away from him in their own research. (Many graduate students, though maybe not Veblen, affectionately called Laughlin "Uncle Larry.")[24]

When Veblen met him, Laughlin too was a newcomer to Cornell. He had joined the faculty as the professor of political economy and finance in 1890, following a brief stint as secretary and then president of the Manufacturers' Mutual Fire Insurance Company, an organization that hired him after he was passed over for tenure in the department of political economy at Harvard. Apart from this time away from the academy, Laughlin's background resembled Veblen's other professors: colonial ancestors, parents of modest means, and an undergraduate degree from a distinguished New England college. In Laughlin's case, that school was Harvard, where he later earned a doctorate in history, working with the German-inspired historian Henry Adams (of the storied Adams presidential dynasty), before backing into a position teaching economics at the university. By the time Laughlin moved to Cornell, where he filled the chair recently vacated by a Younger School economist, he was widely known for authoring two Older School textbooks and for his abridgment of the bible of classical economics, John Stuart Mill's *Principles of Political Economy,* which he brought out in many revised editions, heavily annotating them to keep the gospel up-to-date.[25]

As Laughlin conveyed the subject in these formulaic textbooks, economics was the study of the production, exchange, and distribution of material goods, with production getting top billing. (Laughlin's texts generally kept the topic of the consumption of goods on the sidelines, although he considered the topic more directly elsewhere.) Retreading Older

School doctrines, he taught that human wants are unlimited and that men and women cannot satisfy them simply by living off the land (or off other natural resources). Instead, people must labor hard, both physically and mentally, to produce the things that will meet their present needs and, in addition, allow some people—those capable of foresight and long-term abstinence—to save toward the future, storing up a portion of products they make today to serve as capital they can draw on in future to make improvements to the production process. From these premises came, for Laughlin, the central proposition that land, labor, and capital (which he took pains to define and parse into categories) are the universal "requisites of production," the "three factors [that] enter into . . . the production of anything we see about us." Moreover, all three material factors operate according to scientific "laws" of increase; these laws determine the quantity of each factor and account for the differential economic returns that accrue to landowners as rent, to laborers as wages, and to capitalists as profit.[26]

This production-oriented economics led Laughlin to advocate the classical "cost of production theory of value," which went to the heart of late nineteenth-century economic theory. (Here I simplify. The "cost of production theory" came in several varieties, most a bundle of fallacies according to later-day economists. In this section, I stick to Laughlin's own uncritical version.) What does it mean, asked Laughlin, to say that one manufactured good, or commodity, has greater economic "value" than another? Only this: "A commodity has more or less value, as it may be exchanged"—using the medium of money—"for more or less of other things." In other words, if one woolen scarf "exchanges for" twenty tallow candles, "it is twenty times as valuable." But why would scarves and candles exchange in this unequal "ratio"? According to Laughlin's theory, that happens because (leaving aside short-term market fluctuations in the supply and demand of the two commodities) scarves cost more to produce than candles. Making scarves requires producers to spend more on the wages of workers to hire a better "quality of labor" and more of it, and also to pay more in interest to secure a greater "quantity of capital" to use for purchasing machinery and other means of production. Laughlin, following John Stuart Mill, called this relationship the "law of normal value" (or "natural value"), appending the qualifier that "normal" was a descriptive term, not a stamp of approval.[27] In his view, the fact that economic value derives from production costs did not cancel out two other social processes that he foregrounded in his edition of Mill's *Political*

Economy: namely, "unproductive labor," or work that adds nothing to a society's "stock of material products"; and "unproductive consumption," which consists of expenditures by and for society's "unproductive classes." Using these concepts, Laughlin's texts discussed "idlers," "waste," and money squandered on "luxuries," such as "buying, furnishing, and sailing . . . pleasure-yacht[s]."[28]

In his role as purveyor of the theoretical resources of classical economics, Laughlin also pushed back against its challengers. For example, although his doctorate was in history, he criticized members of the German historical school for assuming they could advance the science of economics on the basis of inductive historical research alone. In his view, which drew on the ideas of his hero John Stuart Mill, inductive methods, unaided, impeded the development within economics of theoretical principles of the kind found in the successful sciences of physics and chemistry. Elaborating, Laughlin asserted—in what he saw as a departure from scholars who advocated inductivism without understanding its true function—that, just as "thermo-dynamics . . . is not a body of *concrete* truth," so too "Political Economy . . . does not pretend to be a statement of facts, or a description of actual conditions."[29] Instead, it is, when properly done, a deductively organized set of theoretical propositions—or, in the best case scenario, of "abstract" explanatory laws—that hold differently under different historical conditions, "depend[ing] upon what the facts are in each case." In agreement with the German historical school (and in deference to John Stuart Mill and to the cult of induction at Cornell), Laughlin conceded that inductive research was indispensable in economics; it enabled economists "to collect accurate data which may serve in the process of verification of economic principles . . . or to demonstrate their divergence from actual facts." Even so, he argued that historical facts, in and of themselves, "give no results ending in scientific laws."[30]

Laughlin was less open to compromise, though, when he confronted assaults on classical economic theory from another rival school of thought, a school even younger than the Younger School (and eventually much more consequential for Veblen). This was what economists were, by the 1890s, beginning to refer to as the school of "marginal utility." Before converging on this brand name, American economists sometimes called it the mathematical school, the hedonistic school, the psychological school, or, most often, the Austrian school, depending on what features they wanted to emphasize.[31] (Again we're talking about a range of approaches, which I'm not differentiating here, rather than a monolithic "school.")

Put forth during the early 1870s by a small group of European econo-mists (working independently in several countries) and elaborated by their disciples in the 1880s, the marginal utility approach shared with the Older School the belief that economics is an abstract theoretical science con-cerned with formulating general laws, not an assemblage of inductive historical findings. Marginalist economists intentionally broke from the classical writers, however, in placing consumption, rather than produc-tion, at the center of the new "marginal utility theory of value" that be-came the school's signature feature.[32] In a nutshell, this alternative theory, as contemporaries construed it, held that the value of a commodity de-rives not from the objective costs (wages, interest) involved in producing the article, but from its "marginal utility" to the individual as a consumer. That is to say: the "cause of value" lies in the importance the individual attaches (for whatever reason) to the article as a means to satisfy his or her subjective wants—or, more specifically, in the importance to the indi-vidual of the final unit (the so-called marginal unit) that he or she is willing to purchase of the article before opting for something else. As American economist Francis Amasa Walker glossed the theory in the mid-1880s, for members of the marginal utility school, value "express[es] the utility to the consumer of the last portion of the commodity purchased, its utility at the point reached just before buying ceases [and the] purchaser would rather keep his money in his pocket"—or spend it another way—"than pay the price for any more of the commodity." Walker's contemporary Arthur Hadley explained that this theory derived from what marginalists saw as the universal "psychological" principle that "increased supplies of any article must give the individual who receives them a diminishing in-crement of utility."[33]

To Laughlin, this theory was the "iridescent dream" of economists who knew nothing about the nature of science. In the late 1880s, he dismissed marginal utility theory as a tangle of circular reasoning; and fifteen years later, when marginalism stood at the center of American economics, he ridiculed it as a fad fueled by economists' "joy at a new abstraction," to the disregard of "truth and accuracy."[34] A body of writing in which "the a priori method is too much in evidence, and the facts have been too much sacrificed," marginalism, as Laughlin saw it, amounted to little more than an unfounded psychological generalization—"the law of [the diminishing] satiety" of individual wants—illegitimately inflated into a one-size-fits-all explanation of the hard material forces that operate in economic life.[35]

Before Veblen moved to Cornell in 1891, he knew next to nothing about the marginal utility theory of value, but with Laughlin overseeing his work, the timing of his move proved fortuitous. Marginalist theory began attracting serious notice in the United States, according to historians of economics, in the late 1880s and early 1890s, and these dates exactly coincided with Veblen's return to graduate school.[36] Back at Carleton in the late 1870s, he had received a little foretaste of marginalist thinking as a student of John Bates Clark (who was making his own way toward marginal utility theory); but it was Laughlin—an indefatigable reader of the European economics literature—who brought Veblen up to speed on the latest theoretical developments coming from abroad. Laughlin's presentation was not neutral, however. Instead, just as Veblen's teachers at Carleton, Hopkins, and Yale had introduced him to classical economics by means of critiques, so Laughlin transmitted marginal utility theory to Veblen with an attitude—an attitude of unrelieved hostility (which Veblen would hold throughout his career).

In addition to teaching economic theory to Veblen, Laughlin also reinforced many of the knowledge-making practices Veblen had been exposed to earlier in his schooling (and was now encountering again in the work of Tyler and Tuttle). We would not expect this, and Veblen might not have anticipated it either, since Laughlin's Older School economics rested on ways of thinking that mostly contrasted with those of Veblen's other teachers. Nevertheless, if we stand back from Laughlin's doctrinal writings and consider his work as a whole, he no longer appears as such an outlier. For one thing, like Veblen's other mentors, Laughlin was an intellectual pugilist. This demeanor is evident in his strong attacks on the historical school and the marginal utility school, and his biographer has discussed Laughlin's almost habitual "manner of using derisive, abusive, derogatory and inflammatory language to refer to those with whom he disagreed." Further, Laughlin relished this persona, bragging to University of Chicago president William Rainey Harper on one occasion, for instance: "In my own special subject of money"—Laughlin's principal field of research—"I have gone so far the other way [from the "classical school"] that I may possibly be called an iconoclast."[37]

Besides presenting himself in this rebellious manner to his audiences, Laughlin resembled Veblen's past teachers as well in his social organicism and historical evolutionism (though he was not always consistent on these subjects). On the first page of his first economics text (in 1885), he instructed readers that human beings are never separate individuals but inextricable parts of a "social organism"; at the start of the book's sequel two years later, he called attention to "what society does for its members" and to how "the social mechanism [operates in ways that are] very ingenious and very powerful."[38] Elsewhere, he spoke of "the social power of a community" and the wide-reaching effects of social "institutions"—expressing thanks to the German historical school for encouraging scholars to pursue the "comparative study of institutions."[39] Heeding this advice, Laughlin's *History of Bimetallism* (1886) examined the changing "institutions" of money, banking, and credit, as well as the shifting uses of gold and silver metals. On the basis of this analysis, he maintained that precious metals functioned as "ornaments of display" under "barbaric conditions," whereas, with "the gradual progress of . . . civilization," they became the foundation of currency. This development caused "vanity to exhibit itself under a different guise," so that "mansions, pictures, and sculpture [came to] take the place [previously occupied by] collections of jewelry" as signals of social "prestige."[40] Along similar lines, Laughlin also defended the Teutonic thesis; he accepted that "the democratic character of German political institutions" during the Dark Ages laid the primitive groundwork for the Anglo-Saxon institutions of law and private property.[41]

Early in his career, Laughlin quietly extrapolated from this thesis the corollary that modern institutions "arose by slow development from the slightest germ," and in his later work this evolutionary way of thinking became more apparent.[42] By the 1890s, he embraced evolutionary principles—and the contributions of Charles Darwin and Herbert Spencer—as a matter of course. What was more, when Laughlin was not preoccupied with the inner technicalities of economic theory, he applied evolutionism to economic life itself, offering fluent remarks about "the unconscious evolution of our modern industrial system," the "onward sweep of th[e] evolution of the fittest instrument[s] of production," and the value of "the evolutional method" for understanding how American banking "has been a distinct growth out of lower forms of banking life."[43] On his account, furthermore, inasmuch as economic conditions evolved, economic thought also underwent a "gradual evolution": the science of political economy originated with the birth of "modern society" in the sixteenth century, and the ideas of economists subsequently changed in step with social changes.[44]

Because of this ongoing process of social evolution, said Laughlin, economists of his era were confronted with policy-related "subjects [such as] transportation, agriculture, socialism, taxation, public finance, banking, [and] monetary systems."[45] Studying these empirical subjects did not, in his view, remove the need to develop the abstract economic theories of classical economics; but economists also had an obligation—to policy makers and the general public—to speak to "practical problems" on the national agenda. (Laughlin wavered over whether economists should confine themselves to providing people outside the academy with relevant facts and theories, or should go further to devise policy recommendations and carry them to the public stage.) For his own part, Laughlin dealt with the problems raised by popular demands for financial reform and socialist reconstruction. Regarding socialism, for example, he observed that, in his own time, "the poor day-laborer jostles the millionaire on the street and wonders"—with "rage and envy"—"what reason there is why he works all day long when the other man is luxuriating in leisure and comfort." "As a remedy for this excessive difference," he pointed out, labor has sought refuge in socialism, advocating a paternalistic "system of appealing to the State, rather than to individual action," without realizing that employment and economic efficiency stagnate when they lack the stimulus provided by privately owned capital. Taking that proposition as settled, Laughlin acknowledged that modern workers (the industrious ones, at any rate) still had legitimate "ground for complaint," and that cooperatives and other nonstatist "forms of socialism," which "people go into . . . of their own free will," might yield improvements for labor that were impossible under both present-day capitalism and "state socialism."[46]

DURING THE YEAR and a half Veblen spent at Cornell, Laughlin's approach to economic knowledge was amplified by other aspects of the university's economics program. Laughlin was not modest: he knew the subject matter of political economy backward and forward. But he also recognized that his discipline, like many of the natural sciences, was fast differentiating into subfields. To keep pace, what was required, he believed, was the "division" of departments of economics into a variety of subjects taught by specialists, some of them theorists, others empirical researchers. As the head of his department at Cornell, Laughlin encouraged this development, although university administrators resisted some of his more sweeping expansion plans.[47] Still, in fall 1891, just as Veblen was starting his second year in the program, the administration added two other economists to the faculty of the School of History and Political Science, both of them young men rising in reputation: Adolph Miller (associate professor of political economy and finance, with a master's degree from Harvard) and Jeremiah Jenks (professor of political, municipal, and social institutions, with a doctorate from University of Halle). Less attached than Laughlin to classical economics, the two men reinforced the institutional and evolutionary themes in Laughlin's other writings: Miller through research on the financial institutions that facilitate the "capitalist organization of industrial society"; Jenks through studies of "capitalist monopolies" and other "great industrial enterprises" (which he treated as components of the "living, growing organism" of society).[48] Miller's and Jenks's courses dealt with these subjects when Veblen was at Cornell, where he also (unexpectedly) became part of a growing cohort of other ambitious graduate students in the social sciences. [49] (A standout among these was Frank Fetter, later a distinguished marginalist theorist with whom Veblen would spar in the years ahead.)

THE COMBINATION OF all these factors—Laughlin, Miller, Jenks, and the growing crop of graduate students—made Cornell a richer site of economic scholarship than Veblen anticipated when he first arrived at the university, and as he realized this he changed his course of study. In November 1891, less than a year after registering at Cornell, he petitioned his supervising committee (Laughlin, Tuttle, and Tyler) to allow him to replace his original minors, American history and English constitutional history, with minors in two subareas within economics, which he listed on his petition as "Socialism and The Science of Finance." ("Political Economy," in the sense of economic theory, remained his major.) "The reason for my petition," he explained to the committee, "is partly the altered opportunities now offered by the University, partly a change of opinion on my own part as to what I had best do" (given the circumstances). The committee members granted this request; but since their consent form is the last official piece of paper preserved from Veblen's time at Cornell, we do not know how he actually availed himself of "the altered opportunities"—whether, for example, he took additional coursework or switched out the members of his doctoral committee (perhaps adding Miller and dropping one of the historians). Nevertheless, with this change of his minors, plus a fellowship in political economy and finance, Veblen was now a student full-time in the department of economics, a budding professional academic with both feet planted, finally, inside the field of political economy. His publications from the period tracked the arc of this change.[50]

3.

Andrew White envisioned Cornell as a place where faculty members and fellows would contribute to the growth of new knowledge, and Laughlin thought the same way. He wanted graduate students in economics to become scholars and "publish investigations," and Veblen was quick to do what was expected of him, just as he had done before at Yale, Hopkins, and Carleton.[51] In the ten months between fall 1891 and summer 1892, he published three articles in prominent academic journals. In all three, he looked out on late nineteenth-century American society through lenses furnished by his academic environment.

The earliest article, "Some Neglected Points in the Theory of Socialism," appeared in November 1891 in the *Annals of the American Academy of Political and Social Science,* a new journal of political science, sociology, and economics, based at the University of Pennsylvania. The month of publication indicates that Veblen wrote the article sometime before he moved into economics full time; the *Annals* was an attractive outlet for him since it had been running articles and book reviews on "industrial evolution," the "organic nature of industrial society," and "wasteful expenditure for the sake of ostentation," as well as on the subject of socialism.[52] Veblen framed his article as an intervention into the "controversy" over the "feasibility" of socialism. Doing so, he took aim (as in the past) at the biggest target in sight; in this case, socialism's arch critic Herbert Spencer, whose recent essay "From Freedom to Bondage" fulminated against socialism as a form of state bureaucracy that would "exercise[e] a tyranny more gigantic and more terrible than any which the world has seen."[53]

Spencer's attack was a hyperbolic version of the critique of socialism Laughlin and Tuttle were pushing at the time, and Veblen dealt with it respectfully (to the point of calling himself a "disciple" of Spencer). He accepted his teachers' contention that the "demands of socialist agitators" rested on something more than the objective material plight of workers; for the capitalist system of production, he agreed, had "brought about . . . the most rapid advance in average wealth and industrial efficiency that the world has seen," along with "an amelioration of the lot of the less favored in a relatively greater degree than that of those economically more fortunate." But material improvements for the "less favored," continued Veblen, had only amped up their "subjective" feelings of "envy" and "jealousy" toward men and women who are better off. (Here he used terms right off the pages of Tuttle and Laughlin.) Living in a highly commercialized "modern society," based on private property ownership, people less well-off seek "the esteem of [their] fellow-men" through an emulative "display" of "token[s] of economic success," with the consequence that the age-old "struggle for existence has . . . been transformed into a struggle to keep up appearances by otherwise unnecessary expenditure" (on wasteful "articles of apparel" and "a show of luxury") that has no ceiling. On Veblen's account, this kind of "economic emulation . . . pervades the structure of modern society more thoroughly" than any other factor and fuels the seething popular "unrest" that finds its voice in the socialist call for the collective ownership of property and the "State control of industry."[54]

Rather than dismiss this call, however, Veblen spoke up for it, but with a qualification. He did so skillfully, chipping away at Spencer's diatribe by drawing on the stock of intellectual tools he had been laying in for years. A fundamental lesson of the long "evolution of existing institutions," Veblen observed, was that "there can be no peace from this . . . ignoble form of emulation, or from the discontent that goes with it, this side of the abolition of private property," such as socialism proposes to accomplish. Contrary to its opponents, though, socialism does not, according to Veblen, necessitate a stifling state bureaucracy. "At least as a matter of speculation, this is not the only alternative" going forward. Instead, a regime of collective ownership might operate by means of a "system of modern constitutional government" and other "free institutions of the English-speaking people"—as he phrased his claim several times, bringing in an idea that had been a staple of his education. If political-economic institutions of this type held sway, the "social organism" would increasingly achieve both "industrial efficiency" and effective "self-government," just the combination Laughlin's social policy work advocated but had associated only with voluntary forms of socialism.[55]

VEBLEN'S OTHER TWO publications from his months at Cornell stayed close to Laughlin the economic theorist. They defended two classical economic doctrines Laughlin had retailed in his edition of Mill's *Political Economy,* and Veblen published both items in a journal Laughlin had cofounded in 1886 when he was still at Harvard, the *Quarterly Journal of*

Economics (QJE).[56] One of the world's first English-language economics journals, the *QJE* was also, by the start of the 1890s, America's leading forum for debates in economic theory. Veblen's short articles appeared in the journal's "Notes and Memoranda" section (hereafter, Notes).

Recondite today, the two pieces still bear notice because they show an unknown historical figure. They show Thorstein Veblen as neither a hostile outside critic of the classical tradition in economics nor an evolutionary, institutionalist thinker, but instead as a junior-level professional economist burrowed deeply inside his academic field *and* at just the spot his mentor identified as demanding attention. Put slightly differently, these articles show Veblen working at the theoretical end of turn-of-the-century American economics and plying its tools—the arguments and technical concepts of classical economic theorists—as he honed his doctrinal skills under the supervision of one of the master craftsmen of the trade. Studying on a full-time basis in Laughlin's workshop from late 1891 onward, Veblen tacitly put into temporary storage some of the knowledge-making instruments he had relied on in other contexts (including in his "Socialism" article) to use equipment better calibrated, according to his adviser, for tackling problems on the agenda of economic theorists writing in mainstream academic journals.

The first result, in January 1892, was "Böhm-Bawerk's Definition of Capital, and the Sources of Wages," in which Veblen upheld one of the pillars of classical economics, the "wage-fund doctrine." When Older School economists discussed the cost of production theory of value, they counted workers' wages as a large item in the total cost equation, a calculation that led them to the question: "Where do wages come from?" Typically, these economists' answer was that wages are sourced by employers, who allocate a portion of their accumulated capital to provide what is, in effect, a fixed "fund" that they then divide up in order to advance to workers the wages that allow them to stay afloat in the interval before the production process ends and finished products bring in revenue.[57] Amid the conflicts between Capital and Labor in the postbellum period, economic writers, academic and lay, frequently cited this theory to justify the profits of capitalists as legitimate returns to them for bankrolling the wage fund. No less frequently, the theory encountered strong pushback, on a variety of counts, from champions of Labor, as well as from a number of professional economists. By the tally of historian Herbert Hovenkamp, the dispute over the wage-fund doctrine constituted the "largest single debate" in the early volumes of the *QJE*.[58]

In his first Note in the journal, Veblen entered this "bitter and sterile controversy" (his words) from a particular angle.[59] He seized on a mild attack on the wage-fund theory that had just appeared in a book by Eugen Böhm-Bawerk, whom economists of the time regarded as "the foremost champion of the Austrian School" of marginal utility theory. In this book, *The Positive Theory of Capital* (1891), Böhm-Bawerk sought explicitly to replace the production-focused wage-fund doctrine with a consumption-focused notion of a "subsistence fund." According to Böhm-Bawerk's critique, the classical economists' conception of wages as production costs, which were borne by capitalists, created a distorted image that put the subsistence wages of workers on par with the upkeep costs that employers spend on "the feeding of the beasts of burden and the stoking of furnaces." But this classical analysis erred, in his view, because workers are active consumers, not mere "machine[s] of production"; as such, what they require is "not simply food, nor even the common necessaries and comforts of life, but all that goes to [their] maintenance, . . . whatever their various levels of comfort." Covering these broader "means of subsistence," argued Böhm-Bawerk, is the true function of "wages," and wages in this sense come "not [from] a certain wage fund, provided arbitrarily by capitalist employers," but rather out of the entire "stock of wealth accumulated in a community"—its "Subsistence Fund."[60]

To Veblen, Böhm-Bawerk's case for "shifting the point of view" of economic theorists from production to consumption was specious. In making this assertion, Veblen did not mean to dismiss consumption itself as a topic for empirical research; his "Socialism" article shows otherwise. But now, in his *QJE* paper, he was writing as an economic theorist under Laughlin's watch, so consumption diminished in importance. Indeed, the central point of Veblen's article was to fault Böhm-Bawerk for elevating the theoretical significance of consumption, making a mistake in reasoning that caused him to conflate "wages"—a production cost that *is* "paid out of capital"—with "earnings," which flow more diffusely to "the laborer [because he or she is] a member of society." Veblen believed that, by differentiating these two concepts, he was offering a concession to the Austrian marginalist (by recognizing that this diffuse flow of income occurred) while still affirming the classical view that capital is the true source of wages. Self-congratulatory about this feat, Veblen judged "that Professor Böhm-Bawerk's discussion does not upset the wages-fund doctrine in any of its essential tenets," and that his own four-page Note had successfully "put at rest" the long-running controversy.[61]

As he laid out this argument, Veblen admitted he was weaving "a web of excessively fine-spun technicalities" about a slender "point of classification." But research of this kind was necessary, he said, for advancing "pure theory" in economics, and he continued along this path in the July 1892 issue of *QJE* in a Note titled "The Overproduction Fallacy." This was another attack piece; it went after Uriel Crocker, an amateur Boston economist who would probably have escaped Veblen's notice but for the fact that, in the April 1892 issue of the *QJE,* Crocker had published an attack on John Stuart Mill's earlier attack on the concept of economic overproduction. What provoked Veblen was Croker's contention that it is possible for an economy to suffer from a problem of "general overproduction," a condition in which a nation's producers, taken as a whole, produce more goods than they can sell at prices that adequately cover costs of production. In Crocker's view, this problem was endemic to modern economies because "machinery . . . has been created with a capacity of production in excess of adequate demand." He (and other writers) viewed this chronic condition as an explanation for the recurring economic crises of the late nineteenth century: falling prices, falling profits, rising unemployment, and so forth. Veblen, though, offered a different interpretation. "Hard times and commercial crises" were happening during this period: that he did not question. But rather than delve into a direct discussion of these hardships, he kept within the bounds of classical theory by arguing that the notion of "general" overproduction is "palpably absurd"; inasmuch as commodity overproduction occurs, it is a "particular" dislocation due to short-term industrial disruptions that eventually right themselves though a normal process of "readjustment." That was Mill's view and Laughlin's—and for the time being Veblen was satisfied with it.[62]

4.

Cornell University's regulations stipulated that students seeking advanced degrees had to complete "two years of graduate study." To comply, Veblen's plan, as of November 1891, was "to continue in the University until June 1893."[63] But this idea proved short-lived, and six months later he was getting ready for another move (temporarily without Ellen), this time to the University of Chicago, which was preparing for its official opening in fall 1892. So, in late May, Veblen sent a request to the secretary to the university's trustees: "I have been assigned to give a course of instruction, in the Dept. of Political Economy, and am anxious to secure rooms in time, so as to be able to enter them a little before the University opens. It would be a great favor to me to let me know what the different classes of rooms are, . . . as well as their price." (How the secretary replied is not known.)[64]

Behind this change of plan was Laughlin, who in early 1892 decided to resign from Cornell to take President William Rainey Harper's offer to found and chair the University of Chicago's department of political economy. In negotiating with Harper, Laughlin set as a condition that he would bring along three of his Cornell subordinates: Adolph Miller (the other professor in his department), William Caldwell (one of Miller's graduate students), and Veblen. The president agreed to the package deal, and the three men joined Laughlin's new department, Caldwell for one year, Miller for ten years, and Veblen for fourteen, until he was just shy of his fiftieth birthday.

A HUNDRED TIMES larger in population than Ithaca at the time, Chicago of the late nineteenth century was a city that provoked outsized reactions from contemporary observers. Arriving there in 1887, Frank Lloyd Wright (who was joining the architectural firm that was constructing the largest and one of the tallest buildings in the United States) saw the metropolis as "murderously actual," a scene of the "grinding and piling up of blind forces."[65] In 1894 John Dewey, moving to town to head the University of Chicago's philosophy department, described the city as "sheer Matter with no Standards at all"; it was "the place to make you appreciate at every turn the absolute opportunity which chaos affords."[66] Dewey's colleague in the English department, future novelist Robert Herrick, provided an international comparison, venturing that "no other city on the globe could present quite [Chicago's] combination of tawdriness, slackness, dirt, and vulgarity." Privately, Veblen may have had similar general impressions, at least if we believe Archibald Maynard, who studied with him in the 1890s and later told Dorfman that Veblen "seemed to think Chicago (the city) a horrible hodge-podge. . . . It was the confusion of things there that he seemed to dislike. He compared it to ancient Rome." What Veblen's scanty published comments about the city brought out when he was living there, however, was less Chicago's distinctiveness than how well it reflected economic changes that were underway everywhere. In *The Theory of the Leisure Class,* he called Chicago the "representative city of the advanced pecuniary culture."[67]

The city held this status, he felt, because it epitomized the era's defining economic features—pioneering them, polishing them, and parading them out on a grand scale. "The greatest railroad center in the world" (as historian William Cronon has called it), the city carried the capitalist marketplace far and wide and helped spur the rise of the corporate form of the business enterprise, along with the development of the specialized financial institutions and instruments (for example, the "futures" market) that enabled it to operate at full speed.[68] The city's landscape bore the pockmarks of stockyards and slaughterhouses, lumberyards, grain elevator warehouses, and massive steel-producing factories, all of them reliant on tens of thousands of German and Eastern European immigrants living on subsistence wages. (Second-generation Norwegians, like Veblen, were also a large presence in the city.) And Chicago's high-end retail stores, gilded theaters and hotels, lakefront mansions, and coiffed residential suburbs blared consumption as a way of life. Together, these developments erected a steep social hierarchy that extended upward from slum dwellers and unskilled day laborers, to midlevel corporate managers, advertising executives, and professionals, to titans of commerce and industry and their families. By 1890, Chicago claimed more than two hundred millionaires, six of them with wealth exceeding $10 million (= $295 million): the "predatory rich" and the "idle rich," as English journalist W. S. Stead described them (in *If Christ Came to Chicago!*) after visiting the city in the early 1890s. Writing in 1893, American novelist Henry Fuller, too, savaged "the encroachments of wealth and privilege" that Chicago's economic elites thrived on.[69]

A SPECIAL POINT OF civic pride for this aristocracy was hosting the World's Columbian Exposition of 1893, an international fair the locals mounted to celebrate the four-hundredth anniversary of Columbus's voyage to the Americas. Lavishly installed on Chicago's South Side, where it towered over the first makeshift buildings of the University of Chicago, the Exposition drew to the area more than twenty-five million spectators during its run from May to October 1893. Enticements included exhibitions of the latest technological innovations (in architecture and transportation, factory and farm machinery, munitions, entertainment, and so on) and avenues with pavilions—"vast department stores"—sponsored by many states, US territories, and foreign countries (among them, Norway).

Attached to the fairgrounds, too, were "congresses" on pressing social problems such as "Labor" and "Women," with addresses featuring prominent reformers such as Henry George, Clarence Darrow, Susan B. Anthony, and Elizabeth Cady Stanton. According to Andrew Veblen's diaries, the Veblen clan (father Thomas included) came to Chicago several times to attend events at the fair.[70]

How often Thorstein Veblen went along on these family outings is unknown; but, whatever the frequency, the Exposition provided a massive echo chamber in which elements from his long-accumulating intellectual repertoire resounded within earshot. Among the fair's final ceremonies, for instance, was a "Congress of Evolutionists," for which the planned speaker was none other than Herbert Spencer, introduced (in absentia) as the "Columbus of the new epoch." But it did not take this late session to showcase that "evolution" was the guiding conceit of the Exposition from the start; so much so that its organizers delegated much of the physical arrangement of the event to groups of professional anthropologists (of neo-Lamarckian, Spencerian, and even Darwinian temperaments). By the time the fair opened, what attendees saw before them were acres upon acres of prehistoric archeological remains; followed by dioramas of tribal artifacts (pottery, dress, weapons, entire villages); juxtaposed with forced encampments of living indigenous peoples relocated to the fairgrounds from Africa, the Pacific Islands, and several Western states. Lest anyone miss the telos, ethnologists configured this mélange to give spectators a millennial walking tour through sites signposted with the names of the "stages" of human evolution—"savage," "barbarian," and "civilized"—signaling the third stage with glistening displays of the material and cultural achievements of modern science.

The exhibitors did not render this account as a saga of the accomplishments of separate individuals. Scientific geniuses, farsighted explorers, and other stock historical heroes factored into the narrative, but chiefly as representatives of collective entities, such as societies, nations, culture areas, or (in the brutal barbarism of the age) "races"—the last depicted by anthropologists at the site using grotesque stereotypes of human beings dark and light in skin color, short and long in skull shape, indolent and industrious in everyday behavior. Daniel Brinton, head of the "Congress of Anthropology," used other holistic terms as well, speaking of how evolutionary "development proceeds rather through institutions, . . . which themselves express the emotions, convictions, and experiences of the human species." Taking in all the tropes, contemporary journalists praised the fair for bringing "the spiral of evolution" to life for Chicago's mass audiences.[71] No less for Veblen: the Exposition took ways of seeing and thinking he had been using in different academic contexts—the practice of cognizing the social world as a ceaselessly changing organic unity, and the practice of valorizing science and other productive activities—and translated them into large, three-dimensional shape.

STILL AND ALL, the Chicago Exposition was a sideshow, as men and women conscious of the economic life of the city realized very well. Four days after the fair started, the already tottering US stock market violently contracted, setting off what became the Panic of 1893 and, in due course, a brutal five-year depression—the most severe in the nation's history up to then—which forced unemployment on millions of workers, shuttered tens of thousands of businesses and banks, and blighted wide swaths of the farm sector. In Chicago, the commercial bubble (and the demand for short-term workers) generated by the Exposition temporarily mitigated the full effects of this implosion, but these hit with intensifying force as the big event wound down. By the second half of 1893, contemporaries estimated that as many as 180,000 people, upward of 40 percent of the city's labor force, were jobless, in many instances homeless, and that at least 10 percent of the population lived on the edge of starvation. What was more, in Chicago as elsewhere, even workers who held on to their jobs experienced sharp wage cuts and deteriorating work conditions.[72]

This economic meltdown swelled many currents of social unrest. During the early months of the panic, downtown Chicago became the scene of mass demonstrations by unemployed laborers, thousands of them, demanding jobs and economic assistance. Heavily covered by the press, these public outcries were minor compared with more organized forms of economic protest that had already erupted in Chicago in the early 1890s and would outlast the period of the depression. These included the growth of labor unions and a resurgence of local labor activism, trends that confirmed Chicago's prior reputation as the hotbed of disputes between capitalists and workers in the United States. These developments brought with them a renewed commitment on the part of labor leaders and union members to what George Detwiler (publisher of *Knights of Labor*, the city's leading labor newspaper) called "the great ethical proposition that society as it is presently constituted is corrupt and vicious, and that its only salvation is a complete reconstruction." He added: "In the minds of the men of labor . . . great changes are impending throughout the world."[73]

Here Detwiler sounded the language of members of Chicago's socialist movement, which had been a robust presence in the town as far back as the 1870s and became even more of one by the century's end. Tied originally to local ethnic communities (German and Scandinavian communities in particular) and sometimes faced with violent opposition in other quarters of the city, socialism commanded much wider audiences by the early 1890s, in part because of the willingness of Chicago's socialist writers and organizers to accommodate a variety of visions: everything from the revolutionary ideals of European socialists in the tradition of Karl Marx to the genteel, reform-oriented ideas of Christian socialists.[74] The latter ideas shaded over, by turns, into the social programs and policy proposals that contemporaries associated with the "Progressive Movement," or the "Progressives": a large collage of reformers who aimed to regulate predatory capitalist institutions by means of state action (antitrust measures, prolabor legislation, public ownership of utility companies, and so on), to clean up corruption and inefficiency in municipal government, and to improve living conditions and opportunities for the destitute through prohibitions against vice—through, for instance, welfare services and educational programs offered at "settlement houses." Chicago churches, philanthropies, and civic associations, often with the assistance of social scientists in the area, engaged in wide-ranging efforts to advance these projects all through the turn-of-the-century period.[75] Well aware of such activities, Veblen put his energies elsewhere.

5.

Like Johns Hopkins fifteen years earlier, the University of Chicago entered the world with extensive coverage in the nation's newspapers and magazines because of the big money and high aspirations behind it. The money came (principally) from John D. Rockefeller, the wealthiest man in the country; the aspirations came from his choice as the institution's first president, William Rainey Harper, an unpolished thirty-five-year-old professor of Semitic languages at Yale. Both Baptists, the men were connected though a group of prominent Chicago Baptists struggling to resuscitate a tiny Baptist college named the University of Chicago that had closed in 1886. But the group's hopes for another denominational college dissolved as plans took form for a new institution, incorporated in 1890 under the same name, which Rockefeller backed with a $1.6 million pledge, the first of many gifts from him that would eventually total $36 million (= roughly $1 billion). Along the way, other wealthy benefactors, mainly from the Chicago area, also chipped in handsomely, though from the start members of the press and other onlookers tagged and ridiculed the school "Rockefeller's University." When John Dewey arrived on campus in 1894, he felt the prevailing sentiment, writing to his family: "I fear Chicago Univ. is a capitalist institution—that is, it too belongs to the higher classes."[76]

Even so, money for building the institution flowed in slowly at first. In 1890, local department store magnate Marshall Field committed to the new school a ten-acre plot of land in the tony residential suburb of Hyde Park, seven miles south of downtown Chicago. But a well-equipped university, up to the standards of Harvard, Yale, and Johns Hopkins, was nowhere in sight. Coming on to the scene a few months before the university's official opening in October 1892—just when Veblen was also arriving—Robert Herrick found himself "gazing at . . . unfinished gray stone buildings scattered loosely over the immense campus which was nothing more than a quagmire with a frog pond."[77] Worse for the school, President Harper failed in his initial efforts to assemble the senior-level faculty he envisioned. His declared aim was to recruit academic stars— "eminent men . . . who had already shown their strength" and would continue to do so—but stars were hard to lure to an unbuilt school in the Midwest. So Harper repeatedly foundered until, in early 1892, he convinced Laurence Laughlin and classicist W. G. Hale to accept offers to leave Cornell for Chicago. Their acceptances encouraged luminaries in several other disciplines to follow, though only after Harper succeeded in piecing together unprecedented academic salaries—as high as $7,000 (= $205,000) a year for "head professors"—by juggling financial accounts in a way that forced him to trim elsewhere in his budget. In an era when jobs for younger academics remained in extremely short supply, however, Harper could always count on a pool of men (and women) willing, as Veblen was, to take subaltern positions at substantially lower salaries. This austerity measure allowed the University of Chicago to start off with a "faculty" of more than a hundred members.[78]

Harper's decision to prioritize the hiring of senior academic stars reflected his ambition to build nothing less than "the greatest university in the world." His goal, he told Rockefeller in 1890, was "to revolutionize university study," and his colleagues praised him for the "iconoclasm" he brought to his presidency by overhauling many already accepted higher-educational conventions.[79] (Compared with East Coast universities, the University of Chicago had a different organizational structure, a different academic timetable, and more comprehensive arrangements for extension work and professional schools; it also admitted women to both its undergraduate and graduate programs.) Fundamental to Harper's administration, nonetheless, was his dedication to the same ideal that had inspired Daniel Gilman at Hopkins and Andrew White at Cornell: the desire to advance the growth of new knowledge. Harper wanted the University of Chicago to surpass the scholarly output of these other institutions; but he shared with their presidents and faculty members the German vision of the university as a community of specialized researchers devoted to original scientific investigation in all domains of human inquiry. Harper's biographers attribute his commitment to this conception to his Yale dissertation supervisor, German-schooled philologist William Dwight Whitney, since, like Veblen, Harper did not himself study in Germany.[80]

This ideal shaped the University of Chicago from the time Harper began planning it. Extolling "science as the greatest factor in modern civilization," Harper reasoned that the university needed "to devote [its] entire energy . . . to pure science," or, in other words, "to make the work of investigation primary, the work of giving instruction secondary." In later years, he would somewhat modify this view (giving more weight to undergraduate teaching), but at the outset he was unambiguous: "The true University is the centre of thought on every problem connected with human life and work, and the first obligation resting upon the individual members which compose it, is that of research and investigation." This belief served as the theme of Harper's speeches and early reports about the university; "'research' and 'investigation,'" wrote Herrick in an 1895 account of the institution, are "words that haunt the place."[81]

Other American university executives of the era frequently made statements like these, but Harper did not stop with utterances. Having extracted from Rockefeller powers that were large even for the imperial university presidents of the late nineteenth century, Harper was able to put considerable organizational force behind his words. In order to promote specialization in scientific research, for example, he established early on what historian William Barber has described as the forward-looking "disciplinary division of labor that was lacking in older institutions," even at schools like Cornell that were starting to carve out separate departments for separate academic fields. By the time the University of Chicago opened, Harper had subdivided it into more than two dozen departmental units, including freestanding departments of political economy and history. At his institution, Harper boasted, "the organization in Departments . . . was effected more rigidly than in any other institution."[82]

Harper insisted that, at his university, the "work of investigation" meant *real work*. An irrepressible micromanager, he stipulated that men and women holding graduate fellowships (as Veblen did in his first year at Chicago) were "required to spend five-sixths of [their] time in original investigation." Further, to spur on faculty members, Harper installed seven ascending faculty ranks: reader (or assistant), associate (or tutor), instructor, assistant professor, associate professor, professor, and head professor (or chairman). He set down that the "promotion of younger men in the departments [into these ranks] will depend more largely upon the results of their work as investigators than upon the efficiency of their teaching." Still further, for continued advancement, faculty members needed to engage in "the work of production" and "to publish the results of their investigation."[83] To do any less was, in Harper's view, to undermine what the professional academic was all about. (The expression "publish or perish" dates from the 1920s, but the principle was already Harper's policy 125 years ago.)

> No man becomes a member of the University staff of whom great things are not expected. The University will be patient; for there is no greater folly . . . than that of making public what is not yet ready for the world to know. The University, I say, will be patient, but it expects from every man honest and persistent effort in the direction of contribution to the world's knowledge.[84]

With Harper reiterating this message in one speech and official bulletin after another, few University of Chicago faculty members, permanent or temporary, were unaware of what he wanted. Describing the university's early years, mathematician E. H. Moore, who also arrived on the scene the year Veblen did, recalled: "Dr. Harper made us all feel his conception of a research institution of the highest grade as the goal of our efforts."[85] In his secure position as a department chairman, Moore found this goal exhilarating, which was John Dewey's reaction too at "the chance to build up the department of philosophy [and] associate with men whose main interest is in advanced research."[86] Shailer Mathews, another 1894 arrival on campus (as an associate professor of New Testament history), wrote in his autobiography: "The air [at the University] was charged with enthusiasm and hope. On the faculty there were men who had already won distinction, [and who] set the highest standard of research and scholarship. . . . A sense of an uncompleted task faced us in the prophetic brick walls of [the unfinished] buildings . . . and in the crudities of our surroundings."[87] Reactions were more mixed, however, among men and women on the lower rungs of Harper's intricate hierarchy of academic positions. For them, the local intellectual excitement was tinged with occupational anxiety, as they watched the president dismiss, year after year, junior staff members who fell short of his work expectations.

Even with these expectations carefully spelled out, however, Harper was not one to leave "work" to run on without some additional guidance. For him, the pursuit of scientific research meant the use of "the scientific method," which he judged to be "the great triumph and the great glory of modern thought." This method, as he defined it, rested on the "observation" of facts, followed by "inductions"—"based upon these facts"—of the "principles" by which the facts operate. Research of this kind, wrote Harper, was essential in all domains of human knowledge: "The word 'science' is very broad, and scientific work, as well as scientific methods, may not be restricted to the physical and biological sciences." Indeed, in his own research, Harper (according to scholars who have studied his academic writings) "accepted unreservedly the scientific method as the only appropriate method for studying the Bible." Not only this, but like Veblen's Yale mentor George Ladd, Harper believed in "the historical evolution of the bible"; he treated the sacred text as "a profoundly historical and historicized document, anchored in the culture of a time and place, [which was] by no means [the] equivalent of nineteenth-century civilization." This holistic, evolutionary stance fit with Harper's conviction that the process of historical change constituted one of the most pressing subjects of scientific research. "The modern man," he wrote, "must know the past, must be in touch with the present, and must anticipate the future," capabilities that demand knowledge of the "stages in the evolution which have been taking place from the beginning of man's history," and which are "the result of the operation of laws of life which antedate the existence of man himself."[88]

IN PART BECAUSE OF favorable timing, Harper's university became saturated with these modes of thinking. Tasked with building his entire faculty from scratch, determined to appoint academic stars in their prime, and bent on staffing his lower ranks with younger scholars who emulated the stars, Harper could, by the early 1890s, hardly avoid hiring a large number of men and women whose intellectual practices resembled his own. In many academic fields by that time, these were the knowledge-making practices of the majority of scholars employed or educated at research universities in the United States and Europe. In this situation, it was almost inevitable that scholars in different corners of his university would ply similar intellectual tool sets.[89]

Within the School of Biology, this equipment was standard operating procedure. According to historians of science, a strong "evolutionary consensus" dominated the biological departments at the University of Chicago throughout the 1890s, when "evolutionism . . . was at the center of [the] research and teaching" of leading figures in the fields of botany, neurology, and zoology, even when they disagreed on major issues such as the mechanisms causing evolution. During this period, as well, "the study of organisms as a whole," in fluid interaction with their particular environments, united specialists from several disciplines, as part of their common effort to replace the static plant and animal classification schemes of the past with dynamic approaches to the analysis of life-forms.[90]

To cite one of the principals in this consensus, Charles O. Whitman, the German-trained chairman of the zoology department, held that the objective of the biological sciences was to investigate, by means of "observation, experiment, and reflection," the "fundamental problems of heredity, variation, adaptation, and evolution," especially those "vital processes [that are] known only in living organisms—processes which are slow and cumulative in effects, expressing themselves in development, growth, life-histories, species, habits, instincts, intelligence." (In identifying these topics, Whitman did not claim exclusive ownership; like many contemporaries, he saw "habits," "instincts," and "intelligence" as subjects large enough for sharing among zoologists, physiologists, psychologists, and others.)[91] Sometimes, argued Whitman, these "cumulative development[s]" take place in accord with Darwinian "natural laws," other times as a result of the species' "mutual dependence," including "the phenomena of symbiosis and parasitism"—phenomena he flagged as a special focus of researchers at the University of Chicago. (Whitman's renown was based in part on his studies of the *Clepsine,* a freshwater leech.) Like his colleagues, too, he drew parallels between "organic and social existence." "On the same ground that the sociologist affirms that a society is an organism," Whitman asserted, "the biologist declares that an organism is a society." The corollary of this equation, he maintained, is that "social evolution" is continuous with "organic evolution." In both spheres of life, evolution leads to increasingly complex forms of "social organization"—to a division of labor—through similar processes, which he described in familiar contemporary language: "Opportunities for the first steps in the division of labor presented themselves fortuitously, [after which its] inherent advantages . . . in the struggle for existence [secured its further growth by] the aid of natural selection."[92]

The few members of the School of Biology who ran against the grain did not diverge very far. The most voluble critic of the local consensus was Jacques Loeb, a German-born physiologist with a medical degree, who considered prevailing evolutionary and organismic approaches too superficial to produce detailed scientific knowledge of the "mechanisms of life." A friend of Veblen's—the two men met at the University of Chicago and kept in professional and personal contact for years—Loeb proudly wore the badge of an "iconoclast." Provocatively, he insisted that "all life phenomena are determined by chemical processes," or by "the chemical activity of the cell"; and he faulted the "theory of evolution" for treating the development of life-forms merely "historically," rather than on the basis of laboratory experiments on the real-time responses, or "reflexes," of animals or plants to different environmental stimuli. Loeb saw these reflexes as expressions of an organism's inherited "instincts" and "tropisms"—its hard-wired movements toward or away from stimuli of certain kinds. (Discussing the human animal, Loeb wrote, more speculatively, about which social conditions might incline an individual toward "workmanship," rather than in the direction of "wrongdoing [and] dissipation.") Through his use of these physiological arguments, Loeb broke with many biological scientists at Chicago and elsewhere; even so, he did not shed their overall intellectual outlook—their dynamic and holistic ways of perceiving and thinking. When examining instincts, for instance, Loeb dealt with how "the animal as a whole reacts" to changing environmental conditions. More broadly, he viewed his lab experiments as steps toward unpacking "processes of growth" intrinsic to life-forms and carrying the study of evolution to a more "foundational" level in order "to gain a deeper and more certain insight into the possibilities for the transformation of species beyond that which we have at present."[93]

CHICAGO'S BIOLOGICAL SCIENTISTS applied their general evolutionary views across a wide stretch of specific empirical topics. Whitman took a special interest in the behaviors of pigeons and Loeb in the gyrations of worms, while their colleagues wrote about the history of rock formations in Indiana and the flora of Texas. Nearby on campus, however, an assortment of other subjects commanded attention, as philosophers, psychologists, historians, political scientists, economists, sociologists, and anthropologists forged ahead with the project of slicing the old terrain of mental and moral philosophy into specialized academic disciplines. As producers of knowledge, nonetheless, all these specialists remained kinsmen. What counted as "knowledge," in one gray building after another, was the study of objects in perpetual motion, not at rest; the study of wholes, not separate parts; and the study of phenomena in accord with the norms of modern science, rather than the teachings of established authorities or the theories of armchair speculators. Insofar as it related to humankind, what qualified as "knowledge" also presupposed the merit of productive activity over other forms of human conduct.

In the philosophy department—which, until 1905, was a composite department of philosophy, psychology, and pedagogy—the chairman John Dewey and his lieutenants, James H. Tufts and George Herbert Mead, devoted themselves, from the mid-1890s onward, to formulating the ideas that would solidify into the Chicago school of pragmatism by the early twentieth century. These ideas centered around the novel postulate that the action of human beings (whether the action is physical, cognitive, evaluative, or a blend) takes two forms: occurring sometimes on the basis of acquired habits that enable people to achieve their purposes in routine situations, and sometimes by a productive process of problem solving, triggered by new situations in which old habits fail to perform successfully.[94] Dewey, Tufts, and Mead developed this dualist conception partly in response to traditional theories of human knowledge and the human mind and partly in fierce opposition to the one-dimensional view of human conduct they associated with classical economics. (This hostile attitude toward British economics reflected, once again, the influence of the German historical school. Tufts and Mead both did postgraduate work in Germany, while Dewey, like Veblen, studied at Hopkins with Germanist George S. Morris).[95]

Considering economists' assumptions about human nature, Dewey, for example, held that "such impulses as love of gain . . . are pure abstractions" that hide the complexity of conduct in the real world. On his account, human actions exhibit great "range and variety," veering sometimes in "selfish" directions, but springing other times from "disinterestedness," as in the instance of hard-driving scientific researchers animated by pure "curiosity" and a "love of knowledge." What is more, according to Dewey, even actions that may look egoistic frequently have larger purposes: "The man's desire for food"—one of economists' favorite examples of self-interest—"has reference to his desire . . . to support his family, to gain a recognized position, to contribute to society." In this way, "interests . . . are social in their very nature." Consequently, understanding them demands "a more organic view of the individual and of society than is logically possible" on the basis of utilitarian and hedonistic conceptions about action. Without breaking loose from these antiquated theoretical straight-jackets, wrote Tufts, a discipline like "psychology is limited to the study of that mythical being [of "individual man"]—its field . . . so narrow as to be scarcely worth tilling."[96]

But break loose from these theories is what Dewey, Tufts, and Mead did, hammering away at them with the interlocked concepts of "social institutions" and "evolution." Three years before moving to Chicago, Dewey was already laying the groundwork, observing that every "individual" is "constituted by its relations and formed by its institutions"; that not only is "the child . . . born as a member of a family" but he or she also quickly runs "upon the institution of property" and "finds the political institutions," the "educational institutions," and the "religious institutions" of his or her society, encountering "everywhere [men and women who are expressing] common wants and proposing common ends and using cooperative modes of action." For Dewey and his Chicago colleagues, moreover, these social arrangements were in perpetual flux. They were moving pieces in an ages-long evolutionary process that occurs (for the most part) according to Darwinian laws, as amended in the case of the human species because the "environment is now distinctly a social one," "fitness" a matter of "social adaptation" to particular historical circumstances. Seen in this light, Dewey continued, the "struggle for existence" involves a contest among different "social structures" and "forms of action," along with the "selection" and "survival" of those best fit for "maintaining the institutions which have come down to us, while we make over these institutions so that they serve under changing conditions."[97]

In similar language, the three Chicago philosophers described the "evolution of morality," the "evolution of the self," the "evolution of mind," and even the "evolution of logic." The last topic provided a natural segue to examine, as well, the development of the modern evolutionary sciences and to extol the superiority of scientific research methods over older, static ways of knowing nature and society. Dewey put the point succinctly, remarking that the "statements arrived at by experimental science are of an historical order; they take their rise in, and they find their application to, a world of unique and changing things: an evolutionary universe."[98]

From the standpoint of American intellectual history, the philosophy department at Chicago was in a league of its own. To this day, the ideas of John Dewey and his pragmatist colleagues remain subjects of academic and popular interest, while the names of most faculty members from the university's social science departments have been long forgotten. During Veblen's own time there, however, Chicago's social scientists stood in high esteem on and off campus, fully aligned with the philosophers' and the biologists' views about the requisites of knowledge.

The largest social science department was the combined department of sociology and anthropology, which was one of Harper's personal favorites, since it gave the University of Chicago a competitive edge over peer institutions.[99] (East Coast research universities were slower to grant departmental status to the oddity of "sociology.") To helm the department, Harper hired Albion W. Small, the sitting president of Colby College in Maine. A historian trained in Germany and at Johns Hopkins (under Veblen's early mentor Herbert Baxter Adams), Small produced during the 1890s a substantial body of work that revolved around the usual indictments of the classical English economists: excoriating the concept of "economic man" for reducing the whole "sum of human pursuits and interests" to the "desire for wealth" alone; and chiding proponents of "abstract economics" for neglecting "actual conditions" in the social world. As an alternative to this approach, Small defended (as if on cue) an "organic concept of society" and the claim that individuals stand in myriad "social relations" as a result of "institutional phenomena," including the "traditions, beliefs, and aims" prevalent in their societies. So far, so pat; but Small then elaborated his critique of economics by explaining that "in our age, the fact of human association is more obtrusively and relatively more influential than in any previous epoch," as the result of changes occurring in the economic sector itself, among them basic changes in "processes of production and consumption." Because of these transformations, "the world of the living Rothschilds and Morgans, Carnegies and Vanderbilts, the world of railroad systems, [and of] trusts and trade unions, is a world in which Adam Smith would not readily find himself"—and one he would not find easy to understand.[100]

Other sociologists on Small's faculty, such as Charles R. Henderson and George E. Vincent, rehearsed these notes at every opportunity. In their popular 1894 text *The Study of Sociology,* for instance, Small and Vincent spelled out how "ideas of the social organism [are] fundamental" to "the study of society," which calls out for the analysis of modern-day "economic institutions" (such as property ownership arrangements, industries, stock exchanges, and banks), side by side with the "institutions of sociability," "ecclesiastical institutions," "educational institutions," "aesthetic institutions," "punitive institutions"—and even "institutions of vice." Probing these in detail, Small said, would enable sociologists to texturize their broad and necessary "generalizations" about human societies with a "precise knowledge of particulars" about specific cases.[101]

In alluding to these necessary generalizations, Small had in mind the laws of "social evolution." These, in his view, demonstrated unequivocally that "the social body 'grows,' [and that] society exhibits a real . . . process of development"—something else Older School economists overlooked, according to his indictment. Small and his colleagues were more ambiguous, however, as to how evolutionary development took place. Mostly, they vacillated between softened Darwinian explanations (for example, the notion of "cooperative" struggles for survival) and well-worn teleological accounts, showing a fondness for accounts that conjured up a future where social scientists would take a lead role in shaping the direction of societal development. These comparatively small differences aside, though, no one on Small's faculty doubted that societies had been evolving since the dawn of time and were still in the thick of doing so.[102]

Occupied with analyzing the historical era that was unfolding immediately in front of them, Small and his fellow sociologists willingly ceded the study of earlier evolutionary epochs to the anthropological wing of their department. This was then in the hands of two scholars with whom Thorstein Veblen became good friends: Frederick Starr and William I. Thomas. Both prolific authors, the two men were also vintage late nineteenth-century comparative ethnologists, locked into the convention of differentiating—and racializing—societies as "savage," "barbarian," and "civilized," and persuaded that these societal types constituted "stages" in a worldwide evolutionary process.[103]

Between the two, Starr had the broader range. His work sought to encompass the historical development of everything from basket weaving to religion, though he gave heaviest emphasis to changes in weaponry, property ownership, and body coverings—or what he liked to call "dress."

In a protest against the economists' view of clothing as a simple, utilitarian response to an individual's "wish to protect [him- or her-] self against weather and harm," Starr proposed that dress is primarily a social form of "adornment," "ornament," and "display." That is to say, dress constitutes a set of "trophies" that serves "to mark a man from his fellows as one who has done what others had not accomplished"; as such, it functions as a "mark of social inequality [that] will exist wherever class distinctions are recognized."[104]

William I. Thomas's writings addressed some of these same subjects, which he liked to associate with a body of research popular in Germany under the name of "folk psychology" (a term Veblen quickly picked up). A student of Jacques Loeb, as well as of Starr, Thomas maintained that "the first expressions of [human] culture . . . are incidental accompaniments of physiological desires [for] nutrition and reproduction." He invoked Darwinian terminology (more insistently than other members of his department did) to describe how these two "instincts" triggered a struggle for existence among primitive tribes, which was followed by the emergence of different customs and, after that, by the "natural selection" of those folkways that enabled tribes to adapt and survive. Thomas showed a particular fascination with the effects of customs such as bride capture and bride purchase on the debased status of women in savage and barbarian societies.[105] From these phenomena, he expanded outward to argue "that our customs, our laws, our arts, our religion, our speech, our minds, are the product of society in common, and that through a comparative examination of the languages, ceremonies, usages, and institutions of primitive peoples, we have means . . . of tracing the laws of the progressive unfolding of the psychical activities of man."[106] In this vein, Thomas held, along with Starr, that it was time for anthropologists to copy the example of nineteenth-century biologists and go beyond merely "classify[ing]" ethnological materials to build a "science" of the "laws of growth" as they relate to the "institutions and usages" of human societies.[107]

IF THE ASPIRATION TO create new scientific knowledge set the dominant tone for the new University of Chicago, the school had other ambitions too. According to Harper, modern universities possessed a unique capacity to serve as a "guide of the people and an ally of humanity in its struggle for advancement," for the fundamental reason that "the truth in any line of thought already known, if practically applied, will contribute greatly to the betterment of life and thought." Imbued with this conviction, Harper opened the university's doors with a freestanding "Extension Division," which offered evening and Saturday lecture courses, as well as correspondence courses, for working men and women throughout the city; in addition, he took an energetic part in more than a dozen local organizations for social reform. The same commitment to the university's public mission was broadly (though not universally) shared among members of his faculty, even as they otherwise differed in their political stances, which ranged across the political spectrum but generally leaned toward some form of Progressivism. With tacit, if not explicit, approval from Harper, scholars in all divisions of the university took an active role in many of Chicago's reform-oriented movements and associations.[108]

All the same, as a consequence of a tangled personnel case that drew heavy attention in the city's newspapers in 1894 and 1895, the University of Chicago had, for many years, a tainted reputation for siding ideologically with the barons of American capitalism, just as the public had expected members of Rockefeller's University to do. The case involved Edward Bemis, an associate professor in the Extension Division and adjunct in the departments of political economy and sociology. As Harper knew when he recruited him in 1892, Bemis was an economist of the Younger School—that is why Harper wanted to bring him on board. Bemis, in fact, had already published articles criticizing corporate monopolies and advocating public ownership of utility companies. (A classmate of Veblen's at Hopkins in 1881, Bemis was a disciple of Richard Ely.) By January 1894, however, Harper, the cost-conscious administrator, had become discouraged because of low student enrollments in Bemis's Extension Division courses, so he suggested that Bemis resign. When Bemis refused, Harper induced him to cooperate by allowing him to remain on the Chicago faculty for two more years while he looked for another job.[109]

By historical coincidence, Harper's request came just before the eruption of a jolting set of events that caused many Americans to believe their country was careening toward open class warfare. This jolt was the Pullman strike and boycott, which occurred within a few miles of the University of Chicago in summer 1894, as part of the surge of social protest unleashed by the Panic of 1893. The protest began when the Pullman Palace Car Company, a manufacturer of deluxe railway cars, imposed a nearly 30 percent wage cut on workers at its Chicago-based factory. Hit hard, workers tried to talk company executives into a compromise, but management would not yield. So, in May 1894, workers walked off their jobs, soon gaining support in huge numbers (eventually in the tens of thousands) from unionized railroad workers in Chicago and elsewhere, who joined the cause by refusing to work on trains that had Pullman cars attached to them. This action paralyzed service on some twenty of the nation's railways, leading President Grover Cleveland to send federal troops to Chicago, where violent, sometimes deadly, street confrontations—involving thousands of soldiers, workers, and sympathizers—broke out for several days, until the militia forced an end to the boycott in mid-July 1894.[110]

Throughout these events, most University of Chicago faculty members looked on nervously from their offices. But Bemis decided to give a public address in which he hurled a few (mild) criticisms at the railroads. Immediately, railroad owners made their displeasure known to the university's trustees, and a few days later Harper rebuked Bemis, warning him to "exercise great care in public utterances about questions that are agitating the minds of the people." Bemis chafed at this, egging on local newspapers when they sought to tie his public critique of the railroads to Harper's demand for his resignation. Angry recriminations then flew back and forth, as the press pitted Bemis and his supporters against Harper and his defenders, portraying Bemis as a martyr to Harper's interest in placating "rich plunderers." Historians have long debated who was in the right and who was in the wrong.[111]

This moot historical question aside, few faculty members at the university interpreted the Bemis affair as a signal they needed to hide their own opinions, for on most days of the year their president was sending signals to the contrary.[112] These reflected Harper's preeminence as one the country's staunchest proponents of academic freedom. While the Bemis drama was still unfolding, for example, Harper articulated the principle that "serious injury will be done to the cause of higher education if . . . there is not the largest freedom of expression—a freedom entirely unhampered by either theological or monetary considerations." In the years ahead, even after public suspicion of his personnel decisions had relaxed, he continued to insist that "the greatest single element necessary for the cultivation of the academic spirit is the feeling of security from interference. . . . Freedom of expression must be given the members of a university faculty even though it be abused, for . . . the abuse of it is not so great an evil as the restriction of such liberty."[113]

In this climate, faculty members at the university did not generally hold back from expressing their discontents and anxieties about the economic status quo. In a campus address at the height of the Bemis affair, for instance, historian Harry Pratt Judson, starchy chairman of the political science department (and later president of the university), spoke up about the "tyranny of aggregated wealth" and "the public be damned" attitude of "great captain[s] of industry" who drive the "soulless corporation": an institution that often resembles "an express train [when it] thunders over the shrinking form of a child who has fallen on the tracks, [and crushes] remorselessly the quivering flesh and the tender bones."[114] Taking a different tack, Shailer Mathews from the Divinity School interpreted the teachings of Jesus as a rejection of "an atomistic, self-centered moral life" and a "denunciation . . . of those men who make wealth at the expense of souls; who find in capital no incentive to further fraternity; who endeavor to use wealth as to make themselves independent of social obligations and to grow fat with that which should be shared with society."[115] For Charles Henderson, as for other sociologists at the university, "great corporations [were] a dark blot on the history of th[e] century," part of the shameful chronicle of "the idle rich"—and other "social parasites"—who live off the "toil of other people."[116] Or, as Small and Vincent put it: "there are idle rich men and women who, by virtue of inheritance, landownership, and other socially sanctioned arrangements are receiving large shares of wealth, for which they make little or no return to society"; their lives are "attempts to 'get something for nothing'" using the latest techniques for "stealing, robbing, and fraud."[117] Even William Rainey Harper sounded alarms. Estimating the future prospects of modern democracy, he opined (in some of his most tortured prose) that "the most interesting problem, perhaps, that confronts the future of democracy is the question: How will she adjust herself to men of wealth," particularly when the "number of wealthy men increases every decade"? The answer, he asserted, depends on the "spirit" with which wealthy men conduct their economic activities. Historically speaking, said Harper, "wherever the industrial spirit has prevailed, as opposed to the predatory, [the] evolution [of democratic institution has continued] and will continue until it includes within its grasp the entire world." When the predatory spirit has dominated economic life, however, democracy has fallen victim.[118]

TO ANYONE AT THE University of Chicago even slightly tuned into the local surroundings, these ways of making sense of the world were palpable. Evolutionism, holism, veneration of science, and a high appraisal of work-oriented activities. One did not have to sit down and read articles by members of the faculty to figure out that these intellectual tools were the instruments the majority of these scholars were using in their research (and exemplifying in their teaching). Harper let all this be known—he was not a subtle man. Advertisement was his gift, and he kept the university's printing presses running at full capacity, turning out one announcement and newsletter after another about the intellectual life of the institution: the *Official Bulletin,* the *Quarterly Calendar,* the *Annual Register,* and the *University Record,* as well as numerous less regular publications.[119]

Picking up any of these, a reader from the mid-1890s would immediately sense the prevalence of holistic ways of seeing. In a campus address abstracted in the *University Record,* for instance, Thomas Chamberlin (of the geology department), spoke of how scientists "are coming to realize, as never before, the intimate dependencies and interaction of all things upon each other, not simply of the living upon the living, nor of the so-called nonliving upon the so-called dead, but of every kind on every kind." In another abstract, Hermann von Holst (of the history department) described "the individual being [as] an organic component part of the people as a social body and a body politic"; while, in yet another, John Dewey depicted the primary school "as a social and political institution, [whose] history . . . correlates with the history of other institutions, [as part of] an organic record of the intellectual development of humanity." This theme recurred when department chairs were called on to describe their departments in the *Annual Register.* Here the social science departments focused their mission statements not on the study of atomized individuals but on the study of collective entities: "great movements and institutions" (history department), "political institutions" (political science department), and "social institutions" (department of sociology and anthropology).[120]

In plain sight, too, for anyone perusing university news sources, was the massive presence on campus of evolutionary science. To cite only a few examples: notices regularly appeared for courses with titles such as The Evolution of Morality, The Philosophy of Evolution, and Plant Evolution, as well as for a course, General Biology, that dealt with "evolution, heredity, variation, parasitism and symbiosis." Further, there were advertisements for campus addresses by researchers from both inside the university and elsewhere who were studying different facets of evolution. Looking at the list of local speakers, a reader could spot a talk by Charles Whitman titled "The Evolution of the Wing-bars of Pigeons" and one by Norman Wyld (of the zoology department), "Some Present Aspects of the

Theory of Evolution"—an address that held, approvingly, that "the essence of Darwinism is [its] insistence on the effects of the natural selection and elimination of the least fitted." Among speakers from outside the university, one could find British psychologist C. L. Morgan presenting "Habits and Instinct, a Study of Heredity," French Nobelist Henri Moissan describing "The Evolution of the Diamond," and *Chicago Tribune* writer Sherwin Cody speculating about "The Evolution of the Novel." In addition, one would be inundated with paeans to the hard work of scientists: perhaps by George Goodale (Bowdoin College botanist) enthusing about how scientific laws are formulated on the basis of painstaking inductive research; perhaps by Camillo von Klenze (of the German Department) extolling "scientific curiosity" and that "science (including the historical sciences) daily increases our intellectual maturity and insight, and invents or discovers physical and ethical antidotes and remedies."[121]

University of Chicago faculty members hardly needed Harper's constant stream of newsletters and other promotional materials to measure the local pulse. The faculty of the 1890s was relatively small and tightly packed into a few buildings; practically everyone knew who was who and what research projects, courses, public addresses, and so forth were going on at the university. When *Popular Science Monthly* ran an article in 1897 on "Science at the University of Chicago," Veblen's friend Frederick Starr, although not a natural scientist himself, supplied the text, describing in granular detail the research underway in zoology, botany, physiology, geology, physics, experimental psychology, and several other fields. And when Andrew Veblen visited Thorstein in Chicago during these years (as he often did), he took note that his brother "knew most of the men [at the university] fairly well" and "talked a good deal" about them. Within just a few steps of Thorstein Veblen's office in Cobb Hall were the offices of James Tufts, Albion Small, Charles Henderson, Harry Pratt Judson, and Hermann von Holst, as well as Starr.[122]

This milieu was the backdrop of Veblen's professional life for thousands and thousands of hours. From 1892 to 1906, it was what he observed when he stepped back from his own academic field and saw what knowledge looked like in other fields at the university. By the time Veblen arrived in Hyde Park, of course, the knowledge practices prevalent at the University of Chicago were nothing new to him. He had already been using them for years as he worked alongside his mentors at Carleton, Johns Hopkins, Yale, and Cornell. With all this past experience, it is not likely that his contacts with Chicago's biologists, philosophers, sociologists, or anthropologists significantly changed his basic intellectual modus operandi—although interaction with these scholars did expand his storehouse of information about subjects such as tropisms, habits, dress, marriage customs, and social institutions. By the same token, Veblen's Chicago colleagues presented no resistance or opposition to the practices he had been accustomed to, so he did not have to retrain and retool to adjust to the local environment. Just the opposite: the university was set up to exert a booster effect on Veblen through the process of repetition-with-variation. Not only were faculty members in many different fields around the university using a knowledge-making repertoire much like the one Veblen had been practicing for years, but they were continually transposing it to fit new situations and adapting, rejiggering, and stretching it to serve new purposes. When Veblen did the same, he was in good local company.

6.

While he was studying at Cornell in 1891, Thorstein Veblen had set his sights on pursuing a career in political economy; and during his first half-dozen years at the University of Chicago, he transitioned from an entry-level neophyte into a full-fledged member of the field. By the late 1890s, he was an accomplished teacher of economics, a well-known contributor to some of its leading subfields, and an active member of his profession. Reaching age forty, his intellectual world was then, first and foremost, the world of late nineteenth-century American economics.

When Veblen arrived in Chicago, he did not envision what was in store. Starting out, he was still Laurence Laughlin's graduate student, only now with the title of "Senior Fellow"—and an annual stipend of $520 (=$15,200).[123] President Harper, following his policy of monitoring the work of graduate fellows, kept a close eye on Veblen's research and teaching, and the two of them had occasional side dealings as well. Before he left Ithaca, for example, Veblen informed Harper that he had finished eighty-seven hours of freelance work for him, preparing what he referred to as a "ms. on 'Salaries'"; for this, Veblen charged the president $34.80 (=$1,020), amiably telling him that he "expect[ed] to be paid for the work only in case you find it answers your purposes." Less courteously, Veblen wrote Harper the following summer (July 1893) to say he was backing out of an agreement to produce lessons for a "correspondence course ... in the Elements of Political Economy" in the Extension

Division, because he felt Harper was underpaying him for taking on this extra assignment. (The episode presaged a more serious quarrel between the two men over Veblen's salary two years later.)[124]

These incidental activities were unrelated, however, to the work Harper expected out of Veblen as the holder of a graduate fellowship in political economy. This work involved (among other things) taking courses in the department of political economy; so during the fall and winter quarters of the 1892–1893 academic year, Veblen continued to train with Laughlin, resuming with one of the two subfields he had minored in at Cornell. In January 1893, he described to Harper that, besides his other projects, he was then "occupied [with] a study of Socialism, under Professor Laughlin's direction, preparatory to giving a course of instruction in the university this coming quarter."[125] (That would have been spring quarter 1893, though, because of logistical complications, Veblen did not actually teach the course until winter quarter 1894.) This goal, as Veblen was probably aware, fit with Harper's plan to have the political economy department regularly offer a course on socialism.[126]

Laughlin, too, supported the idea of having Veblen teach such a course; for, like Harper, he wanted Chicago's department of political economy to stand apart from its competitors elsewhere by providing a wide assortment of courses taught by a staff with inclusive intellectual interests. When Harper originally designed the department, his intention was to bring together scholars from both the classical and the German historical schools of political economy; in fact, before he offered the department chairmanship to Laughlin, devoted member of the Old School, he came close to offering it to Richard Ely, acolyte of the Younger School. Regardless, once Laughlin took up his duties at Chicago, he too was quickly drawn toward Harper's more catholic conception of an economics department, announcing, as early as 1892, that one of the "chief" aims of his program would be "to foster a judicial spirit" among different approaches to the study of political economy.[127]

Whether Harper and Laughlin achieved this ideal over the long run has been the subject of debate among historians of economics. Observers on the scene during the 1890s, however, scored the efforts of the two men a definite success, praising the "diversity of outlook [that] characterized the department of economics" as a site of teaching and research.[128] While at Chicago, this was the outlook Veblen regularly encountered as he became involved, more and more deeply, in the internal life of the political economy department following an accelerated change in his academic status: the end of his limbo-life as a graduate student and the start of his professional career as a faculty member. This transition—which Veblen had been hoping for since he registered in the graduate program at Hopkins a decade earlier—took place in summer 1893, when President Harper promoted him from the position of senior fellow to the junior faculty rank of reader. (The promotion carried a raise of $80 [= $2,400], enough to bring Ellen to Chicago and support her.)[129] Because of Harper's and Laughlin's efforts to maintain a pluralistic department of economics, Veblen spent his years on the Chicago faculty among economists whose writings and courses cut across the partisan divisions of fin de siècle economics. Nonsectarians (for the most part), these colleagues did not require him to conform to any particular economic creed, let alone to the doctrines of classical economics. To the contrary, in their own work they drove home to him many of the same intellectual practices he brought with him to Chicago and was now witnessing in other departments of the university.

This was another instance where historical circumstances worked in favor of the development of Veblen's economics. During the early 1890s, most American universities did not have economics departments that were hubs of faculty research activity. Yet, at the University of Chicago, Laughlin refused to settle for anything less, as he made explicit to Harper when he began staffing his department.[130] In the late nineteenth century, however, staffing a department with researchers almost invariably involved (as I noted earlier) appointing young scholars who carried strains of evolutionism and organicism, as well as a deep commitment to the project of science—and Laughlin had a lot of appointments to make. Because of Harper's policy of bringing people onto the faculty in low-level positions, at low salaries, and with slim chances of promotion, faculty turnover was a chronic problem. In the department of political economy, departures and arrivals occurred annually; between 1892 and the end of the century, fourteen different men (not counting Veblen) held faculty positions there. An administrative headache for Laughlin, this heavy turnover also meant that Veblen not only had colleagues in step with his own ways of thinking but also encountered successive cohorts of short-term appointees of similar makeup—each reinforcing the ideas of previous cohorts, as well as the ideas of the corps of permanent department members.

Among the temporary employees, most relevant for Veblen was Carlos Closson, a master's degree holder from Harvard, who taught economics at the university in 1894 and 1895 and also produced a body of research Veblen tracked for several years afterward. This research related to Veblen's interest in ethnology; what especially appealed to him was Closson's effort to extend Darwinian evolutionary laws of natural selection to cover the process of "social selection" that had occurred among different European racial "stocks." These Closson classified using contemporary anthropological terminology, such as "dolichocephalic blond," a stock indigenous to Germany, Scandinavia, and the British Isles; and "brachycephalic," a stock native to other areas of Europe. Associated with each of these "races," argued Closson, was a different "psychological character," such that dolichocephalic-blond ethnic groups were "more active," "more enterprising," and "more self-reliant" as compared with "more passive" brachycephalic groups. This association, according to Closson's reasoning, dealt a severe blow to classical economics by demonstrating that the attributes of "economic man" were not universal but race specific; or, in other words, that "the economic efficiency of a population is largely dependent on its ethnic composition, that concretely an advanced stage of industry and great wealth-producing capacity are characteristic of populations in which [the dolichocephalic element] forms the predominant, or at least the controlling element."[131]

Besides its short-term appointees (and Veblen), Chicago's department of political economy had three continuing members, all of them men with whom Veblen stayed on good terms and to whom he turned for letters of recommendation in later years. (All three obliged with glowing letters.) These were Laughlin himself; Adolph Miller, who became a professor of finance following his move from Cornell to Chicago; and William Hill, another Harvard master's degree holder, who entered the department as an tutor in 1892 and inched up the faculty ladder until his departure from the university two decades later.

During their years together with Veblen, none of the three men fit the standard profile of a classical economist. Laughlin held most loyally to Older School tenets, but even he explicitly pulled back from defending the theoretical principles of John Stuart Mill to devote his energies to research on economic topics of the day, including the institutions of money and credit. Laughlin's strong interest in contemporary institutions (rather than in whether an economist passed a litmus test for theoretical orthodoxy) was actually what motivated him to hire Miller and Hill: Hill because he specialized in the study of railroads, and Miller because of his research on national finance and taxation. All three scholars shared, moreover, the conviction that these economic institutions were historical products, features of the evolving entity they called the "present industrial system." Miller illustrated this point when he discussed the temporal "relativity of the idea of capital" and the historical fact that, "like every other process of social life, [methods of taxation have] been a product of slow growth." What was more, according to all three economists, "slow growth" involved, under modern conditions, class conflicts that pitted workers, who were denied the advantages of the capitalist system, against capitalists, who benefited from the system because of their "unscrupulous pursuit of wealth" (Miller), their use of "shrewd promoters and financiers" (Hill), and their acts of "political brigandage" (Laughlin). This picture of the status quo led the threesome to disavow socialism, at the same time as they hoped to tame the predatory aspects of capitalism through social reform measures, such as the social settlement houses Laughlin set up on Chicago's South Side.[132]

For Laughlin, Miller, and Hill, understanding the modern industrial economy demanded that economists pay more attention to the phenomenon of economic consumption. In this, the Chicagoans converged with exponents of the marginal utility theory of value (which I described earlier), although their reaction to marginalism was otherwise split, with Laughlin remaining hostile to the new approach and Miller more appreciative of its importance. Yet they all made consumption a topic in their research. Laughlin, for example, analyzed "the shifting and unreliable whims of fashion" among women, while Miller examined national taxation methods as the foundation for "the consumption of the State." Throughout their work, furthermore, the trio held fast to the view that, like the natural sciences, economics should aim to build explanatory theories—although all three warned against tendency of economists to give "too much attention to the abstract and general and not enough to the concrete and particular" (as Miller put the point in 1897).[133]

THE CURRICULUM LAUGHLIN set up for the political economy department covered both sides of the picture. Organized to furnish "a complete training . . . over the whole field of economics," the program had two components. The first consisted of "theoretical courses," which dealt with "economic principles and their historical development"; the second was coursework on "practical economics"—Laughlin's catchall for courses on "descriptive topics," such as "transportation, agriculture, public finance, banking, [and] monetary systems," along with courses on "statistics" (or "the collection of facts and the weighing of evidence"). As the department taskmaster, Laughlin expected most faculty members to offer courses in both categories, as well as to update them to include recent theories and empirical evidence. For much of the 1890s, for example, Veblen taught Problems of American Agriculture, a "practical" course, and Socialism, one of the department's five designated "theory" courses. Colleagues and students regarded these two courses as "his," although, as short-term faculty members came and went in the second half of the decade, Laughlin handed over to Veblen three more of the theory courses: Scope and Method of Political Economy, History of Political Economy, and Economic Factors in Civilization. Laughlin clearly valued Veblen's teaching, telling Stanford president David Starr Jordan in 1899 that Veblen "has given the courses on Socialism here [at Chicago] with a breadth, depth, and discretion that have always commanded admiration. . . . I might say much the same of other topics which he has taught here for seven years. And he gets a great deal of work out of all his students, keeping also a close personal relationship with them."[134]

Of these five, the Socialism course has left us the fullest paper trail in the lecture notes of Sarah McLean Hardy, a graduate student who took the two-part course when Veblen launched it in the winter and spring quarters of 1894. This dating places the course roughly fifteen months after his move to Chicago and suggests it was probably his first teaching assignment at the university. Hardy's notes show that, at this early point in his professional career, Veblen was already a skilled economic knowledge maker: confronting a new task—the job of teaching graduate students and advanced undergraduates about "recent socialistic developments"—he reached for and applied tools he had learned to use in previous situations. In a purposeful departure from many existing ways of thinking about socialism, for instance, Veblen's lectures presented the phenomenon in holistic and evolutionary terms. Socialism was, he informed his students, a "social institution" that aims for the "deliberate, conscious control of industrial functions by the community in its corporate capacity"—a social institution that is a "matter of growth" and that will emerge, if at all, only through "a process of evolution" that unfolds according to Darwinian principles. Set in this dawning light, he continued, the prospects of socialism belong among those "econ questions [that are] questions of evolution, of social natural selection," because "all econ & Indus. Institutions = a question of natural selection."[135]

Veblen conveyed this way of thinking in all his other courses too, underscoring the dynamic aspect of his subject, whatever it happened to be.

According to published course descriptions, Problems of American Agriculture centered on the "changing conditions of agriculture"; Scope and Method of Political Economy on the "origin and development" of different schools of economic thought; and Economic Factors in Civilization on "the origin of some phases of our present Industrial System," including "the Teutonic invasion of Europe, the Roman land system, the Feudal system, the rise of commerce, [and] the history of the condition of laborers, processes of production, and changes in consumption."[136] And there were many points of overlap between the substance of these courses and the content of Veblen's scholarly publications, although it is an open question whether his teaching or his scholarship took temporal precedence in the development of his ideas during the 1890s. As with most academics, then and now, the two activities likely influenced each other. All the same, insofar as sufficient documentary evidence exists to allow for chronological dating, it appears that Veblen's lectures—except for his course American Agriculture—preceded his writings on topics where the two sources correspond.[137]

LIKE ACADEMICS OF more recent times, Veblen also had organizational responsibilities. (Harper and Laughlin made sure the professional academic came into the world with plenty to do.) Some of these were light. For several years after it opened, the University of Chicago had a skeletal centralized library; although the research of faculty members (outside the natural sciences) remained mostly library-based, library materials were located mainly in separate departmental libraries. These were overseen by department members, and in his first year at Chicago, Veblen served as his department's "attendant" for the History, Political Science, Social Science, and Political Economy Library—an ideal assignment for a voracious reader. In addition, he took part in the Political Economy Club, a colloquium where faculty members, graduate students, and speakers from outside the university regularly gathered to present and discuss papers about recent research in economics. As a result of his role in the club, Veblen was also the official department delegate to the University Union, where representatives of some twenty departmental clubs met for similar purposes. Although none of these activities was especially time-consuming by itself, in combination they functioned to deepen Veblen's involvement in his local intellectual surroundings, as well as his immersion in some of the bigger debates about science, history, and society that were ongoing in the field of political economy and neighboring disciplines.[138]

Much more engrossing of his energies, however, were his obligations at the *Journal of Political Economy* (*JPE*), which was another brainchild of Harper's. Believing the goal of scholars was to discover new knowledge and then to disseminate it, Harper expected every department at his university to provide a vehicle for publishing scientific research in its field, and once again Laughlin was quick to do what the president wanted. In December 1892, he brought out the first issue of the *JPE*, dedicating the new quarterly to topics in "practical economics," while also agreeing to consider articles on economic theory that came his way. (Here Laughlin was offering a compromise to his former colleagues at Harvard's *QJE*; by allowing them first dibs on theoretical articles, he sought to stake for the *JPE* the "free field" of research on "practical economic problems.")[139] As head of his department, Laughlin became the titular editor of the journal, which he assured Harper would be open to authors "of any shade of economic belief, who can present their results in the ablest and most meritorious way."[140] After setting down the *JPE*'s mission and policies, however, Laughlin's interest in the day-to-day job of a journal editor waned (Harper had him busy on other fronts), and he increasingly gave it over to Veblen. While still a graduate student fellow, Veblen became the journal's "working editor," according to an eyewitness account by Robert Morss Lovett, Veblen's novelist colleague from the English department, who would "meet him on his way to his chief's sanctum [Laughlin's office], a long, lean, cadaverous figure" marching off to his editorial duties. The next year (1894–1895), this de facto arrangement expanded further into the official position of managing editor, by which point Veblen was largely running the journal, as Andrew Veblen explained to Dorfman: "Though [Thorstein] was Managing Editor of the Journal of Pol. Economy, I gathered that he was virtually in entire charge, and did practically all the work of editing. I often talked with him about this work, and I feel sure I understood the matter." Veblen continued in this capacity until at least 1904, although along the way his colleagues and correspondents (and he himself) often dropped "Managing" in favor of simply "Editor."[141]

Regardless of its title, the task was immense, dwarfing the work of most editors of academic journals in our own time. Under Veblen's editorship, the *JPE* published some fifty articles and Notes each year, plus roughly the same number of book reviews, and Veblen orchestrated the process. Authors corresponded with him to float ideas and get his go-ahead for articles and Notes; he advised them on their manuscripts; he personally solicited book reviews; and when short of material to publish, he wrote articles and Notes as well. (In this era, journals often paid authors a small sum for publishing their articles; and at *JPE*, Veblen also decided, on a case-by-case basis, whether authors would receive $25, $30, or another sum for their contribution.) These activities kept Veblen in regular communication, for more than a decade, with a wide range of American and European economists—famous figures and little-known ones—and gave him a position of almost unrivaled professional centrality. Indeed, as compared with Veblen, most fin de siècle economists were isolated from one another. Occasionally, they might attend the annual convention of the American Economic Association; but without today's whirlwind of academic conferences and deluge of electronic communications, the majority had relatively limited interaction with other men and women in the discipline. Exceptions were few: elected officers of the American Economic Association, chairmen of large departments, editors of the few other extant economics journals. In the 1890s (as since), well-established scholars usually held these positions, so rookie Veblen was highly unusual. Taking on the managing editorship of the *JPE* shortly after he joined the University of Chicago faculty brought him extensive contacts with economists nationally and internationally when he was still a junior member of the field.[142]

Even more, the job engulfed him in the intellectual life of the field at its theoretical and empirical ends both. Just as Laughlin envisioned, articles concerned with theoretical issues continued to appear primarily in the *QJE*. But the *JPE* still garnered a good number of these, publishing during Veblen's tenure articles by several leading figures in the debate over marginal utility theory—among them his former teacher John Bates Clark, the Italian marginalist Vilfredo Pareto, and the English antimarginalist Joseph Nicholson—plus papers by neophytes (all connected to the University of Chicago) with a range of views on the theory. These pieces included Langworthy Taylor's analysis of marginalist assumptions about "economic man," Henry Stuart's attack on the "hedonistic" premises of the new theory, and Herbert Davenport's friendly effort to reformulate the theory.[143] Besides these articles, the *JPE*—in order to deliver on its commitment to "practical economics"—also ran a slew of studies and reviews on agriculture, transportation, factory conditions and wages, national and state finance, and (Laughlin's special favorites) banking, credit, and currency. Readers of volume 3, from 1894–1895, for instance, could find fare with titles such as "Belgian Monetary Legislation," "Public Ownership of Mineral Lands in the United States," "State Aid for Railroads in Missouri," and "Taxation in Chicago and Philadelphia," among many other items heavy with specifics of place and time and larded with discussion of changing economic "institutions." During his years at the University of Chicago, Veblen brought out volume after volume of this type, always keeping abreast of the latest developments in the field of political economy.[144]

7.

Still, Veblen knew that Harper and Laughlin both valued research and publication over teaching and administrative service, and here too he hit the ground running. In his first year at Chicago, Veblen published two substantial research articles and two book reviews. These earned him his rapid promotion onto the faculty as a reader—an upward move Harper authorized for none of the other holders of graduate fellowships in the political economy department. In his second year, Veblen followed this auspicious beginning with two more (shorter) articles, six book reviews, and an eight-hundred-page translation into English of a high-profile German economic treatise. And again, Harper quickly rewarded him, elevating Veblen to the rank of associate (or tutor), despite the president's reluctance to advance anyone up the ladder, let alone to approve two promotions in two years for one junior member of his faculty.[145]

But the promise of Veblen's scholarship and his successful completion of the German-to-English translation caught Harper's favorable attention. The book Veblen translated as *The Science of Finance* was *System der Finanzwissenschaft* (hereafter, *Finanzwissenschaft*) by Gustav Cohn, a German economist then acclaimed on both sides of the Atlantic for two connected reasons. For one, economists regarded Cohn's writings as embodying a "golden mean" between the Older School's commitment to abstract theory and the Younger School's emphasis on historical research. In addition, economists saw Gustav Cohn's work, particularly his *Finanzwissenschaft* of 1889, as addressing what Veblen's colleague Miller spoke of as an acute need for a "systematic treatise covering the subject of public finance"—a subject with urgency in the United States and Europe during the 1880s and 1890s because of changes taking place in the ways nations and states taxed their populations to pay for government spending. At Cornell, this subject had been one of Veblen's two minors in political economy, and Laughlin and Miller made it a core part of the economics program at Chicago, even as they lamented the shortage of English-language works on public finance. In this context, the three men hatched the idea of translating Cohn's *Finanzwissenschaft* into English, and of making this volume the first entry in a monograph series Laughlin had just launched, Economic Studies of the University of Chicago. Responsibility for the translation devolved onto Veblen, and it occupied him intensively from mid-1892 to mid-1894—with the approval of Harper and Laughlin both. (Sometime translators themselves, the two men viewed translation as a serious form of scholarship.)[146]

This project was a smart career move on Veblen's part, whether or not he thought of it this way. It hitched his name to that of an internationally renowned writer and to a topic of pressing academic and lay concern; and the positive reactions that contemporaries showed to the translation— which appeared in 1895 as *The Science of Finance*—redounded to Veblen at a time when his own scholarly reputation was still in the making. More important, Cohn's book fed the reservoir of knowledge practices Veblen had been building up, absorbing him in the use of these practices during the hundreds of hours he spent painstakingly moving between Cohn's German text and the one he was constructing in English. Concretely, this meant a sentence-by-sentence enmeshment in Cohn's ways of thinking, including his assault on the classical economists' "rationalistic, atomistic theory of . . . man" and their "egoistic, individualistic conception" of human nature as a "fixed datum" impelled by pleasure and pain. As a treatise on public finance, moreover, Cohn's *Finanzwissenschaft* focused not on economic production but on the dynamics of consumption: on how "the collective needs of [the] community" have (or have not) been met by the ever-changing institutions of taxation that governments establish to collect revenues. It is because of these dynamics, according to Cohn, that the study of taxation demands an analysis of the "evolution of the State" and an examination of the "long historical development of institutions." These arguments, set out at length in *Finanzwissenschaft*, gave Veblen material that aligned his work translating Cohn's volume with many other lessons in knowledge making he had had up to this point.[147]

Veblen's early book reviews from his time at the University of Chicago were much slighter performances, some as short as two paragraphs, none longer than nine.[148] All of them appeared in the *JPE*, most likely at Veblen's own initiative; they dealt with books he probably wanted to read because of their close connection to his articles and course offerings during this period. As synopses of works by European authorities on socialist thought or agrarian economic conditions, the reviews show Veblen defining himself as a "student of economic institutions" and commending social scientists who used detailed empirical observations to formulate "broad generalizations" that left room, nonetheless, for the "idiosyncrasies" of individual cases. In the same vein, the reviews criticized socialist writers whose rigid theoretical preconceptions prevented them from examining the changing historical relationship between economic and political institutions and from grasping "that [socialism] will be reached if at all by *an evolution from existing forms* of social organization."[149] Running through his reviews from mid-1893 onward, these judgments evidence how institutionalist-evolutionary ways of thinking already provided Veblen with his metric for assessing the contribution of other political economists.

THE FOUR ARTICLES Veblen published in his first two years at Chicago were more scattershot. Different from one another in subject matter and method of argument, they show him bouncing around intellectually, reacting to immediate external prompts in the manner of a junior scholar, rather than pursuing a cohesive and original line of work of his own. In fact, of the four articles, only two shared so much as a topic: "The Price of Wheat since 1867" and "The Food Supply and the Price of Wheat."[150] These Veblen completed during his fellowship year, when he continued to train under Laughlin's supervision; and the time he devoted to working on them prolonged the detour into Older School economics that he had been drawn toward at Cornell. By examining the economics of American wheat farming, the two articles related directly to Laughlin's interest in practical economic problems. In addition, the *JPE* was explicitly calling for empirical studies of agriculture, which Veblen's colleagues regarded as the "leading national industry."[151]

So, right away, Veblen responded to the call, stepping up with two substantial articles on American wheat prices: a subject remote from his evolutionary and institutional concerns, but falling squarely within the boundaries of classical economics, which foregrounded questions about commodity production and the attendant costs of production. In the first of these, Veblen presented charts and graphs, based on data he culled from statistical reports of government bureaus and regional boards of trade, to describe postbellum movements in wheat prices in relation to fluctuations in the cost of the factors that go into wheat production, such as farm machinery and railway freight charges. In the second article, he engaged in a short exercise in mathematical forecasting, extrapolating from data on current price levels what wheat prices would likely be ten years into the future if costs of grain production remained stable. In both articles, Veblen's attention was on economic change but in the very limited sense of the swings in supply and demand that occurred in the "normal course of things."[152]

Veblen's next article did not appear for another year (June 1894). He wrote it around the time he was finishing his translation of Cohn's opus, and it took the form of a Note in the *JPE* commenting on a situation the nation's newspapers were tracking closely. A sharp contrast with his purely descriptive, data-heavy articles on wheat prices, the Note marked the only time during his Chicago years that Veblen penned an "opinion piece" on current events, although the *JPE* often published articles in this genre by other economists. Laughlin was a master of this type of writing, and Veblen's intervention resembled his mentor's work in its iconoclastic tone and unsympathetic stance toward popular proposals for economic reform.

Veblen's target was a short-lived social movement that fell among the many labor protests that followed the Panic of 1893. This was the Army of the Commonweal, a band of several hundred unemployed workers (from Massillon, Ohio, and surrounding regions) that marched on Washington, DC, in spring 1894, to demand the federal government create a public works program funded by issuing paper currency—a scheme hatched by the army's leader, populist businessman Jacob Coxey. More peaceful than the Pullman strike a few months later, Coxey's Army was no more successful, and Veblen used his Note partly to dismiss Coxey's currency plan as an "articulate hallucination," ill-adjusted to "modern industrial evolution." This reproach of Coxey was incidental, however, to the polemic Veblen then let loose against Americans' growing "conviction that society owes every honest man a living"—"life, liberty, and the *means* of happiness"—and against the companion belief that the state should fulfill this sweeping demand. In Veblen's opinion, statist measures of this kind, although endorsed by German economists and their American followers, wrongly assumed "the feasibility of paternalism, or socialism, on a scale that is not borne out by the experience of the past."[153]

Six months later, Veblen went in still another direction with "The Economic Theory of Woman's Dress."[154] Among modern-day readers, this short article is the best known of Veblen's early writings; more than any other, it prefigured arguments about "conspicuous consumption" that he developed in his later work. When he wrote the article in 1894, however, what mainly concerned Veblen was laying out the "economic theory" named in his title. This was his goal because the subject of "dress" itself had already generated a flurry of research by social scientists, some of it reported in the *Popular Science Monthly,* the same periodical in which Veblen's article appeared. In fact, this journal had previously run his friend Frederick Starr's long series on "Dress and Adornment," among other apropos pieces. These articles—plus one Laughlin had just published on "fashion"—spurred Veblen not to hunt down more factual information about dress but to shape information that was easily available on the topic into something more.[155] That something was a "theory," by which Veblen meant, here and going forward, a set of the principles—or causal laws— that scientists arrive at by induction: by formulating generalizations on the basis of "brute facts" drawn from observation (whether firsthand or secondhand).[156] This was not the kind of knowledge-making work Veblen had tried his hand at in any of his publications up to this point, but once again he was game to shift gears.

The result was a theory that drew on familiar observations to set forth three "cardinal principles" to explain what makes an item of woman's apparel into a socially visible sign or "index of the wealth" of the household the woman belongs to. These are the apparel's "expensiveness" (the more costly an item, the more it serves as evidence of the householder's economic success), its "novelty" (the more modish an item, the more it does likewise), and its "ineptitude" (the more "cumbrous" a garment, the more it displays economic success by showing the woman wearing it "is manifestly incapable of doing anything that is of any use"). According to Veblen, these principles are not universally valid; widely applicable, they nonetheless hold to different degrees at different stages of "social evolution." All the same, the high value consumers attach to commodities that are expensive, novel, and incapacitating illustrates that real-life purchasing decisions look beyond buying items that will increase a household's "productive efficiency," since buyers also seek to acquire objects that announce themselves as "waste": as "conspicuously unproductive expenditures." This complicated illustration was consequential because Veblen knew that, whereas classical economists recognized, at least to some degree, *both* "productive" *and* "unproductive" economic activities (which he believed was the right thing to do), theorists from the new marginal utility school elided the "unproductive" in order to assert that all economic action is "productive"—period. (I will elaborate on this point in Chapter 8.) Veblen's article showcased "dress" to drive home the economic significance of the "unproductive," repeating this loaded adjective again and again, lest readers miss the message.[157]

AND THEN HE STOPPED. After taking off fast down the publication track in his first two years at the University of Chicago, Veblen published nothing aside from book reviews for the next three-and-a-half years. This hiatus, which ran from late 1894 until mid-1898, occurred just at the point in time when one would expect a junior faculty member to publish more, not less, particularly at a university where the president based reappointment and promotion decisions heavily on scholarly productivity. Unlike in the mid-1880s, Veblen had no debilitating health problems holding him back. So why the pause in publications?

True, this was not a complete halt; some of Veblen's book reviews from the period had heft.[158] Ten in all (and all published in the *JPE*), these reviews mainly discussed books on socialism by prominent European writers, although, as Veblen's teaching portfolio grew, he also took up books on the different schools of economic thought. In most cases, the reviews were little more than capsule summaries. Even so, Veblen made a few of them opportunities to elaborate his views on social evolution and to suggest that the faux-scientific approaches of existing economic schools needed to give way to a genuine "science of economics."[159]

Still, the reviews added up to a slim thirty-five pages, unaccompanied by a single article, to say nothing of a book—the thinnest publication record among the regular members of the political economy department. But, then again, several surrounding circumstances, some more pressing than others, were slowing Veblen down, especially in the way he handled them. For one, there was his belief—dating to the 1894–1895 academic year—that, under Harper, he could not trust that publishing would bring him a future at the university, let alone a financially secure future. To what degree this belief was based on how Harper was treating Veblen personally, and to what extent it reflected the general anxiety rippling over an institution where the president left everyone in a state of uncertainty, we do not know. Describing the mood on campus in these years, novelist Herrick recalled "much grumbling and growls [about the] false promises" Harper had made to those on the faculty about their promotion prospects, salaries, and so forth.[160] Yet, as Veblen realized, he himself had, early on, been among the fortunate few; during his first two years at the university, Harper had not only promoted him twice but also frequently commended his work. In a November 1895 letter, Veblen reminded Harper: "Your repeated expressions of good will and appreciation have encouraged me to look with some confidence for an advance."[161]

By that date, however, the relationship between the two men had changed for the worse. Among other issues, they were feuding over what Veblen regarded as an overdue pay increase; and it seems that this salary dispute initially precipitated his drop-off in publications. In later years, Veblen spoke frankly of the connection between academic pay and productivity, pointing out that "the more scantily paid grades of university men" necessarily face constant economic and social pressures that "divert their time and energy" from their "scholarly or scientific pursuits."[162]

This statement carries the ring of Veblen's personal experiences; but, be that as it may, when Harper promoted Veblen from the position of reader to associate with the start of the 1894–1895 academic year, Veblen received no salary increase. In Harper's universe, this was not unusual, as Veblen knew, but it was galling to him all the same. In fact, as early as April 1895, Edward Bemis was reporting to Richard Ely (then at the University of Wisconsin) that "Veblen wants to leave" the University of Chicago because of his disagreements with Harper.[163] This exit scenario proved to be a nonstarter, however, and the following academic year, 1895–1896, Harper left Veblen's salary as it was. This decision inflamed Veblen's frustrations, provoking him to badger Harper over "the apportionment of salaries for the coming year"—a gutsy reaction considering Veblen was not sure the president would even keep him on the faculty for another year.[164] Summarizing the situation to Sarah Hardy in November 1895, Veblen wrote, "I don't know what the chances of my reappointment for next year may be. It is not altogether improbable that I may be dropped from the budget . . . when it is made up next month. To make the way plain and smooth, *I have struck for higher wages.*"[165]

This was a risky gambit to try with Harper, who held the stronger bargaining position. But Veblen "struck" nonetheless—he stopped publishing articles—and he got the result he wanted. Harper relented and agreed to promote him (for the third time in four years) *and* to increase his pay, moving him up, as of the 1896–1897 academic year, to the rank of "instructor" at an annual salary of $1,500 (= $48,300), which was a giant hike in compensation of 150 percent.[166] Why Harper responded this way is unclear. In light of Veblen's able teaching and service work, Harper may simply have wanted to end the strike. As well, he may have been aware, through Laughlin, that Veblen was working on a promising longer-term project. Following these improvements in his job situation, though, Veblen did not see another boost in salary or rank until 1900, after he had resumed (in 1898) writing articles on a regular basis and had published (in 1899) a widely noticed book that was selling well.

Veblen's grievances over pay were exacerbated by his departmental workload, which started increasing shortly before his publications trailed off. Part of this increased load was due to his growing teaching obligations: four new courses, with four new sets of lectures, to prepare between the fall quarter of 1894 and the winter quarter of 1897. In addition were the responsibilities that came with his enlarged role as managing editor of the *JPE;* in letters from 1895, Veblen described, for example, how his editorial duties were eating into his writing time. On top of this, it seems that Laughlin, at some point in the period, began transferring other administrative tasks to Veblen, as historian of economics Charles H. Hull, who knew Veblen at the time, explained to David Starr Jordan in 1905: "It is the common gossip [among professional economists] that Veblen does much of the work of the Chicago Department of Economics and does not receive there the recognition which he deserves." This treadmill of mundane organizational demands provided the context for Veblen's biting (and perhaps not outdated) 1904 comment: "No infirmity more commonly besets university men than this going to seed in routine work and extra-scholastic duties."[167]

Nevertheless, Veblen's salary discontents and departmental obligations were smaller impediments to publishing than a drama happening at the same time in his private life, in which the academic and the personal blurred into one another. The drama revolved around Sarah McLean Hardy (whom I have already mentioned several times).[168] A graduate of the University of California at Berkeley, Hardy (1870–1959) came to the University of Chicago for the fall 1893 term to study under Laughlin. Her interests were in practical economics (monetary questions in particular), and faculty members and fellow graduate students immediately identified her as a rising intellectual star—a status magnified by her ability to combine her academic work with extracurricular activities that ranged from volunteering at settlement houses to attending parties with members of

Chicago's elites (where she was hounded by wealthy suitors). In the winter and spring quarters of 1894, Hardy took Veblen's Socialism course; and during the two years that followed, their professor-student relationship grew into long talks and long walks—and into a correspondence that was, from Veblen's side, increasingly intimate and fevered. Hardy perhaps guessed where things were heading when, in January 1896, Veblen sent her letters saying, for example: "a previous engagement . . . prevented my seeing or appreciating, until it was too late, the Napoleonic opportunity I had of carrying you off and keeping you to myself for the best part of the afternoon"; or, "assuming then that you need advice [about economics], and assuming also the larger assumption that I am at liberty to thrust myself upon you with it."[169] In a letter dated February 24, 1896, Veblen removed the veneer, telling Hardy flat out: "I love you beyond recall," and "ever since the first time I saw you, in the library, you have gone with me as a vision of light and life and divine grace"; and "my life since then has centered about you."[170]

This was an admission, not a proposal. By the time Veblen sent the letter, Hardy was already engaged to her future husband, and Veblen's relationship with her stayed within the bounds of the platonic. But not wanting to deceive (or further to deceive) his wife, in March 1896 Veblen confessed his love of Hardy to Ellen, expressing deep remorse to her over his wayward affections, and asking her for a divorce.[171] When Ellen refused this request (as she continued to do until 1913), the couple's daily living situation became so painful, according to Ellen, that it sapped "every vestige of youth" from her and Thorstein both. In a letter in April 1897, she described his condition late into his fifth year at Chicago: "Mr. Veblen's health is entirely broken down. He says often that he will not live through the year, [and] he to whom existence was pleasure enough knows no joy, and I believe no ambition. *He speaks of resigning his position here, which means that he will drop out of University life and do no more work.*"[172]

Because these are Ellen Veblen's words, we cannot simply take them at face value. Ellen exaggerated in the best of circumstances, and here she was bleeding as she described her failed marriage in a letter to Sarah Hardy (by then, Sarah Hardy Gregory), of all people. Still, Thorstein Veblen *was* emotionally distraught at the time, agonizing—in overwrought Victorian fashion—that his love for Hardy was "the cry of a lost soul" and grieving that his life had turned upside down, decaying into "deterioration" and "death." People who imagine themselves in this way, as lost souls, do cut back on the amount of work they do (publishing academic articles in

Veblen's case); they do resign their jobs; they do abandon their career paths. So it is plausible that Veblen's future as an economist teetered at the brink during this "untoward episode" with Hardy, especially at moments when his dissatisfactions with the university were running high.[173]

Pushing him even close to the edge, moreover, was a predicament of another kind. Besides a stillborn love, a shattered marriage, an enervating workload, and salary frustrations, intellectual problems were stymieing Veblen. For, although he ceased publishing between 1894 and 1898, he did not stop thinking during these years about questions in economics or abandon his interest in advancing scientific knowledge—the reason for life itself at the University of Chicago. In no sense were these years an intellectual time-out: editorial work and graduate student teaching kept Veblen constantly informed about developments at the frontiers of his field—and he kept writing all the while. In fact, as early as November 1895, and on three occasions in the following three months, Veblen told Sarah Hardy that he was writing a "monograph" titled *The Theory of the Leisure Class*. Yet, on the last two occasions, he was downcast about the future of the book, worrying that he had "achieved nothing beyond [adding] sheets of handwriting to the waste basket" and speaking with uncertainty: "*if* the ms. ever comes to anything," which he said was "doubtful." "It disappoints me and puzzles me," he confided to Hardy, "that I am unable to say what I want to in the way I want to say it." [174] Before he could resume publishing, Thorstein Veblen had to break through this impasse. Without yet realizing it, he was very close to doing just that.

CHAPTER 8

WORKING IN THE FIELD

1.

Whether or not Ellen Veblen was right when she said her husband came close, in 1897, to "drop[ping] out of University life and do[ing] no more work" there, once he decided to stay the course Thorstein Veblen was clear about what he was choosing to do.[1] "The university man's work," he wrote is 1904, "is the pursuit of knowledge," and "no man whose energies are not habitually bent on increasing and proving up the domain of learning belongs legitimately on the university staff." With his fondness for synonyms, Veblen sometimes swapped out the words "knowledge" and "learning" for "research," "scholarship," and (most reverentially) "science," but his credo held firm: "Scientific and scholarly inquiry . . . is the primary and indispensable" job that falls to people in the "academic community."[2]

Or, more precisely, "the advance in science and scholarship" is the defining task of members of the academic community in the modern age—the age of "civilization" (to insert Veblen's ethnocentrism). In times past, "among the savage and lower barbarian peoples," for example, a different attitude held sway. These peoples did not deliberately seek "to *advance* knowledge" and, aside from accumulations of technical know-how, what passed as knowledge were "myths and legends."[3] In the era of modern civilization, however, what counts as knowledge is theoretically organized "matter-of-fact knowledge," which derives from "closer observation and more detailed analysis of facts." Producing this knowledge is, according to Veblen, the "calling" of modern scientists and scholars. "Civilized mankind looks to this quest of matter-of-fact knowledge as its most substantial asset and its most valued achievement," cognizant that science is the "most perfect flower of the western civilization." Still further, "the current scheme of civilization" purposefully affords a social space for this intellectual quest by attaching it to institutional foundations: to universities in their modern form. "It is," Veblen asserted, "the university's particular office in this scheme to conserve and extend the domain of knowledge."[4]

The passages I have just quoted might just as well have been written by President Harper at the University of Chicago, or President Gilman at Johns Hopkins, or President Porter at Yale, or President White at Cornell—or by any number of other late nineteenth-century champions of the university as the best arrangement for advancing scientific knowledge. In fact, throughout the speeches and writings of these university builders, statements almost identical to Veblen's were standard fixtures, and over the course of his education Veblen encountered these statements again and again. All the same, they are *not* statements we would expect Veblen to condone, let alone endorse, in view of his scalding critique elsewhere of higher-educational institutions. In *The Theory of the Leisure Class*, for instance, Veblen painted universities as resorts for scions of the leisure class who were devoted to useless scholastic rituals and resistant to the growth of science. But it is important to realize that he leveled this attack primarily against higher-educational institutions of the premodern era and later survivors of these relics, rather than against modern universities, at least insofar as they broke loose from the past and made way for scientific research.[5] The trouble was, as Veblen continued in *The Higher Learning in America*, that the presidents of the country's new research-oriented institutions—men whom he called the "captains of erudition"— often allowed "business principles" of organizational management to impinge on their decisions and to "divert the universities from the pursuit of knowledge." That, Veblen complained, was exactly the sad state of affairs he witnessed at the University of Chicago, where Harper, through his "ravenous megalomania" and chasing after resources from conservative businessmen, "c[a]me substantially to surrender the university ideal."[6]

But the failings of Harper and other captains of erudition did not lead Veblen to give up on this research ideal or deny that it could be realized institutionally. Instead, he felt the University of Chicago had actually lived up to this promise in its earliest years, when Harper still evinced a "sincere devotion to the cause of scholarship" and "let the academic policy be guided primarily by scholarly ideals." This idyll was "very brief," though, and Veblen longed for "remedial measures" that would ensure the pursuit of "disinterested science and scholarship." In this sense, his legendary criticisms of American universities actually reflected an uncompromising dedication to the "university ideal" rather than a rejection of it. More than a half century ago, the distinguished historian of American higher education Laurence Veysey rightly singled Veblen out in exactly this respect: as a critic of the university who was more loyal to the cause than the loyalists were and who embodied the "extreme case . . . of academic men [of the period] who viewed *research as their primary goal.*"[7]

This view carried with it something more that Veblen shared with President Harper and other university builders of the era: the belief that advancing knowledge under modern conditions necessitates intellectual specialization. Because Veblen was so broadly read, and because his writings subsequently influenced—and continue to influence—scholars in so many areas of the social sciences and the humanities, it is natural for us to envision him as a generalist rather than as a specialist. But Veblen did not characterize himself as a generalist during most of his academic career—and it was not how he characterized university faculty members who succeeded as knowledge makers. To "extend the bounds of knowledge," the professional academic "must be a specialist," he said, continuing:

> But no one is a competent specialist in many lines. . . . One line, somewhat narrowly bounded as a specialty, measures the capacity of the common run of talented scientists and scholars for first-class work, whatever side-lines of subsidiary interest they may have in hand and may carry out with passably creditable results. The alternative. . . . is amateurish pedantry, with the charlatan ever in the near background.[8]

Unusual among writers of his time, Veblen anticipated the language of social scientists of our own time by speaking, as I have been doing in this book, of academic disciplines as "fields of knowledge" (or "fields of learning"). These, he asserted, are the organic divisions that properly make up the university, in which each "specialty"—or "line of adventure"—corresponds to the "special segment of [a particular] field of knowledge" in which scholars carry out their research.[9] Applying these terms to his own work, Veblen explicitly located himself in the "field of economics," and he did so just at the time when "economic theory" was solidifying as one of its distinct specialties. In his view, "scientists and scholars [are] occupied . . . with the keeping and cultivation . . . of a special line of inquiry." As an academic of the era, this was what Veblen wanted to accomplish in the field of economics.[10]

2.

During the 1890s, when Veblen was coming into his own as an economist, most scholars active in the discipline agreed that American economics was in churning intellectual disarray. The consensus on this score was, in fact, one of the rare points of agreement among economists, although their opinions diverged over whether the disorder was more a benefit or a drawback for members of the field.

The upside of the disarray was the growth of intellectual inclusiveness: the emergence and spread among economists of a willingness to tolerate different ways of practicing economics. This attitude contrasted with the uncompromising division that marked American economics during most of the 1880s, when representatives of the Older (classical) School and the Younger (historical) School contended for all-out victory, each side battling to eliminate the other once and for all. By the decade's end, however, the two warring parties learned that their doctrinal extremism came at a heavy price: it discredited economic knowledge in the judgment of university administrators and the general public. Faced with this life-threatening reaction, economists of both schools abandoned polarization in favor of intellectual pluralism. They did so not by letting go of controversies among themselves—"When did one economist ever agree entirely with another?" asked one economist in 1901—but by making space in the discipline for a fuller range of theories, methods, and substantive topics and accommodating these different approaches as they mingled at meetings of the American Economic Association (AEA), in the pages of economics journals, and on the faculties of political economy departments.[11] As early as 1892, for example, Edwin Seligman (of Columbia University) was welcoming the arrival of economic studies that were "catholic in temper"; and in 1899, when Jacob Hollander (of Johns Hopkins University) looked back over the decade as a whole, what stood out was that "eclecticism has become the dominant note in economic writing."[12] According to historian of economics William Barber, this "tolerance for diversity" that pervaded American economics in the 1890s was among the factors that enabled Veblen "to press his ideas forward."[13]

Even so, diversity had a downside that alarmed most American economists of the time. It exploded their discipline into a scattershot of disconnected fragments, bringing it to the brink of "general catastrophe," in the words of cool-headed Francis A. Walker, then the president of the AEA. Walker gave this assessment in 1891 (the year Veblen returned to graduate school to study political economy). During the two decades that followed, many other economists vented similar anxieties about the turmoil and uncertainty they saw afflicting their field.[14]

A large part of the reason for the chaos was the erosion of classical economics as the structure that held the theoretical, empirical, and policy branches of economics together, as it had done for American political economists up through the late 1870s. From that date onward, and more with each passing year, the center ceased to hold. In college textbooks, watered-down versions of classical teachings appeared well into the twentieth century, and Older School loyalists, like J. Laurence Laughlin and William Graham Sumner, continued to defend certain traditional doctrines (such as the concept of a wage fund) throughout the fin de siècle era. But by the 1880s, the classical monopoly was over, and most people in the field of economics knew it. Not unusual, for example, was Simon Patten (of University of Pennsylvania) when he casually tossed into an 1896 letter to Frank Taussig (of Harvard University) a remark the two economists took as a matter of common knowledge: "We all have broken the bonds that held us to the old classic system, each in our way"—the last phrase a telling indication of disunity of practices that accompanied the decline of the Older School.[15] Contemporaries pinned this shift (correctly, in the view of modern historians) not on any one shortcoming in the classical approach but on successive defections from classicism by scholars of many different persuasions, as well as by members of the public increasingly uneasy with laissez-faire social policies.

One of these defections came as a result of the proliferation within economics of specialized subfields devoted to research on empirical topics rather than to theoretical questions. Historian of economics Joseph Persky has documented this development in a study of the 173 articles that appeared in the *Quarterly Journal of Economics* (*QJE*) and the *Journal of Political Economy* (*JPE*) between 1897 and 1902. Analyzing the content of these articles, Persky found that barely 8 percent dealt with issues in economic theory, whereas more than 60 percent were "descriptive" articles on subjects including banking and currency regulations, public utilities, transportation and railroads, labor and unions, taxation, tariffs, and trusts and corporations. Many of these articles came from a source that was rapidly expanding as part of the growth of research universities, and that was a wellspring of monograph-style doctoral dissertations, the majority of them produced by the inductive methods of the German historical school. In turn-of-the-century American economics, dissertations on specialized empirical topics formed the basis of scores of articles; and young scholars who earned their doctorates by carrying out this kind of research often continued along the same lines in their later careers.[16]

Because most of these scholars (lacking the present-day luxury of financial grants to collect new economic data) had to rely on existing documents they could easily access—statutes, reports by government agencies and commissions, newspaper collections, and miscellany from local libraries and historical societies—their research had a strong historical coloring, sometimes overtoned with evolutionary terminology. In a typical empirical article, the economist would track his or her subject—say, a contemporaneous form of banking, transportation, or taxation—back a generation or two or three, identifying changes that occurred along the way. The modest result, as Jacob Hollander summarized it, was a collection of studies on the "historical evolution of economic institutions" depicted in local contexts and over relatively short time periods.[17] Concurrently, studies of broader economic changes migrated out of the discipline of economics and into the discipline of history, where they spawned the new subfield of economic history. The pioneer behind this movement in the United States was Englishman William Ashley, professor of economic history at Harvard, whose books (well known to Veblen) plumbed the medieval roots of modern industrial society. In doing so, Ashley acknowledged the inspiration of the German historical economists and the evolutionary theories of Herbert Spencer.[18] Meanwhile, a still lengthier time perspective overran the field of anthropology, where ethnologists marshaled reports on "savage" and "barbarian" societies, and on the social and psychological characteristics of the "races" that peopled them, to repudiate traditional notions of economic man and propose more mutable conceptions of economic life.[19]

Adding to this empirical jumble of specialized research topics and temporal perspectives was the clamor within the increasingly specialized area of economic "theory" itself—the "unmistakable ferment" sparked in the subfield by the eruption of many "radical reconstructions" (to quote Laurence Laughlin's description).[20] "In these days," deplored Thorstein Veblen's University of Chicago colleague William Caldwell in 1893 (just months after Veblen joined the political economy department), "so much is unsettled in theory."[21] In a leading textbook four years later, Charles Bullock (of Williams College) used similar language; he depicted economic theory as the chaotic scene of "many controversies on fundamental points of theory" which are "unsettled at the present time."[22] Latching on to the same adjective, Frank Fetter (of Stanford University, and previously a student at Cornell when Veblen was there) went further, as he sized up the situation at the start of the twentieth century: "At no time since Adam Smith . . . have opinions upon important questions of economic theory been more unsettled."[23] And John Bates Clark, in a book review in the 1897 volume of the *JPE*, volunteered a diagnosis: "Essential parts of old theories have been abandoned; and yet of the theories that are to take their places, no one has as yet won universal acceptance."[24] To expect this high degree of consensus was to set a very high standard, but one that Clark and many other economists hoped economic theory would, nonetheless, meet at some point in the not-too-distant future.

With classical economics on its last leg and German historicism diverted into empirical monographs, the leading contender for eventual success in the theory area (and the alternative Clark bet on) was the marginal utility theory of value. A novelty in American economics as recently as the 1880s, marginalist theories—which American economists associated, at first, mainly with the "Austrian school"—stood at the forefront of many of the major debates in economic theory by the 1890s.[25] In 1894, for instance, Arthur Hadley (of Yale) observed that "almost all economists have been somewhat affected by . . . the writings [of the] 'Austrian School'"; while David Green (of Hartford Seminary) reported the following year that "the young men whose ideas upon economic theory have been formed since the Austrian writings became accessible" (which was the late 1880s) "have quite generally adopted the leading conceptions and nomenclatures of the Austrian school."[26] By 1897, Veblen's Chicago associate Langworthy Taylor, writing in the *JPE*, remarked (with only slight exaggeration) that "marginal theory" had gained such prominence "in [economic] science that other theories are now always regarded as adjuncts."[27] The theory's adoption and prominence, to be sure, brought no end to the intellectual chaos in the field. Austrian marginalism was not the only variety of marginalism; as American economists of the 1890s knew from Clark's own work, as well as from the work of European authors like Alfred Marshall, William Stanley Jevons, and Leon Walras, marginalist theories took different forms, which sometimes clashed with one another and almost always faced severe criticism from economists who were not among its aficionados. Even so, by the mid-1890s, marginalism, according to Hadley, was being "applied in detail to an endless variety of topics, [ranging from] the phenomena of the market . . . to the problems of distribution of wealth."[28]

AMONG THESE TOPICS, it was the "distribution of wealth" that arched over all the others. When Scottish theorist William Smart wrote in the *Annals of the American Academy of Political and Social Science* in 1892 that "almost every economist is just now engaged on the subject of distribution," he made an observation that economic theorists on both sides of the Atlantic would have agreed with.[29] The subject had a distinguished lineage. More than a century earlier, Adam Smith had introduced it when he discussed how the wealth of a nation is "naturally distributed among the different ranks of the people" in a society—namely, laborers, landowners, and capitalists. Smith's concern lay with explaining the level of wages, rents, and profits (or interest, a concept not yet sharply distinguished from the concept of profit) that flowed to members of these groups as a result, respectively, of performing labor services for hire; leasing their land to people who wanted to work it; and using their saved-up financial resources to lend to producers of commodities so they could hire workers, buy raw materials and manufacturing equipment, and so forth.[30]

After Adam Smith, the topic of distribution coursed in and out of writings of the classical school. Economists fought over the definition of basic terms like "wages," "rent," "interest," "profits," and "capital"—to say nothing of the concepts of wealth and income (still poorly differentiated). So tangled did this in-house vocabulary become by the last quarter of the nineteenth century that one of the AEA's first initiatives was to establish a Committee on Economic Theories in 1885 to sort through "the wide range of meanings now attached to particular terms," especially those that formed part of the economics of distribution.[31] (Unable to reach agreement among its members, the committee disbanded after a few years.) Compounding the confusion, economic theorists wavered over whether the study of distribution should concentrate on explaining the absolute gains and losses in wealth that accrued to the different social classes or, instead, on figuring out the "natural laws" that determined the relative "shares" of national income netted by Labor, Land, and Capital—the so-called "agents" or "factors" of production.[32]

As to the content of these laws, political economists differed further, although they shared a tendency to attribute the returns to each factor to the operation of a distinguishable distributional principle. According to one typical formulation, for example, wages were determined by the size of the "wage fund" that capitalists maintained to cover labor costs; rent by the prices landowners were able charge lessees (mainly farmers) as a result of the scarcity of fertile lands; and interest by the amount of financial reserves capitalists had available to lend because they had abstained from unnecessary consumption.[33]

By the late 1880s, European and American theorists began to abandon this convoluted and splintered approach to the analysis of distribution. They knew that physics and astronomy rested on a simple set of theoretical laws (Newton's laws of motion), while the biological sciences were moving, in different ways, toward integrated laws of evolution. So economists, aspiring for scientific legitimacy, veered away from separate laws of distribution, embarrassed that this practice was, as Frank Fetter eulogized it, a scientific "anachronism" and "laughing stock."[34] What theorists needed—or so they said to one another in growing numbers—was to undertake "the construction of a . . . consistent theory of distribution" so as "to reach a common law" that could explain, in symmetrical terms, the income shares received by workers, capitalists, and landowners; and to formulate "an economic law which will, from its beauty and simplicity, commend itself to universal acceptance," as laws in the natural sciences do.[35]

Giving urgency to the task of finding this common law was an upwelling of voices beyond the academy consumed by the subject of economic distribution. Sounding out from newspapers, magazines, and popular books, commentators from across the political spectrum railed against toxic patterns of wealth and income distribution they saw as emerging and entrenching themselves during the fin de siècle era. In substance, many of these fulminations foreshadowed economic debates in the first two decades of our own century—with the twist that nineteenth-century discussions of distribution were heavily inflected by a belief in a deep cleavage between Labor and Capital as social classes (as contrasted with our own prevalent notion of more graduated class divisions).[36] At stake were contending factual claims about which of these two classes was the main beneficiary of the economic transformations underway in the country, plus contending normative claims about which class deserved to be the beneficiary. Viewed from the angle of writers on the side of Labor, economic change was robbing hard-pressed workers of their rightful entitlement to the fruits of their labor, as the growth of corporations and monopolies enabled predatory owners of capital to amass enormous fortunes. In contrast, capitalists' spokespersons held that Capital was the real victim, its well-deserved profits constantly shrinking as Labor solidified substantial wage gains by unionizing and striking.[37]

Writers easily mobilized statistics in support of both arguments. Defending the pro-Capital position with data from the 1880 census, Edward Atkinson, businessman and amateur economist, estimated that only 10 percent of the "annual product" of the nation was going to people whose livelihoods derived mainly from "rent, interest, profit, or savings, [while] nine tenths [of the product] constitutes the share of the laborer, [as] expressed in personal wages." On Atkinson's interpretation, these percentages proved that, at a time when "capital [has been receiving] a diminishing portion of, or profit from . . . an increasing [national] product, . . . organized labor [has been securing] an increasing share."[38] Countering this finding from the pro-Labor side, Charles Spahr, another businessman and lay economist, presented evidence showing that, because of special legal protections for corporations, "the wealthiest ten per cent of American families received approximately the same income as the remaining ninety per cent."[39] Academic economists who joined this public debate wanted a consistent, uniform measure by which to adjudicate these contrary claims: a single law of economic distribution.

HERE, MARGINAL UTILITY theory reentered the picture. Previously used by economists in the United States to explain the "value" of economic goods (see Chapter 7), marginalism took on a highly visible second life in the 1890s as a way for economic theorists to think about the distribution of wealth and income.[40] Richmond Mayo-Smith (of Columbia) spotted this trend in the field as early as 1894: "The whole world of economic theorists is groaning and travailing over a theory of distribution based on marginal utility; economists are tumbling over each other in the race to be the first in applying the doctrine" to explain the division of shares of national income between capitalists and workers.[41] (By this date, landowners were fast disappearing into the woodwork of economic debates.)

These gymnastics brought forth different arguments, but here it suffices to consider the claim by several marginalists that the same principle of diminishing returns that governs consumer spending (and the value of commodities) extends to commodity producers when they spend to acquire factors of production. According to this principle, producers, as they buy units of capital and labor to make their products, receive decreasing gains from each additional increment of capital or labor until they arrive at the "final increment" that will contribute (by their rough calculations) to their output. The interest rate or wage rate needed to acquire this last, marginal unit sets the standard for the rate employers spend on interest and wages overall.[42]

What does this recondite account of the spending behaviors of employers have to do with the distribution of income shares among the agents of production? Marginalists in Europe dealt with this issue in a variety of ways; but to Veblen's American contemporaries, the answer to the question was most fully worked out by John Bates Clark in articles he published during the late 1880s and throughout the 1890s, and then amplified in his 1899 opus *The Distribution of Wealth: A Theory of Wages, Interest and Profits*. (By this point, Clark's focus had shifted from what it was at Carleton when he was teaching Veblen.)[43] In these writings, Clark systematized the marginalist theory of distribution by incorporating the concept of "productivity." Doing so enabled him to argue—with great fanfare—that income shares are legitimate "rewards" to workers and capitalists alike for their differential "contributions" to the production of economic goods.[44]

To support this argument, Clark built on marginalist ideas about employers when they are in the course of adding the final marginal increment of labor or capital to their production processes. (In this specific context, "capital" was a shorthand for the monetary funds employers borrow at interest from owners of capital—capitalists—in order to purchase raw materials, facilities, tools, and other instruments that make manufacturing possible.)[45] Clark integrated these ideas into the "law of final productivity," which held that after producers arrive at this final increment of labor or capital, they have nothing to gain by using their resources to add more units of the same because those additional units will make no further productive contribution. What this means, he reasoned, is that Labor and Capital receive wages and interest payments—their legitimate share of national income—to the extent that additional increments of labor or capital continue to increase productivity. "Each unit"—whether of labor or of capital—"is worth to its employer what the last unit produces," asserted Clark, drawing from this proposition the inference that, in the "normal" or "natural" course of things, "labor tends to get, as its share, what it separately produces," and "capital does the same." Or, in slightly different wording: "The share of income that attaches to any productive function"—labor, capital—"is gauged by the actual product of it," because economic life "tends to give to labor what labor creates [and] to capitalists what capital creates," in a synchronized upward movement that "is perpetually gaining in efficiency" and carrying "the individual members of it to higher planes of life." In epigram: "We get what we produce—such is the dominant rule of life."[46]

Among younger economic theorists, Clark's "marginal productivity theory of distribution" (as they named it a few years later) gave rise to a maelstrom of highly technical debates about calibrating, measuring, and comparing "marginal units" of capital and labor. But beyond the technicalities, several larger points stood out. First was Clark's unrelenting emphasis on the "productive contributions" of all factors of production.[47] This was a principle that ran square against critics on both sides of the controversy about the distribution of wealth between Capital and Labor. In the context of this controversy, Clark's productivity thesis constituted a strong defense of the economic status quo; he used his notion that capitalists and workers "get what they produce" explicitly to assail the "socialist," "revolutionist" contention that "the laboring classes . . . are regularly robbed of what they produce."[48] Simultaneously, Clark's productivity argument voided the classical economists' distinction between productive and unproductive labor. According to Clark's reasoning, "unproductive labor" was a contradiction in terms because an employer will add increments of labor to the production process only up to the marginal point where those increments continue to be productive of output; otherwise, the employer will stop acquiring more of those units. The same argument, Clark believed, refuted the claim by pro-Labor advocates that capital is an "unproductive" force. "*True labor*," held Clark, "*is always productive, [and] in the same way, true capital is always productive*"; thus, "in the case of laborers, . . . the marginal line separates persons who represent true labor from persons who do not, and in the case of [manufacturing] instruments"—insofar as manufacturers buy those instruments with funds borrowed from capitalists—"the marginal line separates those that embody true capital from those that do not."[49]

Finally, Clark's productivity thesis made a secure place for a figure who had long hovered on the sidelines of theories of distribution: the "entrepreneur." (Some economists simply used the term "businessman" or "employer," while others preferred "undertaker"—no humor intended.) The same factor of production as the capitalist, according to many classical economists, the entrepreneur began to assume an independent identity in economic writings during the late nineteenth century, as the ownership of business firms shifted from individual capitalists to consortia of capitalist shareholders reliant on hired executives and managers.[50] Economists argued over whether these newly differentiated economic agents were organizational assets or liabilities, but Clark did not wonder. Consistent with the rest of his theory, he depicted entrepreneurs as vital contributors to the production process, who "render [economic] service by coordinating labor and capital." In return, they receive "the share of income that attaches to . . . what the coordinating function creates"; and, he explained, this justified the "reward . . . we shall call profits"—the amount of a firm's income that remains after its managers have paid wages to workers and interest to capitalists.[51]

Clark's defense of entrepreneurial profits, his assertion that labor and capital are inherently productive, and his glorification of the economy as a kingdom of just rewards for productive contributions were not particular to Clark. By the turn of the century, these ideas were implements in the marginalist's intellectual tool kit, and to some extent they would retain this place long into the future.[52] All the same, Clark himself stood out at the time (as he has since) for his comprehensive integration of these powerful claims. And, for synthesizing them, he received unrestrained praise from contemporaries who were critical of the doctrines of classical economics. Henry Seager (of Columbia) described Clark's *Distribution of Wealth* as "mark[ing] an epoch in the history of economic thought in the United States," while Fetter canonized John Bates Clark as "the Columbus of economic theory." By the century's end, American economic theorists widely regarded Veblen's old college teacher as the great, forward-marching revolutionary in their field.[53]

Even as Clark was solidifying this accomplishment and looking to the future of economic theory, however, he and other marginalists understood they were marching backward as well, resuscitating a way of economic thinking that had been all but buried by then. Intentionally, they were reviving some of the principal knowledge-making practices of classical economics, fomenting a movement that became in time one of the great counterrevolutions in the modern history of the social sciences.[54] Clark instigated this movement, ironically, at the same moment he was breaking with the Older School over questions of value and distribution. For, to make this break, he reverted to using the same intellectual tools he had previously condemned in his critique of classical economics: namely, abstract, deductive theorizing designed to formulate universal scientific laws.[55] Clark, the marginalist, made no effort to conceal this rearguard action. Instead, he openly built his theory of distribution on a small number of abstract assumptions—the "law of final productivity," in particular—which he invoked to explain the rewards that accrue to Labor and Capital under "normal" conditions of "perfectly unobstructed competition." Clark took this step knowing that such assumptions frequently deviated from the realities of modern economic life, which could give rise to "a disturbed and abnormal state." He recognized, for example, that corporate monopolies—"the very antithesis of competition"—could "vitiate the action of natural economic law" and "infuse . . . into [income] distribution an element of robbery" as businessmen engaged in "predatory work" toward competitors, and even "filch[ed] something for nothing out of the returns of the corporation" that employed them.[56]

From Clark's perspective as an economic theorist, however, such deviations were small interferences with the normal state of economic affairs. More important for him (and for other American and European marginalists) was setting down "a distinct set of economic laws, the action of which is not dependent on [social] organization." These "static" laws, as Clark contentedly called them, "act in the economy of the most advanced state, as well as in that of the most primitive"; they operate "in all stages of social evolution." In this sense, they "are fundamental [and] universal," analogous to the transhistorical "laws of mechanics" formulated by physicists (rather than to biologists' laws of organic growth and development). Clark believed economists could attain scientific knowledge of the basic laws of economics only by (mentally) subtracting history, evolutionary change, and organic social processes: that is, only by "sweep[ing] out of existence the industrial institutions of modern society" and postulating the abstraction of the isolated "individual [who is] making a living by his efforts and [by nature's] bounty"—and who experiences diminishing satisfactions from any given type of economic good. To be sure, "dynamic" laws also played a part in Clark's work, but this role tended to remain secondary. Foremost, he trained his sights on "natural, normal, and static" laws, acknowledging their "imaginary" character, yet insisting that knowledge making in economics depended on them. Besides, in his judgment, "one can hardly assert too emphatically the dominance of the static forces in real and dynamic societies."[57]

To Clark's marginalist contemporaries, these ways of thinking were seductive and compelling, although economists from other corners of the fragmented discipline responded with reactions that ranged from apathy to scorn. Regardless of this difference, few members of the field failed to notice some of the backward features of the marginalist approach to knowledge production. Committed marginalist Frank Fetter observed, for instance: "The sudden revival of abstract or deductive economics, just as such studies seemed to be growing into discredit, is one of the most remarkable chapters in economic theory." Fetter made this remark, ambivalently, in a paper on the state of economic theory that he presented in a session at the annual meeting of the American Economic Association in December 1900. Fetter was preceded on the scheduled program by invited speaker Thorstein Veblen, who had his own opinions on the contemporary state of the field.[58]

3.

Thorstein Veblen knew the field of economics inside out because he was involved in it from the inside, not looking down on it from Olympus as a detached spectator or iconoclastic outsider.[59] Chiseled into historical legend as the quintessential "marginal man," estranged from the mainstream, Veblen was, rather, a solidly anchored professional academic of the modern day: a knowledge specialist with top-of-the-line educational credentials, working in an established academic field at a major research university, carrying out his academic duties (scholarship, teaching, and organizational service), and sparring back and forth with other specialists over the intellectual issues that collectively concerned them as field members.

By the standard of their era and of ours, there is little out of the ordinary here. The figure of the professional academic is one we all recognize when we step inside a twenty-first-century university and hear faculty members talk about their work. They do much of what Veblen and his peers were already doing, at the birthing hour of the professional academic, in their role as knowledge makers participating in the intellectual life of their particular fields. True, no more than now were academic fields hermetically sealed; typically, their boundaries were porous, allowing specialists in any one discipline to keep in contact with those in other academic fields and in fields beyond the university. But the nature of these out-of-field contacts has varied; and (as pointed out in Section 1) Veblen epitomized the type of scholar whose overriding mission, as he understood it, was to advance the existing state of knowledge within his own academic field. Bearing this in mind, recalling his lengthy education under the mentorship of economists from all the major economic schools of his time, and realizing, too, that he spent *not one* of his adult years (until he was nearly sixty years old) in a position *outside* of the academy, and Veblen emerges as the consummate academic insider.[60]

His insider status shows in his work, almost all of it addressed mainly to economists. As I discussed in Chapter 2, research by contemporary sociologists who study social fields has found that new entrants to an academic discipline gravitate in one of two directions: either they agree with some existing theory or line of empirical investigation and seek to extend it, or they disagree and try to develop alternative ideas. Veblen went in both directions in succession. As Laughlin's graduate student at Cornell and Chicago, he followed on Laughlin's heels, defending the tenets of classical economic theory against critics like Böhm-Bawerk and carrying out studies of American wheat prices that fit with Laughlin's program for practical economics. Around the time of his promotion to a faculty position at Chicago in mid-1893, however, Veblen ambitiously changed course, ceasing his efforts to extend the approach of the Older School (or of the historical school, or of the Austrian school) and breaking out on his own.

The change fit with President Harper's expectation that the members of his faculty would engage in original research to create new knowledge. Further, the timing of the change coincided with growing feeling among economists, including those in Veblen's department, that their field had dissolved into disarray, brought down by "unsettled" questions that cried out for new answers. This uproar was one of the factors that pushed theories of wealth distribution to the center of the discipline in the early 1890s and, in the process, made way for the ascendance of marginal productivity theories by the end of the decade.

A man at the margins of his field would probably have ignored these frontline developments, but that was not Veblen, who was attracted to the hot spots—just as he had been in the past. At Carleton, during a period when Sir William Hamilton was regarded as "the greatest metaphysician of the age," Veblen devoted his valedictory to the Scotsman's theories; at Johns Hopkins, at a time when political economists were engrossed by the redistributive tax plans of John Stuart Mill and Henry George, Veblen presented a critical analysis of their plans; at Yale, with the "back to Kant" movement in high gear, Veblen tackled the great philosopher's "hardest" treatise; at Cornell, Veblen controverted the arguments of Herbert Spencer, the "Columbus of the epoch," and Eugen Böhm-Bawerk, whom contemporaries ranked among the "foremost" economists of the day. [61] And he held to this modus operandi at Chicago: with "almost every economist then engaged on the subject of distribution" and "the whole world of economic theorists groaning and travailing over a theory of distribution," Veblen was not wired to retreat to the periphery, certainly not when there were new icons—new economic theories and theorists—to contend with. Besides, he had already spent years practicing his skills as an iconoclast—though, again, not because he was alienated from the mainstream. In the Age of Iconoclasm, mainstream academics *were* iconoclasts. The field of economics was a battleground full of them.[62]

Still, Veblen entered the field with his own accumulated gear. "Distribution theories" were not a monolithic entity that all economists parsed in the same way. To members of the dwindling classical school, distribution theories looked one way; another way to adherents of the German historical school; yet another way to representatives of the marginal utility school. These differences triggered different reactions, some friendly, some not, depending (in part) on the intellectual equipment of the particular economist trying to navigate the swampy terrain of American economics in the 1890s.

It is useful here to recall the pragmatist theory of human conduct (described in Chapter 2), and to consider two family situations in which I might find myself. In the first, my spouse and I are driving to the home of friends for dinner, and we get a flat tire. This is aggravating, but it is a routine problem, one we have dealt with in other circumstances, and we solve it by using the tools in the trunk to change our tire, so we can get to dinner roughly on time. But the second situation is not so cut-and-dried. One summer, our daughter and her husband have to leave unexpectedly for a business meeting, and they drop their two teenagers off for us to look after for a week. My wife and I had planned to take a few days off work to enjoy some quiet time, but now what are we going to do? We take mental stock of our resources (money, time) and our accumulated skills (we are experienced long-distance cyclists but unskilled campers), and we try to shape the shapeless, out-of-the-ordinary situation facing us into some more tractable problems: keeping the kids away from video games and getting them out for a few bike rides; or encouraging them to visit college websites and start studying for the SATs; or arranging what could be a memorable family getaway. Each choice will lead to a different solution, which we do not initially have worked out, but toggling between the skills and resources at our disposal and these more defined problems, we finally land on a solution that satisfies us: a road trip, with a couple of days spent cycling, plus tours of a few college campuses.

Like the paths cut by many other original knowledge producers, Veblen's road to the wealth of economic knowledge he created resembled the second of these cases. At the turn of the century, there was a chaotic situation in the field of economics, with many theorists wrapped up in theories of wealth distribution and also in disagreement. Veblen grasped that the tool set of practices and resources he had accustomed to using during his decades-long education equipped him with a knowledge-making repertoire that was multipurpose and malleable, adaptable to a variety of new situations. This stockpile also contained implements that enabled him to configure emerging theories of distribution into a set of defined problems he could try to solve, as he rejiggered—readjusted, recalibrated, even redesigned—both the tools and the problems until they fit together, like a key in a lock, to serve his crystallizing goal of developing a new theory of distribution—a *nonproductivity theory* (as I will call it). Along the way, Veblen formulated other novel ideas too, some ancillary to his theory, some relatively independent; and later writers, down to the present, have imaginatively tapped into this large reserve of ideas to address problems that were not his. Constructing a new theory of economic distribution, however, constituted the core of Thorstein Veblen's work inside the field of economics of his day.

OF COURSE, getting there took time. We see glimmerings of Veblen's academic attraction to the topic of wealth distribution in his Johns Hopkins paper on George and Mill; his Note on Böhm-Bawerk; and his early articles on Spencer, Coxey's Army, and woman's dress, but these were bare inklings. More substantial was his Socialism course at the University of Chicago, discussed in Chapter 7. Offered during winter and spring quarters 1894, the course carried a warning that was printed in the university's *Annual Register:* "Those who have not carefully examined questions of *value and distribution* will be at a disadvantage in this course." This was his way of telling graduate students the course would deal with the topic that was at the top of the agenda of late nineteenth-century economic theorists; and the forewarning may have surprised them, since studying socialism did not ordinarily require prior knowledge of the fine points of modern economic theory.[63] But Veblen hoped his course would bring the two subjects together; so—to judge from Sarah's Hardy's course notes—he interspersed class sessions on the ideas of major socialist thinkers of the past, such as Karl Rodbertus, Karl Marx, and Ferdinand Lassalle, with lectures on the "Austrian school" and contemporary distribution theorists like Böhm-Bawerk and Clark.[64]

Even further, he made the course an occasion to contest these new theories. This he did by drawing on an 1874 treatise by classical economist J. E. Cairnes, who had outlined several abstract principles of economic distribution, one of them a forerunner of Clark's productivity theory. Cairnes called this the "works-principle," by which he meant the idea that the distribution of economic rewards (among workers, capitalists, and other agents of production) "ought to be regulated by the degree to which *each has contributed* by his effort to the fund available for distribution."[65] Veblen's lectures sought to show that, in the light of empirical facts about capitalist society, the abstract works-principle breaks down before something whose empirical workings are actually observable: the "princ. of ostentatious waste!!!!"—as Hardy quoted an apparently emphatic Veblen. From her sketchy notes, Veblen's circuitous argument is difficult to pin down but seems to have run as follows: because members of modern society believe in the works-principle, they regard people with wealth enough to afford lavish displays of consumption as people who have merited rich economic rewards by making productive contributions. Wanting to appear economically successful themselves, the less well-off members of society emulate the behaviors of the wealthy by engaging in "excessive consumption"—consumption beyond what they require for their needs and "comforts." The prevalence of these spending behaviors causes a misdirection of social resources; and, in this way, "waste" becomes the ruling economic principle—not "productivity," as distribution theorists were wrongly asserting. In Veblen's view, the "waste" principle also serves to demonstrate the need for economists to look beyond the capitalist economy, for the "great advantage [of socialism is that it] would do away with prin. of ostentatious waste & emulation, [which is] ultimately at bottom of conspicuous waste" as an economic fact—or so he intoned in one of the last lectures in the course.[66]

AS LEAST AS FAR AS Hardy's notes indicate, Veblen's lectures did not contain the expression for which he is best known: "leisure class." Since the expression was already in popular circulation, it is likely that he or someone else in the course mentioned it. Still, the phenomenon of the leisure class was not yet his explicit focus. And it remained off site even as late as his December 1894 article on woman's dress, in which he continued to offer observations about ostentatious spending and waste, now in order to fault productivity theorists for overlooking the presence of the non-productive in economic life.

Sometime in 1895, however, Veblen began to refer to the "leisure class" by name. In a November 1895 letter to Hardy, he spoke of a multipart book he was writing on socialism, saying that "the first volume [of the book] is *The Theory of the Leisure Class*."[67] The following month he told her, "*The Theory of the Leisure Class* is back on the boards again." Here he boasted the manuscript had a "high theoretical structure" and contained "an excessive invention of unheard-of economics doctrines, [especially] the doctrine of conspicuous waste, which is of course to constitute the substantial nucleus of this writing."[68] In neither of these letters, though, did Veblen say anything more—anything tangible—about the leisure class itself. (Possibly he did so in previous conversations he and Hardy had about the book.) As in his socialism course, his concern was, instead, with analyzing economic doctrines, particularly with developing a theory of waste that would defeat the marginalist theory of distribution. But Veblen remained inductivist in his outlook; he felt a theory of waste required a solid foundation in empirical facts and, to him, "woman's dress" probably seemed too narrow a subject to provide enough empirical material for an entire book. The leisure class—a wider topic, with larger implications—did not have this drawback.

These late 1895 letters to Hardy preceded Veblen's dispirited letters from January and early February of the following year, where he told her he was at a standstill with his book and doubted it would "ever come to anything."[69] What got him going again, we do not know. His correspondence with Hardy shows, nonetheless, that it was precisely in the midst of this period of uncertainty that he began to draw, more heavily than in his publications up to this point, on the intellectual repertoire he had been amassing and practicing in different contexts all his academic life. Veblen described his position at this juncture in what is probably the most intellectually revealing letter he ever wrote: a letter to Hardy, dated January 23, 1896, where he momentarily stepped back from the details of his book project to offer an aerial view of "the probable fate of economic science in the immediate future."

I have a theory [regarding this fate] which I wish to propound. . . .
My theory touches the immediate future of the development of

economic science, and it is not so new or novel as I make it out to be. It is to the effect that the work of the [current] generation of economists . . . is to consist substantially (so far as that work is to count in the end) in a rehabilitation of the science on modern lines. Economics is to be brought into line with modern evolutionary science, which it has not been hitherto. The point of departure for this rehabilitation, or rather the basis of it, will be the modern anthropological and psychological sciences, perhaps most immediately . . . folk psychology. . . . The science, taken generally, is to shape itself into a science of the evolution of economic institutions.[70]

Here, explicitly laid out, was Veblen's program for economic knowledge making, every part of it an item right out of the storehouse of intellectual resources and practices he had been building up. His program at Carleton; his training with Adams, Ely, Morris, and Peirce at Johns Hopkins, with Sumner, Porter, and Ladd at Yale, and with Tuttle, Tyler, and Laughlin at Cornell; and his immersion in the quadrants of the University of Chicago: through all of these experiences coursed evolutionary modes of knowing, which were repeatedly celebrated. The same was true of "institutions" and the allied idea of society as an organism; at each stop along Veblen's itinerary, beginning with the communities of the Upper Midwest and continuing at every school he attended, organic thinking—thinking in terms of social institutions, rather than atomized particles—was inextricable from the very act of thinking, whether the academic field was philosophy, history, or political economy. (All of Veblen's mentors in economics emphasized the significance of economic institutions.) And modern science? Admired in the farmlands and common schools of Wisconsin and Minnesota, in best-selling novels and populist tracts, and at World Fairs, scientific ways of producing knowledge had no equal in American higher education in the late nineteenth century. Indeed, they essentially defined the intellectual milieus during Veblen's time at Hopkins, Yale, Cornell, the University of Chicago, and even remote Carleton College.

This is not to say that Veblen was rifling deliberately through the storage boxes of his education when he wrote to Sarah Hardy about the needed "rehabilitation of the science [of economics] on modern lines." Not more than any of us when we are faced with a baffling problem and rummaging around for implements that might help deal with it did Veblen, in January 1896, stop to recollect where he got each of his intellectual tools, or when he first learned to use it, or how he figured out it applied to a range of tasks. For him, this was not the time to review his educational life history but to try to push ahead past his writing impasse. Even so, he recognized that the program he was proposing was "not so new or novel as I make it out to be." From his editorial work at the *JPE,* he could scarcely miss, for example, that younger economists were turning out monographs dealing with the "evolution of economic institutions."[71] Still, as his letter to Hardy continued, most of these empirical studies were too descriptive to speak to the theoretical problems of the hour—although, he added, eventually studies of this type "will have to come into an organic relation with . . . theoretical work." What was more, he saw signs theoretical progress was happening:

> This generalization [about the future of economics] may strike you as pretty fantastic, . . . but there is so much of a foundation for it all as that economic speculation and writing is visibly taking on such a cast today. This happens, if nowhere else, in the writings of some of the "cranky" economists. It might also be argued that this was the meaning of the movement called the Historical School; but the Historians . . . ran off into inanities. On the other hand, the Austrians and their followers in other countries have been groping out instinctively and blindly into the domain of psychology, . . . but as they were out of date in their psychology, besides not knowing what they were about, the result has not had the value which it otherwise might.[72]

As Hardy understood, "cranky economists" referred to classical economists like Laurence Laughlin. Among existing schools, this group was the only one he explicitly cited in evidence of his claim that there was already "so much foundation" for the renovation of economic theory. (This positive view reflected Veblen's own past writings in the classical vein, as well as his attachment to Laughlin.) In contrast, Veblen accused the German historical school of "inanities," while reserving his harshest comment for the Austrians and their followers: the "blind" marginalists.[73] As in his Socialism course a year earlier, this group was his main foil, guilty this time of impeding the development of economics into a "science of the evolution of economic institutions."

AFTER THIS INSIGHT INTO what he wanted to accomplish, Veblen broke through his writing impasse, completing a draft of his book sometime prior to fall 1896.[74] In mid-September 1896, the head of the New York office of the British publisher the Macmillan Company, a leading publisher of works on economic theory, asked Veblen, on the recommendation of economist Herbert Davenport, to submit the manuscript for review. (A major figure in Veblen's career, Davenport was a graduate student at Chicago during the 1897–1898 year, by which point he had already published two pro-marginalist theory texts with Macmillan. Despite their intellectual differences, he and Veblen became lifelong friends.) Responding to this invitation, Veblen referred to a draft he had written entitled "The Theory of the Leisure Class"; but now he added a subtitle that announced the arrival of the kind of economics he had envisioned in his letter to Hardy: "A Study in the Evolution of Economic Institutions." Still, Veblen told the publisher he needed time to revise the manuscript, which he finally submitted in June 1897. By then, however, Macmillan waffled; it first rejected the manuscript (raising sales concerns), then reconsidered when Veblen pushed back, until eventually accepting it on the double condition that Veblen would make stylistic revisions and pay half the cost of any losses the publisher incurred. Agreeing to these stingy terms, Veblen sent the publisher a final version in September 1898. Macmillan published the book in February 1899, steeply priced at $2 (= $65) per copy.[75]

What alterations he made to the book between mid-1896, when Davenport read the first draft, and September 1898, we do not know. Veblen told Macmillan the final revision was "appreciably more readable" and shorter than the version he first submitted, and that he had made "considerable changes" to its content, though he did not elaborate.[76] During this interval, he was in regular contact with Davenport, whose marginalist thinking may have heightened marginalism's immediacy for Veblen; also, he was reading his manuscript aloud, chapter by chapter, to his evolutionist friend Frederick Starr, and their discussions may have reinforced Veblen's interest in ethnological research.[77] But these inferences are guesswork. More certain is evidence from Veblen's book reviews during this period. These, as historian of economics Geoffrey Hodgson has pointed out, show Veblen working out an antiteleological, Darwinian stance in regard to the mechanisms of social evolution.[78] The book reviews also indicate Veblen's strong dissatisfaction with the arguments of distribution theorists. In a review from summer 1898, just as he was finalizing his book manuscript, Veblen denounced English economist William Mallock for defending the theory that that "owners of capital and directors of business [merit a] large share of the product of industry" because of their "productive" contributions.[79] These themes carried directly over into the book.

4.

All the expressions in the revised title Veblen finally settled on—*The Theory of the Leisure Class: An Economic Study in the Evolution of Institutions*—mattered to him, and he thought of them as forming a unity.[80] As a microscopic dissection of the leisure class, the book has no equal. But Veblen saw it no less as an analysis of economic institutions and their evolution—and as a critical and constructive contribution to economic theory. Before the book's publication, a sizable literature already existed on the leisure class, and the topic was part of the regular diet of readers of fin de siècle publications, both popular and academic, nonfictional and fictional. Inevitably, though, contemporaries had different opinions; some Americans admired the members of the leisure class and sought to emulate their lifestyles, while others ridiculed them as nonproductive social parasites. Veblen knew all this: voices on both sides of the conversation were loud and pervasive, and all his life he had been listening to diatribes against indolence and wasteful extravagance.

Veblen did not write his book, however, to dust off and rephrase the words of writers on the subject stretching as far back as Juvenal, Luther, and other canonical authors familiar to Veblen from his school days. He was neither a Roman satirist nor a religious reformer, any more than he was an aggrieved midwestern farmer or a futuristic novelist in the tradition of Edward Bellamy. He was a late nineteenth-century American economist, and his four-hundred-page anatomy of the leisure class was, from first to last, an "economic study" that had a scientific "theory" to offer. And just in case readers missed these words in the book's title, the first page of the preface spoke explicitly of the book's "theoretical premises," its "theoretical position," and (twice) its direct ties to "economic theory." To fasten on the theoretical argument of Veblen's book is not, however, to take away from its insights into the blood and guts of modern society. Just as his article on women's dress used commonplace information to build fresh theoretical generalizations that, in turn, cast a new light back on mundane articles of clothing, *The Theory of the Leisure Class* set out to theorize on the basis of "data ... drawn from everyday life" and "familiar to

299

all men" in order also to change how we see and understand the "homely facts" of ordinary social life that we take for granted.[81]

VEBLEN ACHIEVED HIS OBJECTIVES by using large parts of the book to make what we might think of as three surgical cuts into the corpus of marginalist economics.[82] (This count is mine, not a tally by Veblen, who was a disorganized writer even at his best—and he was not at his best in *The Theory of the Leisure Class,* partly because he was still feeling his way as a book writer, partly because of the difficult personal circumstances he was going through.) Veblen's first incision, appearing in the book's early chapters, involved an attack on the theory of value espoused by the marginalists, or, as he called them, "those economists who adhere with least faltering to the body of modernised classical doctrines."[83] To recap: marginalist theory postulated a direct link between consumer purchasing behavior and the "value" of the goods available for purchase. This consumptionist postulate was the theory's hallmark feature, as economists widely recognized. In this context, to write a book about the leisure class meant entering into marginalist territory; for, as Veblen understood it, what defined the leisure class was its pattern of consumption—its "consumption of goods" and its "consumption of time," as he said at several points in the book.[84] However, while marginalists examined the consumption of goods in terms of their marginal utility to the individual consumer, Veblen rejected this approach, countering it in *The Theory of the Leisure Class* with arguments that drew on the ways of understanding his education had instilled in him, particularly the practice of thinking in social rather than individualistic terms.

According to Veblen, the value of an object derives, foremost, not from the importance an individual consumer attaches to the last unit she or he acquires, but from the object's social significance: its function within a society whose members behave in accord with a dynamic psychology of reputation seeking, interpersonal emulation, and public display, rather than a hedonistic psychology of the satisfactions associated with additional units of the same object. (This difference in approach was part of what Veblen was getting at when he told Hardy in 1896 that he wanted to rehabilitate economics by using the "modern psychological sciences," not the "out of date psychology" of the Austrian school.)[85] Primarily, according to Veblen, objects of consumption are possessions by which men in society—and here he meant men, *not* women—signal their "pecuniary success," as they engage in "pecuniary emulation" and strive to outdo one another in a never-ending game of "invidious comparison." In this game, "the display of goods"—specifically, the "conspicuous consumption of valuable goods"—becomes a chief "means of showing pecuniary strength, and so of gaining or retaining a good name," or "reputability." Indeed, it is the capacity of some goods to confer reputability that gives "value" to these goods, *not* their utility for "serv[ing] the consumer's physical wants, [nor even] his so-called higher wants—spiritual, aesthetic, intellectual, or what not." "No class in society, not even the most abjectly poor, forgoes all customary conspicuous consumption," observed Veblen. But it is men of wealth who carry this process the farthest, since whispered wealth does not satisfy. What counts to them is exhibiting "evidence of wealth" through "unproductive consumption": that is, "conspicuously wasteful expenditures" on "superfluities" that run the gamut from high-priced clothing and ornate dinnerware (such as hand-wrought silver spoons) to gardens of exotic cottonwood trees and "grotesque" breeds of pets, including various "canine monstrosities." (Veblen was obviously having fun here.) This rollout of illustrations laid the ground for Veblen's later reputation as a satirist and an iconoclast who debunked the conventions of his society.[86]

More central to Veblen's analysis than the unproductive consumption of goods, however, was leisure: the "non-productive consumption of time." Unlike wasteful goods consumption, however, wasteful time consumption had, in his view, a narrower social class basis. To meet their needs, the members of the "lower classes [cannot] avoid labor"; life requires them to engage in "productive labor," or what Veblen termed "industrial employments." (He used the latter expression to mean all human activities that go to create a material product, not only work that occurs in the industrial sectors of modern societies.) Under the duress of this requirement, "labour becomes irksome" and "correspondingly odious" in repute, causing men—men with sufficient wealth (or property) that they are not compelled to work—to withdraw from "productive employments," for what better way to publicly display "pecuniary strength" in the contest for "invidious distinction"? Veblen explained:

> Conspicuous abstention from labour . . . becomes the conventional mark of superior pecuniary achievement and the conventional index of reputability; and conversely, since application to productive labour is a mark of poverty and subjection, it becomes inconsistent

with a reputable standing in the community. [This situation] dis-countenances participation in productive labour.[87]

From this insight followed Veblen's disquieting assertion about the lei-sure class: "The characteristic feature of the leisure-class life is a *conspic-uous exemption from all useful employment.*" The reality and pervasive-ness of this "exemption" did not deny, Veblen conceded, that leisure-class men sometime pursue nonproductive, "non-industrial occupations," such as warfare, politics, and law, because these activities bring social esteem—and, in some cases, additional wealth. Regardless, "the leisure-class canon demands strict and comprehensive futility" (rather than usefulness), even to the point of expecting class members—leisured women especially—to wear constrictive clothing that "make[s] plain to all observers that the wearer is not engaged in any kind of productive labour." Here, Veblen returned to one of his favorite illustrations, though he cited many others as well: part of his ingenuity was combing through the lifestyles of mem-bers of the leisure class for more and more instances that reveal this basic disconnect between possessing wealth and working productively. By piling on these examples, and inserting criticisms of contemporary economic theorists for neglecting them, Veblen hoped to break the core premise of marginalist productivity theory: Clark's notion that "we get what we pro-duce." By Veblen's account, the leisure class gets plenty, consuming with abandon, all the while doing nothing even remotely productive for the larger "human collectivity."[88]

Pressing these points, Veblen made use of practices, long familiar to him, that he had plied in his early articles and lectures. These included the practice of viewing the world in organic terms (rather than in atom-istic categories), the practice of valuing conduct that is socially produc-tive (rather than wasteful), and the practice of training attention on the evolutionary movement of societies (rather than their ahistorical features). Without hesitating, he then stretched all of these practices further in *The Theory of the Leisure Class,* adjusting them as necessary, to carry out a second, deeper incision into marginalist doctrines: one that went directly to marginalism's empty approach to temporal change.

Marginal productivity theorists, like Clark in the 1890s, although they did not dispute the raw fact of historical change, prioritized the "static" analysis of economic life. Their stated plan was to postpone the study of dynamics until they had formulated the timeless, universal laws of eco-nomics; to do so, their practice was to regard economic life as it operated before their eyes, at their own hour in history, as the template for what was "normal" for economies in all times and places. In the aftermath of his education, however, Veblen found this marginalist way of knowledge making indefensible. To his thinking, economists needed visual distance; they needed to stand back from the immediacy of the present to bring their subject matter into proper focus. Without this distance, they were left viewing the "current situation [as] a permanent state of things" and "accept[ing] things as they are," thus succumbing to a myopia at odds with modern science, which seeks "theories of the genesis and causation of the present-day state of things."[89]

This temporal myopia, Veblen believed, was responsible for the marginalists' obliviousness to the leisure class and conspicuous consumption, along with other lacunae in their work. Reaching into his toolbox for a concept that captured these neglected phenomena, Veblen referred to them en masse as "institutions"; but again he singled out "economic institutions," which he now defined succinctly as "habitual methods of carrying on"—in evolving ways, some successful, some not—"the life process of the community in contact with the material environment in which it lives." In the first sentence of the book's first chapter, he applied this collective concept to the subject of his study, characterizing the leisure class as an "institution" that had "developed" in "stages" over many centuries. And following this opening move, he immediately set off to examine the "savage," "barbarian," and "civilized" stages of human history, making use of ethnologists' familiar evolutionary trichotomy, which he intermixed with Herbert Spencer's distinction between "militant" and "industrial" societies. By Veblen's account, "the institution of a leisure class . . . emerged gradually during the transition from primitive savagery to barbarism; or, more precisely, during the transition from a peaceable to a consistently warlike habit of life," as found in "higher barbarian culture"; when this "predatory stage" subsequently gave way to the "earlier stages of the quasi-peaceable development of industry, . . . the leisure class in its consummate form" crystallized, though only to undergo further mutations with the later evolution of industrial society.[90]

A striking feature of this account was Veblen's flexible attitude toward the reigning notion of evolutionary stages. Accustomed to thinking of scientific laws as probabilistic statements, Veblen did not try to squeeze the development of economic institutions into a one-size-fits-all evolutionary scheme. In his view, the typifying features of any evolutionary stage manifested to different degrees in different societies at that same stage, depending on the historical specifics of individual cases. Discussing savage societies, for example, Veblen observed that "unequivocal instances of a primitive savage culture are hard to find"; looking across "communities that are classed as 'savage,'" such as the "tribes of Andamans," the "Bushman and Eskimo groups," and "some Pueblo communities," he saw major developmental differences. He also contrasted the consumption patterns of the leisure class of "civilized Europe" with those of the modern American leisure class, which he differentiated further into the leisured classes of southern and northern states.[91] In these ways, Veblen gave historical texture to his institutional-evolutionary analysis, following the repeated example of his teachers.

But Veblen was not done of this score. Scientists during Veblen's era expected proponents of evolutionary theory to specify the mechanisms by which social evolution occurs. Halfway into *The Theory of the Leisure Class*, Veblen came around to this question. [92] With biological scientists then divided over what they referred to as "Darwinian" and "neo-Larmarckian" explanations of how evolution takes place, Veblen (like Charles Darwin himself) recognized the operation of both mechanisms, giving both a part in his analysis of the development of social institutions. We see this in one of the most frequently cited passages in *The Theory of the Leisure Class*:

> The life of man in society, just like the life of other species, is a struggle for existence, and therefore a process of selective adaptation. The evolution of social structure has been a process of natural selection of institutions, . . . a natural selection of the fittest habits of thought to a process of enforced adaptation of individuals to an environment which has progressively changed with the growth of the community and with the changing institutions under which men have lived.[93]

Within a page of this statement about the evolution of institutions, however, Veblen complicated the story by tacking on (in a clumsy manner) a subplot involving the evolution of "ethnic types." For Veblen, as for his contemporaries (in ethnology and elsewhere), this expression referred to "aggregates of human subjects . . . with more or less definite physical and intellectual" traits, like those associated with the "dolichocephalic blond" and "brachycephalic-brunette" racial "stocks" of Europe (and, after colonization, of the Americas as well).[94] The first "stock" Veblen characterized as more "predatory" in temperament, the second as more "peaceable or anti-predatory," a distinction that reflected his general interest in undermining economists' one-dimensional depiction of economic actors as utility seekers. Veblen linked these speculations about ethnic types directly to his views on the mechanisms of social evolution: "For the immediate purpose [of the book] it need not be a question of serious importance whether [the evolutionary] process is a process of selection and survival of persistent ethnic types, or a process of individual adaptation and an inheritance of acquired traits."[95] Before saying more on this contested issue, however, Veblen had still another mechanism he wanted to introduce into his evolutionary narrative.

Doing so was part of Veblen's third incision into the body of marginal productivity theory, the last of his three cuts and probably the most critical (both for his time and for ours). To assert, as Veblen did, that the wealthy leisure class abstains from productive labor, yet indulges richly in consumption, laid bare a question that did not (and could not) arise for marginal productivity theorists: How do those who do nothing productive acquire the wealth they need to support lives centered on the conspicuous consumption of goods and time?

Veblen's evolutionary theory gave him a plain explanation: nonproductive people command wealth because they are predators, securely situated in "predatory institutions."[96] Adroitly, for a thoroughly nonreligious man, Veblen paraphrased John 4:38: people of the leisure class "reap where they have not strewn." Veblen wrote this in regard to men in "barbarian" societies, but he did not stop there; one of the lessons he drew from his long study of social evolution was that predation always finds a way. In the barbarian stage, men took to "exploit," by raw warfare and seizure, coercing women (who were often their captured slaves) to shoulder the burden of productive labor for the tribe. Under the impetus of invidious distinction, this form of exploit evolved into the institutions of private property ownership and wealth accumulation, although, at first, these still rested on the forced seizure of objects from the people who labored to produce them.[97] However, as the barbarian stage slowly mutated into the industrial stage of evolution, predation reinvented itself in the (slightly) disguised form of "pecuniary institutions" and nonproductive "pecuniary employments," as Veblen coldly observed:

In the early barbarian or predatory stage, [status in the leisure class was based on] massiveness, ferocity, unscrupulousness, and tenacity of purpose. These were the qualities that counted toward the accumulation and continued tenure of wealth. . . . But the methods of accumulating wealth, and the gifts required for holding it, have changed in some degree since the early days of the predatory culture. . . . Life in a modern industrial community, or in other words life under the pecuniary culture, acts . . . to conserve the barbarian temperament, but with the substitution of fraud and prudence . . . in place of that predilection for physical damage that characterizes the early barbarian. This substitution of chicane in place of devastation takes place only to an uncertain degree.[98]

Illustrating "chicane," Veblen wrote of the efforts by members of the pecuniary class—particularly by entrepreneurs involved in "management and financiering"—to craft organizational "changes affecting bankruptcy and receiverships, limited liability, banking and currency, coalitions of labourers or employers, trusts, and pools": "institutional furniture [designed to facilitate] peaceable and orderly exploitation."[99] (Veblen expanded on some of these points in later writings, as I will discuss.) An economy with these features, as he knew, was the antithesis of the economy presupposed by productivity theorists like Clark, who minimized the role of predation in the acquisition and preservation of wealth.[100]

The conviction that society was a vicious scene of predation was part of the tool set that Veblen learned to use while growing up on the farmlands and in schools of the Upper Midwest and that he practiced again under his mentors at Johns Hopkins, Yale, Cornell, and Chicago. (At Yale, Sumner could scarcely put this idea aside, no matter what the topic.) But now Veblen was applying it, in combination with other tools, to achieve a new purpose: to deliver the coup de grâce to marginal productivity theory with his own nonproductivity theory. Predation, said Veblen, was "parasitism" by another name, "parasitic" an expression that accurately captured the behavior of the modern leisure class. Further, these descriptors accorded with the research of evolutionists who were then studying the mechanisms of parasitic symbiosis (discussed in Chapter 6). An institution burrowed deep inside the social body, "exempt from productive labor," "sheltered from the stress of those economic exigencies which prevail in any modern . . . industrial community," and enabled to reproduce the "dolicho-blond type of man" with his predatory/pecuniary methods, the leisure class has it as its "office," according to Veblen, "to retard the movement [of] social evolution" toward adaptation and readjustment to changes in the economic environment, particularly "advance[s] in technical methods, in population [size], or in industrial organisation."[101] Articulating this same point in terms more familiar to some of his readers, Veblen inverted teleological accounts of evolution to suit the specifics of social evolution:

> The leisure class . . . consistently acts to retard that adjustment to the environment which is called social advance or development. . . . The law of natural selection, as applied to human institutions, gives the axiom: "Whatever is, is wrong." Not that the institutions of to-day are wholly wrong for the purposes of the life of to-day, but they are, always and in the nature of things, wrong to some extent. . . . The institution of a leisure class, by force of class interest and instinct, and by precept and prescriptive example, makes for the perpetuation of the existing maladjustment of institutions, and even favours a reversion to a somewhat more archaic scheme of life.[102]

In this retardant role, "the institution [of the leisure class] acts to lower the industrial efficiency of the community," Veblen argued, repudiating the marginalist claim that society's productivity-based system of wealth distribution *leads to* efficiency. In Veblen's view, the social parasite's enervating effect on its host precludes the marginalists' fantasy scenario. To support itself in its wonted style, the leisure class depends on "an underfed class of large proportions," and so it "withdraw[s] from [the lower classes] as much as it may of the means of sustenance, [reducing] their available energy, to such a point as to make them incapable of the effort required for the learning and adoption of new habits of thought."[103]

Productivity theorists' disregard of this massive efficiency drain was, to Veblen's way of thinking, a further instance of their ignorance of historical movement: a void that extended beyond their blindness to the nonproductivity of the leisure class to a flawed understanding of "the entire existing system of the distribution of wealth" that underpinned the leisure class. For Veblen, the distribution of wealth between social classes was not an eternal fact of nature; it, too, was an evolving "social institution," born in the barbarian stage and gradually transformed thereafter. Veblen regarded the leisure class as an "archaic institution" that would not survive the long march of history; however much the leisure class retarded "social advance," it could not thwart all "change and development," particularly not the expansion of the "industrial process" through the productive labors of men and women engaged in "industrial employments."

This expansion, combined with the eventual automation of the organizational practices devised by the pecuniary class, would, said Veblen, ultimately render this class "superfluous" and show "the dispensability of the great leisure-class function of [wealth] ownership"—in an evolutionary development inconceivable within the static boundaries of the marginalist productivity theory of distribution. Veblen's book did not specify what the next evolutionary stage would be and when it would arrive, aside from gesturing to "an indefinite future," which he was careful not to name "socialism."[104] *The Theory of the Leisure Class* grew out of Veblen's 1894 course on Socialism and his 1895 plan to write a series of books on socialism, only to result by 1899 in an "economic study" that mentioned socialism not once.

REACTIONS TO THE BOOK were mixed. In October 1899, after the book had been out eight months, Veblen wrote, self-mockingly, to brother Andrew: "Reviews of *The Theory of the Leisure Class* are coming in, for the most part quite severe. Opinion seems to be divided as to whether I am a knave or a fool, though there are some who make out that the book is a work of genius, I don't know just how." To judge from the known reviews, however, the first notices the book received were favorable. Mostly, these were brief summaries (largely accurate and somewhat amused) in the popular press, although the book also scored a long review by novelist William Dean Howells—"the Dean of American Letters"—who applauded Veblen for his sharp, satirical observations on the conventions of America's elite class.[105]

Critical assessments soon followed, however. In August 1899, D. Collin Wells, an economist from Dartmouth College writing in the prestigious *Yale Review,* archly ridiculed just about everything Veblen said in his book, calling its main arguments "vicious." Two months later, the *JPE* ran a more serious review in which Harvard economist John Cummings attacked *The Theory of the Leisure Class* from a marginalist standpoint. This attack provoked a lengthy reply by Veblen, which I will discuss later.[106] Counterbalancing these negative reviews were complimentary reactions by natural scientists at the University of Chicago, at least when they talked to Veblen in person. In a December 1899 letter, Veblen told Stanford economist-cum-sociologist E. A. Ross (who himself regarded the book as "masterly") about what he was hearing: "You will pardon a bit of conceited garrulity. One of the surprises, and not the least flattering, that has come to me in connection with the 'Leisure Class' is the fact that several of the men in the natural sciences here speak of it as an example of true scientific method!"[107]

The next year, sociologists weighed in, with Samuel Lindsay (of the University of Pennsylvania) criticizing Veblen's use of ethnological evidence, but Lester Ward (of the US Geological Survey) enthusing that *The Theory of the Leisure Class* was so analytically astute that it almost "contains too much truth." Writing in the popular magazine *The Dial,* Veblen's University of Chicago colleague Charles Henderson discussed the "great merit" of the book, adding in the comment: "The word 'socialism' is scrupulously avoided [in the book], but the arguments made familiar by the socialists gleam through the sentences of every chapter." Veblen did not welcome this interpretation, as Chicago philosopher George Herbert Mead recounted in May 1901: "Had a pleasant call upon Veblen, who is pained because [some reviewers say that] his book is good Socialism."[108]

Whatever opinions about the book reviewers had, not one suggested that its author was an alien outsider, lofted high above the academic mainstream. Instead, most the reviewers described *The Theory of the Leisure Class* matter-of-factly as an "economic study" that fell inside the bounds of economics. Ward elaborated this point, observing (with approval) that Veblen's "point of view is strictly economic, and he deals with a subject within his own specialty, and has not seen fit to branch out into wider fields, as economic writers are so much in the habit of doing. *Ne sutor ultra crepidam*" ("shoemaker, not beyond the shoe"—the classical warning about going outside one's sphere of expertise).[109] A few commentators did remark that *The Theory of the Leisure Class* was also a contribution to sociology, but its relevance to economics was uppermost for all of them. What was more, although some reviewers lacked the knowledge needed to identify exactly what Veblen brought to the study of economic theory, the cognoscenti spotted this right away. They singled out Veblen's distinction between "productive and non-productive employments," with Cummings's review objecting to how Veblen (unsuccessfully) used this dichotomy to undercut existing theories of wealth distribution. Cummings (among others) criticized Veblen's distinction, while other reviewers commended it. Either way, they acknowledged Veblen was making his novel arguments from inside his field.[110]

PROBABLY FOR THIS REASON, Veblen's stature in the field rose following the book's publication. In 1901, for example, he was invited onto the governing Council of the American Economic Association, where he served two consecutive three-year terms.[111] More significantly, his employment situation began to improve, partly because of a job opening at Stanford University, the University of Chicago's West Coast counterpart. (Both schools opened in the early 1890s with large endowments from very wealthy men.) At the time, Stanford's president was ichthyologist David Starr Jordan, another micromanager in the style of Harper, who planned to make an appointment in his department of economics and sociology.[112] When word of this plan got around (as it quickly did), Jordan was inundated with advice and applications, including one from Veblen, who wrote him, very formally, in March 1899: "I am told that a vacancy may presently be expected in your faculty of Political Economy. . . . If such is the case, and if the work required is of the kind for which I am equipped, it is my desire to be considered as a candidate for the place." Veblen mailed this inquiry a few days after he had had his publisher send Jordan a copy of *The Theory of the Leisure Class,* with a letter pointing him to the chapter on parasites—a subject of Jordan's own research. Apparently, Jordan liked the book and initially encouraged Veblen's application.[113]

All this occurred while Veblen was smarting over Harper's continuing unwillingness to boost his rank or salary, despite (as he reminded Harper in January 1899) "the expressions of cordial appreciation of my work which have from time to time been vouchsafed both by Professor Laughlin and by you."[114] So Veblen asked three major-league figures in his field to recommend him to Jordan: Harvard's classically inclined theorist Frank Taussig, Cornell's historically oriented researcher Jeremiah Jenks, and Laughlin himself. All three agreed and sent strong letters of support, accompanied in Laughlin's case with an explanation.

> Dr. T. B. Veblen, of our staff wishes me to write you of him. Under the circumstances my only hesitation is in saying things which might lose him to us. For I must say that he is one of the brainiest, deepest economists we have. . . . Speaking for myself alone, I should not think of allowing him to go. . . . But, in President Harper's view, there is not just now income enough to grant Dr. Veblen the promotion which he has deserved. Consequently, he is moved to think he should look elsewhere. I cannot find fault with him in this; and it is my duty to say the truth of him when requested. But I have a hope that he will not be tempted away from us until we can honor him as I think he deserves.[115]

Figure 8 Thorstein Veblen, early 1900s

In the end, Jordan decided to hire marginalist Frank Fetter, although Veblen remained on his attention screen. For the time being, though, Jordan's expression of interest gave Laughlin leverage to push Harper to raise Veblen's salary by 33 percent, to $2,000 (= $64,200) and to promote him to the rank of assistant professor, starting in 1900. (An entry-level position today, "assistant professor" at Chicago in 1900 was a mid-tier rank Veblen shared with several other major scholars who were roughly his age.)[116] These changes in status were his material reward for publishing his first book.

5.

As he was putting the finishing touches on *The Theory of the Leisure Class* and in the period shortly afterward, Veblen wrote several related articles. Since the best remembered of these appeared in print before the book, interpreters have often seen them as laying the book's groundwork, although Veblen actually drafted the better part of the book *before* composing the articles. Because of this sequencing, we should see these other writings as offshoots of the book project rather than the other way around (with allowances for feedback, since Veblen carried some of the ideas he developed in the articles back to the book manuscript as he was finalizing it).

In substance, these offshoot writings clustered in two groups, both complements to the economic argument of *The Theory of the Leisure Class*. One group drew on research in the area of ethnology, and the second group consisted of critical analyses of schools of economic thought. Both strands became regular features of Veblen's oeuvre, continuing during his remaining years at the University of Chicago and extending through his time at Stanford.

Of the two strands, the ethnological demonstrates again how deeply immersed Veblen was in this branch of anthropology. In an 1899 review of a book by Simon Patten, for example, he referred confidently to recent research on the "Aleutian and Alaskan tribes," the "Yucatanese and Mexican civilizations," and the customs of the Ainu, the Austrians, the Bushmen, the Fuegians, the Haida, and the Pueblos. Veblen gestured to this research to urge economists to build theories that accommodated societies unlike their own; for good measure, he also recommended they take account of studies of the different "racial stocks" of Europe.[117]

Fluent in this ethnographic literature, Veblen effortlessly appropriated it in the service of his own nonproductivity theory of distribution. We see this in a trio of articles that originated in an address he gave to a graduate student club at the University of Chicago in April 1898. During the months that followed, they ran in back-to-back issues of the Chicago-based *American Journal of Sociology* (*AJS*), where they alternated with related pieces on folk psychology by one of the journal's editors, Veblen's friend W. I. Thomas.

In these articles, Veblen filled in some of the evolutionary background for *The Theory of the Leisure Class*. As in the book, he centered his analysis on the binary of productive versus unproductive labor, contrasting the status of work in "savage" versus "barbarian" societies. Given the limited length of a journal article, Veblen got immediately to the point, letting readers know he had productivity theories of distribution as his aim. In the first paragraph of the second article in this ethnological series, for example, Veblen wrote:

> In the accepted economic theories, the ground of ownership is commonly conceived to be the productive labor of the owner. This is taken, without reflection, to be the legitimate basis of property. . . . [This axiom made it hard for classical economists] to explain how the capitalist is the "producer" of the goods that pass into his possession. [Nevertheless, even now,] the main position is scarcely questioned, that in the normal case wealth is distributed in proportion to—and in some cogent sense because of—the recipient's contribution to the product.[118]

Veblen's last few words here were a transparent allusion to John Bates Clark and other marginalists, whose theory of wealth distribution sought to avoid the classicists' stumbling block by demonstrating that "capital" and "labor" both contribute actively to the production process. On Veblen's account, this marginalist claim did not square with the facts of evolution, which showed that, as the economic environment of societies changed during the "barbarian" stage, productive labor came to be a "tainted" activity—something "unworthy," "debasing," and "shunned by self-respecting men." From that stage forward, men preferred to live by "predatory exploit," amassing wealth by "the practice of plundering—of seizing goods [and] persons" from groups they could overpower.

This thesis foreshadowed Veblen's argument in *The Theory of the Leisure Class,* but in the articles he presented it as part of a more linear chronology. He also considered in fuller ethnological detail the long, peaceable, "savage" stage of evolution, introducing in this context a new concept that was indebted to folk psychologists' notions about human instincts. This concept was "the instinct of workmanship," by which Veblen meant humankind's hereditary "proclivity to purposeful action," with the human being "an agent seeking in every act the accomplishment of some concrete, objective, impersonal end." (Conferring on the human species a "great advantage over other species in the struggle for existence," this trait, according to Veblen, manifested more in some "races" than others.) At the "savage" stage, according to Veblen, the instinct of workmanship exerted a controlling influence in group life. In the "barbarian" stage it receded, though never to the point of disappearing.[119] This was an idea Veblen wove into *The Theory of the Leisure Class*. Going forward from there, ethnological materials continued to inform his writings and lectures. For instance, in "Economic Factors in Civilization"—his signature course at the University of Chicago from 1899 to 1906—he referenced monograph after monograph dealing with the economic institutions of "savage" and "barbarian" societies in order to equip his students to understand modern industrial civilizations. When his interest as an economist segued from the leisure class to the business enterprise (discussed later), he culled the research of ethnologists to locate the early beginnings of the institution of "trusts" in the "barbarian" age of the Vikings. And when he was in his fifties, Veblen submitted a proposal to the Carnegie Institution to carry out a multiyear, firsthand ethnological study, situated primarily in Denmark and Sweden, of "Baltic and Cretan Antiquities."[120]

The second cluster of articles from the period just before and after *The Theory of the Leisure Class* did not have the same direct overlap with the book as Veblen's 1899–1900 ethnological articles. Over the past fifty years, however, this second cluster—made up of critical studies of the leading schools of economic thought—has acquired a large reputation in its own right, particularly among present-day readers dissatisfied with "mainstream economics" (as they construe it). Veblen published this set of four articles in Harvard's *Quarterly Journal of Economics,* where it was a natural fit because the journal was a magnet for expository essays on the different kinds of economic theory.

In the eyes of many of his contemporaries, Veblen's *QJE* articles were admirable journeyman contributions, but no more than that. They covered ground that was mostly familiar, particularly to economists interested in the meta-analysis of different economic schools. For Veblen himself, on the other hand, the *QJE* pieces were an occasion to go public with the program he had foreshadowed in his January 1896 letter to Sarah Hardy: his program for the "rehabilitation" of economics into "a science of the evolution of economic institutions." In the articles, Veblen elaborated on this program by drawing on material he had just worked up for two graduate-level courses he was assigned to teach after he finished drafting *The Theory of the Leisure Class:* History of Political Economy (which he first taught in the fall quarter of 1896), and Scope and Method of Political Economy (which he first taught in the winter quarter of 1897).[121]

The starting point of the four essays was Veblen's observation that "economics is helplessly behind the times and unable to handle its subject-matter in a way to entitle it to standing as a modern science." Veblen knew this accusation was not new. Scholars in the natural sciences, in the neighboring social sciences, and in economics too had been raising the complaint for years, although their complaining had not taken them much beyond asserting that "modern sciences are evolutionary sciences." So, in the title of the first article (from July 1898), Veblen posed the question: "Why Is Economics Not an Evolutionary Science?" In this and the three articles that followed (between January 1899 and February 1900) under the title "The Preconceptions of Economic Science," he answered by arguing that economics was stymied by misguided methodological assumptions. These prevented economists from offering what a genuine evolutionary science offered—namely, a "matter-of-fact" analysis of phenomena "in terms of cause and effect," where each effect becomes, in sequence, the cause of another effect in a continuous process of "cumulative causation."[122]

The rehabilitation of economics, by Veblen's reckoning, required extending this view of science to the study of economic phenomena, with the objective of producing "a genetic account of the economic life process."[123] But in the *QJE* articles, Veblen was less concerned with doing so himself than with identifying the reasons why economists of the past had *not* done so—an analysis he carried out by means of a dense exegesis of the work of some dozen canonical writers, from worthies like Adam Smith to the marginalists of his own time.[124] Read today, this exegesis, which ran for more than one hundred pages, seems abstruse and ponderous, although it showcases Veblen in fine iconoclastic form, as he combines detailed textual exposition with a direct assault on the ideas of generations of his predecessors.

To organize his attack, Veblen held to the standard partitioning of the history of economics into the classical school, the German historical school, and the Austrian school. Along the way, he folded in a few additional subdivisions, plus some remarks on the socioeconomic contexts that spurred the development of these different schools. Veblen's analysis of the historical school was minimalist, however; that he saved for a future publication. In his 1898–1900 *QJE* articles, his primary interest was to identify what handicapped the classical economists (and their descendants down to the marginalists) from engaging in evolutionary thinking. In technical, theoretical detail, he argued that the obstacle was their adherence to "taxonomic" methods, practices of "classification" long since discarded in the evolutionary sciences.

This was artful and compelling labeling on Veblen's part, since "taxonomy" and "classification" were words with strong negative valences (as the work of Ely, Thomas, and many natural scientists attested). These terms connoted timeworn efforts, widely discredited outside of economics, to pigeonhole life-forms: to assign them to fixed, static categories rather than to treat them as subjects of evolutionary growth and change. Yet, on Veblen's account, taxonomy—and the hair-splitting definitions and gnarled nomenclatures that were part of it—went to the core of the classical heritage, which labored to distinguish separate factors of production (with hard-and-fast boundaries dividing labor, capital, and land) and to differentiate "normal" from "abnormal" economic phenomena (with regard, in particular, to wage rates, interest rates, and rents).[125]

To readers of the *QJE*, these examples immediately conveyed that Veblen was targeting the marginalists just as much as the classical economists, and at several points he said so explicitly (while admitting, reluctantly, that a few marginalists were beginning to see the light). He explained that for theorists steeped in taxonomic ways of thinking, economic change (insofar as it occurred at all) consisted of little more than the teleological movement of an abnormal economic phenomenon toward its normal, or natural, condition—with the movement's teleological direction set by whatever the economist decided to designate as an economy's "normal" state. John Bates Clark's distribution theory was, to Veblen, just the latest version of this Austrian-style economic reasoning.[126] Indeed, Veblen himself had practiced it in the Laughlin-influenced articles he wrote at Cornell and during his first year at the University of Chicago. But now, with his evolutionary tools recharged by daily involvement in the intellectual life of the university, he ripped into taxonomists; first, for postulating classification schemes that had little or no basis in observable facts, and then for drawing deductions about production, consumption, and distribution from these a priori categories.[127]

Veblen's discussion of these theoretical-cum-methodological defects gave him an opportunity to take up ideas that traced back to Carleton, Hopkins, and Yale, where Clark (in his earlier years), Ely, and Sumner had all initiated him into the field of political economy by way of the historical school's attack on the fiction of "economic man" as a selfish, atomized, and ahistorical being.[128] Now, Veblen returned to these points, flavoring them with the word "hedonistic," a slander that economists of the 1890s often associated with marginal utility theory (because of its focus on utility-maximizing individuals). He wrote:

> The reason for the Austrian failure seems to lie in a faulty conception of human nature, [which] is conceived in hedonistic terms. . . . The hedonistic conception of man is that of a lighning [*sic*] calcu-

lator of pleasures and pains, who oscillates like a homogeneous globule of desire of happiness. . . . He has neither antecedent nor consequent. He is an isolated, definitive human datum . . . self-poised in elemental space.

Or in another formulation:

In hedonistic theory the substantial end of economic life is individual gain. . . . Moreover, society, in [this] philosophy, is the algebraic sum of individuals; and the interest of society is the sum of the interests of the individuals.[129]

Later admirers of Veblen, bypassing the first sentence in the first of these passages, have often praised such statements for their unique insight into classical economics and its sequels. For Veblen himself, however, in the academic milieu of the 1890s, the function of these passages was to transpose directly onto marginalist theory a critique of economics that he (and most of his contemporaries) knew by heart. That making this move was Veblen's purpose is signaled in his unequivocal opening statement about "the Austrian failure" and its "faulty conception of human nature."

Where he went next, though, involved applying a range of tools to repair the damage caused by the marginalists. These included the Darwinist idea, voiced most strongly to him by Sumner (and echoed by Peirce and Tuttle), that there is no grand telos steering the overall course of history; the ethnological idea, common to Clark (the early Clark), Summer, Tyler, Starr, and Thomas, that the makeup of humankind—its habits, propensities, instincts, and so forth—differs in different times and places (as well as across races); and the psychological idea, broached by Ladd and Porter (and developed by Dewey's and Veblen's other pragmatist colleagues at Chicago), that human conduct is teleological, an active process in which men and women seek to attain their ends or purposes.[130] In the 1898–1900 *QJE* articles, Veblen spliced these points together in several overloaded passages, to the following effect:

The modern sciences [have] narrowed the range of discretionary, teleological action to the human agents alone, . . . compelling our knowledge of human conduct [to make use of] teleological terms. . . . *Economic action must be the subject-matter of the science if the science is to fall into line as an evolutionary science. . . . According to this conception, [man] is not simply a bundle of desires, . . . but rather a coherent structure of propensities and habits. . . .* [These] are the products of his hereditary traits and past experience, cumulatively wrought out under a given body of traditions, conventionalities, and material circumstances; and *they afford the point of departure for . . . further development of the methods of compassing the ends sought and for the further variation of ends that are sought to be compassed.* In all this flux there is no definitively adequate method of life and no definitive or absolutely worthy end of action, so far as concerns the science which sets out to formulate a theory of the process of economic life. . . . *What, in specific detail, [humans] seek, is not to be answered except by a scrutiny of the details of their activity; but, so long as we have to do with their life as members of the economic community, there remains the generic fact that their life is an unfolding activity of a teleological kind.*[131]

Veblen saw this analysis as the abstract counterpart to his empirical attack in *The Theory of the Leisure Class* on the marginalist notion that labor is "always productive." For, inasmuch as men and women are other than "homogeneous bundles of desire," and are teleologically oriented actors seeking ends that are heterogeneous and ever more varied, any economic theory that rested on "always" statements was, according to Veblen, untenable. And that, he said, was exactly the case with distribution theories in which "productivity is . . . presumed [as the defining feature] of any occupation or enterprise that looks to a pecuniary gain," and in which it is assumed "that the remuneration of . . . persons engaged in industry coincides with their productive contribution."[132] In Veblen's view, the alternative to these distorted assumptions was an economics that recognized that, in the "flux" of history, there arose different kinds of economic activities, chief among them the divergent industrial and pecuniary activities found in modern society—the former productive, the latter nonproductive. The contrast between the two was the linchpin of his critical attack on the picture of economic life offered up by productivity theories of distribution.

"Why Is Economics Not an Evolutionary Science?" and the three installments of "The Preconceptions of Economic Science" impressed *QJE* editor Frank Taussig, who encouraged Veblen to widen his critique to include other leading schools of economic thought. Sometime in 1900 or 1901, Taussig asked Veblen to write an extended review essay on the latest opus from the German historical school, Gustav Schmoller's *Grundriss der allgemeinen Volkwirtschafslehre (Outline of General Eco-*

nomics). Probably Taussig was aware of Veblen's interest in the German intellectual tradition, because Veblen had just translated and published one of the classics of German socialist thought, Ferdinand Lassalle's 1863 address, *Die Wissenschaft und die Arbeiter (Science and the Workingmen)*.[133] In any event, Veblen accepted Taussig's invitation and prepared for the *QJE* a twenty-five-page essay that discussed Schmoller in relation to the earlier history of the historical school. Following Laurence Laughlin and other American critics of the school, Veblen attacked the German historicist tradition for its theoretical barrenness and its reduction of economic research to nothing more than "narrative, statistics, and description," which were misused to lend support to political programs that rested on indefensible premises about society's final destiny. Bringing Schmoller himself into the story, Veblen lauded the younger economist for attempting to depart from this older historicist tradition by building a "causal theory" of economic evolution—"a Darwinistic account of the origin, growth, persistence, and variation of institutions." Still, according to Veblen, Schmoller's work fell seriously short; it duplicated the principal failings of Schmoller's forebears, especially their urge to dispense "reformatory advice" and indulge in normative questions about "what ought to be and what modern society must do to be saved." From Veblen's perspective, this teleological backsliding violated the protocols of Darwinian science.[134]

During Taussig's editorship of the *QJE*, Veblen subsequently published a pair of long exegetical articles on the Marxist school of economics. These were outgrowths of a series of lectures Taussig and his colleagues arranged for Veblen to present at Harvard's department of economics in April 1906. (This invitation was a good sign of Veblen's professional standing, since the Harvard department, the center of academic economics in the United States, did not host lecturing gigs for marginal men.) Veblen gave these lectures just as he was making plans to leave the University of Chicago and accept a position at Stanford University, and the lectures appeared in the *QJE* shortly afterward. Highly critical of Marxist economists for combining the worst of the German historical school (teleological reasoning about the progressive direction of history) and the classical school (hedonistic psychology), Veblen rebuffed the Marxist school, just as he had rejected the others, as pre-Darwinian: "unfit . . . for the purposes of modern science" and an obstacle to scientific "inquiry into the evolution of institutions."[135]

Attacking Marxism was only an interlude for Veblen, however. During his three years at Stanford (1906–1909), critical analyses of the theories of the marginal utility school—particularly its productivity theory of distribution—remained at the forefront of his exegetical writings.[136] In fact, of the seven articles and review essays Veblen published in this period, six consisted, in part or all, of the exposition and dismantling of the work of leading members of the school, including John Bates Clark himself. Because Veblen's Stanford years fall outside the time frame of this book, I will not discuss these articles, except to note one striking feature. Even more than Veblen's previous expository articles, those from his time at Stanford are extremely technical, and aimed at experts (and very few others). In them, Veblen plumbed marginalism's canonical texts to such depths—and with such tortured language—that even professional economists sometimes balked.

In 1909, for example, when Veblen submitted his capstone paper on marginalism, "The Limitations of Marginal Utility," to the *Political Science Quarterly,* its editor, economist Edwin Seligman, who had just published Veblen's essays on marginalist Irving Fisher, demurred. He explained to Veblen: "We all agree that it is an admirable article, quite up to the level of the excellent work which you always do; [but] we try to avoid technical articles and pure theory as much as possible, as we have an arrangement with the *Quarterly Journal of Economics* whereby we usually send such articles to them, and they send articles of a more concrete character to us."[137] This is what Seligman did; and the *QJE,* still edited by Taussig (who still welcomed Veblen's work), accepted the article in what amounted to a routine transaction among academic insiders: a friendly exchange between the editors of two elite journals over a paper by the past editor of another leading journal (*JPE*), written for academic economists about the latest theories of other academic economists. As Taussig and Seligman knew, Veblen's article had a message that mattered to economists of the time (even if they might disagree with it)—namely, that marginalist theory was "a consistent and comprehensive failure." Or, as Veblen said more acerbically: "It is a long time since puerility or absurdity has been a bar to any supposition in the arguments on marginal utility."[138] For Veblen, the judgment was corroborated by research he had recently completed in his ongoing effort to develop his own nonproductivity theory of distribution.

6.

As these things go, the interval between Veblen's first book and his second, *The Theory of Business Enterprise,* was short. He completed the first in

September 1898, the second in February 1904; and he had major parts of the argument of the second down on paper as early as December 1899, and more by December 1900.[139] Still, even allowing for the detours involved in the writings considered in the previous subsection, the path between the two books was not as straight as these dates suggest. In July 1900, with *The Theory of the Leisure Class* as his reference point, Veblen wrote to Sarah Hardy that "the 'next book" has been named." He explained: "It is to be called 'The Instinct of Workmanship,' [and] I have no doubt [it] will be written before long, but I confess . . . I don't know what or what kind of things will go into the new book." Veblen soon put these worries aside, however; the *Instinct of Workmanship* did not appear for fourteen more years. Shortly after writing to Hardy about it, he decided another project would come first.[140]

What altered Veblen's course was, as on previous occasions, partly the result of unanticipated circumstances arising at the top of the academy. I mentioned earlier John Cummings's thirty-page review of *The Theory of the Leisure Class,* which appeared—in the spotlight, as the lead article— in September 1899 in the *JPE*. In this essay, Cummings (who, before joining the Harvard faculty, had been Veblen's colleague at Chicago) defended the high earnings of "captains of industry," assailing *The Theory of the Leisure Class* for the "unreal character" of the distinction Veblen drew between productive, industrial employments and nonproductive, pecuniary employments. Rather than separable from one another, industrial and pecuniary activities, according to Cummings, necessarily combine in the work of people involved in the process of production, such that "the labor which the manufacturer performs is exactly the same sort of labor that is performed by every workman in his factory, only it is of a higher order."[141] Because this marginalist assertion directly collided with the argument of *The Theory of the Leisure Class,* Veblen pushed back hard in a long reply in the December 1899 issue of the *JPE*. Here he condescendingly granted that the industrial-pecuniary distinction—lost on Cummings, he said—was "recondite" and might benefit from a clearer, fuller exposition.[142]

Veblen's chance to provide this came, barely a month later, when Frank Taussig, Cummings's Harvard colleague, contacted Richard Ely, then the president of the American Economic Association, to propose inviting Veblen to speak at the December 1900 meetings of the AEA on a particular "theoretic subject" that Taussig wanted to hear more about. Wrote Taussig: Veblen "has done some writing of late on what he calls the difference between 'productive' and 'pecuniary' activity. This distinction is a novel one, [and] I think a paper by Veblen, setting forth his conclusions, would be a fresh contribution and would stimulate interesting discussion."[143] Ely agreed and proceeded to invite Veblen, who accepted his former teacher's offer and prepared, by the December 1900 due date, his milestone paper, "Industrial and Pecuniary Employments."[144] Pleading illness, Veblen did not show up to deliver it in person when the conference assembled; but he followed through and, as the AEA required of invited speakers, published the paper in its volume of conference proceedings early in 1901. (In what follows, I refer to this paper as Veblen's AEA article.)

By July 1901, Veblen had enlarged this article into a short book manuscript titled "The Captain of Industry and His Work." When he submitted this to Macmillan, however, the publisher declined it, causing Veblen to expand the manuscript again over the course of the next two years. At this stage (March 1903), Laurence Laughlin intervened on Veblen's behalf, recommending the revised manuscript to his own publisher, the distinguished house of Charles Scribner's Sons, which accepted it a year later, under a new title: *The Theory of Business Enterprise*.[145] (In this form, the book was published in September 1904, priced at $1.50 [= $45] a copy.) Veblen, by this date, had tightened the manuscript, cutting out a long final chapter in which he had applied his analysis of the business enterprise to modern universities. From the leftover material, Veblen then build a freestanding book, which Scribner's rejected as "too highly specialized."[146] Perhaps worn down by the drawn-out submission process, or perhaps too absorbed by more pressing problems, professional and personal, Veblen then decided to set aside the remnant for the time being, eventually shelving it for more than a decade. Slightly revised, it was finally published in 1918 as *The Higher Learning in America*. Chronologically speaking, this late publication date places the book outside the time limits of my study, but because Veblen seems to have composed most of it earlier, I include it in the following discussion, along with his other Chicago-period writings on the business enterprise. Together, they show Thorstein Veblen as the academic economist he had become by his late forties.

AT THE TURN OF the last century, the large corporation—the "business enterprise" as contemporaries called it—was a highly visible, highly charged topic in American culture, dwarfing the leisure class as a subject of public controversy and academic debate. According to economic historians, the corporation was born in the years between the end of the Civil War and the start of the new century; and during these years, it assumed several different organizational forms (cartels, trusts, mergers, and so on), which contemporaries often referred to en bloc as "trusts" or "monopolies." In tandem with this institutional transformation, impassioned discussion about the benefits and the dangers of the corporation erupted in the press and other popular outlets, in which negative reactions typically outnumbered the positive. The research of historian Louis Galambos has found, for example, that "by 1901, an entire generation of Americans had acquired distinctive attitudes toward big business," among which "the most general pattern [was] one of mounting hostility"— "anger against the trusts and syndicates that were remaking the structure of industrial society."[147] Fueling these attitudes were headlining public events, such as the star-studded Chicago Trust Conference in September 1899, and searing exposés of major corporations by muckraking journalists like Henry Demarest Lloyd (in 1893) and Ida Tarbell (in 1904).[148]

Publications directed at more specialized audiences also appeared almost daily. Taking stock in 1901, Charles Bullock (soon to join the Harvard economics department) reported that the previous two years alone had brought nearly thirty books and scores of articles on the business enterprise by scholars in several academic fields. As we would expect, economists were the heaviest producers of this work, which compiled data on the makeup and workings of modern corporations, sometimes as part of research on the evolution of economic institutions.[149] For instance, in books from the 1880s and 1890s, Yale's Arthur Hadley examined the growth of corporations in the transportation industry, while Cornell's Jeremiah Jenks published in 1900 a set of studies on the consolidation of firms in the sugar, whiskey, and petroleum industries. (I mention Hadley and Jenks, rather than other figures, because Veblen knew them personally from his time at Yale and Cornell.) Like other empirically oriented economists during this period, Hadley and Jenks both aimed for an evenhanded treatment of their topic. They credited trusts and other large business enterprises with increasing productivity and efficiency but worried that corporations were enlarging the zone of "unscrupulousness" in business dealings. Both scholars discussed the new, often shady, techniques of profit-making that corporations were devising (complex financial instruments, mass advertising campaigns, and so forth) and some of the shifty new characters who were joining the cast of capitalists, workers, and entrepreneurs in the saga of the modern corporation: specifically, financiers, promoters, and speculators (their exact names and roles were still in flux). Hadley and Jenks were neither alone among economists in noticing the appearance of these techniques and characters nor in attempting to identify their "productive contributions." As the literature on the business enterprise grew at the turn of the century, so did writings by economists on these accompanying developments.[150]

Academics from other social sciences (sociology, political science) and from the humanities (philosophy, history) also examined these omnipresent economic changes, as we have seen in my earlier discussion of Veblen's teachers and his University of Chicago associates. Further, when Veblen looked beyond his local circles, he encountered scholars in other fields who were tackling the phenomenon of the corporation: case in point, his colleague at-a-distance Lester Ward, the "patriarch of sociology" (as Veblen and others called the first president of the American Sociological Society). As early as 1883, in his *Dynamic Sociology,* Ward drew attention to "monopolies" and other "combinations"; on his account, these institutions exacerbated society's already severe maldistribution of wealth. Ward used the growth of monopolies and combinations to illustrate his "Law of Acquisition," which posited a distinction between the activities of "getting" wealth and "producing" wealth, adding the corollary that human beings prefer the first alternative over the second. Historically, this preference gave rise, Ward held, to changing "modes of acquisition," on the basis of which society's "non-producers"—its "non-industrial or parasitic classes"—contrived to wrest the lion's share of wealth away from its actual producers. Ward classified these methods of acquisition as "robbery, theft, war, statecraft, priestcraft, and monopoly," associating his own evolutionary era with "the monopoly of capital, which denies to the true producer the product of his labor, [while deriving] large profits from the manufacture"—the business enterprise—for the capitalist. Inventive, this argument made little impression on economists, though that was probably fair; Ward was neither writing for them nor speaking to recent intellectual developments in their field.[151]

IN CONTRAST, Veblen wrote *The Theory of Business Enterprise* mainly for economists. He said so explicitly, telling his friend E. A. Ross in October 1905 (a year after the book came out) that, in publishing it, he did so with "some misgivings, chiefly that it would pass unnoticed by the gild [*sic*] of economists to whom it is addressed."[152] If Ross had asked, Veblen would have said the same about the articles he published in the lead-up to the book. But the title of the book—identical in form to *The Theory of the Leisure Class*—sent the clearest signal that, once again, Veblen's uppermost purpose was to develop a scientific "theory." And, in historical context, that made sense, because empirical information about the modern corporation was already easily accessible.

This accessibility probably explains Veblen's claim to Sarah Gregory (nee Hardy) in 1903 that the "business enterprise [is] a topic on which I am free to theorize with all the abandon that comes of immunity from the facts"; for, as they both knew, he was not at all immune to widely known "facts" about the corporation.[153] Furthermore, the *JPE*, which Veblen was still editing, regularly published empirical articles on big business, and he was teaching courses called "Trusts" and the "Organization of Business Enterprise."[154] Veblen's footnotes in *The Theory of Business Enterprise* brimmed with citations to academic research on the subject, as well as to pertinent government documents, including the thick *Report of the Industrial Commission on Trusts and Industrial Combinations*. This contained firsthand testimony by business leaders who were witnesses in a federal inquiry into the workings of the American corporation.

This factual material informed Veblen's theory, and one of his aspirations was that, in return, the theory would lay bare ugly folds, not yet spotted by contemporaries, in the underbelly of corporate America. Formulating a correct economic theory took precedence, however, and in *The Theory of Business Enterprise* Veblen announced that his "present purpose [was] to outline an economic theory of current business enterprise"—a theory that would undo the distortions of marginal productivity theorists.[155] In the 1901 AEA article that anticipated the book, Veblen identified these economic distortionists, pointing once again to John Bates Clark and the Austrians. He then homed in on Clark's foundational productivity thesis: that "the several participants or factors in the economic process severally get"—in terms of income or wealth share—"as much as they produce; and conversely, in the normal case they severally produce as much as they get." For easy reference, Veblen labeled this thesis the "theorem of equivalence," mildly remarking that he wanted to enter a "possible correction [to this] point in the theory of distribution." But this comment was false modesty on his part. For, as he and his readers in economics knew full well, his "correction," if it stuck, meant an end to the productivity theory of distribution, the hot spot for economic theorists at the time.[156] Nothing to be modest about here.

In *The Theory of the Leisure Class,* Veblen's target had been exactly the same theory, but in *The Theory of Business Enterprise,* he fired from a different angle. Provoked by Cummings's critique of *The Theory of the Leisure Class,* Veblen shifted away from the institution of the leisure class, going so far as to nearly eliminate "leisure" and the "leisure class" from *The Theory of Business Enterprise* and his subsequent writings.[157] (This elision perhaps explains why later commentators on Veblen, captivated by his earlier ideas about the leisure class, have been fairly indifferent to these later writings.) In place of leisure, Veblen now centered his analysis on *work*—leisure's very opposite. For Veblen, this change of focus did not come out of the blue. Already in *The Theory of the Leisure Class,* he had observed (briefly) that, whereas "conspicuous leisure" and "conspicuous consumption" were fused in times past, "the modern transition" to the corporation meant the uncoupling of the two—that is, a historical movement *away from* the primacy of leisure. Years later, Veblen put this cardinal point succinctly:

> Probably . . . no class of men have ever bent more unremittingly to their work than the modern business community. Within the business community there is properly speaking *no leisure class,* or at least no idle class. . . . The business community is hard at work, and there is no place in it for anyone who is unable or unwilling to work at the high tension of the average. . . . This high tension of work is felt to be very meritorious in all modern communities.[158]

On the surface, this was an enormous concession to marginalists like Clark, who justified high economic rewards precisely on the basis of merit or productive work contributions. But Veblen then threw an iron wrench into the marginalist account by foregrounding and amplifying the distinction he had made in *The Theory of the Leisure Class* between two fundamentally different kinds of work or, as he called them, "employments": "Leaving aside the archaic vocations of war, politics, fashion, and religion, the employments in which men are engaged may be distinguished as pecuniary or business employments on the one hand, and industrial or mechanical employments on the other." Elaborating, Veblen defined pecuniary employments as "concerned primarily with the phenomena of value—with exchange or market value and with purchase and sale" (of commodities, securities, and so forth). In contrast, industrial employments "begin and end outside the higgling of the market; their proximate aim and effect is the shaping and guiding of material things and processes."

As such, these industrial employments depend on the "machine process"—Veblen's shorthand for "mechanical contrivances" and other technological advances—and revolve around the "production of goods and services."[159]

As far back as Adam Smith, classical economists had presaged Veblen's distinction when they differentiated productive and unproductive labor, a contrast they interpreted to lend support to their own theories.[160] But Veblen advanced a new interpretation—an interpretation conditioned by the mode of knowing he had been practicing most of his life. Construing the social world in organic terms, conceptualizing it as constantly changing, juxtaposing productive activity to inferior forms of human conduct: operating with these engrained ways of thinking, Veblen parsed pecuniary and industrial employments in a manner different from marginalists, such as Cummings, who plied other knowledge-making tools. So, where these other economists discounted the contrast between the two employments, Veblen heightened the distinction by means of a three-pronged attack that he hoped would invalidate the productivity theory of distribution.[161] (These prongs correspond to the three incisions Veblen performed on marginalism in *The Theory of the Leisure Class;* to spare more surgery, I am changing the metaphor.)

First came the organic prong. Considering economic actors through the individualistic lens of marginalists, there is not much difference between industrial and pecuniary employments. Both are activities in which a person labors, either physically or mentally, and receives an economic return for his or her contributions to the production process. But switch the marginalist lens for one that encompasses the wider community in which the person is situated, and suddenly the picture changes, according to Veblen, because we now observe that some activities function "to suit the needs or the conveniences of the community at large," while others seek to gratify the private "quest for gain." In this difference lies, in his view, the rationale for differentiating industrial and pecuniary employments, and for concluding that the former are productive and the later are nonproductive. Industrial employments "bear . . . upon the welfare of the community" in a material sense, because "it is to the interest of the community at large [to have] the best and largest possible output of goods or services." Conversely, pecuniary employments "are lucrative without necessarily being serviceable [in this sense] to the community." These employments confer "gains" on the people engaged in them that "*must plainly be accounted for on other grounds than their productivity, since they need have no productivity*"—contrary to the assertions of productivity theorists of distribution. True, continued Veblen, pecuniary employments entail work—long, stressful hours in the office—on the part of pecuniary actors, who are often locked in tough competition with one another. But activity of this sort aims at netting individual profit—an objective rooted in the social institution of private property ownership.[162]

Keeping to this organic perspective, Veblen mapped these two employments onto specific occupations in the modern division of labor. Broadly speaking, he equated nonproductive, pecuniary activities with the jobs of business managers and "undertakers" (Clark's entrepreneurs), corporate promoters and speculators, bankers and stock brokers, lawyers and real estate agents: the despised rogues' gallery that Veblen had heard farmers in the Upper Midwest complain about since his youth. Industrial activities, on the other hand, Veblen associated with inventors, mechanical and civil engineers, industrial chemists and mineralogists, mining experts and electricians, foremen and skilled mechanics, and farmers. Veblen knew, of course, that most of these jobs lay on the upper rungs of their respective occupational ladders; and he now and then glanced lower down, including unskilled manual laborers in the industrial category and "accountants and office employees" and "clerks and subalterns" in the pecuniary. He also recognized that some occupations straddled these categories and others combined the features of both, as in the instance of businessmen whose goals were shaped more by the "instinct of workmanship" than by the pursuit of profit. Most important for Veblen, though, were the "great captains of industry," the leading capitalists and entrepreneurs, who took charge of industrial employments and diverted the machine process away from "serviceability for the needs of mankind" and toward business ends. On Veblen's account, this hijacking made "pecuniary activities . . . the controlling factor about which the modern economic process turns." In his view, productivity theorists were unable to see, let alone understand, this takeover.[163]

Here Veblen moved to the second prong of his attack on marginalism. Wondering how marginalists could miss, while staring directly at it, the hard fact that nonproductive, pecuniary activities dictate modern economic life, he again faulted economists' static, ahistorical thinking. In his view, productivity theories were premised on ideas about economic activity that had been formulated in the late eighteenth and early nineteenth centuries by classical economists as they looked out at the economy of *their* time, when industrial and pecuniary employments had yet to split off from one another. Veblen patiently schooled Cummings on this historical point:

> In the earlier phases of modern industry, where the owner was at the same time the foreman of the shop and the manager of the "business," . . . the distinction does not obtrude itself on the attention because the separation of employments is not marked. Probably on this account the distinction is . . . not made in the received discussions of economic theory which have for the most part taken their shape under the traditions of a less highly developed differentiation of employments than the existing one.[164]

This transformation, said Veblen, reflected the separation in modern society between the ownership and the management of productive enterprises, as well as interrelated institutional changes such as the expansion of the "credit economy" and the "capital market" at the expense of the older "money economy" and "goods market."[165]

Veblen analyzed these institutional developments—and their "cumulative" causal effects on one another—by drawing on monographs of German, British, and American economic historians. He did this in a flexible manner, reaching backward in some cases to American society a century earlier, in other cases to England between the sixteenth century and the eighteenth century, and in other instances to continental Europe during the Middle Ages. He also examined the cross-national movement of institutions, adopting a version of the Teutonic thesis that Herbert Baxter Adams and others had taught him years before: "The perfected system of business principles," wrote Veblen in reference to the United States in the early twentieth century, "rests on the historical basis of free institutions, and so presumes a protracted historical growth of these institutions," as they were bequeathed to North America by the British, building on Germanic foundations. (Veblen's attachment to this thesis was part of his continuing insistence that Western institutions, including those that were forerunners of the business enterprise, originated with "the dolicho-blond racial stock [in the region of] the North Sea and Baltic.")[166]

In speaking of the "historical growth of institutions" and "cumulative causation," Veblen summoned the terminology of his earlier articles, in which he had identified the phenomena economists needed to study to reinvent their field as a dynamic, evolutionary science. Otherwise, however,

Veblen's analysis of the business enterprise often gives the impression that he has retreated from the expansive evolutionism of his previous writings. In *The Theory of Business Enterprise,* Veblen's time orientation resembles that of the economic historians whose work he was drawing on. His book takes readers back several centuries, but it did not go back vast epochs, as social evolutionists and ethnologists did, or as Veblen himself had done in *The Theory of the Leisure Class* when he examined the so-called savage, barbarian, and civilized stages of human history.

This difference did not mark a fundamental shift in Veblen's thinking about time, however, because—unlike many later scholars—he did not decouple economic history from evolutionism. Like his teachers (Adams, Sumner, Tuttle, Tyler), he again saw these perspectives as two halves of a whole, two complementary ways of incorporating change into social-scientific thinking: on the one hand, by considering time in century-sized units; on the other hand, by considering time in millennial units—with the understanding that smaller units are nested in larger units and that all units are in perpetual motion. Compatible with this outlook, Veblen kept in sight, even as he examined the epoch of the business enterprise, that this era was infinitesimal on the world-historical clock: "some ninety-nine one-hundredths of [the] course of [economic] development had been completed before the ownership of the mechanical equipment came into undisputed primacy as the basis of pecuniary domination."[167] From this fact it followed, for Veblen, that classical and marginalist economists seriously erred in assuming that the economic laws they formulated when writing in their own moment held across the board. Rather, according to Veblen, even the best theoretical generalizations—say, his own regarding productive and predatory activities—applied only with greater or lesser degrees of probability to individual historical cases, such as the development of "specifically modern economic phenomena."[168] Writing in a period when university administrators in the United States were splitting up ethnology, economic history, and studies of the modern-day evolution of economic institutions and allocating these topics to different academic fields, Veblen built eclectically on all these lines of research to mount his assault on the statics of marginal productivity theory.

And then he greatly raised the stakes of his historical critique. Because marginalists failed to set the economy in motion, and because they neglected the widening separation between industrial and business occupations, they faltered before what Veblen regarded as one of history's great riddles. Their theories could not address the paradox that, even though the growth of industrial activities had enormously increased the capacity of modern society "to suit the needs [and] convenience of the community at large," the community at large never reaped these benefits but instead suffered great deprivation.[169] By Veblen's reckoning, this productivity paradox stood behind many anguishing questions:

> Why do we, now and again, have hard times and unemployment in the midst of excellent resources, high efficiency and plenty of unmet wants? Why is one-half our consumable product contrived for consumption that yields no material benefit? Why are large co-ordinations of industry, which greatly reduce cost of production, a cause of perplexity and alarm? . . . Why are large and increasing portions of the community penniless in spite of a scale of remuneration which is very appreciably above the subsistence minimum? . . . These and the like questions, being questions of fact, are not to be answered on the ground of normal equivalence [between what a person produces and what he or she gets in return]. Perhaps it might better be said that they have so often been answered on those grounds . . . that the outlook for help in that direction has ceased to have a serious meaning. These are, to borrow Professor Clark's phrase, questions to be answered on dynamic, not on static grounds.[170]

In all of Veblen's writings, no passage matches the first part of this one in feeling.[171] Here his words disclose sentiments, both compassionate and angry, about turn-of-the-century American society that Veblen almost always kept to himself. Yet, even as he lets his passions break through, we see him speaking to his contemporary economists. The emotions shown in the passage are feelings he might have expressed in any number of venues, but Veblen chose to reveal them in the *Publications of the American Economic Association* (of all arid places). And there he attributed his society's failure to unravel the productivity paradox to none other than the economists' productivity theory of distribution—as his mention of John Bates Clark made clear, with heavy irony. For although Clark admitted the importance of a dynamic economics, he did not offer one; his theorizing at the time, as readers of the *Publications* were well aware, eschewed dynamics in favor of a static analysis of economic distribution. In Veblen's opinion, that kind of analysis left the productivity conundrum still awaiting a resolution.

So he proceeded to the third prong of his attack. He circled back to the theoretical argument about predation he had laid out in *The Theory of the Leisure Class* and pushed that argument further. In his 1901 AEA article, Veblen described pecuniary employments as "lucrative"; and in *The Theory of Business Enterprise,* he observed that business occupations, in the postbellum era, had grown so extremely lucrative they resulted in "accumulations of wealth" that "surpass all recorded phenomena of their kind" and have no equivalent in "the history of human culture." Dissenting from the explanation of Clark and other marginalists, however, Veblen denied that these accumulations were rewards for productivity. In his view, the new wealth-conferring occupations still belonged in the category of "unproductive work." Reflecting on his own time and place, he asserted that "success in business affairs . . . comes only by getting something for nothing," and that "the great mass of reputably large fortunes in the country are of such an origin." (The "something for nothing" barb, which many of his teachers and colleagues had also hurled at the wealthy, was one Veblen lobbed frequently from here on out in his work.)[172]

But how is it possible, under the high-tension "regime of competitive business," for people to get "something for nothing"—especially when that something is a large accumulation of wealth, perhaps even a megafortune? Veblen had raised a similar question in *The Theory of the Leisure Class,* but, because he was absorbed in the analysis of consumption, he did not detail the ways economic predation operates in modern society. While pointing out that, in the industrial age, predatory activity assumes the form of pecuniary employments, he offered little specificity about what pecuniary occupations involve. By the time he wrote *The Theory of Business Enterprise,* however, he stepped up with a fuller answer. He examined an arsenal of economic arrangements and institutions that executives at large business enterprises were devising to boost their profits, including mass advertising (and misinformation blitzes), loan credit (and intricate debentures), and corporate consolidation (trusts, mergers, and other combinations).[173]

More important than any of these institutions singly was the totality they created as the result of what Veblen saw as the "close interdependence of [nearly all] lines of industrial activity in a comprehensive system," whose component parts demand constant coordination and "interstitial adjustment." These tasks necessitate "pecuniary transactions," and "it therefore rests with the business men to make or mar the running adjustments of industry." The consequence of this situation is a golden profit-making opportunity for business managers because, counterintuitively, managers do not ordinarily want "interstitial adjustment." Faced with competition, the typical businessman instead seeks—through manipulating commodity prices, as well as "through shrewd [stock] investments and coalitions with other business men"—to set off "disturbances": strategic disruptions that benefit his corporation (and his person) and inflict damage on competitors.[174] Wrote Veblen:

> [In] the modern industrial system, . . . a disturbance of the balance at any point means a differential advantage (or disadvantage) to one or more of the owners of the sub-processes between which the disturbance falls; and it may also frequently mean gain or loss to many remoter members in the concatenation of processes, for the balance throughout the sequence is a delicate one, and the transmission of a disturbance often goes far. It may even take on a cumulative character, and may thereby seriously cripple or accelerate branches of industry that are out of direct touch with those . . . upon which the initial disturbance falls.[175]

In these circumstances, largely unknown prior to the 1870s (said Veblen), lay the seed of recurrent industrial crises, cycles of economic expansion and contraction, and "the oscillation between good times and bad." Criticizing other economists for regarding these upheavals as abnormal, Veblen snidely turned their privileged word "normal" back at them; "brisk times, crises, and depressions, follow[ing upon] one another with some regularity"—that was "the normal course of business," the standard way people on the upper rungs of the pecuniary hierarchy reaped their profits. "It is, in great part, through or by force of [such] fluctuations . . . that large accumulations of wealth are made," and "the great gains of successful promoters of corporations and the like come in this manner usually."[176]

Despite the economic gains that accrue to pecuniary employments, however, these occupations still have nothing productive about them—nothing "serviceable to the community." According to Veblen, the entrepreneurs' "gains (or losses) are related to the magnitude of the disturbances that take place, rather than to their bearing upon the welfare of the community."[177] Furthermore, when disturbances come, their toll lands not on businessmen themselves, but on men and women in industrial occupations:

> Unproductive work directed to securing an income may seem to be an idle matter in which the rest of the community has no substantial interest. Such is not the case. In so far as the gains of these unproductive occupations are of a substantial character, they come out

of the aggregate product of the other occupations in which the various classes of the community engage. The aggregate profits of the business . . . are drawn from the aggregate output of goods and services; and whatever goes to the maintenance of the profits of those who contribute nothing substantial to the output is, of course, deducted from the income of the others.[178]

This proposition brought Veblen back to the phenomenon of parasitism, leading him to assert that business was "parasitic" on industry. And that assertion—which he had heard repeated to him, in strong tones, throughout his long education—gave him the explanation he sought for the paradox of productivity: the economic scourges of his era existed and lasted because the incumbents of nonproductive occupations leeched on those in productive occupations, with the result that productive people often experienced "a degree of privation" nearly on par with "industrially less efficient people on a lower level of culture." Veblen depicted this situation in strong Darwinian language once again. Writing about competing business enterprises, he held that "the ground of survival in the selective process [among them] is fitness for pecuniary gain, not fitness for serviceability at large"; yet it is fitness in the latter sense that matters for the long-term "vitality of the community." For this reason, "a persistent excess of parasitic and wasteful efforts over productive industry must bring on a decline" of a society dominated by business enterprises— although businessmen might stave off this collapse, for a time, by ratcheting up the "output of goods by modern methods" of production and laying "added strain [on people] engaged in the productive work" of the group.[179]

Here, Veblen's iconoclasm showed its range, as he simultaneously exposed modern corporations as hives of swarming parasites, derided marginalism for disingenuously sanitizing these infested sites by rebranding nonproductivity as productivity, and attacked economists for failing to situate themselves historically. On Veblen's account, the business enterprise was no more immune from historical change than any other economic institution. As the controlling force in modern civilization, the business enterprise too would necessarily undergo "natural decay" and prove "transitory." Where history was heading next, however, Veblen felt he could not say, because no teleology was steering the evolutionary process as a whole, only (as he had said before) the "discretionary action of the human agents," whose institutionally shaped choices were still unformed. Nevertheless, limiting himself to the "calculable future"—to what, in light of existing scientific knowledge, seemed probable in the near term—Veblen pointed to two contrasting possibilities, both beyond the ken of productivity theories.[180]

One alternative was militarization and war—barbarism redux. According to Veblen, the business enterprise, as its grows, spills over national boundaries and fosters the expansion of a world market in which "the business men of one nation are pitted against those of another and swing the forces of the state, legislative, diplomatic, and military, against one another in the strategic game of pecuniary advantage." As this game intensifies, competing nations rush (said Veblen presciently) to amass military hardware that can easily fall under the control of political leaders who embrace aggressive international policies and "warlike aims, achievements, [and] spectacles." Unchecked, these developments could, he believed, demolish "those cultural features that distinguish modern times from what went before, including a decline of the business enterprise itself."[181] (In his later writings from the World War I period, Veblen returned to these issues.)

The second future possibility was socialism, which interested Veblen (for the time being) not only as an institutional alternative to the business enterprise but also as a way of economic thinking that nullified the productivity theory of distribution. In cycling back to the phenomenon of socialism, which he had bracketed in *The Theory of the Leisure Class*, Veblen zeroed in on men and women who held industrial occupations, in which he observed a growing dissatisfaction with the bedrock institutions of the modern age. This discontent was socially concentrated, found not so much among laborers who were "mechanical auxiliaries"—manual extensions—"of the machine process," but "among those industrial classes who are required to comprehend and guide the processes." These classes consist of "the higher ranks of skilled mechanics and [of people] who stand in an engineering or supervisory relation to the processes." Carrying out these jobs, with their distinctive task requirements, inculcates "iconoclastic habits of thought," which draw men and women into trade unions and, as a next step, "into something else, which may be called socialism, for want of a better term."[182]

This phrasing was vague even for Veblen, but he felt hamstrung because "there was little agreement among socialists as to a programme for the future," at least aside from provisions almost "entirely negative." Even so, two planks stood out for Veblen. One was that socialism aspired to be "radically democratic" and to eliminate the state, in the conviction that "the community can best get along without political institutions." This proposal fit with Veblen's view that the state was a deep pocket of non-productivity. (It accorded, as well, with his long-standing rejection—after the fashion of Sumner, Tuttle, and Laughlin—of state paternalism, whether in the form of populism, state socialism, or other top-down reformist measures then in the public eye.) Still more important to Veblen than socialism's stance toward political institutions was its central economic plank: its opposition to "all pecuniary institutions [and its] demand for the abrogation of property rights"—an all-out end to the institution of private property ownership.[183]

In this demand, Veblen saw signs of a mode of thinking about economic life that dealt another hard blow to productivity theories. For the most part, Veblen's critique of the marginalist approach to wealth distribution focused on the productivity side of the theory; Clark and others postulated that economic actors are productive, whereas Veblen—in line with his commitment to inductive science—sought to show empirically that economic conduct is often nonproductive. In so doing, he bypassed another side of the theory: the assertion that productive contributions bring commensurate income rewards and equitable shares of a nation's wealth. When John Cumming described *The Theory of the Leisure Class* as an attack on this claim, Veblen shot back that the book was not concerned with "the equity of the existing distribution of property and of the incomes that accrue to the various classes"—"just deserts" [*sic*] was a subject for the "the moralist," not "the economist."[184]

For Veblen, what actually was relevant for the economist here was to grasp, as marginalists did not, the time-bound nature of the entire issue of the distribution of wealth. Elaborating points foreshadowed in *The Theory of the Leisure Class,* Veblen argued that only with the development of the institution of individual property ownership did questions about the distribution of wealth shares arise for economists and for the public. And not until those questions were in play could reformers advocate for the *redistribution* of shares away from people who held them and toward individuals who better merited them on the basis of their productive contributions. (Different reformers had different ideas about who these people were.) As Veblen viewed modern socialism, however, the young trade union movement, whatever its long-term prospects, was upending economic theories built on this ahistorical "business proposition" about who gets shares of what size. "Such is not the trend of socialistic thinking, [which] looks to the disappearance of property rights rather than their redistribution." As such, socialism gave expression, he said with satisfaction, to an emerging way of economic thinking that lay beyond "the entire range of doctrines covered by the theory of distribution in the received economics." In his opinion, these doctrines could not keep pace with the movement of human history.[185]

7.

Thorstein Veblen was acutely aware of his own place in the onrush of history. More than anyone, he knew that the fundamental distinction he drew between "industrial" and "pecuniary" employments omitted the very activity that he himself was involved in and had not existed before the coming of "modern civilization." That activity was science, or, more accurately, the advancement of scientific knowledge. In his final publication before leaving the University of Chicago, an article actually titled "The Place of Science in Modern Civilization," Veblen, invoking his Latin again, extended a thirteenth-century statement by Pope Alexander IV: "*Quasi lignum vitae in paradiso Dei, et quasi lucerna fulgoris in domo Domini* [As the tree of life in God's paradise, and as the lamp of light in the house of the Lord], such is the place of science in modern civilization."[186] This proposition was Veblen's conviction, as he again channeled a belief that had followed him from the humble flatlands of Minnesota to the citadels of the country's new research universities.

Yet his dichotomy—the divide between industrial and pecuniary employments—did not include scientific activity. We can search *The Theory of Business Enterprise* and the text of his 1901 AEA article, we can scour the list of job titles he associated with the two types of employments, but scientific knowledge producer is simply not there, and neither is professional academic—Veblen's own métier. Admittedly, inasmuch his main subject in these writings was the business enterprise, Veblen's exclusion of scientists made some sense (especially when his editors were insisting he cut words). In Veblen's view, scientists were rarely found in "industrial" occupations; they were neither supervisors of the epoch-defining "machine process" nor skilled mechanics, let alone manual laborers. (Hard to imagine Noah Porter, George Sylvester Morris, William Graham Sumner, or Veblen's other mentors holding down any of these jobs.) But even less did scientists typically fall into Veblen's category of "pecuniary" occupations, except for men and women who were scientists in job title only.

Veblen certainly acknowledged that inventors and people trained in engineering and other "mechanical sciences" often played a significant role in the design and redesign of the machine process; but they did so at the behest of business managers trying to appropriate scientific knowledge for the pecuniary end of profit making.[187]

When Veblen spoke about science, he was not talking about these activities. As he made plain in *The Higher Learning in America,* science—whether natural science or social science—was "detached and dispassionate knowledge"; it had no "ulterior purposes of expediency"; it was "without afterthought as to the practical or utilitarian consequences." Provoking readers with the question, "What is the use of [scientific] learning?," Veblen answered by summoning America's most admired Protestant layman: "Benjamin Franklin—high-bred pragmatist that he was—once put away such a question with the rejoinder: What is the use of a baby?"[188]

Veblen did not forget that children, when they reach adulthood, often do things that are useful, productive, or "serviceable to the community at large." (The latter remained Veblen's definition of "productive.") Seen not statically but dynamically, not in terms of immediate individual returns but in terms of longer-run social benefits, the results of scientific research could be productive. When put into application by people engaged in industrial rather than pecuniary employments, "scientific knowledge," Veblen maintained, had advanced, "besides the machine industry proper, such branches of practice as engineering, agriculture, medicine, sanitation, and economic reforms."[189]

Even so, whether or not advances like these actually take place "is a wholly fortuitous and insubstantial coincidence," because "useful purposes lie outside the scientist's interest," which is "the pursuit of knowledge for its own idle sake." Keeping to this note, Veblen insisted that science, bona fide science, mainly finds its root in the instinct of "idle curiosity"—an attribute "closely related to the aptitude for play"—and is, for this reason, "a species of leisure." In the modern world, torn between industrial and pecuniary work, this type of leisure requires a strong institutional shelter; it necessitates research universities freed of practical objectives, profit-making in particular. (On Veblen's assessment, that was the historical lesson William Rainey Harper and his lieutenants at the University of Chicago opted to disregard.)[190]

This productivity contrast was a deliberate part of Veblen's analysis of modern society, although readers who reduce his oeuvre to a critique of the leisure class have overlooked it. In his attack on marginal productivity theory, Veblen observed that many people on the top rungs of the business world forgo leisure for unremitting work; yet they are not productive, because they strive after self-serving pecuniary goals that add nothing in serviceability to the community at large. Inversely, given favorable institutional conditions, scientists with the leisure to follow the play of their idle curiosity may—fortuitously—make contributions that are productive. With no eye to practicality, they do create, now and then at least, socially beneficial knowledge. Such ideal institutional conditions were not, however, something every academic man or woman could count on, as Veblen knew.

CHAPTER 9

CONCLUSION

1.

Thorstein Veblen was a man of his place and era, a prototype of the academic professional in the period when American research universities were emerging, and a member in high repute of the nascent field of economics. During his fourteen years on the faculty of the illustrious department of political economy at the University of Chicago, he authored two major books directed mainly at professional economists, published dozens of articles and book reviews almost exclusively in journals of economics, translated books for audiences of economists, and held positions of responsibility in his discipline. Inside the field of economics, he knew everyone of intellectual stature, and they all knew him, at least through his prolific writings. An iconoclast in the Age of Iconoclasm, he was not an academic outsider.

What was more, most of his fellow economists, even his critics, understood the thrust of his economics: the novel nonproductivity theory of the distribution of economic rewards that he built to right the productivity theory of distribution, which a battalion of economists armed with ideas about marginal utility was spreading throughout the field. Still further, economists took his theory seriously. Rather than push Veblen to the periphery, opponents kept his theory on the front lines. (Opposition attracts attention.) That was the effect, for example, of John Cummings's 1899 attack on *The Theory of the Leisure Class*. Quarreling with Veblen's antimarginalist thesis that besides so-called productive ("industrial") employments there exists a predatory and parasitic counterforce of nonproductive ("pecuniary") employments, Cummings gave the thesis wide currency among economists of all stripes. Writing in the *Quarterly Journal of Economics* (*QJE*) four years later, economist (and sociologist) E. A.

Ross, then at the University of Nebraska, praised Veblen for bringing to light the "great gulf between . . . pecuniary as contrasted with industrial employments." In a 1905 review of Veblen's *Theory of Business Enterprise,* Harvard economist T. N. Carver (a marginalist, no less) "heartily commended" the book, remarking that "the author's contention that the large business man is primarily an acquirer, and only incidentally a producer of wealth, is undoubtedly correct." In 1911, Harvard's Frank Taussig, after situating Veblen in the rarefied company of Adam Smith and John Stuart Mill, judged that "among modern discussions"—of "productive and unproductive labor"—"none is more deserving of attention than [Veblen's distinction] of 'industrial' and 'pecuniary' employments." That same year economist Alvin S. Johnson (of Stanford) characterized Veblen as a "profound critic . . . of the marginal-utility doctrines"—a judgment frequent among contemporary observers in the field of political economy.[1]

BY THE TIME THESE assessments started appearing, however, Veblen was already halfway out the gates of the University of Chicago, his relationship with the institution and President Harper nearly over. The reasons behind this final rupture have been the subject of scholarly speculation for more than a century; but for Veblen himself, two causes stood out, as he explained in a detailed February 1905 letter to his friend and former Chicago colleague, physiologist Jacques Loeb.[2]

The first related to gossip circulating around Hyde Park during spring and summer 1904 about an extramarital affair between Veblen and Laura McAdoo Triggs, an occasional student at the university who had attended one of his courses and who was married to a friend of his recently dismissed by Harper from the Extension Division. Based on the known facts of the case, most modern biographers have acquitted Veblen of this adultery charge, and Veblen himself—an honest man, according to accounts from the time—strenuously denied it. But Harper, constantly worried that the university's corporate and Victorian sponsors would cut off financial support if the moral misdeeds of his subordinates went ignored and unpunished, made it a policy to police the private lives of faculty members. He turned to Ellen Veblen and questioned her about the Triggs story, and Ellen (perhaps in reaction to her husband's earlier enchantment with Sarah Hardy) fueled Harper's suspicions, provoking him to demand that Veblen "sign a promise to have nothing more to do with Mrs. Triggs."[3] Because a promise like that would have amounted to an admission of wrongdoing,

Veblen refused, at which point Harper told him he "need look for no recognition or advancement [at the University of Chicago], but may be
dropped whenever it can be done without inconvenience."[4] This confrontation occurred sometime in the second half of 1904.[5]

The incident left Veblen bitter for many years—understandably. To
him, Harper's conduct was a disingenuous act of character "assassination," a smoke screen set up to divert attention from an issue largely un-
connected with Triggs.[6] This issue—the second of the two causes Veblen
saw behind the breakdown of his relationship with the president—was
his vitriolic attack on the control of universities by corporate executives,
which was the centerpiece of the chapter he had removed from *The Theory
of Business Enterprise* and was then trying to publish as a stand-alone
book. Harper had previously tolerated a milder version of this attack in
The Theory of the Leisure Class. But Veblen's offending new chapter apparently pushed the president to his limit, probably because the university's finances had hit bottom and he could not risk alienating donors by
subjecting them to criticism by a member of the department of political
economy. (The university closed the 1904–1905 year with only $25
[= $760] in its coffers, a striking contrast to its $8.5 billion endowment
in 2020.) Veblen summed up the situation in a letter to Loeb:

> I had left over from the manuscript of the book on Business Enter-
> prise a somewhat long chapter which offered an analysis of the
> working of business enterprise in the administration of a univer-
> sity. This chapter I proposed to publish as a separate small volume,
> and in the search for a publisher the manuscript came into the hands
> of the president, [who] was apparently not pleased with it and seems
> to have seen in it some reflection on the regime here.

According to Veblen, Harper latched onto the alleged affair with Triggs
to prod him to resign. In this predicament, Veblen told Loeb: "I should be
glad to leave this place."[7]

Veblen immediately began looking for another job. In January 1905
he applied for the position of chief of the Documents Division of the Library of Congress, completing a formal application requiring him to provide the names of a dozen references, six to vouch for his "character" and
another six for his "capacity." Even today, a dozen would be a large number
of references for an established academic to supply, but Veblen rolled out
a list that included present and former colleagues in his department at the

University of Chicago (Laughlin, Adolph Miller, William Hill, and Herbert Davenport), big-name economists outside Chicago (Frank Taussig, Jeremiah Jenks, Bernard Moses, and the ever-loyal John Bates Clark), and, in order to attest to his intellectual breadth, luminaries in other disciplines (Lester Ward, J. F. Jameson).[8] Some years earlier, as I mentioned previously, Veblen had considered leaving the academic world, and his application to the Library of Congress shows that he was willing to do so again. His Chicago colleague William Hill told Herbert Putnam, the librarian of Congress, that "Dr. T. B. Veblen desires to change the field of his activities." But the point was moot, because Putnam found Veblen ill suited for the position, which required knowledge of "library science" and the "general care of documents."[9]

Passed over by the Library of Congress, Veblen's next step was to ask Jacques Loeb, who had left Chicago in 1902 to join the faculty of the University of California, Berkeley, to prime the university pump. "You might do me the best possible service by speaking to Mr. Jordan in my behalf," he wrote, referring to Stanford University president David Starr Jordan, to whom Loeb was connected. Equipping Loeb with a selling point, Veblen suggested Loeb let Jordan know "my endeavor is to make Economics a science in the same sense of the term as the material sciences"—the natural sciences—"with which Mr. Jordan himself is chiefly occupied."[10]

To leave no doubt about what he had in mind, Veblen wrote Loeb: "There is no university in America that I should prefer to Stanford."[11] Jordan had come close to appointing Veblen back in 1899 and was now seeking to rebuild his department of economics, which had experienced major setbacks in the interim. Knowing this, Loeb, along with Adolph Miller (who was by then the chair of Berkeley's economics department) and Wesley Mitchell (Veblen's former student, now a junior member of Miller's department), pushed the idea of hiring Veblen to Jordan, who (according to Mitchell) had already read and "expressed enthusiasm" for Veblen's books and "said he would like to have Veblen at Stanford." Before he could act on this idea, however, Jordan needed to find a new chairman for his economics department. For this position he soon recruited Allyn Young of the University of Wisconsin, who was also keen on appointing Veblen. In April 1906, Jordan himself "renewed his favorable impressions" of Veblen (after the two had dinner together in in Chicago) and immediately made him a job offer—only to discover that Veblen bargained hard, especially when it came to salary.[12] Wrote Veblen on April 9, 1906:

343

In replying to your very kind offer, . . . I am very sorry that no more liberal terms are possible at present. I have, of course, thought the matter over since meeting you in Chicago the other day, and my liking for Leland Stanford [University] and for California is no less decided than it has been, but I have come to think that I can not [sic] afford to accept any academic rank lower than the highest assigned to any member of the department or any salary less than the highest paid to any member of the department. I shall be very sorry if this reservation bars me out, but I do not see any way to forego it.[13]

He continued a week later:

The reservation which I made in the terms on which I could afford to . . . accept your offer may have seemed somewhat gratuitous and may need a word of explanation. . . . My acceptance of an inferior grade would be looked on by my friends in the science as something in the nature of a "reduction to the ranks." This I could not afford. I know by experience that such a circumstance would handicap me in my work and at the same time contribute to my discomfort.[14]

Coming from a thinker who derided "invidious comparison" when other men and women engaged in it, Veblen's concern about how he would "be looked on" by his friends if he took a "salary less than the highest paid to any member of the department" is a surprising stance. But be that as it may, Jordan talked Veblen down, persuading him to accept less than Young's salary of $3,000 (= $90,000) by reminding him that Young, as the department chairman, carried extra administrative work. Still, before accepting Jordan's offer of an associate professorship at $2,500 (= $74,000), Veblen let the president know he would agree to this lower salary only for his first year.[15] On May 13, 1906, he accepted Stanford's offer. A month later, on June 19, he resigned from the department of political economy at the University of Chicago.[16]

Veblen's time at Stanford was brief. Following his resignation at Chicago, he left for California almost immediately, though with a detour along the way to Hood River, Oregon, where Ellen Veblen had settled in 1904. Aiming to reconcile, Thorstein convinced her to move with him to Palo Alto, and the two of them did in late summer 1906. (This was right after his father died, in August 1906, and shortly before his mother died, in February 1907.) But their rapprochement lasted less than a year, and before long Veblen was embroiled in another episode of "domestic infelicitude" (as he called it). That imbroglio notwithstanding, by summer 1907 Veblen's friends found he "was his old humorous self" again.[17] He also continued to be productive on the job, publishing during his time at Stanford seven long articles and review essays (in addition to book reviews) in leading academic journals. In April 1909, he fended off the offer of a distinguished professorship of economics and sociology from his old friend Herbert Davenport at the University of Missouri.[18]

Far more consequential for him in the long run was the arrival in the San Francisco area, in fall 1907, of Ann Fessenden Bradley Bevans, a woman whom Veblen first met near the end of his time at the University of Chicago, where she attended one of his courses. Twenty years his junior and on the verge of divorce, she and Veblen formed a friendship which, according to acquaintances of hers, quickly developed into a sexual relationship, probably around mid-1905. Subsequently, a year after Veblen's move to Palo Alto, Bevans left her children in Chicago to relocate to the Bay Area, for the stated reason of studying economics at Berkeley. From that point on, she and Veblen conducted a discreet love affair that continued until 1914, when the two were finally able to marry. (Veblen had to wait for Ellen to grant him a divorce.) Most modern Veblen scholars believe this was Thorstein Veblen's one sexual relationship during his marriage to Ellen Veblen.[19]

Even so, in the eyes of Stanford's administrators, Veblen's private life was beyond the pale, and Ellen made sure they saw it that way. Beginning in May 1909, she besieged President Jordan, via letters and in person, regarding her husband's infidelities with Bevans and (in Ellen's version of events) with Sarah Hardy and Laura Triggs as well. By early October, Jordan felt he needed to take protective action, as Veblen described to Herbert Davenport a few weeks later: "From fear of scandal [Jordan] asked me to resign, which I have done."[20] Jordan's own account ran along the same lines: "The whole matter [with Veblen and his wife] is a kind of Bohemianism which is inconsistent with the requirements of life outside Bohemia. . . . When the details became known to me, I had a talk with Dr. Veblen, who tendered his resignation, a matter unavoidable under the circumstances."[21]

To tide Veblen over financially, Jordan agreed to pay his salary through the end of the 1909–1910 academic year. This grace period gave Veblen a chance to recuperate from another bout of illness (pneumonia) and to prepare a grant application to a new research foundation, the Carnegie

Institution of Washington, for an "Inquiry into Baltic and Cretan Antiquities." The project was something he had already had in mind before his resignation, but now he elaborated it into a plan of ethnological research that would take him to Europe to study the "early growth of those free institutions which have marked off European civilization" from other civilizations. The project would, he explained, deal especially with the "native endowment of the races" of different societies, as well as with "such industrial and pecuniary facts as are reflected by the available archeological sites and exhibits." For a scholar in his fifties who had never done hands-on research of this kind, the plan was ambitious, even as it carried over themes from his earlier work. That the research would take time—three years' time, by Veblen's estimate—did not concern him, since he felt he had time to spare, though not the resources, so he included in his application a request for an annual salary of $3,000 [= $90,000], pointing out that his "retirement from university work leaves me without an income." But the Carnegie officials were not convinced. Coming from the natural sciences and dubious about economics, they did not fund the proposal, despite letters strongly supporting it from Veblen's A-list of recommenders. As it turned out, however, Veblen was not yet at the stage of "retirement" from university life.[22]

WHAT HIS RECOMMENDERS WROTE about him attests to Thorstein Veblen's high standing in his field at this advanced stage of his career. (We need to bear in mind, of course, that people who agree to write reference letters generally have positive things to say; during the 1905–1910 period, there were also academics critical of Veblen's work, though theirs was not the prevailing opinion.) Endorsing his application for the position as chief of the Documents Division at the Library of Congress, Lester Ward, for instance, wrote to Librarian Putnam: "Veblen has shown himself to be one of the ablest men in the country in various lines. I regard his *Theory of the Leisure Class* as one of the most brilliant productions of the country and now his *Theory of Business Enterprise* sustains his high character as a writer and thinker." Similarly, John Bates Clark, overlooking Veblen's attacks on him, let the librarian know his "high estimate . . . of Professor Veblen's ability and attainment," and of his "keen analytical power." Summing up the judgment of the discipline of economics as a whole, Carl Plehn, respected professor of finance at Berkeley, informed Putnam also that Veblen "is held, as a scholar, in high regard among all American economists."[23] The following year, right after David Starr Jordan hired Veblen at Stanford, Allyn Young sent the president a similar report saying that, based on conversations with economists at Yale and the University of Wisconsin, "there is general agreement that no better selection could have been made" for the job than Veblen. That was Young's own view too: "I do not think that [Veblen] has an equal among American economists in the breath of scholarship and subtlety of analysis." And three years later, when Young heard Veblen was leaving Stanford, his reaction was to tell Jordan that "Veblen's resignation will leave a big hole [in the economics department] on the side of productive scholarship."[24]

Assessments like these also ran through the letters Veblen's backers sent on his behalf to the Carnegie Institution in 1910. Regarding Veblen's plan to study European antiquities, J. Laurence Laughlin explained to mathematical physicist Robert S. Woodward, the foundation's president, that "the scientific importance of such an investigation, which would combine the anthropological and economic point of view, can scarcely be exaggerated, [while] Professor Veblen's fitness to make the investigation has been proved by the books he has already published."[25] More expansively, Allyn Young stated:

> I feel no hesitation in saying that Veblen is the most gifted man whom I have known. His scholarship is extraordinary, both in range and thoroughness. . . . His special competence in such subjects as economic theory and psychology is matched by his exceptional acquaintance with the fields of anthropology and ethnology. . . . Professor Taussig of Harvard recently wrote me that he regarded Veblen as one of the very few men who have given distinction to American work in the field of economics.[26]

Speaking for himself, Frank Taussig, supportive as always, declared Veblen a "brilliant and many-sided scholar." He added: "A brother economist, in whose judgment I have much confidence, once remarked . . . that Veblen came as near to being a genius as any economist we have; and I am inclined to think that the remark was just." And President Jordan, the same man who had fired Veblen just seven months earlier, told Woodward that Veblen "has a mind that, in certain lines of subtlety and keenness of apprehension, has no superior in this country. . . . He is one of the highest living authorities in certain specialized lines," one being "the origin and development (especially economic development) of primitive man," the other being "economic theory."[27]

Turn-of-the-century academic movers and shakers, such as these men, were frugal with encomiums; they did not hand them out to strangers or to men (or women) marginal to their academic fields. But, plainly, that was not how they perceived Veblen as late as the date of his resignation from Stanford. To the contrary, their opinion, as Allyn Young expressed it to Herbert Davenport, was that Veblen needed to secure a new academic job for precisely the reason that he "would be peculiarly helpless outside the academic field."[28] In their view, Veblen belonged inside that field.

LIKE ALL REPUTATIONS, HOWEVER, intellectual reputations are mutable. As matters of group opinion, they run hot and cold, turning one way today, another tomorrow.[29] In the period after he left Stanford, perceptions of Veblen gradually changed, transforming his image from that of an academic insider to that of an outsider—although this shift occasionally reversed itself. Why these fluctuations occurred is a question beyond the scope of this book, but several factors may be part of the answer.

One was Veblen's public persona. Throughout his life, many people—colleagues, acquaintances, students—found Veblen shy, detached, and hard to read in social situations. Recalling Veblen's years at the University of Chicago, to take one example, philosopher James Tufts, an admirer of Veblen's work, observed that he "played largely a lone hand"; likewise, historian J. F. Jameson (Veblen's friend from his days at Johns Hopkins) commented that he "kept to himself largely." More vividly, John Bates Clark, after visiting Chicago's political economy department for several weeks in 1903, wrote to Edward Seligman at Columbia: "Veblen is, if I can judge, the ablest of the six economists here. [He] is a quiet mouse-like man who has such a gift of reticence that one has to force things out of him in order to get any impression of what he is capable of." Questioned by Joseph Dorfman about Veblen's political views, Charles Merriam, Veblen's contemporary in Chicago's political science department, said that "it often seemed to me that he was almost wholly detached," refusing to take sides or show his hand in any political argument. In the classroom, students found the same inscrutable riddle standing in front of them, clothed in the demeanor of the introvert. According to Stephen Leacock (an economics graduate student in the early 1900s and later Canada's leading humorist), Veblen "had no manner, no voice, no art," and "he lectured into his lap, with his eyes on his waistcoat." Observations like this were commonplace among students.[30]

On the one hand, there was nothing especially unusual about Veblen's behaviors. In his era, scholars acted in these ways all the time (as many still do). But rarely do personality traits like these give rise, in and of themselves, to the perception that academics with these characteristics are misfits for their jobs. (When academic heavyweights show these quirks, their colleagues and students often find them endearing eccentricities—and the butt of good-natured jokes.) On the other hand, attributes such as shyness and reclusiveness do provide grist for the mill of interpreters who (for whatever reason) want to depict a scholar as alienated from his or her surroundings, as many commentators have done with Veblen. Among people who knew Thorstein Veblen personally, however, these attributes told only a small part of his story.

At all the stages of his career discussed in this book, Veblen had many professional friends. To them, his shyness and detachment were mannerisms that faded once he and the other person were on more familiar terms. Scholars who knew him one-on-one described him as a "regular guy" and "whole-heartedly congenial," as well as "spontaneous, humorous to the point of being 'smart alecky,' rather boyish, fairly talkative." At the University of Chicago, he made, according to Herbert Davenport, several "strong friendships" (in and out of the department of political economy), some of them men who later stepped up to help him find employment when William Rainey Harper (and then David Starr Jordan) sacked him. Veblen saw himself as having friends; he told Sarah Hardy that "friends" were reading *The Theory of Business Enterprise,* and he explained to Jordan how a low salary offer "would be looked on by my friends."[31] As part of Veblen's application to the Carnegie Institution, Jordan wrote to Robert Woodward: "Dr. Veblen. . . . has a number of strong friends in this institution [Stanford] and the Universities of Chicago and California."[32]

Apropos of these relationships, documents from the time show that, rather than being holed up alone in his office, Veblen was frequently out and about: attending annual meetings of the American Economic Association, giving talks at other universities, and participating at lunches and dinners with his colleagues. (When living in Hyde Park, however, he apparently avoided the "socialist" parties that Ellen Veblen liked to throw in their apartment.) He did keep his political views in soft focus, but that was because, as Charles Merriam elaborated in the letter quoted earlier, Veblen's "chief interest was that of a scientist"—an objective observer.[33]

Moreover, despite rumors about his poor teaching, he was popular with graduate students, who were impressed by the depth of his knowledge

349

(and liked his dry humor). A. P. Winston told Dorfman that Veblen, while at Chicago, had an "immense influence over his students, [who had] an unbounded reverence of him" and that Veblen took a "friendly interest in [their] welfare."[34] To the Librarian of Congress, colleague William Hill remarked: "No other one in the department has been so stimulating and helpful to our graduate students as Dr. Veblen."[35] In their own research, graduate students cited his work heavily; and some of them—including stars like Herbert Davenport and Wesley Mitchell—remained in close touch with him to the end of his life. Still further, Veblen stood out favorably for his supportiveness of female graduate students, who saw him not as the Lothario of legend but as "rather shy of women" and "always a gentleman" (quoting contemporaries Edith Abbott and Katharine Davis, respectively). Future social reformer Sophonisba Breckinridge commented that, aside from John Dewey, no University of Chicago social scientist so successfully "developed the situation of a master with disciples as was the case with Mr. Veblen."[36]

But all this evidence only deepens the mystery of Veblen's reputation as an academic *outsider*. If Veblen was detached in some settings and engaged in others, then reclusiveness does not go far to explain the reversal of his insider status during his post-Stanford years. More relevant is that Veblen's academic career went into a tailspin after he resigned from Stanford. The fact that he landed a faculty position at Stanford in the first place, after being driven out at Chicago (and battered by "character assassination"), was a testament to economists' unusually high regard for his work. Nevertheless, for an academic to survive a second discharge from a top university was unheard of in 1910—and, magnifying the problem in Veblen's case was that, for a second time, he had been handed a dishonorable discharge for moral offenses. (Even today, few untenured academics would get a third chance if their personal indiscretions became public scandals that required university presidents to contain the institutional damage.) Following back-to-back forced resignations, Veblen was a marked man, stamped with a stigma of shame that Ellen Veblen kept fresh by her relentless efforts to incriminate Veblen in academic circles. In a letter he sent on October 21, 1909, to Davenport, who had been trying to gin up a job for him at the University of Missouri, Veblen described the crisis he had reached:

I am fully persuaded that I could not get any kind of appointment at your place, nor indeed at any other university. So I thank you for all your kind efforts in my behalf, and regret that it should all be of no effect. I am sorry, but I have no doubt. [Mrs. Veblen appears] to have written the cabinet [of major figures] in Chicago . . . to help do me up, and also to Columbia (N.Y.), perhaps also elsewhere. If she knew of negotiations at Missouri she probably would have written to Hill also, which would explain his change of sentiment.[37]

Veblen's reference to Hill was to Alan Ross Hill, the president of the University of Missouri, an academic backwater in the country town of Columbia, Missouri (population ten thousand). Earlier in 1909, Hill had supported Davenport's plan to recruit Veblen to the university as a distinguished professor. But after Veblen was pushed out at Stanford, Hill would go no further than to allow Davenport to appoint Veblen as a lecturer, on an annual renewable contract, at a salary less than half what he had been earning at Stanford. To make things even harder for Veblen, this offer was coming from an institution that his contemporaries looked down upon as outside the league of top-tier research universities. When science writer Edwin Slosson, for example, published his 1910 study of "great universities" (as measured by faculty resources, faculty productivity, and so forth), his list included the University of Chicago, Yale, Stanford, Cornell, and Johns Hopkins—all of them schools that formed part of Veblen's biography—as well as Harvard and the Universities of Pennsylvania, California, Illinois, Michigan, Minnesota, and Wisconsin. The University of Missouri did not make the list.[38]

Stuck without alternatives, however, Veblen had little choice but to take Missouri's offer and to remain on the faculty there from early 1911 to early 1918. (His new wife, now Ann Bradley Veblen, joined him in Columbia in 1914, bringing along her two adolescent daughters, whom Veblen had adopted.) Initially, this position required Veblen mainly to teach undergraduate economics courses, although his assignments changed somewhat in 1914, when Davenport became the founding dean of the School of Business and Public Administration (a professional school designed mainly for college seniors), and Veblen's appointment moved along with his boss's.[39]

There, Veblen reconnected with some of his former students from Chicago and Stanford, who had taken positions at Davenport's new school.[40] Yet, neither the welcome presence of these colleagues, nor the admiration he encountered on campus from people who had heard of his books, did much to soften the occupational blow. An outspoken critic of small country towns, state universities, and business schools for their "pecuniary" outlook, these settings now constituted Veblen's daily world—a place to get some writing done, but a marginal academic outpost nonetheless. Worse still, his occasional efforts to return to a position at a research-oriented university brought no results. For example, hoping he was "not persona non grata" with University of Minnesota president George Vincent (a friend from his Chicago days), Veblen in 1913 proposed, through Wesley Mitchell, that "he give me an appointment on his faculty (in Economics, Sociology, Ethnology, or at large)," but the fanciful idea came to nothing.[41] The same thing happened with the more realistic plan hatched by Davenport, after he moved to Cornell in 1916 to head its economics department, to add Veblen to his own faculty roster for the 1918–1919 year. This proposal too fizzled when Cornell authorities checked with officials at Stanford, only to hear back the following from David Starr Jordan's successor as university president, geologist John Branner (whom Ellen Veblen also had contacted):

> [Veblen] seems to be recognized by scholars in his specialties, but scholars are doing mankind no service when they back for a professorship in our colleges a person who is unfit to associate with decent men, to say nothing about decent women, and least of all with young people. [He is not] proper company for man or beast. I have been told that he has reformed. I do not believe that such men reform, . . . they simply change their bases of operations, cover up their moral rottenness, and manage to divert attention from it by the devices practiced by such people. At bottom [he] is a Hun and will remain one.[42]

Writing to Dorfman in 1933, feminist Charlotte Perkins Gilman recalled the heavy occupational cost Veblen had to pay because of his "Bohemian" relationship with Ann Bradley: "It seemed to me a needless piece of sex extravagance, and it certainly did him great harm in professional standing."[43]

And there was more of the same to come, as this rolling stone entered his sixties. Following his time at the University of Missouri, Veblen spent a year and a half entirely outside the academy, working at jobs arranged in part by his friends: first as a "special investigator" for the United States Food Administration, in Washington, DC (where he relocated in late 1917); next, as an editor and writer for *The Dial*, the New York–based literary magazine, which was then branching out into topics related to postwar social reconstruction. After these stints, Veblen joined with several prominent academics (from the "progressive" side of the ideological spectrum) to launch, in fall 1919, the New School for Social Research—an experiment in higher education designed to eliminate traditional requirements and credentials for students and to promote the free discussion of contemporary social issues.[44] Operating on a shoestring budget, the school nearly dissolved in 1922, although Veblen stayed on for a few more years, teaching occasionally, his salary subsidized by a small fund set up by former students. In 1925, he retired from this position, eventually resettling near Palo Alto, California. Here he died of heart disease on August 2, 1929, a few months before the start of the Great Depression. (His wife Ann had died in 1920.)[45]

VEBLEN'S MOVE TO the periphery in terms of employment after departing Stanford was mirrored in his decision to pull back, more and more over time, from the academic field of economics. Following his move to Stanford, Veblen's work resumed right where he left off in Chicago, as he shifted his base of operations from one major department of political economy to another. His earlier program to make economics a science of the evolution of economic institutions—thereby closing the book on marginalism and its productivity theory of distribution—continued to define his thinking. Using the knowledge practices that had long been part of his intellectual repertoire, his Stanford writings delved further into problems that had been on his worktable for years.

We see this in the meaty articles on the marginalist concept of "capital" that he published in 1908 and 1909. In these, Veblen returned to the assertion by John Bates Clark and others that capital makes a "productive contribution" that warrants a corresponding economic return. Again adopting an evolutionary and organic viewpoint, Veblen maintained that modern industrial production rests heavily on something generally omitted from the marginalist treatment of capital. That something is the "intangible assets of the community" and, in particular, its storehouse of "knowledge," by which he meant (in this context) the "technological knowledge of the ways and means" of producing goods and services. On Veblen's account, such knowledge is, at once, the "creative"—and serendipitous—"contribution of the inventor" (and of other scientists, motivated by idle curiosity) *and* an outgrowth of the "community's common stock" of previously accumulated knowledge. For this reason, knowledge making constitutes "industrial" work, inasmuch as production always depends on knowledge. Conversely, the business enterprise is (as he had asserted before, using a somewhat different argument) a "predatory" rather than "productive institution": an institution that wields its "strong arm" to expropriate society's stock of knowledge for private pecuniary gain, diverting knowledge from serviceability to the community at large.[46]

After Veblen's ouster from Stanford, however, this subject all but vanished from his work. Up to then the author of articles for economics journals and of books aimed at "the gild of economists," Veblen—as soon as he exited the research hothouses of Chicago and Stanford—stopped writing in these genres almost completely.[47] No more technical articles in professional economics journals, no more books—shouting out "theory" from their titles—intended to intervene in academic debates in the field of economics: he was done with these ways of speaking. (Below I will add a small qualification to this statement.)

This shift in focus shows as early as Veblen's first post-Stanford book, *The Instinct of Workmanship and the State of the Industrial Arts,* which he began writing shortly after arriving in Columbia, Missouri. The book's title derived from an article he had written in 1898 and a vague book plan he had floated in 1900. But in the decade afterward, he recast that plan, producing by 1914 a book that scholars today regard as the closest Veblen ever came "to a general statement of his evolutionary system."[48] To this end, Veblen repurposed materials from his earlier writings, moving issues of psychology and ethnology front and center, allotting greater space to decisive moments in the economic history of Europe, but sidelining economic theory to such an extent that he eliminated any and all discussion of "nonproductive" economic activity—the economic phenomenon at the very core of the nonproductivity theory of distribution he formulated in *The Theory of the Leisure Class* and *The Theory of Business Enterprise.* Reviewers noticed the change; they gave the book mostly positive reviews but classed it as a contribution to disciplines other than economics. Ulysses Weatherly (economist-sociologist at Indiana University), for instance, wrote that "no more stimulating essay on the psychology and sociology of work has appeared in recent years," while economist Alvin S. Johnson (who five years earlier had praised Veblen for his attack on marginalism) described the book as "thoroughly characterized by the sociological point of view." And the best economist E. H. Downey (of the University of Wisconsin) could do for this book of seven chapters was to say: "To students of economics, the interest of the present work will center in chapters vi and vii."[49]

But Veblen was undaunted by this reaction. Off in a business school at the University of Missouri (and subsequently situated in one-of-a-kind positions on the East Coast), Veblen was not seeking to strengthen his ties to economics as an academic field. By this point, his sights were set on a broader readership in hopes of turning the light of economic knowledge onto topics of contemporary interest, such as industrial production in Germany (*Imperial Germany and the Industrial Revolution,* 1915), the dim prospects for peace in postwar Europe (*Inquiry into the Nature of Peace and the Terms of its Perpetuation,* 1917), and the role of engineers in social reconstruction (*The Engineers and the Price System,* 1921).[50] In all these writings, Veblen retained his interest in the evolution of economic institutions, as well as in the divide between the industrial and pecuniary sectors of modern society. But advancing his attack on the ideas of professional economists lost its appeal, except briefly in his valedictory book (*Absentee Ownership: Business Enterprise in Recent Times; The Case of America,* 1923), where he again jabbed at the "folklore of Political Economy" for treating the modern corporation as "a creative force in productive industry," rather than as an institution designed by the country's "kept classes" in order to "get something for nothing" from the larger community.[51] Despite this encore, Veblen was now writing mainly for popular periodicals like the *New Republic,* the *Public,* and *The Dial,* not for the academic outlets like the *Journal of Political Economy* or the *Quarterly Journal of Economics.*[52] We see the unintended consequences of this shift in the behavior of some of his newfound lay readers, who were taking his words to practical extremes, as journalist H. L. Mencken observed, with mocking exaggeration, in 1919:

> A year or so ago [Veblen] dominated the American scene. All the reviews were full of his ideas. A hundred lesser sages reflected them. Every one of intellectual pretensions read his books. Veblen was shining in full brilliance. There were Veblenists, Veblen clubs, Veblen remedies for all the sorrows of the world.[53]

Nevertheless, this popular craze was short-lived, and Veblen did nothing to prolong it. Before the bubble burst, he had, in any case, already withdrawn from the field of economics.

Coincidentally, just as Veblen was retreating, a new generation of economists was coming onto the academic scene, bringing its own ideas about where the discipline of economics should head now that the 1910s had arrived. By this point American economics hardly resembled the field Veblen had entered in the 1890s, or the one he began studying back in the 1870s. Indicative of the change was Wesley Mitchell's anecdotal report, shortly after the 1909 meeting of the American Economic Association, on the reception of John Bates Clark, whom the past generation of economists had likened to Christopher Columbus. Wrote Mitchell: "Despite the authority of his eminence and the charm of his personality, John B. Clark seemed to have no following, [and] of any other type of economic theory there seemed no comprehension in the general mind."[54] Mitchell was overstating his observation for effect, but he was right in grasping that economic theory—marginalist or otherwise—was no longer the big intellectual hot spot it had been for several decades before this. (Empirical research based on marginalist theory still had a very long future ahead of it, but that is a separate matter.)[55] This intergenerational change, strong enough to push even the Columbus of economists to the sidelines, took a heavy toll on Veblen's standing inside the field of economics. To the extent Veblen's writings from his time at the University of Chicago (and Stanford) offered a critique of marginal productivity theory, by the 1910s the market for that critique was dwindling among his younger contemporaries.

This is not to say that the newcomers opposed Veblen's assault on atomistic and ahistorical economic thinking or his agenda to study the evolution of economic institutions. Some economists still found Veblen's agenda compelling, while others did not; American economics of this era was pluralistic in outlook. In 1918 economists sympathetic to Veblen's program launched "institutional economics" as a reform movement within the discipline, and the movement continued strong until after World War II. During the interwar period, most institutionalists acknowledged Veblen as one of their principal forebears, whereas members of the increasingly visible neoclassical school took their inspiration from Englishman Alfred Marshall. Going forward in time, opinions about the substantive value of Veblen's ideas reflected further divisions within the field of economics, and divergent assessments appeared in neighboring disciplines as well. (In sociology, reactions to Veblen's theories swung from largely positive during his lifetime, to mostly hostile during the three decades following the Depression, to scattershot in the time ever since.)[56]

Veblen's reputation as an academic outsider extended across all these divisions. Tracing back to the years after he lost his job at Stanford and was marooned in Missouri, the marginal-man image took hold and fed on itself. To some extent, Veblen himself even promoted it (probably sub-consciously) by introducing in his post-Stanford writings the trope of the long-suffering loner, a hero defined by attributes just like those he increasingly wanted to project publicly.[57] In a 1919 essay on the "intellectual pre-eminence of Jews in modern Europe," for example, Veblen portrayed innovative Jewish scientists as "renegades," "iconoclasts," and "wanderers" with "no secure place"; they were "aliens of the uneasy feet"—socially detached and gifted with objectivity of vision—who gave themselves over to the "thankless quest for unprofitable knowledge, . . . especially in the field of scientific theory."[58] In keeping with this identity, Veblen, when offered the presidency of the American Economic Association in 1925, declined, telling the AEA's nominating committee that he was in "failing health," but alluding to other professional grievances when he said privately (according to his stepdaughter Becky Veblen Meyers) that "he was really too done up" to assume the position.[59] His final request was to obliterate all tangible evidence of academic (and other) connections:

> It is my wish, in case of death, to be cremated . . . as expeditiously and inexpensively as may be, without ritual or ceremony of any kind: that my ashes be thrown loose into the sea, . . . that no tomb-stone, slab, epitaph, effigy, tablet, inscription or monument of any name or nature, be set up in my memory . . . that no obituary, me-morial, portrait or biography of me, nor any letters written to or by me be printed or published, or in any way reproduced, copied or circulated.[60]

For academics (and members of the public) who built their impression of Veblen mainly during the last decade of his life, this unmoored man of letters, shy in personality as always, *was* Thorstein Veblen. Then, by reit-eration and with the fading and rewriting of memories, this image super-seded the earlier picture, even among some of the women and men, such as Wesley Mitchell, who knew Veblen during his heyday as an academic economist.[61] In one of the earliest obituaries for Veblen, John Maurice Clark (Columbia economist and the institutionalist son of John Bates Clark) went so far as to ask: "Was Veblen an economist?" This was a ques-tion he dodged by locating Veblen more outside of the field than inside it.[62] Other assessments in this vein followed, appearing right at the time Joseph Dorfman was at work on *Thorstein Veblen and His America*. Writing his book in this historical context gave Dorfman a license to construct history in reverse, to narrate the past from the angle of the present (his), to stretch fifty years backward in time the image his own contemporaries had formed of Thorstein Veblen and his work, and to project that snapshot from Veblen's sunset years onto the long span of his career. In this way was a social thinker, a scholar who spent most of his life inside the halls of major American universities and most of his professional career deep inside the academic field of economics, miraculously reincarnated as the quintessential academic outsider.

2.

If the type of economic knowledge Thorstein Veblen produced carried the stamp of his location on a field-map, if he created his theory so he could intervene into debates within the discipline of economics, it also bore the heavy weight of time—life time. Before his ideas could be scored by fellow economists as original contributions to the specialized field of economics, Veblen needed time (years) to enter onto the field; and before he could enter the field and make his mark there, he needed time (years, months) to gain command of the knowledge practices and resources that enabled him to do so; and before he could command those practices, he needed time (years, months, weeks, days) to use them over and over in different contexts. The story of the development of Thorstein Veblen's ideas—like the story behind many major intellectual achievements—is one that involves fields, field entry, knowledge practices, and the process of repetition-with-variation. Yet, contemporary studies by sociologists and other researchers concerned with the development of new knowledge often forget about time—not in the sense of historical dates but in the sense of the cumulative force of years, months, weeks, and even days.

Veblen's theory, as his contemporaries (correctly) saw it, was a direct assault on the central claim of the marginal productivity theory of distribution. That was the idea that an economy metes out its rewards—legitimately—in exact proportion to the productivity of the men and women who constitute the economy, and that people who receive the greatest economic rewards do so because their productive contributions greatly exceed the productive contributions of people who receive lesser rewards. This notion has had a long history that continues today; Americans, at least, never seem to be done with it. But in Veblen's day, with arguments about the distribution of wealth and income raging in public discussions and among professional economists, the idea gained the imprimatur of a new breed of marginalist economists who had pushed to the forefront of these debates. Marginalist John Bates Clark, Veblen's one-time teacher, gave the idea perhaps its most memorable expression: "We get what we produce—such is the dominant rule of life."[63]

To Veblen, this marginalist assertion was groundless. It relied on fallacious a priori, atomistic, and ahistorical preconceptions, which flew in the face of the principles of modern science. His strident writings on this topic ripped into deduction-based economic theories built on premises that cast economic actors as separate individuals pursuing economic goals under conditions that did not change fundamentally over time. This was the iconoclastic side of Veblen's work.

Complementing it was the constructive side of Veblen's thinking. This involved rejecting a priori deduction for induction; discarding assertions about self-propelling individuals and replacing those assertions with the empirical study of social institutions; and renouncing the notion that economic life operates according to timeless laws in favor of a dynamic mode of analysis that enfolded, inside the long-term movement of societies across evolutionary epochs, shorter-term changes in economic institutions during specific historical periods. With this upending of the tenets of marginalism, Veblen brought to light the cold fact that, over the evolutionary course of history, economic productivity has gone together with nonproductivity. In opposition to marginalist productivity theory, he characterized those in society who reap the greatest rewards not as productive men (and women) but as unproductive predators—parasites who, in order to "get something for nothing," leech on the productivity of people who are left with pitiable rewards. And Veblen revealed how these social relations of acquisition mutate as that unearned "something" continually takes new forms, as predation reinvents itself, as the unproductive parasites of one era evolve into those of the next. He witnessed this pattern, in live action, in the nonproductive consumption practices of members of the leisure class and in the nonproductive financial practices of executives in modern business enterprises (to sound the titles of his two major books). He saw this pattern, too, in the split between the industrial and pecuniary institutions of his time. In these insights lay Veblen's nonproductivity theory of economic distribution.

Behind this theory was Veblen's repertoire of knowledge-making practices. In the intellectual tool kit he had in hand when he encountered the marginalists' theory of distribution was the practice of viewing phenomena as constantly in flux, the practice of thinking in organic terms, and the practice of elevating science-based knowledge over other ways of knowing. Also among Veblen's tools was the practice of attaching high value to productive work that was serviceable to the community and distinguishing it from forms of human action that were unproductive, even predacious. Had the marginalists' logic not collided with these practices, their productivity theory of distribution might not have looked problematic to Veblen. But it did, and he parsed it into problems he could take on by recalibrating and recombining the knowledge tools he had available. Using this equipment, he deftly crafted his critique of marginalist theory as an attack on apriorism, atomism, ahistoricism, and the erasure of nonproductivity; and, inversely, he framed his own theory as inductive, institutional, evolutionary, and structured around the opposition between productive and unproductive activity. (Critiques by some of Veblen's contemporaries homed in on other defects of marginalism.)

This project attracted Veblen's attention after he entered the field of economics. Landing in that field took years—years full of false starts, unplanned detours, and serendipitous bends in the road. Thorstein Veblen was not born an economic theorist or even an academic. He was a bright farm boy living in a rural county where there happened to open up a new college with a newfangled curriculum and a young faculty, including a young faculty member who was just entering the field of political economy. The field intrigued Veblen, but initially it took a back seat to his interest in the field of philosophy, a subject in which he decided to pursue a doctoral degree—an unusual objective in this era of American history. Earning that degree took him several years (during which time he also studied political economy, history, and psychology), but, once he had his doctorate, the scarcity of academic positions in the discipline of philosophy brought him up short.

This professional setback was followed by a long health setback, after which he made several attempts to find work teaching economics, or political science, or just plain "social science" at small local colleges. When all these efforts failed, he decided to take the unheard-of step of seeking a second doctorate, this time in economics (with minors in American and English history). On track for this degree, Veblen's course veered again when his faculty adviser accepted a job to create a department of political economy at a start-up research university and brought Veblen along on a graduate fellowship. From this short-term position, Veblen then inched up a rung to the low-level faculty rank of reader in political economy. This advance occurred more than a dozen years after his college graduation;

and at this point his relationship to the field of economics was still tenuous, both because reader positions were temporary appointments and because he himself was slow to commit. On the brink of the publications that would establish his place as an original economic thinker, Veblen considered leaving academia altogether. In the end, he stayed in economics (until his subsequent exile), but his entry into the field was bumpy, to say the least.

Even so, the fits and starts were time well spent for Veblen's intellectual development. For, at every stop on his educational itinerary, he was (without intending to) receiving training in the knowledge practices he subsequently plied to construct his economic theory. In the course of his education, Veblen did more than read notable books in the areas of philosophy, political economy, history, psychology, and so forth. He worked directly with eleven of America's leading social thinkers, interacting with most of them for hours on end and often one-on-one, as they did *their work*—as they lectured and mentored, tossed around their ideas, discussed the literature of the day, carried out new research, wrote books and articles, and fought iconoclastic battles with other scholars—using the same knowledge-making repertoire Veblen would use. All espoused the inductive methods of modern science, upheld holism against atomism, and adhered to evolutionary and historical reasoning rather than to static ways of thinking. When examining human conduct, all these teachers consistently contrasted any kind of unproductive activity invidiously with productive work that is serviceable to the community.

These practices Veblen himself practiced again and again, in a cumulative process of repetition during which each iteration amplified previous iterations. Furthermore, his teachers' practices echoed throughout his surroundings: in other academic fields at the schools he attended, in the work of professional colleagues, and in discussions in the farming areas where he lived when he was not in the academic world. To be sure, Veblen was not the only budding academic of his generation who encountered these knowledge-making instruments. Contemporaries of Veblen who attended the same new or remodeled universities he did (or who studied abroad, particularly at German universities) were also familiar with these tools. But Veblen's apprenticeship was in a category of its own, temporally speaking. It began relatively early in life (because his local college offered a state-of-the-art curriculum); it ran continuously, uninterrupted by discordant learning experiences (because, after college and when he was not subsequently back home, Veblen was always situated in major research university operating at the same forefront of knowledge); and it extended over an unusually long period of more than twenty years (because of his prolonged entry into the field of economics).[64] By the end of this apprenticeship, Veblen commanded not just a pliant toolkit, but a deep well of long-amassed know-how, an intellectual reservoir, vitalized and revitalized by many converging streams.

In Veblen's case, moreover, repetition was more than duplication. His apprenticeship was not with a single mentor situated at one school and in one intellectual field. Not only did Veblen study at several higher-educational institutions, but he also chose universities that contemporaries regarded as organizational contrasts—with Johns Hopkins perceived as a design for the future, Yale as a model from the past. And, most important, Veblen studied with professors in different disciplines: philosophy, history, psychology, and sociology, as well as economics. (Veblen's education also sprawled across geographical locations: the small towns of Minnesota, Connecticut, and New York; the explosive cities of Baltimore and Chicago.) Too, his studies encompassed a range of topics, running from George Sylvester Morris's Hegelian saga of the evolution of human knowledge and Noah Porter's Kantian rejoinder, to the Darwinist psychological doctrines of Charles Sanders Peirce and George Trumbull Ladd, to the historical-institutional teachings of Herbert Tuttle on the Prussian state and Moses Coit Tyler on colonial American literature. Within the field of political economy itself, Veblen trained both with the country's leading representatives of the classical school (William Graham Sumner, J. Laurence Laughlin) and with the school's leading historicist critics (Richard T. Ely, Herbert Baxter Adams, and the young John Bates Clark). What was more, his work under the guidance of the critics occurred first in the lineup, inclining him against classical theory when he later met it personified. The knowledge practices that Veblen accustomed to through repetition, as he traversed varied sites of knowledge production, exhibited reach; they were multipurpose and versatile, stretching now to this problem, now to that one. When Veblen finally entered the unsettled field of economics and confronted the marginal productivity theory of distribution, he had at his disposal malleable tools that he transposed onto another set of intellectual problems.

There are different ways of understanding Thorstein Veblen, the knowledge maker; the spatial and temporal aspects of his development went together with other features of his intellectual biography. We might try a little mental experiment, however. We might think away Veblen's movements through academic fields and the thousands of hours he spent mastering the intellectual tools of his trade. Immediately, we realize this experiment is unnecessary. It has been run often in studies of intellectual innovators. Like Thorstein Veblen, the men and women who formulate novel ideas have frequently been described apart from their circuitous field movements and the moving clock of their daily intellectual lives. But when we efface place in this particular sense, elide time in this particular sense, we flatten and abbreviate much of the process by which new knowledge arises. Examining the time-space coordinates of social life opens up that historical process for our viewing.

NOTES

1. Introduction

1. Joan Robinson, *Collected Economic Papers,* vol. 5 (Oxford: Blackwell Publishing, 1979), 95.

2. Here and throughout the book, when I myself speak of someone as "original" or "innovative," I am situating the person's work in a particular historical context. What is original by this metric is what informed contemporaries see as a new addition—whether theory, concept, argument, bundle of information, or whatever—to a historically specific conversation. I realize that there are other—more transhistorical, but defensible—metrics of originality. In particular, when I quote statements from post–World War II scholars who apply the term "original" to Veblen's work, I am quoting statements often based on less historical conceptions than my own. That is the case, for example, with the remark by Joan Robinson cited earlier.

3. More accurately stated, I am unaware (after many years of working on this project) of any other person who clocked more years than Veblen.

4. JD*TV,* 12, 29, 21, 316.

5. Varying his word choices slightly, Dorfman reiterated this characterization of Veblen throughout his long career (see Chapter 2). Joseph Dorfman, *The Economic Mind in American Civilization,* vol. 3, *1865–1918* (New York: Viking Press, 1949), 455; Joseph Dorfman, "Background of Veblen's Thought," in *Thorstein Veblen,* ed. Carlton C. Qualey (New York: Columbia University Press, 1968), 106–130, 109.

6. C. Wright Mills, "Thorstein Veblen," in *The Politics of Truth: Selected Writings of C. Wright Mills,* ed. John H. Summers (New York: Oxford University Press, [1953] 2008), 63–78, 63, 66.

7. John Kenneth Galbraith, "Who Was Thorstein Veblen?," in *The Essential Galbraith,* ed. Andrea D. Williams (Boston: Houghton Mifflin, [1973] 2001), 200–221, 212.

8. Cornel West, *Keeping Faith: Philosophy and Race in America* (New York: Routledge, [1993] 2009), 200.

9. David Riesman, *Thorstein Veblen: A Critical Interpretation* (New York: Scribner's, 1953), xii.

10. Theodor W. Adorno, *Prisms,* trans. Samuel M. Weber (Boston: MIT Press, [1967] 1983), 89.

11. John Patrick Diggins, *Thorstein Veblen: Theorist of the Leisure Class* (Princeton, NJ: Princeton University Press, 1999), xiv, xxi.

12. "Inscrutable misfit": Diggins, *Thorstein Veblen*, xxii. "Stranger" is one of the most common descriptors throughout the entire literature on Veblen. On the relation between depictions of Veblen and the politics of commentators who have written about him, see Rick Tilman, *Thorstein Veblen and His Critics, 1891–1963: Conservative, Liberal, and Radical Perspectives* (Princeton, NJ: Princeton University, 1992).

13. I discuss this revisionist scholarship in Chapter 2.

14. Stephen Edgell, *Veblen in Perspective: His Life and Thought* (Armonk, NY: M. E. Sharpe, 2001), 54.

15. The notion of "academic man" came into use at the end of the nineteenth century, and by the middle of the twentieth century it was the subject of many books and articles on US higher education. However, it is obviously a gendered term, and I have seen no need to perpetuate it in this book. Granted, professors at research universities were uniformly men (with perhaps a half-dozen equivocal exceptions). But this was not true of staff members at small teaching colleges, as my section on Carleton College will indicate. In substituting "professional academic" for "academic man," however, I am not denying the prevalence of male-gendered practices and beliefs in the American academy in Veblen's time (or subsequently). To make this point clear in later chapters, I will, when it seems important to signal the heavily male composition of the academy, revert to male-gendered pronouns. Although I am uneasy about doing so, I also do not want to misrepresent the historical situation that was in front of Veblen.

16. The qualifier here is that this description holds for the years in Veblen's career that are the subject of this book, not for subsequent years.

17. These were the generation of his teachers, his own generation, and the generation that followed.

18. My count here includes Veblen's writings immediately before and during his time at the University of Chicago. I could make the same statement about his work during the three-year stint at Stanford that followed his departure from the University of Chicago.

19. In later chapters, I will come back to the following three quotations.

20. J. Laurence Laughlin to David Starr Jordan, April 29, 1899, Box 21, Folder 211, DSJP.

21. Allyn A. Young to Jordan, May 16, 1906, Box 49, Folder 494; and Young to Jordan, May 16, 1906, Box 49, Folder 489, both in DSJP.

22. David Starr Jordan, fellowship recommendation for Veblen, to Carnegie Institute, 1911, Box 62, "J" file, JDP.

23. I would add to this generalization, however, that these recent studies cover a historical period when "philosophy" itself was a broader area than it is today. Including both mental philosophy and moral philosophy within its boundaries, it dealt with a wide range of subjects we would now locate in psychology, political science, and sociology. My comment here pertains to synthetic studies of the intellectual life of the period. There are, however, many specialized monographs on turn-of-the-century thinkers who were not philosophers.

24. Louis Menand, *The Metaphysical Club: A Story of Ideas in America* (New York: Farrar, Straus and Giroux, 2001), x–xi. Books on Dewey and James have been particu-

larly numerous and, although very valuable for understanding this period, have inadvertently tilted the picture in the direction of philosophy.

25. I would qualify this statement by mentioning the recent work of scholars who have brought economists, though not Veblen himself, into the broader story, see Michael A. Bernstein, *A Perilous Progress: Economists and Public Purpose in Twentieth-Century America* (Princeton, NJ: Princeton University Press, 2001); Thomas C. Leonard, *Illiberal Reformers: Race, Eugenics and American Economics in the Progressive Era* (Princeton, NJ: Princeton University Press, 2016). Backhouse and Fontaine have attributed intellectual historians' neglect of economists to a felt lack of "the technical skills needed to discuss economics." Roger E. Backhouse and Philippe Fontaine, "Contested Identities: The History of Economics since 1945," in *A Historiography of the Modern Social Sciences,* ed. Roger E. Backhouse and Philippe Fontaine (New York: Cambridge University Press, 2014), 183–210, 185.

26. Insofar as they touch on Veblen's upbringing, most accounts dispense with his formal education in a paragraph or less, as I elaborate in Chapter 2. For a comprehensive review of the secondary literature on Veblen during the last two decades of the twentieth century, see Solidelle Wasser and Felicity Wasser, "Veblen References 1983–1996," *Research in the History of Economic Thought and Methodology* 9 (1999), 275–315.

27. The descriptor appears in a book review signed "W," most likely the abbreviated in-house signature of William Caldwell, Veblen's colleague at the time at the University of Chicago. W., review of *Die Enstehung Volkswirtschaft* by Karl Bucher, *JPE* 2 (1894): 304–308, 305. The review ran during Veblen's tenure as the managing editor of the journal.

28. John Bates Clark, *The Distribution of Wealth: A Theory of Wages, Interest and Profits* (New York: Macmillan, 1899), v.

29. This interpretation is not new. That Veblen's work was a critique of marginalism, and marginal productivity theory in particular, has been remarked on by many scholars. Christopher Brown, "Is There an Institutional Theory of Distribution?," *Journal of Economic Issues* 39 (2005): 915–931, 915–919; Guglielmo Forges Davanzati, *Ethical Codes and Income Distribution: A Study of John Bates Clark and Thorstein Veblen* (New York: Routledge, 2006), 53–72; William M. Dugger, "Radical Institutionalim: Basic Concepts," *Review of Radical Political Economics* 20 (1988), 1–20; Mary O. Furner, *Advocacy and Objectivity: A Crisis in the Professionalization of American Social Science, 1865–1905* (New Brunswick, NJ: Transaction Books, [1975] 2011), 191n37; Abram L. Harris, "Veblen and the Social Phenomenon of Capitalism," *American Economic Review* 41 (1951), 66–77; Ken McCormick, "Veblen on the Nature of Capital," *Revista Internazionale di Scienze Economiche e Commercials* 36 (1989), 609–622; David Reisman, *The Social Economics of Thorstein Veblen* (Northampton, MA: Edward Elgar, 2012); Dorothy Ross, *The Origins of American Social Science* (Cambridge: Cambridge University Press, 1991), 204–216; Malcolm Rutherford, *The Institutionalist Movement in American Economics, 1918–1947: Science and Social Control* (Cambridge: Cambridge University Press, 2011), 35; and Rick Tilman, *Thorstein Veblen and the Enrichment of Evolutionary Naturalism* (Columbia: University of Missouri Press, 2007), 169–173. In Chapter 8, I describe how Veblen's contemporaries offered a similar interpretation.

30. Paraphrasing *TLC*, 40.

31. This view was commonplace among members of the classical school of political economy. I will return to it in the glossary to Chapter 4.

32. Kloppenberg does not associate this "historical sensibility" with American economists of the period—or with Veblen, whom his massive study dispatches in a single sentence. James T. Kloppenberg, *Uncertain Victory: Social Democracy and Progressivism in European and American Thought, 1870–1920* (New York: Oxford University Press, 1986), 107–114.

33. Ross and Hodgson provide important exceptions to this statement. More briefly, Tilman has done the same. Ross, *Origins;* Geoffrey M. Hodgson, *The Evolution of Institutional Economics: Agency, Structure and Darwinism in American Institutionalism* (London: Routledge, 2004); Tilman, *Enrichment of Evolutionary Naturalism,* xiii.

34. Wesley C. Mitchell, *Types of Economic Theory: From Mercantilism to Institutionalism,* vol. 2, ed. Joseph Dorfman (New York: Kelley, 1969), 601. To avoid the distraction of quoting Mitchell's statement with multiple brackets and ellipses, I here dispense with these and streamline the passage. I would also note that the date that I attach to his statement, 1969, is misleading; it suggests that Mitchell was writing at a long remove in time from his contact with Veblen. But 1969 is merely the publication year of notes from a lecture course that Mitchell taught on and off between 1913 and 1937.

35. I am referring again to JD*TV.*

36. For a valuable collection of scholarship in this vein, see Erik S. Reinert and Francesca Lidia Viano, eds., *Thorstein Veblen: Economics for an Age of Crises* (New York: Anthem Press, 2012). More generally, the *Journal of Economic Issues,* the official publication of the Association for Evolutionary Economics, contains scores of articles on the present-day relevance of Veblen's economic ideas. See also the many volumes in two major book series: *Routledge Advances in Heterodox Economics* (London: Routledge) and *New Horizons in Institutional and Evolutionary Economics* (Northampton, MA: Edward Elgar). Several of these volumes include discussions of the differences between the "old institutionalism" of Veblen and today's varieties of "new institutionalism."

37. AV to JD, March 19, 1925, JDP.

38. AV to JD, April 21, 1931, JDP.

39. Quoted in Stephen Edgell, "Dorfman's Veblen: A Problematic Intellectual Legacy" (paper presented at the 4th Conference of the International Thorstein Veblen Association, The New School, New York, NY, May 11–12, 2002).

2. Theoretical and Historical Scaffolding

1. For this trip, as for any other, there are dozens of ways of packing, some more useful, others less, depending on what the traveler wants to accomplish. I believe these four concepts offer an enlightening way of understanding the development of Veblen's economic ideas, but there are many other perspectives, sociological and otherwise, that I might have used instead. The question of how new knowledge develops is not only one for the sociologist; it has also been addressed by theorists and researchers in psychology, education, organizational and management studies, computational science, philosophy, literary and performance studies, as well as in Science Studies and in scholarship on the history of science, the history of the social sciences, and the history of the

humanities. Sifting and sorting through even a fraction of this massive literature would have pulled me away from my travel plan.

2. I capitalize Science Studies to distinguish books and articles associated with this particular field of scholarship from literatures that "study science" mainly from the point of view of other disciplines and academic traditions. I draw no distinction between Science Studies and Science and Technology Studies (STS).

Shapin provides a comprehensive discussion of the rise and fall of the internal/external distinction in the history and sociology of science. Steven Shapin, "Discipline and Bounding: The History of the Sociology of Science as Seen Through the Externalism–Internalism Debate," *History of Science* 30 (1992): 333–370. On the place of the distinction in sociology, see Charles Camic and Neil Gross, "The New Sociology of Ideas," in *Blackwell Companion to Sociology,* ed. Judith R. Blau (Malden, MA: Blackwell, 2001), 236–249. The assault on the internal/external distinction occurred at the point when Science Studies researchers were mainly occupied with analyzing the *production* of scientific knowledge. Since that time, their interest has extended as well to questions about the *circulation* of knowledge beyond the walls of scientific institutions. Steven Epstein, "Culture and Science/Technology: Rethinking Knowledge, Power, Materiality, and Nature," *Annals* 619 (2008): 165–182, 167. Because this book is concerned with the development of Veblen's economic ideas, however, my own focus is in keeping with the older STS focus on knowledge production.

3. To avoid misunderstanding, a definition of "discipline" is probably useful. For this purpose, Pierre Bourdieu's definition is conveniently thorough: "A discipline is a relatively stable and delimited field [which is] easy to recognize: it has an academically and socially recognized name (. . . such as sociology as opposed to 'mediology,' for example); it is inscribed in institutions, laboratories, university departments, journals, national and international fora (conferences), procedures for the certification of competences." Pierre Bourdieu, *Science of Science and Reflexivity* (Chicago: University of Chicago Press [2001] 2004), 64–65. Historically, as Abbott has observed, disciplines have been more a feature of US higher education than of academic institutions elsewhere in the world. Andrew Abbott, *Chaos of Disciplines* (Chicago: University of Chicago Press, 2001), 122–126. Also worth noting in this regard is that subject matter associated with the name of any particular discipline has varied historically, as Abbott continues: "There are in fact no given bodies of academic work [that fall inevitably to a given discipline]. Bodies of academic work are perpetually being redefined, reshaped, and recast by the activities of disciplines trying to take work from one another or to dominate one another" (137). In this sense, the "relatively stable" condition that Bourdieu's statement mentions is only *relatively* stable.

4. When I want to refer to academic disciplines en bloc, I will speak of "knowledge fields"; in some contexts, I will also speak of intellectual fields and academic fields—trying to make clear how these notions relate to one another. Bourdieu's work put several of these concepts into circulation in the social-scientific literature, though without clarifying their connection to one another, as I have discussed elsewhere. Charles Camic, "Bourdieu's Cleft Sociology of Science," *Minerva* 49 (2011): 275–293; Charles Camic, "Bourdieu's Two Sociologies of Knowledge," in *Bourdieu and Historical Analysis,* ed. Philip Gorski (Durham, NC: Duke University Press, 2013), 183–211.

5. The same individual may occupy a position in more than one field.

6. I refer here and later to the work of Bourdieu, as well as to that of Randall Collins, because their theories are widely known among social scientists and thus require less introductory exposition. Randall Collins, *The Sociology of Philosophies: A Global Theory of Intellectual Change* (Cambridge, MA: Harvard University Press, 1998); Randall Collins, "A Network-Location Theory of Culture," *Sociological Theory* 21 (2003): 69–73; Randall Collins, *Interaction Ritual Chains* (Princeton, NJ: Princeton University Press, 2004). Their writings also encapsulate the main themes in the immense social-scientific literature on fields insofar as it relates to this book. In drawing on these two theorists, I am mindful of shortcomings in their work. I discuss these elsewhere. See Camic, "Cleft Sociology"; Camic, "Two Sociologies"; Charles Camic, "Das Verschwinden des 'Charakters': Eine Fallstudie der neue Ideensoziologie," in *Soziologiegeschichte: Wege und Ziele,* ed. Christian Daye and Stephan Moebius (Berlin: Suhrkamp Verlag, 2015), 310–337. My present aim, however, is not to exposit or critique but only to tap these theories to the degree necessary to build the theoretical platform for my treatment of Veblen. For the same reason, my discussion presents an eclectic blend of their ideas. I interchange concepts that Bourdieu and Collins do not themselves view as equivalent; and I gloss over major differences between the two theorists. My understanding of Bourdieu has been heavily informed by *Bourdieu and Historical Analysis,* ed. Philip Gorski (Durham, NC: Duke University Press, 2013).

7. Neil Fligstein and Doug McAdam, *A Theory of Fields* (New York: Oxford University Press, 2012), 9.

8. Bourdieu describes an academic field as "the site of permanent rivalry for the truth," while Collins describes knowledge fields as organized "under the guiding banner of 'truth,'" or truth-seeking. Pierre Bourdieu, "Preface to the English Edition," in Pierre Bourdieu, *Homo Academicus,* trans. Peter Collier (Stanford, CA: Stanford University Press, [1984] 1988), xi–xxiv, xiii; Collins, *Sociology of Philosophies,* 25. (In different ways, the fields of medicine, law, and journalism are also sites of struggle over truth claims.)

9. To secure this support, field members sometimes conceal their internal disagreements in order to present a unified public front.

10. Bourdieu also emphasizes the importance of newcomers. Pierre Bourdieu, *The Field of Cultural Production: Essays on Art and Literature* (New York: Columbia University Press, 1993), 55–61. We should recognize, however, that at certain points in time, fields may not actually have newcomers and also that old-timers can produce new knowledge as well. I focus here on field newcomers because I am looking ahead to Veblen at the start of his academic career.

11. Collins, *Sociology of Philosophies,* 38–39.

12. Bourdieu, *Field of Cultural Production,* 176.

13. Earlier, I commented that the traditional "internalist" approach viewed new ideas as outgrowths of the "preexisting state of knowledge" in some area of scholarship; and my description of field theory's approach to the development of new knowledge has just used some similar language. The words mean something different, however, in the contexts of the two approaches. An internalist approach premises that knowledge is on a course of development that leads naturally toward a particular goal; internalist historians portray thinkers from the past as relay runners, each one going some distance along the track until she or he hands off to the next person, who then runs the next leg of the course. Field theorists reject this teleological conception. For them, the "state of knowledge" at any one time is a heterogeneous mix of the positions of con-

tending field members as they struggle among themselves—not advancing toward some natural outcome but hewing out divergent pathways.

14. I take the metaphor "string" from Preda. Alex Preda, "STS and Social Studies of Finance," in *The Handbook of Science and Technology Studies,* ed. Edward J. Hackett, Olga Amsterdamska, Michael Lynch, and Judy Wajcman (Cambridge, MA: MIT Press, 2008), 901–920, 907. Knorr Cetina discusses the pre-1980s conception of knowledge more fully, contrasting it with the practice-based conception of knowledge that I am about to describe. Karin Knorr Cetina, *Epistemic Cultures: How the Sciences Make Knowledge* (Cambridge: Cambridge University Press, 1999).

15. Different scholars use somewhat different terminologies here. I take the "resources" and "practices" formulation from Pickering's early discussion of the subject. Andrew Pickering, "From Science as Knowledge to Science as Practice," in *Science as Practice and Culture,* ed. Andrew Pickering (Chicago: University of Chicago Press, 1992), 1–26. Epstein provides a valuable later treatment. Steven Epstein, "Culture and Science / Technology: Rethinking Knowledge, Power, Materiality, and Nature," *Annals* 619 (2008): 165–182. Regardless of the words used, dozens of monographs in Science Studies have made the general argument that knowledge consists of more than statements (or ideas). For an overview of this large body of research, see Edward Hackett, Olga Amsterdamska, Michael Lynch, and Judy Wajcman, eds., *The Handbook of Science and Technology Studies,* 3rd ed. (Cambridge, MA: MIT Press, 2008); Ulrike Felt, Rayvon Fouche, Clark A. Miller, and Laurel Smith-Doerr, eds., *The Handbook of Science and Technology Studies,* 4th ed. (Cambridge, MA: MIT Press, 2017).

16. While the distinction between "resources" and "practices" is useful theoretically, my emphasis in the following chapters falls more heavily on the latter, because the types of knowledge practices I will discuss presuppose the presence of correlative knowledge-making resources—obviating the need for me to discuss resources separately (except in regard to a few episodes in Veblen's education). In foregrounding "practices," my analysis corresponds (I believe) not only with a great deal of research in Science Studies, but also with the large literature associated with the "turn to practice" that has occurred in the social sciences and the humanities over the past three decades. See Theodore R. Schatzki, *Social Practices: A Wittgensteinian Approach to Human Activity and the Social.* (Cambridge: Cambridge University Press, 2001); Theodore R. Schatzki, Karin Knorr Cetina, and Eike von Savigny, eds., *The Practice Turn in Contemporary Theory* (London, UK: Routledge, 2001). For a review of this work and an effort to extend it to the study of practitioners of the social sciences, see Charles Camic, Neil Gross, and Michèle Lamont, introduction to *Social Knowledge in the Making,* ed. Charles Camic, Neil Gross, and Michèle Lamont (Chicago: University of Chicago Press, 2011), 1–40.

17. Ann Swidler, "Culture in Action: Symbols and Strategies," *American Sociological Review* 51 (1986): 273–286, 277; Ann Swidler, *Talk of Love: How Culture Matters* (Chicago: University of Chicago Press, 2001), 19. Swidler characterizes these "cultural materials"—and "culture" at large—"as a bag of tricks or an oddly assorted tool kit . . . containing implements of varying shapes that fit the hand more or less well, are not always easy to use, and only sometimes do the job." Swidler, *Talk of Love,* 24.

18. Swidler, *Talk of Love,* 25. Over the past twenty years, this idea has played a major role in several other areas of sociology, including political sociology, the sociology of social movements, and the sociology of evaluation. The central figures in these

developments have been Michèle Lamont (and her collaborators) and Charles Tilly, but the literature on the subject has ballooned rapidly. By now, it has become too extensive to address explicitly in this chapter, although this literature implicitly informs my analysis. Michèle Lamont and Laurent Thévenot, eds., *Rethinking Comparative Cultural Sociology: Repertoires of Evaluation in France and the United States* (New York: Cambridge University Press, 2000); Charles Tilly, *Regimes and Repertoires* (Chicago: University of Chicago Press, 2006).

19. Hans Joas, *The Creativity of Action*, trans. Jeremy Gaines and Paul Keast (Cambridge: Polity Press, [1992] 1996), 128–129, 141.

20. The pragmatist tradition predates contemporary field theory by a nearly a century, so pragmatists do not themselves use the expression "knowledge fields." Because their work is concerned with the development of knowledge in social contexts, however, inserting "knowledge fields" does little damage to their theory. John Dewey, *Human Nature and Conduct* (New York: Dover, 1922), 25.

21. Dewey, *Human Nature*, 244. Implements that cannot be adapted and improved are often discarded, and the same holds for pieces of intellectual equipment that are difficult to move from tool set to tool set. Fitted to one repertoire, the same tool may clash inside other ensembles, to the point where the problem solver stops using the implement and tosses it aside, as Joas has explained. Joas, *Creativity of Action*, 131.

22. There is no hard and fast boundary between these phases of field entry, or between them and phases that come afterward. I would add that social scientists have a long tradition of empirical research on the factors that affect people's employment status and their entry into different occupations and careers. As of yet, researchers who study knowledge production have been slow to build on this tradition.

23. Bourdieu and Collins both state explicitly that internal field dynamics are the linchpin to their theories of knowledge production. Bourdieu writes, for instance, that "the essential explanation of [the intellectual innovation of field members] lies . . . in the objective relations which constitute this field"; "the most important properties of each producer are . . . outside him, in the relationship of objective competition" that characterizes the field where he (or she) is situated. Bourdieu, *Field of Cultural Production*, 30; Pierre Bourdieu, *Sociology in Question* (London: Sage, [1984] 1993), 51. Collins makes the same claim, using the word "network": "It is not individuals [who] produce ideas, but the flow of networks throughout individuals"; that is to say, "the network is the actor on the stage" of intellectual history. Collins, "Network-Location Theory of Culture," 70. These claims have to do with fields, not field entry.

24. Pierre Bourdieu, *Distinction: A Social Critique of the Judgement of Taste*, trans. Richard Nice (Cambridge, MA: Harvard University Press, [1979] 1984), 109–168. Elaborating on this observation, Bourdieu carried out several well-known studies, including one on how the different social backgrounds of would-be French academicians produced different sets of dispositions, which fitted them for different academic fields, different positions within those fields, and different patterns of mobility during their careers. Bourdieu, *Homo Academicus*.

25. Bourdieu, *Homo Academicus*, 39–40.

26. Collins, *Sociology of Philosophies*.

27. Examining the networks of more than a thousand philosophers, Collins sidesteps the question of how these figures initially got into their networks. The result is that

his philosophers become parachutists of sorts, dropping onto their intellectual field from out of nowhere. Collins, *Sociology of Philosophies*. In some of his other work, however, in which he is not dealing with knowledge fields, Collins shows considerable awareness of the significance of prefield experiences.

28. Collins, *Sociology of Philosophies*, 68–74, 71.

29. David Kaiser, "Training and the Generalist's Vision of the History of Science," *Isis* 96 (2005): 244–251, 245; Cyrus Mody and David Kaiser, "Scientific Training and the Creation of Scientific Knowledge," in *The Handbook of Science and Technology Studies*, ed. Edward J. Hackett, Olga Amsterdamska, Michael Lynch, and Judy Wajcman (Cambridge, MA: MIT Press, 2008), 377–402, 381.

30. Gerald L. Geison, "Research Schools and New Directions in the Historiography of Science," *Orisis*, 2nd ser., 8 (1993): 226–238, 235.

31. The emphasis on learning by drill and discipline goes back to the work of Thomas Kuhn, but during the past three decades the subject has received further attention within Science Studies. Thomas S. Kuhn, *The Structure of Scientific Revolutions*, 2nd enl. ed. (Chicago: University of Chicago Press, [1962] 1970). Aside from the sources above, I draw in this paragraph on the following works: Kathryn M. Olesko, *Physics as a Calling: Discipline and Practice in the Konigsberg Seminar for Physics* (Ithaca, NY: Cornell University Press, 1991); Robert E. Kohler, *Lords of the Fly: Drosophila Genetics and the Experimental Life* (Chicago: University of Chicago Press, 1994); John L. Rudolph, *Scientists in the Classroom: The Cold War Reconstruction of American Science Education* (New York: Palgrave, 2002); John W. Servos, "Research Schools and Their Histories," *Osiris*, 2nd ser., 8 (1993): 2–15; Andrew Warwick, *Masters of Theory: Cambridge and the Rise of Mathematical Physics* (Chicago: University of Chicago Press, 2003).

32. The most important modern-day sociological treatment of temporality is Andrew Abbott, *Time Matters: On Theory and Method* (Chicago: University of Chicago Press, 2001).

33. Social-scientific research on the life course has been extensive. My summary description here draws on the foundational work of Harvey J. Graff, *Conflicting Paths: Growing Up in America* (Cambridge, MA: Harvard University Press, 1995); Glen H. Elder Jr. and Rand D. Conger, *Children of the Land: Adversity and Success in Rural America* (Chicago: University of Chicago Press, 2000); Michael J. Shanahan, "Pathways to Adulthood in Changing Societies: Variability and Mechanisms in Life Course Perspective," *Annual Review of Sociology* 26 (2000): 667–692; and the collection by Jeylan T. Mortimer and Michael J. Shanahan, eds., *Handbook of the Life Course* (New York: Springer, 2004).

34. Glen Elder, Monica Johnson, and Robert Crosnoe, "The Emergence and Development of Life Course Theory," in Jeylan T. Mortimer and Michael J. Shanahan, eds., *Handbook of the Life Course* (New York: Springer, 2004), 3–19, 7.

35. Obviously, different intellectual biographers have different reasons for writing their books, and I'm not suggesting that analyzing the field-entry process is (or should be) at the top of everyone's list. Even so, we might ask to what extent intellectual biographies do shed light (at least incidentally) on this process—the question discussed in the remainder of this section.

36. Malachi Hacohen, "Rediscovering Intellectual Biography—and Its Limits," *History of Political Economy* 39 (2007): 9–29, 9. On the contemporary status of intellectual

biography in the humanities, see Anthony Grafton, "The History of Ideas: Precept and Practice, 1950–2000 and Beyond," *Journal of the History of Ideas* 67 (2006): 1–24; Lloyd E. Ambrosius, ed., *Writing Biography: Historians and Their Craft* (Lincoln: University of Nebraska Press, 2004); and the special issue on biography in *Isis*, particularly the articles by Joan L. Richards, "Introduction: Fragmented Lives," *Isis* 97 (2006): 302–305; and Mary Terrall, "Biography as Cultural History of Science," *Isis* 97 (2006): 306–313.

37. Biography still remains an unpopular genre in Science Studies and in sociology. For example, the most recent *Handbook of Science and Technology Studies* (2017) contains not one reference to biography in its twelve hundred pages, even though there are scholars affiliated with the area who have made major biographical contributions. Felt, Fouche, Miller, and Smith-Doerr, *Handbook*. Important exceptions to this generalization include Donald Mackenzie, *Statistics in Britain, 1865–1930* (Edinburgh: Edinburgh University Press, 1981); Theodore M. Porter, *Karl Pearson: The Scientific Life in a Statistical Age* (Princeton, NJ: Princeton University Press, 2004); Steven Shapin and Simon Schaffer, *Leviathan and the Air-Pump* (Princeton, NJ: Princeton University Press, 1985); Richard Swedberg, *Schumpeter: A Biography* (Princeton, NJ: Princeton University Press, 1991); Neil Gross, *Richard Rorty: The Making of an American Philosopher* (Chicago: University of Chicago Press, 2008). In sociology, biography has been a highly suspect form of analysis since the 1930s, despite the fact that sociologists had previously held a more favorable view. See Elder, Johnson, and Crosnoe, "Life Course Theory," 3–4. At the middle of the last century, C. Wright Mills mounted an effort to revive the genre, but this proved unsuccessful. C. Wright Mills, *Sociology and Pragmatism* (New York: Oxford University Press, 1966). Today, sociologists mainly confine biography to life course studies, with the exceptions found in the Science Studies biographies just mentioned and in biographical studies of major sociological theorists, most notably W. E. B. Du Bois, Emile Durkheim, and Max Weber. See Aldon D. Morris, *The Scholar Denied: W. E. B. Du Bois and the Birth of Modern Sociology* (Berkeley: University of California Press, 2015); Marcel Fournier, *Emile Durkheim: A Biography* (Cambridge: Polity Press, 2013); Joachim Radkau, *Max Weber: A Biography* (Cambridge: Polity Press, 2009). Otherwise, contemporary sociologists, almost instinctively, view the study of single subjects as asociological—although one might think that sociologists, of all people, would know better. Indeed, as sociologist (and Science Studies scholar) Steven Shapin has asked: "What could be more sociological than a claim that an individual worked with, and artfully reworked, the material given by his culture?" Steven Shapin, "Personal Development and Intellectual Biography: The Case of Robert Boyle," review essay on John T. Harwood, *The Early Essays of Robert Boyle*, *British Journal for the History of Science* 26 (1993): 335–345, 334. On the topic of biography, Bourdieu's work shows mixed tendencies. Frequently, Bourdieu invidiously contrasts "the biographical method" with his own field-oriented account of intellectual production. Bourdieu, *Field of Cultural Production*, 180. He also ridiculed "the biographical illusion." Pierre Bourdieu and Loic J. D. Wacquant, *An Invitation to Reflexive Sociology* (Chicago: University of Chicago Press, 1992), 207–208n169. In other writings, however, Bourdieu has explicitly focused on the lives of individual producers of culture, Heidegger and Flaubert in particular. Pierre Bourdieu, *The Political Ontology of Martin Heidegger* (Cambridge: Polity Press, [1975] 1991); Pierre Bourdieu, *The Rules of Art: Genesis and Structure of the Literary Field*, trans. Susan Emanuel (Stanford, CA: Stanford University Press, [1992]

1996). On more recent biographical studies in the history of economics, see D. E. Moggridge, "Biography and the History of Economics," in *A Companion to the History of Economic Thought,* ed. Warren J. Samuels, Jeff E. Biddle, and John B. Davis (Malden, MA: Blackwell Publishing, 2003), 588–605. Also see a special 2007 issue on biography in *History of Political Economy,* particularly the articles by Robert W. Dimand, "The Creation of Heroes and Villains as a Problem in the History of Economics," *History of Political Economy* 39 (2007): 76–95; Hacohen, "Rediscovering Intellectual Biography"; E. Roy Weintraub and Evelyn L. Forget, "Introduction," *History of Political Economy* 39 (2007): 1–6.

38. To be fair, there are biographies that avoid these problems, most notably (among recent biographies of economists) Roger E. Backhouse, *Founder of Modern Economics: Paul E. Samuelson,* vol. 1, *Becoming Samuelson, 1915–1948* (New York: Oxford University Press, 2017). In the following paragraphs, however, I focus on examples that *do* exemplify these problems because I am looking ahead to the biographical literature on Veblen, not offering a general survey of recent intellectual biographies.

39. Parents, and fathers in particular, fare much better when they are historical figures in their own right. Hence the prominence that Brent gives to Benjamin Peirce in his biography of Charles Sanders Peirce, and the large role played by Henry James Sr. in Richardson's biography of William James. Joseph Brent, *Charles Sanders Peirce: A Life,* rev. and enl. ed. (Bloomington: Indiana University Press, 1998); Robert D. Richardson, *William James in the Maelstrom of American Modernism* (Boston: Houghton Mifflin, 2006).

40. John Milton Cooper, Jr., *Woodrow Wilson: A Biography* (New York: Vintage, 2009), 22, 31, 36. Typical for biographies of this type, Cooper has little to say about Wilson's studies even during his Hopkins period. In these years, Wilson studied with Herbert Baxter Adams and Richard T. Ely, scholars with whom Veblen also studied. As Chapter 5 will show, these two men both produced a substantial body of relevant work. Cooper, however, does not examine any of Adams's or Ely's writings.

41. Robert Westbrook, *John Dewey and American Democracy* (Ithaca, NY: Cornell University Press, 1991), 4.

42. Louis Menand, "Lives of Others: The Biography Business," *New Yorker,* August 6, 2007.

43. Robert Skidelsky, *John Maynard Keynes* (New York: Penguin 2003); Thomas K. McCraw, *Prophet of Innovation: Joseph Schumpeter and Creative Destruction* (Cambridge, MA: Harvard University Press, 2007).

44. Menand, "Lives of Others."

45. For example, see Peter Groenewegen, *Alfred Marshall: Economist, 1842–1924* (London: Palgrave Macmillan, 2007); Jorg Guido Hulsmann, *Mises: The Last Knight of Liberalism* (Auburn, AL: Ludwig von Mises Institute, 2007).

46. Jeremy Adelman, *Worldly Philosopher: The Odyssey of Albert O. Hirschman* (Princeton, NJ: Princeton University Press, 2013), 116.

47. Brent, *Peirce;* Philip J. Pauly, *Controlling Life: Jacques Loeb and the Engineering Ideal in Biology* (New York: Oxford University Press, 1987); Glenn Jacobs, *Charles Horton Cooley: Imagining Social Reality* (Amherst MA: University of Massachusetts Press, 2006).

48. The leading advocate in sociology for this type of explanation was Lewis Coser, whose argument was actually anticipated by Veblen, "The Intellectual Pre-eminence of

Jews in Modern Europe," *Political Science Quarterly* 34 (1919): 33–42. Lewis A. Coser, *Men of Ideas* (New York: Free Press, 1965); Lewis A. Coser, *Masters of Sociological Thought,* 2nd ed. (New York: Harcourt Brace Jovanovich, [1971] 1977); Lewis A. Coser, *Refugee Scholars in America* (New Haven, CT: Yale University Press, 1984. For a discussion of subsequent literature, see Neil McLaughlin, "Optimal Marginality," *Sociological Quarterly* 42 (2001): 271–288. Levine, Carter, and Gorman long ago criticized sociologists' tendency to conflate the concepts of "stranger" and "marginal man." Donald N. Levine, Elwood B. Carter, and Eleanor Miller Gorman, "Simmel's Influence on American Sociology," Parts I and II, *AJS* 81 (1976): 813–845 and 1112–1132. In the text I do not distinguish these concepts because I am describing a body of scholarship that does not do so.

49. Sociologist Anthony Giddens has written: "Repetition means time—some would say that it *is* time." Anthony Giddens, *In Defence of Sociology: Essays, Interpretations and Rejoinders* (Cambridge: Polity Press, 1996), 14.

50. Gilles Deleuze, *Repetition and Difference,* trans. Paul Patton (New York: Columbia University Press, [1968] 1994), 1. For discussion of Deleuze's views, see Sarah Gendron, *Repetition, Difference, and Knowledge in the Work of Samuel Beckett, Jacques Derrida, and Gilles Deleuze* (New York: Peter Lang, 2008).

51. The humanist literature on repetition and repetition-with-variation is enormous, spanning the distance from ancient works on rhetoric to the writings of postmodern philosophers, and it is still on the increase in many humanistic fields, including cultural anthropology and cultural history (see notes 50 and 52). Under the label of "replication," the phenomena of repetition and repetition-with-variation have also been strong presences in the Western scientific tradition since Newton's time. On these points, see Charles Camic, "Repetition with Variation: A Mertonian Inquiry into a Lost Mertonian Concept," in *Concepts and the Social Order: Robert K. Merton and the Future of Sociology,* ed. Yehuda Elkana, Andras Szigeti, and Gyorgy Lissauer (Budapest, Hungary: Central European University Press, 2011), 165–188. In contrast, sociologists' interest in "repetition" has long been and continues to be almost nil, aside from the work mentioned above in notes 32 and 49 and in studies of religious and political rituals. (I base this statement on an earlier analysis I carried out, with my research assistant Iga Kozlowska, of the use of "repetition" in all sociological journals included in the JSTOR database for the years 1965 to 2012. For later evidence for the lack of scholarship on repetition, see Stephanie L. Dailey and Larry Browning, "Retelling Stories in Organizations: Understanding the Functions of Narrative Repetition," *Academy of Management Review* 36 (2014), 22–43.

52. Just as in the arts, however, what qualifies as the "same" practice, as a "variation" on that practice, or as neither depends on the practitioner and the audience. Writing about painting, for instance, philosopher and novelist Umberto Eco has remarked: "We know very well that in certain examples of non-Western art, where we always see the same thing, the natives recognize infinitesimal variations." Umberto Eco, "Innovation & Repetition: Between Modern and Post-Modern Aesthetics," *Daedalus* 134 (2005): 191–207, 201. This ambiguity appears as well when we consider knowledge practices historically: we recognize what are or are not variations only insofar as we situate ourselves in the knowledge maker's own historical context—as I have tried to do in this book.

53. In emphasizing the significance of place, I am drawing on a large body of research in Science Studies. For an overview, see Christopher R. Henke and Thomas F. Gieryn, "Sites of Scientific Practice: The Enduring Importance of Place," in *The Handbook of Science and Technology Studies,* ed. Edward J. Hackett, Olga Amsterdamska, Michael Lynch, and Judy Wajcman (Cambridge, MA: MIT Press, 2008), 353–376.

54. As will become clear in later chapters, I am speaking here from the point of view of the historical figures involved in the story that will unfold, not from some ahistorical perspective. The mentors, disciplines, and institutions that Veblen and his academic contemporaries regarded as "different" might well appear "all the same" to men and women in other times and places.

55. Here I am citing Giddens, *Defence of Sociology,* 19; Collins, *Interaction Ritual Chains,* 43; Abbott, *Time Matters,* 273. To quote Giddens in full: "Tradition is repetition, and presumes a kind of truth antithetical to ordinary 'rational enquiry'—in these respects it shares something with the psychology of compulsions." Giddens, *Defence of Sociology,* 19.

56. Robert K. Merton, *Mass Persuasion: The Social Psychology of a War Bond Drive* (New York: Fertig, [1946] 2004). I have elsewhere examined Merton's use of the concept of repetition with variation, as well as the historical sources of the concept and its subsequent disappearance in sociology and neighboring fields. Camic, "Repetition with Variation."

57. Humanists have also drawn attention to a relationship between repetition and creativity, although not from the angle of knowledge-making practices, as evidenced by Eco, "Innovation & Repetition."

58. My understanding of reservoir geophysics is based on Richard Schatzinger and John F. Jordan, eds., *Reservoir Characterization: Recent Advances* (American Association of Petroleum Geologists, 1999).

59. JDTV, 247, 35, 319, 42. Dorfman attributes the first two and last two quotations in this sentence to some of his interviewees, citing their words in this way to corroborate his own interpretation of Veblen. Edgell provides a more comprehensive listing of passages where Dorfman, speaking for himself, describes Veblen in similar terms. Stephen Edgell, "Rescuing Veblen from Valhalla: Deconstruction and Reconstruction of a Sociological Legend," *British Journal of Sociology* 47 (1996): 627–642; Stephen Edgell, *Veblen in Perspective: His Life and Thought* (Armonk, NY: M. E. Sharpe, 2001).

60. Joseph Dorfman, "Background of Veblen's Thought," in *Thorstein Veblen,* ed. Carlton C. Qualey (New York: Columbia University Press, 1968), 106–130, 109, 127–128. Joseph Dorfman, *The Economic Mind in American Civilization,* vol. 3, *1865–1918* (New York: Viking Press, 1949), 455.

61. JDTV, 7–13.

62. JDTV, 12, 29, 271.

63. JDTV, 247, 316; Dorfman, *Economic Mind,* 455.

64. Dorfman, "Background," 127–128.

65. For information on Dorfman's career, I rely on Russell H. Bartley and Sylvia E Bartley, "Stigmatizing Thorstein Veblen: A Study in the Confection of Academic Reputations," *International Journal of Politics, Culture and Society* 14 (2000): 363–400; Edgell, "Rescuing Veblen"; Edgell, *Veblen in Perspective;* Rick Tilman, *The Intellectual Legacy of Thorstein Veblen: Unresolved Issues* (Westport, CT: Greenwood Press, 1996).

See also Warren J. Samuels, "The Veblen-Commons Award: Joseph Dorfman," *Journal of Economic Issues* 9 (1975): 143–146.

66. In an early letter to Andrew Veblen, Dorfman implies that he *spoke* to Thorstein, but that he did not manage to interview him for the purpose of his research. (Like most of Dorfman's letters to Andrew Veblen, this one is undated. Going by the date of Andrew's reply, however, Dorfman had to have written him in spring 1925.) Raising with Andrew a long list of biographical questions about his younger brother, Dorfman adds: "You might ask why I haven't asked Veblen himself these questions? Well, the primary reason is that when speaking to Veblen, it is . . . impossible to act like a reporter. You listen to him and forget why you came." JD to AV, 1925, JDP. Noticeably missing from the awkward second and third sentences here is the first-person pronoun—raising the question whether Dorfman met personally with Veblen to talk about his life or Dorfman is slyly paraphrasing someone else who met Veblen and found it "impossible to act like a reporter."

67. After Dorfman's death in 1991, his heirs donated the letters and other materials that he accumulated when writing his book on Veblen to Columbia University, where they are now archived as the Joseph Dorfman Papers (JDP). Scholars who have compared the originals of these letters with statements in Dorfman's book have identified many discrepancies. See Bartley and Bartley, "Stigmatizing Thorstein Veblen"; Edgell, "Rescuing Veblen"; Edgell, *Veblen in Perspective;* Tilman, *Intellectual Legacy.*

68. C. Wright Mills, "Thorstein Veblen," in *The Politics of Truth: Selected Writings of C. Wright Mills,* ed. John H. Summers (New York: Oxford University Press, [1953] 2008), 63–78; Theodor W. Adorno, *Prisms,* trans. Samuel M. Weber (Boston: MIT Press, [1967] 1983); John Kenneth Galbraith, "A New Theory of Thorstein Veblen," *American Heritage Magazine* 24 (1973): 33–40; Cornel West, *Keeping Faith: Philosophy and Race in America* (New York: Routledge, [1993] 2009).

69. Robert Heilbroner, *The Worldly Philosophers: The Lives, Times, and Ideas of the Great Economic Thinkers,* rev. 4th ed. (New York: Simon and Schuster, [1953] 1972), 210; Daniel Bell, introduction to *Thorstein Veblen, The Engineers and the Price System* (New Brunswick, NJ: Transaction Publishers, [1983] 1990), 1–35, 34. Dorothy Ross, *The Origins of American Social Science* (Cambridge: Cambridge University Press, 1991), 204.

During the sixty-year period from the mid-1930s to the mid-1990s, other voices in the Veblen-as-outsider chorus included Myron W. Watkins, review of *Thorstein Veblen and His America, American Economic Review* by Joseph Dorfman, 25 (1935): 284–286; Robert Weidenhammer, review of *Thorstein Veblen and His America* by Joseph Dorfman, *Annals* 178 (1935): 205; John Dos Passos, *The Big Money* (New York: Harcourt, Brace, and Company, 1936); Paul H. Douglas, review of *Thorstein Veblen and His America* by Joseph Dorfman, *Economic Journal* 47 (1937): 529–531; Abram L. Harris, review of *Thorstein Veblen and His America* by Joseph Dorfman, *JPE* 44 (1936): 109–111; Max Lerner, "Editor's Introduction," in *The Portable Veblen,* ed. Max Lerner (New York: Viking, 1948), 1–52; Louis Schneider, *The Freudian Psychology and Veblen's Social Theory* (New York: Kings Crown Press, 1948); Lewis S. Feuer, "Thorstein Veblen: The Metaphysics of the Interned Immigrant," *American Quarterly* 5 (1953): 99–112; David Riesman, *Thorstein Veblen: A Critical Interpretation* (New York: Scribner's, 1953); Bernard Rosenberg, *The Values of Veblen: A Critical Appraisal* (Washington, DC: Public

Affairs Press, 1956); George M. Frederickson, "Thorstein Veblen: The Last Viking," *American Quarterly* 11 (1959): 403–415; Max Eastman, *Love and Revolution: My Journey through an Epoch* (New York: Random House, 1964); Coser, *Masters of Sociological Thought;* Herbert Hovenkamp, "The First Great Law and Economics Movement," *Stanford Law Review* 42 (1990): 993–1058; Stjepan G. Meštrović, "Introduction to the Transaction Edition," in *Thorstein Veblen: A Critical Interpretation,* by David Riesman (New Brunswick, NJ: Transaction, 1995), ix–xxx. I have found Tilman (*Intellectual Legacy*) and Bartley and Bartley ("Stigmatizing Thorstein Veblen") valuable guides to this extensive literature.

70. John Patrick Diggins, *Thorstein Veblen: Theorist of the Leisure Class* (Princeton, NJ: Princeton University Press, 1999), xv, xxii, 34, 38, xxv, 32. In this period, Eby and Meštrović continued to uphold versions of this interpretation. Clare Virginia Eby, *Dreiser and Veblen, Saboteurs of the Status Quo* (Columbia: University of Missouri Press, 1998); Stjepan G. Meštrović, "Appreciating Veblen without Idealizing or Demonizing Him," *International Journal of Politics, Culture, and Society* 16 (2002), 153–157; Stjepan G. Meštrović, introduction to *Thorstein Veblen on Culture and Society* (Thousand Oaks, CA: Sage, 2002).

71. I quote here from Rick Tilman, "The Utopian Vision of Edward Bellamy and Thorstein Veblen," *Thorstein Veblen: Critical Assessments,* vol. 1, ed. John Cunningham Wood (London: Routledge, [1985] 1993), 321–338, 333; Sidney Plotkin and Rick Tilman, *The Political Ideas of Thorstein Veblen* (New Haven, CT: Yale University Press, 2011), 19. On Bellamy, see Tilman, "Utopian Vision"; on Loeb, see Charles Rasmussen and Rick Tilman, *Jacques Loeb: His Science and Social Activism and Their Philosophical Foundations* (Philadelphia: American Philosophical Society, 1998). See also Rick Tilman, "Thorstein Veblen: Incrementalist and Utopian," *Thorstein Veblen: Critical Assessments,* vol. 1, ed. John Cunningham Wood (London: Routledge, [1973] 1993), 171–184; Rick Tilman, "Dewey's Liberalism versus Veblen's Radicalism: A Reappraisal of the Unity of Progressive Social Thought," *Thorstein Veblen: Critical Assessments,* vol. 1, ed. John Cunningham Wood (London: Routledge, [1984] 1993), 285–306; Rick Tilman, *Thorstein Veblen and His Critics, 1891–1963: Conservative, Liberal, and Radical Perspectives* (Princeton, NJ: Princeton University, 1992); Tilman, *Intellectual Legacy;* Rick Tilman, "Thorstein Veblen and the Disinterest of Neoclassical Economists in Wasteful Consumption," *International Journal of Politics, Culture and Society* 13 (1999): 207–223; Rick Tilman, *Thorstein Veblen and the Enrichment of Evolutionary Naturalism* (Columbia: University of Missouri Press, 2007); Stephen Edgell and Rick Tilman, "The Intellectual Antecedents of Thorstein Veblen: A Reappraisal," *Journal of Economic Issues* 23 (1989): 1003–1026; Stephen Edgell and Rick Tilman, "John Rae and Thorstein Veblen on Conspicuous Consumption: A Neglected Relationship," *History of Political Economy* 23 (1991): 731–744. Edgell presents another comprehensive river-style account. See Edgell, *Veblen in Perspective.* For earlier interpretations in this vein, see W. M. Dugger, "The Origins of Thorstein Veblen's Thought," *Thorstein Veblen: Critical Assessments,* vol. 1, ed. John Cunningham Wood (London: Routledge, [1979] 1993), 237–244. For discussion of Tilman's work, see Daniel H. Borus, "Sui Generis Veblen?" *International Journal of Politics, Culture and Society* 11 (1998): 607–615.

72. On the "influence" on Veblen of these particular thinkers, see, for example, Hugh J. Dawson, "E. B. Tylor's Theory of Survivals and Veblen's Social Criticism," *Journal*

of the History of Ideas 54 (1993): 489–504; E. Anton Eff, "History of Thought as Ceremonial Genealogy: The Neglected Influence of Herbert Spencer on Thorstein Veblen," in *Thorstein Veblen: Critical Assessments,* vol. 1, ed. John Cunningham Wood (London: Routledge, [1989] 1993), 413–428; Ann Jennings and William Waller, "The Place of Biological Science in Veblen's Economics," *History of Political Economy* 30 (1998): 189–217. For other instances of this style of approach, see Blake Alcott, "John Rae and Thorstein Veblen," *Journal of Economic Issues* 38 (2004): 765–786; Donald R. Stabile, "The Intellectual Antecedents of Thorstein Veblen: A Case for John Bates Clark," *Journal of Economic Issues* 31 (1997): 817–825. The following chapters will furnish additional examples.

73. Edgell, along with Bartley and Barley ("Stigmatizing Thorstein Veblen"), use "pathography" as they describe—and then upend—Dorfman's depiction of Veblen as a stunted personality. Stephen Edgell, "Thorstein Veblen: The Mistaken Marginality of the Man from Marx," paper presented at the Inaugural Conference of the International Thorstein Veblen Association, February 1994, The New School, New York, NY; Stephen Edgell, "Dorfman's Veblen: A Problematic Intellectual Legacy," paper presented at the 4th Conference of the International Thorstein Veblen Association, May 11–12, 2002, The New School, New York, NY; Edgell, *Veblen in Perspective.* Together with Tilman, these scholars have also taken the lead in the successful effort to overhaul Dorfman's provincializing description of Veblen's family. Tilman, *Intellectual Legacy,* 30. See also Russell H. Bartley and Sylvia E. Yoneda, "Thorstein Veblen on Washington Island: Traces of a Life," *International Journal of Politics, Culture and Society* 7 (1994): 589–613; Russell H. Bartley and Sylvia E. Bartley, "In Search of Thorstein Veblen: Further Inquiries into his Life and Work," *International Journal of Politics, Culture and Society* 11 (1997): 129–173; Russell H. Bartley and Sylvia E. Bartley, "In the Company of T. B. Veblen: A Narrative of Biographical Recovery," *International Journal of Politics, Culture and Society* 13 (1999): 273–331; Russell H. Bartley and Sylvia E. Bartley, "Revising the Biography of Thorstein Veblen," *International Journal of Politics, Culture and Society* 13: (1999): 363–374. This line of research began with Carlton C. Qualey, introduction to *Thorstein Veblen* (New York: Columbia University Press, 1968), 1–15. It continued with John Kenneth Galbraith ("New Theory of Thorstein Veblen"), ironically in the same article in which he endorses a version of the outsider thesis. It has been continued as well in J. R. Christianson, "Thorstein Veblen: Ethnic Roots and Social Criticism of a 'Folk Savant,'" *Norwegian-American Studies* 34 (1995): 3–22; Jonathan Larson, "Speculations on the Origins of Veblen's Aesthetic Criticisms: As Revealed by the Restoration of the Veblen Family Farmstead," http://elegant-technology.com/SSpecor.html; Jonathan Larson, "A Restoration of Significance," *Journal of Economic Issues* 29 (1995): 910–915; Jonathan Larson, "Joseph Dorfman's Many Errors from a Minnesota Perspective," http://elegant-technology.com/SSjoDrME.html; William C. Melton, "Thorstein Veblen and the Veblens," *Norwegian-American Studies* 34 (1995): 23–56; William C. Melton, *The Veblens in Wisconsin: A Progress Report* ([location unknown]: Melton Research Inc., 2004). These revisionist studies about the conditions under which Veblen grew up have been complemented by research on his later years, which amends the popular stereotype (accepted by Dorfman) that Veblen was a serial womanizer. See JJTV; Tony Maynard, "A Shameless Lothario: Thorstein Veblen as Sexual Predator and Sexual Liberator," *Journal of Economic Issues* 34 (2000): 194–199. In later chapters, I will return to this stereotype.

74. I here quote Tilman, *Intellectual Legacy*, 30; Bartley and Bartley, "Company of T. B. Veblen," 282; Edgell, *Veblen in Perspective*, 49–55. In his most recent work, Tilman has toned down emphasis on the outsider stance in his interpretation of Veblen. See Plotkin and Tilman, *Political Ideas*. The same goes for Edgell, "Dorfman's Veblen."

75. To be sure, some accounts avoid this problem, because they *are* focused on the development of specific ideas in Veblen's work. In later chapters, I make use of this research.

76. Veblen scholars do not themselves use the expression "knowledge-making practices." Most of them would just say "ideas."

77. Dorfman's 1934 perfunctory, and generally misleading, description of Veblen's schooling actually compares favorably with many later, highly abbreviated treatments of the topic, including those of Diggins (*Thorstein Veblen*), Edgell (*Veblen in Perspective*), and Tilman (*Intellectual Legacy*); but see Plotkin and Tilman (*Political Ideas*), who offer a somewhat fuller account. In the past two decades, revisionist accounts of Veblen's years at Carleton and Cornell have also begun to appear: Russell H. Hartley and Sylvia Erickson Bartley, "The Formal Education of Thorstein Veblen: His Carleton Years, 1874–1880," paper presented at the 4th Conference of the International Thorstein Veblen Association, May 11–12, 2002, The New School, New York, NY; Eric Hillemann, "Thorstein Veblen and Carleton College, and Vice Versa," paper presented at the 5th Conference of the International Thorstein Veblen Association, June 3–6, 2004, Carleton College, Northfield, MN; Francesca Lidia Viano, "Ithaca Transfer: Veblen and the Historical Profession," *History of European Ideas* 35 (2009): 38–61.

78. On the migration of American students to German universities and the effect of their return migration on the organization of America's new research universities, I draw on Carl Diehl, *Americans and German Scholarship* (New Haven: Yale University Press, 1978); Jurgen Herbst, *The German Historical School in American Scholarship: A Study in the Transfer of Culture* (Ithaca, NY: Cornell University Press, 1965); Daniel T. Rodgers, *Atlantic Crossings: Social Politics in a Progressive Age* (Cambridge, MA: Harvard University Press, 1998), 76–111. Diehl enters the important qualifier that, in adopting German models, American university presidents also modified them to suit academic conditions in the United States; Diehl, *Americans and German Scholarship*, 50.

79. Respectively, Peter J. Bowler, *The Earth Encompassed* (New York: Norton, 2000), 305–334; Randall Collins and Michael Makowsky, *The Discovery of Society*, 8th ed. (New York: McGraw, 2009); Daniel T. Rodgers, *The Work Ethic in Industrial America, 1850–1920* (Chicago: University of Chicago Press, 1974), xii; Daniel Patrick Thurs, *Science Talk: Changing Notions of Science in American Culture* (New Brunswick, NJ: Rutgers University Press, 2007), 85, quoting contemporaneous sources.

80. Historians have used "Age of Iconoclasm" to describe many earlier periods, among them the Renaissance and the Reformation. As far as I am aware, they have not yet picked up on this theme when examining American culture in the late nineteenth century.

81. George Rogers Howell, "Modern Solution of Old Problems," address delivered to the Livingston County Historical Society, January 15, 1895. In associating iconoclasm with philosophy and the physical sciences, Howell neglected to mention that contemporaries in areas ranging from literature to medicine were also portraying theirs as the "Age

of Iconoclasm." Describing the era, freelance essayist Laurence Hutton spoke of "these days of literary iconoclasm." Laurence Hutton, "Literary Notes," *Harper's New Monthly Magazine* 84 (1892): B-001. Meanwhile, Rose Cleveland (former US first lady), in a study of George Eliot's poetry, drew attention to "this scientific age—this age of iconoclasm." Rose Elisabeth Cleveland, *George Eliot's Poetry, and Other Sketches* (New York: Funk and Wagnalls, 1885), 192. In an analysis of heredity, Dr. John Dickey offered a more elaborate statement. He wrote: "The last quarter of the nineteenth century is the age of iconoclasm. It is natural that it should be for it is the period of the most marked progress in all lines of human knowledge and experience that the world has yet witnessed. Oldest beliefs have been dimmed by the passing clouds of doubt, biggest idols have toppled uneasily on their pedestals, darkest corners of ignorance and superstition have been illuminated by the searchlights of science. [And] in no realm of knowledge has there been more decided advances and more readjusting of seemingly well establish theories than in that of medicine." John L. Dickey, "The Significance of Heredity," *Medical Examiner and Practitioner* 10 (1900): 167. Commenting from inside the academy, historian and Cornell University president Charles Kendall Adams wrote simply: "This has sometimes been called the Age of Iconoclasm." Charles Kendall Adams, *A Manual of Historical Literature* (New York: Harper and Brothers, 1888), 13. From 1890 to 1897, a magazine titled the *Iconoclast* achieved an estimated circulation of fifty-thousand readers throughout the Midwest and the South. See Charles Carver, *Brann, The Iconoclast* (Austin: University of Texas Press, 1957).

82. Irving Browne, *Iconoclasm and Whitewash, and Other Essays* (New York: James Osborne Wright, 1885), 25.

83. Percy Douglas, "Iconoclasm Necessary to Progress," *North American Review* 148 (1889): 768–769.

84. As the quotations in the two preceding paragraphs show, contemporaries did not see iconoclasm ("spirit" that it was) as something distinct from scientific research. To the contrary: they considered the scientific method as the one of great tools of iconoclasm; and they regarded the natural sciences—inasmuch as they were based careful empirical research in laboratories and elsewhere—as the premier sites of iconoclastic work. According to this metric, it was the non-research-based knowledge fields that lagged behind, because they often made do, according to observers at the time, with speculative "armchair" scholarship. See H. ten Kate, "On the Alleged Mongolian Affinities of the American Race: A Reply to Daniel G. Brinton," *Science* 12 (1888): 227–228, 228. That said, Sera-Shriar has shown that nineteenth-century "armchair" scholarship frequently amounted to more than untamed speculation and actually involved its own distinctive set of methods and practices. Efram Sera-Shriar, "What Is Armchair Anthropology? Observational Practices in Nineteenth-Century British Human Sciences," *History of the Human Sciences* 27 (2013): 26–40.

85. *HL*, 132, 138.

86. Traweek provides a present-day analogue when she describes how graduate students in physics learn, by the repeated example of their professors, that they are expected to be "brash" in demeanor. Sharon Traweek, *Beamtimes and Lifetimes: The World of High Energy Physicists* (Cambridge, MA: Harvard University Press [1988] 1992).

3. Beginnings

1. The literature on the Norwegian migration to the United States, on conditions in Norway at the time, and on Norwegian settlements in the Midwest is enormous. I have found especially useful Theodore C. Blegen, *Norwegian Migration to America: The American Transition* (Northfield, MN: Norwegian-American Historical Association, [1931] 1940); Jon Gjerde, *From Peasants to Farmers: The Migration from Balestrand, Norway, to the Upper Middle West* (Cambridge: Cambridge University Press, 1985); Jon Gjerde, *The Minds of the West: Ethnocultural Evolution in the Rural Middle West, 1830–1917* (Chapel Hill: University of North Carolina Press, 1997); John Gjerde and Carlton C. Qualey, *Norwegians in Minnesota* (St. Paul: Minnesota Historical Society Press, 2002); Odd S. Lovoll, *The Promise of America: A History of the Norwegian-American People*, rev. ed. (Minneapolis: University of Minnesota Press, [1984] 1999); Carlton C. Qualey, *Norwegian Settlement in the United States* (Northfield, MN: Norwegian-American Historical Association, 1938); Carlton C. Qualey and Jon Gjerde, "The Norwegians," in *They Chose Minnesota: A Survey of the State's Ethnic Groups,* ed. June Drenning Holmquist (St. Paul: Minnesota Historical Society Press, 1981), 220–247; Ingrid Semmingsen, *Norway to America: A History of the Migration,* trans. Einar Haugen (Minneapolis: University of Minnesota Press, [1975] 1978); Lowell J. Soike, *Norwegian Americans and the Politics of Dissent, 1880–1924* (Northfield, MN: Norwegian-American Historical Association, 1991).

2. This one-sentence description of the social class structure in Norway is obviously an oversimplification, glossing over large regional and temporal differences and, with them, differences in the spread of status differences within these class categories. Historians argue over all these issues as well.

3. Cited in Blegen, *Norwegian Migration,* 199.

4. Gjerde and Qualey, *Norwegians in Minnesota,* 2–4; Terje Mikael Hasla Joranger, "Valdres to the Upper Midwest: The Norwegian Background of the Veblen Family and Their Migration to the United States," in *Thorstein Veblen: Economics for an Age of Crises,* ed. Erik S. Reinert and Francesca Lidia Viano (New York: Anthem Press, 2012), 67–87.

5. Joranger, "Valdres," 69; Knut Odner, "New Perspectives on Thorstein Veblen, The Norwegian," in *Thorstein Veblen: Economics for an Age of Crises,* ed. Erik S. Reinert and Francesca Lidia Viano (New York: Anthem Press, 2012), 89–98, 93.

6. Soike, *Norwegian Americans,* 19–21.

7. Lovoll speaks of this period as the era of "government by elite." Lovoll, *Promise of America,* 3.

8. Odner, "New Perspectives," 93.

9. Peter A. Munch, "Authority and Freedom: Controversy in Norwegian-American Congregations," *Norwegian-American Studies* 38 (1973): 3–34.

10. Quoted in Odner, "New Perspectives," 95.

11. Munch, "Authority and Freedom," 12.

12. AV to JD, November 23, 1931, JDP.

13. AV-*Gen,* 102.

14. Except as indicated, the information is this paragraph is from AV-*Fam,* 1–3; AV-*Gen,* 59–62, 60.

15. AV to JD, February 7, 1926, JDP.

16. Laurence M. Larson, *The Changing West and Other Essays* (Northfield, MN: Norwegian-American Historical Association, 1937), 69–70.

17. Joranger, "Valdres," 73.

18. Thomas Veblen's own recollections of this journey are contained in two short translated documents. See Erik S. Reinert, "Veblen's Contexts: Valdres, Norway and Europe," in *Thorstein Veblen: Economics for an Age of Crises,* ed. Erik S. Reinert and Francesca Lidia Viano (New York: Anthem Press, 2012), 17–50, 43–44. The fullest account is AV-*Fam,* 3–5. Also useful are two of Andrew Veblen's letters to Dorfman: AV to JD, November 9, 1929, and February 4, 1930, both in JDP.

19. Throughout the text, I use the website measuringworth.com to convert nineteenth-century dollar amounts, largely meaningless in themselves, into their approximate equivalents in purchasing power for 2020. (For simplicity's sake, I will show these equivalents by giving the 2020 amounts in parentheses following the nineteenth-century figures.) As the authors of the site explain, however, purchasing power is only one of several conversion metrics that one might use, most of which translate the nineteenth-century figures into enormous equivalents in today's terms. I use "purchasing power" because it produces relatively conservative adjustments and is fairly intuitive in its meaning.

20. My understanding of these currents is beholden, especially, to Jeremy Atack and Peter Passell, *A New Economic View of American History,* 2nd ed. (New York: Norton, 1994); Daniel Howe, *What Hath God Wrought: The Transformation of American Society, 1815–1848* (Oxford: Oxford University Press, 2007); Walter Licht, *Industrializing America: The Nineteenth Century* (Baltimore: Johns Hopkins University Press, 1995).

21. In speaking of the "Upper Midwest," I'm speaking somewhat anachronistically, since this expression was rarely used before the twentieth century. In the nineteenth century, the region—which we now think of as including Michigan, Wisconsin, and Minnesota (plus or minus northern Illinois and Iowa), and which was carved out of the old "Northwest Territory"—would usually have been called the either the "North" or the "West," depending on the geographical and cultural location of the writer, as well as the date when he or she was writing. For much of the time period dealt with in this book, for example, the "West" began in Chicago and fanned out from there. Later historians who cover the period sometimes use the nineteenth-century language, while others use the twentieth- (and now twenty-first-) century terminology. I have found it less confusing to do the latter, except when I'm quoting directly from scholars who follow a different practice, as Atack and Bateman do (see note 23). To reduce tedium, I sometimes shorten "Upper Midwest" simply to "Midwest."

22. For 1774, see Carole Shammas, "A New Look at Long-Term Trends in Wealth Inequality in the United States," *American Historical Review* 98 (1993): 412–431, 424. For 2016, see Edward N. Wolff, "Household Wealth Trends in the United States, 1962 to 2016: Has Middle Class Wealth Recovered?" National Bureau of Economic Research (2017), 44, http://www.nber.org/papers/w24085. Data from 2020, grouped differently, are given at: https://www.federalreserve.gov/releases/z1/dataviz/dfa/distribute/table/#quarter:122;series:Net%20worth;demographic:networth;population:all;units:shares.

23. Jeremy Atack and Fred Bateman, *To Their Own Soil: Agriculture in the Antebellum North* (Ames: Iowa State University Press, 1987), 270 (emphasis added). In this passage, the researchers speak of the "rural North" as including both the Northeast and

the Midwest. But in their analysis, they present a more complete table that reports percentages for these two regions separately; these percentages show an even (slightly) less unequal distribution in the Midwest than in the Northeast. This table is the source of the percentages that I include in the preceding paragraph. On the basis of these figures, Atack and Bateman write: "Nowhere were conditions riper for realizing this goal"—the goal being "economic parity with [one's] neighbor"—"than *in the antebellum Midwest* with its small farms, rural communities, and abundant lands." Atack and Bateman, *Their Own Soil*, 88, 86 (emphasis added). See also Jeremy Atack and Fred Bateman, "Yeoman Farming: Antebellum America's Other 'Peculiar Institution,'" in *Agriculture and National Development: Views on the Nineteenth Century*, ed. Lou Ferleger (Ames: Iowa State University Press, 1990), 25–51; Lee Soltow, *Patterns of Wealthholding in Wisconsin since 1850* (Madison: University of Wisconsin Press, 1971). Steckel offers a critique of Atack and Bateman's analysis, but it does not bear on the portions of their work that I am drawing on. Richard Steckel, "Poverty and Prosperity: A Longitudinal Study of Wealth Accumulation, 1850–1860," *Review of Economics and Statistics* 72 (1990): 275–285.

24. I draw this formulation from Atack and Bateman, *Their Own Soil*, 11–12; Atack and Passell, *New Economic View*; Hal S. Barron, "Listening to the Silent Majority: Change and Continuity in the Nineteenth-Century Rural North," in *Agriculture and National Development: Views on the Nineteenth Century*, ed. Lou Ferleger (Ames: Iowa State University Press, 1990), 3–23; Allan Kulikoff, "Households and Markets: Toward a New Synthesis of American Agrarian History," *William and Mary Quarterly*, 3rd ser., 50 (1993): 342–355. Midwestern farming is another topic surrounded with a vast literature. In addition to the sources just listed, I build on Kathleen Neils Conzen, "Immigrants in Nineteenth-Century Agricultural History," in *Agriculture and National Development: Views on the Nineteenth Century,"* ed. Lou Ferleger (Ames: Iowa State University Press, 1990), 303–342; Joseph P. Ferrie, "The Wealth Accumulation of Antebellum European Immigrants to the U.S., 1840–60," *Journal of Economic History* 54 (1994): 1–33; Steven Hahn and Jonathan Prude, introduction to *The Countryside in the Age of Capitalist Transformation: Essays in the Social History of Rural America*, ed. Steven Hahn and Jonathan Prude (Chapel Hill: University of North Carolina Press, 1985), 1–21; Wayne D. Rasmussen, introduction to *Agriculture and National Development: Views on the Nineteenth Century*, ed. Lou Ferleger (Ames: Iowa State University Press, 1990), xiii–xx; Dorothy Schweider, "Agricultural Issues of the Middle West, 1865–1910," in *Agriculture and National Development: Views on the Nineteenth Century*, ed. Lou Ferleger (Ames: Iowa State University Press, 1990), 97–115; Donald L. Winters, "The Economics of Midwestern Agriculture, 1865–1900," in *Agriculture and National Development: Views on the Nineteenth Century*, ed. Lou Ferleger (Ames: Iowa State University Press, 1990), 75–95. As we would expect, there are debates in this literature over issues of fact and interpretation. Because these issues are largely incidental to my discussion of Veblen's upbringing, I have tried to steer clear of them or to take a nondenominational position.

25. Atack and Bateman, *Their Own Soil*, 11–12.

26. Barron, "Silent Majority," 7.

27. Harriet Friedmann, "World Market, State, and Family Farm: Social Bases of Household Production in the Era of Wage Labor," *Comparative Studies in Society and History* 20 (1978): 545–586, 548, 560.

28. Bachelor farmers had a long history in Norway. See Gjerde and Qualey, *Norwegians in Minnesota,* 13. For part of Kari and Thomas's time in Sheboygan, they also shared their home with Kari's mother and her second family (Kari's own father had died young). This branch of the family emigrated from Norway after the Veblens did, and it later resettled in Minnesota, where the Veblens then relocated. AV-*Fam,* 14.

29. AV-*Fam,* 23.

30. William C. Melton, *The Veblens in Wisconsin: A Progress Report* (n.p.: Melton Research Inc., 2004), 13.

31. Between 1850 and 1855, the population of Manitowoc County grew by 10,000, bringing it to 13,050. Ralph Gordon Plumb, *A History of Manitowoc County* (Manitowoc, WI: Brandt Printing, 1904), 36.

32. Thorstein Veblen is sometimes identified as his parents' sixth child, sometime as their fifth child, depending on whether one includes (as I have done) Kari and Thomas's first child, who died in infancy before the couple left Norway for America. In choosing a name for their sixth child, Kari and Thomas followed Norwegian naming conventions: Bunde was Kari's maiden name; Tosten (Thorstein) was the name of her father—hence, Thorstein Bunde Veblen, AV-*Fam,* 50.

Perhaps to enhance their depiction of Veblen as an "outsider," Veblen scholars often refer to him using the full name of "Thorstein Bunde Veblen." But so far as I am aware, this was not how Veblen referred to himself or was referred to by his contemporaries. To his parents and siblings (when he was growing up), he was always "Tostein." According to Andrew, "It was on coming to Carleton that he adopted the spelling Thorstein and took as a 'middle' name, Bunde." After that, however, he (and others) did not actually use "Bunde." In the annual catalogues of Carleton and Yale, he was "Thorstein B. Veblen," and in the *Johns Hopkins University Circulars* he was "T. B. Veblen." On his oldest surviving letters, from the early 1880s, he signed "T. B. Veblen," which was the form he also used on most of his publications before 1897, when he switched over to "Thorstein Veblen." Asked in 1928 by the registrar of Yale University how he wanted his name to appear in the *Alumni Directory,* Veblen said "Thorstein Veblen," telling the registrar *not* to include the "B." Postcard stamped March 10, 1928, TV-YU.

33. AV to JD, January 14, 1931, JDP.

34. Melton, *Veblens in Wisconsin,* 13–14.

35. Gjerde, *Peasants to Farmers.*

36. AV-*Fam,* 15. On soil conditions, see Louis Falge, ed., *A History of Manitowoc County, Wisconsin,* vol. 1 (Chicago, Il: Goodspeed Historical Association, 1912), 37.

37. AV-*Fam,* 25.

38. AV-*Fam,* 64–66; William C. Melton, "Thorstein Veblen and the Veblens," *Norwegian-American Studies* 34 (1995): 23–56, 36–38; Melton, *Veblens in Wisconsin,* 14–15. In taking in these men, the Veblens were following a Norwegian custom, as Andrew explains: "All the settlers who could find room in their house for newcomers were obliged to give them shelter until they could find homes for themselves. Those that had built commodious houses invariably had newcomers living with them during the first months after their arrival." AV-*Fam,* 64.

39. AV-*Fam,* 75; Melton, "Thorstein Veblen and the Veblens," 37.

40. William Cronon, *Nature's Metropolis: Chicago and The Great West* (New York: Norton, 1991). Aside from Chicago, the cities of Milwaukee, Minneapolis, and Kansas

City also served as major trade and commercial centers of the Midwest. Cronon, *Nature's Metropolis*, 284.

41. Plumb, *Manitowoc County*, 37–39.

42. Nuba Pletcher, "Early Railroading in Rice County," *Rice County Historian* 24 (no. 1) ([1936] 1988): 2–4.

43. Cronon, *Nature's Metropolis*, 97–147.

44. Quoted in Cronon, *Nature's Metropolis*, 140.

45. "Norwegian-Americans" were not, of course, a monolithic group, and I do not want to "essentialize" them. Among themselves, they differed considerably, particularly by region of origins. For understanding the Veblen family, however, examination of these differences would lead too far afield.

46. Melton, *Veblens in Wisconsin*, 4–6; Johan Reiseren's popular *Veiviser for Norske Emigranter til De forende nordamerikanske Stater* (Guide for Norwegian Emigrants to the United States of North America).

47. Larson, *Changing West*, 73.

48. The Veblens were regular subscribers to the Norwegian-American weekly paper *Emigranten*. AV-*Fam*, 42–43. For a thorough treatment of the content of this paper, see Odd S. Lovoll, *Norwegian Newspapers in America: Connecting Norway and the New Land* (St. Paul: Minnesota Historical Society Press, 2010).

49. Melton, *Veblens in Wisconsin*.

50. AV to JD, March 13, 1930, JDP.

51. AV-*Fam*, 21–22.

52. In this way, Manitowoc mirrored the general situation in the Midwest, which Gjerde describes as "one of the most ethnically and culturally diverse areas of antebellum U.S." Gjerde, *Minds of the West*, 6. See also Conzen, "Immigrants."

53. On the Norwegian settlement of Manitowoc, see Robert A. Bjerke, introduction to "Memoirs of Two Eccentric Personalities of Manitowoc's Norwegian Community," by Andrew A. Veblen and C. John M. Gronlid, *Manitowoc County Historical Society Occupational Monograph* 60 (1986): 1–3; Robert A. Bjerke, "The Manitowoc Norwegians," *Manitowoc County Historical Society Occupational Monograph* (n.d.).

54. Joranger, "Valdres"; Melton, *Veblens in Wisconsin*.

55. On the interplay of these two goals, see Gjerde, *Peasants to Farmers*; Gjerde, *Minds of the West*. See also Kenneth O. Bjork, preface to *A Voice of Protest: Norwegians in American Politics, 1890–1917*, by Jon Wefald (Northfield, MN: Norwegian-American Historical Association, 1971).

56. Lovoll, *Promise of America*, 62–63.

57. On the history of these controversies, both before and after the Norwegian migration, see August Suelflow and E. Clifford Nelson, "Following the Frontier, 1840–1875," in *The Lutherans in North America*, ed. E. Clifford Nelson (Philadelphia: Fortress Press, 1975), 147–251.

58. John Useem and Ruth Hill Useem, "Minority-Group Patterns in Prairie Society," *AJS* 50 (1945): 377–385, 378n5.

59. Gjerde, *Minds of the West*; Gjerde and Qualey, *Norwegians in Minnesota*. In in the early twentieth century, the German sociological theorist Georg Simmel called attention to the way in which internal group conflict can produce social solidarity.

60. Lovell, *Promise of America,* 145.

61. Lovell, *Promise of America,* 88.

62. Andrew Veblen, "Old Berger," trans. Robert A. Bjerke, *Manitowoc County Historical Society Occupational Monograph* 60: 1–3 [1915] 1986), 1; AV-*Fam,* 84.

63. AV-*Fam,* 35, 81.

64. Blegen, *Norwegian Migration,* 163; AV-*Fam,* 40. Critical of the "Yankee Spirit," Ottesen said of America, "Here is neither art, poetry, nor science; here are dollars and steam—that is all." Quoted in Munch, "Authority and Freedom," 13.

65. AV to JD, May 18, 1930, JDP.

66. R. Laurence Moore, "What Children Did Not Learn in School: The Intellectual Quickening of Young Americans in the Nineteenth Century," *Church History* 68 (1999): 42–61, 42–43. Moore illustrates his claim through the examples of Richard T. Ely and William Graham Sumner, both of whom were Veblen's teachers in graduate school. Writing without reference to the historical context of Moore's analysis, Greenblatt also observes how religious controversy teaches that "religious doctrines are open to inquiry and argument." Stephen Greenblatt, *The Swerve* (New York: W.W. Norton, 2011), 27.

67. On the motives behind the Veblens' move, see Joranger, "Valdres," 76–77; Melton, "Thorstein Veblen and the Veblens," 24–25. On the area into which they moved as it was in 1860, see Anonymous, "Norwegians in Rice County," *Rice County Historian* 17, no. 2 (1989): 1–2.

68. On the economic preeminence of wheat, see William E. Lass, *Minnesota: A History,* 2nd ed. (New York: Norton, 1998), 155. See also Atack and Passell, *New Economic View,* 293–294.

69. EVOM, available in printed form as "Memoirs of Emily Veblen Olsen," http://elegant-technology.com/resource/EMILY, PDF, 9. A century later, John Kenneth Galbraith agreed with Thomas's view, saying of the land in this area that "there can be no farming country anywhere in the world with a more generous aspect of opulence." John Kenneth Galbraith, "A New Theory of Thorstein Veblen," *American Heritage* 24 (1973) 33–40, 34.

70. On the economic boom in Rice County and surrounding towns, like Faribault, see Franklyn Curtiss-Wedge, ed., *History of Rice and Steele Counties, Minnesota* (Chicago: H. C. Cooper, 1910); Joan R. Gunderson, "Before the World Confessed," in *All Saints Parish, Northfield, and the Community, 1858–1985* (Northfield, MN: Northfield Historical Society, 1987).

71. Also after the move to Rice County, Minnesota, Kari gave birth to three more children. This brought the Veblens' total to eleven children born in the United States. However, immediately following the move, an infant son, who had been born in Cato, died. Subsequently, one of the three children born in Rice County (when Kari was forty-eight) also died in infancy; and subsequent to that, another son born in Cato died (in 1885) at age twenty-three. Kari and Thomas thus raised nine children to adulthood. Of these, eight children—four sons, four daughters—were still alive when Andrew completed his family genealogy in 1925. AV-*Fam,* 143–145.

72. Melton, *Veblens in Wisconsin,* 15–16.

73. Joranger, "Valdres," 78, citing unpublished research by William Melton.

74. These downturns included the Panic of 1857 (and, later, the Panic of 1873), as well as the general slump in commodity prices after the Civil War. Atack and Passell, *A*

New Economic View; Ferrie, "Wealth Accumulation." There is considerable debate among economic historians, however, on the state of the American economy in this period. I return to this subject in Chapter 6.

75. AV to JD, February 17, 1926, JDP.

76. Melton, "Thorstein Veblen and the Veblens."

77. AV to JD, December 7 1931, JDP.

78. AV to JD, January 11, 1932, JDP.

79. In both cases, it took time for Thomas and Haldor to build, so in the interim the family lived in inferior, makeshift quarters. Emily Veblen, who took part in the family's move to Rice County, explained to Dorfman: "When my parents came to a new place and were getting settled, there they had hardship and hard work, but pretty soon prosperity and comfortable circumstances came to reward them for their labors." Emily Veblen Olsen to Dorfman, September 18, 1934, CCA; AV-*Fam*, 64; Jonathan Larson, "A Restoration of Significance," *Journal of Economic Issues* 29 (1995): 910–915, 912. Melton elaborates on the design of the Rice County house, characterizing it as a unique combination of a Greek Revival exterior—popular among Americans at the time—and a Norwegian interior. Melton writes that "throughout the house, the standard of carpentry and cabinetmaking skill is extremely high," involving "tremendous" effort. Melton, "Thorstein Veblen and the Veblens," 31, 34.

80. Erling Ylvisaker, *Eminent Pioneers: Norwegian-American Pioneer Sketches* (Freeport, NY: Books for Libraries Press, [1934] 1970); AV-*Fam*, 59–64.

81. Ylvisaker, *Eminent Pioneers*, 11–12; Blegen, *Norwegian Migration*, 66.

82. AV-*Fam*, 59–64.

83. For Emily's account, see EVOM; for Mary's, see Ylvisaker, *Eminent Pioneers;* for Ed's, see John Edward Veblen to JD, undated, JDP.

84. AV to JD, February 17, 1926, JDP.

85. AV-*Fam*, 73–74; EVOM, 8; Ylvisaker, *Eminent Pioneers*, 4–5. Remembering life in the Veblen household when he was growing up, John Edward Veblen told Dorfman that his older brother Thorstein "always favored the Indians whereas all others I heard talk about such things were against the Indians and I noticed he was always on the side opposite to all others." John Edward Veblen to JD, undated, JDP.

86. *IW*, 25, 48, 27.

87. AV to JD, February 17, 1926, JDP. As adults, the children quarreled about the *kinds* of intelligence that Thomas and Kari had.

88. *JJTV*, 10; *IW*, 97.

89. Thorstein Veblen, "The Price of Wheat since 1867," *JPE* 1 (1892): 68–103, 82, 91, 83, 85.

90. *TLC*, 87.

91. *AO*, 132, 139, 135. Chapter 6 will further consider Veblen's views on midwestern farmers.

92. *AO*, 168–169.

93. *IG*, 318.

94. *AO*, 132.

95. As Chapter 8 will explain, "serviceability" is the *summum bonum* in Veblen's scheme of values.

96. Blegen, *Norwegian Migration*, 240; Semmingsen, *Norway to America*, 11; Lovoll, *Promise of America*, 161–169.

97. Edward Ehlert, "The History of 'Learnin' in Manitowoc County," *Manitowoc County Historical Society Occupational Monograph* 14 (1971): 1–8, 2.

98. AV to JD, February 8, 1932, JDP.

99. In saying that Emily "was the first Norwegian-American woman" to graduate from an American college, I am repeating a claim that has often been made—and is highly probable. I am unaware, however, of hard evidence in support of the claim.

100. AV to JD, February 25, 1930, JDP.

101. Andrew Veblen, "Old Berger," 2. These in-home classrooms were a common feature of Norwegian-American communities at this time. Christianson, "Ethnic Roots," 4.

102. In a letter to Dorfman, Andrew mentions the presence of a parochial school in Rice Country, though he writes dismissively of it. "The parochizl [*sic*] school of the Nerstrand community [in Rice County] was a woe-begone affair that led a precarious existence. Thorstein's attendance might be said to have been spasmodic—somewhat more so than the course of the parochial school itself. It dodged in irregularly when the children might be available between the district school and the seasons when . . . the children could help in farm operations." AV to JD, February 25, 1930, JDP. Elsewhere, Andrew refers to a short-lived "Norwegian" school in Cato. Andrew Veblen, "Fat Rode," trans. Robert A. Bjerke, *Manitowoc County Historical Society Occupational Monograph* 60 ([1915] 1986): 3–4, 3. This, too, was probably a parochial school, since "Norwegian" schools were almost always parochial schools.

103. Bjorn Sandvik, "'Suffered under Pontius Pontoppidan' or 'Good, Old Pontoppidan'?" in *Crossings: Norwegian-American Lutheranism as a Transatlantic Tradition,* ed. Todd W. Nichol (Northfield, MN: Norwegian-American Historical Association, 2003): 57–71.

104. Paraphrased from Ernst Troeltsch, *The Social Teaching of the Christian Churches,* 2 vols., trans. Olive Wyon (Chicago: University of Chicago Press, [1911] 1931), 547. On the presence of these themes in the Bible itself, see Michael Barton, "The Victorian Jeremiad: Critics of Accumulation and Display," in *Consuming Visions: Accumulation and Display of Goods in America, 1880–1920,* ed. Simon J. Bronner (New York: Norton, 1989), 55–71.

105. This aspect of Lutheranism stands in contrast to what Troeltsch described as the "viral individualism" of Calvinism. Troeltsch, *Social Teaching,* 534.

106. *Dr. Martin Luther's Small Catechism explained in Questions and Answers,* 1885, 27–30.

107. Heinrich J. Maurer, "Studies in the Sociology of Religion. I. The Sociology of Protestantism," *AJS* 30 (1924): 257–286, 268–270.

108. For Emily's statement, see EVOM, 3; for Andrew's, see AV to JD, February 25, 1930, JDP. In the recent scholarly literature on Veblen, this aspect of Dorfman's narrative has been convincingly challenged. See Bartley and Bartley, "In Search of Thorstein Veblen"; *JJTV;* Stephen Edgell, *Veblen in Perspective: His Life and Thought* (Armonk, NY: M. E. Sharpe, 2001).

109. AV to JD, March 13, 1930, JDP. In this letter, Andrew tells Dorfman that Thorstein always had a slight Valdris accent. In contrast, Rudolf von Tobel, who knew Thorstein during his years at Carleton College, told Dorfman: "He was a master of as correct and precise English, without a trace of foreign accent, as anyone in college, unless his habitual drawl might be so considered." von Tobel to JD, February 28, 1930, JDP.

Possibly Veblen, like many people, spoke somewhat differently within his family and outside of it.

110. Emily Veblen recalled: "My father and mother learned to understand and talk English a short time after they came from Norway, though, of course, they did not pronounce it very well. My father transacted business with Americans and Germans in English, and read English newspapers." Emily Veblen Olsen to JD, September 18, 1934, CCA.

111. Larson, *Changing West*, 16–38; Frank C. Nelson, "The School Controversy among Norwegian Immigrants," *Norwegian-American Studies* 26 (1971): 206–219; James S. Hamre, "Norwegian Immigrants Respond to the Common School: A Case Study of American Values and the Lutheran Tradition," *Church History* 50 (1981): 302–315; Ehlert, "'Learnin' in Manitowoc County," 2.

112. AV-*Fam*, 47.

113. The controversy over schooling continued after the Rice County move. In neighboring Goodhue County, the pastor was B. J. Muus, one of the Midwest's strongest proponents of parochial schools. Muus's "views were often extreme and he stated them without any view to conciliation or accommodation." Larson, *Changing West*, 131.

About the common school that the Veblen children attended in Rice County, Emily Veblen offered two recollections that were not entirely consistent—although in both instances she was writing in the mid-1930s, which was seventy years after the situation she was recalling. In her 1934 letter to Dorfman, she contrasted the Rice County school with the Cato school, saying that while English was spoken in the latter (which was attended by Germans and "Yankees"), in the former "it so happened that all the children in our district were Norwegian, which accounts for the Norwegian speech in our school." Emily Veblen Olsen to Dorfman, September 18, 1934, CCA. But in her jottings in the margins of Dorfman's book, Emily wrote that there "never was a time when the school in our district was taught by any but American teachers." Quoted in Bartley and Bartley, "In Search of Thorstein Veblen," 132. It may be that the second quote refers only to the schools in Cato, in which case there actually is no inconsistency. But it is more likely that, in Rice County, while students did typically speak Norwegian among themselves, the teacher spoke English to them. Regardless, the textbooks would have been in English, so this would have been the language of instruction.

114. Falge provides a first-hand account of the cavalier approach to schooling in Manitowoc during the time the Veblens lived in the area. Falge, *Manitowoc County*.

115. Ruth Miller Elson, *Guardians of Tradition: American Schoolbooks of the Nineteenth Century* (Lincoln: University of Nebraska Press, 1964); Carl F. Kaestle, *Pillars of the Republic: Common Schools and American Society, 1780–1860* (New York: Hill and Wang, 1983); Louise L. Stevenson, *The Victorian Homefront: American Thought and Culture, 1860–1880* (New York: Twayne, 1991); Paul Theobald, *Call School: Rural Education in the Midwest to 1918* (Carbondale: Southern Illinois University Press, 1995); William J. Reese, *America's Public School: From the Common School to "No Child Left Behind,"* updated ed. (Baltimore: Johns Hopkins University Press, 2011).

116. AV to JD, March 19, 1925, JDP.

117. On the recitation method, Elson, *Guardians of Tradition;* Theobald, *Call School.* For contemporaneous discussions, see Herbert B. Adams, "Progress in the Study and the Teaching of History," *Chautauquan* 9 (1889): 240. Elson adds: "In many classrooms the memorization technique was reinforced by the monitorial system, whereby older students

were designated to hear the recitation of the younger ones." Elson, *Guardians of Tradition*, 9.

118. Elson, *Guardians of Tradition*, 10.

119. AV to JD, February 25, 1930, JDP.

120. My reasoning here follows the standard template: all men are mortal, Socrates is a man, Socrates is mortal. That is to say, all common-school students read textbooks of this type, Thorstein Veblen was a common-school student, Thorstein Veblen (must have) read textbooks of this type.

121. For later research, see Kaestle, *Pillars of the Republic;* Theobald, *Call School;* Reese, *America's Public School*.

122. A Minnesota law of 1881 directed teachers to give lessons that emphasized "industry, order, economy, punctuality, patience, self-denial, health, purity, temperance, cleanliness, honesty, truth, justice, politeness, peace, fidelity, philanthropy, patriotism, self-respect, hope, perseverance, cheerfulness, courage, reflection, self-reliance, gratitude, pity, mercy, kindness, conscience and the will." John N. Greer, *The History of Education in Minnesota* (Washington, DC: Government Printing Office, 1902), 53. The legislative passage of this law occurred seven years after Veblen left the Rice County District School, but—barring the possibility that Minnesota legislators in 1881 differed in their expectations from legislators of the 1860s and 1870s—this list gives some idea of what parents in the state wanted common schools to transmit to their children.

123. On William McGuffey's hugely popular readers, see John H. Westerhoff III, *McGuffey and His Readers: Piety, Morality, and Education in Nineteenth-Century America* (Milford, MI: Mott Media, [1978] 1982); Dolores P. Sullivan, *William Holmes McGuffey: Schoolmaster to the Nation* (Teaneck, NJ: Fairleigh Dickinson University Press, 1994).

124. On private property, see Elson, *Guardians of Tradition*, 26, 29, 256, 254.

125. Elson, *Guardians of Tradition*, 46.

126. Quoted in Elson, *Guardians of Tradition*, 68–69.

127. Quoted in Elson, *Guardians of Tradition*, 122–123.

128. Quoted in Elson, *Guardians of Tradition*, 143, 161, 207, 222, 264, 292.

129. Elson, *Guardians of Tradition*, 21, 33–34, 152, quote from 17.

130. *TLC*, 388. Chapter 6 will explain why Veblen placed midwestern farming communities in the category of "advanced industrial communities."

131. Joseph J. Rappel, *A Centennial History of the Manitowoc County School Districts and its Public School System, 1848–1948* (Manitowoc, WI: Manitowoc, Engraving, 1948); Ehlert, "'Learnin' in Manitowoc County."

132. AV to JD, March 13, 1930, JDP. In this letter, Andrew added: "It was taken as a mild scandal that he spelled down the teachers."

133. Greer, *History of Education in Minnesota*, 28. In this context, "political economy" was, most likely, the practical subject of home economics.

134. AV to JD, March 18, 1930, JDP; *TLC*, 388.

135. Jeremy Agnew, *The Creation of the Cowboy Hero* (Jefferson, NC: McFarland & Co, 2015).

136. AV to JD, February 25 and March 13, 1930, JDP. On Veblen's poetic efforts during his college years, see John Bates Clark to JD, March 19 and April 18, 1930, JDP.

137. Brian W. Downs, *Modern Norwegian Literature, 1860–1918* (Cambridge: Cambridge University Press, 1966), 21–24, 45–46.

138. AV to JD, May 14, 1931; and AV to JD, July 18, 1925, both in JDP. On Veblen's saga translation, see Chapter 6. Among the books Veblen toted with him when he retired to Washington Island, Wisconsin, were several Norse sagas. See Russell H. Bartley and Sylvia E. Yoneda, "Thorstein Veblen on Washington Island: Traces of a Life," *International Journal of Politics, Culture and Society* 7 (1994): 589–613. Speaking more generally, Lovoll has observed: Norwegian "peasant tales gained great favor with Norwegian immigrants [to the United States]. They were part of creating a glorious past, as were the historical narratives from the Age of the Vikings. . . . Viking heroes symbolized the strength embodied in the Norwegian people and their expansive powers." Lovoll, *Norwegian Newspapers in America*, 41.

139. On the long time horizon of the Norse-Icelandic sagas, see John Lindow, *Norse Mythology: A Guide to the Gods, Heroes, Rituals, and Beliefs* (Oxford: Oxford University Press, 2001); Margaret Clunies Ross, *The Cambridge Introduction to the Old Norse-Icelandic Saga* (Cambridge: Cambridge University Press, 2010). Writing in the mid-1880s about methods for teaching history as an academic subject, G. Stanley Hall (who nearly overlapped with Veblen at Johns Hopkins a few years earlier) classed the "Norse sagas" among the literatures valuable for "stimulating the historical sense." G. Stanley Hall, introduction to *Methods of Teaching History*, vol. 1, ed. G. Stanley Hall (Boston: Ginn, Heath & Company, 1884),v–xiv, xii.

140. On the specifically "Nordic" elements in Veblen's later work, see Jonathan Matthew Schwartz, "Tracking-down the Nordic Spirit in Thorstein Veblen's Sociology," *Acta Sociologica* 33 (1990): 115–124; Edgell, *Veblen in Perspective*; Kåre Lunden, "Explaining Veblen by His Norwegian Background: A Sketch," in *Thorstein Veblen: Economics for an Age of Crises*, ed. Erik S. Reinert and Francesca Lidia Viano (New York: Anthem, 2012), 53–66.

141. Colin B. Burke, "The Expansion of American Higher Education," in *The Transformation of Higher Learning, 1860–1930*, ed. Konrad H. Jarausch (Chicago: University of Chicago Press, 1983), 108–130, 111.

142. Alan I. Marcus, "The Ivory Silo: Farmer–Agricultural College Tensions in the 1870s and 1880s," *Agricultural History* 60 (1986): 22–36; Theobald, *Call School*, 51, 96–97.

143. Blegen, *Norwegian Migration*, 240; see also Gjerde and Qualey, *Norwegians in Minnesota*, 38.

144. AV to JD March 13, 1930, JDP; AV-*Fam*, 47.

145. L. M. Biørn, writing to "School Board for the Norwegian Lutheran School in Decorah" (i.e., Luther College), September 9, 1865 (letter in Norwegian, translated by David Natvig), LCA. After graduating Carleton College in 1877, Andrew Veblen joined the Luther College faculty for four years. Andrew A. Veblen, "At Luther College, 1877–1881," *Palimpsest* 56 ([1918] 1975): 150–160.

146. On economic conditions in Northfield, see Lynn Carlyn, ed., *Continuum: Thread in the Community Fabric of Northfield, Minnesota* (Northfield MN: City of Northfield, 1976).

147. The standard history of Carleton College is Leal A. Headley and Merrill E. Jarchow, *Carleton: The First Century* (Northfield, MN: Carleton College, 1966). Two

useful older works are M. McG. Dana, *The History of the Origin and Growth of Carleton College* (St. Paul, MN: Pioneer Press, 1879); Delavan L. Leonard, *The History of Carleton College: Its Origin and Growth, Environment and Builders* (Chicago: Revell, 1904).

148. *CarltAC* 1874–1875, 8; *CarltAC* 1877–1878, 7.

149. Andrew explained to Dorfman: "I went to Carleton because it was recommended by good, well informed academic friends as being a good college, and because of all schools it was the most accessible, and I could live in Northfield more cheaply than anywhere else, while being at the same time in close touch with home, etc." AV to JD, November 29, 1929, JDP.

150. Roger L. Geiger, introduction to *The American College in the Nineteenth Century,* ed. Roger L. Geiger (Nashville, TN: Vanderbilt University Press), 1–36; and Geiger, "The Era of the Multipurpose Colleges in American Higher Education, 1850–1890," *American College,* 127–152; John R. Thelin, *A History of American Higher Education,* 2nd ed. (Baltimore: Johns Hopkins University Press, [2004] 2011), 74–109.

151. James W. Strong, "The Relation of the Christian College," *Journal of Proceedings and Addresses, National Education Association* 31 (1887): 152–157, 151; Dana, *Origin and Growth of Carleton College,* 29. Years earlier, before studying for the ministry, Strong had worked intermittently as a common-school teacher and briefly as the superintendent of schools in Beloit, Wisconsin.

152. Eric Hillemann, "Thorstein Veblen and Carleton College, and Vice Versa," paper presented at the 5th Conference of the International Thorstein Veblen Association, June 3–6, 2004, Carleton College, Northfield, MN, 5.

153. Strong, "Christian College," 152.

154. Geiger, "Multipurpose Colleges."

155. Of the twelve members of the 1879–1880 faculty, three did not cover academic areas: one taught music, another "voice culture," a third English (writing, presumably). *CarltAC* 1879–1880, 4–5.

156. Of the nine faculty members who were teaching academic subjects in 1879–1880, seven had A.M. degrees and one an M.D. Only President Strong, who held an honorary D.D., lacked these higher-educational credentials. Of the nine, only Strong and George Huntington, professor of logic and rhetoric, were clergymen. (Huntington also had an A.M.) For useful sketches of several of these faculty members, see Russell H. Bartley and Sylvia Erickson Bartley, "The Formal Education of Thorstein Veblen: His Carleton Years, 1874–1880," paper presented at the 4th Conference of the International Thorstein Veblen Association, May 11–12, 2002, The New School, New York, NY. I do not name or discuss them individually because they were primarily college teachers, not research-oriented scholars. A few of them had minor academic publications, but none produced a body of work from which we might glean their own views on the larger issues I examine. For that purpose, the books they assigned to their students provide a better guide.

157. Hillemann provides an excellent discussion of Veblen's time at Carleton. Hillemann, "Carleton College." See also Bartley and Bartley, "Formal Education."

158. Over the course of this period, Carleton's *Annual Catalogue* renamed these tracks several times.

159. In Chapter 4, I elaborate on what Veblen's parents may have been envisioning for his career.

160. Walter R. Agard, "Classics on the Midwest Frontier," *Classical Journal* 51 (1955): 103–110.

161. Robert D. Richardson, *William James in the Maelstrom of American Modernism* (Boston: Houghton Mifflin, 2006), 42.

162. The expression "from word to worlds" is from Caroline Winterer, *The Culture of Classicism: Ancient Greece and Rome in American Intellectual Life, 1780–1910* (Baltimore: Johns Hopkins University Press, 2002), 3; Porter is quoted in Winterer, 132. In a similar vein, Grafton speaks of "worlds made by words." Anthony Grafton, *Worlds Made by Words* (Cambridge, MA: Harvard University Press, 2009). For a longer-term perspective on the influence of the classics on America social thought, see Carl J. Richard, *The Founders and the Classics* (Cambridge, MA: Harvard University Press, 1994).

163. I based these statements on entries in Anthony Grafton, Glenn W. Most, and Salvatore Settis, eds., *The Classical Tradition* (Cambridge, MA: Harvard University Press, 2010); Susan Sorek, *Ancient Historians* (New York: Continuum, 2012).

164. Because Smith's texts went through multiple editions, I have used those dates of publication that fall closest to the years when Veblen was assigned Smith's books. On "political institutions" and "religious institutions," William Smith, *A Smaller History of Rome* (New York: Harper and Brothers, 1869), 12. (Here Smith speaks also of the "institution of slavery," 128.) For "national institutions," William Smith, *Smaller History of Greece* (London: John Murray, 1866), 11.

165. Cicero quoted in J. P. Toner, *Leisure and Ancient Rome* (Cambridge: Polity Press,1995), 28. On "parasites" in the ancient texts, see Cynthia Damon, "Greek Parasites and Roman Patronage," *Harvard Studies in Classical Philology* 97 (1995): 181–195.

166. Smith, *Smaller History of Rome,* 126–127, 314.

167. Smith, *Smaller History of Greece,* 38, 42, 215; Smith, *Smaller History of Rome,* 126.

168. W. H. D. Rouse, trans. *Great Dialogues of Plato* (New York: New American Library, 1984), 435; John M. Cooper, *Pursuit of Wisdom* (Princeton, NJ: Princeton University Press, 2012), 36–38.

169. My description of Juvenal's work may look like a sleight of hand that projects Veblen's words two thousand years backward into Juvenal's mouth, anachronistically inflating the similarity between the two thinkers. The terms I have just associated with Juvenal are not my own interpolations, however. I draw them from scholars writing about Juvenal's texts in and of themselves. Kenneth Weisinger, "Irony and Moderation in Juvenal XI," *California Studies in Classical Antiquity* 5 (1972): 227–240; Mark Morford, "Juvenal's Fifth Satire," *American Journal of Philology* 98 (1977): 219–245; Patrick Kragelund, "Nero's *Luxuria,* in Tacitus and in the *Octavia,*" *Classical Quarterly* 50 (2000): 494–515; Catherine Clare Keane, "Theatre, Spectacle, and the Satirist in Juvenal," *Phoenix* 57 (2003): 257–275. A more general discussion of the classical authors' negative view on luxury is provided in Leslie Dunton-Downer and Kris Goodfellow, *The English is Coming* (New York: Simon and Schuster, 2010); M. Gwyn Morgan, "Tacitus, Histories, 2, 7, 1," *Hermes* 125 (1995): 33–340.

170. Peter Gay, *The Enlightenment: An Interpretation,* vol. 1, *The Rise of Modern Paganism* (New York: Knopf, 1966), 85.

171. Smith, *Smaller History of Rome,* 222–223; Winterer, *Culture of Classicism,* 184–192.

172. From this point onward (and continuing into Chapter 4), my listing of the courses that Veblen took and the books he used involves some conjectures because, in some instances, Veblen's (handwritten) college transcript omits the titles of the courses he took. Further, his transcript does not indicate which faculty member taught which courses. These problems are discussed by Hillemann, who convincingly interpolates course titles and instructor names by working from Carleton's *Annual Catalogue,* which lists the courses required for each year in its program. Hillemann, "Carleton College." Since the number of course offerings were few, the number of faculty members fewer, and each faculty member's subject area relatively well defined (for example, mathematics/astronomy, English literature/modern languages, and so on), inferring which courses Veblen took and with whom follow fairly straightforwardly. The same applies with regard to the textbooks he used. These are listed in editions of the *Annual Catalogue* and map fairly directly onto course titles. Nonetheless, conjectures are conjectures, and they can be wrong. For the purposes of my account, however, this is not an especially serious problem. The *Annual Catalogue* lists a fairly small number of books and, in terms of the themes pertinent to my analysis, there is considerable duplication in content from one subject-area text to the next. What this means is even if I've "assigned" to Veblen a book he did not read, his takeaway message from the one he did read would have been much the same.

173. Truman Backus, *Shaw's New History of English Literature* (New York: Sheldon and Company, 1874); John Hart, *Manual of American Literature* (Philadelphia: Eldredge, 1875). Veblen likely also read Butler (which shared with Backus and Hart the features I'm about to mention). Frederick Butler, *A Complete History of the United States of America Embracing the Whole Period from the Discovery of North America down to the Year 1820,* 3 vols. (Hartford, CT: [no publisher information], 1821).

174. Hart, *American Literature,* 140, 544, 549.

175. Backus, *New History of English Literature* 10–11, 193–194.

176. Marcus, "Ivory Silo"; Thelin, *American Higher Education,* 81–83; A. J. Angulo, "The Initial Reception of MIT, 1860s–1880s," *Perspectives on the History of Higher Education* 26 (2007): 1–28.

177. *CarltAC* 1879–1880, 21–22.

178. *CarltAC* 1879–1880, 29–30. On the observatory, see Delavan, *The History of Carleton College,* 201–204; William W. Payne, "Carleton College Observatory," *Publications of the Astronomical Society of the Pacific* 3 (1891): 85–87. On time standardization (in relation to the growth of corporate capitalism in nineteenth-century America), see Jack Beatty, *Age of Betrayal: The Triumph of Money in America, 1865–1900* (New York: Vintage, 2007).

179. "Biology" was not yet a recognized scientific field. Students encountered its (eventual) subject matter spread across courses in botany, zoology, and geology. Edward J. Larson, "Before the Crusade: Evolution in American Secondary Education before 1920," *Journal of the History of Biology* 20 (1987): 89–114, 92.

180. Andrew Veblen described the situation to Dorfman: "Laboratory work and field work was employed at Carleton in subjects where they regularly came in. Physical and chemical laboratories were quite generally established in western institutions early in the '70's and even before. Of course field work in surveying, botany, and geology, was required everywhere." AV to JD, March 13, 1930, JDP. Andrew vouched for Thorstein's

interest in such work. "He took the prescribed course in botany in college. . . . As he was observant, this beginning gave him the means of noting plants in a methodical manner and would naturally stimulate accuracy. . . . He kept up the interest in growing things, largely, I think, because he was perforce in close touch with them, living in the country, as he did." AV to JD, January 11, 1928, JDP. Emily Veblen remembered collecting woodland specimens with Thorstein for a botany course they took together at Carleton. EVOM, 11.

181. *CarltAC* 1877–1878, 32. This description of final exams is only one of many references in the catalogue to the place of repetition in the curriculum. Contemporaries often complained about the role of recitation in college education. Ephraim Emerton, "The Practical Method of Higher Historical Instruction," *Methods of Teaching History,* vol. 1, ed. G. Stanley Hall (Boston: Ginn, Heath & Company, 1884), 31–60; J. R. Seeley, "The Teaching of History," *Methods of Teaching History,* vol. 1, ed. G. Stanley Hall (Boston: Ginn, Heath, 1884), 193–202; Herbert B. Adams, "Progress in the Study and the Teaching of History," *Chautauquan* 9 (1889): 240. These sources provide good contemporaneous descriptions of the method. For more recent treatments, see Louise Stevenson, *Scholarly Means to Evangelical Ends: The New Haven Scholars and the Transformation of Higher Learning in America, 1830–1890* (Baltimore: Johns Hopkins University Press, 1986); Thelin, *American Higher Education.* Although the details varied from institution to institution, Veysey gives a good sense of its workings in classic language instruction: "The recitation was not a discussion group in the twentieth-century sense; it was utterly alien to the spirit of Socratic byplay. Rather it was an oral quiz, nearly an hour in length, held five times per week through the academic year. Its purpose was to discover whether each student had memorized a grammatical lesson assigned him the day before." Laurence R. Veysey, *The Emergence of the American University* (Chicago: University of Chicago Press, [1965] 1970), 37.

182. C. W. Eliot and F. H. Storer, *The Compendious Manual of Qualitative Chemical Analysis,* 17th ed. (New York: van Nostrand, [1869] 1891), iii; Lyman H. Atwater, *Manual of Elementary Logic,* rev. ed. (Philadelphia: Lippincott, [1867] 1879), 34; Alphonso Wood, *The American Botanist and Florist: Including Lessons in the Structure, Life, and Growth of Plants* (New York: Barnes, 1870), 145; Simon Newcomb and Edward S. Holden, *Astronomy for Schools and Colleges* (New York: Holt, 1879), 1.

183. Newcomb and Holden, *Astronomy for Schools and Colleges,* 131.

184. Arnold Guyot, preface to *Physical Geography* (New York: n.p., 1873); Atwater, *Elementary Logic,* 189.

185. Sociologists and historians of science have extensively debated the role played by these religious beliefs in the overall development of modern science. Shapin overviews this debate, which goes back to Robert Merton's classic argument that seventeenth-century English Protestantism gave a great "spur" to modern scientific investigation. Steven Shapin, "Understanding the Merton Thesis," *Isis* (1988): 594–605; Robert K. Merton, *Science, Technology, and Society in Seventeenth-Century England* (Atlantic Highlands, NJ: Humanities Press, [1938] 1970).

186. Sidney A. Norton, *The Elements of Physics* (New York: Wilson, Hinkle & Co., 1875), 15; Wood, *American Botanist and Florist,* 124; Newcomb and Holden, *Astronomy for Schools and Colleges;* James Orton, *Comparative Zoology: Structural and Systematic,* rev. ed. (New York: Harper and Brothers, [1876] 1883), 209. On Wood, see Elizabeth B.

Keeney, *The Botanizers: Amateur Scientists in Nineteenth-Century America* (Chapel Hill: University of North Carolina Press, 1992). On Orton, see Robert Ryal Miller, "James Orton: A Yankee Naturalist in South America, 1867–1877," *Proceedings of the American Philosophical Society* 126 (1982): 11–25.

187. James D. Dana, *Manual of Geology*, 3rd ed. (New York: American Book Company, [1863] 1880), 591; Newcomb and Holden, *Astronomy for Schools and Colleges*, 131, 500–501; Joseph LeConte, *Elements of Geology* (New York: Appleton, 1877), 264–265.

188. Dana, *Manual of Geology* 1, 826; LeConte, *Elements*, 264–265, 396, 557, 553–554; Newcomb and Holden, *Astronomy for Schools and Colleges*, 131, 501. On Dana, see William F. Sanford Jr., "Dana and Darwinism," *Journal of the History of Ideas* 26 (1965): 531–546. On LeConte, see Lester D. Stephens, "Joseph LeConte's Evolutional Idealism," *Journal of the History of Ideas* 39 (1978): 465–480; Lester D. Stephens, *Joseph LeConte: Gentle Prophet of Evolution* (Baton Rouge: Louisiana State University Press, 1982).

189. Dana, *Manual of Geology*, 593, 2; Orton, *Comparative Zoology*, 201, 210. In an oft-cited and celebrated passage, Veblen later criticizes economists for treating a human being as a "homogeneous globule of desire." Thorstein Veblen, "Why Is Economics Not an Evolutionary Science?," *QJE* 12 (July 1898): 389. "Homogeneous globule" had broad currency in nineteenth-century scientific literature.

190. Guyot, *Physical Geography*, 111–116; LeConte, *Elements*, 268, 560–567.

191. Peter J. Bowler, *Darwin Deleted: Imagining a World without Darwin* (Chicago: University of Chicago Press, 2013), 94.

192. Joel F. Yoder, *Herbert Spencer and His American Audience*, unpublished dissertation, Loyola University, Chicago, 2015.

193. Edward Larson, "Before the Crusade: Evolution in American Secondary Education before 1920," *Journal of the History of Biology* 20 (1987): 89–114.

194. James R. Moore, *The Post-Darwinian Controversies: A Study of the Protestant Struggle to Come to Terms with Darwin in Great Britain and America, 1870–1900* (Cambridge: Cambridge University Press, 1979).

195. I return to this point in Chapter 4.

196. AV to JD, July 12, 1930, JDP. Andrew did not say which evolutionary theory or theories he was referring to.

197. *CarltAC* 1874–75, 23; *CarltAC* 1878–1879, 25.

198. To put this figure in perspective: Thorstein's award was equal in amount to fourteen times the cost of his tuition for six years at Carleton. It was larger than the total amount of tuition that Thomas and Kari paid in years when they had, as they sometimes did, three children enrolled at Carleton. At $8 per term for tuition, for three terms per year, the family's annual tuition total would have been $72 (= $1,835).

199. How Veblen managed to combine two years of coursework into one is not clear. Hillemann discusses the logistical possibilities. Hillemann, "Carleton College," 11–13.

200. John Bates Clark to JD, March 19 and April 18, 1930, JDP.

201. AV to JD, February 17, 1926, JDP.

202. *CarltAC* 1874–1875, 28. Usually spelled "Philomathean," similar societies existed at other American colleges.

203. Another example of this side of Veblen was his seventy-eight-line poem of parody: "The Following Lines are Respectfully Dedicated to the Class of '82 by One who Sympathizes with Them in Their Recent Bereavement" (printed in JD*TVR,* 587–591). At other times, however, Veblen opted for the heavy. Following his death in 1929, the *Carleton Circle* ran an obituary in which the author quotes from Benjamin Buck, one of Veblen's classmates: "I can recall Veblen's philosophical papers and discussions on our literary programs. On one program he used forty minutes in reading one of his abstruse papers which was not understood by the members of the society. If I remember correctly it was on John Stuart Mill's philosophy." Hillemann, "Carleton College," appendix E-4.

204. Rudolf von Tobel to JD, February 28, 1930, JDP.

205. *TLC* 373. On the Veblens in relation to the robbery, see Hillemann, "Carleton College," 10.

206. Nell Irvin Painter, *Standing at Armageddon: A Grassroots History of the Progressive Era* (New York: Norton, [1987] 2008), 27. The statement from the *Rice Country Journal* appears in Hillemann, "Carleton College," appendix D-2.

207. On Ellen Rolfe's family background, see Russell H. Bartley and Sylvia Bartley, "In the Company of T. B. Veblen: A Narrative of Biographical Recovery," *International Journal of Politics, Culture and Society* 13 (1999): 273–331, 286–291. I return to this subject in Chapter 6.

208. von Tobel to JD, February 28, 1930, JDP.

209. Ellen Veblen to Sarah Hardy Gregory [undated, but probably 1897, following JJ*TV,* 201], TV-UoC; reproduced in JJ*TV,* 202.

210. Hillemann describes the construction of the house. Hillemann, "Carleton College," 4–5. For Emily's account, see EVOM, 14.

211. On Andrew's graduation address, see Hillemann "Carleton College," appendix D-1. Andrew's *Northfield Standard* article is located in Vol. 44, AVP.

212. *TLC,* 394–397.

213. With no irony, Veblen made use of classical expressions and allusions when he leveled his attack on the classics in *TLC,* 395—a point Lester Ward observed in an early review of the book. Lester F. Ward, review of *The Theory of the Leisure Class* by Thorstein Veblen, *AJS* 6 (1900), 829–837, 836. Veblen's later writings also contained many Latinate terms and phrases, whose meanings would not have been obvious to readers unschooled in Latin. (When Geoffrey Hodgson and I annotated *Essential Writings of Thorstein Veblen,* we needed the help of a professional classicist to guide us through, and to translate, Veblen's frequent Latin phrases. Charles Camic and Geoffrey M. Hodgson, eds., *Essential Writings of Thorstein Veblen* [London: Routledge, 2011].) More generally, as Conroy has pointed out, "the word stock of . . . Veblen's vocabulary is overwhelmingly Latinate; a review of the origins of words in a sample list of favorites reveals that about 85 per cent of them are of Latin origin." Stephen S. Conroy, "Thorstein Veblen's Prose," *American Quarterly* 20 (1968): 605–615, 609. In addition, Veblen could not have followed the philosophical literature of his time (as he had to do to pursue a doctorate in philosophy) had he not been fluent in Latin and Greek.

214. *HL,* 92.

215. Again, though, Carleton was actually better off than many colleges in this category. In full, the second sentence of this passage in *HL* reads: "This holds true, in a

general way, in spite of the fact that the smaller schools are handicapped by an inadequate equipment, are working against the side-draft of a religion bias, with a corps of under-paid and over-worked teachers in great part selected on denominational grounds, and are under-rated by all concerned." As Veblen knew, Carleton itself did not suffer from inadequate equipment and a weak teaching corps. It had the resources to pedagogically outperform its peer institutions. Still, in his view, resources were less decisive than the kind of teacher–student relationships he would have experienced at Carleton. Reflecting further on the ongoing transformation of higher education, Veblen hoped college "would return to that ancient footing of . . . personal communion between teacher and student that once made the American college, with all its handicap of poverty, chauvinism and denominational bias, one of the most effective agencies of scholarship in Christendom." *HL,* 207–208. See also Agard, "Classics on the Midwest Frontier."

216. TV to Hiram Scriver, October 10, 1917, Hiram Scriver Correspondence, 1907–1917, President's Office, Donald J. Cowling, Series POF3, CCA. In an earlier sign of affection for Carleton, Veblen (uncharacteristically) attended and spoke at an 1893 gathering in Chicago of Carleton alumni. See the *Carletonia,* January 23, 1894, in Hillemann, "Carleton College," appendix E-2. Even earlier, it seems that Veblen wrote the Latin refrain for the Carleton class song. (Dorfman stated this in a letter to Andrew Veblen, and Andrew, who did not hesitate to correct Dorfman's errors, did not contradict the statement. JD to AV, June 17, 1926, JDP.)

4. Entering and Leaving

1. Louise L. Stevenson, *The Victorian Homefront: American Thought and Culture, 1860–1880* (New York: Twayne, 1991), 101–102.

2. The fact that none of the Veblen brothers went into law, medicine, government, or the ministry probably reflected their parents' attitude—and the attitude of the Norwegian American immigrants in general—toward the traditional professions. Then, too, as I mentioned in Chapter 3, Thomas and Haldor Veblen had had, when they were in Cato, Wisconsin, particularly bad experiences with lawyers and government officials. As to the ministry, brother John Edward (who, admittedly, was not the most reliable source) later recalled: "Neither mother nor any one else expressed or showed in any way any desire to have a minister in the family." John Edward Veblen to JD, August 4, 1930, JDP.

3. When Thorstein Veblen's second oldest brother, Orson, left Carleton (after two years), he also taught school for five years in the local village of Nerstrand. Albert Nelson Marquis, ed., *The Book of Minnesotans: A Biographical Dictionary of Leading Living Men in the State of Minnesota* (Chicago: Marquis, 1907), 527.

4. Roger Geiger, introduction to *The American College in the Nineteenth Century* (Nashville, TN: Vanderbilt University Press, 2000), 1–36.

5. James H. Fairchild, *Moral Philosophy; or, The Science of Obligation* (New York: Sheldon & Company, 1869); Mark Hopkins, *Evidences of Christianity* (Boston: Marvin, [1863] 1893); D. H. Meyer, *The Instructed Conscience: The Shaping of the American National Ethic* (Philadelphia: University of Pennsylvania Press, 1972), 71–86, 149–151.

6. Fairchild, *Moral Philosophy,* 30, 47, 206, 291–293. Fairchild here uses "industry" in the sense of "work," not industrial production. The instincts he mentions

bear comparison with the "parental instinct" and the "instinct of workmanship," which Veblen will later discuss. (This, of course, is not to say that Fairchild "influenced" Veblen.)

7. Fairchild, *Moral Philosophy*, 296–299, 238, 286, 248, 246, 249, 243, 293.

8. Fairchild, *Moral Philosophy*, 324,160–161; Mark Hopkins, *Evidences of Christianity* (Boston: Marvin, [1863] 1893), 243. Likely Veblen read the work of John Bascom as well, which also laid stress on the "social." John Bascom, *Aesthetics or, The Science of Beauty* (Boston, MA: Crosby and Ainsworth, 1872).

9. George Bancroft, *History of the United States of America, from the Discovery of the American Continent,* vol. 1 (Boston: Little Brown, [1834] 1882), 445, 84, 555, 59, 335, 397, 314, 604. For a discussion of Bancroft and other "gentleman historians," see Garry Wills, *Henry Adams and the Making of America* (Boston: Houghton Mifflin, 2005). In quoting the word "institutions" here, I leave open what Bancroft meant by the term. The same holds elsewhere in the chapter when I quote nineteenth-century authors using the word. In the following chapters, I will discuss how Veblen used the concept.

10. Calvin Townsend, *Analysis of Civil Government,* rev. ed. (New York: American Book Company, 1868–1869), 227.

11. François Guizot, *General History of Civilization in Europe, from the Fall of the Roman Empire to the French Revolution,* 9th American ed. (New York: Appleton, [1828] 1863); L. L. Bernard, and J. S. Bernard, "A Century of Progress in the Social Sciences," *Social Forces* 11 (1928): 488–505, 490–491.

12. Guizot, *Civilization in Europe,* 15–18, 34–35, 65–68, 138, 158, 164, 187–188, 301 (a few of these quotes are slight paraphrases). The Carleton curriculum in Veblen's junior/senior year included two German works in the same vein as Guizot: Frederick Schlegel, *Lectures on the History of Literature, Ancient and Modern,* trans. from German (London: Bohn, 1859); George Weber, *Outlines of Universal History from the Creation of the World to the Present Time,* trans. from German (Boston, MA: Swan, Brever, and Tileson, 1860).

13. On these aspects of the history of American philosophy, I draw on Bruce Kuklick, *A History of Philosophy in America, 1720–2000* (Oxford: Clarendon, 2001).

14. To say that "philosophy" commanded this authority is not to say that "theology" lacked it. Throughout the Christian era, theology and philosophy were tightly integrated, rather than separate, undertakings. This fusion continued in the United States deep into the nineteenth century, though with modifications. Writing about academic philosophy in the United States in the midcentury, Kuklick has observed: "Philosophy and theology moved along similar but distinct courses, the former vaguely but stubbornly thought to undergird the latter." Kuklick, *History of Philosophy,* 65.

15. I base the following account mainly on Elizabeth Flower and Murray G. Murphey, *A History of American Philosophy,* vol. 1 (New York: G. P. Putnam's Sons, 1977); Bruce Kuklick, *The Rise of American Philosophy: Cambridge, Massachusetts, 1860–1930* (New Haven, CT: Yale University Press, 1977); Bruck Kuklick, *Churchmen and Philosophers: From Jonathan Edwards to John Dewey* (New Haven, CT: Yale University Press, 1985); Kuklick, *Philosophy in America;* Herbert W. Schneider, *A History of American Philosophy,* 2nd ed. (New York: Columbia University Press, 1963). Because these studies are *histories* of American philosophy, they usefully depict the schools I am about to characterize as they were understood in the United States in the mid-nineteenth century.

Obviously, my goal here is not to describe the complex ideas associated with these schools, but only to fill in some information relating to Veblen's education.

16. Lyman H. Atwater, *Manual of Elementary Logic,* rev. ed. (Philadelphia: Lippincott, [1867] 1879), 197.

17. The statement is that of James McCosh, quoted in Anonymous, "Sir Wm. Hamilton's Philosophy," *Literary World* 6 (November 1870), 87. I base the following short sketch of the Hamilton-Mill debate on the sources listed in note 15, which describe the debate at it appeared in the United States in Veblen's time.

18. William Hamilton, *Lectures on Metaphysics and Logic,* vol. 1 (Boston: Gould and Lincoln, 1860), 93; William Hamilton, *Philosophy of Sir William Hamilton, Bart.* (New York: Appleton, 1857), 457. See also Edward H. Madden, "Sir William Hamilton, Critical Philosophy, and the Commonsense Tradition," *Review of Metaphysics* 38 (1985): 839–866.

19. John Stuart Mill, *Examination of Sir William Hamilton's Philosophy,* 2 vols. (Boston: Spencer, 1865). See John Skorupski, "Nineteenth-Century British Philosophy," in *The Columbia History of Western Philosophy,* ed. Richard H. Popkin (New York: Columbia University Press, 1999), 575–586, 578–581; Nicholas Capaldi, *John Stuart Mill: A Biography* (Cambridge: Cambridge University Press, 2004).

20. And it is all the more telling if Veblen's Carleton transcript is right. According to Veblen's transcript (made available to me in its handwritten version by Eric Hillemann), his grade in Mental Philosophy was 7.7 out of 10—one of the lowest grades he received at Carleton. If correct, the grade would indicate that Veblen chose the philosophical topic of his graduation address *despite* his poor performance in the subject area. The same puzzle would pertain to Veblen's decision to attend graduate school in philosophy. As we know from our experiences today at least, students do not usually go to graduate school to study a subject in which they received one of their lowest college grades.

These anomalies raise the question whether there was some kind of error in the recording of Veblen's grade, either by whoever entered the grade onto Veblen's official transcript or by the faculty member—presumably J. B. Clark—who transmitted the grade to the recorder of grades. The possibility that Veblen received a higher grade would square with the fact that Clark, who graded Veblen's final exam, remembered years later that Veblen "passed an exceptionally good examination." Clark to JD, March 19 and April 18, 1930, JDP. Moreover, Clark encouraged Veblen to go to graduate school, and (in the 1884 recommendation quoted earlier) he particularly praised Veblen's talents in philosophy. So either the transcript is incorrect or Veblen had good reason to believe his low grade did *not* reflect his philosophical abilities.

21. The later address was by Thomas Hughes, who bested Veblen for the honor of class valedictorian. See Program of Carleton College Commencement, June 24, 1880, Vol. 46, AVP.

22. Quoted by Eric Hillemann, "Thorstein Veblen and Carleton College, and Vice Versa," paper presented at the 5th Conference of the International Thorstein Veblen Association, June 3–6, 2004, Carleton College, Northfield, MN, Appendix D-3.

23. Again I rely on the sources listed in note 15. As I will point out in Part 2 of this chapter, Veblen's study of political economy under Clark gave him additional reasons to keep his distance from Mill.

24. On the other hand, without mentioning Hamilton (or Kant) by name, Veblen later wrote dismissively of philosophical arguments that posit the "unknowable." *TLC*, 365–366. That, however, was twenty years after his commencement speech.

25. G. Stanley Hall, "Philosophy in the United States," *Mind* 4 (1879): 89–105, 105. Hall made his comment specifically in reference to American philosophers.

26. Mill, *Hamilton's Philosophy*, 3, 513. See Don Habibi, *John Stuart Mill and the Ethic of Human Growth* (The Netherlands: Springer, 2001), 244.

27. I briefly return to the subject of Veblen's personality in Chapter 9.

28. Referring to Veblen's junior/senior year, Clark wrote to Dorfman: "I had, at that time, the classes regularly taught by President Strong—those called 'Mental and Moral Philosophy.'" Clark to JD, March 19, 1930, JDP.

29. AV to JD, January 11, 1928, JDP. Thirty years after studying with Clark at Carleton and a decade after publishing his first critiques of Clark's theories, Thorstein Veblen continued to admire Clark, writing that he has "in a singular degree the gift of engaging the affections as well as the attention of students in his field." Thorstein Veblen, "Professor Clark's Economics," *QJE* 22 (1908): 147–195, 148.

30. The American Economic Association annually recognizes Clark's achievements by awarding the prestigious John Bates Clark Medal.

31. A summarizing question-and-answer session with Clark is in Seligman et al., "Report of the John Bates Clark Festschrift Committee," *American Economic Review* 18 (1928), 296.

32. Because the course list in Carleton's *Annual Catalogue* does not associate the names of instructors with the names of courses (discussed in Chapter 3), and because Clark was teaching at least some of President Strong's courses during Veblen's junior/senior year, it is difficult to give an exact count of the number of courses Veblen had with him. In a letter to Dorfman, Carleton Registrar Peter Olesen states clearly that Veblen "had a course in Political Economy during his senior year, the instructor being Professor J. B. Clark." Oleson to JD, February 28, 1930, JDP. Adding this one course to the three courses mentioned earlier brings the total to four. In addition, because Clark was the only social scientist on the Carleton faculty, he almost certainly taught two more required courses that Veblen apparently took: Analysis of Civil Government and History of Civilization. If this reasoning is correct, the total would be six courses (or five if Clark did *not* teach Evidences of Christianity).

Except for Analysis of Civil Government, all these courses would have been in Veblen's crowded junior/senior, and it is unclear how many he physically "attended." It is possible that he studied the material for some of them more or less on his own, with occasional recitation meetings with Clark. In light of Veblen's strong performance on his final exams in these areas, however, it is evident he mastered these materials one way or another.

I am grateful to Eric Hillemann for helping me sort through these details. Hillemann (personal correspondence) suggests that Clark may also have been Veblen's instructor when he took Rhetoricals. Hillemann observes, too, that Clark and Veblen probably interacted as a result of Clark's position as the college librarian. Finally, Hillemann notes that Veblen's membership in the Philomathean Society (see Chapter 3), at whose meetings Clark occasionally spoke, would have afforded further contact between the two.

NOTES TO PAGES 115-117

This much contact between a student and one specific faculty member would, of course, be highly unlikely in most colleges in more recent times. Given the small size of Carleton's faculty in the late 1870s, however, the situation is much more plausible.

33. Quoting Clark's standard letter (dated April 11, 1884) recommending Veblen for an academic job, Vol. 46, AVP. On Clark's and Veblen's later intellectual relationship, see the following chapters. Writing to Dorfman about his brother, Andrew Veblen commented: "I think he kept in touch with Clark for many years after Carleton." AV to JD, February 17, 1926, JDP. The loyalty and kindness Clark showed to Veblen were traits he showed also to other students and colleagues. See James T. Shortwell, "John Bates Clark, 1848–1938: A Tribute," *Political Science Quarterly* 53 (1938): 239–248, 248; and remarks of Frank A. Fetter, in Edwin R. A. Seligman, ed., "Dinner in Honor of Professor John Bates Clark," *American Economic Review* (Supplement) 17: (1927): 1–18, 11–13.

34. I base this biographical sketch on Paul T. Homan, *Contemporary Economic Thought* (London: Harper and Brothers, 1928); Shortwell, "John Bates Clark"; Joseph Dorfman, *The Economic Mind in American Civilization*, vol. 3, *1865–1918* (New York: Viking Press, 1949); John F. Henry, *John Bates Clark: The Making of a Neoclassical Economist* (London: Macmillan, 1995).

35. In the year in between, Clark applied for a graduate fellowship at Johns Hopkins University, but he did not receive one. Hugh Hawkins, *Pioneer: A History of the Johns Hopkins University, 1874–1889* (Ithaca, NY: Cornell University Press, 1960), 82–83.

36. On the teaching of political economy, see A. W. Bob Coats, "The Educational Revolution and the Professionalization of American Economics," in *Breaking the Academic Mould: Economists and American Higher Learning in the Nineteenth Century*, ed. William J. Barber (Middletown, CT: Wesleyan University Press, 1988), 340–375; John B. Parrish, "The Rise of Economics as an Academic Discipline: The Formative Years to 1900," *Southern Economic Journal* 34 (1967): 1–16. I say that Yale's professorship in the subject is somewhat ambiguous because the holder of the position (William Graham Sumner) actually had the title professor of political and social science, although teaching political economy was his main assignment.

37. Henry Fawcett, *Manual of Political Economy*, 5th ed., rev. and enl. ed. (London: Macmillan, [1863] 1876), 47; *CarltAC* 1879–1880, 23.

38. The words "works of English Economists" are from Clark's "Lectures on Political Economy." Which edition of John Stuart Mill's book Clark used at this time is unknown. Mill's *Principles of Political Economy, with Some of their Applications to Social Philosophy* was first published in 1848; but it subsequently appeared in many other editions, partly because Mill kept revising and updating the book, partly because publishers issued it in various abridgements. After 1884, when J. Laurence Laughlin (Veblen's future mentor) brought out what he called a "text-book" edition, this version became the standard in American colleges and universities. Because this version did not exist when Veblen was at Carleton, it is likely that Clark relied on the 1864 Appleton edition of Mill's book. (Unless otherwise indicated, it is volume 1 of this 1864 edition that I will refer to, citing it as Mill, *Principles of Political Economy*.)

39. On this tradition and other traditions of economic thought, see "Glossary on Economic Schools" at the end of this chapter. From early on in his own career, Clark

periodically shed the "political." In an 1878 publication, he spoke of "economic science." In his "Lectures on Political Economy" (see note 40), he spoke of "economists."

40. The John Bates Clark Papers in the Rare Book and Manuscript Library at Columbia University contains three sets of Clark's lecture notes from this period. Unfortunately, these have not been carefully dated or titled, so I have had to make some inferences.

First, in Series II, Box 4, JBCP, there is Folder 6, titled "History Lectures, given at Carleton College, circa 1877–1881." In this case, the label seems accurate, and I will refer to these as "History Lectures."

Second, in Series II, Box 6, JBCP, there is Folder 6, with the name "Lectures on History and Economy, Possibly from Smith College, circa 1881–1895." The content of these lectures suggests that they date (at least in part) from Clark's time at Carleton.

Third, in Series II, Box 5, JBCP, there is Folder 5, labeled "Political Economy and Social Science, circa 1877–1880s." Written on the folder, in a nineteenth-century script that differs from Clark's own, is "Early Lecture Notes given by J. B. Clark around the time the 'Philosophy of Wealth' was being got together." The last comment would date these notes from 1877 to 1886 (Clark's first book, *The Philosophy of Wealth,* was published in 1886). Based on their content, however, these too would seem to come from the first part of this period. I refer to these as "Lectures on Political Economy." It is on the outlines for these lectures that we find the scrawl of Veblen's name. This would place them in 1880—though Clark might have used them before and after this date also.

41. I quote (with slight paraphrasing) from Wilhelm Hennis, "A Science of Man: Max Weber and the Political Economy of the German Historical School," in *Max Weber and His Contemporaries,* ed. Wolfgang J. Mommsen and Jurgen Osterhammel (London: Allen & Unwin, 1987), 42–49, who provides a modified translation of Knies's writings.

42. John Bates Clark, "Unrecognized Forces in Political Economy," *New Englander* 36 (1877): 710–724, 710–717; John Bates Clark, "The Philosophy of Value," *New Englander* 40 (1881): 457–469, 457; "History Lectures"; "Lectures on Political Economy." Historian of economics Mary Morgan has said of Clark in this phase of his career that he "looks remarkably like an early American institutionalist." Mary S. Morgan, "Marketplace Morals and the American Economists: The Case of John Bates Clark," in *Higgling: Transactors and Their Markets in the History of Economics,* ed. Neil De Marchi and Mary Morgan (Durham, NC: Duke University Press, 1994), 229–252, 248. Years earlier Paul Homan drew attention to the similarities between the aspects of Clark's work that I have just described and the work of Veblen. See Homan, *Economic Thought,* 45. Also useful on this subject is Donald R. Stabile, "The Intellectual Antecedents of Thorstein Veblen: A Case for John Bates Clark," *Journal of Economic Issues* 31 (1997): 817–825, 825.

43. According to Schumpeter, this theoretical project was also an aspect of Knies's writings. Joseph A. Schumpeter, *History of Economic Analysis* (New York: Oxford University Press, 1954). Considered from some angles, these two strands in Clark's early work—the historical and the theoretical—may appear at odds with one another, though evidently this is not how Clark saw them at this time or subsequently. In Chapter 8, I briefly return to a variant of this issue: the inconsistency between Clark's early and later work, which has been called the "John Bates Clark problem."

44. Clark, "Philosophy of Value," 169; Mill, *Principles of Political Economy,* 76–80, 257 (emphasis added). Smith and Mill were not alone, as Birken has pointed out: "The distinction between productive and unproductive consumption, intimately connected to the distinction between productive and unproductive labor, seems to be one of the universal features of 'classical economics' in the broadest sense." Lawrence Birken, "From Macroeconomics to Microeconomics: The Marginalist Revolution in Sociocultural Perspective," *History of Political Economy* 20 (1988): 251–264, 252–253n7. Also useful on this point is Rhead S. Bowman, "Smith, Mill, and Marshall on Human Capital Formation," *History of Political Economy* 22 (1990): 239–259; David Leadbeater, "The Consistency of Marx's Categories of Productive and Unproductive Labour," *History of Political Economy* 17 (1985): 591–618. In the 1870s, philosopher John Bascom voiced mild objections to the distinction between productive and unproductive labor, John Bascom, *Political Economy: Designed as a Text-book for Colleges* (Andover, MA: Draper, 1874), 62–64. In 1877, Bascom became the president of the University of Wisconsin, and Veblen met him during his year in Madison. AV to JD, March 28, 1930, JDP.

45. "Lectures on Political Economy"; John Bates Clark, "The New Philosophy of Wealth," *New Englander* 36: (1877): 170–186, 175–183.

46. Clark combined this critique with comments about his society that were more positive in tone.

47. "Lectures on Political Economy."

48. John Bates Clark, "How to Deal with Communism," *New Englander* 37 (1878); 533–542, 540.

49. Clark, "How to Deal with Communism," 533, 534, 540.

50. Clark, "How to Deal with Communism," 541.

51. Clark, "New Philosophy of Wealth"; John Bates Clark, "Business Ethics, Past and Present," *New Englander* 39 (1879): 157–168; John Bates Clark, "Non-competitive Economics," *New Englander* 41 (1882): 837–846.

52. "Lectures on Political Economy"; John Bates Clark, "The Scholar's Duty to the State," *Carletonian,* June 1878.

53. Contemporaries would not, of course, have phrased his ambition in exactly this way.

54. One year older than Veblen, Woodrow Wilson, who began his own career practicing law but soon shifted gears, described a situation that was otherwise much like Veblen's. In an 1885 letter to his future wife, Wilson explained that the intellectual pursuits "for which I was best fitted . . . were not legitimate in a law office, and I was compelled . . . to seek some profession in which they would be legitimate. Evidently, however, there was small latitude of choice. A professorship was the only feasible place for me, the only place that would afford leisure for reading and for original work, the only strictly literary berth with an income attached. True, professorships were scarce and hard to get." Quoted in Ray Stannard Baker, *Woodrow Wilson: Life and Letters,* vol. 1, *Youth: 1856–1890* (New York: Doubleday, 1927), 170.

55. AV to JD, February 17, 1926, JDP.

56. Laurence R. Veysey, *The Emergence of the American University* (Chicago: University of Chicago Press, [1965] 1970), 6. Veysey quotes William Graham Sumner (with whom Veblen would later study at Yale) writing in 1870: "There is no such thing yet at

Yale as an academical *career.* There is no course marked out for a man who feels called to this work, and desires to pursue it." Veysey, *American University,* 6.

57. A. M., 1880. Andrew's master's degree was from Carleton itself, and he received it at the same time Thorstein received his A.B. The requirements for the degree were slight, as the school regulations explained: within three years of completing the college program, Carleton graduates "who have been engaged in literary or professional pursuits, and have sustained a good moral character, may, on application, receive the degree of Master of Arts, Master of Literature, or Master of Science." *Annual Catalogue* 1879–1880, 33. Teaching at Luther College for three years qualified Andrew for the degree, which he took in Science, to suit his developing interest in physics.

58. The cost of studying abroad may have factored into Veblen's thinking about going to Europe. Speaking about conditions in the United States in the 1870s and 1880s, G. Stanley Hall, Veblen's contemporary, recalled that there were many academically inclined college graduates "who wished to go on and could not afford to do so abroad." G. Stanley Hall, *Life and Confessions of a Psychologist* (New York: Appleton, 1923), 230. On the other hand, historian Daniel Rodgers has stated: "So cheap were [German university] fees that in 1889 it was estimated that the cost of a year in Germany, transatlantic travel included, was fully a third less than a year's study at Cornell, Harvard, or Johns Hopkins." Daniel T. Rodgers, *Atlantic Crossings: Social Politics in a Progressive Age* (Cambridge, MA: Harvard University Press, 1998), 85. Whether this bargain price applied a decade earlier, and was known to Upper Midwest families like the Veblens, is unclear. On the development of doctoral program and degrees in the US, see Robert E. Kohler, "The Ph.D. Machine; Building on the Collegiate Base," *Isis* 81 (1990) 638–662.

59. Clark had close ties to Yale. Most of his early articles appeared in the *New Englander,* a Yale-based journal. For discussion of the journal, see Louise L. Stevenson, *Scholarly Means to Evangelical Ends: The New Haven Scholars and the Transformation of Higher Learning in America, 1830–1890* (Baltimore: Johns Hopkins University Press, 1986).

60. Hall, "Philosophy in the United States." I take these data from Thomas Lloyd Malone, "A History of the Doctor of Philosophy Dissertation in the United States 1861–1930" (PhD diss., Wayne State University, 1981), 63; Parrish, "Rise of Economics," 6–11. When I speak of doctorates in "philosophy," I am speaking of degrees awarded for work specifically in the field of philosophy. Since PhD literally means doctor of philosophy, every recipient of the degree technically received a degree in philosophy, though not, of course, in philosophy as a specialized field. See also Ralph P. Rosenberg, "The First American Doctor of Philosophy Degree: A Centennial Salute to Yale, 1861–1961," *Journal of Higher Education* 32 (1961): 387–394.

61. Hall, "Philosophy in the United States," 91. On the job situation in philosophy, I draw more generally on Daniel J. Wilson, *Science, Community, and the Transformation of American Philosophy, 1860–1930* (Chicago: University of Chicago Press, 1990).

62. AV to JD, April 21, 1931, JDP. On Veblen's year in Madison, see J. R. Christianson, "Thorstein Veblen: Ethnic Roots and Social Criticism of a 'Folk Savant,'" *Norwegian-American Studies* 34 (1995): 3–22. Always interested in Veblen's comings and goings, the *Rice County Journal* included the following in its "College News" section for September 10, 1880: "T. B. Veblen is teaching in a Scandinavian academy in

Madison, Wisconsin. May he meet with the highest success." Hillemann, "Carleton College," appendix D-3.

63. Christianson, "Thorstein Veblen," 11. On Norwegian-American academies, see B. H. Narveson, "The Norwegian Lutheran Academies," *Norwegian-American Studies* 14 (1944): 184–226.

64. This particular definition of the doctrine of predestination follows the Norwegian word for the doctrine: *Naadevalget*. Odd S. Lovoll, *Norwegian Newspapers in America: Connecting Norway and the New Land* (St. Paul: Minnesota Historical Society Press, 2010), 131.

65. On these doctrines and the controversy they provoked, see Lovoll, *Norwegian Newspapers*, 131–135; John Gjerde, *The Minds of the West: Ethnocultural Evolution in the Rural Middle West, 1830–1917* (Chapel Hill: University of North Carolina Press, 1997), 118–123.

66. Lloyd Hustvedt, *Rasmus Bjørn Anderson: Pioneer Scholar* (Northfield, MN: Norwegian-American Historical Association, 1966), 42, 89.

67. Ramus B. Anderson, *Life Story of Rasmus B. Anderson* (Madison, WI: n.p., 1915), 210; Ramus B. Anderson, *America Not Discovered by Columbus: A Historical Sketch of the Discovery of America by the Norsemen in the Tenth Century,* 5th ed. (Chicago: Scott, Foresman and Company, [1874] 1901), 3, 43–45.

68. As part of his efforts to promote this project, Anderson organized public lectures by visiting Norwegians, including Bjørnstjerne Bjørnson, whose writings Veblen had known about from his youth. A firebrand in the mold of Anderson, Bjørnson used his controversial American lecture tour to attack the religious, political, and economic status quo and preach evolutionary doctrines. In January 1881, Bjørnson visited and lectured in Madison, where Veblen would have met him. Eva Lund Haugen and Einar Haugen, general introduction to *Land of the Free: Bjørnstjerne Bjørnson's American Letters, 1880–1881,* ed. Eva Lund Haugen and Einar Haugen (Northfield, MN: Norwegian-American Historical Association, 1978), 1–23.

69. Roger E. Backhouse and Steven G. Medema, "Retrospectives: On the Definition of Economics," *Journal of Economic Perspectives* 23 (2009): 221–234; Peter Groenewegen, "'Political Economy' and 'Economics,'" in *The World of Economics: The New Palgrave,* ed. J. Eatwell, M. Milgate, and P. Newman (London: Macmillan, 1991), 556–562.

70. Richard T. Ely, "The Past and the Present of Political Economy," *Johns Hopkins University Studies in Historical and Political Science,* ser. 2, 3 (1884): 143–202; J. Laurence Laughlin, "Sketch of the History of Political Economy," *Principles of Political Economy,* ed. John Stuart Mill, abr. and supp. J. Laurence Laughlin (New York: Appleton, [1884] 1888), 1–42; William Graham Sumner, *Problems in Political Economy* (New York: Holy, 1885).

71. Laughlin, "Sketch of the History of Political Economy," 13–14.

72. John Elliot Cairnes, *Some Leading Principles of Political Economy Newly Expounded* (New York: Harper & Brothers, 1874); John Elliot Cairnes, *Character and Logical Method of Political Economy,* 2nd ed. (New York: Macmillan, 1875).

73. Mill, *Principles of Political Economy,* 17, 55. Referring to Mill's contemporaries, Capaldi writes: "It was generally agreed that Mill wanted to emphasize the element of production in the definition of political economy and to eliminate both con-

sumption and distribution." Nicholas Capaldi, *John Stuart Mill: A Biography* (Cambridge: Cambridge University Press, 2004), 206.

74. Mill, *System of Logic*, 568, 586–593.

75. On historical economics in England, see Gerard M. Koot, *English Historical Economics, 1870–1926: The Rise of Economic History and Neomercantilism* (Cambridge: Cambridge University Press, 1987); Keith Tribe, "Historical Schools of Economics: German and English," in *A Companion to the History of Economic Thought*, ed. Warren J. Samuels, Jeff E. Biddle, and John B. Davis (Malden, MA: Blackwell Publishing, 2003), 215–230.

76. Frederick C. Beiser, *The German Historicist Tradition* (Oxford: Oxford University Press, 2011), 2. On German historicism as a movement, I draw on Frederick C. Beiser, *German Idealism: The Struggle against Subjectivism, 1781–1801* (Cambridge, MA: Harvard University Press, 2002); Beiser, *German Historicist Tradition*; Georg G. Iggers, *The German Conception of History: The National Tradition of Historical Thought from Herder to the Present*, rev. ed. (Middletown, CT: Wesleyan University Press, [1968] 1983); Thomas E. Willey, *Back to Kant* (Detroit, Michigan: Wayne State University Press, 1978).

77. On the German historical school of economics, I build on Herbst, *German Historical School in American Scholarship*; Erik Grimmer-Solem, *The Rise of Historical Economics and Social Reform in Germany, 1864–1894* (Oxford: Clarendon, 2003); Peter Koslowski, ed., *The Theory of Ethical Economy in the Historical School* (Berlin: Springer-Verlag, 1995); David F. Lindenfeld, *The Practical Imagination: The German Sciences of State in the Nineteenth Century* (Chicago: University of Chicago Press, 1997); Heath Pearson, *Origins of Law and Economics: The Economists' New Science of Law, 1830–1890* (Cambridge: Cambridge University Press, 1997); Rodgers, *Atlantic Crossings*, 76–111; Axel R. Schafer, *American Progressives and German Social Reform, 1875–1920: Social Ethics, Moral Control, and the Regulatory State in a Transatlantic Context* (Stuttgart: Franz Steiner Verlag, 2000); Keith Tribe, *Strategies of Economic Order: German Economic Discourse, 1750–1950* (Cambridge: Cambridge University Press, 1995); Tribe, "Historical Schools of Economics."

78. The quote is from Wilhelm Roscher, in Tribe, "Historical Schools of Economics," 219.

79. The idea of the "general welfare" of the population was common among German historical economists. See Lindenfeld, *Practical Imagination*, 2.

80. W. E. B. Du Bois quoted in Rodgers, *Atlantic Crossings*, 88–89.

81. Iggers, *German Conception*, 132.

82. While references to the school of "marginal utility" trace back to the early 1890s, the term "marginalism" itself does not seem to have appeared until the work of J. A. Hobson in 1914. See Peter Groenewegen, "English Marginalism: Jevons, Marshall, and Pigou," in *A Companion to the History of Economic Thought*, ed. Warrens J. Samuels, Jeff E. Biddle, and John B. Davis (Malden, MA: Blackwell), 246–261, 246.

83. Veblen's "neo-classical" makes its first appearance in Thorsten Veblen, "The Preconceptions of Economic Science: III," *QJE* 14 (February 1900): 240–269, 261. Immediately after introducing the term, Veblen added: "The so-called Austrian school is scarcely distinguishable from the neo-classical, unless it be in the distribution of emphasis." Both Marshall and the Austrians were also indebted to the historical school, but the evolutionary institutional current in their thought did not draw Veblen's notice.

84. See Malcolm Rutherford, *The Institutionalist Movement in American Economics, 1918–1947: Science and Social Control* (Cambridge: Cambridge University Press, 2011).

85. Tony Aspromourgos, "On the Origins of the Term 'Neoclassical,'" *Cambridge Journal of Economics* 10 (1986): 265–270.

86. The last four sentences are broad strokes that do not even begin to touch the surface of these long, complicated developments. The history of economic theory during the twentieth century constitutes an enormous topic, which has been open to many interpretive disagreements, including disputes over dates and categories (for example, "modern neoclassical" and "mainstream"). Invaluable in orienting me have been the relevant chapters in Warren J. Samuels, Jeff E. Biddle, and John B. Davis, eds., *A Companion to the History of Economic Thought* (Malden, MA: Blackwell, 2003); David Colander, "The Death of Neoclassical Economics," *Journal of the History of Economic Thought* 21 (2000): 127–143. For an examination of the vicissitudes of the Austrian school in America, see Karen I. Vaughn, *Austrian Economics in America: The Migration of a Tradition* (Cambridge: Cambridge University Press, 1994).

5. Young Philosopher

1. Wilson quoted in Ray Stannard Baker, *Woodrow Wilson: Life and Letters,* vol. 1, *Youth: 1856–1890* (New York: Doubleday, 1927), 173. I take "real university" from the Baltimore native and writer Sophie B. Herrick, who spoke of Hopkins as "one of the very few real universities in America," but then chipped away at the claims to this title by any university other than Hopkins. Her article's placement in a popular highbrow magazine is a good indicator of the general level of public interest in the changes then underway in American higher education. Sophie B. Herrick, "The Johns Hopkins University," *Scribner's Monthly* 19 (1879): 199–208, 199.

Writing to Hopkins's president in 1878, philosophy Charles Sanders Peirce said: "You are the only real university in America." Quoted in Joseph Brent, *Charles Sanders Peirce: A Life,* rev. and enl. ed. (Bloomington: Indiana University Press, 1998), 121. Peirce's father, Benjamin, the Harvard astronomer, described Hopkins "as a great advance in the university system of this country, and as the only American institution where the promotion of science is the supreme object." Quoted in Hugh Hawkins, *Pioneer: A History of the Johns Hopkins University, 1874–1889* (Ithaca, NY: Cornell University Press, 1960), 77. Since the Peirces had an interest in securing a faculty position for Charles at Hopkins, their statements may be somewhat suspect, though father and son both, infamously, spoke their minds.

2. The first quotation in this sentence is from John Milton Cooper, Jr., *Woodrow Wilson: A Biography* (New York: Vintage, 2009) 41; AV to JD, April 21, [1931], JDP. Thorstein Veblen presumably got some of the information he had about Hopkins directly from Rasmus Anderson, who had lectured there; and from Clark, who had applied for a fellowship there (discussed in Chapter 4). Apparently, he also read one or more issues of the *Johns Hopkins University Circulars.*

3. Today's situation is discussed in Chapter 3. See also Thomas Piketty, *Capital in the Twenty-First Century,* trans. Arthur Goldhammer (Cambridge, MA: Harvard Uni-

versity Press, 2014), 348; Edward Pessen, "The Egalitarian Myth and the American Social Reality: Wealth, Mobility, and Equality in the 'Era of the Common Man,'" *American Historical Review* 76 (1971): 989–1034; Sherry H. Olson, *Baltimore: The Building of an American City* (Baltimore: Johns Hopkins University Press, 1980), 155, who is quoting an article from 1865.

4. This strike quickly spread throughout the Northeast and Midwest in the violent series of events that constituted the Great Railroad Strike of 1877.

5. Quoted in Nell Irvin Painter, *Standing at Armageddon: A Grassroots History of the Progressive Era* (New York: Norton, [1987] 2008), 16.

6. AV to Laur. Larson, November 20 1881, Laur. Larson Papers, LCA; EVOM, 16; J. R. Christianson, "Thorstein Veblen: Ethnic Roots and Social Criticism of a 'Folk Savant,'" *Norwegian-American Studies* 34 (1995): 3–22, 12–13.

7. The best history of Johns Hopkins University is Hawkins, *Pioneer*. I also draw on Charles C. Bishop, "Teaching at Johns Hopkins: The First Generation," *History of Education Quarterly* 27 (1987): 499–515; John C. French, *The History of the University Founded by Johns Hopkins* (Baltimore: Johns Hopkins University Press, 1946); Keith R. Benson, "American Morphology in the Late Nineteenth Century: The Biology Department at Johns Hopkins," *Journal of the History of Biology* 18 (1985): 186–205; Keith R. Benson, "H. Newell Martin, W. K. Brooks, and the Reformation of American Biology," *American Zoologist* 2 (1987): 759–771; Keith R. Benson, "From Museum Research to Laboratory Research: The Transformation of Natural History into Academic Biology," in *The American Development of Biology*, ed. Ronald Rainger, Keith R. Benson, and Jane Maienschein (New Brunswick, NJ: Rutgers University Press, 1988), 49–83; James D. Ebert, "Why a Symposium on Biology at Johns Hopkins?" *American Zoologist* 27 (1987): 751–758; Jane Maienschein, *Transforming Traditions in American Biology, 1880–1915* (Baltimore: Johns Hopkins University Press, 1991); Daniel C. Gilman, "Inaugural Address," in *Addresses at the Inauguration of Daniel C. Gilman as President of the Johns Hopkins University* (Baltimore: Murray, 1876), 17–64, 44; Philip J. Ethington and Eileen L. McDonagh, "The Common Space of Social Science Inquiry," *Polity* 28 (1995): 85–90. Extremely valuable also are biographies of Gilman, especially Fabian Franklin, *The Life of Daniel Coit Gilman* (New York: Dodd, Mead, 1910). I have also used Francesco Cordasco, *The Shaping of American Graduate Education: Daniel Coit Gilman and the Protean Ph.D.* (Totowa, NJ: Rowman and Littlefield, 1973); Brooks Mather Kelley, *Yale: A History* (New Haven, CT: Yale University Press, 1974); John K. Wright, "Daniel Coit Gilman, Geographer and Historian," *Geographical Review* 51 (1961): 318–399. Illuminating contemporaneous accounts are Nicholas Murray Butler, "President Gilman's Administration at the Johns Hopkins University," *American Monthly Review of Reviews* 23 (1901): 49–53; Charles W. Eliot, "Congratulatory Address," in *Addresses at the Inauguration of Daniel C. Gilman as President of the Johns Hopkins University* (Baltimore: Murray, 1876), 7–13; William Rainey Harper, "Remarks," 58–62, and Woodrow Wilson, "Remarks," 37–43, both in *Celebration of the Twenty-Fifth Anniversary of the Founding of The [Johns Hopkins] University* (Baltimore: Johns Hopkins Press, 1902); Herrick, "The Johns Hopkins University"; Josiah Royce, "Present Ideals of American University Life," *Scribner's Magazine* 10 (1891): 376–388.

8. Trustee George William Brown quoted in Hawkins, *Pioneer*, 6; Gilman, "Inaugural Address," 55–57.

9. Peirce quoted in Max H. Fisch, "Peirce at the Johns Hopkins University," in *Peirce, Semeiotic, and Pragmatism: Essays by Max H. Fisch,* ed. Kenneth Laine Ketner and Christian J. W. Kloesel (Bloomington: Indiana University Press, 1986), 35–78, 35.

10. Aside from these scientific fields, there were also language departments (English; Greek, Sanskrit, and Latin; German; Romance languages), plus a unit devoted to elocution. *JHCir* December 1881, 154–157.

11. AV to Laur. Larson, November 20, 1881, Laur. Larson Papers, LCA.

12. Royce, "Present Ideals," 383. For a contemporaneous description of the philosophy department, near the time when Royce studied, see Anonymous, "Philosophy at Johns Hopkins University," *Journal of Speculative Philosophy* 16 (1882): 430–433.

In a letter dated January 1877, Henry Carter Adams, one of the university's first graduate fellows (and the recipient of the first PhD in political economy from an American university), wrote: "There seems to be such a free independent spirit here that it does not seem presumptuous in the least to say so. Everyone is trying to do something that no one ever did before." Quoted in A. W. Bob Coats, "Henry Carter Adams: A Case Study in the Emergence of the Social Sciences in the United States, 1850–1900," in *British and American Economic Essays,* vol. 1, *On the History of Economic Thought* (London: Routledge,1968), 365–385, 371.

13. Hawkins, *Pioneer,* 68–69; Benson, "American Morphology." On the Hopkins science program in this period, I have also benefited from Benson, "H. Newell Martin, W. K. Brooks"; Benson, "Museum Research to Laboratory Research"; Ebert, "Why a Symposium on Biology?"; Maienschein, *Transforming Traditions.*

14. *JHCir* March 1882, 190. TV to Gilman, December 9, 1881, JDP. Andrew Veblen was one of the few other graduate students studying in two departments (physics and mathematics).

15. Herbert W. Schneider, *A History of American Philosophy,* 2nd ed. (New York: Columbia University Press, 1963), 400. Here and in the following three paragraphs, I draw on Elizabeth Flower and Murray G. Murphey, *A History of American Philosophy,* vol. 1 (New York: G. P. Putnam's Sons, 1977); Bruck Kuklick, *The Rise of American Philosophy: Cambridge, Massachusetts, 1860–1930* (New Haven, CT: Yale University Press, 1977; Bruce Kuklick, *Churchmen and Philosophers: From Jonathan Edwards to John Dewey* (New Haven, CT: Yale University Press, 1985); Bruce Kuklick, *A History of Philosophy in America, 1720–2000* (Oxford: Clarendon, 2001). The standard biographies of Morris are R. M. Wenley, *The Life and Work of George Sylvester Morris* (London: Macmillan, 1917); Marc Edmund Jones, *George Sylvester Morris: His Philosophical Career and Idealism* (Philadelphia, PA: Washington Square, 1948).

16. George S. Morris, *Kant's Critique of Pure Reason: A Critical Exposition* (Chicago: Griggs, 1882), 27; George S. Morris, *Philosophy and Christianity* (New York: Carter, 1883), 161; George S. Morris, "The Philosophy of the State and of History," in *Methods of Teaching History,* vol. 1, ed. G. Stanley Hall (Boston: Ginn, Heath & Company, 1884), 149–166, 150.

17. Morris, *Philosophy and Christianity,* 285–286.

18. Morris, "Philosophy of the State and of History," 149–152.

19. Morris to Gilman, January 31, 1885, Series 1, MS. 1, Box 1.32, Folder 33, DCGP.

20. TV to Gilman, December 9, 1881, DCGP.

21. Dewey quoted in George Dykhuizen, *The Life and Mind of John Dewey* (Carbondale: Southern Illinois University Press, 1973), 30–31; AV to JD, October 1, 1926, JDP.

22. Christine Ladd-Franklin, "Charles S. Peirce at the Johns Hopkins," *Journal of Philosophy, Psychology and Scientific Methods* 13 (1916): 715–722, 716–717. Also on Peirce's teaching, see Joseph Jastrow, "Charles S. Peirce as a Teacher," *Journal of Philosophy, Psychology and Scientific Methods* 13 (1916): 723–726.

23. For information on Peirce's career, I draw on Brent, *Charles Sanders Peirce;* Fisch, "Peirce at the Johns Hopkins University"; Louis Menand, *The Metaphysical Club: A Story of Ideas in America* (New York: Farrar, Straus and Giroux, 2001); Daniel J. Wilson, *Science, Community, and the Transformation of American Philosophy, 1860–1930* (Chicago: University of Chicago Press, 1990).

24. Dewey quoted in Dykhuizen, *Life and Mind of John Dewey,* 30–31.

25. Charles Sanders Peirce, "Introductory Lecture on the Study of Logic," *JHCir* November 1882, 11; Charles Sanders Peirce, "How to Make Our Ideas Clear," in *The Essential Peirce: Selected Philosophical Writings,* vol. 1, *1867–1893,* ed. Nathan Houser and Christian Kloesel (Bloomington: Indiana University Press, [1878] 1992), 124–141, 125. In his writings from this period, Peirce also made critical comments about economic knowledge. See James R. Wible, "The Economic Mind of Charles Sanders Peirce," *Contemporary Pragmatism* 5 (2008): 39–67. These comments were sufficiently fleeting that it is unlikely they registered with Veblen.

26. Peirce's relationship to Darwinism was complex; some elements in his thinking ran counter to Darwin's theories and led him to embrace non-Darwinian schools of evolutionary thinking as well. Wilson, *Science, Community,* 25–26. Also see Arthur W. Burks, "Peirce's Evolutionary Pragmatic Idealism," *Synthese* 106 (1996): 323–372; Menand, *Metaphysical Club,* 272–280.

27. Charles Sanders Peirce, "The Order of Nature," in *The Essential Peirce: Selected Philosophical Writings,* vol. 1, *1867–1893,* ed. Nathan Houser and Christian Kloesel (Bloomington: Indiana University Press, [1878] 1992), 181.

28. Peirce, "Some Consequences of Four Incapacities," in *The Essential Peirce* [1868] 1992, 52–54.

29. Peirce, "The Doctrine of Chances," in *The Essential Peirce* [1878] 1992, 149.

30. Peirce, "The Order of Nature," 170.

31. Peirce, "The Fixation of Belief," in *The Essential Peirce* [1877] 1992, 111.

32. Michael Ghiselin, "The Darwinian Revolution as Viewed by a Philosophical Biologist," *Journal of the History of Biology* 38 (2005): 123–136, 126–127. Hull has argued: "Peirce was one of the few [nineteenth-century philosophers] who recognized and emphasized the statistical nature of evolutionary theory." David L. Hull, *Darwin and His Critics: The Reception of Darwin's Theory of Evolution by the Scientific Community* (Cambridge, MA: Harvard University Press, 1973), 33. The following scholars have all discussed other ways in which Peirce may have "influenced" Veblen. Stanley Matthew Daugert, *The Philosophy of Thorstein Veblen* (New York: King's Crown Press, 1950); Alan W. Dyer, "Veblen on Scientific Creativity: The Influence of Charles S. Peirce," *Journal of Economic Issues* 20 (1986): 21–41; Robert Griffin, "What Veblen Owed to Peirce—The Social Theory of Logic," *Journal of Economic Issues* 33 (1998): 733–757; John Hall and Oliver Whybrow, "Continuity and Continuousness: The Chain

of Ideas Linking Peirce's Synechism to Veblen's Cumulative Causation," *Journal of Economic Issues* 42 (2008): 349–355; Martin Suto, "Some Neglected Aspects of Veblen's Social Thought," *Social Science Quarterly* (1960): 439–453.

33. Veblen's coursework at Hopkins is described in a letter to Dorfman from the Hopkins's registrar: R. M. Dempster to Dorfman, July 24, 1931, JDP. On Adams's life and career, I draw on Raymond Cunningham, "Is History Past Politics? Herbert Baxter Adams as Precursor of the 'New History,'" *History Teacher* 9 (1976): 244–257; Raymond Cunningham, "The German Historical World of Herbert Baxter Adams, 1874–1876," *Journal of American History* 68 (1981): 261–275; John Higham, "Herbert Baxter Adams and the Study of Local History," *American Historical Review* 89 (1984): 1225–1239; John Martin Vincent, "Herbert Baxter Adams," in *American Masters of Social Science: An Approach to the Study of the Social Sciences through a Neglected Field of Biography*, ed. Howard W. Odum (New York: Holt, 1927), 97–127. For Ely, I used Benjamin G. Rader, *The Academic Mind and Reform: The Influence of Richard T. Ely in American Life* (Lexington: University of Kentucky Press, 1966). On Adams and Ely in relation to their German training, a valuable source is Jurgen Herbst, *The German Historical School in American Scholarship: A Study in the Transfer of Culture* (Ithaca, NY: Cornell University Press, 1965).

34. Quoting Adams's standard letter, this one dated April 28, 1889, recommending Veblen for an academic job, Vol. 46, AVP.

35. Gilman, "Inaugural Address," 44; Ethington and McDonagh, "Social Science Inquiry," 380. On the Adams-Ely program, I also draw on William J. Barber, "Political Economy in the Academic Setting before 1900: An Introduction," in *Breaking the Academic Mould: Economists and American Higher Learning in the Nineteenth Century*, ed. William J. Barber (Middletown, CT: Wesleyan University Press, 1988), 3–14; Philip J. Ethington and Eileen L. McDonagh, eds., "Conference Panel: The Intellectual Legacy of the Johns Hopkins Seminary of History and Politics: Reconsidering the Genealogy of the Social Sciences," *Studies in American Political Development* 8 (1994) 375–408; Deborah L. Haines, "Scientific History as a Teaching Method: The Formative Years," *Journal of American History* 63 (1977): 892–912.

36. Wilson quoted in Baker, *Woodrow Wilson*, 174; on Turner, see Ray Allen Billington, *Frederick Jackson Turner: Historian, Scholar, Teacher* (New York: Oxford University Press, 1973), 73; J. Franklin Jameson Diaries for 1881–1882, entry for December 13, 1881, Container 2, JFJP; Jameson letter to Albert Shaw, November 5, 1882, in Elizabeth Donnan and Leo F. Stock, eds., *An Historian's World: Selections from the Correspondence of John Franklin Jameson* (Philadelphia: American Philosophical Society, 1956), 22. There is, however, probably some exaggeration in these statements. Recounting an 1883 conversation with Adams, Woodrow Wilson wrote that he "readily freed me from his 'institutional' work, and bade me go on with my 'constitutional' studies, promising me all the aid and encouragement he could give me." Wilson quoted in Baker, *Woodrow Wilson*, 180.

37. Veblen did *not* take the other course Adams offered in the same semester, "Institutional History," which dealt with "the origins of Local Self Government in the United States." *JHCir* December 1881, 162.

38. Adams left several sets of lecture notes for "Sources of Early European History," but they are hard to construe. Adams taught the course multiple times, and as he

went along he kept revising, penciling in changes, pasting in new material, and starting over several times, but giving no dates to the different versions. In quoting from his lectures, I am using the iteration that appears, from internal textual clues, to most closely correspond in time to the period when Veblen took the course. "Sources of Early European History–Class Lecture Notes," Series 2, Boxes 27 and 28, HBAP.

39. Herbert B. Adams, "Village Communities of Cape Anne and Salem," *JHS*, ser. 1, 9, 10 (1883): 3–81, 4. Adams elaborated this thesis in several other articles from this period. See Herbert B. Adams, "The German Origin of New England Towns," *JHS*, ser. 1, 2 (1882): 5–38; Herbert B. Adams, "Saxon Tithingmen in America," *JHS*, ser. 1, 4 (1883): 1–23; Herbert B. Adams, "Norman Constables in America," *JHS*, ser. 1, 8 (1883): 3–38. In historicizing the "disposition to truck and trade," Adams played off against Adam Smith's famous claim that human beings universally exhibit a "disposition to truck, barter, and exchange." Adam Smith, *An Inquiry into the Nature and Causes of the Wealth of Nations*, vol. 1 (Oxford: Clarendon, [1776] 1869), 14.

40. On the "Teutonic thesis," see J. W. Burrow, "The 'Village Community' and the Uses of History in Late Nineteenth-Century England," in *Historical Perspectives: Studies in English Thought and Society*, ed. Neil McKendrick (London: Europa Publications, 1974), 255–284; Peter Novick, *That Noble Dream: The "Objectivity Question" and the American Historical Profession* (Cambridge: Cambridge University Press, 1988); Gary Wills, *Henry Adams and the Making of America* (Boston: Houghton Mifflin, 2005).

41. Adams to Gilman, May 11, 1881, Series 1, MS. 1, Box 1.1, Folder 20, DCGP. Adams did not view Darwinism as incompatible with his own Christian reformism.

42. Richard T. Ely, "The Past and the Present of Political Economy," *JHS*, ser. 2, 3 (1884): 143–202, 148, 152, 171–173, 183, 188, 173, and 177. In the next to last passage, Ely is quoting Belgian economist Émile de Laveleye.

43. Ely, "Political Economy," 44. Jameson is quoted in Benjamin G. Rader, *The Academic Mind and Reform: The Influence of Richard T. Ely in American Life* (Lexington: University of Kentucky Press, 1966), 29–30.

44. Ely, "Political Economy," 156, 202; Richard T. Ely, "Recent American Socialism," *JHS*, ser. 2, 4 (1885): 5, 71.

45. Richard T. Ely, *French and German Socialism in Modern Times* (New York: Harper, 1883); Ely, "Recent American Socialism."

46. Richard T. Ely, "A Brief Sketch of the Railway History of Germany," *Papers Relating to the Foreign Relations of the United States, Transmitted to Congress* (Washington, DC: Government Printing Office, 1880), 408–422, 420.

47. Richard T. Ely, "German Cooperative Credit-Unions," *Atlantic Monthly* (February 1881), 207–223, 207, 212.

48. Ely, "Political Economy, 187; Ely, "Recent American Socialism," 21, 51, 61, 67–69, 72. Not all of Ely's work in this period was hortatory. He also published research articles on several German social programs. See Ely, "Railway History"; Ely, "Credit-Unions"; Richard T. Ely, "Bismarck's Plan for Insuring German Laborers," *International Review* (May 1882), 504–526.

49. Gilman, "Inaugural Address," 30. In this famous manifesto, he continued, switching from "less" to "more": university research "means more study of nature, more love of art, more lessons from history, more security in property, more health in cities,

more virtue in the country, more wisdom in legislation, more intelligence, more happiness, more religion." He added: "Remote utility is quite as worthy to be thought of as immediate advantage," 36.

50. Herbert Baxter Adams, "The State and Higher Education," *Annual Report of the Board of Regents of the Smithsonian Institution* (Washington, DC: Government Printing Office, 1890), 709.

51. *JHCir* December 1881, 162.

52. *JHCir* February 1882, 176.

53. John Stuart Mill, ed., *Principles of Political Economy,* abr. and supp. J. Laurence Laughlin (New York: Appleton, [1884] 1888), 411–414.

54. Henry George, *Progress and Poverty* (New York: Cosimo Classics, [1879] 2005), 183, 288–289. See also Henry Fawcett, *Manual of Political Economy,* 5th ed., rev. and enl. ed. (London: Macmillan, [1863] 1876), 569–574.

55. While Veblen's reading of Mill's *Political Economy* at Hopkins familiarized him with this technical terminology, it is unlikely he accepted the point because of Mill per se; Mill's formulation resonated what Veblen had already been learning about the role of predation in human history. The last quotation is from Thorstein Veblen, *HL,* 52 (emphasis added), a text he wrote in 1904. Among Veblen scholars, only David Riesman has, so far as I am aware, drawn attention to this important quotation. David Riesman, *Thorstein Veblen: A Critical Interpretation* (New York: Scribner's, 1953), 147.

Veblen's later commentary on landlord compensation is at *TBE,* 342, where he observed, with approval, that "confiscation of proprietary rights is growing gradually less repugnant to the industrial populace, and the question of indemnity for eventual loss is more and more falling into neglect."

How close Veblen's later thinking stayed to his 1881 abstract appears in his 1915 statement: "Typically [the country town] is a product and exponent of the American land system. In its beginning it is located and 'developed' as an enterprise of speculation in land values; that is to say, it is a businesslike endeavor to get something for nothing by engrossing as much as may be of the increment of land values due to the increase of population and the settlement and cultivation of the adjacent agricultural area." Thorstein Veblen, *IG,* 317.

56. TV to Jameson, February 12, 1883, Container 33, JFJP; TV to Gilman, December 9, 1881, DCGP.

57. "Free enlightened controversy" paraphrases Royce, "Present Ideals," 384.

58. On the clubs and associations, see *JHCir* December 1881, 153. The Metaphysical Club was Peirce's brainchild; he took the name from an earlier "club" he and his friends had created at Harvard. See Menand, *Metaphysical Club,* 272–274. On "dull," see Jameson diary, entry for December 21, 1881, Container 1, JFJP.

59. Gilman, "Inaugural Address," 44; Ethington and McDonagh, "Social Science Inquiry"; Barber, "Political Economy"; Ethington and McDonagh, "Conference Panel"; Haines, "Scientific History as a Teaching Method." For an insightful critique of the Hopkins seminar through a gender lens, see Bonnie G. Smith, "Gender and the Practices of Scientific History: The Seminar and Archival Research in the Nineteenth Century," *American History Review* 100 (1995): 1150–1176.

60. *JHCir* July 1882, 231; Herbert B. Adams, "New Methods of Study in History," *JHS,* ser. 2, 1–2 (1884): 25–137, 64.

61. Edward A. Freeman, "An Introduction to American Institutional History," *JHS* 1 (1882): 13–39; Edward A. Freeman, *Lectures to American Audiences* (Philadelphia: Porter & Coates, 1882); Edmund Ions, *James Bryce and American Democracy, 1870–1922* (London: Macmillan, 1968); Herbert B. Adams, "Cooperation in University Work," *JHS*, ser. 1, 2 (1882): 39–57, 39–40. The *Johns Hopkins University Studies in Historical and Political Science* series continues to this day.

62. Andrew added: "As a security [Thorstein] took out a life policy in their favor" ("their" referring to Thomas and Orson Veblen). Andrew also explained that, at the time he went to Hopkins, "Th. had not had opportunity to save anything probably. It would have to be from his small salary at Madison." AV to JD, February 17, 1926, JDP.

63. Veblen's fellowship appeals to Gilman, dated October 5, October 25, and December 9, 1881, all in JDP.

64. AV to JD, August 5, 1931, JDP. On fellowships at Hopkins, see Hawkins, *Pioneer*, 79–82.

65. A. B. Maynard to JD, February 1933, JDP.

66. AV to JD, July 18, 1925, JDP.

67. Jameson diaries for 1881–1882, entries for February 4, 1882, and March 8, 1882; and TV to Jameson, May 16, 1883, Container 33, JFJP.
Despite this last statement, there were notes of regret in some of Veblen's comments about Hopkins. A few months after arriving in New Haven, he told Jameson, "I miss Prof. Morris." Several months later, he asked Jameson, "Do you hear any of Dr. Ely's lectures? If so, perhaps you could tell me what he is doing." (This remark suggests a more positive attitude toward Ely than the statements quoted earlier.) TV to Jameson, April 2, 1882, and October 9, 1882, Container 33, JFJP.

68. When speaking of "Yale College" here and throughout this section, I mean only the undergraduate liberal arts unit of the institution we now call Yale University. I will not use "University," however, because it was only in 1886 (two years after Veblen left Yale) that the school's trustees adopted the name Yale University. Before then, the operative term was Yale College, which was used inclusively to refer to the school's undergraduate liberal arts program *along with* several affiliated "schools" and graduate "departments" that had been grafted onto that program. Since this wider (pre-1886) sense of "College" differs from the later, narrower sense of the word, which is still in use today, I will—to avoid confusion—hold to the narrower usage.

69. TV to Jameson, April 2, 1882, and June 2, 1882, Container 33, JFJP. On economic conditions in New Haven, see Bruce Clouette, "New Haven, an Industrial City," in *Carriages and Clocks, Corsets and Locks: The Rise and Fall of an Industrial City—New Haven, Connecticut,* ed. Preston Maynard and Marjorie B. Noyes (Hanover, NH: University Press of New England, 2004), 1–16; . Rollin G. Osterweis, *Three Centuries of New Haven, 1638–1938* (New Haven, CT: Yale University Press, 1953); Douglas Rae, "Technology, Population Growth, and Centered Industrialism: New Haven, 1850–2000," in *Carriages and Clocks, Corsets and Locks,* ed. Maynard and Noyes, 73–92. On the local political conditions, see Robert A. Dahl, *Who Governs? Democracy and Power in an American City* (New Haven, CT: Yale University Press, [1961] 1970), a classic in the literature of political science.

70. The words belong to Yale philosopher George Ladd. See Editors of *Science,* with George T. Ladd, "Professor Ladd on the Yale Curriculum," *Science* 156 (1886): 103–105.

As I will discuss later, Ladd was one of Veblen's mentors. On the national press coverage given to debates about Yale's curriculum, I draw on Peter Dobkin Hall, "Noah Porter Writ Large?," in *The American College in the Nineteenth Century*, ed. Roger L. Geiger (Nashville, TN: Vanderbilt University Press, 2000), 196–220.

71. *HL* 207; AV to DC, February 17, 1926, JDP. In *TLC*, 363–400, Veblen elaborated this critique of gentlemen's colleges.

72. TV to Jameson, April 2, 1882, and June 2, 1882, Container 33, JFJP.

73. William J. Barber, "The Fortunes of Political Economy in an Environment of Academic Conservatism: Yale University," in *Breaking the Academic Mould: Economists and American Higher Learning in the Nineteenth Century*, ed. William J. Barber (Middletown, CT: Wesleyan University Press, 1988), 132–168, 141. More generally, see Stevenson, *Scholarly Means*. On the Sheffield School, see Russell H. Chittenden, *History of the Sheffield Scientific School of Yale University, 1846–1922*, vol. 1 (New Haven, CT: Yale University Press, 1928). Here and in the following paragraphs, I draw also on the two standard histories of Yale: Brooks Mather Kelley, *Yale: A History* (New Haven, CT: Yale University Press, 1974); George Wilson Pierson, *Yale College: An Educational History, 1871–1921* (New Haven, CT: Yale University Press, 1952).

74. Stephen G. Alter, *William Dwight Whitney and the Science of Language* (Baltimore: Johns Hopkins University Press, 2005), 95.

75. Alter, *William Dwight Whitney* 174–206; Kelley, *Yale*, 245.

76. Porter to Hubert Newton, September 24, 1882, HNP. Porter's handwriting is sometimes difficult to decipher, so I had to infer his words from the context. Where I've done so, I've used brackets and question marks.

77. On Sumner's life and work, I draw on Robert C. Bannister, *Social Darwinism: Science and Myth in Anglo-American Social Thought* (Philadelphia: Temple University Press, 1979); Robert C. Bannister, foreword, in *On Liberty, Society, and Politics: The Essential Essays of William Graham Sumner*, ed. Robert C. Bannister (Indianapolis: Liberty Fund, 1992), ix–xxxvi; Donald Cecil Bellomy, "The Molding of an Iconoclast: William Graham Sumner, 1840–1885," unpublished dissertation, Department of History, Harvard University, 1980; Bruce Curtis, *William Graham Sumner* (Boston: Twayne, 1981); Harris E. Starr, *William Graham Sumner* (New York: Holt, 1925). I also draw on plus two brief autobiographies: William Graham Sumner, "Autobiographical Sketch of William Graham Sumner," in *Essays of William Graham Sumner*, vol. 1, ed. Albert Galloway Keller and Maurice R. Davie (New Haven, CT: Yale University Press, [1889] 1934), 3–5; William Graham Sumner, "Sketch of William Graham Sumner," in *Essays*, vol. 2 (New Haven, CT: Yale University Press [1905] 1934), 3–13. Bannister (*Social Darwinism*) and Bellomy ("Molding of an Iconoclast") usefully analyze the development of Sumner's thought and its internal contradictions, issues I paper over in this chapter.

78. Sumner, "Lectures on the History of the U.S. [of] America, 1824–1876," and "Lectures on Political Economy," J. C. Schwab notes for 1886–1887, Group 219, Series 2, Box 67, WGSP. Schwab himself was a future economist.

79. Sumner, "Lectures on Political Economy."

80. Sumner, "Lectures on Political Economy"; William Graham Sumner, "Sociology," in *On Liberty, Society, and Politics*, 183–200, 183–184, 192–193. Not only Sumner, but also contemporaneous members of the Yale faculty in history, art history, political science, and several other fields, espoused organicism and institutionalism, as Stevenson has shown.

Speaking of the group of faculty members that she calls the "New Haven Scholars," Stevenson writes that they "propounded theories that elaborated on the value of institutions to society. They saw man as a social." Stevenson, *Scholarly Means,* 5.

81. For a discussion on Sumner's ideas in relation to Spencer's, see Bannister, *Social Darwinism;* Bellomy, "Molding of an Iconoclast"; Curtis, *William Graham Sumner.* In October 1882, Spencer, on a much publicized trip to the United States, made a half-day stop in New Haven. His description of his visit does not mention Sumner, though the two certainly met the next month at a banquet in New York, where Sumner lavished praise on Spencer's ideas. Herbert Spencer, "Social Evolution and Social Duty," in *Various Fragments* (New York: Appleton, [1893] 1904), 130–134; William Graham Sumner, "Professor Sumner's Speech," in *Herbert Spencer on the Americans* (New York: Appleton, [1882] 1904), 35–40. Veblen, who was in New Haven in October 1882, was no doubt aware of Spencer's stopover, though there is no evidence that Veblen encountered Spencer directly. On Spencer's American visit and his huge American celebrity, see also the more recent account by Barry Werth, *Banquet at Delmonico's* (New York: Random House, 2009). The best recent treatments of Spencer's thinking are Mark Francis, *Herbert Spencer and the Invention of Modern Life* (Ithaca, NY: Cornell University Press, 2007); John Offer, *Herbert Spencer and Social Theory* (London: Palgrave Macmillan, 2010).

82. William Graham Sumner, "The Administration of Andrew Jackson," in *The Forgotten Man and Other Essays,* ed. Albert Galloway Keller (New Haven, CT: Yale University Press, [1880] 1918), 337–367, 337–338; William Graham Sumner, "The Challenge of Facts," in *Essays,* vol. 2, 87–122, 119; Sumner, "Sociology," 184; William Graham Sumner, "The Science of Sociology," in *The Forgotten Man* ([1882] 1918), 401–405, 39; William Graham Sumner, "Sociological Fallacies," *North American Review* 138 (1884): 574–579, 579.

83. For the more historical side of Sumner's thought, see Roscoe C. Hinkle, *Founding Theory of American Sociology, 1881–1915* (Boston: Routledge & Kegan Paul, 1980).

84. Sumner, "Lectures on the History of the U.S."

85. William Graham Sumner, "Socialism," in *On Liberty, Society, and Politics,* 159–182, 164–167; William Graham Sumner, *Protectionism: The–Ism which Teaches that Waste Makes Wealth* (New York: Holt, [1885] 1888), 48. For a discussion of whether and to what degree Sumner was a "social Darwinist," see Bannister, *Social Darwinism;* Bellomy, "Molding of an Iconoclast"; Curtis, *William Graham Sumner;* Geoffrey M. Hodgson, "Social Darwinism in Anglophone Academic Journals," *Journal of Historical Sociology* 17 (2004) 428–463. In attacking government programs on the grounds of "paternalism," Summer drew on a strain of American political discourse associated with the mugwump faction of the Republican Party in the 1880s. For a discussion on this discourse, see Richard Schneirov, *Labor and Urban Politics: Class Conflict and the Origins of Liberalism in Chicago, 1864–1897* (Urbana: University of Illinois Press, 1998), 260–263.

86. William Graham Sumner, "The Challenge of Facts," in *Essays,* vol. 2, 87–122, 117; William Graham Sumner, "The Philosophy of Strikes," in *On Liberty, Society, and Politics,* 127–132; William Graham Sumner, *Problems in Political Economy* (New York: Holy, 1885), 52; Sumner, *Protectionism,* 8, 21, 45, 56, 79. For "jealousy of wealth," see Sumner, "Lectures on the History of the U.S." As I will point out in Chapter 8, the notion of industrial "exemption" was central to Veblen's economics.

87. AV to JD, July 18, 1925, JDP; TV to Jameson, April 2, 1882, May 16, 1883, Container 33, JFJP.

88. "A very important thesis" and "over some very strong competitors" are statements in Sumner's letter, dated September 3, 1889, recommending Veblen for an academic job, Vol. 46, AVP. The "John A. Porter University Prize" announcement ran in *Yale Literary Magazine* (December 1883): 121. In the competition, Veblen bested Edward Bourne, whose essay for the prize was published a short time afterward. Edward G. Bourne, *The History of the Surplus Revenue of 1837* (New York: G. P. Putnam's Sons, 1885).

89. TV to Sumner, August 22, 1889, Group 291, Series 1, Box 29, Folder 796, WGSP. Veblen, "Application of Graduate Student," January 9, 1891, TV-CU. This application is reproduced in Francesca Lidia Viano, "Ithaca Transfer: Veblen and the Historical Profession," *History of European Ideas* 35 (2009): 38–61, 56–57.

90. Morris Hadley, *Arthur Twining Hadley* (New Haven, CT: Yale University Press, 1948), 45–52. Ralph P. Rosenberg, "The First American Doctor of Philosophy Degree: A Centennial Salute to Yale, 1861–1961," *Journal of Higher Education* 32 (1961): 387–394. On doctorates supervised by Sumner, see Bannister, *Liberty, Society, and Politics,* xxxiii.

91. Ladd brought out in English several volumes of Lotze's writings, apparently enlisting Veblen, who had a strong command of German, to translate one of these, possibly Lotze's *Outlines of Metaphysics,* which appeared in 1886. Years later, University of Chicago philosopher James Tufts (who had studied at Yale with Ladd about the time Veblen did) told Dorfman that Veblen "translated one of the series of Lotze's Lecture Notes which Ladd edited," J.H. Tufts to JD, October 21, 1932, JDP.

92. AV to JD, March 5, 1930, and March 18, 1930, JDP. On Ladd's teaching assignments, see Eugene S. Mills, *George Trumbull Ladd: Pioneer American Psychologist* (Cleveland, OH: Case Western Reserve Press, 1969), 110.

93. George T. Ladd, *The Doctrine of Sacred Scripture: A Critical, Historical and Dogmatic Inquiry into the Origin and Nature of the Old and New Testaments,* 2 vols. (New York: Scribner's).

94. Ladd, *Doctrine of Sacred Scripture,* vol. 1, 15–17, 275–285.

95. Ladd, *Doctrine of Sacred Scripture,* vol. 2, 699–700. For Ladd's disputes with the Bible, see Ronald L. Numbers, "George Frederick Wright: From Christian Darwinist to Fundamentalist," *Isis* 79 (1988): 624–645, 631.

96. George T. Ladd, *Elements of Physiological Psychology: A Treatise of the Activities and Nature of the Mind from the Physical and Experimental Point of View* (New York: Scribner's, 1887). On biblical literalism, see Mark A. Noll, *Between Faith and Criticism: Evangelicals, Scholarship, and the Bible in America* (Vancouver, BC: Baker Publishing Group, 1991). On the new psychology, see Chapter 6. On the dating of Ladd's laboratory research, see George T. Ladd, "Letter to the Editor," *Science* 45 (1895): 626–627; J. McK. Cattell, "Early Psychological Laboratories," *Science* 67 (1928): 543–548; J. McK. Cattell, "Psychology in America," *Scientific Monthly* 30 (1930): 114–126.

97. George T. Ladd, "Psychology as So-Called 'Natural Science,'" *Philosophical Review* 1 (1892): 24–53, 50–51.

98. Ladd, *Physiological Psychology,* 527–528, 573–574, 588–589, 616–618, 622; Mills, *George Trumbull Ladd,* 9.

99. William James, *The Principles of Psychology* (New York: Holt, 1890). On Ladd in relation to James, see Thomas Dixon, "The Psychology of the Emotions in Britain and America in the Nineteenth Century: The Role of Religious and Antireligious Commitments," *Osiris,* 2nd ser., 16 (2001): 288–320.

100. On Porter's life, see Kuklick, *Churchmen and Philosophers;* Stevenson, *Scholarly Means;* and especially George Levesque, "Noah Porter Revisited," *Perspectives on the History of Higher Education* 26 (2008): 29–66.

101. Kelley, *Yale,* 271.

102. Stevenson, *Scholarly Means,* 66.

103. Spencer, *The Study of Sociology,* 268. On the Sumner-Porter controversy, see Hall, "Noah Porter Writ Large?"; John D. Heyl and Barbara S. Heyl, "The Sumner-Porter Controversy at Yale: Pre-paradigmatic Sociology and Institutional Crisis," *Sociological Inquiry* 46 (1976): 41–50; Werth, *Banquet,* 216–219.

104. Noah Porter, *The Human Intellect* (New York: Scribner's, [1868] 1886), 5, 8, 13–14, 615; Noah Porter, *The Elements of Moral Science: Theoretical and Practical* (New York: Scribner's, 1885), 3; Noah Porter, *Evolution* (New York: Bridgman, 1886), 5–6. On Porter's psychology, I have benefited from Graham Richards, "Noah Porter's Problem and the Origins of American Psychology," *Journal of the History of the Behavioral Sciences* 40 (2004): 353–374.

105. Noah Porter, *Books and Reading; What Books Shall I Read and How Shall I Read Them?* (New York: Scribner's 1871), 126, 160, 180; Noah Porter, "Address," in *Addresses at the Inauguration of Professor Noah Porter, D.D., L.L.D., as President of Yale College* (New York: Scribner's, 1871), 27–65, 53; Noah Porter, *Science and Sentiment, with Other Papers, Chiefly Philosophical* (New York: Scribner's, [1882] 1883), 290; Porter, *Moral Science,* 432; Porter, *Evolution,* 5–6.

106. Porter, *Books and Reading,* 160, 180.

107. Porter, *Moral Science,* 39–41, 349, 356–357, 374, 411, 432–435, 439–440.

108. James's description of Porter is in his August 5, 1883, letter to Charles Renouvier. William James, *The Letters of William James,* ed. Henry James, 2 vol. (New York: Atlantic Monthly Press, 1920), 231–232.

109. TV to Jameson, April 2, 1882, Container 33, JFJP. On the courses Porter taught, see *YaleCat* 1881–82, 50. We get a sense of how often Veblen and Porter interacted in another letter to Jameson, in which Veblen explained why he was reapplying for a fellowship at Hopkins: "The notion of a fellowship would never have entered my head but for the suggestion of Pres. Porter. Some two or three weeks ago the President spoke of it, and . . . I was induced, by his repeatedly speaking about it and advising it, to send an application." TV to Jameson, May 16, 1883, Container 33, JFJP. Porter's insistence that Veblen apply for the Hopkins fellowship reflected, most likely, his concern with Veblen's finances.

110. TV to Jameson, February 12, 1883, Container 33, JFJP.

111. Most useful for understanding Porter's view on Kant is Noah Porter, letter, in "The Centennial of Kant's *Kritik* at Saratoga, N.Y.," compiled by John W. Mears, *Journal of Speculative Philosophy* 15 (1881): 293–302, 436. On his ideas about induction, see Porter, *Books and Reading.* On Porter's epistemology, I draw on Stanley Matthew Daugert, *The Philosophy of Thorstein Veblen* (New York: King's Crown Press, 1950); Robert L. McCaul, "Dewey in College, 1875–1879," *School Review* 70 (1962): 437–456;

and the brief comments in Flower and Murphey, *History of American Philosophy;* Kuklick, *Rise of American Philosophy;* Kuklick, *Churchmen and Philosophers;* Kuklick, *History of Philosophy;* Schneider, *History of American Philosophy.*

112. The statements from Robinson, Coyle, and Porter appear in John W. Mears, "The Centennial of Kant's *Kritik* at Saratoga, N.Y.," *Journal of Speculative Philosophy* 15 (1881): 293–302, 298–299. On the announcement for the Griggs series, see Anonymous, "German Philosophy for English Readers," *Journal of Speculative Philosophy* 15 (1881), 323–324, 324; Robert Adamson, *On the Philosophy of Kant* (Edinburgh: David Douglas, 1879), 127.

113. Veblen, "Kant's *Critique of Judgment,*" *Journal of Speculative Philosophy* (July 1884): 260–274. Veblen's interest in Kant lasted throughout his career. His late book, *An Inquiry into the Nature of Peace and The Terms of Its Perpetuation* (New York: B. W. Huebsch, 1917) was, he said, intended both to echo the title of Kant's famous 1795 essay "Perpetual Peace" and to extend Kant's ideas. We see these themes as well in an article Veblen wrote two years later, "Immanuel Kant on Perpetual Peace," *The Dial* 66 (May 17, 1919), 469.

114. Veblen, "Kant's *Critique of Judgment,*" 262, 267, 270–272. Porter, *Human Intellect,* 452–457. Although Veblen was following Porter, he did not name him in this article. The best discussion of this article is Daugert, *Philosophy of Thorstein Veblen.* On Veblen in relation to Kant, I have also found useful John Patrick Diggins, *Thorstein Veblen: Theorist of the Leisure Class* (Princeton, NJ: Princeton University Press, 1999); Rick Tilman, *The Intellectual Legacy of Thorstein Veblen: Unresolved Issues* (Westport, CT: Greenwood Press, 1996).

115. AV to JD, July 18, 1925, JDP. Mitchell's statement is quoted in Wesley C. Mitchell, *Types of Economic Theory,* vol. 2 (New York: Kelley, 1969), 621n11. On the doctrine of retribution, I have consulted Edward Beecher, *History of Opinions on the Scriptural Doctrine of Retribution* (New York: Appleton, 1878); James Freeman Clarke, *The Christian Doctrine of Forgiveness of Sin* (Boston: American Unitarian Association, 1867); William Jackson, *Eight Lectures* (London: Hodder and Stoughton, 1875).

116. *Doctors of Philosophy of Yale University, 1861–1915* (New Haven, CT: Yale University Press, 1915).

117. *YaleCat* 1883–1884, 48.

118. Because the topics for the Porter Prize competition were not announced until December 1883, and submissions were due by mid-May 1884, Veblen's work on "The Distribution of Surplus Revenue" necessarily fell during this five-month period.

119. Bellomy, *Molding of an Iconoclast,* 377; Richard T. Ely, *Ground under Our Feet: An Autobiography* (New York: Macmillan, 1938), 111; Charles Sanders Peirce, "Grounds of Validity of the Laws of Logic: Further Consequences of Four Incapacities," in *The Essential Peirce: Selected Philosophical Writings,* vol. 1, *1867–1893,* 56–82, 57; Ladd quoted in Eugene S. Mills, *George Trumbull Ladd: Pioneer American Psychologist* (Cleveland, OH: Press of Case Western Reserve University, 1969) 83; Jameson Diaries for 1881–82, entry for October 12, 1881, Container 2, JFJP.

120. This is not to say Veblen's professors never used these alternative practices. Rarely are knowledge makers so stubbornly fixed in their ways that, when the situation requires, they refuse to apply tools different from those they ordinarily prefer. This flexibility was true of Veblen also.

121. Here I draw especially on Lowy, whose analysis describes a dynamic similar to the one I am describing. Ilana Lowy, "The Strength of Loose Concepts—Boundary Concepts, Federative Experimental Strategies and Disciplinary Growth: The Case of Immunology," *History of Science* 30 (1992): 371–396. The literature in Science Studies on the broader issue is enormous, going back to the classic work of Fleck and Kuhn. Ludwig Fleck, *Genesis and Development of a Scientific Fact* (Chicago: University of Chicago Press, [1935] 1979); Thomas S. Kuhn, *The Structure of Scientific Revolutions*, 2nd enl. ed. (Chicago: University of Chicago Press, [1962] 1970). I draw the concept of "trading zones" from Peter Galison, "Computer Simulations and the Trading Zone," in *The Disunity of Science: Boundaries, Contexts, and Power*, ed. Peter Galison and David J. Stump (Stanford, CA: Stanford University Press 1996), 118–157.

122. Regarding Veblen's teachers' commitment to graduate training: on Adams, see Hawkins, *Pioneer*, 173; Allan G. Bogue, *Frederick Jackson Turner: Strange Road Going Down* (Norman: University of Oklahoma Press, 1998), 44; W. Stull Holt, *Historical Scholarship in the United States, 1876–1901: As Revealed in the Correspondence of Herbert B. Adams* (Baltimore: Johns Hopkins University Press, 1938), 15. On Ely, see Billington, *Frederick Jackson Turner*, 76; John R. Commons, *Myself* (New York: Macmillan, 1934), 42–43; Rader, *Academic Mind and Reform*, 18. On Morris, see Dykhuizen, *Life and Mind of John Dewey*, 29; Wenley, *Life and Work of George Sylvester Morris*, 320. On Peirce, see Fisch, "Peirce at the Johns Hopkins University," 84; Jastrow, "Charles S. Peirce as a Teacher"; Ladd-Franklin, "Charles S. Peirce at the Johns Hopkins." On Ladd, see Mills, *Ladd*, 100, 110. On Sumner, see Curtis, *William Graham Sumner*, 48; Barber, "Political Economy," 150.

123. I am referring to the support Veblen received from Ely and Adams for his "Taxation of Land" paper, from Sumner for his "Distribution of Surplus Revenue" paper, and from Porter for his research on Kant.

124. In making this statement, I am leaving out of the picture students from the natural sciences and from areas of the humanities apart from philosophy and history.

6. Transition

1. For an examination of the poor job market in philosophy in the United States in the 1870s and 1880s, see Daniel J. Wilson, *Science, Community, and the Transformation of American Philosophy, 1860–1930* (Chicago: University of Chicago Press, 1990). For a contemporaneous account, see G. Stanley Hall, "Philosophy in the United States," *Mind* 4 (1879): 89–105. When I say Veblen was one of five who received a doctorate in philosophy in 1884, I am counting only scholars who wrote dissertations in the area of philosophy, not those who earned "doctor of philosophy" degrees in other fields. Aside from Veblen and Dewey, the other three 1884 philosophy PhDs were James Darlington and Charles Klein, both of whom pursed careers in the ministry outside the academy, and Nicholas Murray Butler, whose doctoral degree was from Columbia University and who went on to a very distinguished career as a philosopher (among other achievements). Butler did not go directly into an academic job because of special circumstances; after receiving his PhD, he followed his advisers' suggestion and went to Europe for a year of additional study. Upon his return, he immediately joined the Columbia faculty. For the names of doctoral recipients, see Thomas Lloyd Malone, "A History of the Doctor of

Philosophy Dissertation in the United States 1861–1930" (PhD diss., Wayne State University, 1981), 63.

2. Quoting Porter's standard letter of recommendation for Thorstein Veblen, Vol. 46, AVP.

3. John Edward Veblen to JD, August 4, 1930, JDP; AV to JD, March 19, 1925, JDP.

4. TV to Rasmus Anderson, May 1, 1890, RBAP. Andrew's words "never mentioned" are from his manuscript, "Comments on Florence Andrus Noble Veblen's Essay on Thorstein Veblen," Vol. 46, AVP.

5. On the other hand, an item in the *New York Times* in December 1883 quoted Noah Porter saying to a Yale alumnus worried about malaria: "In respect of the college's healthfulness there was no occasion for apprehension. Not a single case of malaria had occurred on the college premises. . . . As for New Haven itself, there was far less of malarial fever than there was 10 years ago." *New York Times*, Historical Archive, entry for December 8, 1883.

6. I owe the diagnosis of Thorstein Veblen's condition as Addison's disease to Dr. Bryan Lassner, Director of Resident Education, Emergency Physicians Medical Group, Chicago, Illinois. Because Addison's disease runs in families, the condition may perhaps explain Andrew Veblen's own perplexing five-year period of inactivity (see Chapter 3). Dr. Lassner raises the alternative possibility that Thorstein Veblen may have been suffering a form of depression—a diagnosis consistent with the stage of life when he experienced his symptoms. The fact that Veblen later recalled these years as enjoyable does not preclude the possibility of depression.

7. TV to Anderson, May 1, 1890, RBAP; John Edward Veblen to JD, March 14, 1930, JDP.

8. TV to Sarah Hardy, October 28, 1895, TV-UoC; reproduced in JJ*TV*, 188. On Iowa City, see Anonymous, *History of Johnson County, Iowa* (Iowa City: [no publisher information] 1882); Clarence Aurner, *Leading Events in Johnson County Iowa History* (Cedar Rapids, IA: Western Historical Press, 1912). On Stacyville, see J. F. Clyde and H. A. Dwelle, eds., *History of Mitchell and Worth Counties, Iowa* (Chicago: S. J. Clarke Pub. Co., 1918); Cheryl Mullenbach, *The History of Stacyville, Iowa: 1856–2006*, http://www.stacyville.com/Pages/HistoryBook.html.

9. Walter Licht, *Industrializing America: The Nineteenth Century* (Baltimore: Johns Hopkins University Press, 1995), 102. I also draw on Jeremy Atack and Peter Passell, *A New Economic View of American History*, 2nd ed. (New York: Norton, 1995), 427–456; Robert Galman, "Economic Growth and Structural Change in the Long Nineteenth Century," in *The Cambridge Economic History of the United States*, vol. 2, *The Long Nineteenth Century*, ed. Stanley L. Engerman and Robert E. Gallman (Cambridge: Cambridge University Press, 2000), 1–55; Jeffrey G. Williamson, *Late Nineteenth-Century American Development: A General Equilibrium History* (London: Cambridge University Press, 1974); Peter H. Lindert and Jeffrey G. Williamson, *Unequal Gains: American Growth and Inequality since 1700* (Princeton, NJ: Princeton University Press, 2016), 166–171.

10. See Williamson, who speaks of "the Great Depression, 1870–96," *American Development*, 93–118. I draw these figures from Licht, *Industrializing America*, 181–194; Lindert and Williamson, *Unequal Gains*, 166–171.

11. I draw this characterization from White, who qualifies it by stressing that political parties of this era were "not ideologically consistent," and that there were significant local variations tied to regional histories in terms of which social groups affiliated with which of the two major parties. Richard White, *The Republic for Which It Stands: The United States during Reconstruction and the Gilded Age, 1865–1896* (New York: Oxford University Press, 2017), 253–254. Both parties supported pro-business policies. The exception was the faction known as the "Liberal Republicans" (and their successors, sometimes called "mugwumps"), which emerged in the 1870s and did uphold a strong intellectual and social commitment to the laissez-faire doctrines of classical liberalism. Nancy Cohen, *The Reconstruction of American Liberalism, 1865–1914* (Chapel Hill: University of North Carolina Press, 2002); Richard Schneirov, *Labor and Urban Politics: Class Conflict and the Origins of Modern Liberalism in Chicago, 1864–1897* (Urbana: University of Illinois Press, 1998). Among Veblen's teachers, William Graham Sumner was a major figure in this tradition.

12. The literature on the development of the corporation is enormous. Alfred D. Chandler, *The Visible Hand: The Managerial Revolution in American Business* (Cambridge, MA: Harvard University Press, 1977) is the ur-source. Here, and throughout this subsection, I also draw on Atack and Passell, *New Economic View,* 457–521; Richard Franklin Bensel, *The Political Economy of American Industrialization, 1877–1900* (Cambridge: Cambridge University Press, 2000); Ballard C. Campbell, "Understanding Economic Change in the Gilded Age," *Organization of American Historians Magazine of History* 13 (1999): 16–20; Neil Fligstein, *The Transformation of Corporate Control* (Cambridge, MA: Harvard University Press, 1990); Naomi R. Lamoreaux, *The Great Merger Movement in American Business, 1895–1904* (Cambridge: Cambridge University Press, 1985); Licht, *Industrializing America;* Glenn Porter, *The Rise of Big Business,* 3rd ed. (Wheeling, IL: Harlan Davidson, [1973] 2006); William G. Roy, *Socializing Capital: The Rise of the Large Industrial Corporation in America* (Princeton, NJ: Princeton University, 1997); Richard White, *Railroaded: The Transcontinentals and the Making of Modern America* (New York: Norton, 2011).

13. On the railway invasion of the Upper Midwest, see William Cronon, *Nature's Metropolis: Chicago and the Great West* (New York: Norton, 1991), 55–93. On bonanza farms, see Harriet Friedman, "World Market, State, and Family Farm: Social Bases of Household Production in the Era of Wage Labor," *Comparative Studies in Society and History* 20 (1978): 545–586. On the iron ore industry, see William E. Lass, *Minnesota: A History,* 2nd ed. (New York: Norton, 1998).

14. Alan Trachtenberg, *The Incorporation of America: Culture and Society in the Gilded Age* (New York: Hill and Wang, [1982] 2007).

15. For a discussion on the development of financial institutions in this period, see Williamson, *American Development;* Licht, *Industrializing America;* Lindert and Williamson, *Unequal Gains;* Rasmussen, *Agriculture and National Development;* Schweider, "Agricultural Issues"; Winters, "Economics of Midwestern Agriculture"; Lass, *Minnesota;* Atack and Passell, *New Economic View;* Williamson, *American Development;* Melton, *Veblens in Wisconsin: A Progress Report* ([location unknown]: Melton Research Inc., 2004). On inventions, see Thomas Hughes, *American Genesis: A Century of Invention and Technological Enthusiasm, 1870–1970* (New York: Viking, 1989). I have also benefited from Sean Dennis Cashman, *America in the Gilded Age: From the Death*

of Lincoln to the Rise of Theodore Roosevelt, 3rd ed. (New York: New York University Press, [1984] 1993).

16. Charles B. Spahr, *An Essay on the Present Distribution of Wealth in the United States* (New York: Crowell, 1896), 69. In interpreting Spahr's data, I have benefited from Nell Irvin Painter, *Standing at Armageddon: A Grassroots History of the Progressive Era* (New York: Norton, [1987] 2008), xv–xxiv. I take the income distribution statistics from Painter (xiv), whose divisions (1 percent, 12 percent) come closest to the divisions I used in previous chapters. As one would expect, other historians, using other divisions, report different figures. Because I am giving a broad-stroke picture, and obviously not a refined econometric analysis, I have made no effort to adjudicate among these scholars or to track back to the (often unspecified) primary sources on which they build. Lindert and Williamson, *Unequal Gains* (171–173), present a more sophisticated analysis, which suggests *less* income inequality than the figures I give in the text. These authors' evidence comes, however, from the early twentieth century.

17. William Leach, *Land of Desire* (New York: Vintage, 1993), xiii.

18. On the spending behaviors of America's wealthiest families, see Sven Beckert, *The Monied Metropolis* (Cambridge: Cambridge University Press, 2001). On class differences in lifestyles, I also draw on Stuart Blumin, *The Emergence of the Middle Class: Social Experience in the American City, 1760–1900* (New York: Cambridge University Press, 1989); Stuart Blumin, "The Social Implication of U.S. Economic Development," in *The Cambridge Economic History of the United States,* vol. 2, *The Long Nineteenth Century,* ed. Stanley L. Engerman and Robert E. Gallman (Cambridge: Cambridge University Press, 2000), 813–863; Michael McGerr, *A Fierce Discontent* (New York: Oxford University Press, 2003); Painter, *Standing at Armageddon;* Mark Wahlgren Summers, *The Gilded Age: or, The Hazard of New Functions* (Upper Saddle River, NJ: Prentice-Hall, 1997). Rebecca Edwards, *New Spirits: Americans in the Gilded Age, 1865–1905* (New York: Oxford, 2006). Edwards also quotes the Macy's ad (93).

19. On the amount of indebtedness, see Edwards, *New Spirits,* 96. On Montgomery Ward and Sears, Roebuck, see Cronon, *Nature's Metropolis,* 336.

20. On leisure time, I draw on Blumin, *Emergence of the Middle Class;* Blumin, "Social Implication"; McGerr, *Fierce Discontent;* Painter, *Standing at Armageddon;* Summers, *Gilded Age;* Edwards, *New Spirits.*

21. Daniel T. Rodgers, *The Work Ethic in Industrial America, 1850–1920* (Chicago: University of Chicago Press, 1974), xii, 99, 211, 217.

22. See Judy Hilkey, *Character Is Capital: Success Manuals and Manhood in Gilded Age America* (Chapel Hill: University of North Carolina Press, 1997); Sulevi Riukulehto, *The Concepts of Luxury and Waste in American Radicalism, 1880–1929* (Saarijarvi, FI: Academia Scientiarum Fennica, 1998).

23. Mark Twain and Charles Dudley Warner, *The Gilded Age: A Tale of Today* (New York: Harper Warner, 1873), 54–55. Charles Dudley Warner, *As We Go* (New York: Harper, 1893). More generally, the paragraph draws on Michael Barton, "The Victorian Jeremiad: Critics of Accumulation and Display," in *Consuming Visions: Accumulation and Display of Goods in America, 1880–1920,* ed. Simon J. Bronner (New York: Norton, 1989), 55–71; Clare Virginia Eby, *Dreiser and Veblen, Saboteurs of the Status Quo* (Columbia: University of Missouri Press, 1998); Edwards, *New Spirits,* 98–99;

David Horowitz, *The Morality of Spending: Attitudes toward the Consumer Society in America, 1875–1940* (Baltimore: Johns Hopkins University Press, 1985).

24. Licht, *Industrializing America,* 166–186. Also see Bensel, *Political Economy,* 209–217; Edwards, *New Spirits,* 201–220; David Montgomery, *The Fall of the House of Labor: The Workplace, the State, and American Labor Activism, 1865–1925* (New York: Cambridge University Press, 1987); Painter, *Standing at Armageddon,* 1–17, 110–140; Elizabeth Sanders, *Roots of Reform* (Chicago: University of Chicago Press, 1999), 45–55.

25. On the plight of Midwestern farmers, see Rasmussen, introduction to *Agriculture and National Development: Views on the Nineteenth Century,* ed. Lou Ferleger (Ames: Iowa State University Press, 1990), Dorothy Schweider, "Agricultural Issues of the Middle West, 1865–1910," in *Agriculture and National Development,* ed. Lou Ferleger, 97–115; Winters, "The Economics of Midwestern Agriculture, 1865–1900," in *Agriculture and National Development,* ed. Lou Ferleger, 75–95. For a more positive picture of the condition of farmers, see Atack and Passell, *New Economic View,* 402–426; Williamson, *American Development,* 146–163. On the finances of the Veblen family, see Melton, *Veblens in Wisconsin,* 36–37.

26. On Populism and these other protest movements, I draw principally from Lawrence Goodwyn, *The Populist Moment: A Short History of the Agrarian Revolt in America* (Oxford: Oxford University Press, 1978); Robert C. McMath Jr., *American Populism: A Social History, 1877–1898* (New York: Hill and Wang, 1992); Robert C. McMath Jr., "Populism in Two Countries: Agrarian Protest in the Great Plains and the Prairie Provinces," *Agricultural History* 69 (1995): 516–546; Charles Postel, *The Populist Vision* (New York: Oxford, 2007). While these protest movements sparked a range of reactions in the Norwegian-American communities of the Midwest, on the whole the reaction was one of strong support. Arlow W. Andersen, *Rough Road to Glory* (Philadelphia: Balch Institute Press, 1990), 57–70; Jon A. Gjerde and Carlton C. Qualey, *Norwegians in Minnesota* (St. Paul: Minnesota Historical Society Press, 2002), 44–46; Lass, *Minnesota,* 202–207; Odd S. Lovoll, *The Promise of America: A History of the Norwegian-American People,* rev. ed. (Minneapolis: University of Minnesota Press, [1984] 1999), 192–204; Odd S. Lovoll, *Norwegian Newspapers in America: Connecting Norway and the New Land* (St. Paul: Minnesota Historical Society Press, 2010), 118–123, 160–166; McMath "Populism in Two Countries"; Carlton C. Qualey and Jon A. Gjerde, "The Norwegians," in *They Chose Minnesota: A Survey of the State's Ethnic Groups,* ed. June Drenning Holmquist (St. Paul: Minnesota Historical Society Press, 1981), 220–247, 236–238; Ingrid Semmingsen, *Norway to America: A History of the Migration,* trans. Einar Haugen (Minneapolis: University of Minnesota Press, [1975] 1978), 149–150; Lowell J. Soike, *Norwegian Americans and the Politics of Dissent, 1880–1924* (Northfield, MN: Norwegian-American Historical Association); Jon Wefald, *A Voice of Protest: Norwegians in American Politics, 1890–1917* (Northfield, MN: Norwegian-American Historical Association, 1971).

27. On cooperatives in the vicinity of the Veblen farm, see Steven Keillor, *Cooperative Commonwealth: Co-ops in Rural Minnesota, 1859–1919* (St. Paul: Minnesota Historical Society Press, 2000).

28. Postel, *Populist Vision,* vii.

29. On "producerism," see McMath, "Populism in Two Countries." On support for Populism in the Norwegian-American press, see Lovoll, *Norwegian Newspapers in America,* 119–125.

30. The Donnelly "Preamble" is easily available online. I used the website History Matters: The U.S. Survey Course, "The Omaha Platform: Launching the Populist Party," historymatters.gmu.edu/d/5361.

31. Sean Dennis Cashman, *America in the Gilded Age: From the Death of Lincoln to the Rise of Theodore Roosevelt,* 3rd ed. (New York: New York University Press, [1984] 1993), 119, quoting a contemporaneous source.

32. Postel, *Populist Vision,* 287. On the populists as intellectuals, see also Goodwyn, *Populist Moment.*

33. Laurence Gronlund, *The Co-operative Commonwealth: An Exposition of Modern Socialism* (London: Sonnenschein, [1885] 1896). On Gronlund's importance, see Postel, *Populist Vision;* Solomon Gemorah, "Laurence Gronlund—Utopian or Reformer?" *Science and Society* 33 (1969): 446–458; P. E. Maher, "Laurence Gronlund: Contributions to American Socialism," *Western Political Quarterly* 15 (1962): 618–624; Mark Pittenger, *American Socialists and Evolutionary Thought, 1870–1920* (Madison: University of Wisconsin Press, 1993); Rodgers, *Work Ethic,* 217–218.

34. Gronlund, *Co-operative Commonwealth,* 35, 53, 102, 26, 55, 8, 71, 81, 79.

35. Sarah Hardy, "Notes for Thorstein Veblen's course on Socialism, Univ. of Chicago, 1894," Series 77, TV-CCA.

36. The literature on the development of American higher education in the late nineteenth century is extensive. Here, and throughout this section, I draw especially on Roger L. Geiger, *To Advance Knowledge: The Growth of American Research Universities, 1900–1940* (New Brunswick, NJ: Transaction, [1986] 2004]). Roger L. Geiger, introduction to *The American College in the Nineteenth Century* (Nashville, TN: Vanderbilt University Press, 2000), 1–36; Andrew Jewett, *Science, Democracy, and the American University: From the Civil War to the Cold War* (New York: Cambridge University Press, 2012); Julia A. Reuben, *The Making of the Modern University* (Chicago: University of Chicago Press, 1996); John R. Thelin, *A History of American Higher Education,* 2nd ed. (Baltimore: Johns Hopkins University Press, 2011); Laurence R. Veysey, *The Emergence of the American University* (Chicago: University of Chicago Press, [1965] 1970). I also make use of Arthur M. Cohen and Carrie B. Kisker, *The Shaping of American Higher Education: Emergence and Growth of the Contemporary System,* 2nd ed. (San Francisco: Jossey Bass, 2010); Christopher Lucas, *American Higher Education: A History,* 2nd ed. (New York: Palgrave Macmillan, 2006); George M. Marsden, *The Soul of the American University: From Protestant Establishment to Establish Nonbelief* (Oxford: Oxford University Press, 1994); Christopher Newfield, *Ivy and Industry: Business and the Making of the American University, 1880–1980* (Durham, NC: Duke University Press, 2003).

37. I arrived at these figures by reworking the data provided in Roger L. Geiger, "The Era of the Multipurpose Colleges in American Higher Education, 1850–1890," *The American College in the Nineteenth Century,* ed. Roger L. Geiger (Nashville, TN: Vanderbilt University Press), 133.

38. To avoid confusion, it is worth adding historian Roger Geiger's observation that up until 1900, "the rubric of 'research university' would have been considered redun-

dant; the province of a true university was then held to be higher learning, graduate education, and the advancement of knowledge through research." Geiger, *To Advance Knowledge*, xix.

39. With regard to the pre-1890 period, Thelin lists only five of these institutions: Johns Hopkins, Harvard, Columbia, Cornell, and Clark (whose life as a research university proved short-lived). I include six because I also count Yale, for the reasons described in Chapter 5. The additions to the list by 1900 were, according to Thelin: the University of Chicago, the University of California, Catholic University, the University of Michigan, Stanford University, the University of Wisconsin, the University of Pennsylvania, and Princeton University. Thelin, *American Higher Education*, 110. In his account of the leading research universities in the period from 1865 to 1920—Veblen's life span, with a few life years added on either end—Geiger identifies a closely overlapping list of fifteen universities, subtracting Clark and Catholic University and adding the University of Illinois, University of Minnesota, and Massachusetts Institute of Technology. Geiger calls attention to the geographical diversity of the institutions on this list, as well as their diverse histories. He notes that five were among the nation's oldest seats of higher education, another five were private institutions founded in the late nineteenth century, and another five were state universities. Geiger, *To Advance Knowledge*, 3–20, 2–3.

40. I take "containers" from Laurence Veysey, "The Plural Organized Worlds of the Humanities," in Alexandra Oleson and John Voss, eds., *The Organization of Knowledge in Modern America, 1860–1920* (Baltimore: Johns Hopkins University Press, 1970), 65.

41. This paragraph draws on Andrew Abbott, *Chaos of Disciplines* (Chicago: University of Chicago Press, 2001); Thomas L. Haskell, *The Emergence of Professional Social Science* (Baltimore: Johns Hopkins University Press, [1977] 2000); John Higham, "The Matrix of Specialization," in *The Organization of Knowledge*, 3–18; Dorothy Ross, "Changing Contours of the Social Science Disciplines," in *The Modern Social Sciences*, ed. Theodore M. Porter and Dorothy Ross, *The Cambridge History of Science*, vol. 7 (Cambridge: Cambridge University Press, 2003), 205–237; and especially Geiger, *To Advance Knowledge*, 20–39.

42. Daniel Patrick Thurs, *Science Talk: Changing Notions of Science in American Culture* (New Brunswick, NJ: Rutgers University Press, 2007), 85.

43. On different understandings of "science," see Thurs, *Science Talk*, 53–89. On fairs and museums, see Edwards, *New Spirits*, 152–155. On government spending on science, Philip J. Pauly, *Biologists and the Promise of American Life: From Meriwether Lewis to Alfred Kinsey* (Princeton, NJ: Princeton University Pres, 2000), 47–64.

44. Thurs, *Science Talk*, 60, quoting a contemporaneous source.

45. Bernard Lightman, "Darwin and the Popularization of Evolution," *Notes and Records of the Royal Society of London* 64 (2010): 5–24.

46. The names of these areas were then in flux, as was the concept of "biology" itself. Garland E. Allen, *Life Science in the Twentieth Century* (New York: John Wiley, 1975); Joseph A. Caron, "'Biology' in the Life Sciences: A Historiographical Contribution," *History of Science* 26 (1988): 223–268; William Coleman, *Biology in the Nineteenth Century: Problems of Form, Function, and Transformation* (New York: Cambridge University Press, 1971). Garland has written: "During the last 40 years of the nineteenth century [virtually every] biological discipline, except perhaps general physiology and

biochemistry, took a second place to, or was actually pressed into the service of evolutionary theory." Allen, *Life Science*, 1.

47. Aside from these two controversies, biological scientists were locked in heavy conflict over the respective merits of older "naturalist" field methods and newer "experimental" (or laboratory) methods, with the latter rising at the expense of the former. Allen, *Life Science*; Hamilton Cravens, *The Triumph of Evolution: American Scientists and the Heredity-Environment Controversy, 1900–1941* (Philadelphia: University of Pennsylvania Press, 1978); Joel B. Hagen, "Experimentalists and Naturalists in Twentieth-Century Botany: Experimental Taxonomy, 1920–1950," *Journal of the History of Biology* 17 (1984): 249–270; Jane Maienschein, introduction to *Defining Biology: Lectures from the 1890s*, ed. Jane Maienschein (Cambridge, MA: Harvard University Press, 1986), 3–50; Pauly, *Promise of American Life*. I do not discuss this controversy because its impact on Veblen was limited.

48. John M. Coulter, "The Future of Systematic Botany," *Botanical Gazette* 16 (1891): 243–254.

49. Richard T. Ely, "The Past and the Present of Political Economy," *JHS*, ser. 2, 3 (1884): 143–202, 195. Cook illustrates how contemporaries defended the practice of classification against charges such as those of Coulter. O. F. Cook, "The Method of Types in Botanical Nomenclature," *Science*, n.s., 12 (1900): 475–481. My discussion of classification builds on Coleman, *Biology in the Nineteenth Century*; Hagen, "Experimentalists and Naturalists"; Sharon E. Kingsland, *The Evolution of American Ecology, 1890–2000* (Baltimore: Johns Hopkins University Press, 2005); Robert E. Kohler, *Lords of the Fly: Drosophila Genetics and the Experimental Life* (Chicago: University of Chicago Press, 2008); and especially Jan Sapp, *The New Foundations of Evolution: On the Tree of Life* (New York: Oxford University Press, 2009).

50. L. H. Bailey, "Neo-Lamarckism and Neo-Darwinism," *American Naturalist* 28 (1894): 661–678, 661.

51. I take the expression "two-step process of variation and natural selection" from Mayr and from Gould, but many other scholars use it as well. Ernst Mayr, *This Is Biology: The Science of the Living World* (Cambridge, MA: Harvard University Press, 1977); Stephen Jay Gould, *The Structure of Evolutionary Theory* (Cambridge, MA: Harvard University Press, 2002).

52. Bailey, "Neo-Lamarckism," 677. On the prolonged dominance of neo-Larmarckian views, see Coleman, *Biology in the Nineteenth Century*; Cravens, *Triumph of Evolution*; Peter J. Bowler, *The Eclipse of Darwinism: Anti-Darwinian Evolution Theories in the Decades around 1900* (Baltimore: Johns Hopkins University Press, 1983); Peter J. Bowler, *Darwin Deleted: Imagining a World without Darwin* (Chicago: University of Chicago Press, 2013); Jan Sapp, *Genesis: The Evolution of Biology* (Oxford: Oxford University Press, 2003); Sapp, *New Foundations of Evolution*. In Chapter 3, I also discuss the Darwinian and Lamarckian evolutionary mechanisms.

53. P. J. van Beneden, *Animal Parasites and Messmates* (New York: Appleton, [1876] 1885), xxii–xix. The phrase "knights of industry" follows the corrected translation of Sapp, *Genesis*, 60. On the subject of mutualism in general, see Jan Sapp, *Evolution by Association: A History of Symbiosis* (Oxford: Oxford University Press, 1994); Sapp, *Genesis*.

54. Jeffrey Sklansky, *The Soul's Economy: Market Society and Selfhood in American Thought, 1820–1920* (Chapel Hill: University of North Carolina Press, 2002).

55. William James, *The Principles of Psychology* (New York: Holt, 1890), 184, 308, 325. On the "new psychology," I draw on Mitchell G. Ash, "Psychology," in *The Modern Social Sciences,* ed. Theodore M. Porter and Dorothy Ross, *The Cambridge History of Science,* vol. 7 (Cambridge: Cambridge University Press, 2003), 251–274. I also draw on Cravens, *Triumph of Evolution;* Merle Curti, *Human Nature in American Thought* (Madison: University of Wisconsin Press, 1980); Robert J. Richards, *Darwin and the Emergence of Evolutionary Theories of Mind and Behavior* (Chicago: University of Chicago Press, 1987); Sklansky, *Soul's Economy.* For an excellent analysis of the "historical sensibility" of James and Dewey, see James T. Kloppenberg, *Uncertain Victory: Social Democracy and Progressivism in European and American Thought, 1870–1920* (New York: Oxford University Press, 1986), 107–114.

56. Peter Novick, *That Noble Dream: The "Objectivity Question" and the American Historical Profession* (Cambridge: Cambridge University Press, 1988); J. Franklin Jameson, *The History of Historical Writing in America* (New York: Houghton, Mifflin, 1891), 141–142. See also Jewett, *Science, Democracy, and the American University,* 48.

57. Stocking wrote, "Turn-of-the-century social scientists were evolutionists almost to a man." George W. Stocking Jr., *Race, Culture, and Evolution* (New York: Free Press, 1968), 112. See also Roscoe C. Hinkle, *Founding Theory of American Sociology, 1881–1915* (Boston: Routledge & Kegan Paul, 1980); Dorothy Ross, *The Origins of American Social Science* (Cambridge: Cambridge University Press, 1991).

58. On the history of anthropology, I draw especially on Lee D. Baker, *From Savage to Negro: Anthropology and the Construction of Race, 1896–1954* (Berkeley: University of California Press, 1998); Stocking, *Race, Culture, and Evolution;* George W. Stocking Jr., *Victorian Anthropology* (New York: Free Press, 1987); Thomas Trautmann, *Lewis Henry Morgan and the Invention of Kinship,* new ed. (Lincoln: University of Nebraska Press, 2008).

59. Trautmann, *Lewis Henry Morgan,* 269; see also Stocking, *Victorian Anthropology,* 46–77.

60. Francis Galton, "Discussion," *Journal of the Anthropological Institute of Great Britain and Ireland* 18: (1889) 270–272, 270; Edward B. Tylor, *On a Method for Investigating the Development of Institutions; Applied to Laws of Marriage and Descent* (London: Harrison, 1889); Lewis Henry Morgan, *Ancient Society Or, Researches in the Human Lines of Human Progress from Savagery, Through Barbarism to Civilization* (New York: Holt, [1877] 1907; J. W. Powell, "From Barbarism to Civilization," *American Anthropologist* 1 (1888): 97–123.

61. Stocking, *Race, Culture, and Evolution,* 122. On the treatment of race in ethnology, I have benefited from Lee D. Baker, *From Savage to Negro: Anthropology and the Construction of Race, 1896–1954* (Berkeley: University of California Press, 1998).

62. Herbert Spencer, *Principles of Sociology,* vol. 3 (New York: Appleton, [1896] 1914), 316.

63. Historian Thomas Leonard writes: "The vital national issues of the late nineteenth century . . . were economic in nature, and public discourse placed economics at the center of a vigorous national debate" over the economic changes that were then underway. Many other historians of the period also emphasize this point. Thomas Leonard, *Illiberal Reformers: Race, Eugenics and American Economics in the Progressive Era* (Princeton, NJ: Princeton University Press, 2016), ix.

64. On the incorporation of economics into colleges and universities, see A. W. Bob Coats, "The Educational Revolution and the Professionalization of American Economics," in *Breaking the Academic Mould: Economists and American Higher Learning in the Nineteenth Century,* ed. William J. Barber, Middletown, CT: Wesleyan University Press, 1988), 340–375; John B. Parrish, "The Rise of Economics as an Academic Discipline: The Formative Years to 1900," *Southern Economic Journal* 34 (1967): 1–16.

65. J. Laurence Laughlin, "The Study of Political Economy in the United States," *JPE* 1 (1892): 1–19, 4.

66. Parrish, "The Rise of Economics"; Mary O. Furner, *Advocacy and Objectivity: A Crisis in the Professionalization of American Social Science, 1865–1905* (New Brunswick NJ: Transaction Books, [1975] 2011), 57.

67. See my discussion of Clark and Ely in Chapters 4 and 5.

68. I have benefited from Furner's discussion of the founding of the AEA and the surrounding debate in *Science.* In this debate, which ran from April to July 1886, Ely, along with Henry C. Adams, Edwin James, Richmond Mayo-Smith, and Edwin Seligman, spoke for the Younger School, while Arthur Hadley, Simon Newcomb, and Frank Taussig spoke for the Older School. Furner, *Advocacy and Objectivity.* Also valuable on these topics is Haskell, who considers the earlier reform-oriented American Social Science Association as well. Haskell, *Emergence of Professional Social Science.*

69. AV to JD. May 3, 1925, JDP.

70. *AO,* 132, 138–139; *IG,* 319. I cite these late works—from 1923 and 1915—because they contain the fullest reports Veblen gave of rural America *and* because the impressions of farmers and townsmen that Veblen builds on in these reports most likely derived from the time he spent in Minnesota and Iowa during the 1880s. After that period, he never again lived in farm country for any sustained length of time.

71. Thorstein Veblen, "The Army of the Commonweal," *JPE* 2 (June 1984): 456–461, 459.

72. AV to JD, March 19, 1925; John Edward Veblen to JD, undated, JDP. I offer no interpretation of "democratic" because it is unclear from Ed's statement how he was using the term. One possibility is that he meant "democratic" abstractly as a way of organizing a society; a second that he was referring concretely to the Democratic Party of the 1880s and its (pro-business) views; a third that he was speaking anachronistically of policy reforms (of the New Deal type) that people at a later date called "democratic." My best guess is that Ed had the last meaning in mind, although the first would be closest to an accurate description of Thorstein Veblen's own position, and the second the most inaccurate.

73. John Edward Veblen to JD, undated, and March 14, 1930, JDP.

74. TV to Sarah Hardy, December 15, 1895, TV-UofC, reproduced in *JJTV,* 191. The university library was at the State University of Iowa, a facility Veblen apparently used extensively when he was staying with Andrew's family in Iowa City in 1885 and 1886.

75. *IW,* 85.

76. JD to AV, September 11, 1925 [date interpolated], JDP. On ghostwriting, Thomas Harry Williams, *P. G. T. Beauregard: Napoleon in Gray* (Louisiana State University Press, Baton Rouge, 1955), 317.

77. TV to Anderson, May 1, 1890, RBAP. Veblen told Anderson that he intended the translation to be "rather popular than scholarly," April 11, 1890, RBAP.

78. *LS*, vi–x, xiii. On the stature of the *Saga*, see Vigfusson (whom Veblen cited). Gudbrand Vigfusson, "Prolegomena," in *Sturlunga Saga*, ed. Gudbrand Vigfusson (Oxford: Clarendon, 1878), xvii–cciii. On popular interest in the sagas, see Henry van Brunt, "The Statue of Leif Erikson," *Atlantic Monthly* 57 (June 1866): 813–815. For a discussion of Veblen's work on the translation in the early 1920s, see Russell H. Bartley and Sylvia E. Yoneda, "Thorstein Veblen on Washington Island: Traces of a Life," *International Journal of Politics, Culture and Society* 7 (1994): 589–613, 594–595.

In terms of anthropologists' distinctions among savage, barbarian, and civilized stages of evolution, Veblen, who largely accepted this stadial model, viewed the Viking age as "barbarian." In *IW* and *IG*, he considers the earlier "savage" period in the history of the Nordic and Baltic peoples, presenting them as peaceful and work-driven. For a valuable discussion of this theme in Veblen's work, see Jonathan Matthew Schwartz, "Tracking-Down the Nordic Spirit in Thorstein Veblen's Sociology," *Acta Sociologica* 33 (1990): 115–124.

79. J. W. Powell, "Letter of Transmittal," *Second Annual Report of the Bureau of Ethnology to the Secretary of the Smithsonian Institution, 1880–81* (Washington, DC: Government Printing Office, 1882), iii. Franz Boas, "The Central Eskimo," *Sixth Annual Report of the Bureau of Ethnology to the Secretary of the Smithsonian Institution, 1884–85* (Washington, DC: Government Printing Office, 1888).

80. Edward Bellamy, *Looking Backward, 2000–1887* (Orchard Park, NY: Broadview Literary Texts [1888], 2003), 47–48, 62, 72, 75, 101, 177, 179. For some of the scholars who have emphasized Veblen's debt to Bellamy, see Stephen Edgell and Rick Tilman, "The Intellectual Antecedents of Thorstein Veblen: A Reappraisal," *Journal of Economic Issues* 23 (1989): 1003–1026; Donald R. Stabile, "Thorstein Veblen and His Socialist Contemporaries: A Critical Comparison," in *Thorstein Veblen: Critical Assessments*, vol. 1, ed. John Cunningham Wood (London: Routledge, [1982] 1993); Rick Tilman, "The Utopian Vision of Edward Bellamy and Thorstein Veblen," in *Thorstein Veblen: Critical Assessments*, vol. 1., ed. Wood, 321–338; Rick Tilman, *The Intellectual Legacy of Thorstein Veblen: Unresolved Issues* (Westport, CT: Greenwood Press, 1996). I have greatly benefited from the discussion of Bellamy in John L. Thomas, *Alternative America: Henry George, Edward Bellamy, and Henry Demarest Lloyd and the Adversary Tradition* (Cambridge, MA: Harvard University Press, 1983).

81. Ellen Veblen to Sarah Hardy Gregory, undated, TV-UoC; reproduced in JJTV, 201–204. The Jorgensens, plausibly, date the letter as 1897. Theirs is the fullest account of these years in the lives of the Veblens, JJTV, 24–28.

82. Ellen Veblen to Gregory, undated, TV-UoC; reproduced in JJTV, 203. On Veblen's absorption in the *Saga*, see AV to JD, July 18, 1925; John Edward Veblen to JD, undated, both in JDP; JDTV, 68.

83. The statement about the Veblen "bohemian" lifestyle is that of Harriet Rolfe Dagg, in a 1933 letter to Dorfman. JJTV, 26.

84. On William Strong, I draw on Richard White, *Railroaded*, 372–378. Bartley and Bartley suggest that the Rolfe family's financial setback proved relatively short-lived. Russell H. Bartley and Sylvia E. Bartley, "In the Company of T. B. Veblen: A Narrative of Biographical Recovery," *International Journal of Politics, Culture and Society* 13

(1999): 273–331, 289. Veblen himself linked the start of his job search with the abatement of his illness, as he explained to Sumner in a letter dated August 22, 1889: "I have now so far recovered as to feel quite safe on that [health] score, in undertaking the work" of an academic appointment. TV to Sumner, Group 291, Series 1, Box 29, WGSP.

85. AV to JD, November 9, 1929, JDP.

86. Letters from Adams, August 28, 1889; from Sumner, September 3, 1889; and from Porter, undated, all in Vol. 46, AVP.

87. This information on Andrew's efforts to find a position for Thorstein is contemporaneous with the events he describes. It comes from his "day books," which are small appointment and account books, for the years in question. Because these books consist mainly of jottings, I have had to reconstruct them to pin down the account I give in the text. Day Books 2 and 3, Vol. 44, AVP. I learned of this information from Bartley and Bartley, "In the Company of T. B. Veblen," which contains an excellent treatment of this period in Veblen's life.

88. TV to Anderson, May 1, 1890, and June 16, 1890, RBAP.

89. AV to JD, February 17, 1926, JDP; John Edward Veblen to JD, April 9, 1930, JDP. The position at St. Olaf was a special case. There, Veblen ran into objections over his religious beliefs (or lack thereof), in an episode discussed in Kenneth Bjork, ed., "Thorstein Veblen and St. Olaf's College: A Group of Letters by Thorbjorn N. Mohn," *Studies and Records* [of the Norwegian-American Historical Association] 15 (1949): 122–130. On the other hand, neither Andrew nor Ed, when discussing Thorstein's efforts to get a position at any of the state universities to which he applied, make any reference to religion as a factor in his lack of success. That Thorstein had the support of Noah Porter perhaps provided bona fides on this score.

90. *HL,* 31.

91. TV to Anderson, May 1, 1890, and June 16, 1890, RBAP.

92. I am not counting here any pieces on economics Veblen may have produced as a ghostwriter.

93. TV to Sumner, April 30, 1891, WGSP; TV to Ball, January 12, 1891, JDP.

94. John Edward Veblen to JD, undated, and March 9, 1931, JDP; AV to JD, May 3, 1925, JDP.

95. Thorstein Veblen to "Registration, Cornell University," November 25, 1890, TV-CU. Reproduced in Francesca Lidia Viano, "Ithaca Transfer: Veblen and the Historical Profession," *History of European Ideas* 35 (2009): 38–61, 54.

7. Young Economist

1. Over the years I have worked on the book, I have not come across anyone else who fits this description, although this absence of evidence is not conclusive proof of the point. In the natural sciences, there may well have been a few exceptions; and in the social sciences and the humanities, there were many American PhD holders who also did some graduate work in Europe (though not enough to earn a doctorate) either before or after receiving their American doctorates.

2. On the history of Ithaca, I draw on Henry Edward Abt, *Ithaca* (Ithaca, NY: Kellog, 1926). I take Adams's quote from A. W. Bob. Coats, "Henry Carter Adams," *British and American Economic Essays,* vol.1, *On the History of Economic Thought,*

ed. A. W. Bob Coats (London: Routledge, 1968), 365–385, 374. On the university's wealth from a combination of state support and a private endowment from Ezra Cornell, see Morris Bishop, *A History of Cornell* (Ithaca, NY: Cornell University Press, 1962), 258.

3. The statement "to teach such branches" is from the federal Morrill Act of 1862, quoted in Bishop, *History of Cornell,* 58.

4. Quoted in Glenn Altschuler, *Andrew D. White—Educator, Historian, Diplomat* (Ithaca, NY: Cornell University Press, 1979), 87.

5. For the history of Cornell, as recounted in this paragraph and the next, I draw mainly on Altschuler, *Andrew D. White;* Bishop, *History of Cornell;* Roger L. Geiger, *To Advance Knowledge: The Growth of American Research Universities, 1900–1940* (New Brunswick, NJ: Transaction, [1986] 2004). For a valuable contemporaneous perspective, see Thomas Waterman Hewett, "The History of Cornell University in the Twenty-Five Years of Its Existence, 1868–1893," in *Landmarks of Tompkins County, New York,* ed. John H. Selkreg (Syracuse, NY: Mason, 1894), 396–596; Thomas Waterman Hewett, *Cornell University, A History,* 4 vols. (New York: University Publishing Society, 1905). Bishop's book and Hewett's 1905 volumes discuss Cornell's heavy emphasis on science.

6. Andrew D. White, "Historical Instruction in the Course of History and Political Science at Cornell University," *Methods of Teaching History,* vol. 1, ed. G. Stanley Hall (Boston: Ginn, Heath & Company, 1884), 73–76, 73–74.

7. According to Harvard philosopher Josiah Royce, who monitored the contemporaneous scene carefully, Cornell (more so than Johns Hopkins even) carried to a "high development . . . the whole departmental tendency of the time." Josiah Royce, "Present Ideals of American University Life," *Scribner's Magazine* 10 (1891): 376–388, 386.

8. On Veblen's enrollment status, I follow the excerpt of Veblen's Cornell transcript that was sent to Dorfman by Bessie E. Otterson, secretary of Cornell Graduate School, December 31, 1929, JDP (hereafter Veblen Transcript). The volumes of *CornlUR* 1890–1891, 1891–1892, and 1892 describe the subdivisions of the School of History and Political Science. Comparing these volumes shows these divisions in considerable flux from year to year.

9. On the organization of graduate education at Cornell, see Bishop, *History of Cornell,* 163–164; Hewett, "History of Cornell University," 428, 565–574; Hewett, *Cornell University,* vol. 2, 126–134, 379–401. On the loan, see John Edward Veblen to JD, undated, JDP.

In a 1928 biographical sketch, Homan told a story about Veblen's funding at Cornell: "Turning up from somewhere at Cornell University in 1891, unkempt and penniless, Veblen impressed Professor J. Laurence Laughlin . . . and was granted a teaching fellowship." Paul T. Homan, *Contemporary Economic Thought* (London: Harper and Brothers, 1928), 110. Dorfman later embellished this (without giving any source for his statement): "Laughlin often told the story of his first meeting with Veblen. He was sitting in his study in Ithaca when an anaemic-looking person, wearing a coonskin cap and corduroy trousers, entered [and] told Laughlin of his academic history. . . . The fellowships had all been filled, but Laughlin was so impressed with the quality of the man that he went to the president and . . . secured a special grant." JD*TV,* 79–80. This account has often been recycled in books about Veblen, but lacks the ring of credibility, even down to the details of Veblen's "unkempt" appearance (see Chapter 9 note 57). Cornell's records contain no evidence to indicate Veblen received a fellowship (or other university funding) until the 1891–1892 academic year.

10. Veblen Transcript; TV, "Application of Graduate Student," January 9, 1891, TV-CU. The latter document is reproduced in Francesca Lidia Viano, "Ithaca Transfer: Veblen and the Historical Profession," *History of European Ideas* 35 (2009): 38–61, 56–57.

11. Compared with the weak job market in philosophy and the social sciences (political economy excepted), employment prospects for historians were encouraging. "Between 1884 and 1894 the number of full-time [college and university] teachers of history skyrocketed, from twenty to more than a hundred"; Ray Allen Billington, *Frederick Jackson Turner: Historian, Scholar, Teacher* (New York: Oxford University Press, 1973), 63.

12. *CornlUR* 1890–1891, 1891–1892, 1892. Callender discusses the changing relationship between the disciplines of economic and history during this period. Guy S. Callender, "The Position of American Economic History," *American Historical Review* 19 (1913): 80–97.

13. On Veblen's intellectual relationship to Tyler and Tuttle, I draw heavily on Francesca Lidia Viano, "Ithaca Transfer: Veblen and the Historical Profession," *History of European Ideas* 35 (2009): 38–61.

14. For information on Tyler's biography, I draw on Herbert B. Adams, "New Methods of Study in History," *JHS*, ser. 2, 1–2 (1884): 25–137; Howard Mumford Jones, foreword to *The Literary History of the American Revolution, 1763–1783*, by Moses Coit Tyler (New York: Frederick Ungar, 1949), v–viii; Michael Kammen, *Selvages and Biases* (Ithaca, NY: Cornell University Press, 1987).

15. Moses Coit Tyler, "The Party of the Loyalists in the American Revolution," *American Historical Review* 1 (1895): 24–45, 26–27; Moses Coit Tyler, *A History of American Literature*, 2 vols. (New York: Putnam, 1878), 85, 207; Moses Coit Tyler, "President Witherspoon in the American Revolution," *American Historical Review* 1 (1896): 671–679, 10; Moses Coit Tyler, *The Literary History of the American Revolution, 1763–1783*, 2 vols. (New York: Frederick Ungar, [1897] 1949), ix. Tyler's two courses are listed on the Veblen Transcript. To what extent Veblen actually "attended" these courses is uncertain, however. Since both were combined undergraduate-graduate courses, the lectures may well have been rather elementary for Veblen. Possibly, therefore, he and Tyler agreed that he would do the work expected without being physically present in the lecture hall.

16. Tyler, *Literary History*, vol. 1, v–vii and 83–92.

17. For biographical information on Tuttle, I draw on Herbert B. Adams, "Biographical Sketch of Herbert Tuttle," in *History of Prussia under Frederic the Great, 1756–1757*, Herbert Tuttle (Boston: Houghton Mifflin, 1896), xi–xlvi. Tuttle's grade book is in Box 1, HTP. In this grade book, dated for the 1890–1891 academic year, Tuttle penciled in Veblen's name and then scratched it out, with no grade indicated. The reasons for this are anyone's guess.

18. Notes for Lecture Courses, Boxes 1 and 2, HTP. These notes are specifically not dated, which is appropriate since Tuttle taught his courses multiple times from his arrival at Cornell in the early 1880s to his death in the early 1890s. However, from in-

ternal evidence (including an examination dated March 1891), it appears that the extant version of the notes broadly coincides with Veblen's time at Cornell.

19. Herbert Tuttle, *History of Prussia,* 4 vols. (Boston: Houghton Mifflin, 1884–1896).

20. Herbert Tuttle, "The Despotism of Party," *Atlantic Monthly* 54 (1884): 374–384, 1, 28, 108, 228; Herbert Tuttle, "Academic Socialism," *Atlantic Monthly* 53 (1883): 200–203, 209. As I discussed in Chapter 5, the charge of government "paternalism" was a thread in Sumner's thinking, as well as in mugwump thought more generally.

21. Clair Edward Morris Jr., "J. Laurence Laughlin: An Economist and His Profession," unpublished PhD diss., University of Wisconsin-Madison, 1972, 16.

22. AV to JD, May 3, 1925, JDP.

23. Laughlin's courses are described in the *CornlUR* 1890–1891, 101. For "laboratory method" and "independent research," see J. Laurence Laughlin, "Teaching in Economics," *Atlantic Monthly* 77 (1896): 682–688, 685–687. For "economic scientists," see Morris, "J. Laurence Laughlin," 18. For "think independently," see Wesley C. Mitchell, "J. Laurence Laughlin," *JPE* 49 (1941): 875–881, 880.

24. On "Uncle Larry," see Lucy Sprague Mitchell, *Two Lives: The Story of Wesley Clair Mitchell and Myself* (New York: Simon and Schuster, 1953), 86. (It would have been odd for Veblen to use the nickname since he was only seven years younger than Laughlin.) For other positive assessments of Laughlin's teaching, see Herbert Davenport, *Value and Distribution* (Chicago: University of Chicago Press, 1908); Alvin S. Johnson, *Pioneer's Progress: An Autobiography* (New York: Viking, 1952); John U. Nef, "James Laurence Laughlin (1850–1933)," *JPE* 75 (1967): 779–781. For more on mixed assessments, see Alfred Bornemann, *J. Laurence Laughlin: Chapters in the Career of an Economist* (Washington, DC: American Council on Public Affairs, 1940); Ellen Fitzpatrick, *Endless Crusade: Women Social Scientists and Progressive Reform* (New York: Oxford University Press, 1990). Fitzpatrick also discusses Laughlin's strong efforts to encourage the research of women graduate students in economics.

25. John Stuart Mill, *Principles of Political Economy,* abr. and suppl. by J. Laurence Laughlin (New York: Appleton, [1884] 1888), 60–64. For Laughlin's biography, see Bornemann, *J. Laurence Laughlin;* A. W. Bob Coats, "The Political Economy Club," in *British and American Economic Essays,* vol. 2 (London: Routledge, [1961] 1993), 225–238; Morris, "J. Laurence Laughlin." On the immediate background to his appointment at Cornell, see Hewett, *Cornell University,* vol. 2, 132–133. Useful on the subject of Laughlin's ideas are Lance Girton and Don Roper, "J. Laurence Laughlin and the Quantity Theory of Money," *JPE* 86 (1978): 599–625; Neil T. Skaggs, "The Methodological Roots of J. Laurence Laughlin's Anti-quantity Theory of Money and Prices," *Journal of the History of Economic Thought* 17 (1995): 1–20.

26. J. Laurence Laughlin, *The Elements of Political Economy* (New York: Appleton, 1887), 11–15.

27. Laughlin, *Political Economy,* 57–58, 117.

28. Mill, *Principles of Political Economy,* 60–64. Laughlin, *Political Economy,* 37. See also Chapter 4 above.

29. J. Laurence Laughlin, "The Study of Political Economy in the United States," *JPE* 1 (1892): 1–19, 6.

30. J. Laurence Laughlin, *The History of Bimetallism in the United States* (New York: Appleton, 1886), 3; J. Laurence Laughlin, "Sketch of the History of Political Economy;" Mill, *Principles of Political Economy,* suppl. by Laughlin, 33–34.

31. For an illustration of this shifting nomenclature, see Arthur T. Hadley, "Recent Tendencies in the Economic Literature," *Yale Review* 3 (1894): 251–260. The "Glossary on Economic Schools" at the end of Chapter 4 provides some context.

32. Historians of economics have often spoken of the international adoption of this approach during this period as the "marginalist revolution." For the purposes of my analysis of Veblen, however, I do not need to enter into the complicated and controversial question whether and to what extent the intellectual developments I am describing amounted to a bona fide "revolution."

33. Francis A. Walker, *Political Economy* (New York: Henry Holt, [1884] 1889), 76; Hadley, "Recent Tendencies," 253.

34. J. Laurence Laughlin, "Marshall's Theory of Value and Distribution," *QJE* 1 (1887): 227–232, 228.

35. J. Laurence Laughlin, "Hobson's Theory of Distribution," *JPE* 12 (1904): 305–326, 309, 310, 326; J. Laurence Laughlin, *Industrial America: Berlin Lectures of 1906* (New York: Scribner's, 1906), 236. Because Laughlin penned his later statements here after Veblen had become a productive scholar in his own right, as well as a sharp critic of marginal utility theory, it is possible that Laughlin may have been echoing Veblen's views at least as much as Veblen was drawing on lessons learned from Laughlin. This reciprocal relationship would have presented Veblen with repetition in another form.

36. On the complex story of the migration of marginal utility doctrines to the United States, I have found most useful two chapters in *The Marginal Revolution in Economics: Interpretation and Evaluation,* ed. R. D. Collison Black, A. W. Coats, and Craufurd D. W. Goodwin (Durham, NC: Duke University Press, 1973): Craufurd D. W. Goodwin, "Marginalism Moves to the New World," 285–304; and George J. Stigler, "The Adoption of Marginal Utility Theory," 305–320. Also useful on this subject are: Robert M. Fisher, *The Logic of Economic Discovery: Neoclassical Economics and the Marginal Revolution* (New York: New York University Press, 1986); Joseph Persky, "The Neoclassical Advent: American Economics at the Dawn of the Twentieth Century," *Journal of Economic Perspectives* 14 (2000): 95–108; George J. Stigler, "Stuart Wood and the Marginal Productivity Theory," *QJE* 61 (1947): 640–649. I return to this topic in Chapter 8.

37. Morris, "J. Laurence Laughlin," 27; Laughlin to William Rainey Harper, August 23, 1902, Box 23, Folder 6, OPR-UoC.

38. J. Laurence Laughlin, *The Study of Political Economy: Hints to Students and Teachers* (New York: Appleton, 1885), 13; J. Laurence Laughlin, *The Elements of Political Economy* (New York: Appleton, 1887): 3–4.

39. J. Laurence Laughlin, "The Study of Political Economy in the United States," 8, note; J. Laurence Laughlin, "Economics and Socialism," *Chautauquan: A Weekly Newsmagazine* 30 (1899): 252–255, 253.

40. Laughlin, *History of Bimetallis*m, 122–124, 129. In the quote running from "vanity" to "jewelry," Laughlin was drawing on the work of English economists, as Viano ("Ithaca Transfer") has pointed out.

41. J. Laurence Laughlin, *Essays on Anglo-Saxon Law* (Boston: Little, Brown, 1876), 183.

42. Laughlin, *Anglo-Saxon Law,* 304.

43. J. Laurence Laughlin, "Economic Effects of Changes of Fashion," *Chautauquan: A Weekly Newsmagazine* 19 (1894): 9–13, 10; J. Laurence Laughlin, "Causes of Agricultural Unrest," *Atlantic Monthly* 78 (1896): 577–585, 580; L. [presumed signature of J. Laurence Laughlin], review of *History of Banking in the United States* by William Graham Sumner, *JPE* 5 (1897): 259–261. According to Morris, although "Laughlin never made any attempt to systematically apply . . . Darwinian principles to economic analysis, . . . he obviously absorbed and accepted [those principles and] his writing . . . is laced through with expressions of convictions and assertions of fact that were consistent with accepted evolutionary doctrines. He was . . . a great popularizer and propagandist for social Darwinian ideas and values in an era that hardly needed more." Morris, "J. Laurence Laughlin," 13.

44. Laughlin, "Sketch," 2; Laughlin, "The Study of Political Economy in the United States."

45. Laughlin, "The Study of Political Economy in the United States," 14–16.

46. Laughlin, *The Elements of Political Economy,* 263–270; J. Laurence Laughlin, "Workingmen's Grievances," *North American Review* 138 (1884): 510–520, 512–513.

47. Laughlin, "Scheme for the Department of Political Economy and Finance in Cornell University," 1891; see http://www.irwincollier.com/cornell-laughlins-scheme-to -expand-economics1891 (accessed July 21, 2020).

48. Adolph C. Miller, review of *An Introduction to English Economic History and Theory* by W. J. Ashley, *JPE* 2 (1893): 103–105; Jeremiah Whipple Jenks "Trusts in the United States," *Economic Journal* 2 (1892): 70–99, 70, 99; Jeremiah Whipple Jenks, "Capitalistic Monopolies and their Relation to the State," *Political Science Quarterly* 9 (1894): 486–509, 486, 506. Wunderlin describes Jenks's "historical-institutional analyses"; Clarence E. Wunderlin Jr., *Vision of a New Industrial Order: Social Science and Labor Theory in America's Progressive Era* (New York: Columbia University Press, 1992), 18–26. On Jenks, see also John Howard Brown, "Jeremiah Jenks: A Pioneer of Industrial Organization?" *Journal of the History of Economic Thought* 26 (2004): 69–89.

49. Veblen did not have extensive contact with Jenks, who wrote a few years later: "I knew Dr. Veblen slightly when he was in Cornell University." Jenks to David Starr Jordon, April 25, 1899, Series I-A, SC 58, Box 20, Folder 210, DSJP.

50. Veblen, "Communication to the Faculty," November 19, 1891, TV-CU. The official administrative consent form, dated November 20, 1891, shows that Tuttle "gave ascent" to Veblen's request "with some reservations," although there are no indications of what those reservations were, TV-CU. These documents are reproduced in Viano, "Ithaca Transfer," 58–59.

51. Laughlin, "Scheme."

52. A. F. Woodford, review of *Introduction to Political Economy* by Richard T. Ely, *Annals* 1 (1890): 320–322, 320; Charles A. Tuttle, "The Wealth Concept: A Study in Economic Theory," *Annals* 1 (1891): 615–634, 626; John Halsey, review of *Luxury* by Emile Leveleye, *Annals* 2 (1891): 123–125, 124.

53. Herbert Spencer, *The Man versus the State* (New York: Appleton, [1884] 1891), 24.

54. Thorstein Veblen, "Some Neglected Points in the Theory of Socialism," *Annals* 2 (1891): 345–362, 345, 348–350, 353–355.

55. Veblen, "Some Neglected Points," 357, 359, 361.

56. This was the third time John Stuart Mill served as Veblen's interlocutor. The previous occasions were, as I have described in earlier chapters, his Carleton commencement address and his paper at Johns Hopkins on land taxation.

57. Capaldi discusses Mill's formulation and subsequent repudiation of the wage-fund doctrine, which Laughlin himself never recanted, as shown in his annotations in Mill, *Principles of Political Economy*, 178–183. See Nicholas Capaldi, *John Stuart Mill: A Biography* (Cambridge: Cambridge University Press, 2004), 353–354. Among Veblen's teachers, Sumner was also a strong proponent of the doctrine. See Herbert Hovenkamp, *Enterprise and American Law, 1836–1937* (Cambridge, MA: Harvard University Press, 1991), 184–195. My understanding of the doctrine is based on Mark Donoghue, "John Elliot Cairnes and the 'Rehabilitation' of the Classical Wage Fund Doctrine," *Manchester School* 66 (1998): 396–417; Robert B. Ekelund Jr. and Robert F. Hebert, *A History of Economic Theory and Method*, 3rd ed. (New York: McGraw-Hill, 1990), 114–117, 170–171; Scott Gordon, "The Wage-Fund Controversy: The Second Round," *History of Political Economy* 5 (1973): 14–35; Hovenkamp, *Enterprise and American Law*, 193–198; Stigler, "Stuart Wood"; Wunderlin, *New Industrial Order*, 3–10. See also the pioneering studies of Stuart Wood, "A Critique of Wages Theories," *Annals* 1 (1891): 426–461; F. W. Taussig, *Wages and Capital* (New York: Appleton, 1896).

58. Quoting Hovenkamp, *Enterprise and American Law*, 196. On the relationship between the wage-fund doctrine and the contemporary class struggle, I draw on Nancy Cohen, *The Reconstruction of American Liberalism, 1865–1914* (Chapel Hill: University of North Carolina Press, 2002), 152–156; John L Thomas, *Alternative America: Henry George, Edward Bellamy, and Henry Demarest Lloyd and the Adversary Tradition* (Cambridge, MA: Harvard University Press, 1983), 102–131.

59. Thorstein Veblen, "Böhm-Bawerk's Definition of Capital and the Source of Wages," *QJE* 6 (1892): 247–250, paraphrasing 249.

60. Eugen V. Böhm-Bawerk, *The Positive Theory of Capital*, trans. William Smart (London: Macmillan, [1888] 1891), 67–69, 419–420; also quoting William Smart's "Translator's Preface," xvi. The "the foremost champion" comment is from James Bonar, "The Austrian Economists and Their View of Value," *QJE* 3 (1888): 1–31, 31.

61. Thorstein Veblen, "Böhm-Bawerk's Definition of Capital and the Source of Wages," *QJE* 6 (January 1892): 247–252, 252.

62. Uriel H. Crocker, "The 'Overproduction' Fallacy," *QJE* 6 (1892): 352–363, 358. Thorstein Veblen, "The Overproduction Fallacy," *QJE* 6 (July 1892): 484–492, 488–490. Several scholars have put overproduction theories in their historical context and discussed the place they occupied in contemporary political debates. See Hovenkamp, *Enterprise and American Law*, 308–312; James Livingston, "The Social Analysis of Economic History and Theory: Conjectures on Late Nineteenth-Century American Development," *American Historical Review* 92 (1987): 69–95; James Livingston, *Pragmatism and the Political Economy of the Cultural Revolution, 1850–1940* (Chapel

Hill: University of North Carolina Press, 1994); Richard Schneirov, *Labor and Urban Politics: Class Conflict and the Origins of Modern Liberalism in Chicago, 1864–1897* (Urbana: University of Illinois Press, 1998), 185–191.

63. *CornlUR* 1890–1891, 140. TV, "Communication to the Faculty," November 19, 1891, TV-CU.

64. T. B. Veblen to Thomas Goodspeed, May 26, 1892, Subseries 7, Box 14, Folder 13, WRHP.

65. A 1932 statement by Frank Lloyd Wright, in Donald L. Miller, *City of the Century: The Epic of Chicago and the Making of America* (New York: Simon and Schuster, 1996), 185.

66. John Dewey quoted in Louis Menand, *The Metaphysical Club* (New York: Farrar, Straus and Giroux, 2001), 298.

67. Robert Herrick quoted in Robert Morss Lovett, *All Our Years* (New York: Viking, 1948), 55; A. B. Maynard to JD, February 1933, JDP; *TLC*, 138.

68. William Cronon, *Nature's Metropolis: Chicago and The Great West* (New York: Norton, 1991), 85.

69. W. S. Stead, *If Christ Came to Chicago!* (London: Office of the Review of Reviews, 1894), 105. Henry Blake Fuller, *The Cliff Dwellers* (New York: Harper, 1893), 162. The figure on the number of millionaires is from Schneirov, *Labor and Urban Politics*, 299. On Norwegian-Americans in Chicago, I rely on Odd Lovoll, *A Century of Urban Life* (Northfield, MN: Norwegian-American Historical Association, 1988). On general economic conditions in Chicago in the 1890s, I draw here and in the following paragraphs on Cronon, *Nature's Metropolis*; Licht, *Industrializing America*; Donald L. Miller, *City of the Century*; Robert B. Spinney, *City of Big Shoulders: A History of Chicago* (DeKalb: Northern Illinois University Press, 2000).

70. Diary notes, Vol. 44, AVP. The secondary literature on the Chicago Exposition is enormous. In this paragraph and the two that follow I draw on John E. Findling, *Chicago's Great World's Fairs* (Manchester, UK: Manchester University, 1994); Chaim M. Rosenberg, *America at the Fair: Chicago's 1893 World's Columbian Exposition* (Chicago: Arcadia Publishing, 2008); and especially Robert W. Rydell, *All the World's a Fair* (Chicago: University of Chicago Press, 1984), 38–71. "Vast department stores" is from Miller, *City of the Century*, 492.

71. On the Congress of Evolutionists, see Rydell, *All the World's a Fair*, 68. Brinton's statement is reported by W. H. Holmes, "The World's Fair Congress of Anthropology," *American Anthropologist* 6 (1893): 423–434, 423–424. The "spiral of evolution" appeared in an article in a November 1893 *Chicago Tribune*, quoted in Rydell, *All the World's a Fair*, 65. On the anthropological displays of evolution and "race" at the fair, I draw also on Lee D. Baker, *From Savage to Negro: Anthropology and the Construction of Race, 1896–1954* (Berkeley: University of California Press, 1998); Burton Benedict, "International Exhibitions and National Identity," *Anthropology Today* 7 (1991): 5–9; Timothy Mitchell, "The World as Exhibition," *Comparative Studies in Society and History* 31 (1989): 217–236; David Jenkins, "Object Lessons and Ethnographic Displays," *Comparative Studies in Society and History* 36 (1994): 242–270. For valuable contemporaneous descriptions, see C. Staniland Wake, "The World's Columbian Exposition, 1893," *Journal of the Anthropological Institute of Great Britain and*

Ireland 21 (1892): 320–321; Frederick Starr, "Anthropology at the World's Fair," *Popular Science Monthly* 43 (1893): 610–621.

72. I do not vouch for the historical accuracy of the figures in this paragraph. The secondary literature offers various numbers, and the source of these is often unclear. However, since my concern is with the situation as it appeared to those observing it, I cite contemporaneous estimates as these were summarized by Veblen's future colleague Carlos C. Closson. Carlos C. Closson, "The Unemployed in American Cities," *QJE* 8 (1894): 168–217. I take the statistic on starvation from Miller, *City of the Century,* 535.

73. This statement, from 1890, is quoted in Schneirov, *Labor and Urban Politics,* 318.

74. On the history of labor movement and socialism in Chicago, I draw primarily on Schneirov, *Labor and Urban Politics.* I have also benefited from James Green, *Death in the Haymarket* (New York: Anchor Books, 2006); Bruce C. Nelson, *Beyond the Martyrs* (New Brunswick, NJ: Rutgers University Press, 1988); David Ray Papke, *The Pullman Case: The Clash of Labor and Capital in Industrial America* (Lawrence: University of Kansas Press, 1999).

75. The Progressive Movement is one of the largest topics in American historiography. For the limited purposes of the preceding sentences, I have relied mainly on Cohen, *American Liberalism;* Steven J. Diner, *A Very Different Age: Americans of the Progressive Era* (New York: Hill and Wang, 1998); Andrew Feffer, *The Chicago Pragmatists and American Progressivism* (Ithaca, NY: Cornell University Press, 1993); Ellen Fitzpatrick, *Endless Crusade* (New York: Oxford University Press, 1990); Louise W. Knight, *Citizen: Jane Addams and the Struggle for Democracy* (Chicago: University of Chicago Press, 2005); Thomas C. Leonard, "Progressive Era Origins of the Regulatory State and the Economist as Expert," *History of Political Economy* 47 (2015): 49–76; Thomas C. Leonard, *Illiberal Reformers* (Princeton, NJ: Princeton University Press, 2016); Michael McGerr, *A Fierce Discontent* (New York: Oxford University Press, 2003); Dorothy Ross, "Socialism and American Liberalism," *Perspectives in American History* 11 (1978): 7–79; Dorothy Ross, *The Origins of American Social Science* (Cambridge: Cambridge University Press, 1991); Schneirov, *Labor and Urban Politics.*

76. I base my account of the founding of the University of Chicago mainly on John W. Boyer, *The University of Chicago: A History* (Chicago: University of Chicago Press, 2015), 78–79; Daniel Lee Meyer, "The Chicago Faculty and the University Ideal, 1891–1929," 2 vols. (PhD diss., University of Chicago, 1994); Willard J. Pugh, "A 'Curious Working of Cross Purposes' in the Founding of the University of Chicago," *History of Higher Education Annual* 15 (1995): 93–126. But I have learned also from the standard older histories. See Thomas Wakefield Goodspeed, *A History of the University of Chicago* (Chicago: University of Chicago Press, 1916); Thomas Wakefield Goodspeed, *The Story of the University of Chicago* (Chicago: University of Chicago Press, 1925); Richard J. Storr, *Harper's University, The Beginnings: A History of the University of Chicago* (Chicago: University of Chicago Press, 1966). I quote John Dewey's letter, dated July 29, 1894, from Menand, *Metaphysical Club,* 298.

77. Robert Herrick, "My Life," 46–47, Box 3, Folder 10, RHP. Local conditions improved with the construction of the Columbian Exposition, but a January 1894 fire destroyed the fairground facilities that remained after the event closed, leaving the area strewn with "blocks of vacant houses and boarded-up hotels." Jean F. Block, *Hyde Park*

Houses: An Informal History (Chicago: University of Chicago Press, 1978), 61. By that point, however, the campus of the university itself was beginning to fill in with some of the Gothic buildings that still stand today. D. J. R. Bruckner and Irene Macauley, *Dreams in Stone: The University of Chicago* (Chicago: University of Chicago Press, 1976).

78. On Harper's difficulties in recruiting senior faculty, see Boyer, *University of Chicago,* 78–79; William Rainey Harper, *The President's Report,* vol. 1, *The Decennial Publications of the University of Chicago* (Chicago: University of Chicago, 1903), xviii. According to Goodspeed, before the university even opened, Harper received more than a thousand unsolicited applications for faculty positions. Thomas Wakefield, Goodspeed, *William Rainey Harper, First President of the University of Chicago* (Chicago: University of Chicago, 1928), 124.

79. "Greatest university in the world" are the words of Lewis Stuart, who was writing to Harper in 1890 about these plans. Quoted in Boyer, *University of Chicago,* 74. On Harper's iconoclasm, see Albion W. Small, "As University President," *Biblical World* (Memorials of William Rainey Harper) 27 (1906): 216–219, 217.

80. I draw biographical information about Harper from John W. Boyer, *Broad and Christian in the Fullest Sense, Occasional Papers on Higher Education,* no. 15 (Chicago: College of the University of Chicago, [2005] 2015); Gale W. Engle, "William Rainey Harper's Conceptions of the Structuring of the Functions Performed by Educational Institutions" (PhD diss., Stanford University, 1954); Maria Freeman, "Study with Open Mind and Heart: William Rainey Harper's Inductive Method of Teaching the Bible" (PhD diss., University of Chicago, 2005); Goodspeed, *Harper;* Meyer, "Chicago Faculty"; George E. Vincent, "William Rainey Harper," in *The William Rainey Harper Memorial Conference,* ed. Robert N. Montgomery (Chicago: University of Chicago Press, 1938), 3–23.

81. William Rainey Harper, "Address of Welcome," *Publications of the American Economic Association,* 3rd ser., 6 ([1899] 1905): 26–28, 240; Harper, *President's Report,* xviii; Robert Herrick, "The University of Chicago," *Scribner's Magazine* 18 (1895): 399–417, 404.

82. William J. Barber, "Political Economy in an Atmosphere of Academic Entrepreneurship: The University of Chicago," in *Breaking the Academic Mould: Economists and American Higher Learning in the Nineteenth Century,* ed. William J. Barber (Middletown, CT: Wesleyan University Press, 1988), 241–265, 245; Harper, *President's Report,* xix.

83. Harper (1892) quoted in Pugh, "Cross Purposes," 112. Harper (1892 and 1894) quoted in Goodspeed, *A History,* 144, 319. Based on my examination of successive volumes of *UoC-AR* for the 1890s, it appears that Harper was somewhat inconsistent in how he distinguished and titled the positions I've just described as reader/assistant, tutor/associate, and instructor. My description represents my best approximation of Harper's usual practice, although he seems to have varied it from time to time.

84. Harper (1894) quoted in Goodspeed, *A History,* 319.

85. E. H. Moore to Alonso Parker, October 25, 1914, Box 4, Folder 12, Thomas W. Goodspeed Papers, Special Collections Research Center, University of Chicago Library.

86. Dewey to Harper, as quoted in George Dykhuizen, *The Life and Mind of John Dewey* (Carbondale: Southern Illinois University Press, 1973).

87. Shailer Mathews, *New Faith for Old: An Autobiography* (New York: Macmillan, 1936), 53.

88. Harper (1894) quoted in Boyer, *Broad and Christian,* 70; William R. Harper, *Elements of Hebrew Syntax by An Inductive Method.* (New York: Scribner's 1888), 6; Harper, in *UoC-QC* 1893, 23. On Harper's biblical work, I quote Boyer, *Broad and Christian,* 29, 35–35; Freeman, "Open Mind," 114.

89. While cautioning against overestimating the influence of the German university on Harper's design of his university, Boyer writes: "The presence of American-born scholars at Chicago who were trained at one or more German universities was extraordinary. Of the 189 members of the faculty . . . in 1896–97, seventy-six had taken degrees or advanced training at a European university, and sixty-five of those had studied at one or more German universities. Thus, over one-third of the faculty members at the new University . . . had direct personal experience with the educational and research practices of the German university system." Boyer, *Broad and Christian,* 134.

90. Philip J. Pauly, *Controlling Life: Jacques Loeb and the Engineering Ideal in Biology* (New York: Oxford University Press, 1987), 91. See also Jane Maienschein, "Whitman at Chicago: Establishing a Chicago Style of Biology?" in *The American Development of Biology,* ed. Ronald Rainger, Keith R. Benson, and Jane Maienschein (New Brunswick, NJ: Rutgers University Press, 1988), 151–182, 168. I am paraphrasing Mitman, who discusses the Chicagoans' deliberate move away from taxonomy. Gregg Mitman, *The State of Nature* (Chicago: University of Chicago Press, 1992), 3, 12–13. For an examination of the "community of Darwinian scientists and social scientists" (Whitman and Loeb included) in relation to Veblen's work, see Emilie Raymer, "A Man of His Time: Thorstein Veblen and the University of Chicago Darwinists," *Journal of the History of Biology* 46 (2013): 669–698. Pauly calls attention to a subgroup of scientists, mainly from the physical sciences and European immigrants, who stood apart from this evolutionary consensus. Pauly, *Controlling Life,* 71.

91. These aspects of Whitman's thinking are discussed in Richard W. Burkhardt Jr., "Charles Otis Whitman, Wallace Craig, and the Biological Study of Animal Behavior in the United States, 1898–1925," in *The American Development of Biology,* ed. Ronald Rainger, Keith R. Benson, and Jane Maienschein (New Brunswick, NJ: Rutgers University Press, 1998), 185–218. Whitman favorably cited the work of leading contemporary psychologists such as James Mark Baldwin, William James, and Conwy Lloyd Morgan, all of whom were reference points for Veblen. Geoffrey M. Hodgson, *The Evolution of Institutional Economics: Agency, Structure and Darwinism in American Institutionalism* (London: Routledge, 2004).

92. C. O. Whitman, "The Naturalist's Occupation," in *Biological Lectures Delivered at the Marine Biological Laboratory of Woods Hole in the Summer Session of 1890* (Boston: Ginn & Company, 1891), 27–52, 46; C. O. Whitman, "Myths in Animal Psychology," *Monist* 9 (1899): 524–537, 524; C. O. Whitman, "Specialization and Organization," in *Biological Lectures Delivered at the Marine Biological Laboratory of Woods Hole in the Summer Session of 1890* (Boston: Ginn & Company, 1891), 1–26, 1–2, 5. I cite two passages where Whitman spoke of "cumulative" development, in anticipation of Veblen's use of the same concept. For further illustrations of research on parasites that was going on at the University of Chicago, see C. M. Child, "Abnormalities in the Cestode Moniezia expansa, I," *Biological Bulletin* 1 (1900): 215–250; Henry Chandler Cowles, "The Ecological Relations of the Vegetation in the Sand Dunes of Lake Michigan," *Botanical Gazette* 27 (1899): 167–202.

93. Jacques Loeb, "On Some Facts and Principles of Physiological Morphology," in *The Mechanistic Conception of Life*, by Jacques Loeb (Chicago: University of Chicago Press, [1893] 1913), 86, 104, 109; Jacques Loeb, *Comparative Physiology of the Brain and Comparative Psychology* (New York, G. P. Putman's Sons, 1900), 6–11, 197–198, 233–34; Jacques Loeb (1903) quoted in Pauly, *Controlling Life*, 112. In speaking of an "instinct of workmanship," Loeb drew explicitly on Veblen, just as Veblen's notions of "tropisms" and "instincts" built in part on Loeb's work. Charles Rasmussen and Rick Tilman, *Jacques Loeb: His Science and Social Activism and Their Philosophical Foundations* (Philadelphia: American Philosophical Society, 1998), 92–121. My discussion of Loeb is heavily indebted to Pauly, who describes the contemporary branding of Loeb as an "iconoclast." Pauly, *Controlling Life*, 102–103.

94. I discussed this pragmatist view of action in Chapter 2; it provides one of the main underpinnings of my argument.

95. Despite their years together at the University of Chicago, Dewey later wrote to Dorfman that, although he was "acquainted" with Veblen and drew on his work, the two did not have much "personal contact." Dewey to JD, January 27, 1930 and September 16, 1932, JDP. For his part, Veblen also drew favorably on Dewey's work.

96. John Dewey, *The Study of Ethics: A Syllabus* (Ann Arbor, MI: George Wahr, 1897), 262–263; John Dewey, *Outlines of a Critical Theory of Ethics* (Ann Arbor, MI: Register Publishing Company, 1891), 127; John Dewey, *Psychology*, 3rd rev. ed. (New York: Harper and Brothers, 1897), 13, 61; James H. Tufts, "Social Psychology," *Psychological Review* 2 (1895): 305–309, 307.

97. John Dewey, "Moral Theory and Practice," *International Journal of Ethics* 1 (1891): 186–203, 203; Dewey, *Outlines*, 169–170; John Dewey, "Evolution and Ethics," *Monist* 8 (1898): 3–23, 10, 17–19.

98. John Dewey, "The Evolutionary Method as Applied to Morality," in *John Dewey: The Middle Works, 1899–1924*, vol. 2, ed. Jo Ann Boydson (Carbondale: Southern Illinois University Press, [1902] 1983), 3–23, 8.

99. On the founding and early development of this department, I draw on Andrew Abbott, *Department and Discipline: Chicago Sociology at One Hundred* (Chicago: University of Chicago Press, 1999); Martin Bulmer, *The Chicago School of Sociology: Institutionalization, Diversity, and the Rise of Sociological Research* (Chicago: University of Chicago Press, 1984); Charles Camic, "Three Departments in Search of a Discipline: Localism and Interdisciplinary Interaction in American Sociology, 1890–1940," *Social Research* 62 (1995): 1003–1033; Steven J. Diner, "Department and Discipline: The Department of Sociology at the University of Chicago, 1892–1930," *Minerva* 13 (1975): 514–553; George W. Stocking Jr., *Anthropology at Chicago* (Chicago: University of Chicago Library, 1979). Abbott analyzes the enormous literature on the "Chicago School of Sociology" in Abbott, *Department and Discipline*. For a discussion on the parallel development of the Chicago's department of political science, see Michael Heaney and John Mark Hansen, "Building the Chicago School," *American Political Science Review* 100 (2006): 589–596.

100. Albion W. Small, "The Relation of Sociology to Economics," *JPE* 3 (1895): 169–184, 170–171; Albion W. Small, "The Organic Concept of Society," *Annals* 5 (1895): 88–94, 88; Albion W. Small, "Static and Dynamic Sociology," *AJS* 1 (1895): 195–209, 204; Albion W. Small, "The Era of Sociology," *AJS* 1 (1895): 1–15, 1; Albion W. Small, Review of *Economics* by Arthur T. Hadley, *AJS* 2: (1897): 739–740, 740; Albion W. Small

and George Vincent, *An Introduction to the Study of Society* (New York: American Book Company, 1894), 15. For Small's biography, I used Vernon K. Dibble, *The Legacy of Albion Small* (Chicago: University of Chicago Press, 1975); Edward Cary Hayes, "Albion Woodbury Small," in *American Masters of Social Science,* ed. Howard W. Odum (New York: Holt, 1927), 149–187.

101. Small and Vincent, *Study of Society,* 87, 165–166; Small, "Organic Concept of Society," 92.

102. Small and Vincent, *Study of Society,* 91. Small lays out his teleological views of evolution in Albion W. Small, *Syllabus: Introduction to the Science of Sociology* (Waterville, ME: Mail Office, 1890).

103. Starr and Thomas both produced work that fell outside the category of comparative ethnology. Thomas, in particular, had ahead of him a career as a sociologist concerned with immigration, personality development, and life histories. In the period when he and Veblen were both faculty members at the University of Chicago, however, Thomas's focus, as Abbott and Egloff have summarized it, was "research and teaching the comparative ethnology of non-industrial societies." Andrew Abbott and Rainer Egloff, "The Polish Peasant in Oberlin and Chicago," *American Sociologist* 39 (2008): 271–258. I have drawn mainly on this article for information on Thomas.

104. Frederick Starr, "Dress and Adornment," *Popular Science Monthly* 39 (1891): 488–502 and 787–801, 787; Frederick Starr "Dress and Adornment," *Popular Science Monthly* 40 (1891): 44–57 and 194–206, 56; Frederick Starr, *Some First Steps in Human Progress* (Meadville, PA: Flood and Vincent, 1895), 136–143.

105. "Barbarian" marriage practices were a favorite subject among late nineteenth-century anthropologists. George W. Stocking Jr., *Victorian Anthropology* (New York: Free Press, 1987).

106. W. I. Thomas, "The Relation of Sex to Primitive Social Control," *AJS* 3 (1898): 754–776, 753; W. I. Thomas, "The Scope and Method of Folk-Psychology," *AJS* 1 (1896): 434–445, 439. Thomas also taught a course titled the "Origin of Social Institutions," which dealt with "origins and developmental relations of invention, trade, warfare, art, marriage, class distinctions, the professions, [and] legal, political, and ecclesiastical institutions." See *UoC-AR* 1899–1900, 191. The Darwinian aspect of Thomas's thought is most fully on display in W. I. Thomas, "On a Difference in the Metabolism of the Sexes," *AJS* 3 (July 1897): 31–63.

107. Thomas, "Folk-Psychology," 435, 439.

108. William Rainey Harper, *The Trend in Higher Education* (Chicago: University of Chicago Press, 1905), 1, 73. On the politics of the University of Chicago faculty members and their commitment to Progressivism, I draw on Mary Jo Deegan, *Jane Addams and the Men of the Chicago School, 1892–1918* (London: Routledge, 1990); Mary Jo Deegan, *Annie Marion MacLean and the Chicago Schools of Sociology, 1894–1934* (London: Routledge, 2014); Diner, *Very Different Age;* Feffer, *Chicago Pragmatists;* Fitzpatrick, *Endless Crusade;* Pauly, *Controlling Life;* Darnell Rucker, *The Chicago Pragmatists* (Minneapolis, MN: University of Minneapolis Press, 1969); Nadine Weidman, "Psychobiology, Progressivism, and the Anti-progressive Tradition." *Journal of the History of Biology* 29 (1996): 267–308.

109. On the Bemis affair, I draw here and in the following two paragraphs especially on Barber, "Political Economy," 249–225; Harold E. Bergquist Jr., "The Edward W. Bemis

Controversy at the University of Chicago," *American Association of University Professors Bulletin* 58 (1972): 384–393. I also found useful Mary O. Furner, *Advocacy and Objectivity* (New Brunswick NJ: Transaction Books, [1975] 2011), 165–198; Meyer, "Chicago Faculty," 174–177; Storr, *Harper's University,* 83–85, 96–98.

110. On the Pullman strike, I rely on Papke, *Pullman Case,* 1–37. Also useful is Menand, *Metaphysical Club,* 289–316.

111. The statement by Harper, in a July 23, 1894, letter to Bemis, quoted in Bergquist, "Bemis Controversy," 387. Union organizer Eugene Debs applied "rich plunderer" specifically to the owner of the Pullman Company, George Pullman. See Papke, *Pullman Case,* 19. Here I use the expression more broadly.

112. True, this is not how some faculty members perceived the situation during the months when the storm was at its height, as Westbrook has argued with reference to Dewey's alarmed reaction to the Bemis affair. Robert B. Westbrook, *John Dewey and American Democracy* (Ithaca, NY: Cornell University Press, 1991), 91.

113. Harper, in UoC-QC 4, no. 1 (1895), 13; Harper, *President's Report,* xxiii. My discussion here follows Meyer, who also refers to statements of Harper that qualified those I have just quoted. Meyer, "Chicago Faculty," 96–99, 169–172. How fully Harper put his support for freedom of academic expression into practice depended, generally speaking, on the specifics of the situation. Always sensitive to the makeup of an audience, Harper was loathe to use ceremonial public events as occasions for faculty members to air views that might offend.

114. Harry Pratt Judson, "Is Our Republic a Failure?" *AJS* (1895) 1: 28–40, 34–35.

115. Shailer Mathews, "Christian Sociology, V: Wealth," *AJS* 1 (1896): 771–784, 784; Shailer Mathews, "Christian Sociology, VII: The Forces of Human Progress," *AJS* 1 (1896): 274–287, 281.

116. Charles Richmond Henderson, *Social Elements: Institution, Character, Progress* (New York: Scribner's, 1898), 132, 401.

117. Small and Vincent, *Study of Society,* 290–291.

118. Harper, *Trend,* 9, 241. My point in this paragraph is to call attention to the critical strand in the work of these members of the University of Chicago faculty, not to present their full views on the contemporary economic order, which were a mix of criticism and apology, including a strong apology for the institution of the leisure class. Harper, in making a distinction between the "industrial" and "predatory" spirit, may have been building on Veblen, who drew a similar distinction in *TLC* and elsewhere (as chapter 9 will show).

119. These publications are complicated stories in their own right, which the following two paragraphs do not tell. In addition to the themes I am about to describe, many others ran through these publications—and, depending on the year and the audience targeted by a particular publication, some of these other themes went counter to the ones I highlight.

120. UoC-UR 1896–1897, 54, 90, 361; UoC-AR 1893–1894, 48, 53, 59.

121. UoC-AR 1893–1894, 43–44, 135; UoC-AR 1895–1896, 186; UoC-AR 1898–99, 179; UoC-UR 1896–1897, 18, 20–22, 283, 397, 403–404; UoC-UR 1897–1898, 92. For a discussion of the importance of Morgan's work for Veblen's development, see Geoffrey M. Hodgson, "On the Evolution of Thorstein Veblen's Evolutionary Economics," *Cambridge Journal of Economics* 22 (1998): 415–431; Geoffrey M. Hodgson,

How Economics Forgot History: The Problem of Historical Specificity in Social Science (London: Routledge, 2001); Geoffrey M. Hodgson, *The Evolution of Institutional Economics: Agency, Structure and Darwinism in American Institutionalism* (London: Routledge, 2004).

122. Frederick Starr, "Science at the University of Chicago," *Popular Science Monthly* 51 (1897): 784–805; AV to JD, July 12, 1930, JDP. I take this information on faculty office locations from *UoC-QC* 2, no. 3 (1893), 23. Obviously, these locations changed from year to year. Robert Lovett (of the English department) recalled how, in the university's early years, "the small faculty, remote from the city, was drawn together by a common feeling of exile." Robert Lovett, *All Our Years*, 62. The research of Jorgensen and Jorgensen suggests that Veblen was part of this milieu, at least on and off. *JJTV*, 65–84.

123. *UoC-AR* 1892–1893, 18, 114. Even with historical adjustment indicated, this stipend figure is considerably lower than today. In 2020, the stipend for a graduate student in the social sciences in the US fell in the range of $25,000 to $35,000 a year. A more apt comparison, however, is suggested by data citied by historian Nell Painter, who points out that in 1893 the poverty line for an American family was $544 per year. Nell Irvin Painter, *Standing at Armageddon* (New York: Norton, [1987] 2008), xvi. At $520, University of Chicago Senior Fellows who had families fell below the poverty line. Living on his own on this small amount, Veblen would have been better off than some of his peers.

124. TV to Harper, September 3, 1892, and July 18, 1893, Box 84, Folder 12, OPR-UoC.

125. TV to Harper, January 23, 1893, Box 84, Folder 12, OPR-UoC. In this letter, Veblen states explicitly: "I am not registered for any of the courses in the university." This statement is worth noting since other sources erroneously state that Veblen did enroll for courses at this time.

126. Furner, among others, has portrayed the University of Chicago administration as resistant to teaching about socialism. Furner, *Advocacy and Objectivity*, 172. But before the university even opened its doors, Harper planned for the political economy department to offer a course on the subject. See *UoC-Bull* April 1891, 14. In 1893, the year before Veblen first taught his course on socialism, Albion Small offered a seminar, The Psychology, Ethics, and Sociology of Socialism, *UoC-AR* 1892–93, 49. Courses on socialism were common in the period in colleges and universities that provided regular instruction in political economy. J. Laurence Laughlin, "Appendix I: Courses of Study in Political Economy in the United States in 1876 and in 1892–93," *JPE* 1 (1892): 143–151.

127. *UoC-AR* 1892–1893, 40.

128. The words are those of Wesley Mitchell, writing in 1945 about Chicago's political economy department during his student days there in the 1890s. Quoted in Mitchell, *Two Lives*, 85. For similar depictions of the department, see Coats, "Political Economy Club"; John U. Nef, "James Laurence Laughlin (1850–1933)," *JPE* 75 (1967): 779–781; Johan van Overtveldt, *The Chicago School* (Chicago: Algate, 2007). Malcolm Rutherford, "Chicago Economics and Institutionalism," in *The Elgar Companion to the Chicago School of Economics*, ed. Ross B. Emmett (Northampton, MA: Edward Elgar, 2010), 25–29.

Barber takes the opposite view, arguing that the efforts of Harper and Laughlin to build a diverse department "ended disastrously," as the result of Laughlin's reluctance to bring onto his staff economists associated with the Younger School. Barber, "Political Economy." But Laughlin's behavior bears another interpretation: because members of the Younger School, Bemis and Ely in particular, were notoriously doctrinaire, bringing them into the department could well have split it into two hostile camps, rather than allowing it to become a place where different approaches comingled—as Laughlin made possible by appointing Miller and Hill (discussed later).

129. I draw this information about Veblen's salary from a letter dated June 10, 1932, from F. E. Barrett, secretary to the dean of faculties at the University of Chicago, to JD, JDP. On Veblen's ranks and titles, and the years he held them, I use J. Laurence Laughlin, *Twenty-Five Years of the Department of Political Economy, University of Chicago: An Economist and His Profession* (Chicago: privately printed, 1916). On Veblen's salary in relation to his peers, see n. 166 below.

130. Laughlin to Harper, November 25, 1892, Box 57, Folder 13, OPR-UoC.

131. Carlos C. Closson, review of *Darwinism and Race Progress* by John Berry Haycraft, *JPE* 3 (1895): 377–381, 379; Carlos C. Closson, "Disassociation by Displacement: A Phase of Social Selection," *QJE* 10 (1896): 156–186, 167–169; Carlos C. Closson, "Further Data of Anthropo-Sociology," *JPE* 7 (1899): 238–252, 239.

132. William Hill, "Changes in Railway Transportation Rates," *JPE* 2 (1894): 282–284; William Hill, review of *Street Railway Franchises* by Lee Meriwether, *JPE* 5 (1897): 403–409; J. Laurence Laughlin, "Causes of Agricultural Unrest," *Atlantic Monthly* 78 (1896): 577–585, 585; Adolph C. Miller, "National Finance and the Income Tax," *JPE* 3 (1895): 255–288, 271, 274.

133. Quoting Laughlin, "Changes of Fashion," 11; Adolph C. Miller, review of *Public Finance* by C. F. Bastable, *JPE* 1 (1892): 133–142, 136.

Laughlin's views of marginalism are discussed earlier in the chapter. On Miller's views of marginalism, see the string of articles and reviews he published in *JPE* between 1894 and 1899: Adolph C. Miller, review of *Growth of English Industry and Commerce in Modern Times* by W. Cunningham, *JPE* 1 (1893): 475–478; Miller, review of *Introduction to English Economic History;* Adolph C. Miller, review of *Natural Value* by Friedrich von Wieser, *JPE* 2 (1894): 308–309; Adolph C. Miller, review of *Progressive Taxation in Theory and Practice* by Edwin R.S. Seligman, *JPE* 2 (1894): 596–599; Adolph C. Miller, review of *Value and Distribution,* by Charles William Macfarlane, *JPE* 8 (1899): 118–119. Just how serious Laughlin was about encouraging historical research is evident in a 1900 letter to Harper. In it, Laughlin, complaining of "the weakness of [the department's] historical collections," wrote: "If we had no modern equipment in science, we could not offer certain advanced laboratory courses; here very expensive laboratories, of which we are proud. But in our group [of social scientific disciplines], the absence of books and materials acts just as an absence of scientific laboratories would in the science group. Our libraries are our laboratories. Without them we cannot do proper research work." Laughlin to Harper, December 12, 1900, Box 23, Folder 6, OPR-UoC.

134. Laughlin to Jordan, April 29, 1899, Series 1-A, SC 58, Box 20, Folder 211, DSJP. In determining which courses fell into the department's "theoretical" and "practical" categories, I have followed *UoC-AR* 1894–1895, 51–52. (The department's classification did, however, vary somewhat from year to year). As to which courses Veblen taught and when, I have done my best to nail this down by piecing together information from successive issues of the *UoC-AR*.

In Chapter 9, I briefly return to the topic of Veblen's teaching, which has been the subject of many misleading statements in the secondary literature. Combined, these statements have created a highly negative view of Veblen's teaching, which is at odds with the positive picture Laughlin drew for Jordan, as well as with several (though not all) contemporaneous accounts. Adding up the criticisms, Veblen has been charged with (1) an indifferent attitude toward teaching in general; (2) a poor classroom manner, complete with haphazard lectures and mumbling speech; (3) low course enrollments; (4) ineptitude at undergraduate teaching; and (5) a cavalier grading policy of giving all students Cs. Except for the mumbling, none of these charges withstands scrutiny, as I have attempted to document elsewhere, building in part on the work of Paul Uselding, "Veblen as Teacher and Thinker in 1896–1897," *American Journal of Economics and Sociology* 35 (1976): 391–399; Solidelle Fortier Wasser, "Veblen in the Classroom: A View from His Students' Notes," *International Review of Sociology* 14 (2004): 535–542; see Charles Camic, "The Rest of the Resume: Veblen's Teaching and Service Activities," in *Institutions and the Evolution of Capitalism: Essays in Honour of Geoffrey M. Hodgson,* ed. Francesca Gagliardi and David Gindis (Cheltenham, UK: Edward Elgar Publishing, 2019): 62–77. Barber provides evidence that Veblen assigned students As and Bs, as well as Cs. Barber, "Political Economy," 423n70.

135. Veblen, Socialism lectures of January 10, January 16, March 15, June 4, and June 11, 1894, in Sarah Hardy, "Notes for Thorstein Veblen's course on Socialism, Univ. of Chicago, 1894," Series 77, TV-CCA.

136. I draw these descriptions from *UoC-AR* 1895–1896, 58–60. It is unclear, however, which of these official descriptions was authored by Veblen himself. At the University of Chicago then, as in most colleges and universities today, published course descriptions were often written by department chairs and then locked in, remaining roughly the same year after year, even when course instructors changed. Because he was the first faculty member in his department to teach the courses Socialism and American Agriculture, Veblen perhaps played a role, along with Laughlin, in crafting their original descriptions—unlike in the cases of the other courses I have mentioned, since these were courses he inherited. But whether he then taught them to conform to their published descriptions is unknown, although comments he made in another context suggest that courses at the university functioned as "uniform packages" that were handed off, as such, from one staff member to another. *HL,* 82n6.

137. See also Chapter 8.

138. *UoC-AR* 1892–1893, 201; *UoC-QC* 2, no. 3 (1893), 97. Abbott discusses the changing role of departmental versus centralized libraries. Andrew Abbott, "Library Infrastructure for Humanities and Social Scientific Scholarship in the Twentieth Century," in *Social Knowledge in the Making,* ed. Charles Camic, Neil Gross, and Michèle Lamont (Chicago: University of Chicago Press, 2011), 43–88, 56–65.

139. Nonetheless, given the strong interuniversity competition in this period between departments in the same discipline, the economists who edited the *QJE* were disturbed when their rival at Chicago launched the *JPE*. A. W. Bob Coats, "The Educational Revolution and the Professionalization of American Economics," in *Breaking the Academic Mould: Economists and American Higher Learning in the Nineteenth Century,* ed. William J. Barber (Middletown, CT: Wesleyan University Press, 1988), 340–375, 362.

140. On Harper's commitment to university publications, *UoC-AR* 1893–1894, 277–278. Laughlin, "Study of Political Economy," 19; Laughlin to Harper, October 22, 1892, as quoted in Vicky Longawa, "Episodes in the History of the *Journal of Political Economy*," *JPE* 100 (1992): 1087–1091, 1087. Longawa provides a useful short history of the *JPE*.

141. Lovett, *All Our Years*, 69. *UoC-AR* 1894–1895, 18; AV to JD, June 23, 1930, JDP. In "Mr. Cummings's Strictures," which appeared in the *JPE*, Veblen referred to himself "as editor of the *Journal*." Thorstein Veblen, "Mr. Cummings's Strictures on *The Theory of the Leisure Class*," *JPE* 8 (December 1899): 106–117; Thorstein Veblen, "The Barbarian Status of Women," *AJS* 4 (1899): 503–514, 106. In the journal's archival records, which run from 1901 to 1905, correspondents addressed Veblen by both titles (*JPER*).

The passage I have just referenced from *UoC-AR* lists Veblen as the managing editor of the *JPE* as early as the 1894–1895 academic year. I stress this point because most sources erroneously give 1896 as the date Veblen assumed this position.

142. *JPER*. Elsewhere I discuss this aspect of Veblen's journal work more fully. See Camic, "Rest of the Resume."

143. W. G. Langworthy Taylor, "Some Important Phases in the Evolution of the Idea of Value," *JPE* 3 (1895): 414–433; Henry W. Stuart, "The Hedonistic Interpretation of Subjective Value," *JPE* 4 (1895): 64–84; H. H. Davenport, "The Formula of Sacrifice," *JPE* 2 (1894): 561–573.

144. In Camic, "Rest of the Resume," I provide a more general analysis of the contents of the *JPE* under Veblen's editorship.

145. In counting the number of book reviews Veblen wrote during this period and subsequently, I include only the reviews he *signed*.

146. I have discussed the circumstances surrounding Veblen's translation of Cohn's treatise more fully elsewhere. See Charles Camic, "Veblen's Apprenticeship: On the Translation of Gustav Cohn's *System der Finanzwissenschaft*," *History of Political Economy* 42 (2010): 679–721.

147. Gustav Cohn, *The Science of Finance*, trans. T. B. Veblen (Chicago: University of Chicago Press, [1889] 1895), 13, 39, 134, 292, 299, 375. These points are elaborated in Camic, "Veblen's Apprenticeship."

148. Thorstein Veblen, review of *A History of Socialism* by Thomas Kirkup, *JPE* 1 (March 1893): 300–302; Thorstein Veblen, review of *Geschichte des Socialismus und Communismus im 19 Jahrhundert* by Otto Warschauer, *JPE* 1 (March 1893): 302; Thorstein Veblen, review of *The Land-Systems of British India* by B. H. Baden-Powell, *JPE* 2 (December1893): 112–115; Thorstein Veblen, review of *Der Parlamentarismus und die Volksgesetzgebung und die Socialdemokratie* by Karl Kautsky, *JPE* 2 (March 1894): 312–314; Thorstein Veblen, review of *A Study of Small Holdings* by William E. Bear, *JPE* 2 (March 1894): 325–326; Thorstein Veblen, review of *Bibliographie des Socialismus und Communismus* by Joseph Stammhammer, *JPE* 2 (June 1894): 474–475; Thorstein Veblen, review of *History of the English Landed Interest (Modern Period)* by M. Garnier, *JPE* 2 (June 1894): 475–477; Thorstein Veblen, review of *L'Agriculture aux États-Unis* by Émile Levasseur, *JPE* 2 (September 1894): 592–596. Hodgson and I discuss several of these one by one in *Essential Writings of Thorstein Veblen*, ed. Charles Camic and Geoffrey M. Hodgson (London: Routledge, 2011).

149. Veblen, review of *The Land-System,* 115; Veblen, review of *Der Parlamentarismus,* 313, emphasis added.

150. Thorstein Veblen, "The Price of Wheat since 1867," *JPE* 1 (December 1892): 68–103; Thorstein Veblen, "The Food Supply and the Price of Wheat," *JPE* 1 (June 1893): 365–379.

151. Miller, review of *Introduction to English Economic History,* 459.

152. Veblen used "normal course of things" in both Veblen, "Price of Wheat," 74; Veblen, "Food Supply," 374.

153. On Coxey's Army, I have relied on Carlos A. Schwantes, *Coxey's Army: An American Odyssey* (Lincoln: University of Nebraska Press, 1985). I also used Diner, *Very Different Age;* Robert C. McMath Jr., "Populism in Two Countries," *Agricultural History* 69 (1995): 516–546; Robert C. McMath Jr., *American Populism: A Social History, 1877–1898* (New York: Hill and Wang, 1992); Painter, *Standing at Armageddon;* Charles Postel, *The Populist Vision* (New York: Oxford, 2007). Quoting Thorstein Veblen, "The Army of the Commonweal," *JPE* 2 (June 1894): 456–461, 456–458, 461.

154. Thorsten Veblen, "The Economic Theory of Woman's Dress," *Popular Science Monthly* 46 (December 1894): 198–205.

155. On Starr's writings, see note 104. Laughlin, "Changes of Fashion." Prior to Veblen, the most synthetic work on the subject was by economist Caroline Foley, "Fashion," *Economic Journal* 3 (1893): 458–474.

156. Here Veblen adopted his teachers' conception of science, topping it off with the influential notion of "theory" put forth by John Stuart Mill, *A System of Logic: Ratiocinative and Inductive* (New York: Harper, [1843] 1858). Unfortunately, Veblen did not pull together all the points mentioned in this sentence in any single passage, leaving readers to piece his views together from comments he sprinkled here and there, particularly in Thorstein Veblen, "Why Is Economics Not an Evolutionary Science?," *QJE* 12 (July 1898): 373–397, 156–157 (where he uses "brute facts"); Thorstein Veblen, "Fisher's Capital and Income," *Political Science Quarterly* 23 (March 1908): 112–128, 493–497. As between the interlinked work of producing observations and building theoretical generalizations, Veblen attached particular importance to the latter, writing: "The objective end [of knowledge production] is a theoretical organization, a logical articulation of things known [into] a comprehensible system." *HL,* 6. Regarding firsthand as well as secondhand observation, see *TLC,* v–vi.

157. Veblen, "Woman's Dress," 203–205.

158. Great heft, according to Hodgson, who uses Veblen's book reviews to argue convincingly that "a revolution took place in his thinking in the years 1896–98," particularly in regard to his views on the process of social evolution. Geoffrey M. Hodgson, "On the Evolution of Thorstein Veblen's Evolutionary Economics," *Cambridge Journal of Economics* 22 (1998): 415–431, 426. See also Geoffrey M. Hodgson, *The Evolution of Institutional Economics: Agency, Structure and Darwinism in American Institutionalism* (London: Routledge, 2004).

159. Thorstein Veblen, review of *Socialism* by Robert Flint, *JPE* (March 1895): 247–252, 252. I return to these issues in Chapter 8.

160. Herrick, "My Life," 50, RHP.

161. TV to Harper, November 22, 1895, Box 84, Folder 12, OPR-UoC. Dorfman, citing Abram L. Harris, misdated this letter to 1898, in *JDTVR,* 16n17.

162. *HL,* 112, 120–121.

163. Edward W. Bemis to Richard T. Ely, April 24, 1895, JDP. In the letter, Bemis attributes Veblen's dissatisfaction not to salary issues but to Harper canceling Veblen's Socialism course "because the subject might be misunderstood." Given that Veblen continued to teach the course, however, there is something off with Bemis's statement. Possibly Bemis was trying to put Veblen in the same political boat as himself, or possibly Veblen soft-pedaled to Bemis the reasons behind his grievances with Harper. It is hard to decide among the possibilities because this letter of Bemis's exists only in a version hand-copied by Dorfman, who appears to have shortened the letter.

Elsewhere, Veblen remarked harshly on the tendency of university administrators to economize by forcing lower-level faculty members to accept "an advance in nominal rank . . . in place of an advance in salary, the former being the less costly commodity for the time being." *HL,* 118n8.

164. TV to Harper, November 22, 1895, Box 84, Folder 12, OPR-UoC. The letter from Bemis to Ely, dated April 24, 1895, is quoted in Clair Edward Morris, Jr., "J. Lawrence Laughlin: An Economist and His Profession" (unpublished PhD dissertation, University of Wisconsin–Madison, 1972), 59n15.

165. TV to Hardy, November 10, 1895, TV-UoC, emphasis added; reproduced in *JJTV,* 190.

166. On Veblen's salary, see letter cited in *UoC-AR* 1892–1893, 40. To support the claim that Harper mistreated Veblen, Veblen scholars have often pointed to the low dollar amount of Veblen's salary. Viewed in the context of the times, however, Veblen's salaries were, at every faculty rank he held, equal to or above the average salary of faculty members at the same rank at a University of Chicago (and peer institutions, such as Stanford University). On salaries at the University during this period, see http://www.irwincollier.com/chicago-instructional-staff-salaries-by-rank-1919/ (accessed May 8, 2020).

167. TV to Hardy, November 10 and December 15, 1895, TV-UoC; reproduced in *JJTV,* 189, 191. Charles Henry Hull to Jordan, April 27, 1905,TV-CU. This document is reproduced in Viano, "Ithaca Transfer," 60–61; *HL,* 121.

168. On Hardy's biography, I rely on Russell H. Bartley and Sylvia E. Bartley, "In Search of Thorstein Veblen: Further Inquiries into his Life and Work," *International Journal of Politics, Culture and Society* 11 (1997): 129–173; *JJTV.* Valuable also are Sarah Hardy's own (undated) letters, which colorfully cover the period when she studied at the University of Chicago. (In these, she makes only one fleeting reference to "Dr. Veblin [*sic*].") Hardy's letters are preserved in GFP, Box 2.

169. TV to Hardy, January 18, January 23, 1896, TV-UoC; reproduced in *JJTV,* 192, 193. The Jorgensens misdate the first of these letters as 1895.

170. TV to Hardy, February 24, 1896, TV-UoC; reproduced in *JJTV,* 198–199.

171. TV to Ellen Veblen, March 31, 1896, TV-UoC; reproduced in *JJTV,* 199–200.

172. Ellen Veblen to Sarah Hardy Gregory, two letters, the first undated [but probably 1897, according to the Jorgensens], the second dated April 1897, emphasis added, TV-UoC; reproduced in *JJTV,* 202, 205.

173. TV to Hardy, February 24, 1896, TV-UoC; reproduced in in *JJTV,* 198–199.

174. TV to Hardy, November 10 and December 15, 1895, and January 18, [1896,] and February 6, 1896, TV-UoC; reproduced in *JJTV,* 190, 191, 192, 196.

NOTES TO PAGES 276–279

8. Working in the Field

1. Ellen Veblen to Sarah Hardy Gregory, April 1897, TV-UoC; reproduced in *JJTV*, 205.

2. *HL*, 12, 13, 199. Aside from his penchant for synonyms, Veblen was often casual, to the point of inconsistency, in his word choices. In *The Theory of the Leisure Class*, he used "scholars" disdainfully to refer to humanists engaged in useless "scholarship" centered on dead languages; as such, they contrasted with "scientists" of modern vintage (113–114, 394–396). However, in several passages from *The Higher Learning in America* (23, 57, 71, 80–85, 121, 146, 193–209), and those I have just quoted, Veblen merged the two groups, allowing that at least some contemporary humanists—some "scholars"—were adopting proper scientific methods in their "scholarship." Because *The Higher Learning in America* is the later of the two books, I take it as expressing Veblen's considered view on the topic.

3. Broadly speaking, the same held true, according to Veblen, in "higher barbarian culture," which marked the arrival of a fully developed leisure class: an institution also resistant to the advancement of knowledge but satisfied with worthless classical scholarship. *HL*, 2–3, 12, 13, 23, 57, 71, 80–85, 121, 146, 193–209, 199.

4. *HL*, 10–11, 89, 121, 199; Veblen, "The Place of Science in Modern Civilization," *AJS* 11 (1906): 585–609, 4, 7–9, 22.

5. *TLC*, 363–374, 386.

6. *HL*, 62, 165, 174, 195.

7. *HL*, 22, 194, 194n11, 198; Laurence R. Veysey, *The Emergence of the American University* (Chicago: University of Chicago Press, [1965] 1970), 37 (emphasis added). See also John W. Boyer, *The University of Chicago: A History* (Chicago: University of Chicago Press, 2015), 144–145.

8. *HL*, 80–81.

9. *HL*, 2, 133; *TLC*, 382. While defending intellectual specialization, Veblen opposed the organizational division of universities into departmental units. *HL* 69–72.

10. *HL*, 2, 28n8, 133–134, 209. In notes he took in 1895 on Herbert Spencer's *Principles of Sociology*, Veblen jotted: "I know little of sociology and am not competent to express opinions"; TV-UoC. At later stages of his career, when he was again in search of academic employment, Veblen associated himself with other fields as well, notably sociology. (See Chapter 9, note 41).

11. Frank A. Fetter, "The Next Decade of Economic Theory," *Publications of the American Economic Association*, 3rd ser., 2 (1901): 236–246, 237.

12. Edwin R. A. Seligman, review of *Public Finance* by Charles Francis Bastable, *Political Science Quarterly* 7 (1892): 708–720, 720; Jacob H. Hollander, review of *Value of Distribution* by C. W. MacFarlane, *Annals* 14 (1899): 123–124, 123. Seligman, Hollander, and Fetter were all economists, as are all the other contemporary authors cited in this subsection.

13. William J. Barber, "American Economics to 1900," in *A Companion to the History of Economic Thought*, ed. Warrens J. Samuels, Jeff E. Biddle, and John B. Davis (Malden, MA: Blackwell, 2003), 231–245, 244. I have elsewhere discussed the eclecti-

cism of turn-of-the-century American economics more fully. See Charles Camic, "Bourdieu's Cleft Sociology of Science," *Minerva* 49 (2011): 275–293.

14. In the experience of these economists, "almost nothing was a given," according to historian Herbert Hovenkamp, in "The First Great Law and Economics Movement," *Stanford Law Review* 42 (1990): 993–1058, 996.

15. Patten to Taussig, September 30, 1896, Correspondence A-Z, FWTP.

16. Joseph Persky, "The Neoclassical Advent: American Economics at the Dawn of the Twentieth Century," *Journal of Economic Perspectives* 14 (2000): 95–108, 97. (The percentage calculations are mine, based on the raw totals that Persky reports.) On monographic studies, see Arthur T. Hadley, "Recent Tendencies in the Economic Literature," *Yale Review* 3 (1894): 251–260, 252; Jacob H. Hollander, "Discussion on an Economic History of the United States," *Publications of the American Economic Association*, 3rd ser., 6 (1905): 186–191, 188–189; Jacob H. Hollander, "The Present State of the Theory of Distribution," *Publications of the American Economic Association*, 3rd ser., 7 (1906): 24–45, 33; Dorothy Ross, *The Origins of American Social Science* (Cambridge: Cambridge University Press, 1991), 200.

17. Hollander, "Economic History," 188.

18. W. J. Ashley, *An Introduction to English Economic History and Theory*, vol. 1 (London: Longmans 1892–93), ix–x. Also in this vein were books Veblen, cited with approval, by Carl Bucher, *Industrial Evolution*, trans. from 3rd German ed., ed. S. Morley Wickett (New York: Henry Holt [1893] 1900] 1901); W. Cunningham, *The Growth of English Industry and Commerce during the Early and Middle Ages*, 2nd ed. (Cambridge: Cambridge University Press, 1890; W. Cunningham, *The Growth of English Industry and Commerce in Modern Times* (Cambridge: Cambridge University Press, 1892). For discussion see Pat Hudson, "Economic History," in *Encyclopedia of Historians and Historical Writing*, ed. Kelly Boyd (Chicago: Fitzroy Dearborn Publishers, 1999): 346–349; Gerard M. Koot, *English Historical Economics, 1870–1926: The Rise of Economic History and Neomercantilism* (Cambridge: Cambridge University Press, 1987). For a discussion on the separation between economics and economic history, see Warren J. Samuels, "Ashley's and Taussig's Lectures on the History of Economic Thought at Harvard, 1896–1897," *History of Political Economy* 9 (1977): 384–411. For a contemporaneous perspective, see Guy S. Callender, "The Position of American Economic History," *American Historical Review* 19 (1913): 80–97.

19. Heath Pearson, "*Homo Economicus* Goes Native, 1859–1945," *History of Political Economy* 32 (2000): 933–989; Sandra J. Peart and David M. Levy, "Post-Ricardian British Economics, 1830–1870," in *A Companion to the History of Economic Thought*, ed. Warrens J. Samuels, Jeff E. Biddle, and John B. Davis (Malden, MA: Blackwell, 2003), 130–147.

20. J. Laurence Laughlin, *Industrial America: Berlin Lectures of 1906* (New York: Scribner's, 1906), 228, 238.

21. William Caldwell, review of *Philosophy and Political Economy* by James Bonar, *JPE* 1 (1893): 601–606, 601.

22. Charles Jesse Bullock, *Introduction to the Study of Economics*, rev. ed. (New York: Silver, Burdett and Company, 1900), 3–4.

23. Fetter, "Next Decade," 242.

24. John Bates Clark, review of *Outlines of Economic Theory* by Herbert Joseph Davenport, *JPE* 5 (1897): 384.

25. In his discussion of why marginalism caught on in American economics in the 1890s, Goodwin draws particular attention to its role in promoting the professionalization of economics. Craufurd D. W. Goodwin, "Marginalism Moves to the New World," in *The Marginal Revolution in Economics*, ed. R. D. Collison Black, A. W. Coats, and Craufurd D. W. Goodwin (Durham, NC: Duke University Press, 1973), 285–304. (The sources cited in Chapter 7 note 36 propose a similar argument.) Other historians, in contrast, give more weight to the ways in which marginalism spoke to the class conflicts of the period. James L. Huston, *Securing the Fruits of Labor: The American Concept of Wealth Distribution, 1765–1900* (Baton Rouge: Louisiana State University Press, 1998); James Livingston, "The Social Analysis of Economic History and Theory," *American Historical Review* 92 (1987): 69–95; James Livingston, *Pragmatism and the Political Economy of the Cultural Revolution, 1850–1940* (Chapel Hill: University of North Carolina Press, 1994); Nancy Cohen, *The Reconstruction of American Liberalism, 1865–1914* (Chapel Hill: University of North Carolina Press 2002); Thomas C. Leonard, *Illiberal Reformers: Race, Eugenics and American Economics in the Progressive Era* (Princeton, NJ: Princeton University Press, 2016); Richard White, *Railroaded: The Transcontinentals and the Making of Modern America* (New York: Norton, 2011). For my purposes, there is no need to choose between these different explanations.

26. Hadley, "Recent Tendencies," 253–254; David I. Green, "Wieser's Natural Value," *Annals* 5 (1895): 52–70, 512.

27. W. G. Langworthy Taylor, "A New Presentation of Economic Theory," *JPE* 5 (1897): 518–528, 524.

28. Hadley, "Recent Tendencies," 253–254. Folwell captured the continuing chaos in the field when he remarked: "In regard to the fundamental doctrines of value, we are still at sea." William W. Folwell, "The New Economics," *Publications of the American Economic Association* 8 (1893): 19–40, 32.

29. William Smart, "The Effects of Consumption of Wealth on Distribution," *Annals* 3 (1892): 1–36, 3. See also Thomas Nixon Carver, *The Distribution of Wealth* (New York: Macmillan, 1904), v. In 1927, Homan, the early historian of American economic theory, observed of this era: "It was a controversial generation, and the controversies were waged mainly around the theory of value and distribution." Paul T. Homan, *Contemporary Economic Thought* (London: Harper and Brothers, 1928), 51. Writing in regard to social scientists more broadly, Ross has stated that, for them, "distribution [was] the core problem of the age." Ross, *American Social Science*, 178. For others who have reached similar conclusions, see Hovenkamp, "Law and Economics Movement"; Joseph Persky, "The Neoclassical Advent: American Economics at the Dawn of the Twentieth Century," *Journal of Economic Perspectives* 14 (2000): 95–108.

30. When the functions of the capitalist and the commodity producer were combined in the same person (as was often true in Smith's account), the lending aspect of this process was not distinct.

31. Richard T. Ely, "Report of the Proceedings of the American Economic Association, Third Annual Meeting," *Publications of the American Economic Association* 4 (1889): 43–95, 62.

32. Ingrid Rima, *Development of Economic Analysis,* 7th ed. (New York: Routledge, 2009), 110–115. For background, I relied on Edwin Cannan, *A History of the Theories of Production and Distribution in English Political Economy from 1776 to 1848* (London: Rivington, Percival & Co., 1894).

33. For example, see Henry Carter Adams, *Outlines of Lectures upon Political Economy,* 2nd ed. (Ann Arbor, MI: Register Publishing House, 1886); Cannan, *Theories of Production and Distribution;* Francis A. Walker, *The Wages Question: A Treatise on Wages and the Wages Class* (New York: Henry Holt, 1876). For contemporaneous discussions of the problem, see Jacob H. Hollander, "Theory of Distribution"; Francis A. Walker, "The Source of Business Profits," *QJE* 1 (1887): 265–286. For historical treatments, see Livingston, "Social Analysis"; Stigler, "Marginal Utility Theory."

34. Fetter, "Next Decade," 238–240.

35. Walker, "Source of Business Profits," 268; John A. Hobson, *The Economics of Distribution* (New York: Macmillan, 1900), vi; Richmond Mayo-Smith, review of *Distribution of Wealth* by John R. Commons, *Political Science Quarterly* 9 (1894): 570–571, 570. For a discussion of economists' near-fixation with finding a unified law of distribution, see Livingston, *Pragmatism,* 57.

36. Here and in what follows, I follow the nineteenth-century practice of capitalizing "Labor" and "Capital" when these words refer to social classes, and removing the capitals when they refer to the inputs to the production process that these classes provide.

37. For a detailed examination of the pro-Labor side of this argument, see Huston, *Securing the Fruits of Labor,* 339–378. For analysis of the pro-Capital side, see Livingston, "Social Analysis," 57–66. This paragraph also draws on Cohen, *Reconstruction of American Liberalism;* Leonard, *Illiberal Reformers;* White, *Railroaded.*

38. Edward Atkinson, *The Distribution of Products* (New York: G. P. Putnam's Sons, 1885), 27; Edward Atkinson, *The Industrial Progress of the Nation: Consumption Limited, Production Unlimited* (New York: Putnam's Sons, 1889), 128.

39. Charles B. Spahr, *An Essay on the Present Distribution of Wealth in the United States* (New York: Crowell, 1896, 123).

40. This was not the first time economists had applied marginalist forms of analysis to the topic of distribution. European economists had been doing so throughout the nineteenth century. See John F. Henry, *John Bates Clark: The Making of a Neoclassical Economist* (London: Macmillan, 1995); John Pullen, *The Marginal Productivity Theory of Distribution* (London: Routledge, 2010). For the classic study of this body of work, see George J Stigler, *Production and Distribution Theories, 1870–1895* (New York: Macmillan, 1941).

41. Mayo-Smith, review of *Distribution of Wealth,* 570.

42. Here and in the following paragraphs, I describe marginal utility theory and marginal productivity theory as American economists generally practiced them during the fin de siècle period. I am not offering a more general description of these theories.

43. For my analysis of Veblen below, I do not need to delve here into the so-called John Bates Clark problem: the question of the relationship between the ideas of the "early Clark" and the "mature Clark," with the divide occurring in the mid-1880s. In the view of some historians of economics, Clark's work underwent major shifts between these two periods, whereas for other scholars, the continuities outweigh the changes. While this issue is immaterial for my purposes, my own view accords with the continuity argument

as spelled out by Guglielmo Forges Davanzati, *Ethical Codes and Income Distribution: A Study of John Bates Clark and Thorstein Veblen* (New York: Routledge, 2006); Henry, *John Bates Clark;* Mary S. Morgan, "Competing Notions of 'Competition' in Late Nineteenth-Century American Economics," *History of Political Economy* 25 (1993): 563–604; Mary S. Morgan, "Marketplace Morals and the American Economists: The Case of John Bates Clark," in *Higgling: Transactors and Their Markets in the History of Economics,* ed. Neil De Marchi and Mary Morgan (Durham, NC: Duke University Press, 1994), 229–252.

44. John Bates Clark, *The Distribution of Wealth: A Theory of Wages, Interest and Profits* (New York: Macmillan, 1899), 5, 168, 211, 367. (For readability, I have here changed some of Clark's singular nouns into plural nouns.) As mentioned in the "Glossary on Economic Schools" in Chapter 4, Clark's version of marginal productivity theory was one of several available during the fin de siècle period. In the twentieth century, still more versions arrived, some of them critical of Clark's approach, which economists faulted (inter alia) for illegitimately drawing macroeconomic conclusions from microeconomic arguments.

45. Clark's conception of capital has been the subject of an extensive secondary literature. My account here draws on Henry's discussion of how Clark defines capital in *The Distribution of Wealth.* Henry, *John Bates Clark,* 80–87.

46. Clark, *Distribution of Wealth,* vii, 3, 21, 56, 177, 180, 189. I have benefited from Pullen's discussion of these issues. Pullen, *Marginal Productivity Theory,* 51–60.

47. The phrase quoted is from Hollander, illustrating how contemporaries interpreted Clark's argument. Jacob H. Hollander, "The Residual Claimant Theory of Distribution," *QJE* 17 (1903): 261–279, 275. See also Herbert Joseph Davenport, *Value and Distribution* (Chicago: University of Chicago Press, 1908), 439–441; J. Laurence Laughlin, *Industrial America,* 233–235.

48. Clark, *Distribution of Wealth,* 4. My understanding of this dimension of Clark's work has benefited from Huston, *Securing the Fruits of Labor;* Livingston, "Social Analysis"; Cohen, *Reconstruction of American Liberalism;* Leonard, *Illiberal Reformers;* White, *Railroaded.*

49. Clark, *Distribution of Wealth,* 353, emphasis added. Contemporaries were very aware of this aspect of Clark's work. As early as 1891, for instance, Charles Tuttle (no relation to Veblen's teacher Herbert Tuttle) commended Clark for "analyses [that] have done away with the sophistical classification [by the classical authors] of labor as productive and unproductive." Charles Tuttle, "The Wealth Concept: A Study in Economic Theory," *Annals* 1 (1891): 615–634, 620. Abandonment of this distinction was a feature of marginalist thinking more generally, as pointed out by Lawrence Birken, "From Macroeconomics to Microeconomics: The Marginalist Revolution in Sociocultural Perspective," *History of Political Economy* 20 (1988): 251–264; Lawrence Birken, "Foucault, Marginalism, and the History of Economic Thought," *History of Political Economy* 22 (1990): 557–569; Mauro Boianovsky, "Anticipations of the General Theory: The Case of F. B. Hawley," *History of Political Economy* 28 (1996): 371–390; John Dennis Chasse, "Marshall, the Human Agent and Economic Growth: Wants and Activities Revisited," *History of Political Economy* 16 (1984): 381–404, 381; Joseph A. Schumpeter, *History of Economic Analysis* (New York: Oxford University Press, 1954), 628–632; Michael V. White and Takutoshi Inoue, "Retailing Poisoned Milk? New Evidence

on Keynes and Jevons's Hostility to John Stuart Mill," *History of Political Economy* 41 (2009): 419–432.

50. I base these statements on William Baumol, "Entrepreneurship in Economic Theory," *American Economic Review* 58 (1968): 64–71; Mark Blaug, *Economic Theory in Retrospect*, 5th ed. (Cambridge: Cambridge University Press, 1996): 439–447.

51. Clark, *Distribution of Wealth*, 3, 5, 27. As Clark abstractly defined it, the entrepreneurial "function itself includes no working and no owning of capital: it consists entirely in the establishing and maintaining of efficient relations between the agents of production." Clark, *Distribution of Wealth*, 3. He granted, however, that in actuality "entrepreneurs usually own capital and perform a kind of labor," often supervisory in nature. Clark, *Distribution of Wealth*, 5. Clark also recognized a major difference between the economic returns entrepreneurs receive in the form of profits and the rewards workers and capitalists receive as wages and interest. In his view, the latter two returns were permanent features of the production process, whereas interfirm competition tends to drive profits to a "no-profit" level. Clark, *Distribution of Wealth*, 70, 179.

52. My understanding of the history of the marginal productivity theory of distribution in the period after Clark's work appeared has been particularly informed by Pullen, *Marginal Productivity Theory*. In accepting one or another version of Clark's claim that "labor is always productive," marginalists were *not* asserting that all members of society are productive. As Leonard shows, many late nineteenth- and early twentieth-century, economists and other social scientists simply "exclude[d] the disabled, immigrants, African Americans, and women from the American work force"—retaining the pejorative "unproductive" for these social groups. Leonard, *Illiberal Reformers*, 2016.

53. Henry R. Seager, review of *The Distribution of Wealth* by John Bates Clark, *Annals* 16 (1900), 121–127, 127. Frank A. Fetter, "The Relation between Rent and Interest," *Publications of the American Economic Association*, 3rd ser., 5 (1904): 176–198, 181–182. Again, however, it is important to distinguish the fact that contemporaries, writing in the moment, saw Clark as a revolutionary from the judgment of intellectual historians who have argued that his views have much older roots. See note 40 above.

54. For a detailed development of this point, see Ross, *Origins*, 172–218; Hodgson, *How Economics Forgot History*, 41–270. For a similar argument, see Robert M. Fisher, *The Logic of Economic Discovery: Neoclassical Economics and the Marginal Revolution* (New York: New York University Press, 1986).

55. Again, I am referring to the way Veblen's contemporaries (and Veblen himself) saw classical economics, not to the way that modern historians of economics would describe it.

56. John Bates Clark, *The Essentials of Economic Theory, as Applied to Modern Problems of Industry and Public Policy* (New York: Macmillan, 1907), 84, 355, 374–375, 394. My understanding of Clark's views of competition and predation is beholden to Morgan, "Competing Notions"; Morgan, "Marketplace Morals." I have also benefited here from Thomas C. Leonard, "'A Certain Rude Honesty': John Bates Clark as a Pioneering Neoclassical Economist," *History of Political Economy* 35 (2003): 521–558.

57. Clark, *Distribution of Wealth*, xiv, 26, 35, 40, 67; Clark, *Essentials of Economic Theory*, 131. Mirowski argues that the sciences of physics and mechanics informed the work of nearly all the pioneers of marginalism. Philip Mirowski, *More Heat than Light* (Cambridge: Cambridge University Press, 1989), 217–222.

58. Fetter, "Next Decade," 237. In the next section, I discuss Veblen's paper and the circumstances surrounding it.

59. My choice of terms here refers back to overhang-style interpretations that have dominated the interpretation of Veblen.

60. In saying "not one," I am leaving out the period from 1884 to 1890, when Veblen lived on his parents' farm recuperating from his mystery illness.

61. The words I quote in this paragraph paraphrase statements quoted earlier in this chapter.

62. So much was this the case that Simon Patten felt the need to caution fellow economists: "We cannot afford to be mere iconoclasts." Simon Patten, "The Making of Economic Literature," *Publications of the American Economic Association*, 3rd ser., 10 (1909): 1–14, 2.

63. *UoC-AR* 1895, 191 (emphasis added). Then again, students may not have been particularly surprised, since the topic of "value and distribution" was part of their training in the political economy department. Of Laughlin's teaching in the department at this time, Bornemann has written: "In his two quarter seminar in theory, [Laughlin] required every student to formulate, write out, and defend . . . a theory of value and distribution." Alfred Bornemann, *J. Laurence Laughlin: Chapters in the Career of an Economist* (Washington, DC: American Council on Public Affairs, 1940), 21.

64. Veblen, lectures on Socialism, April 9–May 10, 1894, in Sarah Hardy, "Notes for Thorstein Veblen's course on Socialism, Univ. of Chicago, 1894," Series 77, TV-CCA (hereafter, Hardy Lecture Notes).

65. J. E. Cairnes, *Some Leading Principles of Political Economy Newly Expounded* (New York: Harper & Brothers, 1874), 264 (emphasis added).

66. Veblen, lectures, May 31–June 4, 1894, Hardy Lecture Notes. Veblen did *not* carry this particular argument into *TLC*.

67. TV to Hardy, November 10, 1895. TV-UoC; reproduced in *JJTV,* 189–190

68. TV to Hardy, December 15, 1895, TV-UoC; reproduced in *JJTV,* 190–191.

69. TV to Hardy, January 23, 1896, TV-UoC; reproduced in *JJTV,* 194.

70. TV to Hardy, February 6, 1896, TV-UoC; reproduced in *JJTV,* 196.

71. The quotation is from Hollander, "Discussion," 188–189.

72. TV to Hardy, January 23, 1896, TV-UoC; reproduced in *JJTV,* 194–195.

73. In a 1901 essay, Veblen elaborated on the "inanities" of the German historical school. Thorstein Veblen, "Gustav Schmoller's Economics," *QJE* 16 (November 1901): 69–93.

74. While the exact dates of the composition of the book do not bear on my argument, my best guess is that Veblen finished this draft in the spring or early summer of 1896, based on two pieces of information. First, Veblen spent some part of summer 1896 in England, away from his office (*JJTV,* 65). Second, Herbert Davenport (whom I am about to introduce) read, or at least perused, the manuscript sometime before Macmillan wrote Veblen about it on September 22, 1896 (JDTVR, 8–10). Putting these details together, the most plausible inference is that Veblen finished the draft before he set sail. Whether this draft included any of the material that Veblen had written in the early part of the year is unknown.

75. The letters that went back and forth between Veblen and the editors at the Macmillan Company are reproduced in JDTVR, 8–15.

76. TV to the Macmillan Company, in JD*TVR,* 9–10.

77. In addition to Davenport, Laughlin's graduate student (and Veblen disciple) Wesley Mitchell was also deeply engaged with marginalism at this time, as indicated by his 1898 paper. Wesley Mitchell, "The Austrian Theory of Value," *UoC-UR* 1898–1899, 222. For a discussion of Veblen in relation to Davenport, see J. Patrick Gunning, "Herbert J. Davenport's Transformation of the Austrian Theory of Value and Cost," in *The Economic Mind in America,* ed. Malcolm Rutherford (London: Routledge, 1998), 99–127. In a letter quoted by Dorfman, Starr stated explicitly that Veblen read the manuscript to him. Starr to Dorfman, JD*TV,* 174. Dorfman wrote that Veblen also read the manuscript to some of his former students.

78. Geoffrey M. Hodgson, "On the Evolution of Thorstein Veblen's Evolutionary Economics," *Cambridge Journal of Economics* 22 (1998): 415–431, 436. Elsewhere, I have speculated that Veblen's move in the antiteleological direction was partly a reaction against the strong teleological strand in Cohn's *Finanzwissenschaft.* See Charles Camic, "Veblen's Apprenticeship: On the Translation of Gustav Cohn's *System der Finanzwissenschaft,*" *History of Political Economy* 42 (2010): 679–721, 708–711.

79. Thorstein Veblen, review of *Aristocracy and Evolution: A Study of the Rights, the Origins and the Social Functions of the Wealthier Classes* by William H. Mallock, *JPE* 6 (June 1898): 430–435, 430.

80. When the publishing house of B. W. Huebsch reissued the book in 1912, however, "in the Evolution" was no longer included in its subtitle, which became simply "An Economic Study of Institutions." Why this change was made is unknown, though it has plausibly been speculated that "deletion of the word 'evolution' was probably based on Veblen's observation that it over-shadowed the modern-contemporary significance" of the book. P. A. Saram, "The Vanishing Subtitle of Veblen's 'Leisure Class,'" *International Journal of Politics, Culture, and Society* 13 (1999): 225–240, 226. Another possibility is that the new publisher, rather than Veblen, insisted on modifying the title, either for the reason Saram suggests or because of some other marketing consideration. Regardless, the text of the book—and its evolutionary argument—remained unchanged.

81. *TLC,* vi–vi.

82. I say "achieved" looking at the situation from a Veblenian standpoint. Naturally, marginalists would see the matter differently and would find ways to punch holes in Veblen's achievement.

83. *TLC,* 24.

84. For example, *TLC,* 240.

85. When Veblen spoke favorably of the "modern psychological sciences," his immediate referents were the writings of Americans William James, J. M. Baldwin, and John Dewey. See Geoffrey M. Hodgson, *The Evolution of Institutional Economics: Agency, Structure and Darwinism in American Institutionalism* (London: Routledge, 2004). Veblen was also familiar with, although critical of, the work of French crowd psychologists Gabriel Tarde and Gustav LeBon, who dealt with social processes such as suggestion and imitation. Thorstein Veblen, review of *Social Laws: An Outline of Sociology* by Gabriel Tarde, *JPE* 8 (1900): 562–563; Thorstein Veblen, review of *Psychologie economique* by Gabriele Tarde, *JPE* (1902): 146–148. Before he came across these French authors, however, Veblen was primed for them by similar ideas in the work of teachers like Ladd and Clark (during his time at Carleton). Writing from a different theoretical

standpoint, Hadley also cited French social theorists in order to criticize marginalism. See Hadley, "Recent Tendencies."

86. *TLC,* 22, 25, 69, 75, 82, 84–86, 139, 142. Veblen's use of "so-called" was a reference to classical and marginalist economists who differentiated lower and higher wants.

87. *TLC,* 10, 17, 35, 38–39, block quote at 41.

88. *TLC,* 266.

89. *HL,* 187. The literature on Veblen's views of evolution is enormous. I have especially learned from the work of Stephen Edgell, *Veblen in Perspective: His Life and Thought* (Armonk, NY: M. E. Sharpe, 2001); Stephen Edgell and Rick Tilman, "The Intellectual Antecedents of Thorstein Veblen: A Reappraisal," *Journal of Economic Issues* 23 (1989) 1003–1026; Hodgson, "Thorstein Veblen's Evolutionary Economics"; Geoffrey M. Hodgson, "The Approach of Institutional Economics," *Journal of Economic Literature* 36 (1998): 166–192; Geoffrey M. Hodgson, *How Economics Forgot History: The Problem of Historical Specificity in Social Science* (London: Routledge, 2001); Geoffrey M. Hodgson, *Evolution of Institutional Economics: Agency, Structure and Darwinism in American Institutionalism* (London: Routledge, 2004); Geoffrey M. Hodgson, "The Revival of Veblenian Institutional Economics," *Journal of Economic Issues* 41 (2007): 325–340; Geoffrey M. Hodgson, "Thorstein Veblen: The Father of Evolutionary and Institutional Economics," in *Thorstein Veblen: Economics for an Age of Crises,* ed. Erik S. Reinert and Francesca Lidia Viano (New York: Anthem Press, 2012), 283–295; Rick Tilman, *The Intellectual Legacy of Thorstein Veblen: Unresolved Issues* (Westport, CT: Greenwood Press, 1996); Rick Tilman, *Thorstein Veblen and the Enrichment of Evolutionary Naturalism* (Columbia: University of Missouri Press, 2007).

90. *TLC,* 7, 38–39, 193.

91. *TLC,* 144–148, 247, 325–326.

92. See discussion in Chapter 6.

93. *TLC,* 188.

94. Most immediately, Veblen was making use here of the work of his former colleague Carlos C. Closson (discussed earlier). Around this time, he also commended to Sarah Hardy several related works: Daniel G. Brinton, *Races and Peoples: Lectures on the Science of Ethnology* (New York: Hodges, 1890); A. H. Keane, *Ethnology* (London: Cambridge University Press, 1893); Gabriel Mortillet, *Le prehistorique* (Paris: Reinwald, 1885); Paul Topinard, *Anthropology,* trans. Robert T. H. Bartley (London: Chapman and Hall, [1877] 1894). TV to Hardy, February 6, 1896, TV-UoC; reproduced in *JJTV,* 196–198. But in back of these works was Veblen's long exposure to similar ideas about race, including the prominent work of European anthropologists of race Otto Ammon and Georges Lapouge. Veblen's attraction to these ideas continued for much his career.

95. *TLC,* 192, 190, 215.

96. The literature on Veblen's views of predation is also very large. I have especially benefited from Edgell, *Veblen in Perspective;* James K. Galbraith, "Predation from Veblen until Now," in *Thorstein Veblen: Economics for an Age of Crises,* ed. Erik S. Reinert and Francesca Lidia Viano (New York: Anthem Press, 2012), 317–328; Sidney Plotkin and Rick Tilman, *The Political Ideas of Thorstein Veblen* (New Haven, CT: Yale University Press, 2011); Malcolm Rutherford, *The Institutionalist Movement in American Economics, 1918–1947: Science and Social Control* (Cambridge: Cambridge University Press, 2011); Tilman, *Intellectual Legacy of Thorstein Veblen;* Tilman, *Enrich-*

ment of Evolutionary Naturalism; John Wenzler, "The Metaphysics of Business: Thorstein Veblen," *International Journal of Politics, Culture, and Society* 11 (1998): 541–574.

97. *TLC*, 4, 12, 14, 40.

98. *TLC*, 236, 238, 240.

99. *TLC*, 210, 229.

100. On Clark, I again have benefited from Morgan, "Marketplace Morals."

101. *TLC*, 194–198.

102. *TLC*, 206–207.

103. *TLC*, 204, 243–244.

104. *TLC*, 207–211, 267.

105. TV to AV, October 17, 1899; Anonymous, review of *The Theory of the Leisure Class* by Thorstein Veblen, *Washington Post* (March 20, 1899): 7; Anonymous, review of *The Theory of the Leisure Class* by Thorstein Veblen, *Brooklyn Daily Eagle* (April 8, 1899): 6; Anonymous [Stephen MacKenna], review of *The Theory of the Leisure Class* by Thorstein Veblen, *Criterion* (March 25, 1899): 26–27; William Dean Howells, review of *The Theory of the Leisure Class* by Thorstein Veblen, *Literature* (1899, April 28 and May 5): 361–362.

106. D. Collin Wells, review of *The Theory of the Leisure Class* by Thorstein Veblen, *Yale Review* (August 1899): 213–218; John Cummings, "The Theory of the Leisure Class," *JPE* 7 (1899): 425–455. Another prominent negative review was by Benjamin Wills Wells, *Swannee Review* 7 (July 1899): 369–374. Tilman analyzes Cummings's review in detail. See Rick Tilman, *Thorstein Veblen and His Critics, 1891–1963* (Princeton, NJ: Princeton University, 1992), 18–25.

107. Edward A. Ross, review of *Die Entwickelung der menschlichen Bedurfnisse und die sociale Gliderung de Gesellschaft* by B. Gurewitsch, *JPE* 10 (1902): 622–625, 625. TV to Ross, December 2, 1899, Correspondence, 1894–1901, Box 2, Folder 2, EARP. A review in the *Popular Science Monthly* classed it in its section on "Scientific Literature." See Anonymous, review of *The Theory of the Leisure Class* by Thorstein Veblen, *Popular Science Monthly* 55 (1899): 557–558.

108. Charles Richmond Henderson, review of *The Theory of the Leisure Class* by Thorstein Veblen, *The Dial* 22 (1900): 437–438; Samuel McCune Lindsay, review of *Evolution and Efforts of Their Relation to Religion and Politics* by Edmond Kelley, *Annals* 6 (1900): 142–144; Lester F. Ward, review of *The Theory of the Leisure Class* by Thorstein Veblen, *AJS* 6 (1900): 829–837, 829; George Herbert Mead to Helen Mead, May 8, 1901, Box 1, Folder 5, GHMP.

109. Ward, review of *The Theory of the Leisure Class*, 831.

110. Cummings, "The Theory of the Leisure Class." Also relevant here is A. M. Day, review of *The Theory of the Leisure Class* by Thorstein Veblen, *Political Science Quarterly* 16 (1900): 366–369.

111. *Publications of the American Economic Association*, n.s. 4, 12–13; 5, 11.

112. On Veblen's interactions with Jordon in regard to a position in this department, see Roxanne Nilan and Karen Bartholomew, "No More 'The Naughty Professor': Thorstein Veblen at Stanford," *Sandstone & Tile* (Stanford Historical Society) 31 (2007): 13–33. On Jordan, see David H. Dickason, "David Starr Jordan as a Literary Man," *Indiana Magazine of History* 37 (1941): 345–358. On the Stanford economics department, see Mary E. Cookingham, "Political Economy in the Far West: The University of

California and Stanford University," in *Breaking the Academic Mould: Economists and American Higher Learning in the Nineteenth Century,* ed. William J. Barber (Middletown, CT: Wesleyan University Press, 1988), 266–289.

113. Jenks to Jordan, April 25, 1899, Series I-A, SC 58, Box 20, Folder 210, DSJP.

114. TV to Harper, January 21 1899, Box, 84, Folder 12, OPR-UoC.

115. Laughlin to Jordan, April 29, 1899, Series 1-A, SC 58, Box 20, Folder 211; Jenks to Jordan, April 25, 1899, Series I-A, SC 58, Box 20, Folder 210. Both in DSJP.

116. See *UoC-UR* 1899–1900, 21–24.

117. Thorstein Veblen, review of *The Development of English Thought: A Study in the Economic Interpretation of History* by Simon N. Patten, *Annals* 14 (July 1899): 125–131, 126–129.

118. Thorstein Veblen, "The Beginnings of Ownership," *AJS* 4 (November 1898): 352–365, 352.

119. Veblen, "The Beginnings of Ownership," 362. Thorstein Veblen, "The Instinct of Workmanship and the Irksomeness of Labor," *AJS* 4 (September 1898): 187–201, 188–190, 200. Two years after he introduced the expression in print, Veblen wrote to Sarah Hardy (by then Sarah Hardy Gregory): "'The Instinct of Workmanship' [is] a phrase which, perhaps without you knowing it, I owe to you." TV to Sarah Hardy Gregory, July 20, 1900, TV-UoC; reproduced in *JJTV,* 207. In Chapter 3, I quote one of Veblen's later definitions of this instinct.

120. Several sets of student notes from Veblen's "Economic Factors in Civilization" are located in Box 67 (Bundle 10) and Box 69 (Bundle 36), JDP. Thorstein Veblen, "An Early Experiment in Trusts," *JPE* 12 (March 1904): 270–279, 270. On Veblen's Carnegie proposal, see Chapter 9.

121. The official description of Scope and Method of Political Economy read: "This course attempts to define the province, postulates and character of Political Economy; to determine its method and to examine the nature of economic truth. [It offers] a critical estimate . . . of the views of leading writers on Methodology." The catalogue listing described History of Political Economy as concerned with "the theoretic development of Political Economy as a systematic body of doctrine," with special emphasis on "schools and leading writers" from Adam Smith and his forerunners to "European and American writers of the nineteenth century." *UoC-AR* 1895–1896, 57–58. When Veblen studied at Johns Hopkins, he had taken a similar course with Ely. See Chapter 5. A fragment of Veblen's History of Political Economy course, based on student notes from a lecture he gave in the mid-1890s at the University of Wisconsin at Madison in a seminar run by Richard Ely, is reproduced in Paul Uselding, "Veblen as Teacher and Thinker in 1896–97: The Hagerty Notes on How the Economist Derived His Criticism of the Structure of Classical Economic Theory," *American Journal of Economics and Sociology* 35 (October 1976): 391–399.

122. Thorstein Veblen, "Why Is Economics Not an Evolutionary Science?," *QJE* 12 (July 1898): 373–397, 378. The other three articles were Thorstein Veblen, "The Preconceptions of Economic Science: I," *QJE* 13 (January 1899): 121–150; Thorstein Veblen, "The Preconceptions of Economic Science: II," *QJE* 13 (July 1899): 396–426; Thorstein Veblen, "The Preconceptions of Economic Science: III," *QJE* 14 (February 1900): 240–269.

123. Veblen, "Preconceptions of Economic Science, I," 122–123.

124. In speaking of the shortcomings of the work of economists of the past, I am describing Veblen's views, not offering what I regard as a correct account of the writings he analyzes.

125. Veblen, "Preconceptions of Economic Science: II," 399.

126. Like his contemporaries, Veblen often lumped Clark together with the Austrians. Veblen, "Preconceptions of Economic Science III," 268 note; Thorstein Veblen, "Professor Clark's Economics," *QJE* 22 (February 1908): 147–195, 149, in which Veblen slightly qualifies his merging of Clark and the Austrians.

127. Veblen, "Economics Not an Evolutionary Science."

128. Veblen had met this attack again in his recent translation of Gustav Cohn's treatise on finance.

129. Veblen, "Economics Not an Evolutionary Science," 389; Veblen, "Preconceptions of Economic Science: II," 419.

130. The last parenthesis here is not, of course, a full account of Veblen's exposure to this view of human conduct, as I have indicated in the previous three chapters.

131. Here I combine two passages that are continuous in theme: Veblen, "Economics Not an Evolutionary Science," 388, 390–391, and Veblen, "Preconceptions of Economic Science: III," 268–269 (emphasis added).

132. Veblen, "Preconceptions of Economic Science: II," 419.

133. This eighty-four-page translation is Veblen's mystery project. As far as I know, no scholars have written anything about it. The fact that the translation was published by the International Library Publishing Company, a publisher of socialist tracts, suggests that Veblen's (loose) ties to Chicago's socialist networks may have had something to do with the publication: someone associated with a publishing company may have asked Veblen to make the translation, or Veblen may have asked the company to publish it. Either guess makes some sense because, within socialist circles, interest in Lassalle was then rising (at the expense of Marx). See G. A. Kleene, "Bernstein vs. 'Old-School' Marxism," *Annals* 18 (1901): 1–29. But, at the time, academic economists were also taking Lassalle's views seriously. See James Bonar, "The Value of Labor in Relation to Economic Theory," *QJE* 5 (1891): 137–164; Hadley, "Recent Tendencies"; Adolph C. Miller, "National Finance and the Income Tax," *JPE* 3 (1895): 255–288; C. W. Mixter, "The Theory of Savers' Rent and Some Application," *QJE* 13 (1899): 245–269; Edward Alsworth Ross, "Seligman's 'Shifting and Incidence of Taxation,'" *Annals* 3 (1893): 52–71. Among Veblen's teachers, both Ely and Sumner had a strong interest in Lassalle's work.

134. Thorstein Veblen, "Gustav Schmoller's Economics," *QJE* 16 (November 1901): 69–93, 81, 85, 89.

135. Thorstein Veblen, "The Socialist Economics of Karl Marx and His Followers II: The Later Marxism," *QJE* 21 (February 1907): 299–322, 304n1.

136. In these writings, Veblen made explicit just how closely he associated marginalism with the theory of distribution. Commenting on "marginal-utility economics," he wrote: "The whole system . . . lies within the theoretical field of distribution, and it has but a secondary bearing on any other economic phenomena than those of distribution." Thorstein Veblen, "The Limitations of Marginal Utility," *JPE* 17 (November 1909): 620–636, 620.

137. Edwin R. A. Seligman to Veblen, May 14, 1909, Catalogued Correspondence, Box 2, JDP.

138. Veblen, "Professor Clark's Economics," 190n1; Veblen, "Limitations of Marginal Utility," 622 (words slightly rearranged).

139. I take these dates from the original correspondence cited in JD*TVR*, 59–63.

140. TV to Sarah Hardy Gregory, July 20, 1900, TV-UoC; reproduced in JJ*TV*, 206–207.

141. Cummings, "The Theory of the Leisure Class," 441, 445, 450. Tilman discusses Cummings's review. Tilman, *Thorstein Veblen and His Critics*, 18–25.

142. Veblen, "Mr. Cummings's Strictures on *The Theory of the Leisure Class*," *JPE* 8 (December 1899): 106–117, 115.

143. Frank Taussig to Richard T. Ely, 1900, JD*TVR*, 59–60.

144. Careful, as always, about the words in his titles, Veblen had asked Ely whether he could change the title Taussig proposed to "The Distinction between Industrial and Pecuniary Activity." TV to Ely, February 3, 1900, JDP. Presumably, Veblen wanted this change in order to hold onto and spotlight the industrial-pecuniary distinction he had drawn in *The Theory of the Leisure Class*.

145. During this period, when Veblen was searching for a publisher, he published a short monograph, "The Use of Loan Credit in Modern Business." This appeared in the University of Chicago's *Decennial Publications*, a series issued to celebrate the university's tenth anniversary. Thorstein Veblen, "The Use of Loan Credit in Modern Business," *Decennial Publications of the University of Chicago*, ser. 1, 4 (March 1903): 31–50. Intended by Harper to showcase the university's achievements, the series included contributions by a number of the leading figures on its faculty. That Veblen's monograph was included, even as the series editors needed to reject the work of several luminaries, is further evidence of his local standing. See "Concerning the Decennial Publications," undated memo, Box 39, Folder 3, OPR-UoC. Veblen recycled this monograph as chapter 5 of *TBE*. He published a related article shortly afterward in the *AJS*. See Thorstein Veblen, "Credit and Prices," *JPE* 13 (June 1905): 460–472.

146. On the basis of a 1905 letter from Veblen to Jacques Loeb, Dorfman states that Scribner's rejected the manuscript after receiving a negative evaluation from Harper. JD*TVR*, 141.

147. Louis Galambos, *The Public Image of Big Business in America, 1880–1940* (Baltimore: Johns Hopkins University Press, 1975), 112. See also Rebecca Edwards, *New Spirits: Americans in the Gilded Age, 1865–1905* (New York: Oxford, 2006), 81–106.

148. Henry Rand Hatfield, "The Chicago Trust Conference," *JPE* 8 (1899): 1–18.

149. Charles Jesse Bullock, "Trust Literature: A Survey and Criticism," in *Trusts, Pools and Corporations*, ed. William Z. Ripley (Boston: Ginn, [1901] 1905), 428–473.

150. Arthur T. Hadley, "Population and Capital," *Publications of the American Economic Association* 10 (1885): 557–566; Arthur T. Hadley, *Railroad Transportation: Its History and Its Laws* (New York: Putnam, 1885); Arthur T. Hadley, *Economics: An Account of the Relations between Private Property and Public Welfare* (New York: Putnam, 1896); Jeremiah Whipple Jenks, *The Trust Problem* (New York: McClure, 1900).

151. Lester D. Ward, *Dynamic Sociology, or Applied Social Science,* 2 vols. (New York: Appleton, 1883), 497, 526, 577–578, 581–583, 594.

152. TV to Ross, October 20, 1905, Correspondence, 1892–1904, Box 3, Folder 2, EARP. That Veblen had an academic audience in mind was something he warned his sales-minded publisher of a year earlier, writing the Scribner's company: "You overestimate the probable sale of the volume to the 'man in the street.' I anticipate that the sales will be practically confined to university circles and to the readers of . . . *The Theory of the Leisure Class.*" Cited in JDTVR, 65.

In an effort to let economists know *The Theory of Business Enterprise* was specifically aimed at them, Veblen even included several heavy footnotes that formulated his arguments using algebraic notations—a telling move at a time when economists (under the influence of Jevons, Walras, and Marshall, among others) were starting to adopt more mathematical ways of expressing their theories. *TBE,* 95, 110, 149–150, 153, 160.

153. TV to Gregory, July 27, 1903, TV-UoC; reproduced in JJTV, 208–209.

154. While at Chicago, Veblen taught "Trusts" three times (in 1904 and 1905) and "Organization of Business Enterprise" once (in 1904).

155. *TBE,* 263. Veblen reiterated this point throughout the book.

156. Thorstein Veblen, "Industrial and Pecuniary Employments," *Publications of the American Economic Association,* Series 3, 2 (February 1901): 190–235, 192.

157. These concepts appear, in passing, only four times in the book. See *TBE,* 375, 389, 396. They make a brief return in his 1917 book *An Inquiry into the Nature of Peace and the Terms of its Perpetuation* (New York: B. W. Huebsch, 1917), 350–355.

158. *IW,* 226–227.

159. *TBE,* 314; Veblen, "Industrial and Pecuniary Employments," 203–205, 307.

160. See Chapter 4, note 44.

161. Again, this count is mine.

162. Veblen, "Industrial and Pecuniary Employments," 204, 207, 214; *TBE,* 29, 37, 157.

163. Veblen, "Industrial and Pecuniary Employments," 197.

164. Veblen, "Mr. Cummings's Strictures," 113.

165. *TBE,* 150–151.

166. Thorstein Veblen, "An Early Experiment in Trusts," *JPE* 12 (March 1904): 270–279, 270.

167. Thorstein Veblen, "On the Nature of Capital I: The Productivity of Capital Goods," *QJE* 22 (August 1908): 517–542, 527.

168. *TBE,* 4.

169. Veblen, "Industrial and Pecuniary Employments," 209.

170. Veblen, "Industrial and Pecuniary Employments, 224–225.

171. With the possible exception of the passage on the "American soul" that I quote in Chapter 3.

172. *TBE,* 167–168; *HL,* 52. "Accumulations of wealth" is a paraphrase.

173. Veblen, "Use of Loan Credit in Modern Business," 41–48.

174. *TBE,* 8, 15, 19, 24–25, 264. This is not to say that Veblen thought that businessmen necessarily favored coalitions and other forms of combination (monopoly, for instance). In his view, businessmen instituted these arrangements only when they brought

strategic advantages over competitors; otherwise, businessmen resisted these organizational forms, even when they meant a "more economic utilization of resources and mechanical contrivances." Veblen observed that "business interests and manoeuvres commonly delay consolidations, combinations, correlations of the several plants and process, for some appreciable time after such measures have become patently advisable on industrial grounds." *TBE,* 39–41. This view contrasted with that of many of Veblen's contemporaries in economics (Clark included) who championed competition and warned against monopoly. See Morgan, "Competing Notions."

175. *TBE,* 25.

176. *TBE,* 25, 178, 189, 207n1.

177. *TBE,* 29.

178. *TBE,* 63–64.

179. *TBE,* 64, 125; Veblen, "Industrial and Pecuniary Employments," 210.

180. *TBE,* 324, 400.

181. *TBE,* 293, 398–400.

182. *TBE,* 312–313, 330–331, 351. Influenced by the research of his student Robert Hoxie, Veblen later modified his view of unions, worrying that their primary concern was with pecuniary gain and questioning their revolutionary potential; Rutherford, *The Institutionalist Movement,* 130–131.

183. *TBE,* 336, 355–356. By the end of the following decade, however, Veblen's views on socialism underwent another about face. Asked by the managing editor of the *Political Science Quarterly* to review a pair of books on European socialism, Veblen replied, "Books on Socialism . . . do not interest me. [In] my opinion Socialism is a dead issue. Too dead to be a live topic, and too lately dead for objective historical treatment." (Underline in original.) TV to Thomas Parker Moon, August 26, 1922, JDP.

184. Veblen, "Mr. Cummings's Strictures," 111.

185. *TBE,* 340–341.

186. Thorstein Veblen, "The Place of Science in Modern Civilization," *AJS* 11 (March 1906): 585–609, 588. Veblen took the Latin phrase from his translation of *Die Wissenschaft und die Arbeiter* by Ferdinand Lassalle, who took the words from Pope Alexander IV, writing in 1255. I thank Carey Seal for translating the Latin. Veblen returned to these issues in "The Evolution of the Scientific Point of View," *University of California Chronicle* 10 (October 1908): 395–416.

187. *HL,* 43–61.

188. *HL,* 1, 28, 56, 147.

189. *HL,* 54; Veblen, "Place of Science, 598.

190. *HL,* 3–4, 15, 95; Veblen, "Place of Science," 590, 597–598. Depending on the context, Veblen described "idle curiosity" as working in tandem with the "instinct of workmanship." *HL,* 3; *IOW,* 39–62, 84–89. I have discussed Veblen's analysis of these two instincts in Chapters 3 and 7.

9. Conclusion

1. John Cummings, "The Theory of the Leisure Class," *JPE* 7 (1899): 425–455; E. A. Ross, "Recent Tendencies in Sociology II," *QJE* 17 (1902): 82–100, 105–106; Thomas Nixon Carver, review of *The Theory of Business Enterprise* review by Thor-

stein Veblen, *Political Science Quarterly* 20 (1905): 141–143, 143; Frank Taussig, *Principles of Economics,* vol. 1, 2nd ed. rev. (New York: Macmillan, [1911] 1917), 110; Alvin S. Johnson, review of Lewis H. Haney, *The History of Economic Thought, JPE* 19 (1911): 709–711, 711. Dorfman provides excerpts from the major reviews of *The Theory of Business Enterprise, JDTV,* 235–238.

2. TV to Jacques Loeb, February 10, 1905, JLP.

3. Ellen Veblen to Lucia Tower, July 3, 1906, in JJTV, 84.

4. TV to Loeb, February 10, 1905, JLP.

5. Russell H. Bartley and Sylvia E. Bartley, "In Search of Thorstein Veblen: Further Inquiries into His Life and Work," *International Journal of Politics, Culture and Society* 11 (1997): 129–173; Clare Virginia Eby, "The Two Mrs. Veblens, among Others," *International Journal of Politics, Culture, and Society* 19 (1999): 353–361.

6. Veblen later referred to the University of Chicago, during his final years there, as a place "where they [Harper and his lieutenants] assassinated me"; Jacob Warshaw, "Recollections of Thorstein Veblen" (c. 1934), JWP, 8.

7. TV to Loeb, February 10, 1905, JLP.

8. TV, "Application for Appointment to the Library Service," JDP.

9. William Hill to Herbert Putnam, January 9, 1905, JDP.

10. TV to Loeb, March 24, 1905, JLP.

11. TV to Loeb, February 10, 1905, JLP.

12. Wesley Mitchell to Sarah Hardy Gregory, April 10, 1908, JDP.

13. TV to David Starr Jordan, April 9, 1906, Series I-A, SC 58, Box 49, Folder 288, DSJP.

14. TV to Jordan, April 16, 1906, Series I-A, SC 58, Box 49, Folder 288, DSJP.

15. TV to Jordan, April 16, 1906, Series I-A, SC 58, Box 49, Folder 288, DSJP.

16. For a fuller account of Veblen's resignation, see Bartley and Bartley, "In Search of Thorstein Veblen," 140–141.

17. Mitchell to Gregory, April 10, 1908, JDP.

18. Herbert Davenport to TV, April 14, 1909, JDP.

19. This is one of the central claims of Jorgensen and Jorgensen, JJTV; and Bartley and Bartley, "In Search of Thorstein Veblen," on whose accounts of this period in Veblen's life I rely in this paragraph. See also Eby, "The Two Mrs. Veblens, among Others"; Tony Maynard, "A Shameless Lothario: Thorstein Veblen as Sexual Predator and Sexual Liberator," *Journal of Economic Issues* 34 (2000): 194–199. On the Palo Alto years in Veblen's life, see R. L. Dufus, *The Innocents at Cedro* (New York: Macmillan, 1944).

20. TV to Davenport, October 21, 1909, JDP.

21. Jordan to James Harvey, January 21, 1910, SC 007, Box 8, OLEP.

22. Dorfman provides a copy of Veblen's Carnegie application and excerpts from some of his letters of recommendations, JDTVR, 575–579, JDTV, 298–300. For the full list of distinguished recommenders, see W.M. Gilbert to JD, March 1, 1932, JDP.

23. Lester Ward to Putnam, December 19, 1904; John Bates Clark to Putnam, January 9, 1905; Carl Plehn to Putnam, 1905, all JDP.

24. Allyn Young to Jordan, April 14, 1906, Folder 489; Young to Jordan, May 16, 1906, Folder 494; Young to Jordan, November 4, 1909, Folder 623, all in DJSP.

25. J. Laurence Laughlin to Robert S. Woodward, May 20, 1910, JDP.

26. Young to Woodward, June 22, 1910, JDP.

27. Frank Taussig to Woodward, quoted by Dorfman, JD*TV,* 299; Jordan to Woodward, May 20, 1910, OLEP.

28. Young to Davenport, November 14, 1909, JDP.

29. Gary Alan Fine, *Difficult Reputations* (Chicago: University of Chicago Press, 2001); Gary Alan Fine, *Sticky Reputations* (New York: Routledge, 2012).

30. James Tufts to JD, October 21, 1932; J. F. Jameson to JD, March 1, 1926, Charles Merriam to JD, September 24, 1932, all in JDP. Clark to Edwin R. A. Seligman, June 1, 1903, ESP; Stephen Leacock, "My Recollections of Chicago," in *My Recollections of Chicago and the Doctrine of Laissez-Faire,* ed. Carl Spadoni (Toronto: University of Toronto Press, [1943] 1998), 6.

31. Jacob Warshaw, "Recollections of Thorstein Veblen" (c. 1934), JWP, 3–4; TV to Sarah Hardy Gregory, June 27, 1903, TV-UoC; reproduced in JJ*TV,* 208; TV to David Starr Jordan, April 16, 1906, Series I-A, SC 58, Box 49, Folder 288, DSJP.

32. Jordan to Woodward, May 20, 1910, OLEP. In connection with his application to the Library of Congress, Veblen mentioned to Lester Ward the support of "some of my friends here [in Chicago], especially Mr. Laughlin and Mr. J.F. Jameson"; TV to Ward, January 4, 1905, LFWP.

33. Merriam to JD, September 24, 1932, JDP. Recalling the years when she and her husband Edward Bemis were friends with Veblen in Chicago, Anne Sargent Bemis later wrote Dorfman: "We both think that Veblen belonged to the American Economic Assn. and the American Academy of Political and Social Science, and there was an eating club at the University of Chicago—perhaps they called it quadrangle club—consisting of professors &c of which he told me he was a member." A.S. Bemis to JD, July 19, 1930, JDP. On Veblen's guest lecturing at the University of Wisconsin and Harvard, see Chapter 8, notes 121, 135.

34. A. P. Winston to JD, October 15, 1932, JDP.

35. Hill to Putnam, January 9, 1905, JDP.

36. Abbott, Davis, and Breckinridge, quoted in Ellen Fitzpatrick, *Endless Crusade: Women Social Scientists and Progressive Reform* (New York: Oxford University Press, 1990), 47, 53.

37. TV to Davenport, October 21, 1909, JDP.

38. Edwin E. Slosson, *Great American Universities* (New York: Macmillan, 1910), x.

39. Bartley and Bartley, "In Search of Thorstein Veblen."

40. Malcolm Rutherford, *The Institutionalist Movement in American Economics, 1918–1947* (Cambridge: Cambridge University Press, 2011), 27–28.

41. TV to Mitchell, February 20, 1913, JDP. This remark contrasts with Veblen's earlier remarks that he knew "little of sociology" (see Chapter 8, note 10).

42. John Branner to E. H. Woodruff, March 28, 1918, SC 34, Box 13, Folder 44; Letter Book 1918, JCBP.

43. Charlotte Perkins Gilman to JD, August 30, 1933, JDP.

44. On the New School, see Luther V. Hendricks, "James Harvey Robinson and the New School for Social Research," *Journal of Higher Education* 20 (1949): 1–11.

45. These final years are well described in Jorgensen and Jorgensen, JJ*TV,* 154–168.

46. In some respects, these views differ from those Veblen formulated in *HL*. Thorstein Veblen, "Professor Clark's Economics," *QJE* 22 (February 1908): 147–195; Thorstein Veblen, "Fisher's Capital and Income," *Political Science Quarterly* 23 (March 1908): 112–128; Thorstein Veblen, "On the Nature of Capital I: The Productivity of Capital Goods," *QJE* 22 (August 1908): 517–542; Thorstein Veblen, "On the Nature of Capital II: Investment, Intangible Assets, and the Pecuniary Magnate," *QJE* 23 (November 1908): 104–136; Thorstein Veblen, "Fisher's Rate of Interest," *Political Science Quarterly* 24 (June 1909): 296–303; Thorstein Veblen, "The Limitations of Marginal Utility," *JPE* 17 (November 1909): 620–636. I quote "strong arm" from Veblen, "On the Nature of Capital I."

47. The phrase "gild of economists" is Veblen's, as discussed in Chapter 8; TV to Ross, October 20, 1905, Correspondence, 1892–1904, Box 3, Folder 2, EARP.

48. The judgment is that of Rutherford, *The Institutionalist Movement*, 140. Veblen's earlier article was "The Instinct of Workmanship and the Irksomeness of Labor," *AJS* 4 (1898): 187–201.

49. Ulysses G. Weatherly, review of *The Instinct of Workmanship, and the State of the Industrial Arts* by Thorstein Veblen, *American Economic Review* 4 (1914): 860–861, 881 Alvin S. Johnson, review of *The Instinct of Workmanship and the State of the Industrial Arts* by Thorstein Veblen, *Political Science Quarterly* 31 (1916): 631–633, 961; E. H. Downey, review of *The Instinct of Workmanship and the State of the Industrial Arts* by Thorstein Veblen, *JPE* 23 (1915): 78–80, 79.

50. *IG;* Thorstein Veblen, *Inquiry into the Nature of Peace and the Terms of its Perpetuation* (New York: Macmillan, 1917); Thorstein Veblen, *The Engineers and the Price System* (New York: B. W. Huebsch, 1921).

51. *AO,* 86, 114–114, 172.

52. The small exception here is his 1925 article, "Economic Theory in the Calculable Future," which did appear in a "supplement" issue of the *American Economic Review. AER (Papers and Proceedings)* 15 (1925): 48–55. Veblen's book, *The Vested Interests and the State of the Industrial Arts* (New York: B. W. Huebsch, 1919) was a compilation of articles that he had previously published in *The Dial*.

53. H. L. Mencken, *Prejudices, First Series* (New York: Knopf, 1919), 79.

54. Mitchell to Sarah Hardy Gregory, January 3, 1909, JDP.

55. On the development of this research tradition in the United States, see *The Marginal Revolution in Economics: Interpretation and Evaluation,* ed. R. D. Collison Black, A. W. Bob Coats, and Craufurd D. W. Goodwin (Durham, NC: Duke University Press, 1973).

56. On Veblen's fortunes in economics, I draw again on Rutherford, *Institutionalist Movement*. With regard to sociology, I discuss elsewhere Veblen's declining reputation, beginning in the 1930s, at hands of theorist Talcott Parsons and his followers. See Charles Camic, "Reputation and Predecessor: Parsons and the Institutionalists," *American Sociological Review* 57 (August, 1992): 421–445.

57. In private, Veblen continued to maintain many close friendships, often with former students. Likewise, he took care with his appearance, at least according to Myron Watkins, Veblen's student at the University of Missouri and later part of his New York circle. Reviewing Dorfman's book, Watkins objected to Dorfman's suggestion that Veblen

was "indifferent to creature comforts and personal neatness." Watkins continued (possibly with some embellishment): "Nothing could be farther from the truth. The reviewer cannot recall a scholar in his whole academic experience more fastidiously neat than was Veblen. . . . [Further,] Veblen was an epicure. Whenever it was feasible, and often at no paltry sacrifice, he obtained the choicest foods, condiments, beverages and fruits. Not infrequently these came on special orders direct from the grower or producer in remote regions: cheeses from Holland, cocoa or chocolate from the East Indies, fruits from the tropics." Myron W. Watkins, review of *Thorstein Veblen and His America* by Joseph Dorfman, *American Economic Review* 25 (1935): 284–286.

58. Veblen, "The Intellectual Pre-eminence of Jews in Modern Europe," *Political Science Quarterly* 34 (1919): 33–42. In several of his post-Stanford books, Veblen also featured the character of the "masterless man," who makes its first appearance in *The Instinct of Workmanship* and continues to show up through *Absentee Ownership*.

59. TV to Edwin Seligman, December 10, 1925, JDP; Becky Veblen Meyers as quoted in JJ*TV*, 260, n. 27. Because Meyers's recollection was long after the event, however, we need to be cautious about putting too much weight on her exact words.

60. Quoted in JD*TV*, 504.

61. We see this change of opinion in Mitchell's two 1929 obituaries, where he lauded Veblen not only because "he brought to economics the detachment of a visitor from Mars," but also because "now and then he would drop a quizzical comment, which came from outer space like a meteor, shocking some bystanders and amusing others"; Wesley Mitchell in JD*TVR*, 601–614, 603, 607. These statements do not claim that Veblen was an academic outsider, but they had the effect (along with a few of Mitchell's other statements) of putting an outer space frame around his friend and former teacher.

62. John Maurice Clark, "Thorstein Bundy [sic] Veblen: 1857–1929," *AER* 19 (1929), 744. British economist J.A. Hobson struck the same note in his obituary. Although he ranked Veblen "as the most considerable thinker in the field of economics that America has yet produced," he continued: "though we speak of Veblen as an economist, he is perhaps better regarded as a sociologist"; J.A. Hobson, "Thorstein Veblen," *The Sociological Review* 21 (1919): 342–345. 342. See also J.A. Hobson, *Veblen* (London: Chapman and Hall, 1936).

63. Clark, *Distribution of Wealth*, 180.

64. My wording here refers back to my discussion in Chapter 2 of the timing, sequencing, and duration of life-course events.

ILLUSTRATION CREDITS

FIGURE 1

Thorstein Veblen's parents, Thomas Anderson Veblen and
Kari Bunde Veblen

PHOTO CREDIT: Courtesy of Carleton College Archives

FIGURE 2

Veblen's Professor at Carleton College, John Bates Clark

PHOTO CREDIT: The Reading Room/Alamy Stock Photo

FIGURE 3

Thorstein Veblen, early 1880s

PHOTO CREDIT: Courtesy of Carleton College Archives

FIGURE 4

Veblen's professors at Johns Hopkins University:
George Sylvester Morris, Charles Sanders Peirce,
Herbert Baxter Adams, and Richard T. Ely

MORRIS PHOTO CREDIT: Gado Images/Alamy Stock Photo

PEIRCE PHOTO CREDIT: National Oceanic and Atmospheric Administration/
Department of Commerce/Wikimedia Commons

ADAMS PHOTO CREDIT: Prints and Photographs Division
Library of Congress, LC-DIG_cwpbh-03589

ELY PHOTO CREDIT: The Reading Room/Alamy Stock Photo

FIGURE 5

Monograph series for research on institutional history

CREDIT: Google Books

FIGURE 6

Veblen's professors at Yale University:
Noah Porter, George Trumbull Ladd, and William Graham Sumner

PORTER PHOTO CREDIT: Reproduced from Timothy Dwight, *Memories of Yale Life and Men, 1845–1899*. (New York: Dodd, Mead, 1903)/ University of Connecticut Libraries/Wikimedia Commons

LADD PHOTO CREDIT: VTR/Alamy Stock Photo

SUMNER PHOTO CREDIT: Images of Yale individuals (RU 684). Manuscripts and Archives, Yale University Library

FIGURE 7

Veblen's professors at Cornell University:
James Laurence Laughlin, Herbert Tuttle, and Moses Coit Tyler

LAUGHLIN PHOTO CREDIT: University of Chicago Photographic Archive, [apf1-03687], Special Collections Research Center, University of Chicago Library

TUTTLE PHOTO CREDIT: History and Art Collection/Alamy Stock Photo

TYLER PHOTO CREDIT: Alpha Stock/Alamy Stock Photo

FIGURE 8

Thorstein Veblen, early 1900s

PHOTO CREDIT: Courtesy of Carleton College Archives

ACKNOWLEDGMENTS

This book is about the extended network of individuals and institutions that shaped the work of Thorstein Veblen. In trying to untangle that network, I became more and more aware of my own dependence on the support of multiple organizations and many people.

This study began with funding from the National Science Foundation, and it has been sustained since then by financial support from the University of Wisconsin–Madison and Northwestern University. Along the way, my research has benefited as well from a residential fellowship at the Russell Sage Foundation and a visiting professorship in the department of sociology at Princeton University. Without the assistance of these institutions, the project would not have gotten off the ground, much less reached completion.

Essential for my research, too, have been materials in several archival collections in the United States. At the end of Chapter 1, I list the collections I cite in subsequent chapters, and I would like to acknowledge and thank the libraries that gave me access to their resources: the American Philosophical Society; Brown University, Manuscripts Division; Carleton College Archives; Columbia University, Rare Book and Manuscript Library; Cornell University, Division of Rare and Manuscript Collections; Harvard University Archives; Johns Hopkins University, Special Collections; the Library of Congress, Manuscript Division; Luther College Archives; Minnesota Historical Society; Missouri State Historical Society; Norwegian-American Historical Association; Stanford University, Department of Special Collections and University Archives; University of California, Berkeley, Bancroft Library; University of Chicago, Special Collections Research Center; Wisconsin State History Society; and Yale University, Manuscripts and Archives Repository.

At all of these libraries I have been helped by knowledgeable and gracious staff members. Among them, I want especially to thank Tara Craig (Columbia Rare Book and Manuscript Library), Eric Hillemann and Nat Wilson (Carleton College Archives), Susan McElrath (Bancroft Library, Berkeley), and Kristina Warner (St. Olaf College, Norwegian-American Historical Association). Eric Hillemann, besides responding to constant requests from me for materials held at Carleton, read and incisively commented on portions of Chapters 3 and 4, sharing his expertise on Thorstein Veblen's college years.

Closer to home, I have had the considerable advantage of the stimulating and congenial intellectual milieus of Northwestern University's Department of Sociology and the Science in Human Culture program at the university. I have benefited from the supportiveness of a succession of Sociology Department chairs, Mary Pattillo and James Mahoney in particular, and of associate chair Susan Thistle. Three graduate students in the department, Elisabeth Anderson, Iga Kozlowski, and Kory Johnson, provided needed research assistance, and the departmental staff, expertly coordinated by Ryan Sawicki and Murielle Harris, solved many logistical and technical problems that threatened to defeat me. My research assistant at the University of Wisconsin, David Nowacek, shouldered the burden of initiating the research into primary sources and chasing down dozens of early leads. At the end of the project, Lila Stromer, Bex Shea, and Jennifer Shea assisted with time-sensitive parts of the production process.

Colleagues near and far—some of whom I've been lucky to know for decades, others newly made e-mail acquaintances who allowed me to steal their time and expertise—have strengthened my theoretical argument and historical analysis many times over. Many generously answered my requests for specific advice and information almost as soon as I asked for help, including Andrew Abbott, Russell Bartley, Thomas Bender, Craig Calhoun, Irwin Collier, Erik Grimmer-Solem, Bryan Lassner, George Levesque, Odd Lovoll, Mary Morgan, Sissel Myklebust, David Natvig, Sophus Reinert, Carey Seal, Rick Tilman, David Swartz, and Francesca Viano. Over the course of years, my work on this project has also been encouraged, enriched, challenged, and abetted in many different and valuable ways by esteemed colleagues and friends who perhaps never realized how much they were helping me nor how very much I appreciated it: Héctor Carrillo, Bruce Carruthers, Mitch Duneier, Joan Fujimura, Neil Gross, Carol Heimer, Gail Kligman, Heinz Klug, Michèle Lamont, Barbara Marwell, the late Jerry Marwell, Aldon Morris, Ann Orloff, Monica Prasad, Gay Seidman, and Franklin Wilson.

When my research finally began to gel into something resembling a book manuscript, my friend Hans Joas carefully read each chapter within days of my finishing the first draft, responding with comments that substantially improved subsequent drafts. When all the chapters came together, I had the windfall of astute critical and constructive advice on the full manuscript from Roger Backhouse, Rogers Brubaker, Steven Epstein, Wendy Espeland, Gary Fine, Daniel Hirschman, Geoffrey Hodgson, Malcolm Rutherford, and George Steinmetz. I am greatly in their debt. I am also deeply grateful for the wise counsel and patience of my editor at Harvard University Press, Ian Malcolm, as well as for the dedicated work of his excellent editorial and production team.

Words start to fail me when I come to the three people I most want to thank. I met my partner, Beth Mertz, when Thorstein Veblen was still on the run from me and the chase was consuming the better part of my time and energy. Beth amiably accepted this intrusion, allowing herself to be pulled into the hunt, mind and heart, even when professional and personal sacrifices fell hard on her. Hauling with me to far-flung archives where Veblen left tracks, puzzling out clues about his lost intellectual whereabouts, excavating the literary remains of his teachers and associates, understanding my frustration as I wrote up my final report on the search, advising me with the sharp insights of an accomplished scholar on how to improve my drafts, she was unflagging in her determination to see this investigation to a close. She did; on my own, it would not have happened. My gratitude is forever.

The two people who have been with this study almost as long as I have are my daughters, Caroline and Susannah. One was in middle school, the other in high school, when I first brought this project home, and it proved to be a constant handful. The sole reason I managed it was because the two of them were always the opposite of that; they made parenting a joyous experience filled with the delights of their high spirits; their developing moral and intellectual capacities; and their ever-deepening generosity, tolerance, courage, and wisdom. By the time the book was nearing completion, and they were counseling me on it and cajoling me to wrap it up, they were large-hearted adults with years of schooling behind them, challenging professional careers, caring spouses, and beautiful, thriving children. In small return for the bounty my daughters have given me, this story of the traveling economist is for them.

INDEX